American Women in the 1960s

CHANGING
THE FUTURE

AMERICAN WOMEN IN THE TWENTIETH CENTURY

Barbara Haber, Series Editor

THE SCHLESINGER LIBRARY ON THE HISTORY OF
WOMEN IN AMERICA, RADCLIFFE COLLEGE

Pulling together a wealth of widely scattered primary
and secondary sources on women's history, *American
Women in the Twentieth Century* is the first series to
provide a chronological history of the changing status
of women in America. Each volume presents the
experiences and contributions of American women
during one decade of this century. Written by leading
scholars in American history and women's studies,
American Women in the Twentieth Century meets the need
for an encyclopedic overview of the roles women have
played in shaping modern America.

Also Available:

Setting a Course: American Women in the 1920s
Dorothy M. Brown

Holding Their Own: American Women in the 1930s
Susan Ware

The Home Front and Beyond: American Women in the 1940s
Susan M. Hartman

Mothers and More: American Women in the 1950s
Eugenia Kaledin

On the Move: American Women in the 1970s
Winifred D. Wandersee

American Women in the 1960s

CHANGING
THE FUTURE

Blanche Linden-Ward
Carol Hurd Green

TWAYNE PUBLISHERS • NEW YORK
Maxwell Macmillan Canada • Toronto
Maxwell Macmillan International • New York Oxford • Singapore Sydney

Twayne Publishers
Macmillan Publishing Company
866 Third Avenue
New York, New York 10022

Maxwell Macmillan Canada, Inc.
1200 Eglinton Avenue East
Suite 200
Don Mills, Ontario M3C 3N1

Library of Congress Cataloging-in-Publication Data
Linden-Ward, Blanche, 1946–
    American women in the 1960s : changing the future / Blanche
Linden-Ward, Carol Hurd Green.
        p.   cm.—(American women in the twentieth century)
    Includes bibliographical references (p.   ) and index.
    ISBN 0-8057-9905-2 (hard).—ISBN 0-8057-9913-3 (pbk.)
        1. Feminism—United States—History—20th century.   2. Women—
United States—History—20th century.   3. United States—Social
conditions—1945–   I. Green, Carol Hurd.   II. Title.   III. Series.
HQ1421.L56   1992
305.4'0973—dc20   92-592
                                                                   CIP

10 9 8 7 6 5 4 3 2 1

Printed in the United States of America

CONTENTS

ACKNOWLEDGMENTS

"With a Little Help From Our Friends"

Elisabeth Sandberg originally joined this project as a coauthor but could only participate at the early stages, providing research and initial drafts for several sections. Valuable research assistance came from Blanche Linden-Ward's students, Leslie Wright and Kathleen Corcoran, and from Cynthia Butler, who worked with Carol Hurd Green in the early stages of the book.

Special thanks are due to friends and colleagues who provided criticism, advice, testimony, and information for various chapters, and/or pointed us to important sources and gave support through a long project: Joan Alden, Rhoda Clugston Allen, Cindy Reppert Ault, Ruth Batson, Alexander Bloom, Joseph Boskin, Joan Brigham, Dorothy Brown, Frances Shea Buckley, Andrew Buni, Rogers Daniels, Angela Dorenkamp, Ellen Fitzpatrick, Toni Frederick, Susan Gill, Jeffrey Grossel, Marilyn Halter, John Hayward, Florence Hoffman, Elinor Langer, Christine Lange Larson, Julia Lindow, Virginia Lowe, Mary McCay, Janet Miller, Kristin Morrison, June Namias, Mary Daniel O'Keeffe OP, Patricia Palmieri, Millie Rahn, Maria Reilly OP, Lois Palken Rudnick, David Sanjek, Henry D. Shapiro, Sarah Way Sherman, Dory Small, Jennifer Tebbe, and Lynn Williams. Barbara Haber's interest in and support of this project and series has been invaluable. Thanks also to the many scholars and sixties friends who read and commented on parts of the manuscript, and to those who responded anonymously to us with their personal testimony in response to our questionnaire distributed at the spring 1990 New England American Studies Association conference, "Out of the Sixties."

Blanche Linden-Ward

Carol Hurd Green

"Woman is still living in the age of man's vengeance."
—*Pearl S. Buck, "The Education of Women," in* To My Daughters, With Love (1967)

INTRODUCTION

Where Women Were in 1960

Mention of the sixties conjures up stereotypical images, bordering on myth, of radical change and discontinuity; yet fifties trends of suburbanization, conformity, complacency, growing prosperity, and a renewed cult of motherhood underlying the "baby boom" persisted for many women well through and past the sixties. For many, the sixties ideal of the middle-class lifestyle remained unattainable, a promise beyond reach. In January 1960, *Look* magazine described America as "a pond of calm and contentment," where the majority of the population expected "a well-controlled, manicured, safe, unspectacular existence of measured material realization." That description of "fifties" America continued to apply to the sixties for middle-class whites, particularly those in suburbs.[1]

The massive post-war demographic movement of "white flight" from cities to suburbs continued. Thousands of young families annually left old neighborhoods for brand new "Cape Cod" or split-level suburban homes. Few new homes were being built in urban areas, so if a family wished to finance a new home through the Federal Housing Administration (FHA), a system established by the 1949 Housing Act, suburbia was often the only option. Many of their peers were moving there, realizing the American Dream of property ownership. Until 1972, veterans could get low-interest federal home mortgages for only one dollar down. Following the example set at the Levittowns, developers nationwide cloned suburbs with easy access to new interstate highways begun in 1956 and largely built in the sixties. Between 1963 and 1973, Americans constructed almost 20 million new domestic units, more than in the fifties. Planner Samuel Kaplan wrote in 1976 that suburbanization was "the greatest migration in our country's history and perhaps one of the greatest migrations in the history of man." By the sixties' end, 40 percent of all Americans, primarily white, about eighty million strong, lived in relatively new houses in over twenty thousand suburban developments, leaving inner cities to blacks and the poor.[2]

Over three quarters of the women interviewed by sociologist Herbert Gans saw suburbia as a place where they could create a "normal family life, being a homemaker." Few expressed interest in a better or more active social, volunteer, or work life outside the home. A 1961 Gallup poll for the *Ladies' Home Journal* found that young women aged sixteen to twenty-one described their goals in terms of consumer goods—a modern kitchen in "a split-level brick" ranch house "with four bedrooms with French provincial furniture." The Future Homemakers of America, a group of teenaged girls and adult sponsors, heard Women's Bureau head Esther Peterson warn of "family breakdown" as a national problem at their 1962 convention in Salt Lake City. After she urged members to "prepare properly for the business of homemaking," delegates defined four national objectives to be achieved by 1965: "(1) discovering myself and my worth to others; (2) contributing to the joys and satisfactions of family living; (3) strengthening my education for future roles; and (4) launching good citizenship through homemaking."[3]

The celebration of domesticity that characterized popular culture in the fifties continued. Doris Day played the middle-class homemaker with four children in *Please Don't Eat the Daisies* (1960). A *Time* magazine article, "The Roots of Home," that year lauded the suburban housewife as "keeper of the American Dream" in language melding praise and disparagement: "She is first of all the manager of home and brood, and beyond that a sort of aproned activist. . . . With children on her mind and under her foot, she is breakfast-getter, laundress, house cleaner, dishwasher, shopper, gardener, encyclopedia, arbitrator of children's disputes and policeman. If she is not pregnant, she wonders if she is. She takes her peanut-butter sandwich lunch while standing, thinks she looks a fright, watches her weight (periodically) and jabbers over the short-distance telephone with the next-door neighbor." The stereotype was that of June Cleaver or Harriet Nelson on popular prime-time television shows. "Ozzie and Harriet," television's longest-running sitcom from 1952 to 1966, depicted a happy family in which the mother played a decidedly supportive but subordinate role.[4]

In popular literature humorist Phyllis McGinley was an unabashed apologist and promoter of the traditional housewife's role. A collection of her poems, *Times Three* (1960), won her a 1961 Pulitzer Prize. *Sixpence in Her Shoe* (1964) compiled her witty verse and essays about kids, husbands, and suburbia. Another domestic humorist, Shirley Jackson (1916–1965) wrote wry and humorous autobiographical prose sketches of homemaking, child-rearing, and the complex relationships between women and houses. Her best-selling novel, *We Have Always Lived in the Castle* (1962), focuses on Mary Katherine, who responds to lack of love with poison and prose. Despite her seemingly light-hearted view of the foibles and pitfalls of the ordinary existence of mother and wife, Jackson suffered from agoraphobia and depression; she died of a heart attack at 47. In her last novel, *Come Along With Me* (1968), the middle-aged widow protagonist enjoys new found freedom.[5]

As Betty Friedan observed in 1963, "The suburban housewife was the dream image of the young American woman. She was healthy, beautiful, educated, concerned only about her husband, her children, her home. She had found feminine fulfillment." The ideal, the "feminine mystique," persisted. As Gans discovered in early-sixties Levittown near Philadelphia, working-class or lower-middle-class suburban women expressed satisfaction with their lives and measured success in material terms. They spoke positively of the "comfort and roominess for family members in a new home," of "privacy and freedom of action in an owned home." Sociologist Mirra Komarovsky found similar attitudes among suburban blue-collar wives. The standard of living was greatly improved from that of their parents or their own childhood memories of the Depression. Discontent was an emotion which most could not afford to express; and if it was contemplated, many considered it akin to evil, ingratitude, haughtiness, and pride.[6]

Likewise, pollsters George Gallup and Evan Hill reported in a 1962 *Saturday Evening Post* that "few people are as happy as a housewife." Of 2,300 interviewed for their lengthy poll, 96 percent declared themselves fairly to extremely happy. Nine out of ten said childbirth was "the most satisfying" moment in their lives. Those working awaited the day when they "could assume the full-time role of housewife and eventually mother." Women testified to traditional values: "Being subordinate to men is part of being feminine." "A woman's prestige comes from her husband's opinion of her." "Women who ask for equality fight nature." The pollsters concluded, "Apparently the American woman has all the rights she wants." A lone dissonant note appeared in the hopes of 90 percent of mothers that their daughters would become more educated, marry later, and not "lead the same kind of life they did."[7]

Suburbanization produced a distinctly new lifestyle for American women. Developers used the isolation and privacy of the suburban home as a selling tool; but it resulted in unprecedented age segregation as well as racial, ethnic, and class homogeneity. For many women, such privacy equaled only loneliness. New houses looked inward, despite picture windows, and had no traditional porches as intermediate space between public and private, where neighbors could talk to neighbors; recreational time was spent on private patios in the rear. Distances demanded a car, if not two; and mother was the chauffeur, her keyring reading "Mom's Taxi." Sociologist Helene Lopata described the era as "one of the few times in recorded history that the mother-child unit has been so isolated from adult assistance. Responsibility for health, welfare, the behavior and ability of the child is basically unshared. The father is not held accountable for what happens to the children because 'he is not home much of the time.'"[8]

Suburban housewives led a grueling schedule. "Every week the average American mother of three children washes 750 dishes and 400 pieces of silver; handles 250 articles of laundry; makes beds 35 times; shops for, carries, sorts, stores, and cooks 175 pounds of food; and walks 35 miles—just in her kitchen! . . . only a small part of what is expected of her." One bank study discovered that the "average" suburban housewife without outside employment still put in a 99.6-hour workweek. Increasingly, however, maintaining such a lifestyle required a second income.[9]

Outside the home, changes in women's social roles were not new in the sixties. After World War II, despite recommendations that women return to domesticity from warwork, female employment escalated. Thirty-five percent of women over age sixteen—about 24 million—held jobs in 1960, and almost a third of these had children. The percentage rose to over half for women aged twenty-nine to sixty-five. Women workers were more mature and—for the the first time, the majority, three out of five—were married. Most were factory workers, secretaries, clerical workers, teachers, and domestics. Although most of these were uninterested in feminism, they were part of a quiet, gradual social revolution. In 1962, the editors of *Harper's* termed this trend "crypto-feminism," women's extension of their spheres beyond the home.

Even middle-class married women sought work to help achieve or maintain family status. Women's earnings contributed to the dramatic rise in family income by 1963, when one-fifth of all families earned over $10,000 a year, with two-thirds of these reporting a wife's income. These women were better educated than previously with three-fifths, depending on class, holding high school diplomas. Married women still risked social stigma in working; and the divorce rate slowly but steadily grew through the decade. The relationship of the two phenomena remains to be proven.[11]

The sixties are also associated with revival of a women's movement and of a level of public criticism about the lack of women's rights that had not existed for many decades. In the fifties, some social scientists scrutinized the "women's question" to inform public policy about the proper roles for women at a time of Cold War international competition. The questions experts posed, however, in no way challenged the status quo and, in fact, aimed to find ways to reinforce it. Still, Eugenia Kaledin found "few areas of awareness during the sixties that had not been set up for action by the group of gifted social critics from the preceding decade."[12]

By the sixties' end, the new feminism attracted proponents and media attention as a national movement. In an important early study of the women's movement, Judith Hole and Ellen Levine define the movement as the "entire spectrum of women's groups from moderate to radical," active from the start of the decade but not coalescing until 1966 and after. "Women's rights" reformists made up a branch "primarily active in attempting to bring about legislative, economic, and educational reforms to eradicate sex discrimination in social institutions . . . through traditional political and legal channels." They formed national organizations and memberships of "moderate and conservative feminists," thriving in the atmosphere of liberal optimism under Kennedy and Johnson. "Women's liberation" was a part of the movement composed of "primarily radical feminists . . . concerned with analyzing the origins, nature, and extent of women's subservient role in society, with emphasis on the 'psychology of oppression'." Through consciousness-raising groups or street theatre, they tried "to educate themselves and others about these issues."[13]

Everyone had her own sixties. Although only a relatively small number defined themselves within a social movement, few lived through the decade without a consciousness of being in history. Since the sixties have turned into myth, with history, memory, and imagination often conflated and, given the phenomenon of selective amnesia, a survey of

American women's lives in that decade is a perilous project subject to correction by participants who experienced and remember it differently. Further, the idea that a ten-year period is a real, not a notional entity, presents challenges; but the sixties lend themselves uniquely to study as self-contained entity: 1960 was a year of remarkable beginnings, 1969 and 1970, of endings. Such easy demarcation does not work so well when considering women. By the decade's end the pace of change and the alteration of relations between the government and the people, between black and white, old and young, women and men, was of a rapidity and extent unparalleled in the experience of those who lived through it, yet most women's lives and expectations remained essentially unchanged.

Nonetheless, the sixties did bring the beginning of crucial changes and new freedoms for some in oppressed social groups. The fifties were not so gray as they have often been painted, and there were shifts in both cultural and political attitudes that presaged the sixties. 1960 witnessed significant beginnings and symbolic endings: A popular television show ended when Lucille Ball divorced Desi Arnaz that May; and an era passed in September with the death of social arbiter Emily Post. Most crucially, in November 1960 a young, glamorous, witty President was elected—the first born in the twentieth century; and the media endeared First Lady Jackie and family to the world. On his inauguration day in January 1961, John F. Kennedy, a potent symbol of what he was calling into being, talked about the promise of the sixties and the idea of a new generation. Before the decade was half over, that generation—Kennedy's—would be attacked by many of its children as the bearer of militarism and capitalism. But in January 1961, exciting and dangerous images were let loose—young, not old; new, not tried; adventurous, not safe—and a climate of expectation began to grow.[14]

The sixties was a time of turbulence and social upheaval, but also one of promise and exhilaration. Amid civil disturbance and an escalating, seemingly endless war, people came together to create new communities and alliances and to say no to old prejudices, to the color line, to acceptance of women's inferior status, to the idea that only a Protestant could be president. Although protests against traditional educational institutions were often anti-intellectual, the sixties was a time of argument and ideas, with conversations seeking and including groups hitherto dismissed as inarticulate. While Marshall McLuhan warned of the demise of the book and while the power of the television image reshaped politics, discussions raged and people everywhere seized on new, cheap printing methods to make their voices heard. The offset press and the copy machine that Xerox began marketing in 1960 improved on the cheaper and more prevalent mimeograph and allowed many who had been silent to tell their own stories in their own terms, to their own audiences. An "underground" press flourished in college towns and large cities. Pamphlets, manifestos, and newsletters appeared in abundance.[15]

This explosion of print, combined with the rapid proliferation of television sets and the lengthened broadcast day, led to yet another paradox—one central to the study of women. Americans perceived social change as happening at a rapid and dangerous pace, while for the great majority, change came slowly if at all. Increased access to the news and pressure on news sources to fill their pages and broadcast hours meant that most Americans saw and heard much more than they experienced. Communications technology allowed arguments and models for social change to spread through the culture more quickly than ever; it gave those distant from the action a sense of nearness. The power of new images—the rebellious youth, the hippie priest, the liberated woman—was enormous, attracting some to new causes and scaring many into a sense that the world they knew was ending. Although the civil rights struggle, women's liberation, and the war in Vietnam directly affected a minority of Americans, most *believed* their lives were changed or threatened by these and other social revolutions; and they made subsequent personal and political decisions based on such belief.

Two groups, especially, sought redress for historical wrongs with expectations heightened by the promise of a new order. Blacks in America, women and men alike, had borne burdens of discrimination and poverty for centuries. White women had first made common cause with oppressed blacks in the mid-nineteenth century. Again in the sixties, white women compared their experience of discrimination to the oppression of blacks; but as a century before the association of these oppressions created problems.[16]

1960 brought events of enormous significance for both the civil rights movement and the nascent women's movement. In February 1960, four black students sat in at a Woolworth's lunch counter in Greensboro, North Carolina, triggering a response that rolled across the South into the North, turning the long campaign for civil rights into a national movement. Without the long struggle that had gone before, without Rosa Parks's 1955 refusal to give up her seat on the bus, the Greensboro sit-in would not have found so many ready to put their bodies into the struggle. Yet, what the students did seemed a new thing, a new generation simply and unarguably demanding justice. The impact was felt across the country.

An event of quite different magnitude and revolutionary implications occurred in 1960 when an oral contraceptive, the "pill," reached the market. After decades of research, an inexpensive, accessible, and apparently safe and reliable contraceptive was available to women. Though the pill was accompanied by warnings, it represented a freedom for women far beyond the symbolic. Some said it signaled the start of the "sexual revolution"; but that was far more complex and rooted in multiple cultural trends, feminist and anti-feminist.

Before they were over, the sixties had been dissected and historical subdivisions had emerged. The usual division is tripartite, following, not surprisingly, the conventional mode of identifying historical periods through presidents. Commentators and political historians have mapped the decade as expansive until Kennedy's death in 1963; chaotic and tumultuous through the Johnson years, with apocalypse in 1968 and the election of Richard Nixon in 1969. Cultural historians have accepted the political division but renamed the parts. Some argue that the sixties did not fully play themselves out until Nixon's resignation in August 1974. Richard Flacks, participant and observer of the student movement, marks the rise and fall by the creation and dissolution of that movement. Morris Dickstein, in *Gates of Eden*, celebrates the cultural changes but ends on a falling note with sections titled "Breaking Out," "Breaking Through," and "Breaking Down." By contrast, the poet Muriel Rukeyser uses the generous metaphor, "breaking open." In the midst of the era's violence, she "came . . . entire to this moment / process and light / to discover the country of our waking / breaking open."[17]

For male political activists, the promise of the sixties ended in 1969 with the collapse of Students for a Democratic Society (SDS) and of organized student resistance to government policies and to the Vietnam war. David Harris saw everything coming together in early 1968; by 1969, it had all "come apart." In 1968, Carl Oglesby, an SDS leader, declared the "decade ready for the dustbin." Much hope, interspersed and followed by much despair—such are the decade's contrasts.[18]

One need not multiply examples to illustrate the oft-made point that women have been left out of history, even out of contemporary history; women's absence has affected the shaping of beliefs about the sixties. When women are left out, the tripartite periodization holds; and the idealistic efforts of the sixties can seem dismissible as a grandiose failure. When women are included, such a conclusion is not so easily made, although the promise of the decade reached partial fruition only later. Examining American women's lives and the events that affected them, reveals neither sharply rising expectations early in the decade nor a dying fall from 1968 on. Rather, at the moment when Carl Oglesby and other male activists were consigning the decade to the dustbin, women were coming together in new groups, raising their voices, publishing manifestos, and demanding justice. Consciousness-raising groups, women's caucuses within professional organizations, women's journals and books—all tumbled into being with breathtaking rapidity from 1968 on. This was a period of anger and rage as women recognized the extent and long history of injustice; but it was also a time of euphoria, hope, self-discovery, and creation of utopian dreams of a new order for women.

The history of rising consciousness is so powerfully attractive as to threaten the skewing of the history of women in this period. The story of women might seem a picture of consistent forward motion, indeed a wave or a rising tide of feminism from the President's Commission on the Status of Women (1961–63) to the triumphant demonstrations for equality made by thousands across the country on 26 August 1970, fiftieth anniversary of the Suffrage Amendment. But to note that by the early nineties women remained egregiously underrepresented in the institutions of power in American society, and were still juggling jobs and families while seeking ever more elusive day care makes it clear that the trajectory of consciousness-raising and hope shot over and beyond millions of American women and underestimated the intransigence of institutions. Feminism gave them a glimpse of the gap between an ideal and their reality and, for some, language to express that understanding; but for the majority of adult American women, life at the end of the sixties was not markedly different from what it was at the beginning.

As with any social movement, the number of women who identified with feminism—through membership in consciousness-raising groups or NOW or by reading women's journals—was small, even at the decade's end. Many women who became politically active chose to put their energies elsewhere, into civil rights or antiwar movements. Most important, for most American women, the dreams and ideas of the movement were far removed from their daily reality.

Americans tend to think of social and cultural developments solely in terms of themselves. As in the nineteenth century, feminism simultaneously grew on foreign soil, inspired by Simone de Beauvoir's *The Second Sex*. French women formed the Mouvement démocratique féminin (MDF) in 1964, two years before creation of NOW. In 1965, legal reform gave French women full civil and economic rights; and in 1967 legal birth control. On 7 November 1967, the United Nations General Assembly proclaimed a Declaration of the Rights of Women.

By the late sixties there was a growing audience able and eager to hear the message of the women's movement, as evidenced by the flood of publications in 1970 alone. But for most adult women and for most of the decade, life went on as before or even became harder. Women who had married in the forties and fifties were raising children born in those years, often in isolated suburban houses to which they had moved for the children's sake. Betty Friedan spoke to these women in *The Feminine Mystique* (1963), identifying their restlessness and dissatisfaction, suggesting paid employment as an antidote; and a steadily increasing number, particularly mothers, sought it. Clearly, however, few went to work for self-expression but because the rising cost of living and accelerated demand for consumption required a second family paycheck. If they sought self-satisfaction they had to find it in traditional women's jobs and for little pay. Less than half the women in the workforce sought or found full-time employment; and women's wages relative to men's dropped from a mid-fifties 63 percent to 58 percent.[19]

The difficulties of keeping up with the effects of inflation and with the social imperative to consume were compounded for many adult women by the increasing difficulty of being mothers. As the rebellion of youth became a national phenomenon, women had to learn to live with children who looked, talked, and acted very differently from what they had expected. Mothers often acted as children's mediators with fathers and grandfathers, even with police, the FBI, and other authorities most had never expected to confront. For better or for worse, "the generation gap" posed special problems for women.

Also, a growing number of women found their marriages splitting up. There were 1,858,000 divorced American women in 1960; 3,004,000 in 1970. Marriages formed in the sixties had a higher divorce rate than those from any previous decade. Women under 25 experienced a 200.2 percent divorce rate increase, but it was a matter of the baby boom age cohort; among women 55 to 64, divorces leaped 200.6

percent. The proportion of divorcées (among whites) was greater in low-income families, leaving increasing numbers of women with high-school educations or less to find ways to support themselves and often their children, beginning a trend later labeled "the feminization of poverty."[20]

The percentage of single and widowed women in the population remained stable overall, although the number of younger single women, the "baby-boomers," increased. Adult single women usually found their opportunities and incomes limited to traditional and traditionally low-paid women's fields, regardless of educational background. As they aged, they were written out of a culture obsessed with youth and whimsy. Older women who were widowed or divorced moved deeper into poverty and isolation. The number of widowed women living alone increased markedly over the ten-year period from 1960 to 1970, from 2,993,000 to 4,685,000. Demographic historians Hugh Carter and Paul Glick cite this figure as evidence of increasing means among widows and that may well have been true for some. For others, isolation was a reflection of family breakups in an ever-more mobile society. Life alone could bring hardship as well as independence. The quarter-million elderly in nursing homes and other institutions for the aged in 1960 grew to half a million by 1970; and most were women.[21]

Black women experienced all these negative changes and at a greater rate than white women. Black women continued to have a higher labor-force participation rate than white women, typically doing jobs least valued by society.

Although there were some changes for the better in black women's lives, improvements were experienced mainly by the few whose education allowed them to take advantage of openings in professional areas. As a group, black women remained low on the economic ladder, and unheard in the councils of business and government. Black marriages broke up at a higher rate than white; and growing numbers of black women headed households. While they struggled for survival for themselves and their children, white men told them that they were matriarchs, their power destructive to black men's ambition. This accusation, first formulated by Harvard sociologist Daniel Patrick Moynihan was disproven again and again but to little avail; the matriarch tag stuck to black women already carrying more than their share of the burden.[22]

The several differentials between black women and white women suggest another reason for seeing women's history in the sixties as a pattern of fits and starts, pauses and surges. Black women's history is central to this decade. The lives of black women were not merely contrast and counterpoint to the majority of women's lives but also the moral measure. The civil rights movement, throughout so dependent on women's work, created the terms and structures that later movements for social justice adopted. The call for women's liberation and the rising consciousness with which the sixties ended could not have come into being if the civil rights movement had not shown the way.

Confronted with the reality of national injustice supported by government, education, business, and churches, many American women, black and white, learned from the civil rights movement to question authority and demonstrate against the illegitimate use of power. They marched along forbidden roads, moved outside the restrictions of home or convent walls, placed their bodies in front of military vehicles. Many women, of all ages, faced hostility and danger for resisting racism and injustice. Many gave up expectations of comfort and security to lead new and unpredictable lives. Some went to the battlefields—as Freedom Riders, teachers, and voter registration workers in the South; as nurses, relief workers, journalists, and peace-seekers in Vietnam. Many found themselves on trial and in prison for their beliefs. Not since the suffrage movement had so many middle-class women chosen to take stands and defy the law. The experience of prison for women had been primarily that of the poor. In sharing it, in discovering injustice and prison's loneliness and degradation, some middle-class white women learned another lesson that poor women and black women had known before them.

While politically active and aware white women realized their debt to black women, the social and economic gap between black and white was slow to diminish. The relation between black and white women provides an important problematic from the sixties on. Black women, with few exceptions, dismissed the call for women's liberation, seeing racism as more critical to overcome than sexism. Rare exceptions came from two important public figures—Shirley Chisholm and Pauli Murray, who both testified to the insidiousness of sexism and paralleled it with racism.

Black women's general refusal to work for women's liberation was a major problem for that movement. Younger white women, who moved beyond the earlier call for equal pay and equal treatment on the job, found it hard to bear the charge of black women that liberation was a luxury. Older white women, too, who worked for civil rights and saw women's liberation as a natural extension of that call for freedom, were troubled by black women's rejection of the newer movement. Their critique could not be ignored but in many ways the dilemma remained unresolved even into the nineties. The challenge for the nascent women's movement was to answer honestly the question: which women were moving?

Just as the rising feminism in the sixties left out black women, it also obscured another important aspect of women's lives—the conditions and culture of adult women. The sixties have become identified with the young, the "baby boom" generation that worked for civil rights, protested against involvement of higher education in the war machine, discovered the depths of injustice, identified itself also as victimized, and founded women's liberation. The story of the young is important, but equally or more so is the story of their mothers, aunts, and grandmothers. Just as young women did not have to wait for men to show the way, so older women did not have to wait for the young. In the decade's peace movements, from protests against nuclear testing to demonstrations against the Vietnam war, in the civil rights movement, in churches, in the labor movement, women well over thirty made an impact and waited for the younger generation to catch up with them.

A few names illustrate this point—civil rights leaders Ella Baker and Fannie Lou Hamer; peace activists Barbara Deming, Dorothy Day, and Dagmar Wilson; writers Eve Merriam and Muriel Rukeyser; sexual reformer Mary Steichen Calderone; labor leader Mildred Jeffrey; theorist and instigator Betty Friedan—all were over forty in 1960. Their work and ideas along with those of many of their contemporaries gave energy and direction to the sixties' movements for social change. According to opinion polls, the public also looked to mature women as models in 1969: Mamie Eisenhower, Indira Gandhi, Pat Nixon, Golda Meir, Jacqueline Kennedy Onassis, Rose Kennedy, Ethel Kennedy, Lady Bird Johnson, Queen Elizabeth II, and Senator Margaret Chase Smith were "most admired." These women were part of the "establishment," however and, in that sense, not part of the proverbial "spirit of the sixties" shared by such groups as women social activists, avant-garde artists, and radical feminists of all ages.[23]

The "spirit of the sixties," like other "spirits," is a myth, but like other myths, one that commanded wide belief then and commands even more today. Made up of intangibles, it was primarily a shift in ideology away from the old secular faith that had kept the nation together during the Depression and war time, and had reigned during the prosperity of the fifties. This faith of an older generation was undermined by multiple forces of conflict and disillusionment, forces that had a special impact often on women, who had been traditionally charged with maintaining continuity of family and community. This book offers several equally impressionistic definitions of the "spirit of the sixties."

The chapters look at women's lives within major American institutions—schools, churches, the workplace, the home, government and politics, the arts. They trace the history of women as they acted in and shaped the movements for social change that were central to the sixties. Although we have attempted to be comprehensive, surveying women's accomplishments in many areas of American culture as well as women's status in ordinary life, this book must remain an introduction. Throughout, we meet women who made a difference, those who understood how much circumstances for women needed to be changed and who tried to shape those changes. Their stories must be understood within the context of the reality of the majority of American women, a reality often far from dramatic, marked by growing economic pressure and by concern over a new order coming rapidly into being and threatening to leave them behind. Their movement was not a wave nor a tide but a number of parallel streams, some shorter, some longer, some steadily advancing, some wavering and stopping, women finding ways to survive and perhaps even to triumph in times of turmoil. In diversity women rediscovered, reaffirmed, redefined, and reframed roles in American society and culture in the sixties; but most of all, they changed the future.

1

Within the System: Women and Politics

The Kennedy Administration

The media took little note of the launching of John F. Kennedy's Presidential Commission on the Status of Women on 14 December 1961 in Human Rights Week. Over the next two years, the public remained unaware of most of its work. Americans took women's social and cultural roles for granted and might have wondered why female status required formal study, but Kennedy had many reasons to scrutinize women's status. Major changes in roles had been underway for over a decade, and political pressure had grown throughout the fifties for passage of an equal rights amendment (ERA); politicians were seeking alternate ways of coping with the changes and pressures. The ERA, first proposed by the National Women's Party (NWP) in 1923, seemed potentially viable with bipartisan support in 1943, then gained momentum under Eisenhower, when over thirty women's organizations supported it, arguing that the Supreme Court repeatedly held that existing constitutional amendments, especially the fourteenth, failed to assure women's rights, and permitted pernicious inequities in federal, state, and local laws. New guarantees were needed.[1]

A coalition of ERA opponents were ready to block the bill. Social feminists, heirs of Progressives and New Dealers, settlement house workers, the National Consumers' League, and the American Civil Liberties Union (ACLU), as well as powerful unions like the AFL-

CIO, had long claimed the ERA would single women out as the only group guaranteed treatment, wiping away protective labor legislation. It might even destroy the American family. NWP officer Emma Guffey Miller (1874–1970) explained the unionists' stance: "The idea of special protection for women is a camouflaged idea gotten up by certain labor leaders who fear women may take their jobs, but their hearts never bled for women who have jobs they do not want."[2]

Opponents had long used counterproposals, such as the Equal Pay for Equal Work and Equal Status bills, to defeat the ERA. Some legislators opposed the ERA because Southerners like South Carolina's Strom Thurmond gave lip service to women's rights in order to deflect attention from black civil rights. When the ERA passed the Senate in 1950 and 1953, Emmanuel Cellar, New York Democrat and Judiciary Committee chairman, blocked it in the House. Yet Eisenhower supported the ERA in 1957 and Women's Bureau head Alice Leopold actively backed it, reversing Labor Department policy since the thirties. By 1960 the NWP found greater ERA support among Republicans than Democrats, but remained confident that it could be passed with either party in the majority. By 1959 the bill had 41 sponsors and 213 co-sponsors in the House.[3]

Anti-ERA forces commanded a larger constituency in the 1960 election. AFL-CIO head Walter Reuther ordered affiliated unions to lobby against the ERA and to report results to Esther Eggertsen Peterson, who had been an active unionist for two decades and was Secretary of the Labor Women's Committee for Kennedy-Johnson. She and a member of the ACLU testified against the "so-called" ERA at both parties' platform hearings. Peterson spoke for 24 unions and other anti-ERA groups, questioning "what constitutes a discrimination," arguing "that orderly legislative revision—specific bills for specific ills—is the practical way to erase unwise discriminations" still in the laws. She claimed the ERA was "unnecessary because most inequalities of which its advocates complain are due to custom and tradition . . . and will and are disappearing in the natural course of social progress."[4]

The 1960 Republican platform reaffirmed a twenty-year endorsement of a constitutional amendment for women's equal rights. Democrats, with a shorter history of rather unenthusiastic support, hedged on the issue. JFK insisted on ambiguity. The Democratic platform's women's plank only supported "legislation to carry forward the progress already made toward full equality of opportunity for women as well as men" and to "guarantee equality of rights under the law, including equal pay for equal work." Kennedy only wanted to protect women workers under the Fair Labor Standards Act, and Democrats carefully avoided mention of the ERA.[5]

After Kennedy's inauguration, Katherine Pollak Ellickson suggested to Peterson that the administration form a commission to study American women's status. Ellickson was associate research director for the CIO and assistant director of the AFL-CIO Social Insurance Department; Peterson was new Assistant Secretary of Labor and Women's Bureau Director, the highest-ranking woman in Kennedy's administration. Women's Bureau sponsorship of a commission might deflect growing ERA support. The idea was not new. The Inter-American and the United Nations Commissions on the Status of Women had been active for years. Domestically, since the thirties, anti-ERA forces proposed studies of female status. The National Manpower Council suggested a study of working women in its report, *Womanpower* (1957). Yet Congressman Cellar's annual attempts to create an anti-ERA Congressional Commission on the Legal Status of Women failed through the fifties and in January of 1961.[6]

Now, Cellar's friend Peterson urged a study as she sensed growing pro-ERA pressure. While questions of women's equality became recurring jokes at presidential press conferences, with Kennedy exchanging jibes with journalist May Craig, administration officials like Peterson saw no humor. She became official bouncer, repeatedly showing aged NWP lobbyists the door with vague assurances of Kennedy's honorable intentions. Peterson's dislike of ERA proponents and concern over their influence in Congress grew. Off the record, beleaguered by being "up against the awful ERA," she characterized NWP lobbyists as elite, teetotaling old ladies, remnants of "the Old Frontier." In a 1961 memo, "The Nuisance ERA," she instructed that the bill "should not [even] be mentioned" and urged Kennedy to launch a formal investigation into women's status. Peterson easily won administration approval for a Presidential Commission on the Status of Women (PCSW) "to set forth before the world the story of women's progress in a free democracy," to highlight positive aspects of women's status, not to enumerate areas of discriminations and legal inferiority, nor to show women as desperately needing constitutional guarantees of rights as pro-ERA groups suggested.[7]

Kennedy's Executive Order 10980 stated that the commission was to identify "all barriers to the full partnership of women in our democracy" and to "demolish prejudices and outmoded customs." Peterson enlisted Eleanor Roosevelt as commission chair; and Roosevelt declared confidence "in achieving full employment and full use of America's magnificent potential," that "with appropriate manpower planning, all Americans will have a better chance to develop their individual potentials, to earn a good livelihood, and to strengthen family life."[8]

Many PCSW findings were a foregone conclusion. Prestige and publicity determined commission membership, "not so diverse that the Commission would be hopelessly divided in discussion and in its final report." PCSW credibility required that dissension not be tolerated but consensus achieved. Peterson made up a roster of five cabinet officials, two senators, and two congresswomen. Other members were nonpartisan from public and private sectors—three-fourths from politics, unions, and academe, along with others from business, law, the press, and from over thirty major national women's groups to encourage grassroots support and to solidify constituencies for its final report. Marguerite Rawalt of the National Association of Women Lawyers was the only pro-ERA member, but Peterson thought her "open to reasonable argument." Still, Peterson protested she did not stack the deck: "It was not to be a political commission," but "to come up with recommendations." As with civil rights, Kennedy favored working quietly and slowly through the courts. Peterson believed change in women's status should come gradually, conforming to Kennedy's approach to social change.[9]

The seven PCSW committees were Civil and Political Rights, Education, Private Employment, Protective Labor Legislation, Federal Employment Policies and Practices, Home and Community, and Social Insurance and Taxes. Ad hoc groups studied problems of widows' benefits, paid maternity leave, private employment, volunteer work, images of women in mass media, and black women. Birth control, abortion, rape, and women's poverty were deliberately avoided. Despite periodic hearings around the nation, news media rarely mentioned them. PCSW news, if any, typically appeared in a newspaper's "Women's Section."[10]

First, the PCSW outlined common beliefs about women's social roles. Sociologist-historian Dr. Caroline Ware's position paper echoed concern that the nation's "industrial society of abundance" use more effectively "the capacities of women to help maintain a growing economy, [to] supply . . . public and private services . . . and [to] achieve the cultural richness and human satisfaction to which our democratic society is dedicated," while not detracting from "their primary responsibility . . . in the home." "Womanpower" would be a national asset, not just a "marginal resource" tapped for paid work and volunteerism in wartime or "times of extraordinary demand" and "discarded when the emergency is past." The idea of women as underutilized resource, not as social group, permeated PCSW studies. Still, national self-scrutiny and growing numbers of working women forced commissioners to study economic and occupational roles outside the home; and post-Sputnik international competition overcame some traditional notions of women's domesticity. America had a shortage of teachers and nurses. Ware and Peterson urged expanding women's roles beyond the home, yet cited only traditionally female jobs and public service.[11]

In one report, *Women in the Defense Decade*, Katherine Brownell Oetinger, Children's Bureau head, noted that "women as a group have discovered that certain of our gifts and strengths have in the past gone largely unused . . . a world as demanding as the one in which we now live requires maximum use of the potentials of all its citizens." Echoing Kennedy's Inaugural, Commissioners repeatedly asked women to consider national interest, not their own, asking American women what they could do to bolster the nation but failing to consider what an ERA could do for women.[12]

Believing women inherently different from men, with particular strengths and weaknesses, commissioners called marriage "a partnership in which each spouse makes a different but equally important contribution," and were not ready to suggest shared responsibilities for family and home care. Reports praising women's roles outside the home still emphasized female nurturing and public moral influence. Kennedy stated that women "have brought into public affairs great sensitivity to human need and opposition to selfish and corrupt purposes." Commissioners urged "selection of women in those areas of government in which the moral tone of the community is directly affected." Such was the view of earlier social feminists, of the network of women in public office during the New Deal, and of Peterson's own circle.[13]

Commissioners publicized a positive view of American women's status to counteract examples of Communist women—in Kennedy's words, "to set before the world the story of women's progress in a free, democratic society." Most shared the philosophy of Undersecretary of Labor James O'Connell: "When a woman comes to be viewed first as a source of manpower, second as a mother, . . . we are losing much that supposedly separates us from the Communist world. The highest calling of a woman's sex is the home." The PCSW, weighing the potential national and international impact of its findings, strove to describe American women's status in such a way as to appeal to the entire Free

World. It was careful not to depict women as deprived of legal rights, yet it claimed honestly to survey discriminations.[14]

The PCSW stressed both the nuclear family as important for a strong society and also women's centrality in the home as wives and mothers, providing crucial cohesion. Peterson worried, "Women are combining activities in the home with outside work to an increasing degree but often without achieving the goals of a warm, secure home and a satisfying job which makes full use of their skills and creative ability." Ware attributed "women's restlessness" to "the lessening of religion as a vital force in our national life." Women, they thought, lacked vocation or motivation "other than self-fulfillment on the purely human and self-centered level." Increasingly, women espoused "the American value system"—individualism and equality—rather than "the Christian tradition of moral values"—feminine selflessness, a modern equivalent of the "cult of true womanhood."[15]

With "widening choices . . . beyond their doorstep," commissioners concluded, women should still be educated for domestic responsibilities. Vocational training "of all ages, educational levels, cultural and economic backgrounds" would help women "fulfill their responsibilities in health, home-making, and family life," with child care and domestic management central. Contradictions existed in trying "to strengthen family life" through traditional roles while "at the same time encouraging women to make their full contributions as citizens" to society at large. The PCSW considered family support services for women who ventured out to work, expressing "increasing recognition of social planning as a function of government at all levels." Yet, it stopped short of urging government support of child care, which was rather to be provided on a limited basis by volunteerism or professional homemaking and child rearing.[16]

When women went to work, public policy and "government responsibility" would have to preserve family by protective labor legislation based on traditional beliefs in women as the "weaker sex." One commissioner declared "real differences, both physical and social, between men and women. Nature cannot be amended." Thus, absolute equality, legal or otherwise, between men and women was impossible, not just a matter of stereotypes and prejudices. Another contended, "the need to protect women remains. Mass production methods cause strain. There is still the temptation to exploit young, inexperienced women." Whether inequalities were inherent in capitalism or gender, assumptions that women's status was and should be different from men's remained central to the PCSW's reason for being, to its opposition to an

ERA that "would destroy the safeguards society has erected around the wife and mother as the center of the family. Equality in family headship would tend to disintegrate the family. . . . If the family is to be preserved, the right of the married woman to support by her husband must be retained." Commissioners believed their work crucial for preserving society itself.[17]

After almost two years of studies, Peterson praised the unanimity in the final report on 11 October 1963, published as *American Women*, and edited by Margaret Mead and Frances Bagley Kaplan. The report summarized PCSW findings, reassuring the nation that its good society was "illuminated by values transmitted through home and church . . . and informed by present and past experience." American women had unprecedented freedoms. Remnants of inequalities and isolated discriminations were anachronisms. There was, of course, some truth in these patriotic generalizations when considered in a global, historic context.[18]

Fear of an ERA informed PCSW conclusions. Sensitive to the need to avoid blatant opposition to the ERA and potential political consequences, Peterson weighted wording carefully: "The Commission does not take a position in favor of" rather than "does not favor" or "does not favor pressing for" an ERA "at this time." But summary ERA rejection did not turn out as planned. At the last session, with all tired and ready to adjourn, Marguerite Rawalt added one small word in two places, preventing categorical rejection: "Since the Commission is convinced that the U.S. Constitution NOW embodies equality of rights for men and women, we conclude that a constitutional amendment need not NOW be sought in order to establish this principle. But judicial clarification [of the Fifth and Fourteenth Amendments] is imperative in order that remaining ambiguities with respect to the constitutional protection of women's rights be eliminated."[19]

Peterson and the Democrats eventually backed the ERA after Title VII of the 1964 Civil Rights Act outlawed discrimination based on "sex" and court cases disallowed protective labor legislation. Later, Peterson claimed Rawalt's additions did not thwart the PCSW's purpose: "We wanted to say that we did believe that women were persons and could be called persons under the fifth and fourteenth amendments . . . what we needed was a definitive case to say that. But, if we didn't get [such a court decision], we should go for the amendment." Peterson's deemphasis of anti-ERA motivations is understandable given the ERA's later history, but her apology also reflects an ambivalence over women's status that developed even while PCSW hearings were underway.[20]

The PCSW marked a watershed—as an index rather than a cause of deep social and cultural change, a landmark as the first official investigation undertaken at a time of a dramatic but quiet transformation in women's status, emerging independent of public policy, social engineering, or feminist activism. It charted changes and provided policymakers and legislators with a glimpse at new and altered gender roles already being fashioned without social theories. *American Women* appeared the same year as Betty Friedan's *The Feminine Mystique*, responding to the same undercurrents of change, the same dissonance between reality and traditional women's roles. Friedan pondered "the problem that has no name." The PCSW described the problem as minor and disappearing in the best of all possible nations. The PCSW studied ways to use women's talents effectively to strengthen the nation; and Friedan explored not only female self-realization outside the family and the home, but development of women's talents which she predicted "may well be the key to our future as a nation and a culture." Inadvertently, both the PCSW and Friedan's book premised the new feminism, yet neither was a catalyst. The growing gap between public policy and the realities of women's inferior legal status made converts to feminism from mid-decade on. PCSW reports did confirm suspicions that Americans discriminated against women overtly and subtly, thus focusing discontent. Indeed, Friedan wrote, "the very existence of the PCSW . . . creates a climate where it is possible to recognize and do something about discrimination against women in terms not only of pay but of the subtle barriers to opportunity."[21]

The PCSW inspired the formation of state commissions to document discriminations, gather data, and make recommendations for legislation to remedy inequalities. A year after *American Women* appeared, 32 state commissions existed; by 1967, all fifty states had one—most of which compiled statistics on inequalities in all areas of women's lives. Many women state commissioners came from national women's organizations. Some were among the few women to have forged prominent professional or political careers. Many believed in working within "the system" for social reforms to extend women's rights incrementally on the state and national level in the absence of an ERA. State commissions received support from the new Interdepartmental Committee on the Status of Women (ICSW) and the Citizens' Advisory Council on the Status of Women (CACSW). The ICSW consisted of top cabinet officers. The CACSW was a body of twenty private citizens appointed by President Johnson, after Kennedy's assassination, to serve as liaison between existing women's organizations, state commissions, and federal agencies; it was advisory only. In 1965, when the CACSW and the ICSW urged the Equal Employment Opportunity Commission (EEOC) to ban gender-segregated employment want ads, the recommendation was essentially ignored, prompting Congresswoman Martha Griffiths (D-Michigan) to decry on the House floor on 30 June 1966 the EEOC's "specious, negative and arrogant" attitude toward sex discrimination, contrary to "an oath to uphold the law." She argued, "I have never entered a door labeled 'men' and I doubt that [a man] has frequently entered the women's room. . . . The same principle operates in the job-seeking process." Ten days later, state commission representatives meeting in their third national conference formed the National Organization for Women (NOW) to fight the institutionalized lethargy.[22]

The CACSW helped highlight major problems in American women's status. Under former Senator Maurine Neuberger, it set up a Task Force on Family Law and Policy, urging revision of property laws to protect the interests of married women in common-law states and equal rights for illegitimate as well as legitimate children. The CACSW tackled controversial issues—married women's domiciles, grounds for divorce, alimony, and child custody. It even advocated decriminalization of abortion and repeal of laws limiting access to birth control.

In this political climate, an Equal Pay Act, first proposed in 1945 and favored by Peterson and the Women's Bureau, finally passed in 1963. Authored by Congresswoman Edith Green (D-Oregon), it amended the 1938 Fair Labor Standards Act. Although it still excluded administrative, executive, professional, domestic, and agricultural employees, it was a triumph for the National Federation of Business and Professional Women (NFBPW), which had long lobbied for it. For the first time, a federal law addressed sex discrimination, requiring that women doing the same work as men be paid the same wages, at least in certain clearly demarcated areas. It negated some state laws mandating a higher male minimum wage.[23]

The Equal Pay Act had many shortcomings. It still did not cover domestic or agricultural work, jobs held by poorer women; and it continued to exclude executive, administrative, and professional workers. It did not compel equality in hiring practices nor did it set up an independent enforcement mechanism, leaving that to the Labor Department's Wage and Hour Division; yet complaints rose from 351 in 1965 to 565 in fiscal 1970. Although to achieve passage of the act supporters eliminated "job comparability," limiting application to a narrow spectrum of jobs performed by *both* women and men, courts occasionally extended the law as in October 1969 when the Dallas federal court ruled "substantially equal" the work of male hospital orderlies and female nurses' aides. The United Auto Workers (UAW) used the law to eliminate hourly wage differentials in only a few job categories. "The act nonetheless bore important signs of tokenism," feminists complained. Indeed, a call for an equal pay law had been a standard anti-ERA ploy.[24]

The Equal Pay Act's shortcomings did serve as catalysts for more sweeping proposals. The International Union of Electrical Workers (IUEW) called for judicial and administrative recognition of "comparable worth" under federal antidiscrimination statues. The proposal that "comparable" job categories, some of which had been gender-segregated as a means of discrimination, should be considered together for federal regulation of equal pay was a radical but necessary concept that would engender great debate but little action through the seventies and beyond.[25]

The Johnson Era: Civil Rights Act of 1964 and Affirmative Action

The Johnson administration took a different approach to the status of women and of minorities, its policies advocating equality in the workplace, education, and the law. A comprehensive Civil Rights bill passed in 1964; but in the House, eighty-one-year-old Virginia Democrat Howard W. Smith tried to discredit it by adding to Title VII a "little amendment," the category of "sex" along with "race, color, religion, or national origin" against which employers could not discriminate in hiring, firing, compensation, benefits, privileges, and conditions of employment. The act contained various "titles," sections prohibiting discrimination in public accommodations, federally funded programs, employment, and other areas. Congresswoman Edith Green was the only woman against the addition, arguing with others that it could destroy the bill. Although the amendment was greeted with laughter on the House floor, it passed, largely through the efforts of Congresswoman Martha Griffiths, with lawyer Pauli Murray (1910–1985) and Mary Eastwood of the Justice Department doing the crucial behind-the-scenes work. A female voice in the gallery rang out: "We made it! God bless America!"[26]

The five-member Equal Employment Opportunities Commission (EEOC), formed to enforce provisions of the Civil Rights Act and adjudicate Title VII complaints, was lax in combating sex discrimination. EEOC member Aileen Hernandez explained, "It's the kind of law that raises the hopes of a lot of people but doesn't provide any means." An amendment let employers differentiate on the basis of sex in wages if, under the Equal Pay Act, exceptions were based on seniority, merit, differences in quantity or quality of production—any factor other than sex, but factors traditionally used as loopholes to women's detriment. EEOC Director Herman Edlesberg dared call the clause against sex discrimination "a fluke . . . conceived out of wedlock." Even Dr. Mary Keyserling, Johnson's Women's Bureau head, and other female federal officials were reluctant to use Title VII to promote women's equality. Actually, all the EEOC could do was negotiate conciliation, recommend that the Attorney General sue on behalf of the aggrieved, or tell the complainant to bring suit herself.[27]

Job discrimination was institutionalized and insidious. Classified job advertisements in newspapers remained segregated into "Help Wanted Male" and "Help Wanted Female" columns. Higher paying commissioned sales, management, and professional positions were listed in the former and lower paying clerical, counter sales, pink collar, and domestic jobs in the latter. Pressed by the new National Organization for Women (NOW) and the National Federation of Business and Professional Women (NFBPW), the EEOC ruled in the summer of 1968 that segregated classified ads have "a discriminatory effect by indicating an employer preference and discouraging . . . the qualified woman job seeker."[28]

Yet Title VII contained a loophole, the Bona Fide Occupations Qualification (*bfoq*) clause permitting employers to reject women for some jobs—like men's clothing model, actor in a male role, men's restroom attendant. Title VII became a joke, dubbed the "bunny law" after a member of the White House Conference on Equal Opportunity in 1965 wondered if the law would force Playboy Clubs to hire male waiters. The press had a field day. In a front-page article, "Can She Pitch for the Mets?" the *New York Times* editorialized, "it would have been better if Congress had just abolished sex itself. . . . Everything has to be neuterized. Housemaid becomes a dirty word. . . . Handyman must disappear from the language. . . . No more milkman, iceman, serviceman, foreman or pressman. . . . The Rockettes may become bisexual, and a pity, too. . . . Bunny problem, indeed? This is revolution, chaos. You can't even safely advertise for a wife any more."[29]

To the horror of unionists, Title VII threatened to overturn state protective legislation applying to women. Through 1968, the EEOC tried to preserve such legislation under the *bfoq* loophole; but it began a case-by-case review of conflicts. Caroline Davis of UAW asked for "a policy saying that state laws affecting women cannot be used as a justification for discrimination." In August 1969, in "Discrimination Because of Sex," EEOC did an about-face, declaring that "state laws and regulations, although originally promulgated for the purpose of protecting females, have ceased to be relevant to our technology or to the expanding role of the female worker in our economy." Thus, the EEOC eliminated a major historical area of objection to an equal rights amendment—that it would negate valuable protective legislation. If those laws were anachronistic, their preservation could no longer be argued as an excuse for rejecting the ERA. Still, change in state laws did not occur overnight.[30]

Aided by NOW, the NFBPW, Human Rights for Women (HRW), and other groups, litigation produced a series of EEOC rulings and lower court decisions. In response to 1968 charges against American Airlines, the EEOC banned firing of stewardesses at a certain age, often 32, establishing the principle "that if all employees in one job classification are members of one sex, any conditions of employment . . . cannot be based on sex." In 1969 alone, 7,500 people filed charges of sex discrimination with the EEOC. The first sex discrimination suit by the Justice Department, *U.S. v. Libbey-Owens-Ford, United Glass and Ceramic Workers of North America, AFL-CIO, Local No. 9*, protesting segregation of women employees in a single plant with less-desirable, lower-paid jobs, did not reach the Supreme Court until 1970; and even at this level it produced a "sellout," a settlement out of court through a consent decree, not a precedent-setting ruling.[31]

In 1967, pressured by NOW, Lyndon Johnson signed Executive Order 11375, prohibiting discrimination by the federal government and its contractors because of sex, although official guidelines were not issued for 17 months. Previously, many federal agencies had had "full discretion" to limit any job to one sex and half of all government notices for administrative and professional positions had stipulated "men only" because of "arduous or dangerous duties, travel, rotating assignments, exposure to hazardous weather, unfavorable geographical locations, bad neighborhood working environments, or contact with the public." Reasons for "women only" jobs had "involved monotonous, detailed, or repetitive duties." Through enforcement by the Labor Department Office of Federal Contract Compliance (OFCC), Executive Order 11375 was used to sue firms with unfair hiring practices or unequal pay policies for equal work; and it forced Departments like Defense and Health, Education, and Welfare to do routine compliance checks on companies before awarding contracts. The OFCC held economic leverage over firms reluctant to comply but did little to end discrimination against women, lacking specific goals and timetables. Executive Order 11375 did expand Kennedy's 1962 directive outlawing discrimination in federal employment, forcing the Civil Service Commission to create the Federal Women's Program with coordinators in each federal agency mandated actively to recruit and promote women. Because of these limitations, women's groups charged "bureaucratic lip service."[32]

In October 1965, Johnson signed an immigration bill, the "family reunification" act instigated by Kennedy in 1963, which reformed federal policy by abolishing the national origins quota system in place for four decades and permitting admittance of more immigrant women and other family members to the United States, particularly from the Third World. In another law signed the following November, he permitted 250,000 Cuban refugees, who had been admitted to the United States as "parolees" after Castro's 1959 revolution and the 1961 Bay of Pigs fiasco, to apply for visas and citizenship; and many quickly became permanent resident aliens. Adjustments to these laws admitted many Greeks, Italians, Portuguese, Chinese, Koreans, and Filipinos, about 60 percent of them women, many of whom filled low-paying garment-industry jobs.[33]

A final advance for women came in 1968, in the last year of Johnson's administration, with amendment of the Internal Revenue Code to permit widows and single women over 35 who had never married or who were separated or divorced for a year or more to claim head of household status and benefits; 13 million women were affected.

The Nixon Years

Nixon did little to implement or expand upon Johnson's actions to improve the status of women. Only pressure by women's groups forced the OFCC to be more proactive, requiring firms doing federal government business to write "affirmative action" plans, detailed schedules for working more women and minorities into middle- and upper-level positions.[34]

Intensely lobbied by Republican Congresswomen Florence Dwyer (New Jersey), Catherine Barnes May (Washington), Charlotte Reid (Illinois), and Margaret Heckler (Massachusetts), Nixon in October

1969 formed the President's Task Force on Women's Rights and Responsibilities, one of 14 groups charged with collecting information for his State of the Union address and, like Kennedy's Presidential Commission on the Status of Women, an exercise in media manipulation. ERA opponents traditionally spoke of "responsibilities" to weaken emphasis on rights. Nixon's short-lived Task Force, ten prominent women and two men, headed by Virginia Allen, the Executive Vice-President of a Michigan drug store chain and a former NFBPW President, detailed discriminations against women and how to combat them. At press conferences, columnist Vera Glaser goaded Nixon for not placing more women in policy-making posts. She wrote that although "some White House staffers pooh-poohed inclusion of the 'woman question,'" the task force was created largely because presidential counselor Dr. Arthur Burns thought the subject important. Although its timely report went to the White House, Nixon failed to mention women in his State of the Union message, tried to suppress the document, and ignored its recommendations.[35]

Yet, bootleg copies of the Task Force report, *A Matter of Simple Justice*, circulated widely and were serialized in 1970 by the *Miami Herald* and other papers with stories of an "administration cover-up" because of "its militant tone and far-reaching recommendations." *Simple Justice* went no further than *American Women*, but it was "stronger and more urgent" than any former federally-sponsored report, charging that the United States "lags behind other enlightened, and indeed some newly emerging, countries in the role ascribed to women," that discrimination against women was "so widespread and pervasive" that it had "come to be regarded, more often than not, as normal." To no avail, it advocated creating a Conference and an Office of Women's Rights and Responsibilities, appointment of women to high-level government jobs, and presidential pressure for the ERA; but Nixon's Executive Order 11478 in August 1969 only suggested that the Labor Department issue guidelines to implement Executive Order 11375, providing no new enforcement plan nor expanded opportunities. After protests from women's groups and Women's Bureau head Elizabeth Koontz, *Simple Justice* was officially released, accompanied by Labor Department sex discrimination guidelines for federal contractors, at the 9 June 1970 Women's Bureau Fiftieth Anniversary Conference. It was Patricia Nixon, not the President, who opened the conference, insisting that her husband favored the ERA. Two days of "brainstorming" workshops attracted a thousand women ranging from "conservative-reformist to radical feminist" and ended with a pro-ERA resolution. *Simple Justice* prompted proposals of several women's bills in the early seventies, but none passed. Koontz was responsible for the only pro-women activism in Nixon's administration, guiding the Women's Bureau into advocacy of the ERA. Her *1969 Handbook on Women Workers* became the movement's "bible, of sorts."[36]

In June 1970, NOW filed a blanket complaint of sex discrimination against more than 1,300 corporations and 300 colleges and universities receiving federal funds. Labor Department Order No. 4 early in 1970 mandated affirmative action programs; but even these had a minimal and slow effect on the workplace, largely because of Labor Department foot-dragging under James Hodgson. The Labor Department suggested, but did not require action, despite goading by NOW President Aileen Hernandez. Throughout the Johnson and Nixon years, however, legislation, executive orders, and litigation began to diffuse traditional ERA opposition. Because of Executive Order 11375 in 1967, Stephen Schlossberg, UAW General Counsel, finally reported to the EEOC that protective legislation was "a millstone around the necks of women at work," although the union did not totally withdraw its opposition to the ERA. Johnson reiterated personal support for an ERA in 1967, as did Nixon in the 1968 presidential campaign. Still, in 1968 as in 1964, both parties omitted for the ERA from their platforms.[37]

On 11 August 1970, amid the growing feminism, generational struggles, and a political turn to conservatism, the ERA was again introduced in Congress after Martha Wright Griffiths (D-Michigan) had used a rare parliamentary tactic, the discharge petition, to dislodge the amendment from the Judiciary Committee. It passed and without the old "Hayden rider" to keep state protective laws intact. The Senate did not vote because the bill did not emerge from the Subcommittee on Constitutional Amendments of the Judiciary Committee, headed by Senator Birch Bayh (D-Indiana), and because of nine riders proposed by Senator Sam Ervin, Jr. (D-North Carolina) to "protect" wives, mothers, widows, and women workers and exempt women from the draft and combat. Bayh gave credit to the effective lobbying of NOW Board Chairman Wilma Scott Heide and other feminists for the hearings that finally brought the bill to the Senate floor in 1971. In October 1971, the House voted 354 to 24 in its favor; and finally on 22 March 1972, after 49 years and by a vote of 84 to 8, the Senate sent the ERA to the states for ratification. Amendment supporters ranged from very conservative Republican women, "some of whom find 'feminism a dirty word,' to the most radical feminists who challenge the institutions of marriage, the family, and in fact define sexual relationships as a political institution to be restructured." Absent from the anti-ERA forces for the first time were the major unions, although most did not work for it actively. The UAW became the first national union to endorse the ERA in 1970; but the AFL-CIO did not lend lip-service to the amendment until 1973. Many unionists still disliked the idea. By 1975, only fourteen states had ratified the ERA, while sixteen rejected it. Opponents included many conservatives and Southern male politicians, some unionists, and some radical New Left women. The Congressional votes had not reflected the extent of persisting ERA opposition nor the lack of fervor in its favor, factors that proved problematic through the seventies and led to the ratification failure.[38]

Of the two possible constitutional means for ratification by the states—by seated legislatures or by elected convention of 38 or three-quarters of all states—ERA framers chose the former, less democratic and less apt to result in ratification. Although the ratification period was extended from 1979 to 1982, anti-ERA forces regrouped and successfully stemmed any momentum the amendment had. It was not ratified and died, although in the meantime several states enacted their own equal rights amendments.

Litigation and Women

By the sixties' end, a body of judicial precedents favoring women's rights had grown sufficiently to have a positive influence on subsequent decisions. The trend in litigation impelled legislative reform: development of the new field of "sex discrimination law," nonexistent in 1965, implied "a stunning achievement for women and for a social movement." The challenge was that traditions and remnants of English common law still deprived married women of rights in many states. Some local laws restricted employment and stipulated maximum sentences for women for certain crimes. In some places, women could not work at hotel desks after six p.m. but could work all night cleaning. The 1964 Civil Rights Act created "a bar of women's-rights litigators," which "developed and immediately began to challenge in court age-old stereotypes" used to deny women jobs. Litigation, thereafter, aimed to apply the Fourteenth Amendment's equal protection clause to women; and many women's organizations supported litigants to win constitutional rights for women through court precedents.[39]

Most decisions pertaining to women were based on race, not gender, since courts held that the Fourteenth Amendment did not apply to women. *McLaughin v. Florida* (1964) tested a Florida statute making it a crime for a biracial, mixed gender couple to "occupy in the nighttime the same room," even without sexual intercourse, punishable for up to a year in jail for each person. The judgment against the law decried "the state police power which trenches upon the constitutionally protected freedom from invidious official discrimination based on race," not on gender, leaving standing many state laws punishing fornication, adultery, and "lewd cohabitation." Also based on race, not sex, *Loving v. Virginia* (1967) declared anti-miscegenation laws unconstitutional.[40]

A late-sixties shift in judicial mentality concerning women's legal status appears in contrasting *Hoyt v. Florida* (1961) and *Billy Taylor v. Louisiana* (1975), both involving jury-selection procedures excluding women. In *Hoyt*, the Court relied on the "myth" of women's fragility and inability to hear gruesome testimony about a wife's murdering her husband with a baseball bat. It rejected the defense argument that because the husband's infidelity caused the attack "women jurors would have been more understanding or compassion than men in assessing the quality of the appellant's act and her defense of 'temporary insanity.'" Florida gave women "the privilege" to volunteer for jury duty but did not require service as for men because "woman is still regarded as the center of home and family life." In 1963, 26 states still exempted women from jury service for excuses men could not claim. Florida rejected its "volunteers only" approach to women's jury duty in 1967. In 1970, only Louisiana retained a statute prohibiting female jury service, not rescinded until the Supreme Court issued the *Taylor* decision. *Hoyt* was the last case in which the Supreme Court applied the traditional "ordinary equal protection scrutiny" approach to women's rights.[41]

In *Taylor*, a male criminal defendant successfully challenged his conviction on the grounds that his jury was not "a fair cross section of the community." Louisiana let women claim an automatic jury service exemption and most did so. The Court concluded that "If it was ever the case that women were unqualified to sit on juries or were so situated that none of them should be required to perform jury service, that time has long since passed."[42]

Landmark cases of the sixties ranged over many issues. In *Griswold v. Connecticut* (1965), the Supreme Court broke new ground in using the "right of privacy" in the Bill of Rights as basis for decisions on marital intimacy, specifically striking down prohibitions on distribution and use of contraception. In 1961, the head of Connecticut's

Planned Parenthood League and a physician at New Haven's public clinic were arrested for giving information to married persons about contraception. Connecticut law made it a crime punishable by sixty days to a year in jail or a $50 fine to use "any drug . . . or instrument for the purpose of preventing conception" or "to aid, abet, or advise someone else" as an "accessory." Although not suggesting that unmarried persons had similar rights to privacy, *Griswold* paved the way for *Eisenstadt v. Baird* (1972), a case in favor of birth-control activist Bill Baird, arrested for passing a package of spermicidal vaginal foam to an unmarried female Boston University student in felonious violation of Massachusetts law, and more importantly for *Roe v. Wade* (1973), legalizing abortion on demand.[43]

By the decade's end, the EEOC was unprepared for the large number of wage and sex discrimination cases brought under Title VII. In *Weeks v. Southern Bell Telephone and Telegraph Company* (1968), the Fifth Circuit Court of Appeals ruled that to prove a "bona fide occupational qualification" (*bfoq*) an employer needed "reasonable cause" and "factual basis for believing, that all or substantially all women would be unable to perform safely and efficiently the duties of the job involved." It undermined state protective labor laws, specifically a Georgia statute limiting weights women could lift on the job, by concluding that "Title VII rejects just this type of romantic paternalism . . . and instead vests individual women with the power to decide whether or not to take on unromantic tasks. Men have always had the right to determine whether the increase in remuneration for strenuous, dangerous, obnoxious or unromantic tasks" was worthwhile; "women are now on equal footing."[44]

Other litigation started in the sixties, and resolved in the seventies, successfully challenged employment discrimination based on sex. In 1971, *Diaz v. Pan American World Airways, Inc.* held that airlines could not use gender as a *bfoq* in hiring only women as stewardesses; and the job title was changed to flight cabin attendant. Also in 1971, *Sproqis v. United Air Lines, Inc.*, the culmination of NOW efforts, overturned policies banning married stewardesses.[45]

Culminating the sixties, 1971 "initiated a new epoch in women's rights litigation" and "a new wave of interpretations of the equal protection clause," first with the seminal Supreme Court judgment in *Reed v. Reed* (1971) that "women as a class had a constitutional right to the equal protection of the law." Over their son's will, Sally Reed challenged her husband and Idaho statutes preferring men over women as estate administrators. The Supreme Court led by Chief Justice Warren

Burger found such sexism "arbitrary" and contrary to the Fourteenth Amendment's equal protection clause. Henceforth, the Supreme Court considered women among other "groups for whom the statutory denial of benefits would be treated as semisuspect," although that policy remained tacit until *Craig v. Boren* (1976).[46]

Women in Politics and Government

The "indefatigable" Eleanor Roosevelt remained a political force behind and in front of the scenes until her death on 7 November 1962—the end of an era; but she had seen in the new and helped set it on firm footing. At the 1960 Democratic convention at age 75, and looking, wrote Norman Mailer, "fine, precise, hand-worked like ivory," she crusaded for a ticket led by Adlai Stevenson, with the young Massachusetts Senator in second place to give him "the opportunity to grow and learn." To her dismay, Stevenson lost the nomination because an influential male coalition, including her three sons, backed John F. Kennedy. Candidate Kennedy courted Mrs. Roosevelt, travelling to Hyde Park as to "a summit meeting of two sovereigns," and won her support. She would be an active campaigner, crucial to his victory, especially by bringing in the black and ethnic vote.[47]

After Kennedy's election, Roosevelt served as his personal counselor on style and as a public commentator through her syndicated column. In 1962 alone, Roosevelt chaired the PCSW, sponsored hearings on the Hill to permit civil rights workers to testify about police and judicial harassment in the South, and lobbied Congress for equal pay laws. She was JFK's "roving ambassador," as she had been for FDR, accentuating her favorite themes—the underprivileged and international peace. Kennedy appointed her to the American delegation to the United Nations General Assembly, the Peace Corps Advisory Council, and the Tractors for Freedom Committee after the Bay of Pigs fiasco. She added her voice to those of the Women Strike for Peace (WSP) in urging him to negotiate a nuclear test ban treaty over Pentagon objections; and he nominated her for the Nobel Peace Prize. Still, she could not persuade him to end America's entanglement in Vietnam or to do more for migratory workers and blacks—or perhaps her death and his assassination cut short that work.

Roosevelt badgered JFK to place more women in responsible administration positions and on the federal bench; but the few he appointed—42 in all—were not egalitarian activists. Kennedy proved as much a gradualist as Eisenhower on civil rights; yet in the year of Eleanor Roosevelt's death, Kenneth issued an order, largely through her urging, nullifying an 1870 federal law barring women from top-level civil service jobs. Esther Peterson, as Assistant Secretary of Labor and Women's Bureau head, was Kennedy's highest ranking woman. In 1962, Kennedy appointed Persia Crawford Campbell (1898–1974), Chair of the Consumers' Union Board, to the President's Council of Economic Advisors. Johnson reappointed her and in 1964 made her the Presidential Representative on International Trade Negotiation. Campbell, specializing in issues of the Pacific rim and Southeast Asia, participated in many international conferences and worked with the United Nations.[48]

Still, Jacqueline ("Jackie") Bouvier Kennedy (1929–) stole the show as the most visible woman public figure from 1960 to 1963 and one of the most charismatic First Ladies ever at a time of intense new media scrutiny of the White House. Her major project was the historic redecoration of the Executive Mansion after she persuaded Congress to declare it a Smithsonian Institution museum. Her televised tour of the result showed her as consummate hostess and connoisseur. She was the beautiful young mother of two toddlers—the quintessential woman in terms of the era's ideals—but far from the typical housewife. She championed the arts, genteel culture, and sophisticated style, but rarely impinged on male political territory. Reporters wondered at her displays of "political naiveté." One commentator felt she had "her own special kind of intelligence, but in the feminine, intuitional sense." A December 1961 Gallup poll on most admired women placed her second to Eleanor Roosevelt. Jackie was not upset; repeatedly she insisted, "I'm *not* Mrs. Roosevelt."[49]

Some historians judge that only Eleanor Roosevelt surpasses Claudia Alta Taylor ("Lady Bird") Johnson (1913–) in importance as First Lady; and LBJ fostered the association, identifying his administration with "that very great, grand, and lovely lady" at a series of memorial tributes; but Lady Bird was her own woman. She was the head of several Texas businesses valued at $5 million, and was adept at getting things done. She was a tireless campaigner in the 1960 election, helping turn Texas Democratic for her husband the vice presidential candidate. As a no-nonsense First Lady, mother of two teen-aged girls, she made three to four national tours annually to promote "Great Society" programs, doing grassroots lobbying for educational programs like the Teacher Corps. She avidly took on social causes, serving as honorary chair of Operation Head Start, which was to educate five-year-olds.[50]

Lady Bird Johnson aggressively championed environmental issues, including social problems in inner city neighborhoods. Under her influence, not just the White House, but Washington itself became more attractive. In addition to park improvements, she urged historic restoration of Pennsylvania Avenue from the Capitol to the White House through her Committee for a More Beautiful Capital; but she also urged beautifying public schools in city slums and passage of the Highway Beautification Act of 1965. Her 1965 White House Conference on Natural Beauty inspired 30 state conferences. In 1966, executives of major oil companies met with Mrs. Johnson to discuss the sightliness of service stations. Helped by the Farmers' Union, she launched Project Green Thumb, which recruited retired farmers who worked three to four days a week to improve highway borders. The media often trivialized her crusades as only removing unsightly roadside billboards and planting wildflowers, programs long championed by the National Association of Women's Clubs. Rather, Lady Bird attracted public attention and energies to environmentalism.[51]

Contemporary commentators Averell Harriman and David Lilienthal praised Lady Bird for her influence on LBJ's policies. On LBJ's inauguration, columnist Doris Fleeson wrote, "We have two Presidents." Yet when LBJ decided not to seek a second term, an aide commented that Lady Bird had exerted no pressure: "She's not that kind of woman." She did, however, help bring into the White House strong women like Elizabeth "Liz" Carpenter, LBJ's Secretary and later a loyal Hubert Humphrey supporter. Carpenter credits Lady Bird with being a positive political force, the "'gentle hand,' often softening the hurts her husband inflicted on his staff members, mediating quarrels between aides, and winning over her husband's opponents."[52]

Lady Bird Johnson gave an unexpected lecture to the American Home Economics Association in 1964, urging women to take more active roles in "The Great Society." Echoing the spirit of the PCSW, she declared, "Today the nation cannot afford to waste the talents of American women. With the lengthening of the life span and the shortening of the hours needed to run the house and raise the children, a great deal of talent and time is available" to women to be used in diverse public causes, particularly those aimed at rooting out poverty on the local level. She urged all to become involved in politics as well as volunteerism: "I am only one of 65 million American women." She lauded disappearance of the "cynical feeling . . . that politics is an ugly business in which no woman should soil her hands. . . . One of the most difficult problems in government today—federal, state or local—is recruiting really superior minds for the highly professional public offices. One solution . . . is to tap the immense reservoir of talent . . . among American women."[53]

Lady Bird Johnson apparently convinced LBJ, for he had a better record than Kennedy in appointing women—an unprecedented 150 in the executive branch alone, 75 percent of whom were married with children. LBJ insisted that their White House welcome reception not be a women-only event, declaring, "Their husbands are prouder of them than anybody else." One of those women was Virginia Mae Brown (1924–1991), a West Virginia lawyer and the state's assistant attorney general, appointed to the Interstate Commerce Commission (ICC). When Brown became ICC Chairman under Nixon in 1969, she was the first woman to head an independent administrative federal agency. Johnson made Margaret Hickey, public affairs editor of the *Ladies' Home Journal*, Chairman of his Citizens' Advisory Council on the Status of Women. He also appointed minority women: Patricia Harris as U.S. ambassador to Luxembourg, Charlotte Hubbard as deputy assistant Secretary of State, Frankie Freeman as U.S. Civil Rights Commission member, and Aileen Hernandez to the EEOC. LBJ made a federal judge of 45-year-old Constance Baker Motley, who rose from being NAACP Legal Defense and Education Fund aide to argue successfully nine NAACP cases before the U.S. Supreme Court by 1964 and later win election to the New York State Senate. Evelyn Harrison helped with the extensive recruiting of women for government work, noting that Johnson wanted "to underline our profound belief that we can waste no talent." In 1964 alone, there were over 70 presidential appointments of women and hiring or promotion of over two thousand to jobs in the then prestigious $10–20,000 per year range, including the first woman on the Atomic Energy and Federal Trade Commissions and the Board of the Export-Import Bank.[54]

Some women had important positions in the Nixon administration beginning in 1969, although First Lady Patricia "Pat" Nixon presented a demure, low-keyed image reminiscent of Mamie Eisenhower. When Nixon named Shirley Temple Black to the U.S. delegation to the United Nations in 1969, journalists joked that she "was clearly marked for a diplomatic career ever since she single-handedly negotiated a truce between rebel Hindu tribes and the forces of the British raj in *Wee Willie Winkie*," a thirties film. Nixon's most activist woman appointee was Women's Bureau head Elizabeth Duncan Koontz (1919–), a Democrat. Through her work for civil rights, improving working conditions for teachers, promoting bilingual education, eliminating discriminatory curricula for minorities like American Indians, and establishing students' rights, she earned her 1968 election as the first black woman President of the million-member National Education Association (NEA), where she started the Center for Human Relations. She insisted on the minimum wage for domestic workers, who were mostly minorities. She took a feminist stance to end various discriminations, many ingrained in protective labor laws for women, and many of which she said "had been used to hold women back." She persuaded the Labor Department to break with its traditional stance and support the ERA.[55]

Yet Nixon's administration harbored reactionary forces, and feminists increasingly read both subtle and blatant signals of unfriendliness. Vice President Spiro Agnew told the American Management Association in March 1969: "Three things have been difficult to tame—fools, women, and the ocean. We are beginning to tame the ocean, but don't have luck with fools and women." Mrs. Agnew proclaimed that in college she had "majored in marriage."[56]

Through the sixties, numbers and percentages of women declined in national electoral politics. In 1961, there were two woman Senators and 15 Congresswomen—9 Democrats and 6 Republicans—an all-time high. The only women in the Senate were Maurine B. Neuberger (D-Oregon), from 1960 to 1966, and Margaret Chase Smith (R-Maine), repeatedly elected after her husband's death. Among those who persisted in Congress were Edith Starrett Green (D-Oregon) and Martha Wright Griffiths (D-Michigan), who entered Congress in 1955 and remained powerful politicians throughout the sixties.

In 1964, Griffiths served on the Banking and Currency Committee and became the first woman on the powerful Ways and Means Committee, helping to frame federal tax policy and working to eliminate economic discriminations against women in social security, insurance, and federal employee benefits; but, like Green, she had little sympathy for welfare recipients. Griffiths was instrumental in passing the 1964 Civil Rights Act that included mention of "sex" in Title VII, and later the ERA. In 1967, she criticized high Defense Department spending. Griffiths, like Patsy Takemoto Mink (D-Hawaii) and Margaret M. Heckler (R-Massachusetts), had legal training; and important to their success were supportive husbands as campaign managers, active advisors, strategists, and sounding boards.[57]

By 1970, despite the PCSW, the state commissions, and rise of feminism, women held less than 3 percent of elective offices. They counted among their numbers only 11 Congresswomen—6 Democrats and 5

Republicans—among 535 Representatives, and one Senator. The number of women in state elective offices—secretaries of states, treasurers, supreme court justices—fell from 41 to 31 from 1960 to 1970; in state legislatures, from 346 to 306, about 5 percent of all seats. The sole woman governor was Lurleen Wallace, elected in Alabama in 1966 as a surrogate for her husband George, who was constitutionally barred by his state constitution from another term.

Women slowly moved into state and local electoral politics—a few aldermen or city council members, city treasurers, recorders of deeds, county and municipal court judges. Blatant sexism made office-seeking difficult. Karen DeCrow, NOW Membership Chairman, remembers that during her 1969 campaign on the Liberal Party ticket for mayor of Syracuse one reporter badgered her for her body measurements; one opponent asked her in a debate, "Why do you hate men so?"; and another sneered, "City Hall had ladies before, but they were there to clean the floor." DeCrow could not muster a women's constituency: "Some women told me we all belong in the kitchen." Others called her "a credit to [area] girls." She was defeated. Women voters proved more apathetic than men; in 1964, 72 percent of registered males cast ballots compared to 67 percent of females. When women voted, it was usually without a feminist consciousness.[58]

Yet Democrat Bella Abzug used her position as national legislative chairwoman of Women Strike for Peace (WSP) as a springboard to Congress from New York's Nineteenth District. Her activist campaign declared, "The Pentagon is still running the country. Yet all the things that really matter to people—like security, health, a decent place to live, and a hopeful future for ourselves and our children—are shoved aside." She pledged "not to vote another penny for military spending until we heal our country's wounds," to fight to abolish the draft, and to "challenge the seniority system that denies the reality of American life." Her promises sounded radical: "I will fight against the discrimination that condemns most working women to low paying jobs, gives women welfare instead of income, keeps them out of the professions, denies them day care facilities and miseducates their children, gives third-rate health care to Black, Puerto Rican and poor women, and forces them to risk their lives by submitting to illegal abortions."[59]

In 1964, Shirley Chisholm (1924–) was elected assemblywoman in New York's 12th Congressional District after a decade's struggle for black representation there. She built upon a sociology major at Brooklyn College, a master's degree in early childhood education at Columbia, a diploma in education administration, and teaching to become in 1968 the first black woman elected to Congress. Other black women won state office: Daisy Elliott and Maxine Young in the Michigan legislature; Daisy Lloyd in Indiana; Willie Glanton in Iowa; De Verne Calloway in Missouri; Grace Towns Hamilton in Georgia, first Negro woman state legislator in the Deep South; and Sarah Anderson, Susie Monroe, and Frances Jones in the Pennsylvania House. Verda Welcome, a Baltimore teacher, won a Maryland Senate seat in 1962 and survived a 1964 assassination attempt.[60]

These successes, and the civil rights movement, encouraged some young black women to enter politics. In 1966, attorney Barbara Jordan (1936–) persisted despite 1962, 1964, and 1966 defeats for state office in Texas and advice of a "friendly" Rice University professor: "You know it's going to be hard for you to win a seat in the Texas legislature. You've got too much going against you: you're black, you're a woman and you're large. People don't really like that image." Jordan became the first black in the Texas Senate since 1882, a springboard to three terms in the U.S. Congress beginning in 1972 and a major role on the House Judiciary Committee investigating Watergate in 1974.[61]

Women continued to work behind the scenes as volunteers in electoral politics and to win positions on state Democratic and Republican committees, although the pattern of a male national chairman and female vice-chairman continued. Mildred Jeffrey (1911–) rose from the Amalgamated Clothing Workers of America in Michigan to the National Democratic Platform Committee in 1960 and then to the National Executive Committee. As head of the new Equal Rights Committee (1965) demanded by the Mississippi Freedom Democrats, Jeffrey insisted in 1968 that all Southern delegations have black members—and a quota of at least 10 percent for states with black populations over 20 percent. She wanted to require all delegations to pledge support for the 1964 Civil Rights Act and the 1965 Voting Rights Act; but Democrats shelved these controversial proposals, fearing it would destroy their old "Solid South."[62]

On the other end of the political spectrum, Phyllis Schlafly (1924–) emerged as the leading right-wing woman. With reactionary credentials as researcher for Senator Joseph McCarthy, she helped nominate conservative Barry Goldwater as the 1964 Republican Presidential candidate. Ivy Baker Priest (1905–1975), having served as U.S. Treasurer in the Eisenhower Administration, only the second woman in that position, worked to increase women's political participation. Although she claimed to retire in 1961 to California, in 1966 she was elected state treasurer, serving two four-year terms under Governor Ronald Reagan. In 1968, she nominated him for the Presidency—the first woman to nominate a man for that office at a major political convention.

All sorts of political organizations urged increased women's participation, although usually only on the grassroots level—bolstering rolls, canvassing, and performing campaign office chores. The ultra-conservative John Birch Society, founded in 1959, charged $24 annual dues for a man and half that for a woman; and even on the far Right, women leaders like Schlafly emerged as influential voices. Friedan and other liberal women worked for Eugene McCarthy's presidential nomination in 1968; yet that year, only one of 108 delegations to the Democratic convention had a woman chair—Oregon's Edith Green. In 1970, the Gallup Poll noted that two-thirds of women would vote for a qualified woman for President.

New reforms in mainstream political parties opened up participation to women, marking the end of the "smoke-filled room" where male regulars and party bosses dominated. Senator George McGovern's Commission on Party Structure and Rules, created at the 1968 Chicago Democratic convention, brought about a "Quiet Revolution" in the party through internal reforms. Delegates to the Democratic national convention would have to be elected on the state level, not chosen in male-dominated caucuses. McGovern's affirmative action guidelines required party representation of women proportionate to the population. These recommendations drew opposition from the likes of Dr. Edgar F. Berman, a close friend of Hubert Humphrey, who testified to the Democrats' Committee on National Priorities in April 1970 that women were unqualified for important decision-making jobs because of "raging hormonal influences" in menstruation and menopause. McGovern's reforms were not adopted until 1971, and did not take effect until 1972, the year of his presidential nomination. Women delegates increased from 13 to 39 percent at Democratic conventions from 1968 to 1972; and representation by women even grew from 17 to 30 percent at Republican conventions in those years.[63]

Intending to further reform rather than simply to rely on the McGovern Commission, several women's state-level organizations arose between 1968 and 1972. The Democratic Farmer-Labor Feminist Caucus in Minnesota tried to promote candidates, especially women, who supported progressive feminist principles. Betty Friedan and Bella Abzug convened about three hundred feminists at a July 1971 organizational conference in Washington to form the bipartisan National Women's Political Caucus (NWPC); but from the beginning, the NWPC was factionalized between those who wanted to support all women candidates and those who insisted on promoting only those with liberal, feminist ideas.[64]

In the short term, the legacy of sixties feminism in mainstream politics was chaotic and divisive. Sissy Farenthold, backed by economist John Kenneth Galbraith, bid unsuccessfully for the 1972 Democratic vice presidential nomination. Gloria Steinem, a long-time McGovern supporter, worked for Shirley Chisholm for the Democratic presidential nomination because she felt that McGovern "still fell short on women's issues." The 1972 McGovern campaign, dubbed "the children's crusade" because of his strong youth support, featured Shirley MacLaine and Jean Westwood in visible roles; but women were not in policy-making positions. McGovern was oblivious, and campaign manager Gary Hart was unreceptive, at best. The NWPC supported McGovern. At the Miami Democratic convention, old-boy politics persisted with conflicts over delegate seating, and many women felt betrayed by McGovernite back-sliding. McGovern opposed abortion on demand but waffled with contradictory statements to placate feminists for whom it had recently become a political litmus test. MacLaine cut the issue of abortion completely out of the platform, thus introducing abortion into the campaign as a partisan issue that helped re-elect Nixon. Shana Alexander editorialized in *Newsweek* that MacLaine amid the Democrats and Jill Ruckelhaus at the Republican convention had each sold her sex "down the river in the name of political expediency." Such was the political legacy of the sixties for women.[65]

2

The Civil Rights Movement

Bernice Johnson Reagon, of SNCC's Freedom Singers, reminds us that the Civil Rights movement gave birth to "not just the Black Power and Black revolutionary movements but every progressive struggle . . . in this country since that time. In all organized struggles coming after the Civil Rights Movement," one finds leaders "who experienced, on more than a cursory level, the energy and transforming dynamics of the Civil Rights Movement. . . . the centering, borning essence of the '60s, and of the New Left." Black women were "at the center" of that movement.[1]

The long struggle for civil rights for black Americans took on new impetus after the 1954 Supreme Court decision, *Brown v. Board of Education of Topeka, Kansas,* outlawing racial segregation in public schools. Culminating a long series of legal battles waged by lawyers of the National Association for the Advancement of Colored People (NAACP), this victory gave hope for other successes. In December 1955, a southern black woman, Rosa Parks (1913–), translated that hope and a profound weariness into definitive action—she would not give up her seat at the back of the bus so a white man could sit down. From her action came the year-long Montgomery, Alabama, bus boycott, the growth of the Southern Christian Leadership Conference (SCLC), the rise to prominence of Reverend Martin Luther King, Jr., a further Supreme Court decision forcing Montgomery to integrate public transportation—the modern phase of the long movement for civil rights. The sixties' idea that injustice was not to be borne but resisted, and the form of that resistance—the interposition of the human body—began with a forty-two year old black woman.

Ten years later, in 1965, Congress passed a Voting Rights Act. The year before, President Lyndon B. Johnson had signed into law the most comprehensive Civil Rights Act in history. Neither banished racism from the country; but each represented a major advance, a public acknowledgment of historic error. In the decade between Parks's refusal to stand at the back of the bus, her subsequent arrest, and the passage of the Voting Rights Act, a powerful movement arose, growing first in the urban and then the rural South, eventually reaching cities across the country.

At every stage, from Montgomery on, women—particularly black women—provided the critical mass necessary for this popular movement to succeed. A few women rose to prominence, but more typically women played supporting roles: swelling mass meetings, marches, and demonstrations; risking arrest and worse out of a profound sense that nothing could be worse than the years of injustice already endured; providing shelter and nurturance to volunteers who spread across the South in the drive to register black voters; and standing on the frontlines themselves. Reagon remembers:

> A majority of the people who were in jail were women
> We were the majority of the people who were in the marches.
> We were the majority of the people who were in the mass meetings.
> It is Black women who are there every night,
> Somehow understanding that in this movement
>   We might be able
>   To increase the space we had to work in
>   In order to deliver the goods
>   So that there will be another day for our folks.[2]

Despite extreme racist violence such as the September 1963 bombing of Birmingham's Sixteenth Street Baptist Church that killed four black girls, the southern civil rights movement blended the Gandhian tradition of *satyaqraha* with ideals of Christian pacifism, enhancing the individual's ability to stand against injustice and giving communal resistance a sacred character. As women interpreted the movement in the South, they sought to place the highest value on leadership that came from the convictions of individuals, not from authorities, and on the strength of people acting together. The idea of autonomy within community marked the organizations in which women felt themselves most effective, and when women sought to create a movement for themselves, that idea was at its center.[3]

A Generation of Women: Rosa Parks and the Montgomery Bus Boycott

When news of Rosa Parks's defiance reached the public, many saw her as a folk hero, a woman of the people who couldn't take it any more and—without ideology—sat firm; but Rosa Parks represented a generation with both a political analysis of the black experience in the South and a longtime commitment to defiance of segregation laws. A department store seamstress, she was also secretary of the Montgomery chapter of the National Association for the Advancement of Colored People (NAACP), then the only active civil rights organization in the South, and a leading member of the St. Paul AME Church, which, along with other Montgomery black churches, was a center for resistance. Her defiance of Jim Crow bus laws provided the Montgomery Women's Political Council (WPC), organized in the late forties by black professional women to "inspire Negroes to live above mediocrity . . . and to register and vote," with the opportunity to realize its long-considered boycott of Montgomery bus lines. WPC President Jo Ann Gibson Robinson issued the call to boycott: "Another Negro woman has been arrested and thrown in jail because she refused to get up out of her seat on the bus for a white person to sit down. . . . If we do not do something to stop these arrests, ... The next time it may be you, or your daughter, or mother. . . . We are asking every Negro to stay off the buses Monday in protest of the arrest and trial."[4]

The boycott lasted 381 days with middle-aged, hard-working women serving as the foot soldiers in this first major civil rights campaign. Some, like Rosa Parks, had jobs in city businesses; more were domestic servants working far from their homes. Yet hundreds accepted the hardship and the risk to their livelihoods; they boycotted. Their employers, mainly white women, were puzzled and angry. One, confiding in her maid because "I know you can keep your mouth shut," revealed that "in the White Citizens' Council meeting, they discussed starving the maids for a month," laying them off, then "they'll be glad to ride the buses again. If they do it, I still want you to come one day a week." "Susie" responded, "Well, Mrs. Powell, I just won't come at all and I sure won't starve. . . . So I'm not worried at all, 'cause I was eating before I started working for you." Only a few white women supported the boycott, augmenting the carpool system set up by blacks.[5]

Rosa Parks both symbolized and found support from many black women of her generation. Earlier in 1955, at the Highlander Folk School in Monteagle, Tennessee, she had met Septima Clark (1905–) who urged her to move beyond her fear that "white people would know she was as militant as she was," to act on her beliefs. A South Carolina school teacher for almost forty years, Clark came to Highlander after being fired by the state for her refusal to give up her NAACP membership. Clark was central to the development of "citizenship schools," forerunners of the sixties Freedom Schools, providing community education. "Literacy means liberation," Clark taught. By July 1962, South Carolina had 40 such schools and double that by 1964, resulting in increased black voting strength, from 57,000 to 150,000, as Clark records. In 1964 she left Highlander to become Director of Citizenship Education for the Southern Christian Leadership Conference (SCLC), formed during the Montgomery boycott.[6]

In Montgomery, Parks turned for support to Virginia Foster Durr (1903–), a white Alabama native and a Wellesley graduate, who had recently returned to the state after her husband, Clifford, lost his Washington job as Federal Communications Commission chairman, a victim of McCarthyism and racism. In Washington, Virginia Durr had worked with Eleanor Roosevelt trying to eliminate the poll tax; she was also a founder of the 1938 Southern Conference on Human Welfare, convened in Birmingham, Alabama. When the Durrs returned home, they encountered hostility for their liberalism. "The South has sort of a ruling class," Durr explained. "If you go against it, as I did on the issues of segregation, you find yourself outside the closed circle . . . And the enemy wasn't a foreign foe, but your mother and your father, your sister and brother." Clifford Durr worked as Montgomery's only white civil rights lawyer. The Durrs knew Rosa Parks through the NAACP; and she occasionally worked for them. When Parks was arrested on 10 December 1955, the Durrs bailed her out and provided assistance and support in her suit and that brought by the Montgomery Improvement Association against city buslines. In 1956, the Supreme Court ordered integration of city buses, the first victory of a large-scale, direct action campaign.[7]

Ella Baker, the Southern Christian Leadership Conference, and the Student Non-Violent Coordinating Committee

Many of the black women who staffed the "front lines of black resistance" in the South were young—the teenage girls of the "Little Rock Nine" who asked to enter Central High School in Little Rock, Arkansas, in 1957; Autherine Lucy, the first black student admitted to the University of Alabama at Tuscaloosa; Charlayne Hunter, who with Hamilton Holmes integrated the University of Georgia; Vivian Malone, who broke the barrier of segregation at the main University of Alabama campus; Diane Nash, a major figure in the Nashville student movement; and Rubye Doris Smith Robinson, the first woman executive secretary of the Student Non-Violent Coordinating Committee (SNCC). But the earliest and most significant women leaders brought long years of experience to the task.[8]

Leading the effort to desegregate Little Rock's Central High School was another woman of Parks's generation. Daisy Bates was president of the state NAACP chapter and, with her husband, publisher of the *State Press*. As white Little Rock became increasingly irrational over school desegregation and disturbed by the presence of the National Guard troops called in to keep order, Bates was under continual threat, her home bombed, the newspaper shut down. She persisted in her work, however, and in 1960 was among the first to respond to the sit-in movement, sending cars to Philander Smith College to pick up students so she could train them for sit-ins.[9]

Of all the politically active women of that generation, however, none had as widespread and long lasting an influence as Ella Baker (1905–1988). In her work with SCLC and, subsequently, with SNCC, Baker brought well-honed organizational skills to the great task of turning groups of dedicated individuals into a movement. Her success was striking: SNCC activist and later Georgia legislator Julian Bond asserts, "Without [Ella Baker] there would be no story" of SNCC.[10]

In 1957, when the young black ministers who made up SCLC called on her, Baker was president of the New York City branch of the NAACP and an active member of In Friendship, a New York organization aiding southern black political activists. A graduate of Shaw University in Raleigh, North Carolina, she had moved to New York in the late twenties and had been organizing for civil rights and for the interests of the poor ever since. Like others in the thirties, she was drawn to radical solutions and began "to identify . . . with the unemployed." In the subdued early fifties, she continued her NAACP work, while seeking something more activist than their legal challenges to segregation laws. When King invited her to take on the task of organizing SCLC, she accepted and returned South.[11]

Typical of women organizers in movements led by men, Baker's work was done outside public notice, behind the pulpits of the black ministers, the charismatic leaders and spokespersons for black southern militancy, and later in the small backstage offices of the student movement. Skeptical of charismatic leaders, Baker shared with Septima Clark the belief that leadership should come from the people. "My theory is, strong people don't need strong leaders." Baker was acutely aware of women's problems in male organizations and of the importance of women's work in the church and the movement. She "knew from the beginning that having a woman be an executive of SCLC was not something that would go over with the male-dominated leadership." Her idea of the appropriate direction for SCLC was different from the ministers'. She recalls, "my personality wasn't right, in the sense that I was not afraid to disagree with the higher authorities. I wasn't one to say 'yes' because it came from the Reverend King."[12]

SCLC leaders believed in a centralized organizational structure and activities focused on large-scale events—mass meetings and demonstrations to attract media and force the attention of public authorities. Baker favored a more decentralized approach, a crusade reaching out to fill "the unmet needs of the people." Searching out and sponsoring indigenous leaders, especially in the "hard core states" of the deep South, would expand voter registration and ultimately political power, she believed. She proposed a gathering of women to create a massive campaign for literacy, combining the forces of the Women's Division of the National Baptist Convention, the National Council of Negro Women (NCNW), and national black sororities. Such a group could allay fears of militancy which could hurt SCLC's fund-raising, she suggested. Understanding the power of nonviolence as a political tactic (but personally skeptical of it as a way of life), Baker envisioned SCLC action teams teaching the people techniques of nonviolence. SCLC rejected Baker's proposals, and they generally neglected her petitions for adequate money and supplies. With her long background as an organizer, however, Baker understood the need for a well-run office and willingly did housekeeping chores to maintain it. Despite her differences with SCLC leaders, she continued until 1960 to provide behind-the-scenes support to establish the movement.[13]

In 1960, Baker convinced the SCLC to let her convene the meeting that led to formation of the Student Non-Violent Coordinating Committee, an organization which would embrace her philosophy of leadership and come close to realizing the popular crusade she envisioned. SNCC grew out of the student sit-in movement which had spread with astounding rapidity across the South and beyond after four male students from the Agricultural and Technical College sat in at a Woolworth's lunch counter in Greensboro, North Carolina, on 1 February 1960. After being refused service they returned, accepted attacks and vilification non-violently, and persisted. By February's end, there had been many sit-ins in the border states of North and South Carolina, Virginia, and in Nashville, Tennessee, where an active Christian Leadership Conference and four black colleges gave the movement impetus. By March, sit-ins had occurred in cities in the deep South with a previous history of civil rights organizing (Birmingham, Montgomery, Baton Rouge), and sympathy demonstrations had begun in northern cities. By April there had been seventy demonstrations. Before the end of 1961, over 70,000 students had participated in sit-ins with over 3000 arrests.[14]

Ella Baker understood the movement's unparalleled potential as well as the need to organize it. With $800 from SCLC, she sent out invitations to the Southwide Student Leadership Conference on Non-Violent Resistance to Segregation for Easter weekend, 15–17 April 1960, at Shaw University. She expected a hundred students; 300 came. Most were black—representing 56 southern colleges, 58 southern communities, 12 southern states. There were also 57 observers from northern campuses and cities.[15]

Baker arranged separate meetings for southern students: "I believed very firmly in the right of the people who were under the heel to be the ones to decide what action they were going to take to get from under their oppression." She encouraged students to create their own organization, not to become the "youth arm" of established organizations: SCLC, NAACP, or the Congress of Racial Equality (CORE). Success depended on developing indigenous leadership and a movement vision. The conference made it "crystal clear" that sit-ins were concerned with "more than a hamburger" (the title of Baker's talk): "Negro and white students, North and South, are seeking to rid America of the scourge of racial segregation and discrimination in every aspect of life." The students' understanding of the "need to avoid leadership" was "refreshing," Baker commented.[16]

SNCC's vision of the transformation of the South through widespread grassroots efforts owed much to Baker, as did the forms the organization developed—voter registration drives in rural communities, Freedom Schools, community organizing, and development of community centers. She brought to SNCC as well the training in nonviolent techniques she hoped to convince SCLC to adopt; while SNCC would later test and reject the ideal of nonviolence, at this initial gathering that commitment was central.[17]

Baker and a young white woman, Connie Curry, were elected as the only non-student members of the SNCC executive committee. Curry, a Greensboro native, had recently returned to the South to observe the sit-ins and organize meetings of black and white students under National Student Association auspices. She remained to assist Baker in planning SNCC conferences and to encourage other young white women to participate. Curry came to interracial concerns from involvement in Methodist youth work; that pattern of church work as a basis for active civil rights participation would also fit many of the young white southern women who joined the movement. Curry was a model for them.[18]

Baker left SCLC to establish SNCC's Atlanta office in the summer of 1960. As SNCC funds were meager, she continued to work for the YWCA, an organization with a long history of encouraging the advancement of black women and interracial cooperation. When SNCC almost broke apart in the fall of 1961, Baker's mediation saved it. Advocates of nonviolent direct action, especially Diane Nash and others from the very active Nashville student contingent, were at serious odds with the faction that wanted SNCC to concentrate on voter registration. The Nashville group mobilized efforts to continue the Freedom Rides (integrated groups riding interstate buses to test implementation of desegregation laws) when terrible violence threatened their cancellation. They also staged a massive demonstration against segregated theatres and moved projects into hitherto unassailably segregated rural communities in Mississippi and Georgia. Voter registration seemed dull by comparison.[19]

Baker suggested a two-pronged effort, with Nash in charge of the direct action component and Charles Jones handling voter registration campaigns. The latter brought its own dangers, she reminded them; the experience of the registration drives of the early sixties more than bore her out. Until 1964, when she left to work for the Southern Conference Education Fund, Ella Baker was SNCC organizer, liaison person, office manager, and healer of wounds: "Where they were going, I had been."[20]

Women and the Student Non-Violent Coordinating Committee

Between 1960 and 1964, SNCC grew from an initial coordinating committee of sixteen to an organization of 350. Numbers of projects and volunteers also grew. "SNCC was in a hurry because SNCC knew it had to move fast if it was not to be destroyed in America." As SNCC moved across the deep South, setting up community projects and conducting voter registration drives, the threat to life was constant, as was exhaustion. "Being beaten and thrown into jail and trying to love everybody while they did it to you . . . was bound to mess you up," Connie Curry recalled. "The toll that was taken in those early days was tremendous."[21]

Women, even young girls, shared the work and danger with men. Although SNCC women were sometimes held back from field work and assigned to "safer" tasks in schools and libraries, often teams were made up of both men and women in hopes that chivalry would ensure some safety; but violence from angry whites was not reserved for men. "Mrs. Marian King was kicked from behind, knocked to the ground while visiting jailed demonstrators in Camilla, Georgia. She was five months pregnant at the time and also carrying her three-year-old daughter." Mrs. King's child was born dead. On another occasion, "sixteen-year-old Shirley Gaines, arrested for seeking access to a bowling alley, was dragged down stone steps by policemen, kicked again and again in her back and side."[22]

Many such incidents occurred. When Anne Moody, then a senior at Mississippi's Tougaloo College, and two black women friends sat in at the Woolworth's lunch counter in Jackson in the spring of 1963, they were thrown from their stools. When the police arrested one of Moody's friends, white Tougaloo student Joan Trumpauer and a white faculty member, Lois Chaffee, joined the group; all four were pelted with food by the mob.[23]

Moody and her friends anticipated greater violence. In Canton, Mississippi, in 1964 she returned to the SNCC Freedom House after a day of registering voters to find her housemates, Lenora and Doris, with guns. "Three young women just don't live in Mississippi alone without any protection," they explained to Moody's distress. To Moody, guns

implied threats of reprisal, seemingly contradicting SNCC's commitment to nonviolence; but threats to the women's safety came nightly. It
was hard to keep up courage. "It had gotten to the point where my
weight was down to nothing. . . . My nerves were torn to shreds and
I was losing my hair." Moody knew she was in danger: she had seen
her photo on a Mississippi Ku Klux Klan pamphlet, and her mother
warned her not to come home because of threats to her family by the
local sheriff. She responded by leading workshops in nonviolent self-
defense for other student activists.[24]

Moody graduated to become a paid CORE activist; she also worked
at the Congress of Federated Organizations (COFO) headquarters in
Jackson on the Mississippi Summer Project in 1964. But she became
increasingly cynical. Hearing Martin Luther King, Jr. deliver his "I
Have a Dream" speech at the 1963 March on Washington, Moody commented, "We never had time to sleep, much less dream." Her memoir
of the movement, *Coming of Age in Mississippi*, appeared in 1968.[25]

Great numbers of SNCC workers from 1960 to 1965 lived in the
homes of townspeople who risked their lives and livelihoods by taking
them in. There were adjustments on both sides: most volunteers were
city-raised college students; most hosts were poor country-bred survivors of a system of racist oppression with deep, tough roots. In a much-
quoted passage, SNCC organizer Charles Sherrod praises the "mama"
who provided nourishment and encouragement to young volunteers:
"There is always a 'mama.' She is usually a militant woman in the community, outspoken, understanding, and willing to catch hell, having
already caught her share." "Mama" for Sherrod and other SNCC workers was Carolyn Daniels—a "young Negro woman who operated a
beauty shop in Dawson" and had a long history as an activist. In December 1963, her home was destroyed, and she was injured by a night-
rider's bomb.[26]

Daniels was relatively young, in her thirties; many "mamas" were
not. In 1962, Sherrod and five other workers, most from northern colleges, stayed with "Mama Dolly" Raines, a "gray-haired old lady of
about seventy who can pick more cotton, chop more wood, and do a
hundred things better than the best farmer in the area." Her home was
regularly threatened. In the 1964 Freedom Summer, when hundreds of
northern volunteers came into Mississippi to assist in voter registration,
a local newscast reported that an offer of $400 had been made to some-
one "to bomb all the houses where volunteers are staying."[27]

The issue of black women's courage and leadership in the dangerous,
often violent search for civil rights was a sensitive one. One student

volunteer observed: "The women make up the lion's share of the movement. This may be partially because they aren't as vulnerable economically but I don't think that factor is very important. Too many women
work and oftentimes a man will get fired for the sins of his wife. Perhaps the major reason is that the women seem to have the calm courage
necessary for a non-violent campaign."[28]

A special 1966 issue of *Ebony* devoted to "The Negro Woman"
stressed her centrality to the movement. "Seasoned by a society that
systematically has denied the Negro male a right to self-assertion," author Phyl Garland explained, women "have had to take the lead in the
struggle for dignity, as well as survival." Older women activists like
Daisy Adams Lampkin (1883–1965) agreed. Fannie Lou Hamer (1917–
1977) explained why three women challenged the Mississippi congressional delegation: it would have been "too dangerous to put men up as
candidates. We were just carrying on until the men could get their
chance, and this year they will."[29]

Rubye Doris Smith Robinson, SNCC's twenty-four-year old Executive Secretary, was skeptical about the reasons given for women's
prominence in the movement. "In the past, Negro women had to assert
themselves so the family could survive. Fortunately, more men are becoming involved with the movement and the day might come when
women aren't needed for this type of work. But I don't believe the
Negro man will be able to assume his full role until the struggle has
progressed to a point that can't be foreseen—maybe in the next century
or so."[30]

Fannie Lou Hamer and Rubye Doris Smith Robinson

The stories of Fannie Lou Hamer and Rubye Doris Smith Robinson
(1942–1967) epitomize black women's work in SNCC. While each
woman was uniquely powerful, both were also striking examples of the
indigenous leadership in which Ella Baker believed. Hamer, youngest
of twenty children of a sharecropper, was herself a timekeeper and
sharecropper on a farm in Ruleville in the Mississippi Delta. Poverty
was endemic there and black sharecroppers, many of them women,
were generally in debt. A 1962 SNCC field worker's report tells, for
example, of the plight of Mrs. Willie Mae Robbinson who "had picked
twenty bales of cotton this season," yet cleared only three dollars for
the entire year. "She had to split her crop with the plantation owner

and pay for her yearly expenses, but as one man told us. . . . 'I know she hasn't eaten what would have come out of ten bales.'"[31]

In August 1962 Hamer attended a SNCC voter registration meeting in a Ruleville church; it changed her life. "If SNCC hadn't come into Mississippi, there never would have been a Fannie Lou Hamer. . . . They treated me for the first time I ever been treated like a human being." The SNCC speakers urged their audience to register at the Sunflower County courthouse: Hamer tried but failed the test to copy out and interpret a section of the state constitution. Such barriers to voting were a common experience for southern blacks; and registrars in county courthouses, many of them white women, were figures of power and fearsomeness. [32]

Returning from the courthouse, Hamer received an ultimatum from her employer: cease her attempts to register or leave the plantation. She left. The house where she took refuge was fire-bombed ten days later, as was a nearby house where SNCC workers stayed.

Other black Ruleville women also suffered economic reprisal for responding to SNCC's encouragement to register. Surplus commodities they needed to get through the winter were made difficult if not impossible to get: "Mrs. Gertrude Rogers . . . heard the mayor of Ruleville . . . say 'most of them with cards ain't going to get any food.' Mrs. Rogers reports that the Mayor also said that those who went down to register were not going to get anything, 'that he was going to mess up the lot of them.'"[33]

As white reprisal continued, Hamer fled to Tallahatchie County. Tired of running, she returned home in December, determined to register. Her model for her courage remained her mother. She had been "a great woman . . . She taught us to be decent and respect ourselves, and that is one thing that has kept me going." Hamer passed the registration test in January 1963. She, her husband, and two adopted daughters resettled in Ruleville. Harassment followed and threats of violence continued. Perry "Pap" Hamer lost his job because of his wife's activities. [34]

In Ruleville, Hamer taught in the SCLC voter education program, then became a SNCC field secretary. Her gifts of energy, language, and a passion for justice, as well as the experience of oppression she embodied, made her a hero for the young. Historian Bernice Johnson Reagon comments: "Fannie Lou Hamer made some decisions during the early part of the sixties that made us stand up and follow—feeling a little stronger and going a little farther because of the price she paid for the stances she took. Mississippi will never be the same. I will never be the same."[35]

With a strong, clear voice and a gift for preaching, Hamer moved audiences to action. For her, as for Ella Baker, the movement became a crusade. While Baker's political roots were in radical movements, Hamer's were in the church. Her exhortations to mass meetings blended Freedom songs, Biblical quotations, and powerful political messages. Mary King testifies to the power Hamer's voice and conviction had on the other civil rights workers: "Whenever she was strongly moved, she would stand spontaneously, radiant, her face glistening, defiant in her compact, rounded physical frame, and lead us in her favorite spiritual: 'This little light of mine, I'm gonna let it shine.' She started singing alone, mellifluously; then our voices would one by one mingle with hers as we let her lead us. The 'light' of the spiritual served as a metaphor for one's life, and 'this little light of mine' was a pledge of her life's purpose." Hamer sang it to express her personal commitment and as a call for others' reaffirmation.[36]

In 1963, returning in a group from a South Carolina voter education workshop, Hamer and other black women used a "white" restroom in Winona, Mississippi. They were arrested, and taken to the county jail. From her cell, Hamer could see fifteen-year-old June Johnson screaming with blood running down her face. She could hear Annelle Ponder, a soft-spoken SCLC worker, quietly refusing to say "yessir" to the white guard, could "hear when she hit the floor and . . . she kept screamin' and they kept beatin' on her." When guards learned Hamer was a registered voter, they warned her: "You bitch, we gon' make you wish you was dead." White guards beat her first, then forced black prisoners to hit her repeatedly with a heavy leather belt, leaving Hamer with permanent injuries.[37]

In August 1964, Hamer told that story to a national television audience, part of her testimony before the Credentials Committee of the Democratic National Convention in Atlantic City. As cofounder, chief spokesperson, and congressional candidate of the Mississippi Freedom Democratic Party (MFDP), she had gone there to demand that the MFDP delegation—not the all-white official state delegation—be seated. The power of Hamer's story and of her presence received an unusual tribute. As she spoke, President Johnson called an impromptu news conference, forcing the networks to turn to him, preempting the live MFDP testimony, although much of it appeared on the evening news.[38]

The MFDP came into existence in April 1964, an outgrowth of SNCC's Freedom Voter Registration campaign the previous fall. More than 63,000 black Mississippians took advantage of this chance to exercise the franchise denied by their state. The new party met early in August in a convention organized by Ella Baker and elected a 68-member delegation to go to Atlantic City. Instead of official recognition and the seating for which they had hoped, the MFDP delegation received only a compromise: the regular state delegation would remain and take a party loyalty oath while two MFDP members were to be seated as delegates at large. Several powerful figures urged acceptance: ACLU lawyer and MFDP legal adviser Joseph Rauh, Dr. Martin Luther King, NAACP's Roy Wilkins, UAW head Walter Reuther, and others argued that the MFDP had won a victory, that it was more important to their cause for Hubert Humphrey to win the vice-presidential nomination than for the MFDP to be seated. Some agreed, but Hamer and a few others were adamantly opposed: the MFDP refused the compromise.[39]

Political realist Baker was not surprised. She clearly knew of Johnson's determination not to risk the loss of southern votes by allowing the MFDP challenge to succeed. For Hamer, the process was disillusioning: "I thought with all my heart that the regular delegation would be unseated. . . . I believed that, because if the Constitution means something, then I knew they would unseat them." Saddened and angry, she nonetheless typically retained some hope: "One day I know the struggle will change. There's got to be a change."[40]

Hamer never gave up her attempt to change the system. On 4 January 1965 she and two other MFDP congressional candidates—Victoria Jackson Gray from Hattiesburg and Annie Devine from Canton—travelled to Washington to challenge the seating of the Mississippi congressional delegation. A businesswoman, Victoria Gray had been a teacher and was a longtime SCLC organizer. Annie Devine sold real estate and insurance in Madison County. When the registration drives began, Devine added voter information as she sold insurance door to door. It was hard to find candidates for MFDP, she explained: "To do something in Mississippi meant your life was out there." She survived in part, she believed, because she was a woman: "The Negro woman does not in many cases have to go through all the things that men go through." And she was careful: "I haven't shouted at people." Her daughter, Monette Devine Travis, was more critical: "It might be a lack of courage on the part of the men—or a lack of opportunity. . . . Those shouldn't have been women who had to go to Washington to challenge the Congress." She added, "Maybe the men, as heads of households, feared they might lose their jobs if they became too active in the movement."[41]

In 1968, Hamer organized Loyal Democrats of Mississippi, a coalition of MFDP members, Young Democrats, the NAACP, the Teachers' Association, and the Masons. She went to the Chicago Democratic convention but found it a discouraging farce: "The People were left out of any real say so," she complained in 1969 to the Democratic Party Committee on Party Structure and Reform. "I told a Congressman I was at the funeral of the Democratic Party, that's how sick that convention was"; but the Committee enacted rules changes that ensured representative delegations in 1972 and later conventions.[42]

While pursuing political change, Hamer also gave enormous time and energy to the problems of poverty in Sunflower County. With passage of the 1964 Economic Opportunity Act, she mobilized efforts to bring Head Start, the successful early childhood education program, to the county. She was also instrumental in founding the Mississippi Freedom Labor Union. With funds from the National Council of Negro Women (NCNW), Hamer began a cooperative pig farm and worked as county coordinator for NCNW's program to fight malnutrition. NCNW backing also enabled her to convert an old building into a garment factory which employed 25 women and provided day care for workers. Dreaming of a "vegetable bank" to improve the health of the county's poor, she launched the Freedom Farm Cooperative, purchasing huge tracts of land for vegetable farming. "Hunger has no color line," she told novelist Paule Marshall in 1970. "What I'm really trying to do, when you get down to it, is to wipe out hunger."[43]

Alliance between NCNW members—mainly urban, northern, and middle-class—and poor women in the rural South is one of the decade's most important stories. Under the strong leadership of Dorothy Height from mid-decade on, the NCNW initiated many self-help programs to address the severe economic needs of blacks, particularly women. The rural women were sometimes skeptical, and differences of class as well as of urban versus rural culture threatened cooperation. Unita Blackwell, a community activist and MFDP member from Mayersville, Mississippi, had learned to come to terms with the young SNCC workers, despite their city styles. She had similar difficulties in her first encounter with the middle-class NCNW women: "We went to the meeting, and I just couldn't stand it, you know. 'Cause it was just . . . what

I call these 'highly elites'. . . . And they didn't know what in the world was going on in the community." Blackwell and some others wanted to leave, but NCNW members persuaded them to stay. Blackwell (later mayor of Mayersville) went on to work with NCNW on such projects as farming cooperatives, Project Home, a turn-key project to help alleviate the state's housing crisis, and Project Women Power, which brought young black women activists to work with Mississippi women.[44]

Many young black women joined the movement. Like many of her SNCC contemporaries, Rubye Doris Smith represented a promise of upward mobility. She grew up in Atlanta, where her mother was a beautician and her father a self-employed mover, and was a sophomore at Atlanta's Spelman College in 1960. With her older sister, a student at Morris Brown College, she joined the Atlanta Student Committee on Appeal for Human Rights, formed for civil disobedience. Rubye Smith was one of 200 chosen for the first demonstration to integrate the state capitol's restaurant. The cashier "refused [her] money [and] the Lieutenant Governor came down and told us to leave. We didn't, and went to the county jail." In April 1960, she attended SNCC's founding meeting.[45]

Smith was jailed again in February 1961 in Rock Hill, South Carolina, having been arrested with Diane Nash and eight other students for sitting in. They refused bail, choosing jail instead, thus launching SNCC's "jail no bail" policy to call attention to the massive injustice of segregation and to clog the courts and jails that abetted injustice. In August 1961 she received another jail sentence for taking part in a Freedom Ride to desegregate the bus terminal in Jackson, Mississippi.[46]

The fourteen participants on the first Freedom Ride, organized by CORE in May 1961, had been dragged from the buses by white mobs in Anniston and Birmingham, Alabama, and brutally beaten while white law enforcement officials simply looked on. Because of the ferocity of the attacks, CORE considered cancelling the Rides; but students in the Nashville Christian Leadership Conference organized under the leadership of Diane Nash to keep them going. The brutality also continued. Lucretia Collins remembers seeing "some men" holding Freedom Rider Jim Zwerg "while white women clawed his face with their nails." Still, a steady stream of students and other Freedom Riders arrived in Jackson in the following weeks. By the end of August 1961, there had been over 500 arrests. The Hinds County jail was overcrowded: Smith was transferred to Parchman State Penitentiary and spent the rest of her two-month sentence in a filthy, bug-laden maximum security cell.[47]

In December 1961, Smith participated in massive demonstrations called by SNCC to end all forms of segregation in Albany, Georgia. The goals of the Albany Movement were broader than those of any earlier phase, and the number of community people and even high school students who went out to demonstrate and to be arrested exceeded those in any other city. Although the massiveness of the organizing task meant that SNCC's goals were not fully realized, its success in mobilizing a community around its oppression was nonetheless significant.

After Albany, Smith worked with a SNCC project in Cairo, Illinois, in summer 1962. That fall, she left college to work for SNCC full-time. In 1966, as the organization began to move away from its original nonviolent ideal toward "black power," Rubye Doris Smith Robinson (she married Clifford Robinson in 1964) became SNCC's first executive woman secretary. She had long since become discouraged with the promise of nonviolence as a tactic against mounting white anger and repression, and she did not resist the direction in which then SNCC chairman Stokely Carmichael and others were taking the organization.

SNCC's rather amorphous structure and philosophy of participatory democracy—"let the people decide"—gave women a better chance to be heard and to lead than did traditionally hierarchical organizations. Smith's career illustrates that point, although her participation in the 1964 office "sit-in," called only half-facetiously to protest relegation of routine and household tasks to women, suggests that she had a double consciousness. She chose to place the continuity of the organization ahead of her own anger; and she discouraged staff members who wanted to do more to call attention to internal difficulties in SNCC.[48]

By 1964, Robinson had taken on enormous responsibilities to keep SNCC functioning. A tough and determined administrator, she oversaw work schedules and expenses of volunteers and kept track of the cars in the crucially important "Sojourner Fleet" on which SNCC depended for voter registration work in remote towns. Volunteers who preferred a more relaxed organizational style chafed under her discipline. For many young black women who joined SNCC in 1964 and 1965, however, Robinson was a model, albeit a difficult one. Gwen Patton remembers that she and other volunteers believed that they were equal to men, but that they also felt they had to be superwomen. Robinson certainly was that.[49]

A trip to Africa in the fall of 1964 with Hamer and other movement veterans proved an overwhelming experience of identity for Robinson and made her even more determined to fight for her convictions. From 1965 on, she combined marriage and raising a child with her exhausting SNCC schedule. Some believed she thus shortened her life. Rubye Doris Smith Robinson died of lymphoma in 1967 at age twenty-six. James Forman, writing of her in *The Making of Black Revolutionaries*, stresses Robinson's centrality to SNCC: she had "brilliant ideas—ideas always more advanced than those of many others in SNCC. . . . Ruby Doris was one of the few genuine revolutionaries in the black liberation movement." Like Ella Baker, Robinson realized that leadership of the people depended on a well-run organization into which they could channel their efforts. And, like Baker, she subordinated herself to the organization without ever giving up her individuality or self-respect.[50]

Many other young black women shared large responsibilities for the success and persistence of the dangerous work of changing the South. In Cambridge, Maryland, Gloria Richardson led the local SNCC chapter and organized a hard-fought series of protests against segregated businesses, defying threats of violence against her and the student activists who had joined her. Diane Nash had come from Chicago to attend Fisk College in Tennessee in 1959; the "blatant segregation" she found there changed her outlook on life. "I began to see the community in sin. . . . Being looked in the eye and told, 'Go around to the back door where you belong' had a tremendous psychological effect on me . . . I didn't agree that I was inferior and I had a difficult time complying with it." By 1961, Nash had seen "raw hatred," had seen her friends beaten, had been a "convict several times," and had begun to feel "part of a group suddenly proud to be called black." Despite what she had seen and experienced, she remained committed to nonviolence as a way of life.[51]

In 1961 Nash married James Bevel, a young minister and close SCLC associate of Dr. King. In April 1962, pregnant, she received a two-year sentence for civil disobedience but refused to use her pregnancy as an excuse to appeal or post bond: "This will be a black baby born in Mississippi," she told the judge, "and thus where ever he is born he will be in prison . . . If I go to jail now it may help hasten that day when my child and all children will be free." She worked for that freedom with SNCC as its first field secretary, and then with SCLC. In 1966, as it was becoming clear to many that the cause of civil rights was linked to the protest against the Vietnam war, Nash and longtime civil rights and peace activist Barbara Deming travelled on a peace mission to North Vietnam, among the first women to make that journey.[52]

White Volunteers—From North to South

From the beginning, whites volunteered in the southern civil rights movement; but their numbers were small. Many early volunteers were southerners themselves, familiar with the ethos of southern life within which the battle was to be fought; a few others were exchange students from northern colleges, such as Anne Moody's friends Joan Trumpauer and Jeanette King and her teacher, Lois Chaffee, who were in the sit-ins. SNCC historian-activist Howard Zinn was teaching at Spelman College, one of many academics impelled by the urgency of events to give up jobs in northern universities. Also, from the 1962 founding of Students for a Democratic Society (SDS), northern campus activists travelled south to learn organizing lessons from SNCC. Tom Hayden, SDS founder and co-author of its initial Port Huron Statement of purpose, came often, married civil rights volunteer Sandra "Casey" Cason, and supported connections between the civil rights and northern student movements like the Economic Rights Action Project (ERAP).[53]

The steady trickle of white volunteers into the South swelled to a wave in the "Freedom Summer" of 1964 and on the Selma to Montgomery march in the spring of 1965. White sympathizers with the civil rights movement stepped up their organizing outside of the South during these years, gradually recognizing that prejudice and segregation were not confined to that region. Across the country, supporters sought ways both to express indignation at injustice and to devise ways to correct it. Some major women's organizations, notably the YWCA and the National Council of Negro Women (NCNW), had long worked against racism and for opportunities for all. In the sixties, others took up those tasks as well. Acting from a belief in the transforming power of education, women from such organizations as the American Association for University Women volunteered in urban classrooms and set up library projects. Others picketed northern branches of businesses that discriminated against blacks in employment and service; and they marched, carrying banners for peace and justice through hostile ethnic neighborhoods in Boston and Chicago.[54]

In a somewhat controversial project, urban, mostly middle-class wo-men, black and white, traveled from northern homes seeking conver-sation and understanding with their southern counterparts through an NCNW-sponsored program called Wednesdays in Mississippi. The idea came from Polly Spiegel Cowan, three of whose children volun-teered in the 1964–65 voter registration drives in the South. Concerned about the lack of adult support for these efforts and about the contrast between the activism of the young and the comfort of their parents' generation, Cowan, working with NCNW President Dorothy Height, initiated a woman-to-woman visiting program. For several months in 1964 and again in 1965, white and black women from Boston, New York, Cincinnati, Washington, and other cities flew to Mississippi, to try to reach mutual understanding on matters of race. Participants in-cluded such notable activists as New York lawyer Florynce Kennedy, Boston black community leader Ruth Batson, and Patti Derian, later a member of the Carter administration. The project was kept secret for most of its duration, for fear of violent repercussion; when it was pub-licized, it drew scorn from younger radical activists who saw it as hope-lessly middle-class and middle-aged.[55]

Wednesdays in Mississippi had considerable success on its own terms, however, and a great impact on individual participants. Report-ing on the Boston team's visit to Canton, Mississippi, from 14–16 July 1964, Ruth Batson described the trip as "the most meaningful thing I have ever done. I had never been South before and had no idea what the problems were, even though I thought I knew. . . . I went South and saw this enormous problem, so big, and I then thought I am not doing so much." On her return to Boston she "immediately got into the Freedom fight with the Massachusetts delegation," single-handedly taking on the task of convincing her state's Democratic delegation to support the Mississippi Freedom Democrat Party challenge. The Wednesdays project led to conversation where none had before existed and to new education initiatives for disadvantaged and black Southern children.[56]

Most of the white women who were deeply involved in the early days of SNCC were southerners who shared the experience of growing up in a racially segregated society. Equally important, as many black student activists, their consciences had been formed by church mem-bership. Interviewing white women who were early participants in the movement, Sara Evans found two consistent similarities: southern her-itage (only Dorothy Miller was a northerner) and entry into the movement through work in the church. Several were minister's daughters. Jane Stembridge, student at Union Theological Seminary and daughter of a Southern Baptist minister, came from New York to the organizing meeting of SNCC in April 1960. She became its first paid staff member, working with Ella Baker to set up the organization's office and work out communications procedures. Mary King, who later co-authored a controversial position paper on women in SNCC, was the daughter of a southern Methodist minister. From early on, she was an invaluable staff member for SNCC, taking on a wide variety of responsibilities.

Another early commentator on women's roles in the movement, Sandra "Casey" Cason (for a time married to Tom Hayden), had a mother who was "divorced, self-supporting intellectual, and liberal." Cason became involved at the University of Texas with religious groups, including the YWCA and the Christian Faith and Life Community, whose members "sought the theological dimension in every aspect of their lives." Her steps toward activism, in both civil rights and feminism, stemmed from YWCA work on race relations and on the changing roles of men and women—"a natural extension of [her] intellectual and moral concerns to join an integrated community, which in turn catapulted her into activism." The YWCA initiated pickets of local restaurants excluding blacks.[57]

Sue Thrasher, in 1964 a cofounder of the Southern Students Organizing Committee (SSOC), a primarily male support group for white student activists, came from a working-class family more liberal in its attitude toward race than most of its neighbors; she was also deeply involved in the Methodist Youth Fellowship while a student at Nashville's Methodist Scarritt College. She took Methodist doctrines "like the fatherhood of God and the brotherhood of man, . . . literally. . . . I was very upset when I found that other people didn't. . . . I was working out my own values within the religious realm, and gradually they provided the foundation for action in every other realm."[58]

Sue Thrasher's search for models led her to two women of an earlier generation. She talked at length with Lillian Smith (1897–1966), whose writings and work on behalf of civil rights had brought her notoriety and vicious attacks in the forties and fifties. Despite ill health, Smith continued to speak out. Her last book, *Our Faces, Our Words* (1964) celebrated the nonviolent crusade for civil rights. Shortly before her death, she resigned from CORE's executive board, distressed by the call for "Black Power" and the turn away from nonviolence. Thrasher also sought advice from Florence Recce, whose husband Sam had been a union leader in Harlan County, Kentucky. Florence Recce wrote "What Side Are You On?," the well-known union song later adapted by the civil rights movement. She helped the younger woman see parallels between the two movements and supported her faith in the rural southerner.[59]

A woman closer to her own age was of special importance to Thrasher and other young white southern activists. Anne McCarty Braden (1924–) was, like Virginia Durr, an Alabama native from an old Southern family. She became a foe of segregation while still a student at Randolph-Macon Woman's College, but her resistance also drew on church experiences. As a journalist covering the courts, she saw clearly the violent injustice of black southern life and became increasingly radical. In 1948, she married journalist and segregation foe Carl Braden. He was jailed for several months in 1954 for selling their Louisville home in a white neighborhood to a black family; both were labeled "communist agitators" and subjected to violence and threats, injunctions and trials. Jail experience "burned their bridges," Anne Braden recalled. The Kentucky authorities' action "hurled" her irrevocably into the southern struggle. "It made life worth living." In 1957, the Bradens became field secretaries for the Southern Conference Education Fund (SCEF), heir to the Southern Conference for Human Welfare, and Anne Braden juggled home, family, and activism. Their home became a center and haven for activists, white and black. SNCC historian-activist Clayborne Carson says the Bradens, "particularly Anne, became part of the small group of whites who gained the trust of most of the SNCC staff."[60]

For many younger women, like Sue Thrasher and Bernice Johnson Reagon, the civil rights struggle in the South provided a unique new experience, the example of women whom they could emulate. Dorothy Dawson Burlage remembers that as a civil rights activist, "For the first time I had role models I could really respect"—women, black and white, old and young.[61]

Freedom Summers

The religious vision with which SNCC began faltered under pressure of violence and discouragement. SNCC had come together as a "redemptive community"; by practicing the philosophical and religious ideal of nonviolence, SNCC founders had believed that they could change the world. By 1964, that faith had been severely tested. Many who accepted nonviolence as a tactic were ready to abandon it or had already; and even some of those who had grounded their lives in the nonviolent ideal were shaken by violence suffered. The organization which faced the arrival of hundreds of untested white northern volunteers in the summer of 1964 was much more skeptical and hardened than when founded four years before. Many movement veterans doubted the usefulness of white volunteers; the prospect of trying to absorb large numbers of people who were far behind SNCC members in the debate over nonviolence, who came with romantic ideas, and who needed protection, was far from welcome. Also opponents argued that the influx of large numbers staying for a short time would enlarge the scope of the work without providing necessary follow-up.

Few of the volunteers who went south in the Freedom Summers of 1964 and 1965 were philosophically committed to nonviolence as a way of life. Most accepted nonviolence tactically and hoped for its transformative power. For men, in a culture which valued meeting fire with fire, adoption of the nonviolent approach demanded a particular kind of courage, embracing not only an openness to one's enemies but also the possibility of being charged with being less than a man. For women, however, nonviolence opened other possibilities, making physical strength almost irrelevant and allowing them literally to embody their courage and their hatred of injustice. Barbara Deming (1917–1985), whose dedication to peace and justice extended from protests against nuclear testing and long marches and jailings for civil rights in the fifties and sixties to the Seneca (N.Y.) peace encampment and the gay liberation movement of the mid-eighties, believed that the unbounded potential of non-violent resistance to evil should have particular appeal for women. "Who better than women should know that battles can be won without resort to physical strength? Who better than we should know all the power that resides in noncooperation?"[62]

Freedom Summer 1964 brought about 650 volunteers to Mississippi; in 1965, recruited by the Freedom Democratic Party, about 750 came to work on voter registration drives, teach in Freedom Schools, and do various tasks to further the movement's goals in several southern states. Most were young, but there were exceptions: 67-year-old Lorna Smith went to Greenwood from California because she "saw on television that they wanted people" and "just had to come." Outspoken and intrepid, she took on the fearful county registrar, Martha Lamb, in direct confrontation; she also challenged white ministers about the validity of a Christianity that denied full rights to blacks.[63]

About half the volunteers were women, and almost all were white. COFO, the umbrella organization of civil rights groups operating in the region, decided that each volunteer had to pay round-trip transportation, have $150 to support themselves plus the ability to post a $500 bond in case of arrest. These rules effectively eliminated black urban students, few of whom had enough money. The decision to recruit large numbers of white volunteers was pragmatic; only if whites were seen to be in danger due to southern racist intransigence would national attention be paid. Danger and death to blacks was not news; danger to children of "a senator or congressman" would be, Ella Baker explained.

Volunteers came mainly from cities, two of every five from the northeast, with most from New York. Almost half of the rest came from the west coast and the midwest. The Free Speech Movement at Berkeley in 1964 mobilized many, who responded to COFO campus recruiters seeking summer volunteers. According to Mary Aickin Rothschild, more white volunteers came from the South than from the mountain and southwestern states combined. Most volunteers were well educated, many from Harvard, Stanford, the University of Wisconsin, and Berkeley. Their parents were also more educated than the average American, and they were generally economically secure.[64]

Particularly among New York participants, there were many sons and daughters of thirties radicals, "red-diaper babies" brought up hearing about America's failure to live up to its promises and believing in their responsibility to try to correct that failure. These parents were no less worried than others about their children's safety in the South, but they supported their decisions to go. Tamar Cole, whose mother, the novelist Helen Yglesias, had long been active in radical causes, went to Mississippi in 1964 without resistance from home. It "seemed natural" to Yglesias that her daughter would want to participate in this most significant social crusade of her times.[65]

Many parents, particularly mothers, were not so supportive; and the prospect of the summer's danger was made more difficult for many volunteers by pressure from home. During training sessions at Western College in Oxford, Ohio, one woman was bombarded by her anxious mother: "She had sent me a telegram signed with my brother's name saying that she had had a heart attack and I must come home immediately (none of which was true). Telephone calls, with her screaming, threatening, crying. . . . Long vituperative letters." Her situation may have been extreme; but several volunteers experienced versions of that pressure as seen in *Letters from Mississippi*, collected by Elizabeth Sutherland. "Bonnie" wrote to her parents from Ohio: "It is very hard to answer to your attitude that if I loved you I wouldn't do this—hard, because the thought is cruel. I can only hope you have the sensitivity to understand that I can both love you very much and desire to go to Mississippi. . . . I hope you will accept my decision even if you do not agree with me. There comes a time when you have to do some things which your parents do not agree with."[66]

For most Freedom Summer volunteers, political action was not new, although the degree of danger was. Most had participated in civil rights actions in the north and developed strength; fifteen percent of the volunteers had worked in peace groups, before the anti-war era. Idealistic "children of the American Dream," most were also "enormously naive about the black community and the terrible pressures that civil rights direct action brought with it."[67]

The danger became clear early: in June 1964 three civil rights workers—James Chaney, a black member of the CORE staff, Michael Schwerner, a white CORE staffer, and Andrew Goodman, a white summer project volunteer—disappeared. Their bodies were found six weeks later, buried under a dam in Philadelphia, Mississippi. Preoccupied by news of that disappearance and its implications, Freedom Summer volunteers took their assignments, which tended to fall along gender lines—men were sent out to more dangerous areas to do voter registration, going in integrated groups into hostile communities. Women also worked on voter registration, but most were teachers or librarians in the community schools or in the volunteers' communication system. Sally Belfrage was a librarian in the Greenwood project. "Margaret" was chief WATS line operator at the COFO headquarters in Jackson. Pleased by the importance of the job, she still felt detached from events: "We in communications have the responsibility of running the telephone system and handling the press, knowing where everyone in the state is. We are the security system. . . . The strange thing is that even here in the heart of the organization and the state, I have a hard time believing what really goes on."[68]

"Pam" taught in a Freedom School whose curriculum had its roots in Septima Clark's community education plans. In the morning, Pam taught the "Core Curriculum . . . Negro History and the History and Philosophy of the Movement." Afternoons, she taught a religion course and one on nonviolence. Mornings, she had fifteen students, girls and young women; afternoons, four to six girls and four boys. Although not true of Pam's class, many students in the Freedom Schools were not young; people of all ages came.[69]

Some of the white women were acutely aware of differences between themselves and those with whom they worked. "Martha" agonized that "as a white northerner I can get involved whenever I feel like it and run home whenever I get bored or frustrated or scared." For "Jo" the differences in education and experience produced resentment on both sides: "Several times I've had to completely re-do press statements or letters . . . It's one thing to tell people who have come willingly to Freedom School that they needn't feel ashamed of weaknesses in these areas, but it's quite another to even acknowledge such weaknesses in one's fellow workers. Furthermore, I'm a northerner. I'm white; I'm a college graduate; I've not 'proven' myself yet in jail or in physical danger. Every one of these things is a strike against me as far as they are concerned."[70]

Black women often resented what they saw as special treatment accorded white women and the sexual relationships developing between black men and white women. Gender distinctions in assignments had not characterized early SNCC years, when black women (and white women like Casey Cason Hayden and Mary King) participated in the danger and expected to be seen as equals. Even the black women who later joined SNCC took on equal assignments. Cynthia Washington, who joined in 1963 and was a project director in 1964, did "the same work as men—organizing around voter registration and community issues in rural areas—usually *with* men." When they returned to town, "the men went with other women," often white women. She realized later that having her own project meant that she was treated differently, but at the time she responded to complaints about women's work contemptuously: "What Casey and the other white women seemed to want was an opportunity to prove they could do something other than office work. I assumed that if they could do something else, they'd probably be doing that."[71]

Every account of the 1964 Freedom Summer stresses its sexual tensions, some resulting from the prurience of local communities, convinced that interracial sex was what the movement was all about: "I was in Jackson overnight Tuesday and had my first brush with Mississippi lawmen. . . . When I told them I was a medical student, they accused me of being down here to do abortions on all the white girls who are pregnant by Negroes. But this seems to be an obsession all across the country." Tensions also arose from the sexual activity of volunteers. Black women were angry at white women; white women feared accusations of racism if they refused a black man. Black-white sexual relations endangered the work by exacerbating local anger. In some cases, white women were removed from field projects for dating black men. Black women, like Cynthia Washington, found exclusion from relationships with black men made an already tense situation worse.[72]

Meridian, Alice Walker's heroine in her 1976 novel of the same name about the movement, listened to Truman Held as he explains that his attraction to the white women was "essentially a matter of sex." For Meridian that was incomprehensible: "She had been taught that nobody wanted white girls except their empty-headed, effeminate counterparts—white boys. . . . White women were considered sexless, contemptible, and ridiculous." Black women were adventurous, "escaping to something unheard of. Outrageous." But Meridian, like Cynthia Washington, discovered her strength and adventurousness were threatening. A male SNCC worker told Washington that some of the black women on the project "made him feel superfluous." Truman Held "did not want a woman who tried . . . to claim her own life."[73]

Older black women, models for younger activists, explained their own lives and the relative lack of male political activism on economic grounds and on the greater danger men faced from whites. Anecdotal evidence suggests that they had been able to challenge traditional gender roles without disturbing the balance between men and women. For younger women, seeking to claim their own lives within the new rules of the sixties' "sexual revolution," things were more difficult. The rhetoric of the times demanded women's availability as a measure of their acceptability. For young black women, who understood the struggle for justice to be their struggle as much as it was the men's, the need to be at once strong and courageous in the political arena and subservient in the sexual created tremendous stress. Richer in female role models than white contemporaries, they continued to do the movement's work.

For young white women in the South, already scared by the work facing them, the contempt of black women, the challenge of black men, and the male-superior attitudes of white men constituted a formidable challenge. Some dealt with the sexual situation by removing themselves from social life entirely. Others sought relationships with white men, risking the loss of themselves in the male shadow. Joanna, the lead character in Rosellen Brown's novel, *Civil Wars*, marries a white "movement hero." The novel shows his failure to grow up from that role and the dissolution of their marriage. Some, against the odds, formed loving and lasting relationships with black men. Some made mistakes.

Despite the sexual tensions and the frustrations of struggling with the white power structure, Freedom Summer 1964 had accomplishments. The report of the Waveland Conference, called in November to assess the results, concluded that it had succeeded in refocusing the nation's eyes on southern civil rights abuses. The six-week search for the three missing men provided a tragic reminder; and the volunteers' work received national coverage, adding new voters to the rolls, calling attention to the ongoing resistance to voter registration, and contributing to a climate of support for federal legislation for civil rights.[74]

Perhaps those who benefitted most were the white volunteers. For a generation of young white Americans, the journey of some to Mississippi provided a measuring stick for idealism and courage and lessons about the burdens black people had long borne in their search for freedom. As Sara Evans makes clear, the young white women who went to Mississippi learned, as had their predecessors, that they could do more than they or their parents ever thought they could. They learned to make connections: Ellen "learned more about politics here from running my own precinct meetings than I could have from any Government professor . . . For the first time in my life, I am seeing what it is like to be poor, oppressed, and hated. And what I see does not apply only to Gulfport or to Mississippi or even to the South. . . . The people we're killing in Vietnam are the same people we've been killing for years in Mississippi."[75]

Freedom Summer also created a proto-feminist consciousness in some. In the fall of 1964, longtime white volunteers Casey Hayden and Mary King, probably working with several other women, presented an anonymous paper "The Position of Women in SNCC," at the Waveland Conference. It equated sexism with racism and criticized SNCC for shutting women out of decision-making. Many assumed that Rubye Doris Smith Robinson had written the paper—an idea that persisted and became a myth, as Evans points out, in accounts of the movement that focused on growing feminism within it. The paper, generally ignored, occasioned Stokely Carmichael's infamous, though, Mary King claims, facetious put-down: "The only position for women in SNCC is prone." Attribution of the paper to Robinson was a tribute to her strong-mindedness and courage, but Mary King recalls that Robinson was wary of the feminist stirrings in SNCC. Concerned about ongoing movement work, she did not want more divisiveness. Hayden and King submitted a second formal complaint to SNCC in 1965 and received another rebuff. Carmichael later claimed that charges of sexual inequality were meant "to stop the movement from going towards nationalism, because [white women] thought they were going to be put out of the movement."[76]

When the time came for the volunteers to return to their lives, many discovered they could not. Despite her earlier anger, "Jo" found by August 1964 that she could "no longer justify the pursuit of a Ph.D. When the folks in Flora have to struggle to comprehend the most elementary of materials on history and society and man's larger life, I feel ashamed to be greedily going after higher learning." She stayed into 1965, by which time the growing impulse toward separatism and black power in the southern movement made the possibility of white effectiveness more remote. With a consciousness formed by her religious training, Jo felt less and less sure of her own authenticity and usefulness: "How honest can one be holding back from people, fearing people and just feeling too tired to open up to people?" Leaving seemed the sensible thing to do, but "still I want to believe in love and disavow violence as a way of life. And still I'm loath to cut myself off from this kind of work and return to academe. I want to be more than I am."[77]

SNCC, too, was trying to assess the future and determine its direction. A conference in Holly Springs, Mississippi, in early 1965, wrestled with issues of personnel and plans for the summer ahead. Minutes of the meeting reflect the continuing importance of women in maintaining the organization and suggest some internal tension. Rubye Doris Robinson complained as the meeting opened that some of volunteers did not seem productive to her: "Some of these people just float and don't do any work." Some of the floaters were volunteers who stayed on after Freedom Summer. Others, like Casey Hayden, were longtime activists seeking some new outlet for their movement work. Stokely Carmichael argued on her behalf, suggesting the stress all felt. "Casey worked," he pointed out. "There must be some reason for her present confusion. Many people who complain about 'floaters' stay in projects without knowing why." The radical programs for which people had come to SNCC were now "lost", and the voting bill would "squash a lot of SNCC work. What then?"[78]

The committee found that hard to answer. SNCC had become a large, sprawling organization, with projects across the South, support offices in Washington, Ann Arbor, and Los Angeles, and Friends of SNCC around the country. Just keeping track of people, cars, money, programs was an enormous task, much of which fell on Rubye Doris Robinson and Betty Garman in the Atlanta office. Decisions had to be made about relations with SCLC, about participation in such large scale demonstrations as the Selma to Montgomery march, and about the need to recruit more white volunteers for the 1965 summer.

The Selma-Montgomery march focused some of the difficulties between SCLC and SNCC. Essentially a grassroots organization, SNCC generally objected to mass demonstrations because they sapped energy from day-to-day work and focused attention on charismatic leaders, especially Dr. Martin Luther King, Jr., of whom they were increasingly critical. The Selma march on 21 March 1965 attracted vast numbers from Mississippi and across the south. Hundreds drove and flew across the country to take part. With Dr. King as its leader, and federal forces marshalled to protect participants, the march engaged nationwide attention. The night it ended Viola Liuzzo, a white community activist and mother of three from Detroit, was shot dead by nightriders.

SNCC's concern over the deviation of effort from the day-to-day work of organizing came not only from the massiveness of work that remained but also from a recognition that the next stages needed a more sophisticated economic analysis than they had done or had the energy to do. In words echoing Ella Baker's warning at SNCC's organizing meeting, Muriel Tillinghast summed up the problem: "What do you do after you finish demonstrating? You stand in front of a hamburger stand for three weeks; but when you get in, you don't have fifteen cents to buy a hamburger. My premise is that Negroes are going to have to fight for everything they get. We'll just have to find a way to keep people producing. Federal programs aren't going to do anything and you know this before you start out. The staff in Mississippi is tired. They just don't have the energy to start knocking on doors."[79]

White volunteers did go south in 1965, working in voter registration drives organized by MFDP and SNCC. The Voting Rights Act was signed on 6 August 1965, and federal marshals went south to protect registrants. The number of blacks on the voter rolls increased dramatically. In Holmes County, fifth poorest in Mississippi, there had been five registered black voters in 1963; over 5,500 by 1967. Freedom Summer 1965 was less intense than in 1964. Projects were more decentralized, and they were not operating under the haunting sense of tragedy that marked the previous summer. Most of those who came for the first Freedom Summer and stayed on were leaving or had left. Exceptions lingered in Holmes County where Susan and Henry Lorenzi stayed until 1969. Slightly older than most summer volunteers, they arrived from Berkeley in 1964, not as students (she was then 23; he, 29) but because they saw that the movement's needs and their own could coincide. They meant to stay because they "needed to feel welcome for more than two months; we were finished with college and seeking to fill our years beyond summer." They served for a year as codirectors of the Holmes County Community Center in Mileston, training a local staff to take over their work. Then they moved to Lexington, to staff the MFDP office there and "for the next four years worked several phases of our transition out."[80]

The Lorenzis lived through the transition in SNCC from the early questioning of nonviolence to the challenge of "black power." The phrase was spoken first by SNCC worker Willie Lee on James Meredith's 1966 march through Mississippi; it came to epitomize the direction in which Stokely Carmichael wanted to take the movement. The time for accommodation and turning the other cheek was past: black power meant that the movement's work should be done by black people for black people, that sympathetic whites should leave the movement and turn their attention to dealing with racism in their own communities. It also meant abandonment of what remained of SNCC's commitment to nonviolence and the establishment of a new commitment to a revolutionary economic and social analysis. For black women, the call for black power became a call for women to take up the role of giving birth and raising children for the black nation that needed to come into being. Some resisted, seeing this as a demand for female subservience; others found themselves caught in the impossible dilemma of trying to choose between allegiance to race or to themselves as women.

As this crucial debate raged, the needs of southern communities remained acute. In Mississippi, the MFDP grew more successful in organizing voter registration drives and in working to develop community leadership. Increasingly, like Fannie Lou Hamer, people in all parts of the movement became aware of the relationship between economic and political issues and of the need to address both. The movement changed direction after 1966, but the urgency remained, as did the centrality of women's work.[81]

Marian Wright Edelman, a young black attorney with the NAACP Legal Defense Fund who was close to Dr. King, testified in 1967 before the Senate Labor Committee's subcommittee on poverty about worsening "survival" conditions in Mississippi at a time when the federal government was shifting over to food stamps from food distribution through the Agriculture Department. The plantation system persisted in some areas; and "the peasants or the tenants on those farms literally could not eat and did not have the most basic survival needs," sinking into even deeper poverty. Edelman conducted Robert Kennedy and other horrified Senators on a fact-finding tour and Kennedy urged Edelman to have Dr. King bring the poor to Washington: "it's time for some visible expression of concern for the poor." The result was the Poor People's Campaign that brought thousands of all races to the Capital just four weeks after King's assassination in Memphis on 4 April 1968. They christened their encampment of 2,500 on the Washington Mall Resurrection City; it remained from 13 May until disbanded by police with tear gas on 24 June. Frustrations over this failure to win support in Washington and anger over King's assassination impelled some to activism that rejected the nonviolence of the civil rights movement and led to escalating radicalism.[82]

Black Power

Radicalization of civil rights began in 1966 when SNCC voted to exclude whites, and Mary King complained that the organization was taken over by newcomers who rejected white veterans like Dottie and Bob Zellner, native Alabamians working in New Orleans' poor white neighborhoods. Mary King felt "dislocated" by the action and went through three years of personal mourning. Rising black nationalism in cities and a shift in focus from the rural South was one cause.[83]

In the wake of the August 1965 riot in the Watts section of Los Angeles, California radicals Huey Newton and Bobby Seale founded the Black Panther Party for Self-Defense, drawing the names and logo from the Lowndes (Alabama) County Freedom Organization. Aiming to counteract local police brutality, its larger agenda was to fight racism deeply embedded in the culture and to replace it with a militant celebration of being black. Elaine Brown, a Black Panther from 1967 on, explains that the movement "reached out mostly to men, to young, black urban men who were on the streets"—gang members offered "some sense of dignity" and "opportunity to make their lives meaningful." Emphasis on the "brothers" did not exclude the "sisters," although feminists criticized Brown for her "return to the community of the black male." She explains the need to recreate black father figures, absent in her experience, "to say, 'Yes, there are men in this world who cared, black men, who cared about the community and . . . were willing to take it to the last degree.'"[84]

Other women joined. SNCC veteran Kathleen Neal married Eldridge Cleaver in 1967 and became a Black Panther. As Communications Secretary, she was the only woman on the Central Committee. The second highest-ranking woman was Connie Matthews as International Coordinator. Iris Shinn became a national spokesperson for the party, appearing on talk shows. Sonia Sanchez and Betty Shabazz, widow of Malcolm X, found asylum at Oakland's Black House, a cultural center like New York's Black Arts Repertory Theatre, a place for cooperative poetry, plays, and art by "a great collage of people from Panthers to so-called cultural nationalists to students." Gloria Abernethy became active in the Richmond branch; Sharla Woods, in San Francisco; and Rosemari Mealy, in Philadelphia—all contributing articles on community concerns to the national newspaper *The Black Panther*. Panther women wore the black berets and leather jackets of the "brothers" but also skirts. Brown remembers their commitment "to surrender something of ourselves, our own lives" because of a belief in the struggle that transcended gender, with a readiness to put their lives on the line if necessary: "It meant really seeing yourself as part of whole, and part of an entire process, and that you were a soldier in the army . . . bringing revolution."[85]

Revolution came of its own accord. In the summer of 1967, violence erupted in the black ghetto of Newark. In Detroit, Carado Bailey and his white wife had been harassed for trying to move into the white suburb of Warren; and false rumors spread that a white policeman had killed a black prostitute. The powder keg erupted following a police raid on a "blind pig," a private after-hours bar. As their neighborhood burned, mothers like Helen Kelly and Daisey Nunley were caught in the middle with a siege mentality, defending children and homes against the dual threat of black gangs and National Guardsmen.[86]

Although primarily focused on urban youth, the black power movement drew upon nascent activism on black campuses like Howard University, where young women experienced particular discontent. Robin Gregory remembers rejecting the advice of the Dean of Women to act and dress in a ladylike manner. She began to wear her hair "natural," copying the Mississippi women she saw at the 1964 Democratic Convention, Stokely Carmichael's girlfriend Mary Lovelace, and her own "radical" aunt from the fifties. The Afro "was an affirmation of being who we were . . . a statement that way." It horrified her parents and provoked public reactions.[87]

Similarly, Adrienne Manns was disappointed to find an upper-middle-class, elitist environment at Howard in 1964, not the black cultural experience she anticipated. Howard's parietal rules strictly regulated women's behavior; and the dominant high-culture, Eurocentric curriculum did not meet her expectations. Manns was more drawn to the black power message of Stokely Carmichael that she heard in the summer of 1966. Paula Giddings had also found Howard lacking in 1965 despite "a period of tremendous ferment"—only speakers on "how to dress, how to speak properly, how to fit into some other kind of occupation or job that had nothing to do with black people" or helping them.[88]

Such discontent came to a head in 1966 with Robin Gregory's campaign for homecoming queen as a way to overthrow the old value system and "to make a statement about the black aesthetic." "Usually they picked someone who was as close to white as they could possibly get." Gregory wore "sharp" but nontraditional women's clothes and an Afro; she campaigned for the title with two silent, handsome men dressed like the Fruit of Islam, Giddings recalls, not in a convertible color-coordinated to her wardrobe. Gregory's popular election sparked a jubilant demonstration to the chant of "Umgawa, Black Power," launching a movement at Howard that resulted in the 1968 take-over of the Administration Building and involved many women.[89]

Through four years of activism, Giddings "got a sense of self, a new sense of my black self, in terms of culture, . . . of politics, . . . of the rights to demand certain things, the right to feel good about yourself . . . as a black person." Similar activism for black studies, black student unions, and reformed admissions at Columbia, Cornell, San Francisco State, Maryland's Bowie State, Northwestern, Tuskegee, and Boston University brought the black power movement to campuses from its base in urban ghettos. Some of the results were positive: a 1968 Howard conference "Toward a Black University," one of several across the nation that fall that explored black studies, drew three thousand and helped spark a black cultural renaissance.[90]

Other activism met with violence. At South Carolina State College in the "Orangeburg Massacre" in February 1968, police killed three protesting black students and wounded 27 others; but the incident received little news coverage. At Ohio State, a demonstration by multiracial students in May 1970 for admission of more black students and an end to ROTC resulted in the calling in of the National Guard. That month, activism ended in tragedy at the all-black Jackson State College when Mississippi Highway Safety Patrolmen and city police killed two students and wounded a dozen others who were protesting expansion of the Vietnam War, which they considered racist, and the killing of four students at Ohio's Kent State a week before.[91]

The ideas of black power articulated by Malcolm X, particularly about education, reached a grassroots constituency independent of the student movement. What happened from 1966–68 in the 98 percent black and Hispanic Ocean Hill-Brownsville neighborhood of Brooklyn was an extreme, nationally known example of problems and trends elsewhere. Parents in the area had been demanding community control over their schools as an alternative to integration. Through the PTA, Dolores Torres and other organized. Frustrated by unanswered complaints about teachers, they took over a meeting of the New York City Board of Education and held a three-day sit-in, winning permission for an experiment to run their school by an eleven-member elected local school board, which included Torres.[92]

Sandra Feldman, with experience from Freedom Rides in 1962, from organizing the 1963 March on Washington, and from Harlem CORE, was named local field representative of the United Federation of Teachers (UFT) in 1967. She tried to persuade the already integrated school staff to cooperate with the experiment; but attempts to force teacher transfers out of the district resulted in a UFT strike met in the streets by angry parents, many of whom staffed classrooms to keep them open. In the fall of 1968, the strike spread through the city, affecting 57,000 teachers and a million students. Only the Ocean Hill-Brownsville schools remained open, staffed by 350 new, nonunion teachers—including many "hippies," about a hundred blacks, and a hundred Jews—hired by the community board.[93]

Meanwhile, children became radicalized. Many gave up their "slave names." Eighth-grader Theresa Jordan renamed herself Nabowiah Weusi, then Karima. Some teachers wore dashikis; bulletin boards bore pictures of Stokely Carmichael and Rap Brown; students read Langston Hughes. Children crossed barricades manned by cops in riot gear and patrolled by helicopters to find "you just can't have a biology class with all the political science going on" outside. Feldman, trying to maintain the peace in the UFT, sympathized with the former teachers "just picked to be symbols." Eventually the UFT won by portraying community activists as anti-Semites. Despite aid from the ACLU and emotional appeals by students like Sia Berhan whose poem "Anti-

Semitism" was read on the radio, the strike and the experiment in black community control of education ended in November 1968 with reinstatement of the old teachers.[94]

The issues at stake included not only quality education but also black culture, an issue addressed by other organizations like Imamu Amiri Baraka's Black Community Development and Defense Organization. Baraka (formerly Leroi Jones) also organized a Black Power Conference in Newark in 1967 that unanimously passed a resolution against birth control and abortion as genocide; and black power women like Toni Cade and Brenda Hyson supported it.[95]

By late 1968, the Black Panther party had chapters in 25 cities but a membership of only about a thousand when FBI director J. Edgar Hoover labeled it "the greatest threat to the internal security of the country" and launched a counterintelligence campaign (COINTELPRO) "to expose, disrupt, misdirect, discredit, or otherwise neutralize" its activities and those of other "Black Nationalist-Hate Groups," including SCLC, SNCC, SDS, and the Nation of Islam. Black Panther rhetoric escalated along with racial violence from 1968 to 1970, blending Marxism and visceral anger against "pigs" and fascist authorities. In an article in the *Black Panther* in early 1970, Elaine Brown called for blacks to take up guns and to fight back, concluding, "WE WILL KILL—ANYONE WHO STANDS IN THE WAY OF OUR FREEDOM!" She responded particularly to the case of Deborah Johnson and Fred Hampton as well as to chronic violence between police and residents in urban ghettos.[96]

Deborah Johnson was recruited to the new Chicago Panther chapter in 1968 when her brother brought home a flyer; she felt their programs should provide free breakfasts, work in medical clinics, and sell newspapers to the community. She watched with fear the violent raid by Chicago police on the Panther office where she worked on 31 July 1969. Johnson became engaged to the charismatic Panther leader Fred Hampton. The "pigs" invaded their apartment in the middle of the night on December 3 to seize Hampton. One tore her robe open and exclaimed, "What do you know, we have a broad here." Another grabbed her by the hair and threw her into the kitchen. Hampton was shot in their bed. Before the police sealed the apartment two weeks later, ten thousand people filed through. One older black woman bemoaned it as "nothing but a northern lynching." Johnson and six other survivors in the apartment that night were charged with attempted murder; but after a federal grand jury found the violence had come from the police, charges were dropped. Meanwhile, Johnson bore Hampton's child.[97]

In 1969, Los Angeles SNCC and Community party member Angela Yvonne Davis (1944–), educated in philosophy with Herbert Marcuse and in Germany, was fired from her UCLA job by the board of regents under orders from Governor Ronald Reagan before she even began teaching. She immediately became "a symbol of black protest," active in the prisoners' rights movement, especially in defense of three black inmates (the Soledad Brothers) who had killed a white guard at Soledad Prison. In August 1970, she became "one of the nation's most wanted fugitives," implicated as an accessory to a raid by the brother of one of the prisoners on a Marin County courthouse, resulting in four dead. Arrested in New York two months later, she was found guilty of murder, kidnapping, and conspiracy. Her story, like so many others, marked the violent end of the decade and the demise of the heroic era of the nonviolent civil rights movement.[98]

Women in the black power movement experienced even more sexist demands than those in the New Left or civil rights movements, especially the male insistence that their mission was giving birth and raising as many children as possible "for the revolution," for the black nation they needed to produce. Women's place was to be "a step behind," perhaps inspired by the rise of the Black Muslims. Some women defended this stance, seeing it as a natural response to the history of their men's suffering under the lingering effects of slavery and heeding a ban on "genocidal" birth control. Others resisted the demanded subservience and resented the discounting of their movement work. Kathleen Cleaver noted that even as a Black Panther Party officer her suggestions were rejected while identical proposals made by a man were implemented. She attributed it to a problem of ego. Cleaver worked the soundtrucks and wrote the first leaflets at demonstrations made up largely by women; but the men insisted that only their voices be heard, that they retain total control. Angela Davis remembered encountering black male chauvinism while organizing in San Diego in 1967: "I came headlong into a situation which was to become a constant problem in my political life. I was criticized very heavily for doing a 'man's job.' Women should not play leadership roles, they insisted. A woman was to 'inspire her man and educate his children.'" Strangely, this pattern replicated the ideal image of women in traditional white society precisely at a time when even mainstream America was beginning to question it.[99]

The American Indian Movement

Similar patterns emerged in the nascent American Indian Movement at the end of the sixties. The Indian population grew by 51.4 percent in the decade, reaching 792,730 in 1970; about half lived in urban ghettos and 28 percent on 115 major reservations. Annual median Indian income of $5,832 in 1970 compared with a national median of $9,590. Indians faced extreme poverty and racism that engendered the American Indian Movement (AIM), drawing inspiration from Black Power and other late sixties radicalism. More militant than the Oglala Sioux Civil Rights Organization (OSCRO), AIM was born in 1968, initially as a coalition of Lakota Sioux men in the Minneapolis-St. Paul Indian ghetto and Ojibways in Minnesota prisons. An unnamed woman proposed the name AIM rather than Concerned Indian Americans, realizing that that reduced to CIA. Like the civil rights movement, AIM was a spiritual and cultural movement—an assertion of native American identity and confrontation with history; and as in civil rights, women of all ages played crucial roles, often behind the scenes but also putting their bodies on the line in public confrontation. In *Lakota Woman* (1991), Mary Ellen Crow Dog, born Brave Bird, tells that story as well as that of her own path toward self discovery through growing native American activism.[100]

As Indians organized across tribal lines, they found unity in the old Cheyenne saying, "A nation is not lost as long as the hearts of its women are not on the ground." Many native Americans had traditions of female leadership—medicine women and sages who determined tribal policy—and creation stories about the First Woman. Women were among those who seized the abandoned prison island of Alcatraz from 1969 to 1971, demanding an Indian cultural center and university on the site. Others tried to take over Fort Lawton near Seattle; some occupied abandoned Army bases in California and Illinois. Micmac Annie Mae Aquash (a.k.a. Brave Hearted Woman) from Nova Scotia joined AIM, participating with Russell Means and 200 militants in burying Plymouth Rock under a ton of sand as a "symbolic burial of the white man's conquest" and taking over *Mayflower II* in 1970. In 1971, a great-grandmother, Lizzy Fast Horse, led a group in scaling Mount Rushmore to reclaim symbolically the Black Hills for her people, whereupon they were seized by police. It was "the older women like Ellen Moves Camp and Gladys Bissonnette who first pronounced the magic words 'Wounded Knee' [site of the 1890 slaughter of Sioux, the last stand in the Indian wars], who said, 'Go ahead and make your stand at Wounded Knee. If you men won't do it, you can stay here and talk for all eternity and we women will do it."[101]

Women's militancy was spurred by escalating incidents of anti-Indian violence in urban ghettos and particularly on reservations where a rash of suspicious "accidents," actually murders, claimed the lives of women like Jancita Eagle Deer and Delphine Peltier. Sarah Bad Heart Bull, her son recently murdered by a white man, was seized and beaten by police during a Rapid City demonstration demanding justice. Indicted on several counts of riot and arson, she served only a few weeks; but justice was not served. Women knew special injustice under the federally controlled system: those who delivered babies at hospitals run by the Bureau of Indian Affairs (BIA) often emerged from anesthesia to find themselves sterilized against their wills.[102]

At Wounded Knee on the Oglala Sioux Pine Ridge Reservation in South Dakota, on 27 February 1973, many women were among the over 2,000 who held defensive bunkers and trenches for 71 days against federal marshalls, the FBI, and a corrupt tribal police force of "goons." There, most women worked behind the scenes, sustaining the warriors, many of whom were also women. Indian nurses worked under fire. Crow Dog found that siege made women stronger. One woman held a bunker singlehandedly after her husband was shot. Afraid to go to the hospital where she might be sterilized and intent on delivering her baby in as traditional a way as possible, the 17-year-old Crow Dog gave birth to a son during the siege, aided by the 72-year-old Potawatomy midwife Josette Wawasik, Ellen Moves Camp, Vernona Kills Right, and Annie Mae Aquash, herself killed by authorities two years later. The birth was greeted by all as a symbol of hope.[103]

Crow Dog remembers, "At one time a white volunteer nurse berated us for doing the slave work while the men got all the glory. We were betraying the cause of womankind, was the way she put it. We told her that her kind of women's lib was a white, middle-class thing, and that at this critical stage, we had other priorities. Once our men had gotten their rights and their balls, we might start arguing with them about who should do the dishes." Native American women did experience sexual exploitation: AIM leaders joked about their "wives of the month" and opposed birth control. Feminism did not shape native activism until the seventies when some formed Women of All the Red Nations. Like many black women, native Americans had more pressing priorities in terms of civil rights and identity.[104]

3

Higher Education

Dr. Bernice Sandler of the Women's Equity Action League testified to a Judiciary Subcommittee of the House of Representatives in 1971 that discrimination against young women permeated all of higher education: "Girls need far higher grades for admission to many institutions. Numerous studies have shown that between 75 and 95 percent of the well-qualified students that do not go on to college are women. And discrimination is one of the major reasons why. In graduate school, the quota system is even more vicious. At Stanford, the proportion of women students has declined over the last ten years, even though more and equally or better qualified women have applied for admission to graduate school. One out of every 2.8 men who applied was accepted; only one woman out of every 4.7 female applicants."[1]

Matters were deepseated, as Betty Friedan pointed out in *The Feminine Mystique* (1963), because at each step in her training a young woman was exposed to ambiguous expectations, with her training for any professional role undermined, if not contradicted, by her training for domestic responsibilities. This precipitated a role crisis: "American girls grow up feeling free and equal to boys—playing baseball, conquering geometry and college boards, going away to college, going out in the world to get a job, living alone in an apartment . . . and discovering their own powers in the world. All this gave girls the feeling they could be and do whatever they wanted to, with the same freedom as boys, the critics said. It did not prepare them for their role as women.

The crisis comes when they are forced to adjust to this role." Also, the messages women received from their chosen professions were blatantly negative, discouraging women from applying for professional training.[2]

Through the sixties, young women in high school and college received mixed signals about academic aspirations. Even at the decade's end, a high school text, *Representative Men: Heroes of Our Time*, highlighted only two women—Jacqueline Kennedy Onassis and Elizabeth Taylor. Young American women had few models of independent professional success, yet they received a boost in their aspirations for higher education from an unexpected source when the 1957 Russian launching of Sputnik precipitated a frantic national reassessment of American education. The National Defense Act of 1958 and early sixties educational acts aimed to recruit talented students, including women, to higher education. Yet in elementary school, girls saw that while 88 percent of their teachers were women very few held positions of authority—only 22 percent of principals were women. In high schools, fewer than half of teachers were women; and it was "almost impossible for a woman—no matter how well qualified—to become principal of a high school"; only 4 percent were women.[3]

Many young women's ambitions to enter the professions were squelched by high school and college counselors, who cautioned them against fields that were "not for girls." Although many of these women earned college degrees, they did not pursue their first professional impulses; and the bitterness and regrets were freely aired at 20th and 25th high school reunions in the eighties.

Despite the traditionalism that encouraged high school women to prepare themselves first for marriage and secondly for clerical jobs or traditional women's occupations, both numbers and percentages of women attending and graduating from college began to rise around 1960, reversing a decline during the fifties in women's higher education, and continuing through the next two decades. In 1960, 38 percent of college-aged women were enrolled as full-time students, compared to 54 percent of their male peers. By 1965, 45 percent of young women matriculated compared to 57 percent of young men; by 1970, 49 percent of young women were in college and 55 percent of young men.[4]

Most women in college were white and middle-class, although the number of black women began to rise. It was not easy to be one of the newly admitted: Patricia Bell Scott remembers her experience as a first-year student at a large, predominantly white university in 1968: "I was part of 'an experiment' that year; about one hundred black freshmen entered a university community of thirty thousand white students. I will remember always my excitement at moving into my dorm room—my first day at chemistry lab—meeting my lab partner, a white male, destined to be a doctor, so he said. I was astonished at how average he was. . . . 'barely above dumb.' And yet I remember how much encouragement he received from the professor, and how much surprise my A scores on tests elicited from the same professor. I received no reinforcement for my excellent performance. . . . I had no one with whom to share these discoveries and anxieties. I eventually learned to accept rejection and not to expect encouragement from anyone except parents for good work."[5]

Despite persistent sexism, there was a resurgence of the movement which a century before had led to the first generation of college educated women—an expansion of co-education, the admission of women into more curricular areas including professional studies, and the equalization of the status of all students by elimination of restrictions on "girls." Philanthropist and birth-control reformer Katharine Dexter McCormick built two women's dormitories at MIT in 1962 and 1968 to silence the administration's spurious excuse that female enrollment had to be low due to lack of housing. Ellen Willis remembers that as a Barnard student in the early sixties she wanted to take a course at Columbia but was told bluntly "that the professor didn't want 'girls' in his class because they weren't serious enough." Still, at decade's end, Jo Freeman considered the university "the most egalitarian environment most women will ever experience."[6]

One Ivy-League male bastion, Yale, admitted female undergraduates in 1969 as 15 percent of the class of 1973. Amy Solomon claims the honor as the first to register in that freshman class—a pioneer across a formidable sex barrier; but prospective male applicants were assured in a recruitment film that busloads of "girls," students from Smith and Vassar, would still be brought into New Haven. Princeton admitted women in 1970. In the 1966–68 academic years, 18 all-male and 35 all-female institutions began gender integration. In 1967, Vassar and Yale had considered a coordinate relationship, but Vassar chose not to move from Poughkeepsie.[7] The movement toward coeducation was rooted in economics, not a recognition of women's rights. All-male institutions, concerned about declining enrollments or encountering financial stress, solved their problem by enlarging the potential applicant pool by adding women to it.

The surge of coeducation brought a decline in women's colleges and a debate about their continued existence. There were 268 single-sex colleges for women in 1960; 146 remained in 1972. The period from June to December 1968 was a landmark in the history of American higher education as 64 women's colleges became coeducational or closed down. The best known, Vassar, admitted men in September 1969. The college's mission, said President Alan Simpson, was not "male-dominated coeducation" but "a college where the sexes are on a footing of genuine equality and where the women are not pushed around by the men." In May 1970, however, visiting Vassar for the Congress to Unite Women, Kate Millett discovered that male students were in authority positions far in excess of their small number and the Women's Liberation group had been marginalized by accusations of lesbianism.[8]

Most women's colleges still not admitting men were Roman Catholic; in 1966 only 17 percent of more than 350 Catholic institutions were coeducational. They had been founded to educate young women apart from the world; most, Rosemary Ruether commented, were "handicapped by that Catholic feminism which decrees subservience as woman's nature and motherhood as her destiny" and hampered by an "anti-intellectualism that stemmed from the way Catholicism has been interpreted as an authoritarian faith."[9]

Many were better than that: exceptions included Immaculate Heart College in Los Angeles, Webster in St. Louis, Manhattanville in New York, Mundelein in Chicago, and the College of Notre Dame in Baltimore. Within the dominant ethos of traditional expectations for women, individual faculty in many women's Catholic colleges struggled to give pre-eminence to intellectual life; and women students had a far better opportunity to see women as professors and presidents in those schools. The women's Catholic colleges also provided educational opportunities for the daughters of working-class families, who could not afford the larger, more prestigious schools. A 1967 study showed that students at the women's colleges ranked "highest on scholarship and awareness" of all Catholic college students, but concluded that although "some of the most radical and creative efforts toward intellectual excellence" were coming from the women's colleges, "even the best" did not rival the Seven Sisters.[10]

Answering the question, "Are Women's Colleges Obsolete?," Ruether argued for their continuation as "natural sources of institutional power for women in society" and their conscious use as such. As small liberal arts institutions they could also "demythologize the work culture which dominates current education" and "capitalize" on their humanistic tradition . . . to hold up a small lamp for the authentic purpose of education."[11]

Traditional dissuasion of women from serious educational aspirations underlies statistics found in a study of a wide variety of male and female college seniors in 1961. While 95 percent of college women expected to work and most were not planning immediate marriage, few (24 percent versus 39 percent of men) planned on going straight on to graduate school. Further figures showed that graduate study drew more average male students while attracting fewer top females. Although more women than men ranked in the top half of their classes, even those near the top were less willing than male counterparts to embark on graduate work right away. Still many women hoped to continue at some future point. Most aspired to be mothers of "highly accomplished children" and wives of "prominent men" but remained a "sympathetic, admiring audience for the small female minority" that was entering masculine fields and winning acclaim for it. Most had been primed by Katharine Hepburn or Rosalind Russell movies, writes historian Barbara Solomon, to look forward to a scenario of "the so-called happy ending in store for the high-powered career woman . . . who renounced her work to ensure the success of her marriage." They realized that "in real life women who had careers had no support from the culture, especially when they combined marriage, career, and motherhood"; and most chose their majors based on such limitations.[12]

In 1960, in the wake of national anxiety over American inferiority in education, *Newsweek* posed the troubling question, "Young Wives with Brains: Babies, Yes—But What Else?" Two years later, the *New York Times* described the "average girl" as viewing her future through a wedding band. "Despite compelling evidence that she will be working at 35, by choice or necessity, today's 21-year-old woman has difficulty looking beyond the ceremonies of her own marriage and her babies' christenings."[13]

Reporting in 1969 on nine years of teaching at Goucher College (then an all-women institution), Florence Howe noted ruefully that things had not changed: "The basic assumption about women's biological inferiority, dealt what one might have expected to be a death blow in the fifties by Simone de Beauvoir, comes to college annually in the heads and hearts of freshmen women." Despite recent events, students and their families assumed that "women who go to college are generally sitting out four years . . . before becoming wives and mothers. . . . Most come without genuine purpose." As early as 1965, Howe, later the founder of the Feminist Press, began to use the "identity of woman" as a theme in a freshman writing class. Predictably, she encountered resistance.[14]

Continuing Education

In 1960 the American Council on Education (ACE) established a Commission on the Education of Women "to direct attention to contemporary problems related to the education of women, to stimulate research on these problems, and to consider methods of practical applications of research findings." The new commission reflected Sputnik-inspired anxiety, as well as "a growing awareness that this nation and society as a whole are seriously in need of the full potential of the brain power available in both sexes." By October 1968, *National Business Woman*, the journal of the National Federation of Business and Professional Women (NFBPW), announced that "special educational programs for mature women amount to a national phenomenon."[15]

A 1967 NFBPW study showed that most women in continuing education programs returned to school to "learn new skills or update skills to compete for employment with the nation's youth." The typical adult coed was married, 35 to 39 years of age, with some previous college work, and "two or three children with the youngest in elementary school and the oldest nearing the age when they will be leaving for college or employment." Annual family income was in the $9–$14,000 range. Her husband tended to be better educated with a bachelor's degree, employed in the professions or semi-professions. Most were white, middle-class women who might be said to have anticipated Betty Friedan's analysis of the suburban malaise and sought a way to escape it; and most sought training for only part-time employment.[16]

Because of national policies and persistent ideas about women's limited ambitions outside the home, most "non-traditional," adult women students were shunted into short-term vocational programs designed to augment, update, and modernize the nation's workforce in clerical, semiprofessional, and technical support with new skills for the rapidly changing, newly automating workplace. The sixties were the heyday of the community or junior college movement, with the number of two-year institutions granting associate degrees increasing from 678 to 912 and enrollments from 748,619 to 1,671,440 between 1961 and 1967, with enrollment and faculty predicted to double between 1968 and 1973 by the American Association of Junior Colleges. These schools, many newly created by states and municipalities, experimented with evening and weekend classes, television courses, storefront classrooms and counseling centers, minicampuses, cooperative work-study programs, innovative curricula, and flexible schedules appealing to housewives or working women. Federal funds came from the 1962 Manpower Development and Training Act, the 1963 Higher Education Facilities and Vocational Education Acts, the 1965 Higher Education Act, and private foundation grants—all intending to increase the worker pool at a time of dramatic technological workplace change and realizing that women were an untapped "human resource."[17]

More academically ambitious continuing education programs for women also arose. In 1960 the University of Minnesota opened the first of these—an extensive program of courses and support services, including "financial aids, babysitting services, counseling and testing, remedial skill training in reading and writing, testing for advanced credit placement and part- and full-time employment counseling." The pioneering Minnesota Plan for Continuing Education for Women, designed by Dr. Virginia Senders, was a "dramatic effort to salvage for society those educated women in whom a large educational investment has been made and whose minds may have 'rusted' with disuse."[18]

In November 1960 Mary Ingraham Bunting, a biologist and president of Radcliffe College, announced a "wholly new exploratory venture beyond orthodox higher education." The Radcliffe Institute for Independent Study was exemplary of the college's belief "that the educated woman has a potential of achievement that she should be allowed and enabled to fulfill." The Institute, first directed by political scientist Constance E. Smith, offered twenty part-time associate scholar fellowships, each with an annual stipend of $3000, primarily for the talented woman in her mid-thirties "who, after marriage, finds it difficult, if not impossible, to continue to be intellectually creative without assistance" or to become "visible professionally." Each year the Institute would invite selected women who had achieved visibility as scholars, professional women, or artists to become resident fellows of the Institute. They would be "given time to reflect, to initiate or consolidate research, to outline and execute new books . . . to work for the future on projects for which their usual commitments may never leave time." Poets Anne Sexton and Maxine Kumin were among many distinguished early resident fellows.[19]

Response to the Institute's founding was "dramatic—indeed almost overwhelming," Bunting reported; almost 200 women applied for the first twenty scholarships. The Institute hosted about 36 fellows a year, most of them married women with children and Boston-area residents. The majority had their doctorates when they came, and planned to use the time to prepare for a return to college teaching or to a profession. In the late sixties, the Institute launched a program to support women in part-time graduate study at Harvard; ninety women "completed their PhDs" and "set a precedent."[20]

Between the Minnesota and Radcliffe programs, hundreds of others appeared with a variety of curricular foci, but with a similar intent: to give women opportunities to develop their skills and talents, to enter or re-enter the workplace. "Prime movers" included the Universities of Michigan and Kansas, UCLA, Claremont, Simmons, and Sarah Lawrence Colleges. From about 20 programs in 1963, the number grew to almost 500 by 1975. In 1961, Rutgers began a program to re-educate women mathematicians after a Ford Foundation survey found that "many women mathematics majors—after years spent in raising families—desired to update themselves in their major . . . . Interest in the program on the part of employers is keen."[21]

The American Association of University Women (AAUW), with a grant from the Rockefeller Brothers Fund, initiated its College Faculty Program in 1962, designed to "prepare mature college women for professional careers in higher education." As an outgrowth, in the summer of 1965, AAUW began a program to train counselors to work with adult women seeking to return to education or employment. A first-of-its-kind inter-institutional community-wide program for women's continuing education began in Miami, Florida, in 1965, sponsored by four local colleges and universities, the Dade County Board of Public Instruction, and twenty community leaders. In 1966–67 "women from 21–79 years of age with educational backgrounds ranging from elementary school to postdoctoral level called on [the Council for the Continuing Education of Women] for a helping hand." The University of Missouri in Kansas City provided training in 1968 under the Department of Labor's New Careers program, designed to create "employment opportunities for the undereducated, unemployed, and underemployed . . . in human and public services."[22]

The Missouri program was one of the few to focus on non-mainstream women's needs, part of a gradual shift in the continuing education movement toward serving "minorities and the disfranchised person." In a critique of the movement, Joy Rice found that continuing education programs were generally "geared . . . to the needs of the 35-

to 55-year old white, urban, middle-class housewife facing the 'empty nest syndrome' and the need to 'retool.'" They were adequate only "as a transitional but largely remedial measure, an interim answer to non-parallel life-styles between men and women." Most movement literature assumed persistence of a pattern of discontinuity in women's educational and work lives, based on the "notion of a woman's accommodation to the needs of others . . . and her precarious attempts to balance those needs with her own"; it "avoided dealing with role equality and the need for role redefinition." Acknowledging the utility of separate continuing education programs for women in providing "an avenue of return to the mainstream of formal higher education," Rice points out that they were not a solution to the problems of role definition: indeed, they may even have been "shortsighted in the sense of circumventing and masking difficult issues that must be confronted before women and men will reach full economic and domestic partnership in our society."[23]

Graduate and Professional Studies

Sex-role expectations took a particular toll on women's graduate school attendance. Mid-twentieth century graduate schools provided the key to the professions, and one element of the great drive to become middle class was the desire also to become a professional." In his "paean to the leaders of the sixties," *The Best and the Brightest*, David Halberstam praised that "unity of intelligence, rationality and tough decisions that supposedly embodied professionalism. Needless to say, all the best and brightest were men." Within higher education, discrimination against women was most blatant in graduate and professional schools. Well through the sixties a number of prestigious graduate and professional schools refused admission to women. In 1963, Harvard began granting Ph.Ds to women who formerly received them from Radcliffe, but Princeton still remained closed to women. Many women who enrolled in graduate school had to drop out because of family pressures and demands; others experienced very difficult years as they faced contempt or neglect by professors who could not take them seriously.[24]

A National Institutes of Health Special Report on Women and Graduate Study recounted the results of a longitudinal study of women graduates of the class of 1961. At graduation, 72 percent had planned to attend graduate school; by 1964, when the study ended, 42 percent had enrolled but only two-fifths attended full-time, and those tended to cluster in medicine and the physical sciences, where financial support was more likely to be available. Only 34 percent of those in sociology and anthropology were full-time students. Four of ten women reported that they wanted to go on to graduate study but could not. Major obstacles were "financial barriers (42 percent), family responsibilities (41 percent), no graduate school available (16 percent), lack of qualifications (13 percent), and disapproval of husband (3 percent)." Commenting on this report, Elizabeth Cless, a leader in the movement for women's continuing education, noted the persistent assumption that women would continue to interrupt their education for family reasons. The study showed that 44.7 percent of those surveyed expected to begin graduate study only after considerable delay. Regretting the loss of women's professional opportunities that this decision caused, Cless also saw the reasons for women's hesitation to educate themselves for nontraditional roles: "Many intelligent women opt out of higher education, rather than risk the emotional punishment incurred by a woman who dares to enter a system built for men by men." She argued that higher education must make space for women's different life pattern by offering greater flexibility in scheduling and in residency requirements and by giving educational credit for life experiences. "Colleges, graduate and professional schools should be the obvious places to learn the flexibility and adaptability that women must find over and over again."[25]

Professional schools, meanwhile, had been deliberately shutting women out. In 1964, women made up only 4 to 5 percent of law students—the same percentage of women admitted to medical schools—deliberately kept low in both fields. Florynce Kennedy had to threaten a law suit based upon racial discrimination to gain admission to Columbia Law School, although the real problem was that she was a woman. A white friend from Barnard with even higher grades was rejected. Kennedy graduated in 1951, having learned from successful confrontations with the administration to use what she called the "testicular approach," applying "the right kind of pressure to the appropriate sensitive area." Conditions did not change for women in the sixties.[26]

Despite a growing national doctors shortage, medical schools still admitted women only as tokens. A Women's Bureau study revealed that female applications to medical school increased over 300 percent between 1930 and 1966 and male applications only 29 percent; but the proportion of women accepted decreased while male acceptances increased. Historian Mary Roth Walsh finds each school had an internal quota system limiting the number of women. In 1961, a journalist elicited blunt confirmation from a medical school dean: "Hell, yes, we have a quota; yes, it's a small one. We do keep women out, when we can. We don't want them here—and they don't want them elsewhere, either, whether or not they'll admit it."[27]

For most of the decade, women constituted 5 percent or less of each class in most medical schools. In 1968, Dr. Charles Phelps claimed in the *Journal of Medical Education* that the presence of 7.7 percent women in medical schools was a sign of remarkable progress since "there were no women in medicine only 100 years ago." Those who went to medical school came generally from very secure financial backgrounds. More women than men medical students had physician parents. For the women who persisted, motivation came more from altruism rather than economics. An interest in people and science, curiosity about the body, and desire to serve were central to women's choice of a medical career; a desire for independence and a need for involvement also ranked high. Maternal support and example were factors; of the women who persisted in medical school, over 15 percent had mothers who were professionals, a percentage considerably greater than the average in American society and three times the rate for male medical students.[28]

In October 1966 the Josiah Macy, Jr., Foundation sponsored a conference "to define the problems of attracting more talented women for the study of medicine, of affording them maximum opportunities for training after medical school, and of keeping them in medical careers after their training has been completed." Dr. Helen Astin reported on the attrition of young women's ambitions for medicine: a study called Project Talent revealed that 51 percent of the boys who had decided to become doctors in the eleventh grade still planned on it one year after graduation from high school, while only 18 percent of the girls had retained their career plans. The attrition in interest was not surprising. Mary Roth Walsh finds "little wonder that so few women are attracted to careers as doctors when all of society's cues are negative. In childhood, the girl is given a nurse's kit, while the boy receives 'Dr. Dan—The Bandage Man.' In high school, boys are encouraged to think of professional careers in science, while girls with scientific talents are directed toward teaching, nursing, and auxiliary jobs as in medical technology. Not surprisingly, women students rejected by medical schools (even those with higher grade point averages than their male peers) are more apt to view their rejections as 'just' and switch to careers with lower educational requirements." Walsh sees bitter truth, not humor, in a cartoon in which a young female student tells her guidance counselor of her interest in medicine, only to hear, "Yes, the medical profession can be a very rewarding career. Why not plan to *marry* a doctor?" Most women entered the medical profession vicariously. Training for doctors' wives was intensive beginning with medical school where they learned how to cope through the Women's Auxiliary to the Student American Medical Association. When husbands received their M.D.s, many medical schools granted wives their own certificate, the P.H.T.—"Putting Hubby Through."[29]

In *Why Would a Girl Go into Medicine?* (1973) Mary Howell, former associate dean of Harvard Medical School, documented "the ways that traditional medical education systematically conditions physicians— both male and female—to feel contempt for women." Using a pseudonym, Dr. Margaret Campbell, to protect her own career, Howell documented the varieties of institutional discrimination against women: the refusal to accept women with children, the absence of lodging and athletic facilities, the lack of gynecological services, and a disregard for affirmative action plans. Female students often heard that they were less intelligent than men, that their place was in the home, that they would never practice, or that they were hysterical. Professors revealed their misogyny by showing nude slides of women to lighten up the lectures for male students; women pretended to turn a deaf ear to comments like "female, forty, fat, and fertile" or "honey, we have to take your womb out, but don't worry, it won't hurt your sex life."[30]

Female students found it difficult to combat the "men's club" atmosphere of medical school because, as one respondent told Howell, "We are brought up to mistrust other women; we learn in the pre-professional years to be individualistic and competitive with our peers; we are urged during professional training to act autonomously; and as women we are forced to compete with each other for 'scarce resource' jobs, research grants, and the favor or approval of our male colleagues." Joni Magee remembers that at NYU's Medical School, "we women did not stick together too much as a group . . . . I had a couple of friends among the male medical students, but mostly it wasn't terribly cordial . . . . they still treated us as freaks." She transferred after two years to the Woman's Medical College where the atmosphere was more supportive.[31]

Despite severe pressures, women medical students persisted at a higher rate than other women seeking higher degrees; about 75 percent of entering women students receiving the M.D. degree. Still, the attrition rate of women students was nearly twice as high as that of men, a problem addressed by the American Association of Medical Colleges in 1966. The study discovered that more than two-thirds of the women dropped out in their first year and most for non-academic reasons but not for marriage or pregnancy; indeed, being married appeared to have a beneficial effect on a woman's progress in medical school.[32]

As the shortage of physicians became significant, however, there was plenty of work for everyone and various schemes were devised to bring women back into medicine. In recognition of the problems facing women medical professionals, the Radcliffe Institute began providing stipends averaging $2,000 annually in 1961, renewable for one year, to women seeking to complete or update their training. Dr. Nancy Hedrie, the first recipient of the fellowship and the first part-time resident in the history of Boston's Children's Hospital was so successful that the hospital agreed to accept several other women with Radcliffe grants on a part-time basis. The Women's Medical College in Philadelphia established a retraining center for women physicians who had been out of the profession for five years or more. In 1966 the San Francisco Presbyterian Medical Center began granting fellowships of six months to a year to women trying to return to medical practice after a period of professional inactivity of ten years or more. In the mid-sixties, however, such retraining programs faced problems resulting from the increasingly rapid advances in scientific and technological knowledge.[33]

In 1970 the Women's Equity Action League (WEAL) filed a class-action suit on behalf of women applicants against all American medical schools. As a result, admission of women grew from 9 percent in 1969–70 to over 20 percent in 1965–76. Between 1969 and 1973, the number of female interns increased over 200 percent. As in other areas of American life, the sixties' nascent feminism did not begin to bear fruit until the seventies.[34]

Women interested in medicine had always been directed into nursing. An influential report by Roberta Brown, prepared in 1948 with AMA backing, had urged baccalaureate preparation, rather than hospital training schools, for nurses. The first associate degree program opened in 1952, but growth was slow. Baccalaureate programs also grew slowly, with only 14 percent of new nurses in 1962 holding the bachelor's degree. Nursing leaders continued to urge greater educational qualifications as a means toward professional respect, and in 1965 the American Nursing Association (ANA) "endorsed the baccalaureate degree for entry into practice." Then, nurses' education "shifted decisively away from the hospital schools . . . by 1970 associate programs claimed over 26 percent of the new graduates, while another 20 percent held graduate degrees."[35]

For black women access to baccalaureate programs remained limited into the eighties, when "more black students [were] enrolled in associate nursing degree programs than in any other type," and access to positions of authority within nursing also remained difficult. At the 1970 ANA conference 150 black nurses met to "discuss ways in which to better articulate the health needs of the black community and to share frustrations with their lack of mobility within the health-care system." Noting that there had been "no black ANA president or vice-president in the 21 years since the [National Association of Colored Graduate Nurses] had dissolved," and the "limited opportunities for black nurses to share in shaping ANA policies and priorities," in 1971 they founded a new organization, the National Black Nurses' Association. The first president was Lauranne Sams, later dean of the School of Nursing at Tuskegee Institute.[36]

The trend toward baccalaureate education was countered by the entry of the Federal government into health care and education. Funding from the Nurse Training Act (1964), the Health Manpower Act (1968), and subsequent government initiatives made available "previously unheard of amounts of financial assistance for nursing schools and students." Cynthia Woods points out that this strengthened diploma and associate degree programs. The government's interest was in responding to the perceived shortage of nurses by providing a "large supply of relatively inexpensive nurses" through expanded associate degree and diploma programs.[37]

Nurses already on the job frequently resisted their leaders' attempts to demand higher qualifications for nurses, seeing in that move an attempt to "isolate a select elite from the general body" and finding in "apprenticeship culture . . . an alternative to professional ideology, a structure within which nurses can affirm their skills and define their work." Baccalaureate nurses were not always welcomed into the "apprenticeship culture" of the hospital where, because of their less extensive clinical experience, they might have to "humble [themselves] to the hospital graduate." A 1969 letter by a college-educated nurse to *RN* defended herself against charges that baccalaureate nurses were incompetent: "I'm tired of being judged as unqualified simply because a few other BSNs haven't measured up."[38]

In other pre-professional training, women comprised under six percent of architecture graduates in 1969; and 8.4 percent four years later.

Degrees in landscape architecture were only slightly higher. Still, women faced fewer problems in architecture than in engineering, a field with less than one percent women at the end of the decade.

At the end of the decade, women law students began to resist the discrimination they faced. At the University of Michigan law school, Noel Anketell Kramer reported that women were working to recruit more women candidates, believing that more female law students would make it harder for law firms to discriminate. Most still faced standard assumptions about their future: if the woman law student was quiet and did not assert herself in class, she was called passive, proving she would never make a good lawyer; but the more assertive were labelled aggressive, castrating females ready to do anything to get ahead."[39]

In 1970 the University of Michigan hosted a symposium on "Women on Campus"; participants confirmed the on-going difficulties for women in graduate and professional schools, although some saw signs of hope. A 1968 study of 25 women in the sociology department at Michigan reported the feeling that the "attitude among faculty [is] that graduate student women won't finish." The number of women in political science was small, as was true elsewhere, but 59 percent of women "entering graduate studies with a B.A. succeeded in earning an M.A., compared with 53 percent of men in the same category." The figures could help lay to rest the longstanding "idea that women are poorer risks, that they are less likely to finish their degrees than men are." For the black woman graduate student, the most profound impact came from racism, experienced by men and women alike. The result was a "very severe energy drain on the resources of the black student who is trying to get an advanced degree . . . . Besides classes, studying, research, there is this necessary involvement in 'black work'," the attempt to make the University "more responsive to the needs of black people." Black women thus did not "have the option to deal with what white females are discussing now in terms of women's liberation."[40]

The Harvard Business School opened to women in 1962. That year the University of Michigan hosted an all-female conference on management that drew thirty-six executives from nineteen states. The conference, costing $500 per person, offered "the same basic study load and lectures generally given to men in such courses—how to motivate people, listening, . . . picking strong followers" and a "few extra pointers on how to adjust to the world of men." General Motors Corporation began admitting women to its engineering school in 1965, and in 1966

Pacific Mutual Life Insurance Company in Los Angeles opened its two top training programs to women. By 1966, according to *Newsweek*, several companies were "actively scouring" women's college campuses for "promising talent."[41]

The issue of women in the professions concerned young women and their parents. When Alice Rossi surveyed University of Chicago women (including professionals, working women, and housewives), she found that "women see their mothers as more congenial to professional achievement than their fathers"; but "both parents are seen as more supportive than other people in the women's lives . . . . It is most interesting to find that women see their fathers as more tolerant and permissive of women entering masculine fields than their husbands, for it suggests a difference between the role of father vis-à-vis daughter and the role of husband vis-à-vis wife. It may be seen that in his father role, a man is freer to encourage his daughter in her pursuits into law, science, medicine, or even engineering, an encouragement he would not extend to his wife or to a woman as a younger courting man, for he would have to live with the consequences."[42]

Academic Women
Teachers and Scholars

Opportunities for women in academe eroded into and through the sixties. Beatrice Hyslop (1899–1973), a historian of France, observed in 1956, "I have seen in my generation the rise and now the beginning of the closing of doors to women." She contrasted this to the brighter conditions she had known in the thirties while working on her doctorate. Causes were multiple. After World War II, so many young men returned to pursue graduate degrees with G. I. Bill assistance that the male-monopolized professoriate exploded in size just as babyboomers entered college. The situation hardened in the sixties. Of 411 tenured professors in Harvard's Graduate School of Arts and Sciences in 1970, only one was a woman and she held a chair restricted to women. At the University of Connecticut, women made up 33 percent of lower level "instructors," but only 4.8 percent of full professors. Figures were comparable elsewhere.[43]

Mary Ellman's *Thinking About Women* (1968) indicted the whole academic establishment, especially graduate literature departments, for systematically excluding women from admission and making professional teaching, creation, and criticism of literature a male domain: "Books by women are treated as though they themselves were women, and criticism embarks, at its happiest, upon an intellectual measuring of busts and hips." At a 1964 MIT conference, physicist Chien-Shiung Wu criticized the male tradition in science and technology for shutting women out.[44]

The problem recurred in all disciplines. Alice Rossi's survey of 188 major sociology departments revealed that women comprised 30 percent of doctoral candidates, 14 percent of assistant professors, nine percent at the associate rank, only 4 percent at full, and less than 1 percent as department chairs. In art history, women made up 30 percent of the doctorates in the sixties and 48 percent by 1970/71; but as late as 1978, only 17 percent of tenured faculty in departments were female. Dr. Bernice Sandler asked, "Where do these qualified women go, for it is clear that very few of them will ever teach in the major universities and colleges." She found many teaching in the new and proliferating junior and community colleges "where the pay, status, and research opportunities are substantially less than in the major universities." Scarcity of women in academic ranks meant that there were even fewer in administrative posts.[45]

National groups like the Modern Language Association (MLA) and American Historical Association (AHA) remained "men's clubs," with jobs for new PhDs located through the "old boy system." Joan Wallach Scott suggests that the pattern in the history profession was especially complex, based in a postwar period when "a new discourse emerged that emphasized masculine qualities of the historian, associating them with the preservation of national traditions and democracy, scholarly activities that evoked renewed commitment to the heroism of the war effort, though now in time of peace and Cold War." Calling for greater valuation of entrepreneurs' role in building America, Allan Nevins suggested in 1951 that "historians abandon 'feminine idealism' and portray businessmen in 'their true proportions as builders of an indispensable might.'" Scott comments, "Representing the typical historical actor as a (white) male made women a particular and troubling exception. . . . Thus, whatever their skills and training, women had the further challenge of repudiating the disabilities assumed to attach to their sex." Typical of this exclusion is John Higham's *History* (1965), a paean that virtually omitted women historians.[46]

Except for the Berkshire Conference, founded in 1929 by professors at eastern women's colleges, not until formation of the Coordinating Committee on Women in the Historical Profession (CCWHP) in 1969 did women have a voice in the historical profession. The CCWHP pressed for a study of women's status which was undertaken by Willie Lee Rose. The Rose Report of 1970 revealed damning statistics—pathetically small numbers of women in full-time, tenure-track history positions and fewer in the AHA. It declared, "The present demand for social justice for women coincides with the permanent interest of the historical profession. To increase the opportunities open to women in . . . history is to advance the quality of the profession itself." The report "opened a new era for women's participation in the AHA"; it generated the Standing Committee on Women Historians (CWH), recognized by the AHA in 1974 and headed by Rose, to end discrimination against women historians and to give them a collective professional identity and entry to policy decisions.[47]

Women in academic medicine also advanced at a much slower rate than their male colleagues. In 1966 of 1047 department heads in 78 American medical schools only 13 were women, and only 105 women held professional rank, compared to 2554 men. Women were disproportionately represented at the lower end of the scale. Even such a prominent figure as Dr. Helen Brooke Taussig (1898–1986), who performed the first "blue baby" operation in 1945, experienced discrimination: while her male colleague was almost immediately elected to the National Academy of Sciences for similar work, Dr. Taussing rose slowly through the ranks at Johns Hopkins Medical School, not becoming a full professor until 1959, the first woman to hold that rank there.[48]

Despite the obstinacy of many academic institutions, several women became publicly recognized scholars in the sixties. One of the most visible was Hannah Arendt (1906–1975), the first female full professor at Princeton (1959), although on a visiting appointment. In 1961 she published *Between Past and Future*, six essays which explore the relation between the social and the public realm and seek a new concept of authority for a modern world in which traditional religious promises of future reward and threats of punishment were no longer available. *On Revolution* (1963) carried on this quest, focusing on American town government as a version of a revolutionary council. Based on Adolph Eichmann's 1961 trial in Jerusalem for Holocaust crimes, which she covered as a *New Yorker* reporter, Arendt published *Eichmann in Jerusalem: A Report on the Banality of Evil* (1963, revised in 1965), drawing the shocking conclusion that the Nazi's acts, performed without due thought, but not his character were monstrous. This very controversial book alienated some friends. Arendt replied to her critics in "Truth and Politics." From 1963 to 1967, she was a member of the influential University of Chicago Committee on Social Thought; she left in 1967 to become a professor at the New School for Social Research. A prolific essayist and lecturer, Arendt's political essays of the sixties and early seventies, which include critical analyses of the war in Vietnam and of domestic policies, are collected in *Crises of the Republic* (1972), dedicated to her close friend, Mary McCarthy.[49]

Women also demonstrated excellence in marginalized research and teaching areas. Lois Mailou Jones (1905–), Howard University professor of painting and design, received a series of research grants to collect and establish a visual and biographical archive on Caribbean and African-American art, particularly that of women artists. Even before the growth of the American Indian Movement (AIM), anthropologist Theodora Kroeber released *Ishi in Two Worlds: A Biography of the Last Wild Indian in North America* (1961) and *Ishi, Last of His Tribe* (1964), which went through multiple editions, reaching beyond an academic readership to contribute to the Native American rights movement. Jean Briggs published her ethnographic studies of Eskimo family life in *Never in Anger* (1970); but the most visible anthropologist remained Margaret Mead (1901–1978), who commented frequently on contemporary culture in such books as *Culture and Commitment: A Study of the Generation Gap* (1970) and *Male and Female: A Study of the Sexes* (1967); she also completed her autobiography, *Blackberry Winter: My Earlier Years* (1972).

Of particular importance was the increasingly rapid development of scholarship about women, and the beginning in the late 1960s of the women's studies movement. Literature on which to build women's studies syllabi grew by mid-decade, especially in history, expanding upon the pioneering contributions of Mary Beard and Alma Lutz. Eleanor Flexner's *Century of Struggle: The Women's Rights Movement in the United States* (1959) became a central text for younger women seeking a usable past. Barbara Welter of Hunter College provided a significant understanding of the socialization of women to domesticity in a path-breaking article, "The Cult of True Womanhood: 1820–1869," in the *American Quarterly* in 1966. Aileen Kraditor published *Ideas of the Woman Suffrage Movement, 1890–1920* (1965), followed by *Up from the Pedestal: Selected Writings in the History of American Feminism* (1968); and William O'Neill contributed *Everyone Was Brave: The Rise and Fall of Feminism* (1969). Both Gerda Lerner and Anne Firor Scott, whose work would teach and inspire a generation of historians of women, wrote their first work in the 1960s. Lerner published a study of the abolitionist Grimké sisters in 1967; her influential anthology, *Black Women in White America* appeared in 1972. Scott's *The Southern Lady: from*

Pedestal to Politics appeared in 1970. By 1968 a Women's History Research Center was open at Berkeley, gathering material on women's liberation for scholarly use.[50]

The Women's Archives at Radcliffe, founded in 1950 with the encouragement of historian Mary Beard, was renamed for Elizabeth and Arthur Schlesinger in 1965. In 1971, publication under Radcliffe auspices of the three-volume *Notable American Women: 1607–1950*, edited by Edward and Janet Wilson James, brought to fruition a thirteen year project. Including scholarly biographies of 1,359 women, the volumes played a major role in shaping the field of women's history and in providing material on which courses could be based.

Contributions from other fields made women's studies interdisciplinary. Alice Rossi, a Goucher College sociologist, analyzed women's status in various societies to criticize pluralist and assimilationist models for achieving equality and to call for a new, more comprehensive ideology. Caroline Bird provided an economic interpretation of women's oppression in *Born Female: The High Cost of Keeping Women Down* (1968). Josephine Carson's *Silent Voices: the Southern Negro Woman Today* (1969) offered a socioeconomic analysis as well as interviews with black women. In *Women and the Law: the Unfinished Revolution* (1969), Leo Kanowitz documented legal discrimination, providing agenda as well as text.[51]

Women's studies courses began to appear late in the decade, primarily in experimental institutions created by the free-university movement rather than in traditional departments. Many of the earliest were in literature, a fact attributed to the "relative accessibility of that field to women." The first "political" women's course at the Free University of Seattle in 1965 grew out of the student movement there. Cathy Cade and Peggy Dobbins offered a women's course in 1966 at the New Orleans Free School. Naomi Weisstein at the University of Chicago and Annette Baxter at Barnard pioneered in the field. Sheila Tobias organized a conference on women at Cornell University in 1969; in 1970 Cornell offerings included an interdisciplinary team-taught course on the "female personality" and enrolled about 400 students. San Diego State launched a five-course program in 1969, which by fall 1970 had become a ten-course curriculum, acclaimed the nation's first official women's studies program. Portland State University in Oregon, City College in New York, Sacramento State University, and the University of Washington also developed programs. A proliferation of black studies courses, inspired by civil rights activists, led newly feminist students to demand that the few women professors develop courses to address women's history and identity. The growth of women's studies courses won national recognition in *Newsweek* in October 1970. Janice Law Trecker proclaimed in the *Saturday Review* in 1971 that "Women's Place Is in the Curriculum," explaining motivations as a "search for ways in which a successful female revolution might be constructed" as well as a "desire for a female heritage" and a "passion for women's history."[52]

Whatever the women's course, required reading often included Simone de Beauvoir's *The Second Sex* (translated in 1952), Caroline Bird's *Born Female* (1968), and Betty Friedan's *The Feminine Mystique* (1963). Carol Ahlum and Sheila Tobias of Cornell compiled syllabi of 16 courses dating from the 1969–70 academic year in *Female Studies I*, published by the newly established feminist press Know, Inc. Almost immediately, Florence Howe, chair of the Modern Language Association Commission on the Status of Women, edited *Female Studies II*, with 66 course outlines and bibliographies. The original term of "feminist studies" was dropped in the seventies for the more objective "women's studies," considered less offensive to traditionalist men who continued to control the academy.[53]

With the increasing awareness generated by scholarship and public activism, inequities of educational opportunity became a major feminist issue at the end of the sixties and through the seventies. As Chair of the Education Committee of the New York City chapter of the National Organization for Women (NOW), Kate Millett authored the pamphlet *Token Learning* (1967), challenging the validity of college and university curricula for women and the shunting of young women into nursing, teaching, and home economics. Millett traced female deprivation of ambition to deep cultural roots and decried the socialization that squelched the ambitions of young women to enter traditionally male professions. "By the time a girl is ready for medical school, she doesn't want to go any more. She never really had a choice. She's been conditioned to her role ever since she got the doll to play with."[54]

In 1968 and 1969, women professors began to react to discrimination in academe and in academic professional organizations. Responding to the women's movement in 1969, the MLA created a Commission on the Status of Women in the Profession. Its first chair was Florence Howe, then teaching at Goucher College. Given the "history of MLA's indifference to women," and the prospect of a new MLA constitution, many women felt the official commission was not enough. In 1970, a small group formed the Women's Caucus for the Modern Languages, gaining 500 members by 1971.[55]

As intellectual historian Dale Spender summarizes, "By the end of the sixties, parameters [in careers of 'women of ideas'] had been forged once again, problems had been named in history, education, psychology, anthropology, sociology, philosophy, literature, the biological sciences and ecology. That future discussion about women was going to break out of disciplinary straitjackets was predictable. That it was the *invisibility* of women in society that was reflected in the disciplines, and not the individual limitations of a particular discipline which was responsible for the exclusion of women from the encoding of knowledge, was soon to be an established and unchallenged assumption of feminist reality."[56]

Beginning in January 1970 and impelled by Dr. Bernice Sandler, the Women's Equity Action League (WEAL) filed charges of sex discrimination under Executive Order 11246 against more than 250 colleges and universities. This action included more than ten percent of American higher education institutions, including the entire state college and university systems of California, Florida, and New Jersey; Columbia University; and the Universities of Chicago, Minnesota, and Wisconsin. Sandler remembers, "WEAL charged an industry-wide pattern of sex discrimination and asked for a class action and compliance review" of all such institutions with federal contracts. She lamented that discrimination against women occurred on all levels—against student applicants encountering "both official and unofficial quotas," against students seeking scholarships and financial assistance, against graduates using placement services, against candidates for faculty positions, against professors seeking promotion or equal pay for rank. Sandler concluded, "The position of women in higher education has actually been worsening; women are slowly being pushed out of the university world." At the end of the sixties, the proportion of women graduate students was less than in 1930, boding ill for women's roles in academe thereafter.[57]

Collegiate Culture

Perhaps because of tradition, perhaps because of the persistent overt and covert discriminations, most women undergraduates through the sixties retained marriage as a primary ambition. Sorority sisters at the

University of Michigan dreamed of finding "HIM" or "Mister Right," admitting they were more concerned with earning their "M.R.S." degree at the end of four years than with completing a B.A. or B.S. A visitor to Vassar in 1962 wrote that the typical student there no longer aspired to make "an enduring contribution to society. Her future identity is largely encompassed by the projected role of wife and mother."[58]

Social events and rituals of collegiate culture still revolved around meeting the opposite sex and finding a marriage partner. Particularly in eastern schools, parties bringing together men and women from separate schools became prototypic. Vivian Gornick remembers attending parties with "bold, quick-witted, sexy" classmates from City College, given to facilitate meeting "the boys from Columbia, urbane, reserved, serious. We all saw ourselves as intellectuals, of course, but the real agenda for the evening was that we would provoke, and they would respond. The point of being a smart girl was that you could arouse the hunger of boys who would tomorrow be men of power . . . . This agenda created energy and excitement, the sexual charge that ran through every party ever given . . . That night on Morningside Heights we were drinking Scotch, up in the Bronx they were drinking beer, and over on the East Side champagne. But the same deal was being cut all over town."[59]

In the short term, many young women aspired to be the "Sweetheart of Sigma Chi" rather than elected to Student Government. The "panty raid" and fraternity serenade were special events defining the status of college women as objects of sex or romance. The Greek system provided rituals to perpetuate mate-seeking and to reward successes. Within the sorority, the ritual of the "circle" was a special event coveted and cherished—the means of announcing to one's group the "status" of being lavaliered, pinned, or engaged, three levels of male commitment. During the "circle," young women stood around in a darkened room, singing the ritual songs while passing a lighted candle, blown out by the lucky one—on the first round for lavaliering, the second for pinning, or the third for engagement—to be greeted with hugs and shrieks of glee. By senior year, many co-eds fell into one of two groups: The lucky ones were engaged with diamond solitaires and gathered regularly to discuss the latest *Bride's Magazine* or *House and Garden*, debating taste in silver and crystal patterns to be listed at department store bridal registries; others were so depressed not to be in the first group that they became anti-social, refusing to be seen in public on weekend nights without a date.

Some sororities were about another kind of status—preserving hereditary lineage as closed clubs—as well as cultivating conventional gender roles. The social consciousness of the sixties eventually influenced sorority life. In 1967 Cornell, Colorado, and Wisconsin administrations forced sororities to minimize alumnae and national organization interference in selecting pledges. At the University of Michigan and other schools, the Panhellenic Council voted to insist on more local control of membership.

College women of the sixties demanded more personal control over their own lives in ways contrary to traditional *in loco parentis* (in place of parents) practices in which administrations framed all sorts of rules. Formerly, students merely ignored or broke rules in secret, occasionally incurring administrative wrath, individually or collectively, as in 1962 when Vassar President Sarah Gibson Blanding decreed that students using alcohol or indulging in premarital sex should withdraw, or as in 1963 when University of Connecticut officials threatened two students with punishment for their "uncontrolled public displays of affection." The young journalist Gloria Steinem reported on the shift in mentality as women students questioned changes in *status quo* because of the Pill in a 1962 *Esquire* article, "The Moral Disarmament of Betty Coed." Dr. Alan F. Guttmacher, Planned Parenthood President, told a press conference in 1967 that public acceptance of women's equality underlay the sex revolution on campuses. "Chastity among women is no longer the great virtue" of a decade before, he declared. "Now women have full equality in sex." He dated the change from the late fifties with general acceptance coming by 1962–63 and approved of the trend, noting only that "No one should be coerced into a sexual relationship to please another, and no pregnancy should result." In 1968 it was a cause célèbre when a Barnard woman was officially disciplined for lying about living "illicitly" with a man.[60]

Increasingly, students organized to protest restrictions in dress codes and curfew hours applying only to women. While detailed dress and grooming standards were breaking down at most institutions, Brigham Young University formalized them in the student honor code deliberately to distinguish itself from the "spirit of rebellion" sweeping other campuses. Still, by 1971 women at the Mormon institution won permission to wear slacks, not just skirts and dresses, although the latter still had to fall below the knee and the administration decreed the "no bra look" unacceptable.[61]

4

Work

Women's workforce participation rose gradually and steadily through the fifties. By 1960, 24 million or 35 percent of American women 14 to 65 were in the labor force, an increase of 19 percent in the fifties. By 1970, women's participation increased to 44 percent of all women, surpassing the World War II rate, when 16 million had worked full time. The percentage of women in the total work force rose from 33 to 38 percent through the sixties. Unprecedented patterns appeared—women working through more life cycle stages, after marriage and childbearing, and in prime fertility years from ages twenty to thirty-five, and at older ages. Major macroeconomic transitions reshaped female workforce participation and gender roles. Economist Valerie Oppenheimer clearly established development of the gender-differentiated dual labor market theory but reported "no evidence that these substantial shifts [increases in all categories] in women's labor force participation were precipitated by prior changes in sex-role attitudes." Ideas "lagged behind behavioral changes, indicating that changes in behavior have gradually brought about changes in sex-role norms."[1]

Labor force participation of white married women nearly doubled: from 21 percent of those married in 1950 to 32 percent in 1960 and 41 percent in 1970. In 1960, in ten million households both spouses worked, although old prejudices against working wives remained. A 1962 study urged that "working mothers would have to be freed of the load of guilt with which society had saddled them"; guilt or not, they increasingly took jobs. Indeed, a 1968 survey found that 10 million women aged 18 to 49 wanted part-time work. The working woman's median age in 1960 was 41, once considered too old for a new hire but now made desirable because of the continuing shortage of young, yet unmarried women; but that age gradually fell through the decade. After the end of the baby boom in 1964, women had fewer children, both delaying childbearing and ending it at a younger age, leaving more prime years for work. The most dramatic trend of the sixties was the growth in the number of working women aged 20 to 24.[2]

Also striking, given persistent public disfavor of working mothers, was the fact that more women with school-aged children (six to 17) entered the workforce—a rise of 50 percent in the decade, from 8 million in 1960, 8.8 million in 1962, 9.7 million in 1965, 10.6 million in 1967, 11.6 million in 1969, to 12.2 million in 1971. In 1960, 39 percent of mothers worked; in 1970, half were employed outside of the home. Numbers of working women with children under six increased dramatically, from 19 percent in 1960 to 28 percent in 1970; young working mothers with children under three doubled, prompting evangelist Billy Graham to preach that sex roles were divinely ordained, calling "the appointed destiny of real womanhood" that of wife, mother, and homemaker.[3]

Employers looked on women not as full-time, long-term employees but as "pink stereotypes." Personnel managers boldly generalized that women often took jobs and left them on "whim"—after working long enough to buy a second car or until they became pregnant; or if divorced or widowed, until they found another husband. Businesses made policy based on such notions. In 1970, Martin-Marietta still refused to hire women with preschoolers, a practice eventually overturned by the Supreme Court. Many employers relied on temporary clerical help, almost exclusively women, from new companies like Kelly Girls.[4]

Throughout the sixties, two-thirds of new employees were women, courted to fill new job categories rather than serving simply as a reserve labor force as before. Clerical work expanded greatly because of automation and the introduction of electronic data processing (EDP), making new jobs to pull women into the workforce. In telecommunications, 96 percent of traffic employees (operators and low-level supervisors) were female while 94 percent of higher paid skilled craftsmen were male, benefitting most from modernized technology. In 1960, one-third of wage-earning women held clerical jobs; and most others held traditional women's positions, thus not challenging existing notions about women and work. Office and factory automation meant fewer jobs for the unskilled, although through the decade the number of all office workers increased by 45 percent. Most were women, increasing employment sex segregation. Along with typing and stenography, vocational training in high schools taught girls new skills like key-punching, required by the growing use of business computers. The job was considered boring and menial, not unlike sewing, just the sort of task fit for women, particularly part-timers.[5]

In 1965, over half of college graduates were employed compared to only about a third of high school graduates; but the college graduate was typically asked first if she could type, not what expertise came with her degree. She was at best given secretarial work, not put into management training. Indeed, the first wave of baby-boom women graduating from college in 1968 found job opportunities only slightly better than those of friends trained in stenography and bookkeeping (not accounting) in trade schools. The greater numbers attending college changed but did not improve the employment situation for women. One study concluded, "as more students attend college, job requirements are upgraded and managerial, technical, and skilled positions require more training than the working-class woman usually receives." Women with four years of high school usually became clerical workers; those with under four years fell primarily into service occupations or factory jobs. In March 1969, 19 percent of the working women with four years of college were employed in nonprofessional clerical, sales, service, or factory jobs far below their abilities. Yet even when hired to positions comparable to men, 1970 female college grads were given starting salaries 3 to 10 percent lower than male peers.[6]

Jobs such as retail salesclerks, private domestic workers, cashiers, and seamstresses remained almost exclusively female through the 1960s and beyond. Three-quarters of women workers clustered in 57 occupations: 30 white-collar, 14 service, and 13 blue-collar or farm work. Women made up over 90 percent of workers in 17 of these occupations and at least 75 percent in the remaining 31, solidifying their occupational ghettoization. From 1960 to 1973, women in service (domestic and corporate) jobs increased over 52 percent, with over a third involved with food—waitresses, cooks, counter workers, cashiers, dish washers, many in the new fast food industry which tripled in the decade, providing low-paying, part-time, flexible-hour jobs particularly for women with young children. The draft for the Vietnam War

drained poorer, less educated young men from the workforce and increased women's lower-level job opportunities. While many employers
courted women workers for these jobs, it was not with wages competitive with men; and women experienced few real gains. Indeed, a gender segregated dual market of jobs developed. Through the sixties,
women earned less and less compared to men.[7]

The median income of a full-time working woman fell from 63.9
cents on the man's dollar in 1955 to 60 cents in 1963 and 58 cents in
1968. Black women earned only about seventy percent as much as
white women. In 1969, women's annual earnings ranged from $2,340
to $7,165, with an average of $5,892 for those with college degrees. In
1967, white women working year-long, full-time jobs averaged $4,152,
non-white women $2,949, white men $7,164, and non-white men
$4,528. Earnings for those with only eight years of school were $1,404
for women versus $4,518 for men. Women with advanced degrees
made $6,114 versus $10,041 for male peers. Median income for female
high school graduates was $2,673 compared to $6,924 for males.
Women with college degrees earned $4,164, less than men with eight
years of school, half that of male peers earning $9,728. One expert in
1971 wrongly explained, "It is not particularly important to a great
many working women whether or not they earn as much as men, or
have equal opportunities for training and promotion."[8]

Even government programs launched by Johnson's War on Poverty
favored males. In 1968, the Job Corps provided vocational training for
32,004 disadvantaged youths, only 9,944 of whom were female. Resistance to the idea of a woman working and achieving financial independence was deep-seated and crossed class lines. Well into the sixties, it
remained conventional for a middle-class girl's parents to ask if her fi-
ancé promised to be a "good provider," to support her "in the manner
to which she had been accustomed" in her father's house; but they sent
her to college, improving her chances on the marriage if not the job
market, enabling her if necessary to support a new husband through
graduate studies. Working-class men were often more rigid in resisting
the idea of *their* wives working, even if it meant material improvements
in their standard of living. Indeed, middle-class women took jobs at a
far higher rate than their blue-collar sisters in the sixties.[9]

Increasingly working women came from the middle class. Sixties
prosperity and the generally low unemployment rate had less impact
on women than the mounting Great Inflation from the Vietnam war
after 1965, which sent more women to work to help make ends meet,

to augment husbands' salaries, to buy the new consumer goods required for the new standards of middle-class status, to help pay mortgages on new homes, to clothe baby-boom children, or to send them to college. Nearly 60 percent of women entering the labor force from 1960 to 1977 were wives of men with above average incomes. In middle-class families with two incomes, the woman earned about a quarter of it. Two-income families became the norm. Two-fifths of women with school-aged children worked, yet often in part-time, temporary, or seasonal jobs, choosing those close to home even if they were overqualified for them.[10]

Publication of Betty Friedan's *The Feminine Mystique* (1963) turned public attention to discontented housewives who wanted fulfillment in jobs; but its focus on middle-class women cast into the shadow the problems of working-class women, black and white, who had been long in the labor force. For them, the issue was not the difficulty of leaving home to work but the lack of freedom to choose to work or not. Studies of women and work subsequent to the publication of Friedan's book made the point repeatedly that growth in numbers of working women came primarily from economic pressure, not from a quest for gender equality. For many working women, the sixties were not good times. Despite working-class women's traditionalism, their contributions helped to raise blue-collar family wages by 30 percent and to maintain a moderate standard of living. Blue-collar males with two children had costs exceeding earnings in 1967 unless wives worked. Female jobs were an alternative or supplement to male "moonlighting," second jobs that kept men away far more than overtime from families. Of those working in 1974, 3.2 million had husbands earning under $5,000 a year; and 2.3 million had spousal paychecks between that and $7,000. If not employed, three-fifths of married female workers would have had family income under $7,000 a year; and an urban family of four required $7,386 to stay above poverty.[11]

By 1974, 8.2 million employed women had never been married and another 6.7 million were widowed, divorced, or separated—working to provide most if not all of their own and dependents' support. 22 percent of household heads were women, many of them minorities, most with children, and most confined to women's work. Because average earnings of full-time female operatives (factory workers) was below $4000, with service workers receiving under $3000, most female-headed families fell below the poverty level. The increase in such families to one in ten by 1969 necessitated women's employment, further undermining the conservative ideology of the "family wage" as male-earned. A third of poor families, 2.4 million in 1967, were headed by a fully employed person, usually a woman. Poverty was more severe among female-headed families, with 45 percent of the families headed by minority women workers in poverty in 1968, compared with 16 percent of those headed by minority male workers. In 1969, 46 percent of all employed black women remained private household or service workers, although these jobs diminished by 600,000 over the decade, perhaps because of the new efficiency of suburban houses but also because of the expansion of clerical jobs. In 1970, 26.9 percent of black women in the workforce were domestics earning a median income of $1,700. Women's unemployment rates remained consistently higher than those of men—4.7 and 2.8 percent, respectively, in 1969. This bill of particulars succinctly outlines problems facing working women. It underlines the cultural lag between the rising consciousness of inequity that marked the sixties and women's social reality of a dual labor market that kept women mired in traditional, lower-paying jobs.[12]

Pressures for change grew as numbers of working women increased steadily, as greater numbers of younger, more educated women entered the workforce, and as aggrieved workers caught the spirit of other movements for rights. Expansion of the female workforce, more than any other single factor, led to a widening circle of voices demanding change and equity. Exploitation had remained unchallenged in many fields. Telephone operators complained: although their positions had "an aura of 'niceness' and while many of them work for extra money in order to consume, their labor is highly industrialized, bureaucratic, and paternalistic. Heavily supervised, in some offices they are permitted to go to the bathroom only two at a time and must petition the supervisor for a space on the waiting list." Supervisors counted heads each half hour "to make sure no one has escaped!"[13]

Women in sales increased from 40 to 42 percent in the sixties but as always were clustered in low-paid, over-the-counter rather than commission sales (as of automobiles or large appliances); they earned only 40 percent of the male sales income. Women had long been successful at difficult door-to-door selling and as insurance and real estate agents, but few companies were willing to add women to their sales forces. Formfit-Rogers, manufacturers of women's undergarments and lingerie, had five women sales representatives outside New York, but the New York office did not plan to hire any: "It's partly social, partly psychological," a vice-president explained. "The big buyers are accustomed to men and they wouldn't like a change." Pressured by Title VII some companies reviewed policies. Olivetti Underwood Corporation, business equipment manufacturers, promoted two women from within into sales. Supervisors reported, "In their first weeks, . . . they were doing well and the company is confident that the girls are going to succeed. Now we're wondering why we didn't try it sooner."[14]

Stewardesses earned about $300 a month in the early sixties and averaged only about two and one-third years on the job. Eighty-five percent had to resign in 1965 because of marriage; but openings were highly competitive due to the job's glamor and stiff appearance criteria. American Airlines required the "wholesome all-American girl type, between ages 20 and 26, 5 feet 2 inches to 5 feet 8 inches in height, with proportionate weight not to exceed 130 pounds. . . . single, in excellent health, attractive, and possess[ing] considerable personal charm as well as a high degree of intelligence and enthusiasm." Western Airlines added "poise, speed, stamina, and smilability." Interviewers prized body characteristics like slender hips, inevitably to be scrutinized by seated passengers, and long arms for easy reaching across seats and into overhead compartments. Only beauty pageant contestants underwent such intensive physical and personal selection. Only four out of every hundred applicants made it to "stew school," an intensive program teaching the fine points of posture and manicuring. Airlines encouraged recruitment publicists like Elizabeth Rich, who wrote *Flying High* to promote the romance of being a stewardess; and *Teen* magazine warned, "DANGER! Keep away from airlines under penalty of finding a zingy, zwingy perfect job!"[15]

Between 1959 and 1974, jobs for women in manufacturing increased 21 percent; the proportion of women industrial workers expanded from 28 to 32 percent, and about 16 percent of all women workers were in factories. There, automation eliminated jobs rather than creating new ones for women, who usually had the "demanding, high-speed, mind-culling, and nerve-racking dead-end jobs for wages lower than those of most male workers"—drilling, spot-welding, soldering, threading, lettering, calibrating, assembling, checking, rechecking, packing, stacking, stamping. About half of women factory workers were clustered in "technologically backward" industries like shoes, clothing, leather, and textiles, all threatened by foreign competition. Women in furniture and fixtures manufacturing grew from 15.6 to 28 percent in the decade but earned some of the lowest industrial wages. Highest paid were petroleum refining, metals, and transportation equipment with 9, 7, and 16 percent women respectively. In 1967, over 75 percent of female "oper-atives" (low- or semi-skilled workers) were full-time, earning under 60 percent of male counterparts; and 39 percent of working-poor women were in blue-collar jobs.[16]

Early in the decade, older women's efforts to improve working conditions brought about important federal legislation. Although its effect was limited, the Equal Pay Act passed in 1963 promised to remedy economic disadvantages in companies doing federal government business; and 36 states enacted equal pay laws covering many employees excluded by the federal law. Unexpectedly, Congress banned discrimination because of sex in Title VII of the 1964 Civil Rights Act; and 23 states followed with similar laws. The decade also witnessed executive orders banning sex discrimination in federal employment and by federal contracts (see chapter one). Five states and the District of Columbia passed "fair employment practices" laws prohibiting sex-based pay discrimination. The Age Discrimination Act (1967), protecting workers from 40 to 65, helped women returning to work after families were grown or when widowed. Yet implementation lagged behind legislation as social change lagged behind the realities of workforce participation. Although media began to recognize that women were in the workforce to stay, it was not until the seventies that some women benefitted from new laws. What distinguishes the sixties is not actual change for the better in women's working conditions, but development of a conversation about inequity.

Younger educated women and older professional women called attention to pervasive patterns of sexual discrimination, but they cannot be credited with starting a movement. Gradually, women from all classes and backgrounds began to understand their condition within a social justice framework, to challenge myths, and to seek redress. Change was, as always, accompanied by resistance—from employers with much to gain from keeping a cheap labor supply, from cultural institutions which saw traditional family values threatened by movement of women into the workforce, and also from women themselves. The women who resisted change reacted against women's liberation's insistence on every woman's right to all of the choices and options men had. Such ideas were frightening and threatening, engendering pain and anger among many women. As they learned their history, younger educated women spoke openly of "rage" against inequities suffered by women; but there was also anger between women, as the less privileged, who knew the realities of discrimination against which their more privileged sisters railed, protested. "Nobody speaks for me," black and working-class women announced as women's liberation rhetoric tried to define the terms in which women's lives would be understood.[17]

Trade union activist Alice Cook complained in 1968 that the women's liberation movement "isn't doing a hell of a lot to help me . . . and when I say me, I mean my kind of people. . . . Women's liberation has to be . . . willing to go out and educate the husbands and the men, and it's got to be involving people like me and the things that are really important to me, like if we've got to work, a job where we can earn a decent salary, or women living alone should be able to support their own families. . . . I'm talking about women who don't go to college. We've never had that experience, and this is the majority of the people."[18]

Congresswoman (later Senator) Barbara Mikulski saw women of her Baltimore ethnic neighborhood "propelled into complicated and confusing roles" that generated anxiety. Lives "were changing faster than our own self image or basic values. New social forces of civil rights, the Ecumenical Council, Watts, Washington, Selma, Vietnam, issues like birth control and busing; new categories of people, like hippies, hard hats, and militants; new problems, like drugs, inflation, crime, the urban crisis—all frightened and astounded us. Our world would never be the same." The women Mikulski knew were often "relieved not to have to spend dreary hours at factories doing work that was tedious, monotonous, and back-breaking, or standing on their feet long hours as shop girls." Dependent on families and husbands for emotional support, they felt threatened by a rhetoric that challenged family values. Some no doubt would have agreed with the male trade unionist who explained, "The way we think, a man should be able to make enough money to take care of things, so that his income doesn't have to be supplemented by his wife having to work. . . . This is one of the roots of evil in this country. Kids running around, because their parents are both out working."[19]

Like such white working-class women, many black women felt excluded from the conversation and protested against having white women, who could not share their experience, speak for them. Struggling to break out of the most demeaning and low-paying jobs, combatting racism, sex discrimination, and poverty, very few black women had the choice to stay at home. Minority employment rates were always higher than those of white women; but their wages were always lower. Black women's options in education and a choice of jobs were severely limited, and their economic needs—in a nation where the only group more excluded was black men—were great. The notion of breaking down barriers in professional and executive employment, the focus of much of the writing and speaking by movement women, could have little meaning for black women for whom erratically paid and unregulated domestic work was often the only option available. It was an official myth that Latina women resisted jobs to stay with family despite economic consequences: 43 percent of Latina women worked but faced even greater obstacles than blacks, both within their communities and at large. Their unemployment rate was 11.5 percent compared to 9.3 percent for Latino men, 11.2 percent for black men, 1.6 percent for black women, 5.4 percent for white men, and 6.8 percent for white women.[20]

Income disparity lessened between white and black women in the sixties. By 1960, black women's median wage was 70 percent that of white women, a drastic improvement on pre–World War II figures; and by 1977, they earned 88 percent of what white women took home. "The convergence of white and nonwhite women's earnings in part reflected a dramatic postwar increase in the number of black women who entered white-collar work—further testimony to the vast expansion of job opportunities in women's fields." By 1960, over a third of black women held clerical, sales, service, or professional jobs—no longer confined to unskilled and domestic jobs. Indeed, by 1960, more black women than black men held diplomas and college degrees. Lessened discrepancies, however, reflect a trend of paying all women less for full-time jobs.

Still, historian Paula Giddings notes that for many blacks "emergence of the women's movement couldn't have been more untimely or irrelevant." Feminism followed the PCSW in concentrating attention on the growing number of middle-class women forced into the labor market in low-skill, low-paid jobs. "*The Feminine Mystique* spoke to middle-class white women, bored in suburbia (an escape hatch from increasingly black cities) and seeking sanction to work at a 'meaningful' job outside the home. Not only were the problems of the White suburban housewife (who may have had black domestic help) irrelevant to black women, they were also alien to them."[21]

Some single women, battling discrimination, also resented overemphasis on suburban middle-class housewives' return to work. A 1968 article in *National Business Woman*, the NFBPW journal, asked whether women are "underestimated by chance or by choice." Angry at married women whom she saw as willing to work for less than fair wages, Elsie Stebbings attacked vehemently. Legislation would not cure this problem, she asserted: women had to change their attitudes toward themselves and their work, especially "the married woman, who, well-educated and skilled, freed from confining responsibilities to home and children to resume her career, fails in her identity of self and in her responsibility to her sex when she seeks less than equal pay with men." Worse yet, women's unemployment rates surpassed men's in 1969 by 4.7 versus 2.8 percent.[22]

In 1970, after five decades of the Women's Bureau, after three decades of a steadily increasing proportion of women in the labor market, and a decade's mounting pressure for women's economic rights, women remained occupationally disadvantaged—indeed worse off than before. Nixon's Women's Bureau Director Elizabeth Duncan Koontz admitted that professional and technical opportunities for women were diminishing, down to only 37 percent of such jobs in 1969 compared to 45 percent in 1940, while the proportion of women service workers (except in private households) increased from 40 to 59 percent; but she declared that "the exploitation of women workers," was no longer a major problem. Protective legislation for women workers remained in place. "No longer do we need to place primary emphasis on the establishment of safety standards or the elimination of long working hours and appalling working conditions"; and federal and state legislation of the decade had made equality of pay and employment discrimination illegal. Koontz was wrong; problems were far from solved. Koontz herself found persisting "serious inequities in the labor market which result in the underutilization of women workers . . . . barriers which deny women the freedom to prepare for and enter employment suited to their individual interests and abilities, and to advance and achieve recognition." She concluded, "Failure to grant women and girls equal opportunities in terms of job training, educational programs, occupational entrance, advancement, and pay creates severe economic hardship, even poverty, for many women and for many families dependent in whole or in part on a woman's earnings."[23]

Conservatives argued that women preferred lower-level jobs, as less taxing on their energy and attention. Margaret Mead observed in 1969 that since an American woman's "work is considered to be subordinate to her home tasks, it is not surprising that women are found overwhelmingly in jobs that require relatively low levels of skill and responsibility: 70 percent of all clerical workers are women, as are 58 percent of all retail sales workers." In addition to traditionalism and discrimination mitigating against all women's job aspirations, placement of women in secretarial, commercial, and service positions also resulted from an immense expansion of such jobs in the sixties. In 1970, only 14.5 percent of working women held professional or technical jobs.[24]

Resistance, anger, and tensions persisted, but finally the logic of the argument that women, no less than men, should have the full benefits of their labors, was stronger than opposition or anxiety. The "feminine mystique" was, after all, a post–World War II bid to revive the nineteenth-century cult of domesticity, which had been undermined first by the women's rights movement and then by the economy and war. Working class and minority women remained skeptical of theories advanced by their white middle-class sisters, but they saw clearly the utility of calling attention to the inequities of the workforce. In Harlan County, Tennessee, Nannie Rainey described the organization by women to fight the injunction against picketing outside the mines: "Well, we seen all those women libbers picketing on television and we didn't see why we couldn't too." In Mikulski's Baltimore neighborhood, women learned to work together—against the havoc being wreaked by wrongheaded urban renewal, and for community betterment—and found strength together.[25]

Unions

Only 3.5 million, or 15 percent, of 24 million working women were unionized in 1960, despite the efforts of women like Angela Bambace (1898–1975), member of the International Ladies' Garment Workers Union (ILGWU) Executive Board, or Esther Peterson, Kennedy's Assistant Secretary of Labor. Those unions that had been largely female—the ILGWU, Amalgamated Clothing Workers, and Communications Workers of America—continued to decline as they had in the fifties because of industrial change. In 1966, women union members earned 80 percent more than non-union women, but the differential fell to 70 percent in 1970, when union men, many in the skilled trades from which women remained excluded, earned 80 percent more than union women. Through the sixties, their percentage of industrial union members shrank to 19 percent from a 1947 high of 27 percent. Overall female union participation increased 37 percent from 1962 to 1972, but only because of growth of Retail Clerks', Electrical Workers', Teachers', Government Employees', and State, County, and Municipal Employees' unions; and women made up three-fifths of the National Education Association and Nurses Association. Many large industrial unions did not truly welcome women or represent their interests, which were often seen by unionists to be at odds with those of the male rank-and-file. After the 1955 merger of the AFL and the CIO, no special efforts were made to organize women workers or to address their needs until a 1970 women's conference in Wisconsin. Indeed, labor officials perpetuated the myth that women were reluctant to organize, that they were complacent about following the male authority of the boss or company and ultimately undermined worker solidarity. Many unionists considered women scab-like in accepting low pay and part-time work that drove up industry profits at the expense of male workers.[26]

Thus, women rarely assumed leadership in the nation's 180 unions. Exceptions were secondary officers in the Stewards and Stewardesses Division of the Air Line Pilots or black activist Addie Wyatt of the Amalgamated Meat Cutters. Only two tiny unions in entertainment fields had female presidents. A few "gifted" women served in shop, local, county, or state offices. Women were most successful in entering the United Automobile Workers (UAW) power structure. In 1960, 68 percent of women auto workers were married, mostly working of necessity and limited to only 24 of 40 job categories in auto parts manufacturing. Many lost jobs because of automation or omission of their names from seniority lists for promotions. At General Motors in 1961, it was considered "sociologically wrong for a woman to have job preference over a man who was a family breadwinner." In that transitional time, international UAW staff member Emily Rosdolsky could still write Walter Reuther that "the traditional concern of the labor movement in this country . . . for protecting women from excessively long hours of work is still valid"; while at the same time, Dorothy Haener advocated "sex blind" treatment and abolition of protective legislation. In 1963 the UAW Women's Department produced the pamphlet, "How to Be Equal though Different—Working Women Today," defending protective laws yet calling for maternity leaves and separate restrooms.[27]

Frances Parks and Nadine Brown campaigned to elect a woman at large to the UAW International Executive Board (IEB) in 1964. Parks accused the union of "practicing personal prejudice against women."

Many men alleged "that women simply were unqualified by nature for union leadership." UAW Secretary-Treasurer Emil Mazey told the *Detroit News*, "Women have equality—plus. They've been seeking equal rights for centuries. One of these days they'll get it and it'll serve 'em right." Others called women "'pussycats' unsuited to the difficult 'manly' work required of board members"—organizing and collective bargaining. In 1964, 170,000 women made up 12.5 percent of UAW membership but only ten percent of 700 international representatives. At the 1964 convention, 200 women and 20 men formed Help Equalize Representation (HER), headed by Joanne Wilson and Elizabeth Jackson, succeeding two years later in winning election from a roster of seven women of Olga Madar to the IEB. Madar held a position at UAW headquarters, Solidarity House, and had experience in directing international departments.[28]

Madar's election signaled a major pro-woman shift in the UAW; and the campaign pointed to a pool of talented and militant women leaders at the local level. The UAW Women's Department, founded in 1944 to increase female participation, had actually served "to ghettoize" and marginalize women in the union. Madar called for women's conferences and workshops "on plant problems such as unequal pay, seniority violations, and maternity leaves" instead of "fashion shows and speeches by local judges on the problems of juvenile delinquency and by international officers on the importance of women stuffing envelopes and answering telephones at campaign headquarters in election years." She favored instruction in the grievance procedure, collective bargaining, and parliamentary procedure. After Madar's election, however, the UAW became more activist on behalf of women, questioning state "protective" laws that applied only to women and often discriminated against them—a dramatic break with American unionist tradition since the Progressive era.[29]

UAW women acutely felt such discriminations as in the August 1966 lay-off of 150 female assemblers in the electronics division of Goodyear Aerospace in Akron, an action based on an old weight-lifting law that kept women from displacing lower-seniority men. UAW unionists Ann Lefebvre, Marlea Stefanski, and Frances Rogers spoke out against protective laws. As Defense Department contracts led to an industry boom in the sixties, women were often left out because of laws restricting their overtime hours. General Motors denied women overtime work and ignored their transfer applications. Many male unionists continued to operate under the ideological slogan, "Women's place is in the home."

Women's grievances grew rather than diminished, especially after 1969–70 when the EEOC and the Michigan Attorney General ruled that state protective laws conflicted with the anti-sex discrimination provision in the 1964 Civil Rights Act, impelling the UAW to renounce the principle of protection.[30]

Attendance at regional UAW Women's conferences doubled from 1966 to 1971. By 1967, after many UAW women joined the new National Organization for Women (NOW), the National Advisory Council (NAC) urged more UAW activism for gender equality in factories. It warned, "the reluctance and resistance to affording them an equal opportunity to advancement in the union is causing many of our sisters to conclude that management men and union men are much alike in their reluctance to promote women." The UAW NAC advocated assigning women in all areas of union activity, not ghettoizing them in the Women's Department; but change was slow. Pressured in 1968 by the conservative AFL-CIO, the UAW withdrew from support of NOW. Dorothy Haener's activism took full effect only in the seventies. In 1970, the UAW endorsed the ERA.[31]

One of the greatest changes for working women and children came among migrant farm workers for agribusiness. Public law permitted *braceros*, Mexican nationals legally imported on contract to growers, to work in the West, undercutting the wages of Chicanos (Mexican-Americans) and Filipino-Americans despite supposed controls. After 1955, Cesar Chavez, with his wife Helen, tried to organize the Mexican-American *barrio* (community) to better abysmal living conditions, founding the Community Service Organization (CSO) with 36 branches in California and Arizona. Dolores Huerta, from a farm worker family yet trained as a teacher, served as a full-time CSO lobbyist in the late fifties, pressuring the California legislature for a minimum wage for farm workers as well as old-age pensionists, for the right to take driver's tests in Spanish, for legality of door-to-door voter registration, and for disability and unemployment insurance. Despite some successes, she knew that legislative change would come too slowly; a union was necessary. Maria Moreno, a Chicana farm worker in California, agreed. Addressing the 1961 AFL-CIO convention, she described "near-starvation conditions she and her 12 children faced"— meals entirely of boiled greens or potato peelings soup.[32]

In 1962, Chavez left the CSO for the AFL-CIO's Agricultural Workers Organizing Committee (AWOC); and Huerta, expecting her seventh child, joined him. Huerta remembers, "I was driving around

Stockton with all those little babies in the car, the different diaper changes for each one. It's always hard, not just because you're a woman but because it's hard to really make that commitment." Chavez founded the National Farm Workers' Association (NFWA), renamed the United Farm Workers (UFW) and made Huerta UFW Vice President and chief negotiator, a post she held for five years, authoring labor contracts in simple, precise language. The UFW used all-woman negotiating teams because, says Huerta, "Growers can't swear back at us. . . . we bring in the ethical questions like how our kids live." Huerta judged that women excelled at negotiations as well as organizing because they had "no big ego trips to overcome" and were "more tenacious." Chavez also urged his wife Helen to learn bookkeeping and head the UFW credit union.[33]

Chavez recruited Jesse Lopez de la Cruz (1919–) and her husband Arnold, migrant worker parents of six, to work as volunteer field organizers. De la Cruz and her family often lived in tents in migrant camps travelling on the annual circuit from Anaheim up to Santa Clara, from the San Joaquin Valley with its vineyards and fruits to Arvin's cotton and north to pick prunes in San José—working in corporate agriculture owned by the Southern Pacific Railroad, Standard Oil of California, or other giants. Winter rest in November or December was in poor areas around Los Angeles. They knew first-hand the malnutrition, hunger, and overwork imposed upon children and mothers without birth control or daycare but with the "double burden" of heavy field work as well as family responsibilities. De la Cruz explained the origins of her activism, "With us, family is very important"; but for the migrant worker, family as well as women were victimized by the agribusiness system.[34]

De la Cruz played a leading role in the UFW, organizing entire extended families that made up the migrant worker community. She picketed growers, only to be sprayed with pesticides and chased by overseers shooting at her and trying to run her down in pick-up trucks. She eloquently argued for issues like shorter hours, higher wages, and health care as well as larger principles of social justice and racial dignity, becoming famous for her "no-nonsense, razor-sharp" style in public debates, taking on powerful growers and their allies. She and her colleagues coopted the names Chicano/Chicana, derogatory terms for Mexican-Americans, by instilling them with a sense of ethnic pride. In 1967, de la Cruz became an official UFW organizer, paid only $5 per week, the same as the workers. She was on the front lines in the campaign to boycott Gallo, then America's major wine producer, as was Maria-Luisa Fangel, mother of eight, who despite minimal English worked with her husband in a Detroit boycott center from 1968 to 1970.[35]

As matters worsened through the decade, marked by the Delano (California) grape strike in 1965, the first UFW action and one that lasted five years, Chavez, Huerta, and de la Cruz won influential support from CORE, SNCC, the Amalgamated Clothing Workers of America (ACWA), and presidential hopeful Senator Robert Kennedy. Huerta and others went to eastern cities to strategize and mobilize a national boycott of California grapes. Danger abounded as deputized growers and Teamsters beat and arrested farm workers. Maximina de la Cruz continued her activism after her husband was killed for his movement work. The first grapes bearing the union label were shipped on 30 May 1970; but widespread victory, once again, did not come until late in the seventies. Meanwhile, Jesse de la Cruz served on the Fresno Economic Opportunity Commission and was appointed advisor to the California Commission on the Status of Women. UFW work educated and empowered her as it did Marie Sabadado, who became director of the Robert F. Kennedy Medical Plan for Migrant Workers.[36]

The growing UFW movement inspired workers of the Farah Manufacturing Company of San Antonio and El Paso to begin a drive in 1969, organized by Anne Kracik Draper (1917–), west coast director of the Union Label Department of the Amalgamated Clothing Workers (ACWA), an AFL-CIO affiliate. Farah, a large producer of boys' and men's pants, operated plants across the Southwest with 95 percent of its employees Chicano and 85 percent women, many working for $1.70 an hour using faulty equipment, lacking maternity insurance, and losing seniority when they took leave to have a baby. Those joining the union were fired. At a September 1970 union parade, cameras caught Rosa Flores raising her fists to the chant "Viva la Huelga!" (Long Live the Strike), making her nationally famous on a poster that inspired a boycott equalled only by that against grapes. The formal strike did not begin until 1972 and was not resolved until 1974.[37]

Wives often suffered non-unionization vicariously. Such was the result of the 1969 Farmington, West Virginia, coal mine explosion that killed 78 miners and stirred women to form the rank-and-file movement that resulted in the Disabled Miners and Widows of Southern West Virginia, which picketed mining companies to illustrate need for the Coal Mine Health and Safety Act. When Joseph "Jock" Yablonsky tried to end the dictatorial leadership of the United Mine Workers (UMW) by Tony Boyle, his wife and daughter were murdered along with him; again, the resulting strike did not end until 1974.

Unions still ignored vast portions of the American workforce, particularly those working in the lowest category of jobs in terms of pay and conditions—cleaning services, hospital workers (orderlies, nurses aides), migrant workers—most of whom were women and minorities. Hospital workers, excluded from protection by the Taft-Hartley Labor-Management Relations Act of 1947 and the National Labor Relations Board, began to organize in 1959. Some women began organizing on the grassroots level. Dorothy Bolden organized maids in Atlanta in 1968, meeting in a Baptist church to form the National Domestic Workers' Union of America. Black women often worked in non-union jobs; but even those unionized encountered particular discrimination. Even the International Ladies' Garment Workers Union (ILGWU) was accused of racism. Women's problems with unions were not truly addressed until the 1974 founding of the Coalition of Labor Union Women (CLUW) by Wyatt, Madar, and Myra Wolfgang, drawing from over fifty unions.[38]

Less important but more publicized was the attempt by Myra Wolfgang, International Vice President of the predominantly female Hotel, Motel, and Restaurant Employees' Union to expose the poor working conditions of Playboy bunnies, who were paid no wages, made all income from tips, and were fired at the drop of a hat for "loss of the bunny image," a euphemism for a range of issues from gaining weight to union activities. Stewardesses and other service employees faced similar difficulties.

At the decade's end, six of every seven working women remained nonunionized and only one fifth of union members were female. But even clerical workers, their ranks swollen through new automated jobs, began to organize, forming local unions like Women Office Workers (WOW), Boston's 9 to 5, Chicago's Women Employed (WE), and San Francisco's Women's Alliance to Gain Equality (WAGE). The *Harvard Business Review* warned employers in 1971: "Your Clerical Workers Are Ripe for Unionization." Indeed, all women workers were.[39]

Business: Executive Women

Difficult conditions for women executives "changed only slightly" in the sixties. The few women managers earned salaries far below those of men, and opportunities for advancement generally remained limited to a few "creative" fields: retailing, advertising, public relations, and sometimes finance. Edith Grimm, first woman vice president of Chicago department store Carson, Pirie & Scott, estimated that the pay scale for women executives was 56 percent that of men. A male CEO told her that a woman had to be "at least ten percent better than a competing man to get any managerial or decision-making post." Grimm warned that "A woman who is determined to play a game so fixed, had better be prepared to 'look like a girl, act like a lady, think like a man, and work like a dog.'"[40]

Tradition and a deeply rooted sense of sex roles were barriers to women's mobility. "Aggressiveness, decisiveness, competitiveness, and risk-taking, . . . normally expected of men but not women," were the "qualities most frequently cited for success." Traditional women's characteristics, "tenderness, submissiveness, nurturance, and emotionality," did not match the "managerial behavioral model." A 1962 article advised women executives "to exercise self-control and not become emotional"; yet that year, another writer urged women executives to bring "the lessons of femininity" to the office, not to resent male antagonism but to exercise "mental and emotional discipline. . . . If women can only maintain their perspective and patience, they will find the obstacle-strewn path more profitable." Social Research, Inc., of Chicago reported in one study that sixty successful women executives "demonstrated greater day-to-day practicality, organizational skill, sensitivity to people and adaptability than men in comparable positions." Such reassuring reports had little effect, however.[41]

Resistance to women managers was widespread. A 1965 *Harvard Business Review* survey of 1,000 male and 900 female executives after passage of Title VII found 65 percent of the men and 20 percent of the women would not like a woman boss. More women urged assessment on a "case-by-case" basis, but 51 percent of the men thought women "temperamentally unfit" for management. Stereotypes prevailed of the "rigid, petty, controlling" female boss meddling in subordinates' private lives. Both men and women executives "strongly agree[d] that a woman has to be exceptional, indeed overqualified, to succeed in management." Assumptions about women's unreliability, absenteeism, and emotionalism continued well past the sixties and in defiance of all available statistics.[42]

The few women who succeeded sometimes found it difficult to fashion an appropriate behavior. Jean Glass, president of a Texas advertising firm, noted that a businesswoman "may become defensive, demanding, mousy, or sexy—all because she's self-conscious about being the one woman in a room with 100 men." The gradual increase in numbers of businesswomen helped: the "problem of how to be aggressive while feminine . . . seems to trouble older executives most; at least, few younger women mention it," *Business Week* reported.[43]

Many women were ambivalent about the costs of success. Married women faced "inner conflict and guilt" as they struggled with the dual responsibilities of home and office. Like other working women, they had to defend themselves against the assumption by other women as well as men that they were "bad mothers" because of the time they spent away from their children. Many successful businesswomen were single or divorced, perhaps, *Newsweek* surmised, because "few men [were] equipped for the strain of having high-powered wives whose business prestige and salary" outstripped their own. A 1967 study of women in senior federal government positions showed that two-thirds were unmarried; similarly, women in male-dominated professions were often unmarried.[44]

Black businesswomen faced both these sexist responses and racism; many called sexism the tougher barrier. They also had to deal with the issue of success for women in a community where men were subjected to systematic discrimination. Some negotiated a delicate balance: Yolande Chambers, a lawyer who became vice president of Davidson department stores in Detroit, and was mother of three children and a minister's wife, felt it important "that a career woman not push her husband to the background . . . especially the wives of Negroes whose manhood [has] been trampled underfoot for three centuries."[45]

Barriers against women were reinforced in many ways. United Airlines ran a 5 P.M. "all male executive flight" from Newark to Chicago; Roslyn Willett, president of her own New York consulting firm, complained in vain to the Civil Aeronautics Board. Public places like the Oak Room in New York's Plaza Hotel and Boston's Locke-Ober's restaurant, where business was done, banned women at lunch time. At Washington's Cosmos Club, women could enter only as guests of members (all men and all white), and they could not come in the front door. These practices persisted until women organized sit-in protests in the early seventies.[46]

Even in the "woman's field" of retailing, the number of women in top-rank positions was "infinitesimal," with only 20 percent in middle management. In 1962, a Michigan State University survey found that

3.3 percent of American executives were women: doors were opening slowly in "creative fields," in "new manufacturing fields . . . not steeped in tradition," in insurance, banking, and real estate. In 1966, no major heavy industry had a woman in a top administrative post; "we don't have ladies' rooms in steel mills," one executive explained.[47]

Traditional employers of large numbers of women continued to maintain gender bias: in 1971, the EEOC called American Telephone and Telegraph "the largest discriminator against women" in the nation. Pressured by Title VII, Bell Telephone started a pioneering program to recruit and train women for "customer contact and management positions"; by 1966, sixty-five local Bell business offices had women managers, and several women were district managers. Such "affirmative action" at Bell and other companies amounted to tokenism to satisfy new laws. More typical was the manager of a business-forms company who explained that "girls just don't have the qualifications" for a job requiring technical know-how: "Our men have to do specifications and layouts, and improve customer's ideas."[48]

Despite formidable barriers, some women were successful. The "best breaks" went to the "wives, widows, daughters, or great good friends of founders or owners." Ruth Handler, who was earning $83,000 in 1966 as president of Mattel Toys, was "typical of this select group" because she had cofounded the company with her husband twenty-five years earlier. Others made it on their own, most often in "creative" or "women's" fields.[49]

One visible success story of the sixties was advertising executive Mary Wells Lawrence, catapulted to industry fame by a $150,000 Braniff Airlines campaign. Already successful, her much vaunted revitalization program brought Braniff remarkable profits in 1965. *Newsweek* praised Wells's "End of the Plain Plane" concept. In addition to company reorganization, she urged repainting airplanes in a vivid "burst of color" and uniforming stewardesses in stylish costumes by Emilio Pucci with "plastic helmets to shield hair-dos from bad weather on the ground." One Wells ad showed stewardesses doing a seductive "air strip" of their new wardrobe.[50]

Mary Kay Ash was another notable success with a $60,000 salary in 1969 from the direct mail skincare and cosmetics empire she launched in 1963 "on a $5,000 shoestring." Ash began as "angry, really angry"— "a divorced career woman in a male-dominated world." Leaving a marketing career after being repeatedly passed over for promotions that went to men, she created a company beginning "with one shelf of skincare products, nine friends who agreed to serve as beauty consultants, and the help of her three children." Her founding principles were "the Golden Rule and an unshakable belief in women." She recruited women to market her products from their homes and lavished them with praise and gifts: diamond and emerald bumblebee pins and pink Cadillacs. The bumblebee was the company symbol because it "isn't supposed to fly but goes right on trying—just like women who didn't know they could fly but they did!" By the late seventies, after a two-for-one stock split, the company was worth $22 million. Ash's secret of success was her ability to foster female loyalty and entrepreneurship; the company was a "forerunner" of the women's movement. Ash wrote that women "want to be, should be, 'soft, gentle, able to make decisions' but ever mindful of their femininity. But, 'in the sense that I want women to succeed, I would call myself a feminist.'"[51]

Beyond the women's fields, the greatest chances for success were in such newer industries as computers where "mushroom growth" and the need for technical expertise outweighed gender considerations. While automation limited women's opportunities at the clerical and operative levels, it opened possibilities for educated women. Younger companies "typically [drew] no distinctions in salaries between men and women professionals." Estill Buchanan, a management consultant and the first woman honors graduate from the Harvard Business School (1962), noted that women were psychologically attuned to the emerging concept of "business team leadership" emphasizing "decentralized organizations in which power accrues to those individuals who can effectively link groups through competence in communication." She believed women also possessed the qualities needed in a modern executive: "a high tolerance for ambiguity and a high threshold for coping with uncertainty."[52]

In newer industries, women more often entered "the executive offices through specialized accomplishment than through the front door of conventional managerial performance." Areas like banking, insurance, and brokerage gave women the chance to prove specific skills. The financial world inadvertently gave women "another edge by favoring a career pattern characteristic of them—rising within a single institution rather than job-hopping." Yet even there, numbers of women in influential positions were small. In 1972 the National Association of Banking Women reported that while 70 percent of banking employees were women only 10 percent were officers, mainly on the junior level. In 1969, the nation's 14,172 banks, had 270 female bank chairmen or presidents, 20 senior vice-presidents, and 50 executive vice-presidents; this was largely due to the fact that top offices were often an inheritance in a family dominated bank.[53]

The securities industry remained a bastion of white men through the sixties. A 1973 article points out that 90 percent of women in that industry were in clerical or bank-office jobs; 5 percent were in sales and management. No large investment banking firm had a woman senior vice president or partner. Of 55,000 registered brokers in New York City only 5,000 were female, including many secretaries who registered so they could take orders when their (male) bosses were absent. Other role limitations existed: women brokers typically dealt with individual customers rather than institutions; women in managerial positions rarely supervised men. The personnel director of the New York Stock Exchange reported that women held sixty of the six hundred managerial positions in the industry, but none of those sixty supervised professional-level men.

In 1965 Julia Walsh and Phyllis Peterson became the first women members of the American Stock Exchange; Muriel Sieber followed in 1967. In 1966, Merrill Lynch, the largest brokerage firm, appointed its first woman vice president. It was 1970 before the Boston Stock Exchange admitted women to membership. In Chicago, Victoria Lynn Sanders progressed from a 1966 job as a research assistant to become in 1971 the city's only black woman stock broker. *Time* magazine noted that "like most black businesswomen, Miss Sanders [believed] that Black Power without green power was meaningless."[54]

In 1969, *Business Week* observed that "the barriers are still up against women at the top executive level. 'Women are assistant to the assistant treasurer, and responsible openings are reserved for men.' . . . Except in industries with special needs, a woman rarely rises beyond middle management—and she has to be better than her male competitor if she wants to go even that far." There were signs of hope: the number of young, entry-level women increased, and they routinely got business posts that had been "closed to their predecessors ten years ago." More women combined careers with family, although no one in the upper echelons of power asked how and at what cost, and the phrase "having it all" had yet to be coined.[55]

At the decade's end, Edith Grimm summed up: "Women aren't at the top because this is still a man's world . . . First, little girls just haven't been brought up to think they're supposed to go into business. And second, they are . . . limited largely by the opinions of men rather than their own inherent ability or inability." In a 1970 study, Cynthia Fuchs Epstein confirmed this pattern: socialization of young women for marriage "seriously" undermined her training for any other role. Epstein explained the ambiguities: "The young girl is asked to be studious and learn, but she increasingly becomes aware that she may not be asked to demonstrate her knowledge. She is asked to be good-looking, and charming and deferential to men." Experts labeled the syndrome "cultural discontinuity or identity stress." Thus, "girls tend to accept the definitions of what they might do; they do not aspire high. . . . women generally have minimal aspirations, choose short-run social and economic advantages" in terms of jobs "and fail to question the social definitions and expectations of their motivation and their capacities."[56]

Daycare

In November 1960, the Women's Bureau, Children's Bureau, Social Security Administration, and Department of Health, Education, and Welfare jointly sponsored the National Conference on Day Care, pointing to a "serious problem" generated by eight million mothers working outside the home—one out of every four mothers with children under 18—400,000 with children under 12. The meeting, headed by Alice K. Leopold, heard Mrs. Randolph Guggenheimer, President of the National Committee for the Day Care of Children, Inc., and representatives of the Child Welfare League of America call for creating centers or group care facilities for children under 12 and for other places for those with special needs, all with licensed professional supervision. But Katherine B. Oettinger, Children's Bureau Head, termed day care services "unique and revolutionary." The conference also considered counseling and homemaker services, pre-school and after-school programs. Participants concluded that without federal funds, child care needs could not adequately be met; and none were forthcoming.[57]

In 1961, Kennedy convened a White House conference to study services for working mothers and children. Its recommendations were even more conservative: "that to maintain the important relationship of infant and mother, children under three should remain in their own homes unless there are pressing social or economic reasons for care away from home" and "that social casework and other counseling services be available both before and during employment of the mother, to help parents decide wisely whether her employment will contribute more to family welfare than her presence in the home." This was, after all, the popular attitude about the importance of mothers as confirmed in Dr. Benjamin Spock's best-selling *Baby and Child Care:* "If a mother realizes clearly how vital this kind of care is to a small child it may make it easier to decide that the extra money she may earn . . . is not so important after all."[58]

In 1962 for the first time since World War II, the federal government appropriated $4 million, a small sum, for day care; but monies were entirely eliminated from the 1965 budget, transferred to the Vietnam buildup. Operation Head Start, inaugurated by the Kennedy administration, provided some child care; but its purpose was remedial early education rather than custodial. *Daedalus,* the journal of The American Academy of Arts and Sciences, devoted an entire 1964 issue to the problems educated women faced in reconciling traditional roles with individual goals. Sociologist Alice Rossi wanted to find ways "to ease the combination of home and work responsibility." Like Charlotte Perkins Gilman half a century before, Rossi advocated professional surrogates for efficient housework and day care to permit women to strive for occupational equality with men.[59]

Studies of the "problem" of working mothers usually focused on potential damage to the child rather than real issues of balancing time and finances. Only occasionally was it suggested that the example of a working mother might acculturate a child to expect gender equality. Emily Hartshorne Mudd, a marriage counselor, was a rare voice in 1964 when she admitted that "no direct relationship between maternal employment and child maladjustment" had been established. Indeed, she said, "some pre-adolescent girls express stronger achievement motivation when they have for a model a productive mother with interests outside the household. Women who enjoy working are warmer and milder in discipline and less rejecting of the housemaking role than many housewives." Sociologist Robert O. Blood observed in 1965, "Employment emancipates women from domination by their husbands, and secondarily, raises their daughters from inferiority to their brothers." Education professor Kate Hevner Mueller noted that mothers entered the job market to fund children's college costs and for "a more satisfying routine," not just to have more luxuries.[60]

On a very limited scale, the 1967 Work Incentive Program (WIN) was one of the first federal programs to provide some temporary, informal supervision of children of recipients of Aid to Families with Dependent Children (AFDC) who were in job training programs. That year, Title IV amending the Social Security Act permitted local welfare departments to fund some child care for clients. Johnson's "war on poverty" did little to advance availability of day care services in any systematic way, even for the underprivileged; and the Nixon administration was even less promising.[61]

Legislators pushed for funding for day care and preschool education for children in the late sixties. Under Albert Shanker's leadership the American Federation of Teachers lobbied for an extension of the public school system to serve early childhood needs. Shanker rationalized his support in terms of maximizing teachers' employment and the use of existing school facilities at a time of declining birthrate. Educators cited successes of the Perry Preschool Project in Ypsilanti, Michigan, which cared for children of impoverished black residents, and a New York City pilot program that educated 750 black children between 1961 and 1970.

Feminists showed little interest in the 1970 White House Conference on Children because they knew that conservative "delegates shared a prior consensus on what constituted an ideal family and what direction social policy should take," a consensus "little different from that articulated at the National Conference on Day Care a decade before. Still, conference members concluded that federal intervention could and should aid American children and their working mothers, adding their voices to those of Marian Wright Edelman, director of the Children's Defense Fund, and Congresswoman Shirley Chisholm. Not until 1971 did Congress pass the Comprehensive Child Development Act, co-sponsored by Senator Walter Mondale and Representative John Brademas; but Nixon vetoed the bill as counterproductive to the need to "cement the family in its rightful position as the keystone of our civilization."[62]

Although by the sixties' end mothers of a third of the nation's preschool children worked outside the home, social conservatives in both political parties did not want to make it any easier for the trend to continue or grow. Nixon declared, "good public policy requires that we enhance rather than diminish both parental authority and parental involvement with children—particularly in those early years when social attitudes and a conscience are formed." Ironically, little reaction came from organized women groups, which had given little attention to child care and other domestic concerns of women.[63]

Absence of child care plagued working women of all classes and professions. For a woman physician subject to emergency calls, solutions included importing domestic help from Europe, placing the children in day-care centers, or setting up medical practice at home. The quality of a practice located at home might suffer due to childrens' distractions however, and she might take longer than other doctors to build up a remunerative clientele. Carole Lopate reports that most female physicians would not use the nurseries available at many large hospitals because they seemed like "the Brave New World picture of depersonalized child care," were often in "lower-class housing projects and/or connected to welfare centers," and were mainly used by "children of janitorial help, aides, and perhaps a minority of nurses." Alternate solutions were very expensive: one $15,000-a-year woman physician added only about $3,300 to the family's net income after taxes, personal expenses, and $5,000 for a housekeeper. Working women in all professions reported at the New York Governor's Conference on Women "that their salaries could barely meet the costs of their going to work" and requested that child-care expenses be tax-deductible" for all, not just to women who were "divorced, widowed, or for some other reason the sole support, or those whose income combined with their husband's [did] not exceed the minimum level of $6,000."[64]

Looking backward in *The Second Stage* (1982), Friedan speculated that "the failure of the women's movement was its blind spot about the family. It was our own extreme reaction against the wife-mother role" that failed to enlist the majority of American women. That blind spot, along with the divisiveness of radical feminism, kept activists from doing something concrete about the absence of quality day care for working mothers of all economic levels.[65]

Associations and Volunteerism

As in the fifties, many married women withdrew from the "public sphere" to the home but remained active in voluntary associations. In 1969, Margaret Mead observed, "American communities still depend on the activities of women volunteers. The churches and hospitals depend heavily on women's organizations." She traced "the success or failure" of most elementary schools to "active participation of women in parent-teacher associations whose members number about 11 million."[66]

Yet some older, mainstream women's organizations found it increasingly difficult to sustain membership; they were "not keeping pace with the growth of population and of the income classes from which they are drawn," Mead warned. The League of Women Voters (LWV), heir to the National American Woman Suffrage Association, dropped to half of its 1920s membership, although it played an increasingly visible role as sponsor of political debates. LWV encouraged women's participation in mainstream political parties but remained nonpartisan and neutral. Sometimes it undercut the more feminist agenda of its Women's Joint Congressional Committee and the small number of members intent on lobbying on women's issues. Its leaders, like those of the National Federation of Business and Profession Women (NFBPW), feared being labeled "feminist" or "militant."[67]

Mead attributed diminishing membership in older groups like the Junior League and the General Federation of Women's Clubs, which had upper-middle-class leadership, to post-war social change: "Today, a large portion of the new middle class has a blue collar background, and women's organizational activities outside the home are largely limited to the church and auxiliaries of fraternal organizations. It is mainly because an increasing proportion of educated women work outside the home that the proportion available for community work is decreasing. The role of the educated woman volunteer has become steadily less appealing as a way of establishing identity, even though those organizations that accord prestige for volunteer work, such as the Junior League, continue to grow." Also, the class of women who founded older organizations and made them work often had more available time because they had domestic help and did not work outside the home, unlike sixties women.[68]

The Young Women's Christian Association (YWCA), with 2.5 million members and 207,000 volunteers of all ages in 7,800 chapters in 6,700 localities, also underwent change in the late sixties. The resolution at its 1970 National Convention reads like that of a radical feminist group: "It is essential that women move beyond being sexual playthings of the male to an affirmation of their role as human beings, with capacity for leadership and contribution in various ways. . . . They need an identity of their own." Based on surveys of program directors, the YWCA concluded, "we're dealing with young people who are activists and agree with many of the platforms of adult contemporary feminists." In response, it set up a National Women's Resource Center to mobilize "our full power as a movement to revolutionize society's expectations of women and their own self-perception," to provide "good role models" through access to films, literature, and other materials, and to reach "the poorer young girls throughout the country and educate them about the options available to them besides marriage."[69]

The U.S. Department of Labor contracted in 1968 with the YWCA to develop a project, called Office Business Culture, for preparing disadvantaged high school graduates and other young women for clerical and sales jobs; and with funds from the Office of Economic Opportunity, the "Y" provided residence for Job Corps women in training programs. Similarly, the Labor Department entered into a jointly sponsored project with the Girl Scouts of America and the Camp Fire Girls to train unemployed or underemployed women to meet needs for community agency personnel in Boston, Dallas, Dayton, Denver, Detroit, and San Francisco. Women in these and other voluntary associations took on projects focused on the problems of poor women in inner cities, thus supporting Johnson's War on Poverty.

Other volunteer women worked to remedy the "urban crisis." In 1967, the Commission on Community Cooperation of the National Council of Negro Women received a Fels Grant to conduct Community Service Institutes to bring together women of various ethnic, racial, religious, and income groups who were raising families in inner cities, to help them communicate across neighborhood boundaries, and by sharing common experiences and problems to minimize tensions. Institutes were held in Newark and Paterson, New Jersey.

In 1968, at her annual Women Doers Luncheon, Lady Bird Johnson called on the nation's women to take action against crime in the streets, which NFBPW President Mabel McClanahan termed "a domestic crisis." Speakers included Margaret Moore, Coordinator of the Model Program of the Indianapolis Women's Crusade Against Crime, Katherine Peden, the only woman on the 11-member National Advisory Commission on Civil Disorders, and Mrs. Charles Coe, a full-time VISTA (Volunteers in Service to America) worker for Project Head Start. The Indianapolis group grew through the mid-sixties from a core of 30 to over 50,000 women. Peden praised the action of Patricia Sheehan, mayor of New Brunswick, New Jersey, who defused an explosive situation by taking "to the streets of the ghetto to listen and talk to the rebelling young people and to ask for a chance to correct the grievous conditions" that led to the brink of riot. McClanahan called on NFBPW members to take similar action.[70]

Women like Helen R. Rachlin developed professional careers as trainers and program directors in the national voluntary organization field; but 13 million of an estimated 22 million nonpolitical and nonreligious volunteers in 1965—18 percent of American women—selflessly donated their time and energies, receiving only intangible gratification. In 1969, the value of their volunteered services totalled $20 billion. They received encouragement from many older women's organizations like the YWCA, AAUW, and Junior League or from newer groups like Washington Opportunities for Women (WOW), a clearinghouse founded by Jane Fleming, Mary Jenny, and Christine Nelson to provide counseling to mature women interested in volunteerism, part-time jobs, or continuing education. Its manual circulated nationwide. In its attempt to minimize federal social programs, the Nixon administration established a Cabinet Committee on Voluntary Action, encouraging an alliance between government and volunteers exemplified by the partnership of Women in Community Service (WICS) with the Office of Economic Opportunity (OEO), and the Labor Department. Under an OEO contract, thousands of WICS volunteers recruited and screened younger women for the Job Corps. WICS also provided recreational activities and budget and job counseling, and housing, legal aid, and health referrals.[71]

Perhaps the furthest American women ventured, literally and figuratively, beyond their traditional cultural roles during the sixties was under the auspices of the Peace Corps, founded in 1961 with policies of welcoming women volunteers equally with men. Even in the Peace Corps, women volunteers were often segregated into "women's work" fields—teaching Pakistani village women about health and home economics or working as nurses in baby clinics in Malaya. The Peace Corps sent volunteers to nine countries in 1961 and to 40 in 1962. The top positions as country directors in six nations were held by men under 30 years of age. A similar gender imbalance characterized Volunteers in Service to America (VISTA), a sort of domestic Peace Corps.[72]

Examples of volunteerism and social consciousness were not always channeled through formal organizations. "Mother" Clara McBride Hale, for instance, began caring for babies of drug-addicted mothers in her Harlem apartment in 1969 when her daughter directed an addict baby to her for foster care. Hale remembers, "Inside of two months I had 22 babies living in a five-room apartment. We hold them and rock them. They love you to tell them how great they are. They're happy, and they turn out well." But they turned out well because of Hale's love, tempered by her personal necessity. She was a widowed mother of two children, aged five and six: "There was no way under the sun that they would give you any other job except domestic jobs. And that meant being away all day from those poor little children who had nobody. So I decided to take in other people's children. I raised 40. Every one of them went to college."[73]

5

Women in the Professions

There were fewer professional women in the fifties than in the thirties; and numbers only began to grow again gradually in the sixties. By 1970, American women still made up only 22 percent of the faculty in higher education, 9 percent of scientists, 7 percent of physicians, 3 percent of lawyers, 2 percent of architects, and less than one percent of engineers. A 1971 study by the Labor Department Women's Bureau concluded: "Occupationally women are more disadvantaged, compared with men, than they were thirty years ago" and "the barriers are still high against employing women in professions other than those traditionally associated with women."[1]

Growing opportunities existed for women only in what sociologist Amitai Etzioni called "semi-professions"—fields like nursing and social work where women had long predominated but where efforts grew to recruit more men "to enhance their professionalization and public image." The semi-professions had shorter training, lesser status, and greater supervision than male-dominated professions. Experts assumed women were meant for these fields because by nature they "on the average are more amenable to administrative control than men" and "less conscious of organizational status and more submissive."[2]

Society still feared the woman who would devote her life to a profession, even if combined with marriage and motherhood, and few models existed for women who wanted such a choice. A 1956 *Life* magazine article on working women insisted on showing the "homemaker-lawmaker" and the "housewife-architect" in their kitchens. When scientist Dorothy C. Hodgkin won a Nobel prize in 1964, the *New York Times* headline announced "Grandmother Wins Award." A few experts and even some feminists blamed women's own fears for blocking their route to professional success. For the few who persisted through prejudice and obstacles to complete professional training, options were limited; and they found themselves excluded formally or informally from professional associations and from advancement opportunities.[3]

Law and the Judiciary

The law was one of the professions most closed to women traditionally and it remained so during the sixties. In 1968 women constituted only 3 percent of American lawyers. By the 1970 census, the number had risen to 4.9 percent. A survey "indicated income of men lawyers to be nearly double that of female lawyers. Only at the bottom of the pay scale did the numbers of women earning a given rate exceed men."[4]

More women stayed in low-paying Legal Aid jobs rather than enter private practice as men typically did; within private firms women much more often entered such "sex-typed" specialities as domestic relations or trusts and estates, those considered by men "less prestigious, challenging, or lucrative." Of the 2700 lawyers in top firms in six major cities at the decade's end, only 186 were women; and they experienced discrepancies in salary and responsibilities, and were often relegated to the lower end of the pay scale. Women in large firms were generally restricted to the "female jobs," functioning as "back room" lawyers, doing necessary research for the more highly-prized male attorney who met the client or went to court.[5]

Through the sixties a number of strong women withstood the odds and refused to conform to the female "ideal" or to succumb to sexism. Margaret Taylor was one of the few women hired by a Wall Street firm—Cahill, Gordon & Reindel. She remembers, "There were so few women lawyers working in the large Wall Street law firms. And everywhere the ideal woman was a housewife and mother . . . glad to be staying home with the kids. If you wanted a career, you were different—and not in a good sense. Some women made a point of talking about their husbands and children to make themselves seem more 'normal.' But . . . this was a man's profession and the harder you worked and the less you acted like a woman . . . the better off you were going to be. That's how you survived. The idea wasn't to change things around . . . it was to make yourself fit in."[6]

Women who wanted to take a fighting posture and tackle larger social problems found models available like Dorothy Kenyon (1880–1972), one of the first women admitted to the New York bar, who served on the board of the American Civil Liberties Union (ACLU) from 1930 until her death, despite attacks by Senator Joseph McCarthy. She was active in the drive to integrate New York's public schools and, from the fifties, in challenges to restrictive abortion laws. With her friend, lawyer Pauli Murray (1910–1985), she crusaded for women's issues through the ACLU. Another ACLU lawyer, Harriet Pilpel, argued the case for reforming New York's abortion laws before the state legislature in 1966, and served on city, state, and federal commissions as well as the committee on political and civil rights of the President's Commission on the Status of Women.[7]

Ruth Bader Ginsburg (1933–), a Harvard Law School graduate and mother of a daughter, taught law at Rutgers in the late sixties when sex discrimination complaints began trickling into the New Jersey ACLU. They were referred to her because "sex discrimination was regarded as a woman's job." Prodded by her students, she wrote the briefs for and argued several precedent-setting cases on sex discrimination before the Supreme Court. In 1971 she became founding director of the ACLU's Women's Rights Project and was later appointed a circuit judge for the U.S. Court of Appeals for the District of Columbia circuit.[8]

Through the sixties, some black women persisted against double odds to achieve distinction as lawyers. In 1965 Marian Wright Edelman became the first black woman admitted to the Mississippi bar; she went on to found and head the Children's Defense Fund to rescue children from poverty. Patricia Roberts Harris (1924–1985), daughter of a dining-car waiter, graduated first in her class at George Washington University Law School, served as professor and dean at Howard Law School, and became a partner in a "prestigious and political" Washington law firm. She won appointment to the 1968 National Commission on the Causes and Prevention of Violence and later became Carter's Secretary of Housing and Urban Development, the first black woman in a presidential cabinet.[9]

In her New York City practice, Florynce Kennedy represented the estates of Charlie Parker and Billie Holiday, but most of her clients were poor, unable to pay her fees. Rather than sacrifice her principles,

Kennedy sometimes moonlighted as a department store salesperson. By the sixties, after a decade of practice, Kennedy was cynical about "how the law was used to maintain the bullshit rather than to change things and that justice was really a crock of shit." She turned to activism rather than litigation to fight racism and sexism, and criticized job discrimination with the observation, "There are very few jobs that actually require a penis or a vagina." To get around the limits of the law, Kennedy organized picketing and street theatre protests—the "Hollywood Toilet Bowl" to spotlight a California television station's refusal to hire a woman media buyer, and a demonstration against anti-abortion laws in front of New York's St. Patrick's Cathedral that featured wire coat-hangers representing underground abortions. Her motto was, "If you want to know where the apathy is, you're probably sitting on it." In 1969, with Diane Schulder and four other women lawyers, she filed a suit for total repeal of the New York state abortion laws.[10]

Other women lawyers shared Kennedy's rage, albeit in quieter, more stoical ways. Denise Carty-Bennia left a Wall Street law firm to teach at Northeastern University Law School after discovering that she was a "two-for," a token black and a token woman, given an office in full public view. She noticed more sexism than racism: "At the law firm, all kinds of outrageous practices were tolerated against women. I was literally ordered not to speak to the secretaries when I met them in the bathroom. . . . I saw that it was fine for women and blacks to drive themselves as associates but unrealistic for them to expect to make partner."[11]

In 1969, influenced by the tide of feminism, women law students from New York University (NYU) and Columbia banded together to protest the blatant sexism of law firm recruiters who either refused to interview qualified women or did so reluctantly, telling candidates "We don't like to hire women," "We don't expect the same kind of work from women as we do from men," or "Women don't become partners here." Law school placement offices "coolly accepted" the unwillingness of employers to hire women. Discrimination occurred on all levels of the profession. The Bar Associations in Brooklyn and the Bronx explained that women lawyers could not join because there were no rest-room facilities for them. The NYU Women's Rights group issued a preliminary report in 1970, challenging "practices that seem strange in a profession that each Law Day reaffirms its belief in equal treatment under the law. What of equal treatment in the Law?"[12]

Columbia and NYU women won funding from the EEOC to create an Employment Rights Project (ERP), headed by attorney Harriet Rabb. ERP filed discrimination complaints with the New York City Commission of Human Rights (NYCCHR) against ten major law firms. NYCCHR Commissioner Eleanor Holmes Norton concluded that "almost without exception women with qualifications equal to or better than male applicants were rejected and that females were never advanced to partnership." Successful class-action suits followed in New York and across the country.[13]

When she became NYCCHR Commissioner in 1980, Eleanor Holmes Norton (1933–) had a reputation as a defender of civil rights and free speech. A graduate of Antioch, she chose Yale Law School because of its sympathy for civil rights. She spent the summer of 1963 working with SNCC in Greenwood, Mississippi, where she had a harsh introduction to the dangers of movement work, spending her first day with civil rights leader Medgar Evers, who was assassinated the next day. In 1964 she helped prepare the legal brief for the Mississippi Freedom Democratic Party's challenge to the state's all-white Democratic National Convention delegation. After graduation, she worked for five years with the New York City ACLU, developed a specialty in civil rights and First Amendment cases, and represented such disparate clients as Julian Bond, the American Nazi Party, and southern segregationist George Wallace in his 1968 free speech case against New York Mayor John Lindsay. When Lindsay was seeking a director for the Human Rights Commission, he remembered Norton's work and offered her the job, which she held until 1977. Norton remembers that she was more fortunate than other civil rights workers because she was "able to participate in institutionalizing the goals of our movements in the place where it counts—government." She traced her success not only to timing and training, but also to her family, particularly her grandmother: "In addition to my own parents, there was this matriarchal figure who considered me the center of the universe and that helped to build self-confidence and the sense of ego that drives a person forward. If you said to me, Did I ever have any doubt that I could get the EEOC running effectively? all I could say was that my grandmother expected me to."[14]

If it was difficult for women in the first stages of the legal profession to gain a foothold, it was nearly impossible at the top, at the level of judicial appointments. In 1960, with election to the Arizona Supreme Court, Lorna E. Lockwood became the first woman seated on a court of last resort in the nation. She remembers arriving at her new courthouse parking space only to be met by an irate guard yelling, "Lady, lady, you can't park there." In 1965, Lockwood became the first woman chief justice of a state court, dubbed "the grande dame of Arizona jurists"; and her name was proposed for the United States Supreme Court seats filled by Abe Fortas and Thurgood Marshall. Only Susie Sharp, appointed to North Carolina's supreme court by Governor Terry Sanford in 1962, held a comparable position.[15]

In 1970, Doris Sassower reported that of almost 10,000 judges in the United States fewer than 200 were women, and all but a very small elite of those sit on "inferior courts of limited jurisdiction." On the intermediate appellate level in the federal court system, there was only one woman out of 92 Circuit Court judges; on the lower district court level there were only three out of 333 district judges. As the first woman ever to address the National Conference of Bar Presidents (in 1969), Sassower highlighted the lack of women on the bench, and made some specific suggestions for concerted effort to rectify the situation. "I was applauded when I said that the time had come for the leaders of the organized bar to recognize their responsibility to open the profession to everyone able to make a contribution to it." But, "no significant action on those recommendations has been taken or announced."[16]

President Kennedy appointed only one woman to the federal bench: Sarah Tilghman Hughes (1896–1985) to the U.S. District Court for North Texas in 1961. After Kennedy's assassination, Judge Hughes administered the oath of Presidential office to Lyndon B. Johnson. Johnson gave three judicial appointments to women, including one to Constance Baker Motley (1921–), the first black female federal judge, the first black woman to argue a case before the Supreme Court (1961), the first black woman in the New York State Senate (1964–65), and the first woman borough president of Manhattan (1965–66). A Columbia Law School graduate, she tried cases in eleven federal courts and argued ten cases in the United States Supreme Court, all crucial segments of the Legal Defense Fund's strategy for desegregating public schools across the nation, which led to the landmark 1954 *Brown v. Board of Education of Topeka* decision. She recalls, "What we Legal Defense Fund lawyers did certainly helped expand the role and significance of the courts. After the *Brown* case, . . . the law could be effectively used as an instrument of major social change." Motley and her colleagues "developed a way in which minorities could successfully deal with the majority" through legal action.[17]

Women learned that lesson as well and increasingly turned to the courts and to political action for redress of grievances. In 1968 Mary Eastwood, who played a significant role in the passage of Title VII of the 1964 Civil Rights Act, and two other lawyers, Sylvia Ellison and Caruthers Berger, joined feminist Ti-Grace Atkinson in chartering Human Rights for Women, Inc., in Washington, D.C., as a non-profit, tax-exempt corporation providing legal aid to promote women's rights, a "kind of ACLU in the area of sex discrimination." It was both a sign of women's understanding of the role of collective action in their own defense and a model for the future.

Medicine: Physicians, Pharmacists, Nurses

Medicine remained a white, upper-class male preserve through the sixties, and women accounted for only 6 to 8 percent of American physicians. A 1970 report to a conference on the status of women in the professions noted a slight improvement in numbers and in attitude toward women. As of April 1970, however, of 279,400 physicians in the United States, only 20,920, well under 10 percent, were female. Getting into and through medical school was only the first of many hurdles.

Options for women in medicine were limited, by custom if not by outright discrimination. Half of all women physicians were certified in three fields: internal medicine, pediatrics, and psychiatry, the latter two having the image of women's specialties. In 1964, when the Women's Medical College of Pennsylvania was resisting coeducation, it chose instead to strengthen the departments of pediatrics, psychiatry, and physiology, hoping to attract more "first-rate women who are interested in these particularly 'feminine fields.'" Female pediatricians were more acceptable because they could be supposed to have personal experience with children, while women fit into psychiatry because they had "traditionally been considered sensitive to the emotional aspects of interpersonal relationships." Women in psychiatry were also assumed to be "able to keep their egos in the background and not compete as directly, so that the clashes of will which sometimes destroy the physician-patient relationship in psychotherapy may occur less frequently with female than with male therapists." Ironically, obstetrics had few women because of "special difficulty in obtaining residencies."[18]

Child psychiatry welcomed women from early in the century. Women often chose psychiatric specialties for practical reasons as well—minimal night and weekend duty during residencies and flexible scheduling once in practice. Surgery had the smallest percentage of women, with 16 percent of all male physicians and only 2 percent of women. Specialties in opthamology, orthopedics, otolaryngology, thoracic, plastic, and neurological surgery had almost no women because department heads in those specialties would "rather pick from the best male candidates than take a chance on a woman" for an internship or residency.[19]

As careers matured, many women entered public health rather than private practice, both because they could thus help a greater segment of the population and because public health offered a salary and regular hours. Male physicians generally avoided salaried jobs which, in 1964, provided an annual (2,000 hour) median income of $16,132 in contrast to $25,879 for the self-employed practice.[20]

The few black women physicians found themselves in somewhat different positions than white women. The proportion of black women to black men in medicine was the reverse of that for white physicians, and community acceptance was less of a problem. One black graduate of the Women's Medical College reported that her practice in upstate New York "grew to full size almost as soon as she set it up, and she had to wait far less for patients than her white classmates." Although her clientele came mainly from the black community, she received more white patients as she became known in the town. The disproportion of women to men was a subject of concern, however. When the Macy Foundation sponsored a conference on "Negroes in Medicine" in 1967, black leaders resolved that future aid for medical education should be given to black men rather than women until a "gender balance" comparable to whites was achieved.[21]

Once in practice, most women physicians put in 60 to 70 hours a week. Part-time work, for greater flexibility in balancing family and professional duties, was rarely available, although by the decade's end the Veterans Administration made efforts to provide part-time positions in its hospitals. Married female physicians relied on supportive husbands more than other professional women did; more than half of the married women physicians had physician husbands. They averaged three children per family—slightly larger than the average for their socioeconomic bracket. The divorce rate for women physicians was slightly higher than the national average, as it was for male physicians.[22]

Women in medicine worried about public acceptance and often felt alienated from other women, particularly those who had chosen to be full-time homemakers. Many women patients or mothers of patients were skeptical about the quality of care they would receive from a "woman doctor," having been acculturated to rank female professionals as inferior to the traditional authority and expert—the male.[23]

Although some found individual sustenance in the new women's movement at the decade's end, few women physicians appear to have identified strongly with it, perhaps, as Mary Roth Walsh suggests, because it seemed a "step away from whatever chance they have for advancement within the medical mainstream." Earlier assertions of women's role in medicine faded. The American Medical Women's Association (AMWA) lost 20 percent of its membership between 1963 and 1967 as younger women rejected it as an "anachronism." The New England Hospital for Women, dedicated since its 1890s founding to advancement of women physicians, closed in 1968; the building became a community health center. In 1969, the Women's Medical College of Pennsylvania began to admit male students, subsequently dropping "Women's" from its name.[24]

Despite personal and professional obstacles, women played increasingly active roles in medicine. The Margaret Sanger Research Bureau continued to be staffed largely by women physicians, who saw 15,000 patients a year and helped to train medical students and other medical personnel in the areas of contraception and fertility. At the Memorial Sloan-Kettering Cancer Center, Dr. Lois Murphy headed the pediatrics department in the clinical unit, as one of the nation's few woman heads of a medical department. There, women physicians worked both in research and patient care. Internist Marguerite Sykes published her chemotherapy research, Doctors Florence Chu and Ruth Snyder specialized in radiation therapy, and Dr. Elizabeth Pickett was known for her work in surgical oncology.[25]

From 1965 to 1971, at Cornell University Medical Center, Dr. Virginia Apgar (1909–1974), a specialist in childbirth anesthesia, held the first medical faculty position that established birth defects as a subspecialty. From 1959 on, she was also an executive with the National Foundation–March of Dimes, developing support for research on birth defects and lecturing on newborn problems. Probably the most dramatic story of accomplishments by women physicians was the work of Helen Taussig and Frances Kelsey in blocking the drug Thalidomide from the United States—a story told in chapter twelve.[26]

Greater opportunities opened for women from 1956 on as pharmacy reprofessionalized, requiring five years study for a B.S. by 1960. In 1958, *American Druggist* worried about future "manpower" and urged "more women to enter pharmacy to make up for the anticipated loss of potential male" students to engineering and medicine. Despite fears about feminizing pharmacy, some schools reversed a policy of a ten percent ceiling for women. By 1957, the National Association of Chain Drug Stores launched a campaign to recruit women, placing ads in *Miss Magazine, Glamour,* and newspapers, publishing brochures like "Why Should a Girl Become a Pharmacist," and mailing "female help wanted" appeals to potential students. One–third of pharmacy schools joined the effort, stressing the "psychic income" of "service to humanity and belonging to a profession" compatible with traditional women's marriage and family goals and responsibilities. The American Pharmacy Association proclaimed in 1969 that the profession needed women and should accommodate them with part-time and flexible schedules, especially in hospitals. Between 1960 and 1970, women studying pharmacy rose from ten to 16 percent and those holding the B.S. from 12 to 19 percent, a trend that continued, aided by federal health policies and programs launched in 1963 to expand the health care industry.[27]

Women made up 98 percent of the nursing profession, most working in hospitals rather than in private duty, a shift that occurred for white nurses in the years between the world wars. For black women, access to hospital nursing did not open until the sixties, a result of the civil rights movement and federal equal opportunity legislation. Otherwise, little changed. Despite demand, nurses' salaries remained relatively low, and nursing was still the only profession "in which the important decisions about what work is to be done and how it is to be done are made by people outside the profession. . . . by doctors." Nurses experienced conflicts between their sense of professional mission and pressures from outdated internalized canons and nostalgic principles.[28]

In 1968, psychiatrist Dr. Leonard Stein described the "doctor-nurse game" as "transactional neurosis" in which "the nurse makes recommendations to the doctor while both pretend she is doing no such thing." Every nurse who Stein interviewed felt that "to make a direct suggestion to a doctor, thus questioning his infinite knowledge, was to insult and belittle him." Doctors could not contend with nurses committed to and taking responsibility for their field. Many women became nurses "by default," not wanting to be teachers or secretaries. Once married, many nurses accepted dead-end jobs compatible with family needs, quitting when home problems arose, with family priorities contrasting to the poor working conditions and low status. "Feminine conditioning explains not only the lack of commitment to nursing but the lack of leadership within it," historian Gena Corea concludes.[29]

Dr. Virginia Cleland observed that with physicians and hospital administrators even nursing directors often acted "like housewives asking for grocery money," fearful of losing their good salaries and positions. Corea explains, "Because of the conditioning of both participants, the [male] doctor-[female] nurse relationship mirrors the male-female one." Martha Fowlkes, a Smith College medical sociologist, found it identical to interaction between boss-secretary, principal-teacher, and husband-wife: "The doctor's handmaiden, the nurse calls him 'Dr. Jones' while he calls her 'Susan.' She obeys his orders, sets up equipment for his performances in the examining or operating rooms and cleans up after him. Only a few years ago, she was even expected to open doors for him, stand when he entered a room and offer him her chair."[30]

The question of nursing's status as a profession had a long history. After World War II, the goal of baccalaureate education for nurses rather than diploma school training surfaced, and the term "professional nurse" came to be applied only to university graduates who earned higher salaries and were differentiated from lower levels of "practical" nursing. These distinctions led to some tensions within the profession and did not diversify its membership. In 1970, women earned 98.6 percent of nursing baccalaureate degrees.[31]

Through the sixties, nursing leaders struggled for professional recognition. In 1962, the American Medical Association (AMA) altered its long held stance of authority over nursing and officially recognized its "separate and distinct professional status." The shift had little impact on nurses' day-to-day lives; concerns over autonomy, role conflict, and the need for greater professional recognition persisted. In a 1968 sociological study of nursing, Fred Katz notes ongoing contradictions in nurses' working lives: "The modern nurse is caught in the throes of change. Medicine has increasingly made her into an administrative specialist, while her heritage is that of bedside care for the individual patient. From her leaders she is under pressure to become a professional, while the physician and she herself are apt to doubt her qualifications as a professional. She is a woman who finds herself in a work situation where the most prestigious positions routinely go to men. She ranks low in occupational prestige and financial rewards." From the mid-sixties on, nurses began gradually to make progress in pay, as some state nursing associations became collective bargaining units and nursing leaders responded more favorably to unionization."[32]

Nurses like Margaret Gene Arnstein (1904–1972), who became Dean of the Yale School of Nursing, led the profession to new frontiers. Working with the Public Health Service (1964–1966), she studied health in developing countries like India, offering valuable advice for foreign aid and the Peace Corps. Many joined U. S. AID Nurses, created in 1966 to enlist American civilians to help Vietnamese civilians needing medical care in war zones. The Vietnamese had only one nurse for every 30,000 people, many afflicted with typhoid, plague, and tropical diseases that would have been daunting enough without the war casualties. AID nursing supplemented military nurses who volunteered for Vietnam service, discussed in the section on "Military and War Service."[33]

Between nurses and women doctors, situations gradually altered. One study found that older nurses maintained "a protective, motherly attitude toward the women on the house staff." The dynamic between female nurse-female physician was quite different than the standard female nurse-male physician relationship characterized by exaggerated deference. Like female physicians, nurses knew what it meant to fight for themselves on the job and were unaccustomed to controlling the nursing profession precisely because it was largely female. By 1970, Corea observed signs of a "revolution" focused on gender in the nursing profession. The *American Journal of Nursing* began to publish articles like "Sex Discrimination: Nursing's Most Pervasive Problem," "Nurses' Rights," "Power: Rx for Change," and "Patient Advocacy or Fighting the System." These reflected the impact of the civil rights and women's movements on some nurses' thinking. Others began preaching their message to colleagues: "As the largest group of health professionals in the country, we have enormous power. If we use it, if we finally take responsibility for our own occupation, we can radically change and improve our health care system." For most of the sixties, however, it was business as usual for nurses—long hours, hard work, low pay, and insufficient respect for professional skills. But an uneasiness was in the air that would lead to later reforms.[34]

The powerful AMA continued to block the professionalization and spread of midwifery, insisting that childbirth was pathogenic and required a physician's supervision. In 1973, there were only 1,300 nurse-midwives, all women and mostly in eleven eastern states, compared to 366,400 general practitioner physicians and 20,500 obstetricians who delivered almost all of the 3 million plus annual births. Several southern states licensed a total of 2,900 lay midwives who handled 0.6 percent of 1969 births there, while 22 states and the District of Columbia had midwife licensing laws and several others issued permits to practice. Only ten nursing schools had midwifery training, and members of the American College of Nurse Midwives affiliated themselves with a hospital or public health service rather than become independent practitioners doing home deliveries.[35]

Military and War Service

After 1965, the Vietnam War increasingly focused the nation's anxiety. Many women, particularly nurses, volunteered to serve, inspired by patriotism; an estimated 193,000 women were in the armed services during the Vietnam era. Women continued to struggle to win positions in the military establishment, fighting for recognition and promotion. Late in 1968, Elizabeth Matthew Lewis, a fine arts librarian, made news when she became the first woman on the U..S Military Academy faculty. After the 1967 repeal of a law restricting military rank for women, Mildred Bailey became in 1974 only the second woman promoted to Brigadier General as Director of the Women's Army Corps (WACS) and only the fourth woman to hold that rank in all the armed services; but Bailey was a rarity.

Sherian Grace Cadoria, who twenty years after Vietnam became a Brigadier General and the highest ranking black woman in the armed forces, remembers, "In Vietnam I interviewed for a protocol job. The colonel told me I couldn't do the job, 'You can't travel, you can't carry luggage, it's too heavy. Women can't do this.' And I said, 'Nobody said I couldn't carry those hundred-pound bags of cotton when I was just a little child.'" She insisted that women could function in the army without losing their femininity: "By Act of Congress, male officers are gentlemen, but by act of God, we are ladies. We don't have to be little mini-men and try to be masculine and use obscene language to come across. I can take you and flip you on the floor and put your arms behind your back and you'll never move again, without your ever knowing that I can do it." Awards of such titles as Miss Fort Campbell or WAC of the Week emphasized beauty rather than competency, to preserve femininity.[36]

Army women, wrote Helen Rogan, "are admitted but not really perceived as soldiers." One of the visible signs of difference was the uniform—white cotton T-shirts and high-waisted green pants, fatigues that "accentuated the curves of their bodies" and which required constant starching and pressing, "Hours slaving in the laundry rooms when they could have been cleaning, practicing their military customs and courtesies for a test, or just resting" like the men who had easy-care, wash-and-wear, synthetic uniforms. Furthermore, they were issued ill-fitting boots designed for male feet, which caused many problems for those undergoing basic training.[37]

Military women had secondary status as part of a support staff, receiving only limited, voluntary training in combat skills. Law forbade them from serving in combat zones, including adjacent seas and sky, and hence there was limited potential for promotion in the Navy and Air Force. Although the Army had no similar law banning female work near combat zones, policy excluded women from units intended "to directly engage the enemy." A first sergeant observed, "Those WACS in Vietnam were really at a disadvantage. It was not fair for them not to know how to defend themselves. If you were in an area that guerrillas had infiltrated, which would you prefer to throw at them—a typewriter or a hand grenade?" The Viet Cong, by contrast, gave many women important positions of combat authority and used their services on all levels of guerrilla warfare.[38]

Commanders were afraid of the impact of female casualties on public opinion. General Kingston, Commander of the Second Infantry Division in Korea, worried, "We're going to get girls, women soldiers, killed, burned, disfigured, amputees, put them home in body bags. That will happen"; and the Pentagon believed such incidents would inflame anti-war sentiments. Of the 58,118 officially dead or missing in Vietnam, eight were women—all nurses, seven from the Army and one from the Air Force—killed simultaneously when an orphans' flight they were accompanying crashed during evacuation of Saigon; their names are on the Vietnam Memorial in Washington. Not counted were twenty civilian female foreign service officers, who died during the fall of Saigon or four Red Cross volunteers, a social worker, and a journalist—all women. In 1968, Lieutenant Jane A. Lombardi, an Air Force nurse, became the first woman to receive Vietnam combat decorations—a bronze star, air medal, and commendation medal for helping evacuate 38 patients from the Da Nang hospital while under attack.[39]

Most women who served "in country" in Vietnam were nurses. Six to seven hundred non-nursing WACS also served there; but although they were qualified to work in 95 percent of Army specialties, restrictions kept them in only 48 percent of Army jobs—primarily secretarial work, dietetics, protocol, cartography, intelligence, air traffic control. Non-medical women were, in the words of Lieutenant Evans who worked in a small Engineering Corps office, "overprotected. We had an eight-foot fence around the compound, topped with barbed wire, and we had a male Marine guard. We had to be in at ten." Army women had beds, air conditioning, and real food, but were issued no weapons and received minimal combat training, although they received "fire pay" equivalent to that of men in a war zone. Evans, although highest ranking NCO, and highest ranking female, remembers, "I think we may have had a pistol locked up in a safe somewhere, but those male guards were the ones with the weapons." Evans had to arrive first at the office each morning because she was a woman and had to make the coffee.[40]

The cavalier attitude of the Pentagon toward military women is evident in its lack of precision in counting the number of veterans. Fragmentary Defense Department figures report between 7,500 and 11,000 women served in Vietnam; but Lynda Van Devanter, nurse-veteran, estimates that there were closer to 15,000 or more American military women in Southeast Asia. Ninety percent were in the Nurse Corps, four-fifths of which was female. They served alongside Department of the Army Civilian Nurses (DACS), Navy nurses, and Red Cross nurses—all affectionately dubbed "round-eyed women" by GIs who too often saw only their concerned gaze hovering over hospital beds or cots in MASH units. Some nurses were very young and inexperienced, 21 or 22, freshly out of training. They "worked night and day with shelling all around them," especially during the 1968 Tet offensive. MASH units staffed by male nurses only were dispatched to combat areas, although according to General Rosemary Parks, female Nurse Corps head, "The commanders just don't like it. They say it does a lot for men to see the women" in field hospitals.[41]

Army psychologist Shad Meshad, who has counseled many nurse veterans, observes: "Women had to be warm fuzzies . . . a wounded soldier's mother, wife, and girlfriend." Women "brought up to nurture and protect others . . . felt like failures because, no matter what they did, the GIs kept dying." The constant flow of casualties was an overwhelming experience recorded by Lynda M. Van Devanter, an army operating room nurse at Pleiku and Qui Nhon, in her memoir *Home Before Morning: The True Story of an Army Nurse in Vietnam* (1983). Her anti-militaristic war stories tell of the immense dissonance between the women's emotional and professional training and what they experienced. She remembers the young man who bled to death under her eyes and "a whole squad that was brought in one day. They had been hung up by their ankles. Their genitals had been cut off and stuffed in their mouths. . . . not the sort of thing a young woman of 21 or 22 expects to see."[42]

Van Devanter said she had volunteered, having imbibed patriotism from Kennedy's invocation for citizens to "ask what they could do for their country." Jane Piper, too short to be an airline stewardess, enlisted to have her tuition paid, not knowing she would learn how to use a .45 and an M-16 during basic training. Charlotte Miller, stationed in Danang, volunteered because it was "the humanitarian thing to do." In addition to soldiers, Miller treated civilian casualties, orphans with "their brains hanging out, their guts opened up," even in monsoon season with five inches of water on the operating room floor. Kathy Gunson, stationed at Phu Bai, served as evaluator, making judgments on who would be "triaged out," and who would be left to die because untreatable. Sharon Balsey remembers, "In U.S. emergency rooms you hardly ever see blast injuries. I just freaked out. Nothing prepares you for it. I never got to the point where the mutilation of bodies didn't bother me." These and other nurses saw an unprecedented quantity and severity of casualties due to the highly developed Medevac system that rushed the wounded to hospitals; and the care they provided, despite grueling 24-, 48-, and even 72-hour shifts, sometimes treating 300 to 500 casualties a day, resulted in a high level of survivals despite massive physical injuries.[43]

Nurses were officers, not supposed to date enlisted men. Many had curfews and were limited to barracks in restricted hours; yet many received prescribed birth control pills even without a physician's exam. To cope emotionally with the horror of the injuries and deaths, nurses had to distance themselves from their profession's intrinsic caring. In the short term, there were R & R (rest and recreation) spells in Bangkok or Hong Kong, shopping for bargains, or idyllic trips to tropical beaches, only an hour or so away from the horror, by air; but inevitably the nurses returned to routines of seven days a week, sometimes round the clock if the "hueys" (helicopters) were bringing in the wounded. Although highly efficient, losing a remarkably small 5 percent of their patients, they personally burnt out quickly. Over half left nursing upon return to civilian life; and many still suffer post-traumatic stress syndrome.[44]

Van Devanter notes several ways in which Vietnam ruined many women's nursing careers: "Like men, many of the women have problems with authority In Vietnam, nurses routinely made life and death decisions; either doctors trusted them or no one else was there. When they came back, they had to fit into the more rigid nurse-doctor relationship," not questioning doctors' judgments nor expressing anger over unnecessary surgery. Stateside, Van Devanter was reassigned to the hemorrhoid room at Walter Reed Hospital, and like other military nurses who had had an extraordinary amount of responsibility and authority under fire, was shocked by her return to "rank-and-file pettiness." There was a personal side as well: "To many in the States, I was either a lesbian or a hooker." Nurses encountered even greater hostility than veterans returning home. One Veterans' Administration (VA) official admitted, "Arch-conservatives often did not recognize the contributions of women because they think women shouldn't serve in the military in the first place. On the other end of the spectrum, there was disdain for anyone associated with Vietnam."[45]

Only at the decade's end did internal protest appear among military women, often in alternative newspapers like *Fun, Travel, and Adventure* (FTA, a.k.a. Fuck the Army) or *WHACK!* or through coffeehouses. But feminism had little impact on the "soldiers in skirts," who were often from working-class backgrounds, and had chosen service to escape from limited opportunities at home.

Many non-military nurses and other volunteers served in Vietnam with agencies like the Catholic Relief Service (CRS), caring for civilian casualties and assisting with other problems. Ann Kidder went to Vietnam to work at Dr. Tom Dooley's hospital in Laos and treated people without asking their politics. Jackie Chagnon, fluent in Vietnamese, performed social work for four years in refugee camps for International Voluntary Services (IVS). She bemoaned how "it didn't take long for a 15-year-old" Vietnamese girl "to understand how she could make money," how "most of the prostitutes would not have been prostitutes had it not been for the war." She blamed the military for setting aside "whore districts" with protected bars and bordellos.[46]

Women volunteers also worked in the Red Cross Recreational Service in Vietnam. Barbara Lynn, touted the first "Negro girl" volunteer, was one of many college graduates bringing wholesome R & R to troops through clubmobiles serving Kool-Aid and cake or offering companionship with puzzles, tricks, quizzes, and games. Such Red Cross and U.S.O. volunteers, dubbed "Donut Dollies," signed on for year-long stints. Joined by performers for the U.S.O., they also worked to raise troop morale, many serving repeatedly and for longer periods than the top stars flying in and out with Bob Hope. Chris Noel, a young actress, made three tours of Vietnam between 1967 and 1969, dancing in white go-go boots and miniskirt atop mess hall tables at firebases, transported from site to site by helicopter. The sultry voiced Noel was also disc jockey on U.S. Armed Forces Radio, counteracting the anti-war propaganda of Hanoi Hannah. In 1969, she married a Green Beret captain, who committed suicide six months later.[47]

An often ignored support group for those fighting the war was made up of military wives and "sweethearts"—over half a million at the height of the Vietnam era. Military wives, like those of doctors and businessmen, had always been treated by institutions as vicarious professionals, responsible for written and unwritten codes of demeanor, support services, and personal giving above and beyond the call of the ordinary wife. Based on traditional assumptions that it was the woman's responsibility to maintain a relationship, they were blamed for statistics of widespread marital problems and a growing divorce rate among veterans. One commentator berated such a wife's need for a husband "to remind her that the daily routine that sometimes seems so meaningless and endless is appreciated and worth all the pain . . . to reassure her of his love" at a time when his very life might be in danger. Compounding their loneliness and isolation, many wives felt their husbands were fighting and dying for an unjust cause. Self-pity and jealousy besieged some women left behind, emotions sometimes muted by babies born in their fathers' absence: "Children keep their mothers going, not simply because they're there to be taken care of, but because they're a reason for being," a contemporary commentator observed. Such encouragement presupposed a traditional, clinging domesticity, a role rapidly being set aside by many women of the Vietnam generation.[48]

Candis M. Williams, wife of a clinical psychologist, formed one of the first women's groups at Denver's Disabled American Veterans (DAV) Center because wives, "bystanders to disaster—are still trying to comprehend a war that happened 13,000 miles away. The partner is not considered to have special problems herself, nor problems related to her husband's poor adjustment. . . . women are products of a culture that views them as the supportive care-givers; they can often be conflicted about seeking help." Media encouraged veterans' wives' feelings that "they had failed to get results with their nurturing, caring, and supportive roles."[49]

Military wives with highest responsibilities were in the "special circle" or corps of officers' wives, which "the Army quaintly referred to as the 'distaff side'" with "the hierarchy and the structured, busy, group-oriented atmosphere" paralleling the male rank structure. Neil Sheehan observed, "The officers' wives had a sense of belonging to a service of their own, because responsibility for most of the social activities of the garrison and its community and welfare work fell to them by tradition"—bridge parties, cocktail parties, dinners, dances, volunteer work, fund-raising. "The women liked the arrangement because it gave them authority and something to do." The Army liked it because their talents and labor were free. "The belief that a wife's attitude and behavior reflected on her husband and either helped or hindered his career also contributed to this sense of membership in an inner group," headed by the commanding general's wife. Wives of senior officers acted like den mothers, coaching younger women in the same way that older officers counseled their juniors. *The Army Wife*, required reading, detailed expectations and a behavior code. Women of such a group formed an important support network for those stationed abroad in unfamiliar surroundings and for those worried about their husbands' safety in Vietnam. Yet stresses associated with both the private and the public aspects of Vietnam resulted in a higher divorce rate among war-service families than in any previous war.[50]

The most stressed women were members of the National League of Families of American Prisoners, women like Pat Mearns, who went to Paris to meet with the North Vietnamese in attempts to win release of their Prisoner of War (POW) husbands from Hanoi. Too many others, widowed young, traded stress for grief—over 20,000 in the sixties. One of the first was Mary Jean Mitchell, who received the grim, formal, military announcement in May of 1963. For them, some service branches like the Navy provided brief psychological counseling; but even more than the women veterans of Vietnam, the widows remain the forgotten casualties.[51]

Journalism

From the turn of the century on, women worked as reporters and editors. By 1960, they represented 37 percent of print media professionals, many of them with decades of experience. As First Lady, Eleanor Roosevelt allowed only women reporters at her press conferences, thus opening many doors for many women journalists and requiring major papers to have a woman on their Washington staffs. But women continued to face rampant discrimination as in the case of Lindsay Van Gelder, rejected for a job at the *New York World-Telegram & Sun* because employers said she "would no doubt run off and get married [her] first day on the job."[52]

Role models emerged for a new generation in difficult times. Eileen Shanahan established herself at the *New York Times* Washington bureau along with only one other woman, Marjorie Hunter. Replacing Bess Furman, who had long covered Eleanor Roosevelt, Hunter was assigned first to White House ladies, then education, and eventually the women's movement. Shanahan, basically an economics reporter, focused many stories on women's issues like the EEOC. Nan Robertson and Betsy Wade also worked for the *New York Times*, Jean Sharley Taylor for the *Detroit Free Press* and the *Washington Post*, and Charlotte Saikowski for the *Christian Science Monitor*. Theo Wilson created her niche by covering a series of nationally important murder trials for the *New York Daily News*. Agnes "Aggie" Sullivan Underwood, a veteran on the *Los Angeles Record*, was finally named assistant managing editor in 1964, the first woman city editor of a major daily. Disappointed at "leaving the trenches," she retired three years later. *Newsweek* was blatantly critical, neglecting her journalistic record to focus on her "baggy black dresses" and hair that "looked as if it was vacuum cleaned."[53]

While many women established or continued prominent careers in print journalism through the sixties, the pattern of the "ghettoization" of women became greater. On newspapers, women were generally assigned, when hired, to the "women's pages," focusing on food and fashion, or to "softer feature" reporting. There were fewer women foreign correspondents in 1968 than in the thirties. Newspapers continued to segregate "women's news" into separate "women's sections," which combined items such as coverage of Kennedy's Presidential Commission on the Status of Women with "Society" items—announcements of engagements and marriages, reports on attendance at Junior League affairs, meticulous descriptions of wedding dresses—mixed with recipes, household hints, gossip columns, the advice to the "love lorn" of "Dear Abby" or Ann Landers, and items of national fashion news provided by the wire service. Emphasis was on the upper classes, "proper" behavior for "ladies," and acquisition of status through consumerism.[54]

By the sixties' end, changes appeared, particularly as the "women's pages" began to include more than food and fashion and editors gradually acknowledged that women wanted to know about serious matters. (They may also have realized that men liked to read about food and even fashion.) By the mid-sixties, a few daring women turned down jobs on the society or women's pages and insisted on covering straight news or reporting in their specialty. Molly Ivins, later a political columnist for the *Dallas Times-Herald*, refused to work on women's sections, "all huff and puff." Only in the seventies did the "women's page" tag gave way to non-gendered titles like "Lifestyle"; and women increasingly found their places in all parts of the newsrooms. In 1974 Carol Sutton became managing editor of *The Courier-Journal* in Louisville; she had begun there as a secretary in the early sixties, had become woman's editor in 1963, and had transformed the women's pages.[55]

Black women found it even more difficult to gain entry to newspaper journalism. American newsrooms were double-barred against minority women entry until those who entered college during (or as a result of) the civil rights movement graduated and sought newspaper work. Charlayne Hunter-Gault, one of two students who desegregated the University of Alabama, became a reporter for the *New York Times*. Dorothy Gilliam, urged by the *Washington Post* after graduating from Columbia Journalism School in 1961 to get some more experience, went to Africa and sent back stories as a free lance. "The times were beginning to change slightly. So when I got back, they offered me a job." She was one of three blacks and the first black woman at the paper.[56]

A graduate of Long Island University, Nancy Hicks Maynard began as a general assignment reporter for the *New York Post* in 1967, moved to the *New York Times* during the city school strike in 1968, staying to cover education and then health and social policy. Editors had "an underlying assumption of incompetence" about the work of black reporters: "One incident cannot make and break a career, but it can make a difference for a person of color. You don't get to make an awful lot of mistakes." All women experienced similar pressure, she knew; except that for white women, "their basic intelligence is not in question. Their ability to cope, their temperament, their toughness—but not their basic intelligence. It's a big moat to get over."[57]

For a small number of women, opportunities began to appear for significant mainstream media jobs. Some worked as foreign correspondents, covering the sixties' battle zones. Writing for the *Herald Tribune*, Marguerite Higgins (1920–1966) was an outspoken anti-Communist, married to the former director of United States Intelligence in Berlin and covering the State Department through her foreign travels. In 1962, Higgins provided an early warning of Soviet military activity in Cuba. Making two trips to Vietnam in 1963, she produced accounts of Buddhist self-immolations as political acts intended to topple the regime of President Ngo Dinh Diem, but called his overthrow the result of American policies and pressure. Her 1965 book, *Our Vietnam Nightmare*, draws from her three syndicated columns a week for *Newsday* from 1963 on, and outlines her investigations and criticism of American policy. Higgins died in 1966 at age 45 of a tropical infection picked up on her last southeast Asian tour.[58]

Other women journalists and writers travelled to Vietnam and one died there. Martha Gellhorn, a veteran war correspondent in Europe, China, and Java, described Vietnamese hospitals and orphanages full of wounded children; and Gloria Emerson went there for the *New York Times* in 1970. Emerson lived in France during the sixties and reported on the civil war in Nigeria in 1968 and on fighting in Northern Ireland in 1969. But she wanted to return to Vietnam, which she had visited in 1956 and which "haunted and held me." Her book, *Winners and Losers* (1976) is a powerful and moving account of the effect of the war on soldiers and other Americans. Photojournalist Georgette "Dickey" Chapelle, 27-year-old veteran reporter and author of *What's a Woman Doing Here*, died from wounds received when covering a Marine engagement in 1965. Controversial but well respected for her toughness and integrity, Chapelle was eulogized by her editor, "She never tolerated favors in the field because of her sex, and personal integrity forced her to write only stories she had 'eyeballed' instead of merely accepting official government handouts."[59]

Although she did not consider herself a journalist, critic-novelist Mary McCarthy also travelled to Vietnam in 1966 for the *New York Review of Books*. She was looking for and finding material damaging to the American interest; but her book, *Vietnam* (1967), although scathing about the war and its effects, is nonetheless sympathetic to all of its victims, on both sides. A second trip in 1967 resulted in another book, *Hanoi.*[60]

While several women wrote syndicated columns on various topics, only three—Elisabeth May Adams Craig (1888–1975), Doris Fleeson (1901–1970), and Mary McGrory (1918–)—were considered serious political columnists. Craig retired in 1965 from a prolific career that included writing columns for the *Washington Times-Herald* and doing a radio program, "Inside Washington." The Washington-based Fleeson was not only the first syndicated woman political columnist (1945); she was also, in McGrory's words, "the only one of either sex to approach national affairs like a police reporter." President Kennedy commented that he would "rather be Krocked than Fleesonized;" unlike Fleeson, influential *New York Times* writer Arthur Krock "startled but seldom wounded." Fleeson held strong convictions and acted on them, helping blacks break the racial barrier in journalism. Despite failing health, she covered Johnson's 1964 campaign, criticizing his character as epitomized by his conduct of the Vietnam war.[61]

Mary McGrory's first work in journalism had been as a secretary and then a book reviewer for the *Boston Herald Traveler.* Moving to a reviewing job at the *Washington Star,* her "great breakthrough" came when the editor asked her to cover the Army-McCarthy hearings in 1954 by writing her account "like a letter to [her] favorite aunt." "All of a sudden, people wanted to adopt me, marry me, poison me, run me out of town." Her column, eventually widely syndicated, covered many important stories: Nixon's defeat (at his "farewell" press conference in 1962, she wrote, he was "like a kamikaze pilot who keeps apologizing for the attack"); the Kennedy campaign and administration, and Kennedy's funeral (one of her only two columns she thought were "OK"); Johnson and Vietnam. Deeply angry at the long brutality of the war, she disagreed with *Star* editorial policy; her tone, she recalls, was "much angrier" than ever, "more opinionated, less reporting"; but when she won a 1975 Pulitzer Prize, the *Star* wondered "why it took so long for her to win it."[62]

Popular columnists in more traditional "women's fields" included sisters Esther Pauline Lederer ("Ann Landers") and Abigail VanBuren ("Dear Abby"), who answered readers' pleas for personal advice with a combination of common sense and humor. Landers compiled her advice in three books during the decade: *Since You Asked Me* (1962), *Truth is Stranger* (1964), and *Teenagers and Sex* (1966). Sylvia Porter pioneered with her widely syndicated financial advice column.

The most powerful woman in newspaper journalism was Katharine "Kay" Graham who took over the *Washington Post* and *Newsweek* in 1963 after the suicide of her husband, its owner. Because of her successful running of one of the nation's major dailies, she became president of the American Newspaper Publishers Association and first woman on the Associated Press Board of Directors.

Although several magazines appealed to women readers, women were seldom in positions of editorial power. In 1969 six women's magazines—*McCall's, Ladies' Home Journal, Woman's Day, Family Circle, Good Housekeeping,* and *Better Homes and Gardens*—ranked with *Life* and *Look* among the top ten popular magazines, each with circulation of over seven million copies per issue. Adolescents read *Seventeen* and *Teen.* Women in their late teens and early twenties favored *Glamour, Mademoiselle* and *Charm.* Young middle-class wives read *Redbook*, which had a circulation over four million in 1970. Working-class women favored *True Confession* (popular since the twenties), *True Story* (with a 1970 circulation of 5,347,000), *Modern Romances,* and similar periodicals emphasizing "female dependence and passivity." In analyzing magazine fiction in 1960, 1965, and 1970, Helen Franzwa found "not one married woman who worked" despite escalating real-world changes. Similar sources provided one basis for Betty Friedan's discussion of "the problem that has no name." All researchers "found no changes between 1940 and 1972" in female images in women's magazines, with the exception of *Cosmopolitan*, discussed in chapter thirteen under "Sexuality," edited by Helen Gurley Brown after 1965. Brown's reshaping of *Cosmopolitan* was so successful that in 1969 Ed Lewis and three other black businessmen launched *Essence* for the fashion-conscious, educated, upwardly mobile, young (18 to 34), single black woman. It quickly became one of the nation's fastest growing magazines, proving under editor Marcia Ann Gillespie that the black ideal of female beauty and status was not as narrow as that of the white "Cosmo girl." It addressed issues such as child care, working mothers' concerns, and the beauty of larger sized women.[63]

News magazines like *Time* and *Newsweek* often had a number of women on the staff, but as researchers, not writers. The more prestigious jobs were reserved for men. Susan Brownmiller, later a leading feminist, spent two years (1963–64) as a *Newsweek* researcher, a "hopeless" job, she recalls. Women had been hired as writers during World War II, but there were none from 1960 to 1970. In March 1970, on the day the magazine ran a cover article, "Women in Revolt," she and 46 women researchers filed an EEOC complaint against *Newsweek*, charging violation of Title VII of the 1964 Civil Rights Act. A similar complaint was brought against *Time* that May. In 1970, all 25 *Newsweek* executives and editors were male and women comprised only 72 of 154 lower level jobs. Similar figures applied to other news magazines, newspapers, and television news outlets.[64]

Still, a number of women had successful magazine careers. Shana Alexander (1925–) began a long association with *Life* in 1951, rising from staff writer to have her own column, "The Feminine Eye," from 1964 to 1969, when she left to become editor of *McCall's;* and Eleanor Rapish was *Life's* "Modern Living" editor. Jane Kramer's cultural criticism began for the *New Yorker* in 1963. She published a number of profiles for the magazine, as well as a book on Greenwich Village, *Off Washington Square* (1963), and *Allen Ginsberg in America* (1969). Pauline Kael began her long career as film critic for *The New Yorker* in the sixties, going there from the *New Republic* in 1968. Diana Vreeland, editor-in-chief of *Vogue*, remained the doyenne of fashion but seemed a figure of an earlier time when the middle-aged rich, social set monopolized fashion. Carmel Snow was also an influential fashion journalist.[65]

Brownmiller's career, like that of several young women journalists, moved through various media jobs en route to feminism. After four years of working as an actress, she became assistant to the managing editor of *Coronet* (1959–60), then an editor for *Albany Report* (1961–62); then a *Newsweek* writer (1963–64), a staff writer at the *Village Voice* (1965–66), and a newswriter for ABC-TV (1966–68). In 1968, the year she cofounded New York Radical Feminists, Brownmiller was a freelance journalist.[66]

Gloria Steinem is probably the best known of the women who went from journalism to feminism. She wrote her first bylined piece for *Esquire* in 1962, "The Moral Disarmament of Betty Co-Ed," about the impact of the birth control pill; and she contributed editorial ideas at the new magazine *Show* for which in 1963 she wrote her infamous "undercover" exposé on the working conditions of a Playboy bunny. Steinem was a founding editor of *New York* magazine, and, in 1972, of *Ms.*, the first general circulation magazine to rise out of the women's movement.[67]

Sara Davidson, whose autobiographical fiction *Loose Change* became a central text of the women's movement, was a staff writer for the *Boston Globe* and free-lanced for magazines. Radical feminist Ellen Willis was rock critic at *The New Yorker* from 1968 to 1975, then an editor of the new *Ms.* magazine in 1972. Betty Friedan had also first established her reputation as a journalist writing for various mass circulation magazines from the fifties on. The *Saturday Review* and *McCall's* excerpted *The Feminine Mystique* in 1963; and Friedan had a regular column, "Betty Friedan's Notebook," in *McCall's*.

Reporting in 1970 on women in communications to the New York University Law School conference on women in the professions, Brownmiller celebrated the "organized discontent" of women in media, especially the continuing battle against exclusion from the National Press Club, which was frequently the site of press conferences by important foreign dignitaries. Women reporters were relegated to the balcony, excluded from questioning speakers and from ready access to telephones for quick filing of stories. Thus, the quality of their work was impeded. After years of pressure, victory came in January 1971 when club members voted 227 to 56 to admit women to full membership. Victors celebrated with a drink at the Men's Bar.[68]

Brownmiller also celebrated on 18 March 1970, when a group of some two hundred women seized the *Ladies' Home Journal*, demanding that women run the magazine. That action was organized by a new professional group, Media Women. During an eleven-hour sit-in, protesters called for all-woman editorial and advertising staffs, an end to exploitative advertising, and redirection of the editorial policy to "support the goals of the modern feminist movement." Jean Hunter points out that the *Journal* was targeted because it was one of the most serious women's magazines and had introduced readers to the idea of working mothers and to Betty Friedan in 1963. A controversial issue in June 1964 had devoted itself to "A Daring New Concept for Women," the idea that "there was more to life for women than housework and children," and had featured an article by Friedan on the "Fourth Dimensional Woman," who added a job to her traditional triad of wife, mother, and homemaker. Under a new editor, John Mack Carter, the magazine in 1965 had continued serious consideration of women's roles but had not covered the burgeoning women's movement. Protestors complained of that neglect and the failure of the magazine's editorial staff to realize the detrimental effect on women of persistently negative or demeaning mass media images. Associate editor Lenore Hershey agreed to include a nine-page supplement section on the women's movement in that August's issue. Eight articles included: "How Appearance Divides Women," "Help Wanted: Female, 99.6 Hours a Week, No Pay, Bed and Bored, Must Be Good with Children," and "Should This Marriage

Be Saved?," a parody of the regular *Journal* feature, "Can This Marriage Be Saved?" The feminists accomplished little in terms of changing long-term *Journal* content, however. A week later, women invaded the male-only Gridiron Club, another media center. A series of protest actions in 1970 and thereafter helped open the field of print journalism to women.[70]

Broadcasting

Network television news remained a male domain for most of the sixties. Reporting to the New York University conference, Lucy Komisar cited statistics that showed men exclusively in charge of main broadcasting outlets, with few if any women on staff: "The usual excuse for not hiring women reporters is 'How can we send her to cover riots?' As if the city were constantly under siege—or male reporters were somehow immune to flying bottles, bullets and fists." There are almost no women announcers, "because television (and radio) executives believe that women's voices don't have 'credibility.' The few women newscasters have daytime shows." An exception, "Meet the Press," on television and radio, regularly featured established female journalists like May Craig.[71]

Already established in journalism as a critic of art and architecture, Aline Bernstein Lochheim Saarinen, widow of the famous modernist architect Eero Saarinen, became a leading television commentator with her 1963 premiere as art and architecture editor of NBC's "Sunday" and as art critic on "Today." She created features, specials, and documentaries on subjects ranging from postage stamp design to city planning. In 1964, Saarinen joined Pauline Fredericks and Nancy Dickerson, becoming NBC's third regular woman correspondent and enlarging her inquiry to topics such as the Presidential inauguration, economic discrimination against women, and environmental quality. She moderated the panel show, "For Women Only," debating with the audience controversial issues like birth control and abortion, until she became chief of the NBC Paris News Bureau in 1971, the first woman to head an overseas television news office.[72]

Morning talk shows featured some women—Dorothy Kilgallen, Betsy Palmer, Betty Furness, and Barbara Walters. Walters worked from 1961 to 1964 as a writer for the "Today" show before becoming a regular and finally, in 1972, co-host. Women appeared occasionally on national evening news in the early sixties. Still, the numbers were poor for women: of 41,000 full time employees in broadcasting only 24 percent were female, and 89 percent of those were in dead-end clerical jobs. Some attempts at change were simplistic: at New York's WABC-TV "the one woman reporter was assigned to cover baseball spring training and report on the first game of the season, while a man did a piece on a maxi fashion show."[73]

Creation of National Education Television (NET) brought opportunities for women like Perry Miller Adato who moved there in 1968 after ten years in the Columbia Broadcasting System (CBS). She remembers, "Because I had a family, I remained a film consultant. . . . If I had been a man, I would have pushed harder or left. But I loved my work and . . . couldn't spend the long hours in the cutting room required of a director without neglecting my family." At NET, Adato created feature-length documentaries like *Gertrude Stein: When This You See, Remember Me*. Similarly, the new Public Broadcasting Service (PBS) permitted innovation by creative women, chief of whom was Joan Ganz Cooney, executive director of Children's Television Network, which aired the first episode of "Sesame Street" in 1969 and other educational series thereafter. As in so many other fields, real opportunities did not begin to appear until the seventies and beyond.[74]

Architecture and Planning

Despite the optimistic article, "A Thousand Women in Architecture," in *Architectural Record* in 1958, sixties women experienced greater difficulties establishing themselves in architecture than they had before World War II, especially as corporate firms came to dominate design. Only two percent of practicing American architects were women, in contrast to 18 percent in Italy in 1969. Whereas Sarah Pillsbury Harkness had been a founder of The Architects Collaborative (TAC) in 1945, "as in other architectural firms of its size and structure, only an insignificant number of women architects" were members of the firm in the sixties and those of the younger generation did not have children. TAC met its affirmative action quota "by hiring a high percentage of women in subsidiary departments, like graphics and interiors."[75]

An older generation had fewer difficulties. Elizabeth Coit was active in public housing on both municipal and federal levels from the late thirties until her 1962 retirement from the position of Principal Project

Planner in the New York City Housing Authority Design Department. Had her suggestions been implemented American public housing "might have turned out very differently," for the better; but her advocacy of public housing was politically unpopular; and, "after all, she was a woman." Still, the American Institute of Architects (AIA) made her a fellow and the New York AIA chapter gave her its Pioneer in Architecture award in 1969.[76]

Natalie de Blois was the only woman of 75 associates at Skidmore, Owings & Merrill (SOM), one of the nation's largest design firms, and from 1944 on designed many of the notable urban buildings with steel-framed glass curtain walls that won SOM an international reputation. Nathaniel Owings, a SOM founder, acknowledged both her anonymity and importance: "only she and God would ever know just how many great solutions, with the imprimatur of one of the male heroes of SOM, owned much more to her than was attributed by either SOM or the client." After twenty years as senior designer, SOM promoted de Blois only to "associate," below twenty-six partners, many with far less talent than hers. Divorced in 1960 and single mother of four children, de Blois "never questioned her subordinate role on the design team. After all, she was already an anomaly by being a professional working mother." In 1974, she left SOM and became active on the AIA Task Force on Women, helping write a landmark report on the prejudices women architects faced in the large, multi-disciplinary firms or "plan factories" that proliferated through the sixties, with corporate structures that impeded women's advancement or recognition.[77]

Older female architects became "very much of the ebullient discourse" of the sixties. Chloethiel Woodard Smith, in her fifties, founded her own firm in 1963 after serving under others in larger offices. Smith designed La Clede Town, a racially and economically integrated, 680-unit community on a 30-acre site near St. Louis in 1967. She authored several important urban planning and design studies for Washington, D.C. and created plans for the New Town of Marshall Hall in Maryland and for Intown in central Rochester. Specializing in multifamily urban and suburban housing complexes and "new towns," Smith fought the modernist trend. Her Acorn Project, an urban-density development in Oakland, California, built by Patricia Avril Coplans, blends dwellings and open space and separates pedestrian and vehicular traffic, harmonizing with traditional landscapes. Unlike the era's suburban developers, she recreated Main Streets and town centers that anticipated postmodernism. Smith's accomplishments earned her election to the College of Fellows of the American Institute of Architects in 1960.[78]

Although fifties anti-urbanism continued and although women have often been identified with suburbanism, several prominent women's voices influenced the planning, design, and preservation of cities, carrying on the ideals of public housing advocate and Berkeley professor of city and regional planning Catherine Krouse Bauer (1905–1964). At thirty, Mary Otis Stevens (1928–) left TAC to join the architectural firm of Thomas McNulty, whom she married in 1958. Together they collaborated on design projects and coauthored *World of Variation* (1969). Her 100-foot-long light mural for the architectural Triennale Exhibit in Milan in 1968 was "visually evocative of . . . urban movements and city rhythms." With the Cambridge Institute in 1969, she designed the New City, a model community based on cooperative property ownership, a nonhierarchical political order, decentralized institutions, and planning by citizens—an innovative social design experiment but never built. In 1969, she founded a press to publish books on the human environment, theory, and criticism. From 1969 to 1971, she applied her theories of urbanism to proposals for Boston's inner city.[79]

In 1960, 40-year-old Anne Griswold Tyng (1920–) collaborated with Louis I. Kahn on the design for the proposed City Tower, exhibited at the Museum of Modern Art (MoMA). She became a well-known lecturer at design schools from the late sixties on. Her "Geometric Extensions of Consciousness," a theoretical blend of perceptual psychology, molecular biology, physics, and philosophy, appeared in *Zodiac 19* in 1969, reflecting the "sixties spirit" as applied to design based on "living geometric form."[80]

Another urbanist, Mary Hommann, developed a Caravan Plan for midtown Manhattan (1965–69), "to convert existing city streets for greater use by people and for more effective public transit." The plan eliminated cars and blended pedestrians with silent, electric, fixed-rail public transit "caravans" on malls. Hommann's plan inspired many cities to close some major inner-city streets to automobile traffic in attempts to revitalize urban activity that was being drained away to suburbs; but the attempts often failed.[81]

The youngest major woman designer, Denise Scott Brown (1931–) earned her master's degrees in city planning and in architecture from the University of Pennsylvania in 1960 and 1965. She taught in Pennsylvania's School of Fine Arts, in the UCLA School of Architecture and Urban Planning (1965–68), then offered an influential design studio at Yale (1967–70). Brown's 1967 marriage to Philadelphia architect Robert Venturi began a long and famous collaboration in design and theory. Their landmark book, *Learning From Las Vegas* (1972), captured the sixties' revaluation of the vernacular and its regard for Pop Art. Drawing design inspiration from commercial automobile "strips," suburban swaths of fast food restaurants, and shopping centers, it provided theoretical inspiration for postmodernism. "A social advocate as well as a formal iconoclast," Brown was hired by a black citizens' committee to create the South Street Project (1968) to block expressway expansion through an inner-city Philadelphia neighborhood; but city fathers blocked her innovative urban design.[82]

Several women became influential critics of the urban environment. Sibyl Moholy-Nagy (1903–1971), an architectural historian at Pratt Institute, reviewed buildings as art objects without concern for social relevance, leading many to call her views outmoded, a judgment disproven by her *Matrix of Man: An Illustrated History of Urban Environment* (1969). As the first architectural critic on a national newspaper, the *New York Times*, in 1963, historian Ada Louise Huxtable (1921–) stirred public opinion to demand aesthetic architecture, to pass zoning laws, to preserve from demolition not only historic landmarks but urban areas embodying a distinct spirit of place. She disliked urban sprawl, which she dubbed the "slurbs"—"cliché conformity as far as the eye can see, with no stimulation of the spirit through the quality of the environment." Huxtable's criticism was characterized by eclectic taste, pragmatism, and elegant language, and won her the first Pulitzer Prize for distinguished criticism in 1970.[83]

Jane Butzner Jacobs (1916–), senior editor of *Architectural Forum* (1952–1962), authored a landmark work, *The Death and Life of Great American Cities* (1961), sounding a note of pro-urbanism in an era that abandoned cities. Her insightful commentary on urban trends continued with *The Economy of Cities* (1969). Jacobs believed "a city cannot be a work of art," because it needs "ugly, discordant, chaotic elements." She applied her theory to activism to correct real problems in New York. She criticized the 1961 zoning resolution that permitted huge skyscraper towers set in empty plazas. She organized opposition to "urban renewal," which really meant destruction of whole neighborhoods for "slum-clearance" for highway expansion. In 1961, her Committee to Save the West Village preserved a 14-block nineteenth-century district, an important part of New York's urban fabric.[84]

Women in architecture and design, like women in other fields, began to organize to scrutinize their status and professional problems. They formed a pressure group within the AIA, gaining more of a voice after the first congress of the International Union of Women Architects in Paris in 1963. Five women in Cambridge, Massachusetts formed the Open Design Office and the Women's Design Center Inc., a non-profit corporation, "to practice, research, and promote the role of women in the environmental professions." In Boston, Women Architects, Landscape Architects, and Planners (WALAP) began a study of the problem of part-time work for women in these professions, publishing their findings in *Architectural Forum* in 1972. A study by the New York Alliance of Women in Architecture (NYAWA) of discrimination found salary discrepancies: the average (mean) income for a male architect was $15,800, for the female, $13,200. Men typically began earning $10,470 per year after graduating from college and received annual increments of $700. Women began earning $8,740 a year, increased annually by only $573.[85]

Sciences and Engineering

The successful launching of Sputnik, the first satellite, by the Soviets in 1957 sent shock waves through America and prompted intense scrutiny of national science education. In 1963 Kennedy's Presidential Commission on the Status of Women pointed to critical shortages of women in science and engineering, a theme echoed at federally sponsored conferences. Alice S. Rossi, research associate for the University of Chicago Committee on Human Development, called for federal programs to help women but saw the need for more sweeping cultural change to encourage women to combine careers and private life: "As long as it is mostly spinsters or widows who are appointed or elected or promoted to a college presidency, a national commission, a senatorship, or a high post in a government agency or scientific institute, we cannot consider that a solution has been found to the problem of women's status in American society." Once women could combine marriage, parenthood, and careers, Rossi felt, more would enter the sciences.[86]

In 1968, the National Register of Scientific and Technical Personnel of the National Science Foundation listed only 27,833 women, nine percent of all scientists (including the social sciences), a proportionate decrease since 1950 despite a great increase in total number of scientists. Women made up about 20 percent or less of those in chemistry, mathematics, biology, and physical chemistry—fields in the medium income range—and under four percent in physics, earth sciences, economics, and sociology. About 37 percent of these had doctorates, three percent medical degrees, 29 percent master's, and 30 percent bachelors'. The average salary was $13,500 for men and $10,000 for women, a higher differential than in 1960. A study of chemists' salaries late in 1968 by *Chemical and Engineering News* revealed that women with Ph.D.s received less than men with B.A.s, even with the same seniority. Although female engineers received 20–40 percent less income than males, the 1000-member Society of Women Engineers remained conservative, only encouraging women to enter the field rather than tackling discrimination or income differentials. Yet in 1968, Dr. Mina Rees became president of the American Association for the Advancement of Science, the largest professional organization, with under one percent women members.[87]

Other women won distinction. Irmgard Flügge-Lotz (1903–1974), a mechanical engineer and author of *Discontinuous and Optimal Control* (1968), was Stanford's first woman engineering professor and the second women elected fellow of the American Institute of Aeronautics and Astronautics (AIAA). She retired in 1968. In 1963 Maria Gertrude Goeppert Mayer shared the Nobel Prize in theoretical physics with Eugene Wigner and Hans Jensen for their *Elementary Theory of Nuclear Shell Structure* (1955)—the first woman to receive that high honor. A condescending article in *McCall's* (July 1964) lauded "An American Mother and the Nobel Prize—a Cinderella Story in Science," although her two children (born in 1933 and 1938) were adults.[88]

In 1960 Jerrie Cobb was the first woman chosen (from a dozen tested) to qualify for NASA's new astronaut program. Newspapers called her an "astronautte," and "America's answer to the Russian cosmonaut Valentina Tereshkova." *Time* declared: "The first astronautrix (measurements 36-27-34) eats hamburgers for breakfast, is an old hand at airplanes with more air time—over 7,500 hours—than any of the male astronauts." Cobb was the nation's leading female pilot, experienced "in everything from crop dusters to B-17s" and employed by Aero Design and Engineering in Arizona. *Life* assured readers that the 29-year-old was "feminine" and "a quiet religious girl with more than the usual pilot's respect for the firmament."[89]

Unfortunately, at Congressional hearings in 1962, John Glenn, America's first man in space in 1961, successfully argued that women be barred from space travel, although "a brutal battery of physical and psychological tests" proved them fit for all stresses. Glenn testified, "Men fly the airplanes . . . and test them. . . . The fact that women are not in this field is a fact of our social order." *Newsweek* described him as "ill at ease and more than a little annoyed" by the committee's questions; but "Blond Jerrie Cobb, 31 . . . was so indignant that, if she hadn't already kicked off her spike-heeled pumps, she could have just stomped." Cobb complained to reporters that NASA "won't let me take the actual training course, but . . . they have a chimpanzee who is being trained to take it." At the decade's end, a *New York Times* writer concluded, "The failure to include women in the NASA pilot program to date appears primarily due to the simple fact that this is . . . a man's world." Such was the case in almost all of the professions.[90]

6

Confronting Institutions

Mention of the sixties brings to mind images of student activism for civil rights, for free speech on political subjects on college campuses, against poverty, and against the Vietnam war. Much sixties activism and women's participation in it did not involve youth only as is often believed; women of all ages played important roles in protesting injustice, and young women had significant roles in campus activism, although their leadership potential was often squelched by male counterparts. Although the most visible and significant activism involved fighting social injustices altruistically in the name of others, women confronted institutional intransigency in all walks of life.

Student Movements

Many young women responded to the "Call to be Human," a sixties campaign slogan that enlisted them in various reform and protest movements. Women were active in the 1960 formation of the Students for a Democratic Society (SDS), which was initially a youth branch of the League for Industrial Democracy (LID), a group of Old Left socialists with dwindling membership. The Port Huron Statement, the June 1962 founding document of SDS, stated that society should "be organized to encourage independence in men." Too often, male SDS leaders interpreted that phrase literally. Sharon Jeffrey, from a UAW activist family, entered University of Michigan in 1959 and joined Alan Haber in organizing a spring 1960 "Human Rights in the North" conference for the Student League for Industrial Democracy (SLID), at which northern students were urged to boycott F. W. Woolworth and S. S. Kresge lunch counters in sympathy with the Greensboro civil rights sit-ins. They reconstituted SLID as SDS, with Jeffrey heading the University of Michigan flagship chapter. Its membership of 45 included Dorothy Dawson and Rachelle Horowitz by December 1961.[1]

Jeffrey studied organizing techniques at a summer 1960 Miami CORE workshop on nonviolent protest, where she met Martin Luther King, Jr. She recruited Tom Hayden, the outspoken editor of *The Michigan Daily*, to SDS, and spent the next summer doing volunteer work in Guinea, learning Third World politics and the problems of African underdevelopment. That fall, she became co-leader of VOICE, a radical campus political party. In the summer of 1962, she joined a National Student Association (NSA) project that was registering black student voters in North Carolina. Jeffrey spent all her free time learning ways to organize or aid the disempowered, disenfranchised, and the poor. She helped author the Port Huron Statement, which emphasized "participatory democracy," and practiced what she preached by lecturing on racial discrimination to university students and tutoring ghetto children in learning skills.[2]

Graduating in 1963, Jeffrey became "research director" for the Northern Student Movement (NSM), founded in 1961 by SNCC-inspired religious activists to give summer courses on "social, economic, and political awareness" in Northern ghettos. She urged SDS to sponsor the Economic Research and Action Project (ERAP), by sending 125 SDS members to slums and ghettos in nine northern cities as part of ERAP's plan to organize "an interracial movement of the poor" as "the new insurgency." Jeffrey herself served on the ERAP Executive Committee. The UAW funded the project with $5000, a "shoestring" budget. Modeled on SNCC community organizing, ERAP drew student activism away from civil rights in the South and from campuses into urban ghettos and other poor areas. It was the only SDS project in which women took most of the responsibility and were more successful organizers than men. Casey Hayden, a SNCC veteran, moved from Mississippi to Chicago in 1965 for ERAP work. Mimi Feingold left CORE in Louisiana for an ERAP project in Cleveland where she found poverty even more depressing than in the rural South.[3]

Charlotte Phillips, a medical student concerned about conditions in Cleveland's near-west-side inner-city neighborhood of Puerto Ricans and Appalachians, urged Jeffrey to set up one of the first ERAP projects there, where mothers on welfare received only 70 percent of Ohio's established standard for decent living. Simultaneously, Jeffrey created a small commune to test the potential for participatory democracy among SDS members in everyday life. Based in a rented apartment for unmarried women and forging ties with older settlement houses and church ministries, it relied on the gentle, non-assertive, non-authoritarian leadership of Jeffrey, Phillips, and Carol McEldowney.

All plans were worked out through the long and tedious process of mutual discussions. Jeffrey described the "group process" as like "a Quaker norm in operation" with "moral suasion through face-to-face discussion," encouraged by Phillips with her strong Quaker background. In the Cleveland ERAP, "rule-by-consensus became an article of faith." Especially given "a very strong feminine component and . . . softer men. . . . Each individual did speak whatever they had to say." One Cleveland ERAP worker remembers letting the poor women decide what they wanted to do, then helping them. Casey Hayden observed, "You can't talk about a kind of democracy unless those who are affected by decisions make those decisions whether the institutions in question be the welfare department, the university, the factory, the farm, the neighborhood, the country." She might have added SDS itself, for the failure of male "leaders" to see beyond their own ambitions and to transcend their impulse to impose control and a system not only contradicted their ideal of participatory democracy, it alienated women and proved a fatal flaw.[4]

ERAP in Cleveland alone registered 400 people on relief to vote, organized community programs on politics, set up a grievance committee for those with welfare problems, and questioned the composition of LBJ's local War on Poverty Committee. Eventually, ERAP confronted opposition to their mobilization of housing project tenants. The "Red Squad Division" of the Cleveland police targeted them as "subversives," taking undercover photographs of ERAP workers and tenants, harassing them with threats; but their work revived the Citizens United for Adequate Welfare (CUFAW). In Newark, ERAP organized rent strikes and seized control of the local War on Poverty Board. Despite the odds, ERAP achieved many local successes.[5]

A Cleveland Conference in February 1965 brought together both organizers and the poor from Baltimore, Boston, Newark, Chicago, Detroit, Mississippi, and Kentucky—including Mary Varela, Nada Ghandler, Nancy Hollander, Mary McGroaty, Sarah Murphy, and others. They broke through old racial animosities, arranging for the poor Appalachian Lillian Craig to host black civil rights activist Fannie Lou Hamer, emphasizing the communality of interests of poor women despite racial barriers. Through ERAP work, from 1963 to 1965, many women learned the philosophy of anti-hierarchical, grass-roots democracy, epitomized by the slogan "Let the People Decide," that they would later apply to feminism; but Sara Evans remembers that due to growing sexism in SDS, successes of women ERAP organizers went unnoticed and unacknowledged. Under the women's influence, ERAP had "changed from a JOIN [Jobs or Income Now] to a GROIN [Garbage Removal or Income Now] approach . . . from men's issues to 'issues which sprang from the women's sphere of home and community life"; but then male SDS leaders lost interest and projects were abandoned. Jeffrey left Cleveland ERAP in 1967 to become executive director of Chicago's Hyde Park-Kenwood Community Conference, remaining one of the nation's major community organizers.[6]

From 1963 to 1965, SDS presidents Todd Gitlin and Paul Potter, both politically ambitious young men, seized power, strategized, and structured an organizational hierarchy to the detriment of grassroots workers, women in particular. Carolyn Craven and San Francisco SDS members complained of frustrations in making West Coast concerns known to the national SDS office and favored decentralization as "the most efficient means of communication, a formally recognized and dependable forum" to disseminate ideas. At the spring 1965 ERAP Institute, Carol McEldowney expressed the consensus that ERAP should have community- not office-centered control "to prevent power from accumulating in any one place or person." The issue centered on whether control should lie with male SDS officers or ERAP women and those they served in poor neighborhoods.[7]

Not all women joined the New Left simply because of social consciousness and personal commitment. Love of SDS activist Sam Melville led young Jane Alpert from a privileged, upper-middle-class life to leftist revolutionary work. She recalls, "I could not have fallen so overwhelmingly in love with Sam if he had not given me such an ideology. Nor could I have accepted the ideology so wholeheartedly if I hadn't been so powerfully attracted to Sam. . . . The combination of sexual love and radical ideology was more than irresistible. It consumed me." Both Melville and Alpert were indicted for bombings, but only he was held without bail. Convicted, he died in the 1971 Attica Prison revolt; and Alpert went underground.[8]

Many women joined movements, remembers one former Harvard student, as a way of "throwing out the past," including materialism— "what the blue jeans and torn clothes and living in communes were all about"; but many, confronted by ideologues found new forms of authoritarianism: "What I would consider liberal now, *we* considered arch-conservative. Someone who wanted to get out of Vietnam but didn't want the NLF (National Liberation Front) to win was a conservative/moderate. People who disagreed weren't permitted to speak; they were shouted down." A new attitude inspired student radicalism: "You put off your depression when you put on your battle jacket."[9]

At the December 1965 SDS "Rethinking Conference" at Champaign-Urbana, where all the speakers were men, the issue of the women's place in the movement surfaced publicly. Helen Garvey asked, "How do we permeate an informal leadership that grew from the days when SDS was a small group of friends? How do we create new leadership, people who know and trust each other and are committed to working to build an organization and a movement? Or, perhaps, how do we minimize leadership rather than merely replacing the old with the new?" SDS leadership exacerbated these problems in the next three years. Sara Murphy, Florence Howe, and other women continued to bring in recruits and train teacher-organizers (TOs) to keep up organization growth, although it had lost many of its initial principles.[10]

Similarly, the 1964 Free Speech Movement (FSM) at University of California at Berkeley, born in a 1960 demonstration against the House Un-American Activities Committee (HUAC) hearings and in support of civil rights activism, involved many women as rank-and-file organizers or protestors; but as in other student movements, young men occupied center stage. Sue Thrasher graduated from the Berkeley movement to manage the Southern Students' Organizing Committee office.[11]

Many reasons existed for women's exclusion from power in student movements. Women's curfew hours and separate campus housing kept them out of the radical version of the "smoke-filled room," the place for making political policy. Barbara Easton recalls that at Harvard-Radcliffe, SDS decisions were made by men at 2 A.M. at Adams House, a male dorm, and announced the next morning in the student paper. Sociologist Wini Breines agrees that "sexism was a powerful ingredient of the New Left." Women were "often afraid to speak up and when they did they were often ignored"; sexual discrimination in the movement replicated that in the larger society.[12]

Male chauvinism was often blatant. Margery Tabankin, a University of Wisconsin student from 1965–69 and first woman President of the National Student Association in 1967, elected on an antiwar platform, recalled how Tom Hayden handed her his dirty laundry when he came to town to speak. She responded as if conditioned, "I'll have it for you tonight." Tabankin coordinated the 1969 Moratorium, "proving I was such a good radical." She remembers, "Most guys didn't take women seriously. . . . They were things to fuck." Sex was "much more on men's terms" within the movement as outside. Tabankin persisted, protesting Dow Chemicals napalm production. Beat up in the demonstration, she reported for the *New York Times* from the hospital.[13]

Being part of the student movement raised many young women's consciousness, schooled them in activist techniques, and empowered them. Through a complex process, by 1967 women began to leave New Left student movements and discover feminism. Intolerable male attitudes pushed them out, and a new consciousness of their own needs pulled them to devote themselves to the cause of women. After official dissolution of SDS in 1969, many female "politicos" became active in its underground revolutionary branch, the Weathermen, who believed violent overthrow of government was the ultimate way to liberate women along with all exploited people. The Weathermen had a higher percentage of women than other New Left groups. This was especially ironic since the ferocity of tactics and a philosophy destructive of personal relationships—the policy that everybody should sleep with everybody—was so masculine. When a Weathermen underground bomb factory in a Greenwich Village town house exploded on 6 March 1970, Diane Oughton was killed; but Kathy Boudin and Cathy Wilkerson escaped into hiding. Oughton came from a wealthy Chicago family but was radicalized by her relationship with Bill Ayers at University of Michigan and by her Peace Corps service. She came to believe that only in revolution could men and women be truly equal.[14]

Another "politico" intent on being "one of the boys" was Susan Stern, the sole Weatherwoman arrested with the "Seattle Seven." Although persuaded by black activist Flo Kennedy to establish a radical feminist group in Seattle, Stern's priorities rested with Weathermen rather than with the splinter Women's Liberation Front. She remembers, "My white knight materialized into a vision of world-wide liberation. I ceased to think of Susan Stern as a woman; I saw myself as a revolutionary tool." She and other women in the Weather underground admitted to being "male-identified": "The vogue was to be tough and macho, and I was as overzealously aggressive and abandoned as a Weatherman as I had been timid and frightened prior to it." Stern's role model was Bernardine Dohrn, "aristocrat" or "high priestess" of the New Left who married Bill Ayers while on the FBI's ten-most-wanted list and was in hiding "underground" in the seventies. Dohrn had little time for or interest in feminism.[15]

The influence of youth in reform movements of the sixties has been exaggerated and mythologized by journalists, participants, and historians. In the heyday of SDS, there were about 100 important activists among the 40,000 students at University of Wisconsin and similar proportions at other major campuses. Many recruited other students to turn out for the fun of it, if not for the issues, at teach-ins and demonstrations. A 1969 Gallup poll reported that 28 percent of college students had participated in some sort of demonstration; but for most, it was a rare event involving little personal commitment. Tabankin denies that there was "a 'generation' that really meant it. Many didn't give a shit, then and now. . . . People want to make it more than it was."[16]

Peace and Environmentalism

Those who think of the sixties' activism exclusively as a youth movement ignore the extensive, intensive efforts of mature women for nuclear disarmament and peace. Pacifism, embraced by older generations of feminists, continued and burgeoned through the fifties, urged on by Eleanor Roosevelt, whose contribution was acknowledged in 1963 when a coalition of groups including the National Committee for a Sane Nuclear Policy (SANE) and Turn Toward Peace (TTP) created the Eleanor Roosevelt Peace Prize. SANE and the Women's International League for Peace and Freedom (WILPF), founded in 1915, staged demonstrations during the August 1961 Berlin Crisis. Following in that tradition, six mature, middle-class housewives in Washington, D.C., gathered in the backyard of Dagmar Saerchinger Wilson (1916–), mother of three and a children's book illustrator, to found Women Strike for Peace (WSP) that September, their fears intensified by the building of the Berlin Wall and the first Soviet test of a hydrogen bomb 3,000 times as powerful as that which had devastated Hiroshima. The WSP worried about ecological consequences, if not total annihilation, from nuclear bombs. Midge Decter explained, "Many people first began concretely to visualize the consequences to themselves and their families of a nuclear attack. The air was filled with expressions of the feelings of powerlessness, and on the other hand, of the will to 'do something.' The government announcement of its shelter program . . . roused people to consider very directly the question of their own survival." The women's goal was to end all nuclear weapons testing and win complete, international disarmament under United Nations controls.[17]

Despite "incredible disorganization and naïveté" and lacking a formal headquarters, president, or board of directors, WSP rapidly spread as a true grassroots movement. Friends recruited friends and whole communities quickly galvanized. Wilson said, "we ran them like we ran our carpools." Eleanor Garst, a WSP founder, recalls, "We came out of our kitchens and off our jobs to cry out against the nuclear threat to the lives of our children and the survival of our planet." The message was "deliberately geared to the lowest common denominator of agreement among the world's women," focused "on unification rather than hairsplitting." Ethel Barol Taylor (1916–), a journalist dubbed the "Rebel in White Gloves" and a mother politicized by Hiroshima, called WSP "more than an organization; it's a state of mind." One California newsletter, the "LA WISP," (Women's International Strike for Peace) denied that "strike" had leftist connotations: "We are Women. We are Ladies, even. We voice a Mother's protective View for the whole world. . . . Stay as lovely as you are, girls." Non-sectarian and non-ideological, WSP was "solidly in the midstream of American life" and aimed to "demolish the notion that peace is only for communists. . . . In this age, the true patriot . . . promotes peace NOW." Midge Decter identified WSP strength in being "ideologically free to act quickly at the same time that it was sociologically in the position to remain respectable." WSP strength was "in the fact that if there is nothing to join and nothing to sign, there are no official policies to approve or disapprove and therefore no internal dissension." Importantly, the movement was "able to hook into the issues of war and peace some of that enormous hoard of civic energy that had been dormant in the U.S. for two decades. . . . quelled by the complicated, gray years of the Cold War or sent into hiding by McCarthyism."[18]

WSP's strength was in adaptability and decentralization; over the decade, various local groups worked alone or in coalitions with diverse politicians, militants, and ordinary Americans who might not otherwise have become activists. They communicated through an informal network, united by local and national telephone trees and, from January 1962 on, by a monthly newsletter simply named the "National Memo," a mimeographed, legal-size, twelve-page publication which local groups copied and circulated. "The Memo" contained an editorial and think-pieces on the social, economic, and spiritual implications of peace work; reports of local activities; announcements, and suggestions for local "actions." For a time, Elise Boulding of Ann Arbor edited the "Women's Peace Movement Bulletin: A Monthly Information Exchange for All Women's Groups in Correspondence with Women Strike for Peace." Local steering committees coordinated actions and occasionally issued their own publications, most simply mimeographed. New England WSP activists joined with the WILPF to publish *Voice of Women* from 1964. By the decade's end, WSP had over 100,000 members in 110 communities in 25 states.[19]

The first big WSP "action" took place on 1 November 1961, drawing an estimated 50,000 in 60 cities with banners reading "End the Arms Race—Not the Human Race" and "No Tests—East or West!" On 15 January 1962, more than 2,000 women and their children boarded a Peace Train in New York, Trenton, or Philadelphia to march on the White House in the driving rain, delivering letters urging the President to negotiate an international agreement to end atmospheric nuclear testing. Signs read: "When it rains, it pours—strontium 90," "Peace is the only shelter," "Peace or Perish," and "Never say die." Another 500 demonstrated at the United Nations, where Mrs. Ruth Gage-Colby of the WILPF presented a similar petition to the General Assembly before moving on to the Soviet embassy and the Atomic Energy Commission. The Mount Vernon, New York, group distributed fact sheets summarizing reports by the Atomic Energy Commission, the Federal Radiation Council, and the Public Health Service. By mid-1962, WSP claimed its contacts in 40 states could mobilize over 100,000 women "at a moment's notice to drop everything and go a-picketing."[20]

WSP reacted quickly to the October 1962 Cuban Missile Crisis. In New York, 800 appeared at the UN to demand intervention and negotiations, not a unilateral solution. Alarmed by the "real possibility of immediate holocaust," 2,000 converged on the White House from across the nation; and 10,000 marched in New York, 4,000 in Los Angeles, 3,500 in San Francisco, 1,200 in Berkeley. These and many smaller local demonstrations received minimal press coverage; but Jerome Wiesner, JFK's Science Advisor, gives credit to WSP along with SANE and Linus Pauling for moving the President—even though he refused to meet with them—to complete the limited nuclear test ban treaty signed with the Soviet Union in 1963.[21] As keynote speaker, Coretta Scott King joined Dagmar Wilson outside the United Nations in celebrating the treaty and WSP's second anniversary.

WSP adapted the tactics of the suffragists and won I. F. Stone's praise for being "flexible and intelligent" as well as "free from stereotypes and sectarianism." The non-partisan WSP remained an "umbrella" movement, without a national hierarchy. Each WSP group retained local autonomy and designed its own innovative programs. These women, mostly married mothers ranging from their twenties on up, repudiated caricatures that they were "busty, grim, and wear hats." They circulated petitions, spoke at PTA meetings, ran study groups, hosted lecturers, distributed leaflets summarizing facts, canvassed neighborhoods, wrote newspaper ads, placed posters on buses, set up tables in shopping centers, and sent numerous letters appealing both to politicians and their wives. A New York group unfurled a block-long petition on a continuous roll of dish toweling. They bombarded Jackie Kennedy with the appeal, "Children Are Not for Burning." At demonstrations like the annual Easter Peace Walk begun in 1963, they often carried large paper flowers with their children's and grandchildren's pictures at the center, shopping bags full of peace pamphlets, and balloons—white for peace or black for mourning, inscribed with slogans like "Stop the Bombing." They wore black armbands and veils, pushed baby carriages, and handed out paper doves, Chinese fortune cookies stuffed with peace messages, and information-packed flyers. They organized motorcades with flying banners to jam busy streets.[22]

WSP sent delegates to establish contacts with international peace groups in Helsinki, Stockholm, Budapest, Frankfurt, Paris, Montreal, London, Athens, and Tokyo. On the first trip to Geneva in April 1962, fifty women, including Mrs. Cyrus Eaton and Coretta Scott King, presented a nuclear test ban petition of over 50,000 signatures to Soviet representatives and visited each delegation of the 17-nation Disarmament Conference. In Geneva, they met with women from Great Britain, France, Norway, Sweden, Switzerland, Canada, Austria, West Germany, and the Soviet Union and thereafter often used the name Women's *International* Strike for Peace (WISP). Some went to Moscow to meet with Mrs. Nikita Khrushchev. Several times, WSP hosted Soviet women in the U.S. In 1964, fifty WSP delegates met at The

Hague with women from 14 nations to lobby NATO against nuclear weapons in general, and in particular their stationing in Germany. That year, WILPF also sent a peace delegation to Moscow, led by Dorothy Hutchinson and Helen Gahaghan Douglas.[23]

These respectable women usually enjoyed a friendly press *when* they received media coverage, and had "respectful and cooperative" relations with government officials. Yet from the start, WSP faced opposition, harassment, threats, and attacks from right wing groups like the John Birch Society and the American Nazi Party. Someone vandalized the WSP Los Angeles office. The CIA paid housewives $100 a week to infiltrate the WSP and scrutinize correspondence.

The greatest challenge came in December 1962, when the House Un-American Activities Committee (HUAC), the group that had institutionalized McCarthyism, subpoenaed WSP founder Dagmar Wilson and eight New York members as part of an investigation of peace groups and an attempt to discredit them. Wilson confronted Chairman Clyde Doyle (D-California) of HUAC, and belittled his red-baiting, dogged attempts to suggest that communists had infiltrated the WSP, because it had few formal leaders, depended on cooperative action, and claimed all were in charge. When Doyle identified "hard-core Communists, pro-Communists, and fellow travelers" among WSP demonstrators in California. Wilson admitted she would not exclude Communists because the disarmament cause required expanding membership as much as possible and "unity for peace." She responded to intensive questions on the pacifists' motives by saying that she found it "very difficult to explain to the masculine mind."[24]

Retired teacher Blanche Posner, like four other New York WSP members, answered all HUAC's grueling questions with the Fifth Amendment, interjecting only one lecture: "You don't quite understand the nature of this movement. . . . inspired and motivated by mothers' love for children. . . . When they were putting their breakfasts on the table, they saw not only the Wheaties and milk, but they also saw Strontium 90 and Iodine 131." Bringing their babies and responding in unison, WSP members packed the hearings and ridiculed the interrogators.[25]

Some journalists were delighted at Doyle's undoing by a group of proper, principled matrons in hats and gloves. Russell Baker reported in the *New York Times* that the three Congressmen "spent most of the week looking lonely, badgered, and miserable, less like dashing Red-

hunters than like men trapped in a bargain basement on sale day."
Women presented each WSP witness with a floral bouquet and a standing ovation. "The three luckless politicians watched the procession of
gardenias, carnations, and roses with the resigned looks of men aware
that they were already liable to charges of being against housewives,
children, and peace and determined not to get caught coming out
against flowers." Taylor described it as "pure theatre." Political cartoons
ridiculed HUAC. Although HUAC admitted that WSP was not subversive, it advised Congressmen to ignore their lobbying.[26]

Not to be undone, in June 1965 the "feds" found Wilson and Donna
Allen, mother of four from WILPF, guilty of four of eight counts of
contempt of Congress for refusal to testify behind closed doors rather
than in open session before HUAC on the subject of their efforts to get
a visa for Japanese peace activist Kaoru Yasiu. The incident was typical
of the era in which writer and peace activist Barbara Deming embarked
with many others on a Walk for Peace and Freedom in October 1963.
The walk originated in Quebec; its goal was Guantanamo, the United
States military base in Cuba, by way of Washington. In January, in
Albany, Georgia, 54 walkers aroused the ire of the local police chief for
their linkage of peace with civil rights. Deming was one of eight women
he arrested and jailed. The women, thrust into a seven-foot cubical cell
built for four in the Albany, Georgia, city jail, served twenty-four days
of dehumanizing treatment and went on a protest hunger strike. Released, their request for a march permit was denied, and they were
arrested again before finally being permitted to proceed on. Deming
tells the story of that experience in *Prison Notes* (1964, reprinted
1985).[27]

WSP activities through 1965 were primarily anti-nuclear. In 1962
they picketed in Las Vegas, at a nearby Nevada bomb-test site, and at
nuclear laboratories. They distributed copies of a pamphlet, "Atom
Bomb Children," detailing mutilation of children at Hiroshima and Na-
gasaki. Ann Arbor WSP members worked on a national program to
collect baby teeth to test for strontium 90 radioactivity in milk; and
they aired a weekly radio program. WSP protested "duck-and-cover"
nuclear drills in schools. They boycotted milk for eight days following
each atmospheric bomb test. Women in a Chicago suburb collected
"Pennies for Peace" to benefit the UN in 1963. Others sponsored a
conference in New York to discuss the papal encyclical *Pacem in Terris*
(Peace on Earth, 1963).

Some activities were prototypes for the protest street theatre later associated with youth activists. On August 6, 1965, women demonstrated at the New York World's Fair on the twentieth anniversary of the Hiroshima bombing. A Connecticut group protested nuclear submarines at Groton. Los Angeles women campaigned against the docking of the U.S.S. Biddle, the nuclear pilot ship of the NATO Multilateral Force (MLF), by dragging a 13-foot rowboat, the "S.S. Biddle-Riddle," through the city with banners that read "Don't Spread Nuclear Weapons." Others fought the ABM program that was developing missiles to deliver nuclear warheads. The WSP wearing of paper daisies on Easter Sunday in 1962 and 1963 to show opposition to nuclear warfare undoubtedly inspired LBJ's controversial Presidential campaign television commercial—a young girl picking petals from a daisy, abruptly interrupted by a nuclear blast—meant to rouse public fears of Barry Goldwater's trigger happiness.

When Kennedy increased United States aid to the South Vietnamese Ngo Dinh Diem against the National Liberation Front, WSP turned to anti-war activities. As early as its second convention in June 1963, WSP resolved to "alert the public to the dangers and horrors" of the Vietnam War and to "specific ways in which human morality is being violated by U.S. attacks on civilian population—women and children." WSP began extensive Congressional lobbying. Deeming legislators "abysmally ignorant" of how the nation was being drawn to war, they distributed packets of articles, booklets, photos, and copies of the Geneva Accords. WSP demonstrated at the 1964 Democratic National Convention in Atlantic City and testified before state and national platform hearings of both parties in 1964, 1966, and 1968 to urge antiwar planks. WSP led letter-writing campaigns, signed petitions, and picketed the White House, the United Nations, embassies, state capitols, and federal buildings. Helen Lamb Lamont followed suit, founding the May 2nd Movement (M2M) for complete U.S. withdrawal from Vietnam and organizing demonstrations in San Francisco, Madison, San Juan, and Boston. Ann Arbor WSP activists helped organize the nation's first anti-war teach-in at the University of Michigan early in 1965. Throughout 1965–66, many women joined marches against the war and presented proxies to Congress.

In 1965, two WSP activists went to Hanoi to arrange the historic, fact-finding meeting that July of ten American women with five from North Vietnam and three from the National Liberation Front (NLF).

That Jakarta (Indonesia) Conference was the first formal meeting of American activists with Vietnamese leaders. A joint declaration accused the United States of committing "military aggression" that violated the 1954 Geneva agreement ending the Indochina War, and of waging a cruel war against the Vietnamese people, testing "new and more horrible weapons" on them. WSP groups in 28 states collected signatures for a petition demanding China's admission to the United Nations. In July 1969 Helen Boston and Jane Spock led a March of Friendship to meet Vietnamese Women on the Canadian side of the Niagara Falls Rainbow Bridge.[28]

In San Francisco, women held silent vigils in front of the armed forces mortuary that was processing bodies from Vietnam. WSP sent Congressmen a "Fact a Week" card detailing information about war costs and quoting antiwar statements by prominent people. Women organized campaigns to bombard Congressmen with Christmas, Valentine, and Mother's Day cards. On 15 December 1965, they delivered over 100,000 cards to LBJ, inscribed "Dear Mr. President: For the sake of our sons . . . for the sake of our children . . . give us peace in Vietnam." Many other church and peace groups copied this idea. In 1966, they staged a Christmas Sing for Peace at New York's Plaza Hotel. Others demonstrated at Internal Revenue Service (IRS) offices to protest use of tax monies for war.

Individual women expressed their desire for peace in a variety of ways. Journalist Carol Brightman began publication of the *Viet Report* in 1965. A newsletter published three times a year in editions of 80,000 (paid circulation 12,000), the *Report* was widely used in teach-ins. Brightman accompanied a delegation to England to attend the Bertrand Russell War Crimes Tribunal, organized to investigate the bombing of civilian sites in North Vietnam.[29]

As the war wore on, other women protested with their bodies. In a tragic example, Helga Alice Herz, a 79-year-old Quaker widow, survivor of Nazi detention camps, set herself afire on 16 March 1965 on a busy Detroit street corner, emulating South Vietnamese Buddhist monks to protest the American bombing of North Vietnam. She left a note to her daughter: "I do this not out of despair, but out of hope." Making a more affirmative gesture of hope, from February to April 1971 dancer and activist Louise Bruyn walked alone for 45 days, carrying her plea to stop the war from Newton, Massachusetts, to Washington.

In 1966, WSP began a campaign against the use of the chemical defoliant called napalm or Agent Orange, which also wounded Vietnamese civilians. Four women, supported by Berkeley and San Francisco WSP and WILPF, were arrested in San José for trying to block napalm shipments from the Dow Chemical Company. Dubbed the "housewife terrorists" and "napalm ladies," they were found guilty. In January 1967, even the usually apolitical *Ladies' Home Journal* ran an empassioned anti-napalm article, "Suffer the Little Children"; and the following month, WSP organized 2,500 protestors to carry huge photos of napalmed Vietnamese children to the Pentagon. Images of the women banging on locked doors with their shoes attracted the international press. That April, women in the New York Mobilization March carried signs, "Children are not for burning!" The WSP Committee on Responsibility organized a boycott of the Dow Chemical Company, producer of various household cleaners as well as napalm.[30]

Women and men of the Society for Friends (Quakers) continued their tradition of pacifism and organized draft resistance through the American Friends Service Committee. WSP joined Quakers in 1966 in directing "the adult movement against the draft," founding the National Council to Repeal the Draft. WSP activists testified at 1967 "People's Hearings" against "inequities of the draft and its damaging effects on the life of our country." Their "Women's Declaration of Conscience" proclaimed: "As mothers, sisters, sweethearts, wives, we feel it is our moral responsibility to assist those brave young men who refuse to participate in the Vietnam war because they believe it to be immoral, unjust, and brutal." Most 1967 WSP activities focused on the draft. That spring the Nassau County WSP created the Long Island Draft Information and Counseling Service to prepare resisters to confront the Selective Service System and to increase community acceptance of conscientious objectors. It counseled over 3,000 a year and served as a model for other WSP Centers across the country, especially after formation of the WSP Anti-Draft Clearing House, chaired by Irma Zigas, who was also on the Executive Board of the National Council to Repeal the Draft, the Board of the War Resisters' League, and the Jewish Peace Fellowship.[31]

In the fall of 1967, WSP marchers left a coffin at General Lewis Hershey's door in a march on the Washington Selective Service Headquarters; and one demonstrator carried a sign, "My Son died in Vain!" They challenged in the courts a new law that no more than a hundred people could picket the White House. WSP picketers turned up at draft boards, induction centers, federal courts, and bus terminals in many cities, closing the Oakland Induction Center for an entire week. In December, WSP played a prominent role in organizing New York's "Anti-Draft Week," supporting Dr. Benjamin Spock, Allan Ginsberg, and others arrested for closing an induction center; and they contributed to defend Spock in his conspiracy trial. In New York, Philadelphia, and Chicago, WSP Peacemobiles stocked with literature on draft alternatives made the rounds of high schools. Boston women held cans at a draft card "turn-in." Other women provided food and clothing for resisters taking sanctuary from Federal marshals, visited "prisoners of conscience" in penitentiaries, and aided deserters in Canada and Sweden. The Washington chapter provided food and blankets for demonstrators at the October 1967 march on the Capitol. WSP groups raised funds for "in-service" military counselers and for GI Coffee Houses and filed suit against the government to end Army surveillance of their civilian activities. Dagmar Wilson traveled to Hanoi in 1969 to facilitate passage of mail to and from prisoners of war, returning with Christmas letters, although the FBI urged families not to participate in a program run by Communist sympathizers.[32]

Creation of the Jeannette Rankin Peace Brigade in 1967, named after the nation's first woman Senator, bridged a gap between several generations of women working for peace, and resulted in "an incongruous coalition of feminists, pacifists, hippies, rock musicians, antiwar students, and assorted radicals" as well as stars like Joanne Woodward and Diahann Carroll. The Brigade appeared in the 1968 march on Washington and enlisted cooperation from members of the nascent women's liberation movement. Rankin (1880–1973), the first woman elected to Congress in 1917 and a veteran pacifist who had opposed United States involvement in both World Wars, came out of a two-decade retirement, hoping to run for a third term in Congress in 1968 at age 88; but facial surgery prevented it, although she continued speaking out against the war until her death. A successor to the Brigade, the Women's Emergency Coalition formed in March 1968 to carry on its anti-war efforts.[33]

WSP had worked with student activists in planning the 1967 Vietnam Summer activities; and in 1968 young SDS women, unlike their male colleagues, reached out to the older pacifists, to explain differences, mend fences, and encourage collaboration. Cathy Wilkerson wrote an open letter to WSP: "As young movement women, we are always proud and pleased to work with and have the support of women in other organizations. Clearly, none of us can win until most of us fight together! Perhaps some of the women in WSP have been upset or dismayed by the resentment and militancy of young people—and young women in particular. We urge you to understand that our resentment is not founded on age or generation gap as 'the man's' media would have us believe. Rather, our sharp edges are the natural effect of our commitment to act in a principled fashion as political human beings. We urgently need and want support, but we must all recognize that our struggle will be wasteful and criminal if it is not fought principally."[34]

WSP became concerned with promotion of militarism through popular culture, and sponsored conferences on the effect on children of militarism and war news. They picketed yearly toy manufacturers' conventions and pressured companies to stop producing guns and war toys. They successfully bombarded retail stores and mail-order companies with letters, demanding that they not stock violent toys; and they awarded "dove of peace" window stickers to those companies that agreed. Because of such efforts, Mattel found the market for its G.I. Joe doll greatly diminished by 1969. WSP protested the equipping of California playgrounds with obsolete military equipment donated by the Army. Chicago women pressured the Museum of Science and Industry to dismantle an exhibit in which children could shoot at a model of a Vietnamese Village from a mock helicopter. The Washington, D.C., WSP contracted with an artist to produce a "peace coloring book"; and another group produced a "Save the Children" LP record of antiwar songs by popular folk singers.

WSP found allies in similar organizations—Voice of Women (VOW), Community Program for Peace (CPP), Women for Peace (WFP), the Fellowship of Reconciliation (FOR, begun in Britain in 1914), Women Speak Out for Peace and Justice (WSOPJ), and Another Mother for Peace (AMP)—all training grounds for a strong female leadership. Louise Peck helped organize WSOPJ and coordinated its efforts with student activists, who unfortunately usually referred to her just as "Sidney Peck's wife," recognizing her longtime activist husband's commitment to the anti-war movement more than hers. Likewise, Cora Weiss of the Socialist Workers Party (SWP), a long-time WSP activist, worked on the WSP Committee of Liaison to forge a network of activists, old and young. She was inevitably a vocal presence at demonstrations.[35]

AMP was founded by Barbara Avedon and others in time for Mother's Day 1967 and was based in Beverly Hills. "Another Mother" bombarded Washington with a half million Mother's Day and Christmas cards reading, "We who have given life must be dedicated to preserving it," and calling for a cabinet-level Secretary of Peace. AMP relied on celebrities for visibility—Joanne Woodward, Debbie Reynolds, Betsy Palmer, Felicia (Mrs. Leonard) Bernstein, Donna Reed Owens, Gloria Vanderbilt Cooper, Bess Myerson, Shelly Winters, Elaine May, and Julie Harris. By 1968 AMP claimed 100,000 members, rivaling WSP, although the overlap was great. They coined and popularized many of the anti-war phrases often attributed to the "flower-power" generation: "All the flowers of all the tomorrows are in the seeds of today," "Now is the time for peace," "Let's make our earth a nuclear-free zone." The AMP logo was "War is not healthy for children and other living things." In 1969, AMP declared a *Pax Materna*, "a permanent, irrevocable condition of amity and understanding among mothers of the world," at the first annual World Mother's Day Assembly.[36]

WSP issued a Children's Bill of Rights in 1968: "When in the course of evolution, the continuance of the human race is threatened, we who give birth must unite to ensure all children a future." Urging that human needs—food, shelter, medical care, and education—be made an international priority, it insisted, "War must be abolished. Military-industrial domination of the world must be ended." Thirty Congressmen joined with WSP in the spring of 1969 as Congressional Action, packing the house gallery to hear speakers on "Special Order of Business on Vietnam" pressure new President Nixon to end the war. WSP also worked closely with National Mobilization, Clergy Concerned, and occasionally with the World Peace Brigade.[37]

Although WSP gave a benefit party in 1970 in New York's Greenwich Village for wives of imprisoned Black Panthers and some members worked with welfare groups to redirect tax revenue from military to social concerns, it resisted enlarging its concerns to address racism, poverty, and pollution. Some realized that projects like the 1966 conferences, "Women's Response to the Rising Tide of Violence," had lessened some WILPF effectiveness against the war. Eleanor Garst judged that the task of promoting peace had become far more difficult at the decade's end because of the Pentagon's missile build-up and State Department intervention in Southeast Asia and Latin America. Mary Clarke, a founder of the Los Angeles WSP, cautioned against jumping "on the popular bandwagon" to "make ecology our main thrust. . . . We must not be detoured into other issues that have substantial movements and groups to wage their campaigns. . . . the fight to end the war and change our foreign policy is 'our thing.'"[38]

While WSP activities spread public consciousness of the environmental hazards of nuclear fallout, one woman's work launched the American environmental movement. *Silent Spring* (1962) by biologist Rachel Carson (1907–1964) was a landmark exposé of the "lethal assault on the biosphere" through fallout from atomic testing, radiation, pesticides, herbicides, and other suspected carcinogens. Responding to an appeal by her friend Olga Owens Huckins, who, based on observations at a Duxbury, Massachusetts, bird sanctuary, worried about the dangers of DDT spraying to control mosquitos, Carson envisioned a future devastated by toxic chemicals. DDT, widely used in agriculture and horticulture, was the worst culprit. She predicted a silenced world, concluding, "No witchcraft, no enemy action had silenced the rebirth of new life in this stricken world. The people had done it themselves." Hers was a lone prophetic voice crying in an impending wilderness, "a quiet, sterile America" created by pollution and industrial greed. Despite chemical industry attacks, *Silent Spring* and Carson's testimony before Congress prompted the 1963 forming of a Pesticides Committee in the federal Office of Science and Technology. Her influence on President Kennedy was great. He established a special panel on the President's Science Advisory Committee to study pesticide effects and evaluate her thesis; and in November 1969 the FDA announced a sweeping ban of DDT use that went into effect in December 1972.[39]

Carson's influence was international. Hers was the first voice to question the chronic irresponsibility of an industrial, technical society toward the natural world. She directed much of her appeal explicitly at women, calling on them to journey toward a new "Spring" of being, an invocation that would inspire a particular direction in the new feminism of the late sixties and after, entering into the feminist environmental theories of Mary Daly, Susan Griffin, and Carolyn Merchant. Rachel Carson died of bone cancer in 1964 at age 57, having sparked a consciousness of ecology that eventually led to development of an environmental movement, launched by celebration of the first Earth Day in April 1970, organized by Marilyn Laurie.

Women, Religious Belief, and Religious Institutions

The sixties was a decade of spiritual as well as political ferment. The two often came together: religious values gave purpose and language to the civil rights and anti-war movements. Like all other established institutions, the churches came under political scrutiny and were often found wanting. In the wake of the suburbanization of American religion and the remarkable growth of the established denominations during the late fifties, they were generally unprepared for challenges. Institutional behavior—almost inevitably—fell short of meeting the expectations of change that contemporary social analysis demanded. For all of the churches the new expectations caused confrontations among members; many, perhaps most, resented or resisted what they saw as the politicization of religion and the struggles were frequently intense.[41]

In religious institutions as elsewhere in American society in the sixties, hitherto marginalized women began to perceive and articulate their distance from the center. The power of law and custom had long enforced silence and subservience on women whose religious faith had to locate itself within hierarchical and patriarchal institutions. The comprehension of marginality, and the chorus of women's voices demanding to be heard, grew as the decade waned.

The effects of the calls for change were widespread. With the growing awareness of the pervasiveness of racial injustice, churchwomen's organizations frequently became involved in civil rights and other activist work. In one such endeavor, a group composed of members of the National Council of Catholic Women, the National Council of Jewish Women, and Church Women United joined with the National Council of Negro Women to serve as a screening and support service for young women entering the Job Corps.

Increasingly, churchwomen framed their concerns about the church within the analysis provided by the developing women's movement. Both Jewish and Catholic women began to question the rigid laws that forbade their full participation in religious life. Those Protestant denominations that had earlier begun the liberalization of gender-restrictive practices found themselves under pressure as women articulated their sense of injustice. In October 1964, responding to the 1963 publication of *The Feminine Mystique*, the Chicago City Mission Society journal, *Renewal*, devoted its entire issue to women and the church. Reverend Peggy Way, a minister in the United Church of Christ, noted the contrast between the secular re-evaluation of women's role in society and the Church's silence. "It is a fact that formal Church leadership (need we state that it is predominantly male?) has counted on women . . . to keep themselves occupied in their own organizations and *out of the sessions, vestries, church councils, presbyteries, etc.,—where the real decisions . . . are made.*" The church treated its professionally trained women, "Christian educators and pastors," as "second class citizens." In 1967 Doris Cole reiterated that charge in *Vanguard*, a bulletin for Presbyterian church officers. In a special 1969 women's liberation issue of *Motive*, the magazine of the Division of Higher Education of the Board of Education of the United Methodist Church, editor and "Token Woman" Joanne Cooke argued that the women's liberation movement was deeply related to the concerns of the church: "All this [the issues and arguments raised by contributors] is clearly Christian. . . . It assumes brotherhood and sisterhood, with a radical call to mutual concern, involvement and commitment. It assumes working for justice and equality; and dignity on earth." Not surprisingly, the special issue raised hackles among conservative readers.[42]

Even within the Mormon (Church of the Latter Day Saints) faith, with its deeply conservative position toward women and its emphasis on the primacy of motherhood, the women's movement had some impact. Church leaders saw the movement as "Satan's way of destroying women, the home, and the family—the basic unit of society"; but Belle Spofford, general president of the Relief Society, while asserting the importance of traditional roles, defended the ideas of equal pay for equal work and the need for women to develop their full potential. Younger Mormon women looked to history for the possibility of diversity. In 1971 a group of Boston women republished old copies of the Mormon journal *Woman's Exponent* in a volume with contemporary poetry and fiction and personal essays on such subjects as mothering, birth control, families and careers, and priestly authority.[43]

In all denominations, women continued as always to form the majority in congregations. In those northern and southern black churches that became centers for the civil rights movement (not all did), women "were the majority in the churches, in the mass meetings"; and women did the daily work of the church. But administrative power remained in men's hands. Writing of the proportionately greater access to authority of women in the Sanctified Church, Cheryl Gilkes notes the general absence from history of the "variety of strong traditions that black women have established in the religious and secular affairs of their community." In fact, she points out that "throughout all varieties of black religious activity, women represent from 75 to 90 percent of the participants." There were also many women in the conservative Black Muslim sect that gained prominence in the sixties. As in the other manifestations of black power and black nationalism, men retained leadership; and the expectation for women was subservience: "Messenger Muhammad teaches us . . . that Mad made Woman for the purpose of his pleasure. He did not need the woman to put one star in the heavens. He wanted the woman for love and companionship. She is the field to produce a nation."[44]

Many women in the mainline churches realized the discrepancy between their numbers and their influence, and some began to organize for change, although progress was slow. In 1970, Jeanne Richie assessed the continuing "systematic subordination" of women in the churches: "The ministry is almost exclusively a male fastness. . . . Although church membership and attendance are predominantly female, the lay boards which make church policy are largely male. . . . A young woman who wants to make a career of religious work will find that about the only opening available to her is religious education, where she will always be in a subordinate and assisting relationship to the minister. . . . For all practical purposes, the ministry is a caste system."[45]

Among the many women concerned about their role in the churches, one woman's voice stood out in opposition to religion itself. Beginning in the late fifties, militant atheist Madalyn Murray (later O'Hair) earned a reputation as "one of the most hated woman in America" for her crusade against prayer in the public schools and her defense of atheism. She became a celebrity when she launched the case of *Murray v. Curlett* in 1960; the Supreme Court ruled in her favor on 17 June 1963, banning Bible reading, saying prayers, and other religious observances in public schools as violations of the First Amendment.[46]

The Ordination Issue

Before 1960 some Protestant denominations had approved access for women to full ministry. The number of ordained women was small, however; and, as Richie suggests, upward mobility was limited. Ordination was an unlikely goal for Roman Catholic women, although the struggle at least to discuss the possibility was joined during the decade. An American section of the British Catholic feminist organization St. Joan's Alliance came into being in 1963, focusing on equal access for women in church and state, including the ordination of women. In 1967 at "probably the first public conference on women and religion in this country," conference organizer Elizabeth Farina condemned exclusion of women from the priesthood and "shocked" her audience by pointing to the "insidious notion that Christ is the redeemer in his maleness." Within Judaism, only the small Reconstructionist group encouraged women to study for the rabbinate. The expansion of the churches in the fifties created a demand for professional leadership and made women's ordination a subject for discussion; the civil rights movement and the early phases of the women's movement added ideology to the practical need.[47]

It was not until the seventies, however, that these changes coalesced into a movement of women into the seminaries and the clergy. Widespread public attention to women's desire for ordination did not come until the summer of 1974, when, against official church policy, three retired Episcopalian bishops ordained eleven women. The result was "an upheaval in the life of the church . . . seldom equaled in American Episcopal history." Behind it lay several decades of debate and some recent developments. In 1958 the Episcopal Theological School (ETS) in Cambridge, Massachusetts, had begun to admit women to candidacy for the Bachelor of Divinity degree, the first professional degree for those seeking ordination. Although not the intent, the result was the appearance of "a body of fully qualified women, many of whom soon found themselves doing a ministry which it seemed could attain its fullness only in the ordained, sacramental priesthood."[48]

In 1964 the General Convention changed the wording of the canon on deaconesses from "appointed" to "ordered." In 1965 controversial Episcopal Bishop James Pike ordained Phyliss Edwards to the diaconate (first of the three orders of ordained ministry). She became the "center of a storm of controversy." In 1970, the American General Convention approved women's ordination to the diaconate "on the same basis as men," while still voting down their ordination to the priesthood. Suzanne Hiatt, under whose leadership an "identifiable movement for ordination actually emerged," was the first American woman ordained to the diaconate under the new canon.[49]

Lay women in the Episcopal church also began to seek a greater role: among their "rank and file" there was a "growing disposition to leave the Christmas bazaars and the overstaffed altar guilds to get on with the work of the church *together* with the men." Women also supported such experiments as team ministries and sought the "relaxing of prohibitions against women in local vestries and in diocesan conventions, and lay involvement regardless of sex at every level of decision making."[50]

Acceptance of women's ordination in other mainline Protestant denominations varied. The Methodist church had permitted the ordination of women since the nineteenth century, although it did not undertake a formal study of women's roles until 1969. Methodist women had a long tradition of active involvement in social and charitable causes; but the number of ordained women working actively in the church was small—246 in 1964, rising only to 278 in 1968. In 1969 Margaret Henricksen became the first woman appointed superintendent of a district of the United Methodist Church (in Bangor, Maine). The tradition of strong participation by women in social and charitable work continued; although, according to Margaret Ermath, among laywomen there was a movement to free themselves of the "good works stereotype."[51]

Within the Southern Methodist Church, the sixties saw a continuation of the kind of women's work for social justice that had characterized that denomination for many years. The Fellowship of the Concerned, an interracial and interfaith women's organization founded in 1949 by Dorothy Rogers Tilly (1883–1970) to promote justice for blacks in the courts, broadened its concerns and was active into the late sixties.[52]

The American Baptist Convention had never restricted ordination to men, but in practice most of its ministers were male. In the late sixties most women pastors were in New England. The 1969 annual meeting noted that "the few women who serve as pastors find themselves limited to a few states with very few choices as to the types of churches served; . . . the numbers of women serving as ministers or directors of Christian Education has been steadily declining; . . . and the pay scale for women who are pastors or directors of Christian Education has been low with little hope of improvement." The assembly passed a resolution urging change in all of these areas.[53]

The Presbyterian Church was the first major American denomination to give full ordination rights to women (1956), and Presbyterian women also held a greater number of positions on boards and commissions than in other large denominations. The numbers of ordained women remained very small during the sixties, however—twenty-four of the 12,216 ordained ministers in 1960, rising only to 76 of 13,125 in 1969. That year, the church's Task Force on Women sent a questionnaire to all women ministers, seeking to discover why more women did not enter the ministry. The primary answer was a lack of professional mobility. Only one of the women surveyed had become pastor of the church she had originally served as assistant pastor. Women ministers were also more likely to be unemployed than their male counterparts, and more likely, therefore, to give up the church as an occupation. Churches did not view their applications in the same light as those of men: a woman waiting for a "call" to a church was told that "since we have a female staff member [the director of Christian education] at present, the committee will not be considering you for this position." The concern about women's role in Presbyterianism during the decade appeared to bear some fruit. In 1970 the number of ordained women rose to 103; and by 1971, there were "213 women ministerial candidates in seminaries."[54]

In 1966, a Lutheran minister described the role of women in that denomination as the "greatest 'hidden' problem in our midst. . . . Ask about the role of women and the response is likely to be smiles and snickers, or devoutly serious assertions that 'no one is interested in pursuing that issue.'" That year, however, a Comprehensive Study of Ministry of the Lutheran Church of America (LCA) urged the opening of greater opportunities for women. A commission charged with studying the problem of ordination announced in 1968 that it could find "no theological or biblical reasons for denying ordination to women." At the end of 1969, more than twenty women were enrolled in LCA seminaries with the intention of seeking ordination. By 1970 Margaret Ermath, who had directed the 1966 study, was able to say that "the problem as problem is recognized; the proportions of it are beginning to be grasped." Nonetheless, women church workers were still "psychologically burdened by attitudes, practices and structures that are culturally archaic and theologically questionable."[55]

Positions varied broadly in the other Lutheran churches. In 1969 the conservative Missouri Lutheran Synod's Commission on Theology and Church Relations finally ended a century-long debate by agreeing that women could vote in congregational meetings. They noted, however, that for a woman to hold "any office in the church at any level that would empower a woman to exercise authority over a man would constitute a violation of the order of creation." At the other end of the spectrum, the faculty of the American Lutheran Church's Theological Seminary certified two women as candidates for ordination in 1970.[56]

At the end of the decade, women's caucuses formed within various Protestant denominations and church groups. In Detroit in December 1969, the women's caucus of the General Assembly of the National Council of Churches described their movement as "a part of the spirit of the '60s which will continue because it is raising crucial issues and pointing to new possibilities for humanity and especially for that portion of humanity which has chosen to gather into the church. Women's oppression and women's liberation is a basic part of the struggle of blacks, browns, youth, and others. We will not be able to create a new church and a new society until and unless women are full participants. We intend to be full participants."[57]

Judaism

The sixties saw the continuation of American Jewish women's long-standing involvement in social service and the development of an increasing commitment to the transformation of American society through the women's movement. Despite resistance from traditional Judaism, Jewish women made major contributions to the new feminism, as organizers, writers, and speakers; in the women's movement as in the student movement, they spoke out clearly for justice. Betty Friedan, Shulamith Firestone, and others articulated new and often revolutionary ideas of equality. Friedan's determination to realize equality for women was rooted in the Jewish experience: it was "really a passion against injustice, which originated from my feelings of the injustice of anti-Semitism."[58]

Historically, Jewish women had been denied any part in public worship. Jewish law excluded women from the study of the Torah and exempted them from many time-bound religious commitments, mainly from communal celebration and prayer. The result was "an identification of women with physical work—childbearing, cooking, cleaning—while men are identified with spiritual activities—prayer, study, rituals." The "underlying motive" was neither the denial to women of the "opportunity to achieve religious fulfillment," nor the proposition that women are inherently more religiously sensitive," but "to assure that no legal obligation would interfere with the selection by Jewish women of a role which was centered almost exclusively in the home." A 1969 study of 400 women, *The Jewish Wife*, found that the "primary responsibility for keeping family ties close falls on the shoulders of the Jewish wife" and that she "insisted on peace in the home at any cost."[59]

The result for women of their exclusion from worship was a concomitant loss of rights: if women were exempted from communal worship they could not then be "counted to the quorum necessary to engage in such worship [the minyan]." In civil matters, if they could not give testimony, they lost the power to compel the court to find the facts to be in accord with their testimony." As the idea of feminism spread, some Jewish women pointed to the discrepancy between the centrality to Judaism of the idea of equality and its refusal to allow women equal participation. For Gail Shulman, "the feminist movement provided me with a context and a supportive community in which to articulate my anger and frustration with patriarchal traditions. Jewish feminists came to see that the treatment of women as 'separate but equal' was the thinly veiled rationalization of a real fear of women."[60]

In 1971 Paula Hyman and a small group of Jewish women, "all of us personally affected by the renascence of feminism," and responding to women's "second-class citizenship" within Judaism, formed a group called Ezrath Nashim ("help of women"). They came before the 1972 American Conservative Rabbinical Convention to ask for the full participation of women in religious observance, synagogue worship, and decision-making bodies; they also sought recognition in Jewish law for women as witnesses, the right of women to initiate divorce, and the general admission of women to schools which trained rabbis and cantors. Although the final decision to admit women to full participation was left to each congregation, the women succeeded in winning many of their points.[61]

The question of women's ordination to the rabbinate began in Reform Judaism when the Central Conference of American Rabbis declared in 1922 that "woman cannot justly be denied the privilege of ordination." In 1956 a Committee on the Ordination of Women reaffirmed the earlier resolution and urged the admission of women rabbinical students. Sally J. Preisand, the first American woman to be ordained a rabbi, began her studies there in 1964. Preisand discovered that, despite Reform Judaism's stated commitment to equality, "they were not yet ready for the spiritual leadership of a woman." Many assumed she was studying to become a rabbi's wife rather than a rabbi: "I had to do better than my classmates so that my academic ability would not be questioned. Professors were fair, but occasionally I sensed that some of them would not be overly upset if I failed. And when, in my fifth year, I was ready to serve my first congregation as a student rabbi, some congregations refused to accept my services." She explained, "[When I] accepted ordination on June 3, 1972, I affirmed my belief in Judaism and publicly committed myself to the survival of Jewish tradition . . . knowing that Judaism had traditionally discriminated against women. . . . I know that there has been a tremendous flexibility in our tradition—it enabled our survival. Therefore, I chose to work for change through constructive criticism."[62]

From the twenties on Rabbi Mordecai Kaplan worked to open Judaism to women's fuller participation. As a Conservative Jew, he had instituted the Bat Mitzvah ceremony for girls in 1922 as a counterpart to the boys' Bar Mitzvah; the ceremony became increasingly popular from the late sixties on. He also early "advocated calling girls to the Torah and counting them in the minyan." Kaplan developed Reconstructionism, a mid-thirties "offshoot" of Conservative Judaism, primarily to "provide a clear and precise ideology for American Jews." In 1948, writing in *The Future of the American Jew*, he urged that women "attain in Jewish law and practice a position of religious, civic, and juridical equality with the man." Kaplan founded the Reconstructionist Rabbinical College, which encouraged women's admission, in 1968; in 1974 Sandy Eisenberg Sasso became the first Reconstructionist woman rabbi. Because of the relatively small size of the Reconstructionist movement, and its essentially secularist stance, Rabbi Kaplan's influence was limited.[63]

Throughout the sixties American Jewish women continued to be active on behalf of social justice and charitable concerns through Hadassah, the National Council of Jewish Women, and American Women's ORT (Organization for Rehabilitation through Training), as well as through temple sisterhoods and in the Council of Jewish Federations (CJF). They thus continued a long and unsung history of philanthropy, one traditionally seen as "a natural extension" of women's proper work. As the concepts of feminism took hold, however, both the nature of the work and participants' perception of it underwent changes. In 1972 Jacqueline Levine, president of the Women's Division of the American Jewish Congress, called upon the General Assembly of the CJF to "grant women access to the 'highest levels of decision and policy making.'" She noted that "progressive child education programs, Head Start, the provision of sheltered workshops for handicapped workers, recreation for women; *all* were begun by women." But they were not allowed to move into leadership positions outside of women's organizations: "Should not the Jewish women volunteers give their expertise and understanding where most needed? At the top. We wish to share, not glory, but responsibility. We wish to offer the independence of our thinking."[64]

The analysis provided by the women's movement was both challenging and troubling to women with a long and significant history of volunteerism. Criticizing American society on the one hand for "ignoring its women volunteers," some feminists also questioned volunteerism as exploitative of women. Jewish-American women, June Sochen comments, "were sensitive to the new message. Those who defended their wifely/motherly/volunteer life found the exploration and the defense to be an energizing, positive experience. Those who accepted the new feminism and rejected the traditional female roles often sought personal rewards in new occupations and professions. . . . [S]till others tried to reform religious Judaism to harmonize with the new feminism. Overall, Sochen believes, "Jewish-organization women . . . integrated the best of the feminist philosophy and rejected" those aspects which were "untenable" in the light of their commitment to their work.[65]

Roman Catholicism

The greatest challenges in the sixties came within Roman Catholicism, the most tradition-bound of denominations. No other American church was so populated with women in positions of responsibility without authority. As teachers, nurses and hospital administrators and workers in church institutions, women—especially nuns—did the work of the church while having little or no voice within it. The decade of the sixties was tumultuous. The Catholic church had to work through both the mandates for change required by the Second Vatican Council (1962–65) and the challenges from social activists. It was experiencing "restlessness," Sister Marie Augusta Neal, S.N.D., told a 1968 symposium on "Religion in America." The restlessness was "experienced as apathy by some, as rebellion by others, and as great expectation by still others." All of the traditions were "up for question."[66]

Traditionally, American Catholic women had not entered theological or jurisdictional debates, their writings typically spiritual reflections or commentaries on the religious education of the young. Increasingly, however, Catholic women thinkers spoke out. Issues of personal relations were central to Sidney Callahan's 1965 book, *The Illusion of Eve*, which suggested ways for young married Catholic women to find fulfillment. While rejecting the feminist solutions of Betty Friedan and Simone de Beauvoir, Callahan also abandoned the traditional assumptions of the Judaeo-Christian churches, which treated women as naturally inferior. In *Sex: Female; Religion: Catholic* (1968), Sally Cunneen drew on a questionnaire sent to subscribers of *Cross Currents*, a liberal Catholic journal, to ascertain their attitudes toward the changes in the Church, particularly as they affected sexual and family life. Unlike Callahan, Cunneen could find no way toward a new synthesis nor any possibility for a single image of the Christian woman; "the differences were too great."[67]

More important theologically was the work of two young women scholars, Rosemary Radford Ruether and Mary Daly, both of whom had roots in Catholicism. Ruether began her teaching career in 1965 at the lively and experimental Catholic women's college, Immaculate Heart, in Los Angeles. She left there in 1966 (in part because of repercussions from a 1962 article in which she questioned traditional church teaching on birth control) to join the faculty of the School of Religion at Howard University. She remained at Howard until her appointment as Georgia Harkness Professor of Applied Theology at Garrett Evangelical-Theological Seminary in Illinois in 1975.[68]

From the beginning, Ruether wrote "in order to integrate the historical and critical perspective into the questions of church practices, on the one hand, and the questions of social renewal on the other." Seeing in the biblical tradition two different perspectives on God, a patriarchal perspective which leads to a "religious sanctification of the existing social order," and the perspective of the oppressed, which leads to a theology of liberation, Ruether has worked to help women to understand the patriarchal nature of the traditional churches and the "role of religion, specifically the Judaeo-Christian tradition, in shaping the traditional cultural images that have degraded and suppressed [them]." In her books since *Religion and Sexism* (1974) Ruether sought to develop a feminist theology to revitalize Christianity and make it a theology of liberation for women.[69]

Mary Daly, a graduate of St. Rose's College in Albany, New York, was a junior member of the theology faculty at Boston College (a Jesuit university) when she published *The Church and the Second Sex* (1968). One of the decade's most influential publications, the book named the sexist attitudes and practices of Christianity, especially of Roman Catholicism, and asked for broad changes. Although moderate by the standards of Daly's later, post-Christian radical feminism, it caused a considerable stir in Catholic circles. *The Church and the Second Sex* is rooted in a response to de Beauvoir's condemnation of the destructive limitations placed on women in the Roman Catholic tradition. Daly agrees with de Beauvoir's analysis but is much more hopeful; at this point she still saw the Church as potentially an institution through which women could come to transcendence: "the seeds of the eschatological community, of the liberating, humanizing Church of the future, are already present, however, neutralized they may be." With "hope and courage" change can occur.[70]

That hope faded quickly, however. In a sermon preached at Harvard Memorial Church in 1971 (the first ever given by a woman at a Sunday service there), Daly attacked the role of the churches "in supporting the sexual caste system," and urged in its place a "new sisterhood [that] is the bonding of women for liberation from sex role socialization." At the sermon's conclusion she led an "exodus" of women from the Church, "to go out from the land of our fathers into an unknown place. . . . [to] demonstrate our exodus from sexist religion." By the time of publication of her second book, *Beyond God the Father: Toward a Philosophy of Women's Liberation* (1973), Daly had abandoned hope for the Church's ability to correct its errors. This volume, and those that followed, have provided a prophetic and radical feminist analysis and rejection of Christianity; their influence on contemporary religious thought has been vast.[71]

While scholars sought to redefine the American Catholic Church, a similar effort at redefinition was being made by its members as groups of laypersons worked to translate belief into activism. At St. Philip's parish in inner city Roxbury, Massachusetts, for example, clerics of various faiths and laypersons of the city and suburbs came together to support the 1968 action of the Milwaukee 14, a group of priests and laypersons who had destroyed files at that city's draft board. Women were at the forefront of organizing support for the 14. Former Sister of St. Joseph Anne Walsh went from support to participation: she later was one of the New York Eight who raided draft boards in Manhattan and Queens. Kip Tiernan, then in advertising, redirected her life as a result of the St. Philip's/Milwaukee 14 experience, later organizing Rosie's Place, the first drop-in shelter for urban women, Up From Poverty, which campaigned to raise the stipends for women on welfare, and the Boston Women's Fund.[72]

In New York City, the Catholic Worker movement and its cofounder, Dorothy Day (1897–1980), regained the attention of many Catholics and others who were in search of a model for combining faith and activism. Throughout the conservative, assimilationist years of World War II and McCarthyism, Day had remained committed to pacifism and the practice of voluntary poverty; and Catholic Worker houses of hospitality in many cities continued to follow the model she and cofounder Peter Maurin had established in the New York houses that had first opened in the Depression years. But the movement's opposition (articulated in its monthly paper, *The Catholic Worker*) first to support for Franco in the Spanish Civil War and then to World War II conscription alienated many supporters.

The charismatic presence of Day and the *Catholic Worker* became in the sixties a source of inspiration and support for a new generation of Catholic antiwar activists. Michael Harrington, whose book *The Other America*, had a profound effect on President Kennedy's understanding of poverty in America, began his social education at the *Catholic Worker*. The earliest destruction of draft cards as a protest against an unjust war was the work of *Catholic Worker* residents. Jesuit resistance leader Daniel Berrigan was an admirer and friend of Day's, as were many others in the "Catholic Left." Day's theology remained much more conservative, however, than that of many who admired her.[73]

True to her historical roots in the cause of labor, Day continued to seek justice for agricultural and other workers outside the ranks of organized labor. In the early sixties she wrote at length in *The Catholic Worker* about Fidel Castro's educational and land reforms in Cuba, while deploring the violence of his revolution. An inveterate traveller, Day went to Cuba in 1962 to see the reforms for herself: "I want to see a country where there is no unemployment, where a boy or a man can get a job at any age, when he wants it, at some socially useful work."[74]

With the boycott against table grapes organized by César Chavez and the United Farmworkers in 1965, Day began her involvement with the UFW. From 1934 on, she pointed out, the *Catholic Worker* had been concerned with the "problem of destitution among farm workers, and we are particularly interested in Chavez because of his emphasis on nonviolence." In addition to her support in the pages of *The Catholic Worker*, Day travelled to California to join the vineyard picket lines. The last of her many arrests for civil disobedience came at a demonstration in 1973 in support of the grape boycott; she was then 77.[75]

Members of the Catholic Left also found the source for political activism in a radical reading of theology. The Catholic Left was a somewhat amorphous group of men and women, mostly young, including many clerics and some nuns, which organized dramatic actions directed against the war in Vietnam. While not immune to the charges of sexism against the Left in general, the Catholic Left enabled many women to act upon their deepest convictions. Among them were Marjorie Melville, who as Maryknoll Sister Marian Peter had worked in Guatemala for several years until her sympathy with revolutionary forces led to personal risk and separation from the order, and Elizabeth McAlister. Melville was one of two women members of the Catonsville Nine, lay and religious protestors who used homemade napalm to destroy files at the Catonsville, Maryland, draft board in May 1968. McAlister, a member of the Religious of the Sacred Heart of Mary and a faculty member at Marymount College, came to political protest through the words and example of Daniel and Philip Berrigan. In 1971, she was indicted with Philip Berrigan (later her husband) and four others on federal charges, accused of plotting to kidnap Henry Kissinger and blow up the heating system of federal buildings.[76]

Increasingly, unrest appeared in the Catholic Left over the discrepancy between men's and women's roles. The first all-women's action, "Women Against Daddy Warbucks," took place on 2 July 1969: five women raided the Manhattan draft board, destroying and removing records and damaging the "1" and "A" on the typewriters. They reappeared at a pre-arranged rally on July 4th, when they tossed shredded draft records to the crowd and were arrested. Historian Charles Meconis sees this event as an important turning point: "[I]t marked the opening round of a struggle within the movement concerning the role of women. The bitterness generated by the subsequent estrangement of these women from the action community was deep." Feelings festered as the pressures of repeated actions, arrests, trials, and jailings were taking their toll. By summer 1971, Anne Walsh remembers, "a more conscious critique of the Catholic Left from the feminist point of view was developing. . . . Unlike the rest of the Left, which had a very up-front kind of sexism, sexism," complicated by the new political roles being taken by priests in the movement, "was more subtle with us."[77]

The extensive involvement of Melville, McAlister, Walsh and others in the actions of the Catholic Left is a vivid comment on the massive changes which had taken place in the lives of women religious since Vatican II. In *The Church and the Second Sex* Mary Daly provides an overview of what she calls the "phenomenon of the emerging sisters." Throughout the sixties, this phenomenon engaged the attention of many writers and journalists, within and without the church. Before women's liberation, women religious debated the role of women within a male-dominated institution and undertook a sweeping and prophetic renewal and transformation of their lives. Nuns appeared on television: popular television host David Frost interviewed four of the "New Breed," all in full religious dress, in 1965; the women spoke seriously of the difficulty of change and the show was generally well received. Books by and about nuns proliferated into the seventies. Some, in a time when large numbers of women left the convent, were of the "I leaped (or I peered) over the wall" school, but many others were thoughtful reflections on the religious life and the meaning of the changes within it. Sister M. Charles Borromeo, C.S.C., editor of a volume of articles on *The New Nuns* (1967), emphasized, "it is becoming legitimate for sisters to be persons, each with her own qualities and faults."[78]

In popular culture, however, stereotypically naive images of nuns proliferated: "phalanxes of rollicking postulants invaded—singing, flying, riding motorcycles, and strumming the guitar." Mary Tyler Moore played a nun in the 1970 movie *Change of Habit*, ending with Moore on her knees deciding between the religious life and Elvis Presley, the doctor in the clinic where she is working (in ordinary clothes). These images were very much at odds with the revolutionary, sometimes painful transformations within religious life.[79]

The fifties had seen the development of the Sister Formation movement, designed to remedy the disturbing educational unpreparedness of the great majority of the thousands of teaching nuns. In the sixties, education for women religious "took a quantum leap forward, particularly in areas theological," and increasing numbers of sisters went out from their convents to attend universities. The many rules of conventual life came under increasing scrutiny from women who were reading such contemporary theologians as Hans Kung and Edward Schillebeeckx and whose American characters had difficulty with kneeling to ask permission of a superior for such necessities as taking a bath. "If Vatican II had not come along, I'd have invented it," one nun commented, reflecting on the increased irritability caused by what had come to seem to many rules for rules' sake.[80]

Many accounts of the upheavals of the late sixties quote Erving Goffman's *Asylum*, with its concept of the total institution, as an explanation of what increasingly seemed a stifling climate. Belgian Cardinal Leon Suenens's *The Nun in the World*, published in the United States in 1963, "stunned the still highly structured religious communities." Suenens urged women religious to move beyond convent walls and to act as "animators" for men and women whose everyday lives needed evangelization. He was also responsible for the invitation to American Sister of Loretto Mary Luke Tobin and fourteen other women to sit as "auditors" at the third session of the Vatican Council, from which women had previously been banned.[81]

A 1966 Vatican document, *Ecclesiae sanctae*, required every order to call a chapter (meeting) of renewal within three years of the end of the Council. Maria Reilly, O.P., a member of the Adrian Dominicans remembers the three summers of the renewal chapter of her progressive order as "a Copernican revolution." By 1969 the habit was gone, traditional structures of authority had been abolished, and the sisters had decided they would not guarantee personnel to parish schools. Although popular response focused on the decision to set aside the habit, the decision that individuals would have to take increasing responsibility for themselves was far more revolutionary. For many, taking responsibility for oneself caused great difficulty: Canon Law had treated nuns officially as children, incapable of independence, and the hierarchical structure of the Church had served to underscore that role. In transforming themselves, "what we were doing, without knowing it, was reflecting on our experience as women in a structure created by men, and saying no."[82]

Change was widespread and rapid. Increasingly in the sixties, members of religious congregations left the safety of convents to participate in demonstrations for social justice, to work, to move into the inner cities; they formed new kinds of communities and many linked their fate to that of the poor. Fifty-two nuns from a variety of congregations, dressed in full habit, confronted armed police during the march on Selma, Alabama, in March 1965; arms linked, they placed themselves between the police and the marchers. Sister Margaret Cafferty was one of eight sisters on a protest march with César Chavez and members of the United Farm Workers in April 1966. Subsequently, she moved from the security of her San Francisco convent into an apartment with two other sisters in a condemned inner city building. In 1967, the Loretto order took an unprecedented "corporate stand" against the Vietnam war by joining Negotiation Now, a national call to action. Women from a variety of orders worked together to improve urban life. In northwest Chicago in July 1965, nuns from the Urban Apostolate founded "The Place," a center for teen-age girls, black, white, and Spanish-speaking. In New York, groups of sisters teamed up to run "Summer in the City," a multi-faceted program for youth; and in 1965, sisters joined the difficult organizing process for a rent strike organized by Christians United for Social Action.[83]

For the small number of black nuns (about 900), the social upheaval of the late sixties also led to reappraisals. Sister Joyce Williams, a Benedictine, left teaching in Minnesota to work in the black community of Cleveland: "'After the assassination of Martin Luther King, I told my superiors that I could no longer work in a white school.'" The

National Black Sisters Conference was founded in 1967 by Sister Martin de Porres Grey, a Sister of Mercy from Pittsburgh and the only black member of her order. As a result of meeting other black nuns through the conference, Sister Yvonne Tucker left her order to join another that would give her more freedom to work among blacks. An account of the 1970 meeting of the National Black Sisters Conference notes that for some a "new black awareness had forced them to ask whether the religious life in the Catholic Church was compatible with involvement with their people"; several, disturbed by racism in the Church, had left. For others, however, commitment to the religious life became stronger. Sister Theresa Perry, a doctoral student in theology at Yale, told an interviewer: "Christianity has been the arm of oppression since early times and that is the ways blacks have experienced it. . . . But the Word of God can also be used as a force for liberation."[84]

As orders of religious women undertook sweeping changes, some ran into serious opposition. The Glenmary Sisters (the Home Mission Order of America), missionaries to the Appalachian poor, had welcomed the freedom to dress informally and to travel more freely as ways to realize their apostolate more effectively. Prompted by complaints from some members of the order who did not like the changes, Cincinnati Archbishop Karl J. Alter (in whose diocese the order was officially located) objected. In September 1965 he ordered them to restrict their freedom of movement, forbade them from starting new houses or accepting postulants into the order, and limited their reading, the hours they could keep (all were told to be in bed by 10 P.M.), and the places where they could study. By the summer of 1967, 40 of the 102 women in the order had left individually; in August close to 50 more announced their attention to leave as a group in order to form a new lay community. A small group of 15 remained to "continue living out their life in very close dialogue with . . . the present canonical structure," as one sister explained, but for most there were other "directions that have to be moved in."[85]

In the summer of 1967, the California Immaculate Heart of Mary (IHM) order concluded its chapter of renewal with a lengthy outline of reforms designed to bring about engagement with the "social, economic, intellectual, and spiritual needs of the family of man." All of the changes had been sanctioned by Rome; but they were objected to by conservative Los Angeles Cardinal James Francis McIntyre, who threatened to remove the nuns from their teaching posts in archdiocesan schools. The struggle became bitter and prolonged, and was eventually turned over to the Vatican Congregation of the Religious. Most members of the order left the schools, and approximately 100 of the 500-member order left religious life. The order split in 1968: 50 of the older nuns agreed with Cardinal McIntyre and remained in traditional dress and roles. Another approximately 300 began plans to form a new order, which developed a communitarian rule and welcomed co-members, both men and women, married and unmarried.[86]

Best known of the IHM order was Sister Corita Kent, whose "colorful, deceptively witty serigraphs, or silk-screen prints, dance with buoyant hope," *Newsweek* noted. This hope was based in a deeply religious vision, a "delight in the greatness of God and all he has made." Corita's work had begun in traditional religious imagery but in the sixties burst into "a combustion of free form," vivid, brilliant collages of words and color. Language drawn from advertising was put into juxtaposition with theology: in one serigraph the advertising slogan "Enriched Bread" appears above a quotation from Gandhi: "There are so many hungry people that God cannot appear to them except in the form of bread," to make "a new whole." At Immaculate Heart College in the early sixties, Corita initiated a celebration of May Day, Mary's Day, that was a prototype of happenings and be-ins: "balloons, huge paper flowers, real flowers, colorful banners, were everywhere. The procession of students and faculty [nuns still in their habits] was led by a student from Hong Kong doing a ribbon dance in native costume."[87]

The IHM sisters was the largest group of nuns to leave an American order since Vatican II, but there had been many women who had reconsidered their vocation in the wake of the questions and re-evaluations prompted by the process of renewal. Some formed new organizations or transformed existing groups to respond to the new spirit. The National Assembly of Women Religious, founded in 1968, wanted to give a voice to the "individual, ordinary sister" and to "link religious identity and social activism." More outspokenly feminist, the National Council of American Nuns came into being in 1969, under the leadership of Sister Margaret Ellen Traxler. The Conference of Major Superiors of Women (CMSW), founded in 1956, commissioned an important study in 1965, directed by sociologist Sister Maria Augusta Neal, S.N.D., to assess the process of renewal in various communities and the "relation between one's religious belief and structural change." A questionnaire was sent to more than 139,000 sisters. The response was large, and the study yielded valuable data by which to measure recent changes. In 1968, in part in response to the survey, the CMSW began a period of reorganization. In renaming itself the Leadership Conference of Women Religious (LCWR), the organization reflected its shift away from the older hierarchical model to the development for all women religious of "'creative and responsive leadership.'"[88]

The significant shifts within the governance of individual communities toward a more personally responsible mode of life and the awakening of the late sixties to the range of untreated social injustices in the United States led to a new understanding of the mission of religious women. For many, the new concept of the role of the sister offered a freedom to do God's work more fully; in 1970, there were still over 167,500 women in religious orders. Sister Elena Malits, one of forty sisters who had conducted the CMSW survey, told an interviewer in 1976: "I live in a convent. But it's not a convent of the mind. I don't have a convent mentality, a fixed way, a confining experience."[89]

For many others, however, the best way to fulfill their mission was not within the confines of conventual life, even in its modern form. Almost 28,000 women left religious life between 1965 and 1970. In 1960 only 765 of 168,527 left their orders; in 1966, "over 2,000 nuns defected." The number "reached its peak in 1970, when 4,337 exited." There was a loss of over 25,000 nuns from the parochial schools; by 1968 lay teachers outnumbered sisters. Between 1958 and 1962 more than 32,000 women, mostly young, had sought admission to religious orders; in the 1971–75 period, that number had dropped to 2590. A study by Helen Ebaugh showed that the highest rate of leaving religious life came in those orders that had made the most changes. In such orders, many women felt that "the order no longer afforded them sufficient reason and meaning for belonging since most of the activities in which they were engaged in the renewed order were possible outside its boundaries."[90]

One of the women who had appeared on the David Frost show left religious life because she felt "hypocritical"; the attention being paid to her as one of the "new breed" of nuns was not matched by her sense of herself. Maryellen Muckenhirn, who was a leader in the renewal process within the Holy Cross Sisters and, as Sister Charles Borromeo, author of three books on the religious life, left the order because she could no longer justify "trying to alternate between secular and monastic patterns of existence." Secular life "seems to be the real life, the place of human growth, the place where the spirit of Christ makes demands on me that are both difficult and genuine."[91]

Like other American women in the sixties, but earlier than many, women religious had to make decisions that challenged their traditional way of life. And, as for other women, change was both painful and exhilarating.

Popular Culture

Mainstream Images of Women: Film and Television

In *The Feminine Mystique* (1963), Betty Friedan contrasted women's real lives with the "image to which [they] were trying to conform." In the fifties, social forces and mass media revived the cult of domesticity; and the ideal of ultra-femininity formed a widespread and influential tyranny of acceptable female images, shaping the behavior and self-image of average women of every age; but in the sixties, before and independent of feminism's revival, new female images emerged to challenge middle-class conventions and shock many women of older generations. Hems rose and fell, and women became more creative and self-expressive in dress. Advertising continued to manipulate women, using images of domesticity and sexuality to sell goods. Despite their talents, women were stereotyped and exploited in film, television, and music, but by 1965, themes in humor about women became less misogynist, as *New Yorker* cartoons turned away from older themes: women as unassertive and deferential to men, as bad drivers, and as unable to think rationally. Increasing liberalization of women's images preceded real changes in women's rights and status and led to the misconception that change was greater than it actually was. After all, how really different were the tragic figures of Marilyn Monroe and Janis Joplin, both questing for fame but self-destructing, whose deaths mark the decade's beginning and the end?[1]

Films and Stars

Blond super-star Marilyn Monroe (born Norma Jean Mortenson in 1926) symbolized ideal femininity of the fifties and embodied mass media's exploitation of sexuality, the marketing of a woman as sexual icon. In the sixties, Marilyn appeared in her last movie, *The Misfits* (1961); divorced playwright Arthur Miller; engaged in a tragic affair with President John Kennedy; and died on 5 August 1962, at age 35, of a sleeping-pill overdose. Death only enhanced the power of her image. Famed teacher Lee Strasberg, her Actors Studio mentor, effused about her epitomization of a classic ideal of femininity: "She stood for a whole kind of feminine sensitivity and sexuality." She was "naive, not sophisticated" and "flirtatious," with "'experience' knowledge, and she always spoke out of that, never pretending to anything that she did not, herself, experience. . . . These qualities keep her alive for so many people." They did not keep her *alive*. She was known simply by her first name; and her trademark vulnerability proved all too real.[2]

Art critic Lawrence Alloway observed, "she was lifted out of the calendar-girl, sexy star context into a liberal drama of comedienne as victim. . . . she became a pitiful creature trapped in the mass media, Hollywood's throwaway." Artists quickly found her image recyclable. Within a year, her death spawned art works by James Rosenquist, Andy Warhol, James Gill, and many other men—an orgy of objectification. A 1963 issue of *Life* noted "The Growing Cult of Marilyn." The Sidney Janis Gallery put on a "Homage to Marilyn Monroe" show, omitting a major work by a woman—Pauline Boty's "The Only Blonde in the World."[3]

Equally sad was the death of Judy Garland (1922–1969), a legendary "cult" figure in her own time. Garland revived her movie career in 1961 in a vignette role as a German *hausfrau* in *Judgment at Nuremberg*, earning an Academy Award nomination for best supporting actress. That year, she gave a Carnegie Hall concert that resulted in a double album and two Grammies. She appeared in *A Child is Waiting* (1962) and *I Could Go On Singing* (1963), based on her life; yet in 1963 her weekly television program was canceled due to poor ratings. Garland drank heavily, took diverse pills, and began to lose her voice. Gossip columnists attacked her personal life—three marriages in the decade. She died in London on 22 June 1969 at age 47 from a barbiturate overdose. Over 20,000 attended her New York funeral.

These deaths coincided with the decline of the "star system," in which film celebrities, properties of major studios, were marketed like movies, their "vehicles." Such exploitation, paradoxically, had had benefits for women in economic leverage, benefits lost in the collapse of Hollywood's "phony glamour industry" in the sixties. Only a few actresses dominated the decade. Audrey Hepburn (1929–) played the materialistic child-whore Holly Golightly in Blake Edward's version of Truman Capote's *Breakfast at Tiffany's* (1961). Mirroring the Jackie Look, she epitomized high style and the gamine, prolonging a prolific fifties career with *The Children's Hour* (1962), *Charade* (1963), *My Fair Lady* (1964), *How to Steal a Million* and *Two for the Road* (1966), and *Wait Until Dark* (1967). Other promising young stars like Kim Novak (1933–) saw their careers fizzle out—in her case after her portrayal of a hooker, Polly the Pistol, in Billy Wilder's slightly salacious sex comedy *Kiss Me, Stupid* (1964), inspired a "blue-nose boycott," one of the last restrictionist attempts to preserve Hollywood's self-censoring Production Code.[4]

The Code, in place since 1930, broke down in the sixties. An early deviation was *A Summer Place* (1959), starring Sandra Dee (1942–) and Troy Donahue as sensuous teen lovers who become unwed parents and have a shotgun wedding. Although many parents forbade teens to see the movie, it grossed almost $2 million in three months. Spin-offs followed with Connie Stevens (1938–) in *Parrish* (1961), Shirley MacLaine (1934–) in *The Apartment* (1960) and *Two for the Seesaw* (1963), and Natalie Wood (1938–1981) in *Splendor in the Grass* (1961) and in *Love with the Proper Stranger* (1963). Wood also appeared in a watered-down farce adapted from Helen Gurley Brown's book *Sex and the Single Girl* (1964). All broke new ground in dealing with extramarital affairs while avoiding censorship.[5]

Films of the sixties still celebrated the innocent ingenue—the formula that brought Debbie Reynolds (1932–) fame as *Tammy* in 1957, and in other fifties teen age roles. Public sympathy for Reynolds furthered her box-office popularity after 1959 when her storybook marriage to singer Eddie Fisher ended and he left her to marry Elizabeth Taylor. But as Reynolds pushed thirty, Sandra Dee (1942–), a wisp of a girl with blond pigtails, famed for *A Summer Place* and the first Gidget film in 1959, replaced her in *Tammy Tell Me True* (1961) and *Tammy and the Doctor* (1963). Dee "presented the most passive, fluttery pink-and-white-ribbons perfection, her ample mouth recalled the petulance of an adolescent [Brigitte] Bardot. By scaling down this image of feline sexuality for the nubile high school set, Dee wove the transition between the fifties' naïveté and the sixties' nymphet, exhibiting a provocative self-awareness, almost a fear of her own sexuality, which in view of the decade's moral expectations, was sensible." Even Dee was expendable as others took on the role—Deborah Walley in *Gidget Goes Hawaiian* (1961), Cindy Carol in *Gidget Goes to Rome* (1963), and Sally Field in a 1965 television series, while Carol Lynley (1942–), Tuesday Weld (1943–), and Yvette Mimieux (1939–) projected similar images. Field then parlayed her perky, pure American girl image into the sitcom "The Flying Nun," temporarily type-casting her and squelching her film career.[6]

Teen described Cindy Carol's 1963 Gidget as a sixties ideal: "She's a pixie, a Peter Pan type with a daybreaking smile and mischief in her eyes, and she's finding it hard to believe that she is living in a real world, what with one fabulous thing after another happening to her!" Gidget was "the consummate perky girl," embodying the "qualities of an all-new up-tempo, happy-go-lucky sixties person who peppermint-twisted her way onto center stage as a curtain rose on a decade that promised to be fun." This image was repeated by Goldie Hawn (1945–) in *Cactus Flower* (1969) and Jane Fonda (1937–) in *Barefoot in the Park* (1967). An exception was Stanley Kubrick's *Lolita* (1962).[7]

Hollywood found a lucrative audience in American teens, the first wave of the post-war baby boom, and produced films aimed at them. In the musical *Where the Boys Are* (1961), four college girls—Connie Francis (1938–), Delores Hart (1938–), Paula Prentiss (1939–), and Yvette Mimieux (1939–), spent spring vacation on the Fort Lauderdale beach with beer, parties, and boys and spawned the beach-party formula film, mass-produced in such variations as *Beach Party* (1963), *Muscle Beach Party* (1964), *Bikini Beach* (1964), *Beach Blanket Bingo,* and *How to Stuff a Wild Bikini* (1967). Former mouseketeer Annette Funicello co-starred with pop singer and heart-throb Frankie Avalon in a series of movies after *Beach Blanket Bingo*. Walt Disney, who still had Annette under contract, forced her to wear bathing suits covering her navel. Even the young writer Gloria Steinem capitalized on the vogue with *The Beach Book* (1963), which gave basic information about sandcastles, suntans, palm reading and back rubbing, all bound in a silver cover to double as sun reflector.[8]

Hollywood also exploited the "bad girl" image. Tuesday Weld (1943–) was repeatedly cast as a sex kitten or nymphet in films like *Because They're Young, Sex Kittens Go to College, High Times*, and *The Private Lives of Adam and Eve* in 1960, *Return to Peyton Place* and *Wild in the Country* in 1961, *Bachelor Flat* (1962), and *I'll Take Sweden* (1965), roles which ignored her acting talents and led to her chronic depression and an unhappy private life. Similarly, Nancy Sinatra, personification of the "tough girl," co-starred in *Speedway* (1968) with Elvis Presley.

Doris Day (1924–), the most popular female star of the fifties and one of the highest paid, graduated to bedroom farces in a box-office formula established by *Pillow Talk* (1959), which depicted her as a slightly flirtatious but not risqué young matron with "neutralized" sexuality. Day appealed to a female audience because she seemed wholesome, not too glamorous, not competition. Hollywood maven Oscar Levant quipped, "I knew Doris Day before she was a virgin." In *Please Don't Eat the Daisies* (1960), based on the popular Jean Kerr novel, she's a housewife with four children in a New York apartment who longs for the suburbs. When she relocates, leaving "hubby" in the city for long days and evenings, the sizzling Janis Paige (1922–) tempts him but infatuation fails. In the end, Doris, epitome of the era's proper young suburbanite, rewins his affection by dancing in the playground with children and directing a community play. Day went on to similar roles in *Lover, Come Back* (1961), *Move Over Darling* (1962), *That Touch of Mink* (1962), *Send Me No Flowers* (1964), and *Do Not Disturb* (1965), remaining a top-ten actress in box-office draw between 1959 and 1966.[9]

Real life was not so easy. When Day's third husband and producer-manager, Marty Melcher, died in 1968 after 17 years of seemingly happy marriage, she discovered her entire $20 million life savings gone, squandered or embezzled. Recovering from a nervous breakdown, she reluctantly starred in her own television series, into which Melcher had booked her without her consent. She flopped on Broadway but won back her fortune by suing her lawyer, Melcher's partner.[10]

Julie Andrews (1935–), although British-born, had an "American-applepie mother image" in musicals like *Mary Poppins* (1964), for which she won the best-actress Academy Award, and *The Sound of Music* (1965), one of the top-grossing films of all time. Andrews' roles trivialized her talent. *Thoroughly Modern Millie* (1967) was "slow and silly," writes one critic. The actress was at less than her best in *Star!* (1968), based on the life of Gertrude Lawrence.[11]

Otherwise, an unprecedented sexuality marked sixties films. Swedish-born Ann-Margret Olsson (1941–) graduated from ingenue to sex-symbol roles, from whimsies like *Bye Bye Birdie* (1964) to *Viva Las Vegas* opposite Elvis and *Kitten with a Whip*, (both 1964), and *The Pleasure Seekers* (1965), and *The Swinger* (1966). Perhaps the greatest exploitation occurred in the James Bond movies, which presented women as sex objects, easily seduced by the glamorous spy or victimized by the bad guys. Bond's women had names like Honeychile Rider, Domino, Fiona

Volpe, Kissy Suzuki, and Pussy Galore. A spin-off with Natalie Wood as female lead was *Penelope* (1966), "the world's most beautiful bank-robber," advertised with a cartoon of the actress, nearly nude, clasping two bulging, round money bags marked with $ signs in front of her breasts, and with a phallic gun holstered in her bikini bottoms.[12]

Raquel Welch (1940–), already a divorced mother of two, took acting classes and had plastic surgery before descending on Hollywood in 1963. With her second husband and press agent, Patrick Curtis, she formed Curtwell Enterprises to market herself as a sex symbol. Based on publicity tours and without a single leading role, she became an international star, acclaimed by many as "the undisputed sex goddess of the sixties and one of the highest-paid women in the business." In *One Million Years B.C.* she plays an impeccably beautiful leader of a band of Amazons. When Welch dissolved her partnership and marriage with Curtis in 1971, "she was firmly entrenched in the Wonder Woman . . . a living symbol of the idealized, unattainable female eternal."[13]

Throughout the decade, Jane Fonda inspired controversy, but more for her politics than for her sexuality. Her prominently quoted declaration that marriage was "obsolete" made her better known than her early films *Tall Story* (1960) and *Period of Adjustment* (1962). Sexual roles in *Walk on the Wild Side* (1962) and *The Chapman Report* (1962) "marked her for daring or, if one disapproved, for turpitude. A billboard advertising *Circle of Love* (1965) displayed her nude on a bed. . . . no one forgave her." Playing the cartoon-like sexual role of *Barbarella* did not help. But it was anti-war politics that lost her an Oscar for *They Shoot Horses, Don't They?* (1969), a Depression era drama. Many believed that word had gone out against her before the voting. It was Maggie Smith who won the Oscar for *The Prime of Miss Jean Brodie*. Fonda did win Best Actress two years later for *Klute*, despite her escalating radicalism. In 1968 she and Donald Sutherland organized the Fuck-the-Army (FTA) review to tour Army bases with politicized entertainment as an antidote to Bob Hope's super-patriotic, hawkish tour. Even some supporters denounced them, however, as "missionaries and fakes." Yet one critic acknowledged Fonda as "the only American woman star who successfully combined a political crusade and a movie career."[14]

Mature actresses fared badly in the sixties, and were often hired to play psychotics—Joan Crawford in *Strait Jacket*, Bette Davis and Crawford in *What Ever Happened to Baby Jane?* (1962), Davis and Olivia De Havilland in *Hush, Hush, Sweet Charlotte* (1964), Zsa Zsa Gabor in *Picture Mommy Dead*, and Tallullah Bankhead in *Die! Die! My Darling.*

Crawford (1904–1977) and Davis (1908–1989) were "turned into complete travesties of themselves," writes critic Molly Haskell. Elizabeth Taylor (1932–) "bounced back and forth from heterosexual fantasy to homosexual nightmare, from hussy (*Butterfield 8*, 1960) to hustler-bait (*Suddenly Last Summer*, 1959) to harridan (*Who's Afraid of Virginia Woolf?*, 1966) to hoyden (*The Taming of the Shrew*, 1967) to hypochondriac (*Boom*, 1968)." Hollywood loved presenting women as "grotesques, villains, mummies, and utter mistakes." Haskell mocks Taylor's role as mummy-to-be in *Cleopatra* (1963). Ava Gardner (1922–) had a solid role opposite Richard Burton in *The Night of the Iguana* (1964) but was consigned to the "cast of thousands" in de Laurentis' epic *The Bible* (1966), after which her career petered out. Agnes Moorhead (1906–1974) was nominated for best supporting actress for *Hush, Hush, Sweet Charlotte* (1964) and also received four Emmy nominations for her role as the witch Endora in television's prime-time series "Bewitched" (1963–1971).[15]

The only strong, mature woman survivor was Katharine Hepburn (1907–), in her fourth decade of stardom and her sixties. Unlike contemporaries Crawford and Davis, Hepburn still received prime roles as the drug-addicted Mrs. Tyrone in *Long Day's Journey into Night* (1962) and Queen Eleanor in *The Lion in Winter* (1968). In her last movie with lover Spencer Tracy, Stanley Kramer's *Guess Who's Coming to Dinner* (1967), for which she won her second Oscar, she played opposite Katharine Houghton, her real-life niece, gently tackling a very contemporary social subject—miscegenation. Hepburn ended the decade in *The Madwoman of Chaillot* (1969) and on Broadway playing the title role in the big-budget musical comedy *Coco* (1969), about fashion designer Chanel.

There were a few strong female roles. Patty Duke (1946–), achieved stardom on Broadway at age twelve for her role as Helen Keller opposite Anne Bancroft (1931–); and they repeated the success in the film *The Miracle Worker* (1962). Bancroft received a best actress Oscar, and Duke became the youngest ever to receive one for best supporting actress; but the dramatic successes did not produce many others. Bancroft had four more major films in the decade, including the role of the unscrupulous Mrs. Robinson who seduces her daughter's boyfriend in *The Graduate* (1967). Duke's three other films of the sixties included *Valley of the Dolls* (1967). For a time, "The Patty Duke Show" was a popular television sit-com about an ingenue's adventures.

As a counterpoint to the sexual revolution, celebration of the life of the nun provided a sub-theme in the sixties popular culture. Even perky Mary Tyler Moore played a plainclothes nun in the Elvis movie *Change of Habit*. Called Soeur Sourire (Sister Smile) and the Singing Nun, the white-garbed Sister Luc-Gabrielle of Belgium and her guitar "Sister Adele" had a number one hit, "Dominique" (1963) and appeared on the *Ed Sullivan Show* just like the era's male rock stars. After Debbie Reynolds portrayed her in *The Singing Nun* (1966), the real-life nun quit the convent but failed to remain popular with her song, "Glory Be to God for the Golden Pill," celebrating the birth control banned by Rome.[16]

Haskell sees the period from 1962 to 1973 "from a woman's point of view" as "the most disheartening in screen history": "There were no working women on the screen, no sassy or smart-talking women, no mature women, and no goddesses either. There were, instead, amoral pinup girls, molls taking guff from their gangsters that would have made their predecessors gag, and thirty-year-olds reduced to playing undergraduates." Faye Dunaway (1941–), as the gun moll Bonnie Parker opposite Warren Beatty in *Bonnie and Clyde* (1967), proved that women could be as convincingly violent as men and flaunt sexuality at the same time, shattering old Production Code prohibitions. Haskell explains the deterioration of women's film roles as a backlash against "the growing strength and demands of women in real life, spearheaded by women's liberation." Women's roles were "Whores, quasi-whores, jilted mistresses, emotional cripples, drunks. Daffy ingenues, Lolitas, kooks, sex-starved spinsters, psychotics. Icebergs, zombies, and ball-breakers." Although there was no Hollywood conspiracy to counteract nascent feminism, feminism developed its radical, cutting edge in reaction to such trends in popular culture.[17]

If American films of the sixties were not liberating for women, many European films were, and had a great effect in America. Haskell credits Roger Vadim's *And God Created Women* with "throwing down the gauntlet on behalf of women's sexual freedom" because of a cultural difference in attitudes about female sexuality: "In America the voluptuous Bardot was regarded as dangerous, pornographic, a crazy nymphet, whereas in France she was applauded, especially by women. Americans were fixated on the idea of nudity, whereas the French saw Bardot as someone who was insolently, charmingly her own woman, powerful and upright (literally—they talked constantly of her wonderful posture). . . . free with her sexuality yet not promiscuous or 'bad.'" Also, Jeanne Moreau in Louis Malle's *Les Amants* deserted her husband, child, and home to run off with a lover. "This daring ending," writes Haskell, "acknowledged a fact that American movies and culture spend a good deal of energy denying: that even a loving woman is capable of going against her supposedly natural maternal instincts when seized by passion. In America Moreau was seen as pure villain, a slut who abandons her child." Haskell cites Catherine Deneuve in *Belle de Jour*, Danielle Darrieux and Antonella Lualdi in *The Red and the Black*, and Moreau in *Jules and Jim* for similar roles. In contrast, in British films starring Julie Christie, Lynn Redgrave, and Rita Tushingham, sexual liberation for the modern woman meant "a glacial aloofness and frightening isolation broken only by moments of fitful promiscuity, moments of instant now sensation—as if sex, the liberator amortizing other emotional aspects of fulfillment, ironically provided brief comfort."[18]

Only two American films stood out for depicting a woman's perspective. The film adaptation of Mary McCarthy's novel *The Group* (1966), about young women college graduates in the thirties, provided a rare opportunity for Joan Hackett, Elizabeth Hartman, Jessica Walter, Kathleen Widdoes, and other relatively unknown actresses. The one film to present a critical view of male "chauvinism" was Frank Perry's *Diary of a Mad Housewife* (1970), in which Carrie Snodgress (1946–) portrayed Tina, a woman imprisoned as the traditional wife of a dictatorial New York lawyer, attempting to live up to his ideas of the perfect mother, lover, hostess, and gourmet cook. Driven to an affair with a young writer, Tina finds only the same sort of manipulation. The film's caustic cynicism presaged the more strident strains of feminism in the seventies.

Television

Television became the nation's dominant popular cultural medium after World War II. In 1950 there were fewer than five million sets; in 1960 there were over 45 million. The 1970 census reported that 96 percent of American homes had at least one television. Media analysts Joyce Sprafkin and Robert Liebert found that "by the time an American child is fifteen years old, she has watched more hours of television that she has spent in the classroom." George Gerbner insisted in 1977, "Television is the new religion. It has to be studied as a new religion, an organic structure of rituals and myths, including the news and documentaries, but primarily serial drama." The power of the medium had proven the undoing of Senator Joseph McCarthy's demagogic, anti-Communist witchhunts; and through the Kennedy-Nixon debates, it provided the crucial margin of victory for the Democrat who set a new and different tone for the sixties.[19]

But television was slow to expand or vary roles for women. Sociologist Gaye Tuchman found that between 1969 and 1972, women had only 28 percent of the leading roles on prime-time television and only 20 percent of roles on televised plays. In 1963 only 20 percent of women on television (from 3:30 to 11 P.M. daily and 10 A.M. to 11 P.M. weekdays) were portrayed as employed, a figure that fell to 18.3 percent by 1971. Even these few were "symbolically denigrated by being portrayed as incompetent or as inferior to male workers." Women were "concentrated" in comedies with 40 percent of the roles. Children's cartoons included even fewer female characters (including anthropomorphized foxes and pussy-cats) than adult prime-time programs. Only on "soaps" aimed primarily at female viewers were there equal numbers of actresses and actors. Tuchman concludes, "The paucity of women on American television tells viewers that women don't matter much in American society. . . . The portrayal of incompetence extends from denigration through victimization and trivialization. . . . Equally important the pattern of women's involvement with television violence reveals approval of married women and condemnation of single and working women. . . . Two out of three television women are married, were married, or are engaged. . . . By way of contrast, most television men are single and have always been single."[20]

Judy Klemesrud concludes that Miss Kitty, saloonkeeper on "Gunsmoke," was "the only woman character on nighttime television who is her own woman, who is successful in her own right and who doesn't bask in the reflection of some man." All others were "unliberated ding-a-lings, sex kittens, kooky housewives, lovable widows, crimefighters' secretaries, and nosy nurses." The quintessential ding-a-lings appeared on the vaguely countercultural comedy, Dan Rowan's and Dick Martin's *Laugh-In*, which premiered on 22 January 1968, breaking previous taboos in taste with such spots as Joanne Worley, dressed to appear pregnant, singing "I Should Have Danced All Night." *Laugh-In* featured many women—Worley, Chelsea Brown, Judy Carne, and Ruth Buzzi—and sparked a lasting career for Goldie Hawn, who later went on to films. Hawn made the most of her caricature as the dumb, giggling blond on *Laugh-In*. She made her first successful film, *Cactus Flower*, 1969, breaking from character to play a would-be suicide, a role that won her an Oscar for Best Supporting Actress.[21]

Daytime rather than prime-time television has always been considered the domain of the female viewer. In the sixties, women chose from a variety of popular game shows like *Queen for a Day*, which lasted for almost a decade from the mid-fifties. Contestants tried to out-do each other with hard-luck stories. The studio audience voted on "the most oppressed," with response measured by an applause meter. Although the meter could reach a score of ten, the most pathetic only earned between eight and nine. Producers knew that housewives watched "to convince themselves that however hard or boring their lot might seem, it was roses compared to what some women suffered."[22]

Kathryn Weibel finds it significant, perhaps evidence of the shift in the culture of the decade, that when *Queen for a Day* left the air "a new type of sexist afternoon game show began. Substituting younger, more beautiful people, programs like *The Dating Game, The Newlywed Game, Dream Girl*, and *Family Game* used laughter and inane repartee as the device to reveal the superficiality, if not the outright suffering, present in relationships between couples and families." There was more than just a generation gap fragmenting American society, and television producers were ready to capitalize on all of its manifestations.[23]

Through the sixties, many women joined the increasing audience for soap operas as a favorite form of afternoon television entertainment and serialized fiction. First becoming popular as radio entertainment in 1932, the serialized "narrative form, cultural product, advertising vehicle, and source of aesthetic pleasure for tens of millions of persons" spread to television and its three major networks in the fifties. Only in the 1960–61 season did television soap operas finally supplant their radio antecedents, bringing about their demise, although in the previous five years, soap operas had remained the most popular radio shows, prime time *or* daytime. Proctor and Gamble, like other advertisers, saw television as a better medium for promoting their products; and it owned three of the highest rated "soaps"—*As the World Turns, Search for Tomorrow*, and *Guiding Light* (the longest running of them all). Another top serial, *Love of Life*, was the property of American Home Products. In 1963, NBC challenged CBS's dominance in soap operas by programming its own sponsor-owned schedule—*The Doctors* (Colgate-Palmolive) and Irna Phillips's *Another World* (Proctor and Gamble). About twelve soap operas aired daily—ranging in length from a half hour to an hour and broadcast from about ten in the morning to four in the afternoon. By 1975, an estimated 20 million Americans—almost 90 percent women of all ages, most with a high school education or more—watched them daily.[24]

From the first, soap operas were women's fiction and were aimed at female viewers from 18 to 49, mostly housewives and mothers. Assumptions about the audience affected the narrative form, as Robert

Allen notes. Unlike "normative (read 'male') categories of art and narrative," soap operas typically "lack any semblance of dramatic unity" and "their lack of ultimate closure renders them narratively anomalous." Soap operas are typically family sagas—or stories of networks of families, intermarrying across classes, providing hope for social advancement and dissipating class conflicts at the same time as they reinforce traditional moral values. Tania Modleski thinks they "provide a unique narrative pleasure which, while it has become thoroughly adapted to rhythms of women's lives in the home, provides an alternative to the dominant 'pleasures of the text.'" The form encourages "identification with numerous personalities," creating a sense of community often lacking in suburban America, and a familiarity with characters over extended periods of time that is increasingly absent from women's lives in an era of great geographic mobility and family fragmentation.[25]

Irna Phillips (1901–1973), "queen of soap operas" and writer-inventor of the serial "family drama" with her thirties radio shows, including *Today's Children*, *The Road of Life*, and *Guiding Light*, continued to be "the single most important influence on television soaps" through the sixties, adding *Another World* in 1964 and *Days of Our Lives* in 1965 to her repertoire. These soaps avoided social issues like civil rights. In *Love Is a Many-Splendored Thing* (1967–73), Phillips tried to capitalize on the popularity of Han Suyin's novel and the film of that name, with its romance between a Eurasian woman and a white American physician, an interracial plot that drew opposition from affiliate stations. New writers simply "moved the woman out of town and focused on new plot lines of romantic relationships among younger (white) characters." Certainly, the Asian character was particularly controversial during Vietnam. Rarely did soap operas of the sixties reflect larger social problems. Phillips served in 1964 as consultant on *Peyton Place*, television's first successful prime-time serial that launched several actresses' careers, and featured Dorothy Malone as Constance MacKenzie, Mia Farrow as her daughter Allison, and Barbara Parkins as Betty Anderson.[26]

Women's roles in situation comedies, though abundant, were limited by conventional expectations. Humor, the occult, the age-old association of women with witchcraft, and the suburbanization of the sixties combined to provide enough material to maintain the sitcom *Bewitched* through eight seasons, beginning in 1964. Elizabeth Montgomery as Samantha uses her benign supernatural powers to control her bungling husband Darren, her meddling mother, her children, neighbors, and even Darren's boss. The successful formula prompted *I Dream of Jeannie* in 1965 with Barbara Eden playing the mischievous genie who keeps house for astronaut Tony Nelson (Larry Hagman). The show ended in 1969 when the characters married. Similarly, in 1965, *My Living Doll* cast Julie Newmar as a sexy, female robot living with a psychiatrist (Bob Cummings). Evening television remained dominated by family situation comedies: *Ozzie and Harriet*, *The Donna Reed Show*, *Make Room for Daddy*, *Father Knows Best*, *Leave It to Beaver*.

On the Emmy-winning *Dick Van Dyke Show* (1961–66), with Mary Tyler Moore, there is a "surrogate family grouping" of Rob Petrie's work associates. Sally is "middle-aged, single, and always on the lookout for a good catch." Viewers rarely saw Buddy's wife, Bubbles, but often heard about the "ups and downs" in their relationship. Rob and Laura Petrie still had a marriage ruled by standards of the old Hollywood Production Code which mandated they sleep in separate beds and never converse in the bedroom without wearing layers of robes over long-sleeved and panted pajamas.[27]

As Kathryn Weibel points out, however, by the mid-sixties sitcoms finally began to reflect the divorce rate that had been escalating since 1950. Shows began to portray single parents with children and "spouse surrogates," male or female, while still implying that "marriage is considered more normal and obligatory for women than it is for men. Women are portrayed in confining relationships with men even when they are single and allegedly career oriented." Men coped perfectly well with family responsibilities without women, however, in *Petticoat Junction*, *The Partridge Family*, *The Ghost and Mrs. Muir*, and *My Three Sons*. From 1958 through the sixties, *Bonanza's* loyal viewers accepted it that Lorne Green's Ben Cartwright didn't need a woman to raise his sons. On *Family Affair* in 1968, Sebastian Cabot played the sophisticated Giles French, male nanny of three rich orphans.[28]

Perhaps the most visible evidence of the divorce rate appeared in the demise of the quintessential fifties family sit-com, *I Love Lucy* (originally titled *My Favorite Husband*), which paralleled the collapse of Lucille Ball's real-life marriage. Ball attempted to carry on alone with *The Lucy Show* (1962) and *Here's Lucy* (1968). Jane and Michael Stern remember, "Scheming wives were passé, so Lucy got . . . unmercifully cute. All of the energy that had gone into making Lucy Ricardo so hilarious was now applied to the Herculean task of playing perky as a middle-aged widow in a polyester pantsuit with a cigarette-ravaged croak of a voice. Lucie Arnaz [her real-life daughter] played her short-skirted, high-booted daughter in 'Here's Lucy,' but like her mom, Miss Arnaz had a sandpaper voice and a belligerent acting style that gave her attempts at perkiness a disturbing bawdy-house quality." Another sitcom featuring a lone woman was *The Ghost and Mrs. Muir* (1969), for which Hope Lange won an Emmy.[29]

Marlo Thomas projected the image of the young, optimistic, perky, young woman of the sixties as Ann Marie in *That Girl* (1966–71). As in all popular culture, "The perky girl's nonstop, heels-in-the air image was everywhere. Suddenly there were hordes of TV sit-com bachelorettes living fantasy lives in kicky apartments all over town." Marlo Thomas paved the way for Mary Tyler Moore, who graduated from being Dick Van Dyke's ditsy but Jackie Kennedyesque wife, in a show bearing *his* name, to her own named show in 1970. In the *Mary Tyler Moore Show*, she played Mary Richards, a temporarily liberated, single, working girl in Minneapolis.[30]

The positive image of the competent young working woman had already proven a successful sit-com formula in 1968 with *Julia*, starring Diahann Carroll, a comedy about a young black nurse in an integrated, middle-class community. This was the first time that a black woman played a leading role, other than as a servant, on a prime-time television series. Only a few skilled professional women had appeared on television previously, mainly in supporting roles such as Barbara Bain's Dana, the lone woman on the special IMF secret crime-fighter team in *Mission Impossible* (1966). There were only three women on the classic science fiction series *Star Trek*, first aired in 1966; and they were in stereotypical support roles as a nurse, the captain's personal yeoman (whose sexiness he found distracting), and the communications officer, Lieutenant Uhura, "evoking subliminal images of women perpetually on the telephone." Uhura's role was "further diminished because Captain Kirk consistently took over the communications function whenever important messages were being received or transmitted. By contrast, he never assumed the controls of the male navigators." Still, Nichelle Nichols, who played Uhura, inspired young black women to enter acting.[31]

Late-sixties "teen-cop" Julie of *Mod Squad* was "the first female sidekick in a crime drama series. Most passive of the adventure heroines, Julie used neither gun nor judo to ward off an antagonist. Commonly she served as a decoy, positioned in the enemy's midst until such time as superteen cops Pete and Linc could rescue her. Slim, blond, and freckled, Julie's success frequently depended on her prettiness and her look of naïveté." This popular formula inspired the seventies hit, *The Rookies*, although the role of female side-kick was diminished.[32]

Programming for children made strides only at the end of the decade with creation of the daily, hour-long *Sesame Street* in 1969 by the Children's Television Network, carried over to the new Public Broadcasting Service (PBS). Executive Director Joan Ganz Cooney aimed the show at three- to five-year-olds, especially at preschool ghetto children, attempting to give them a "head start" through early learning of numbers, letters, and language concepts. Some educators, however, criticized the frenzied pace of the program which, they argued, did not expand the audience's attention span.

Popular Fiction

Romance novels became a commodity and part of mainstream women's popular culture in the sixties as large communications conglomerates took over independent publishing houses. This takeover was "the most significant development in American publishing," according to Janice Radway. In 1954, Mary Bonnycastle, wife of the publisher of Canada's mass-market paperback empire Harlequin Enterprises, shifted her own operations from reprints of mysteries and adventure stories to reprints of romance novels purchased from British publishers; and in 1958 Harlequin itself made the formal shift. Marketed at first only in Canada, Harlequin sold almost 19 million romance novels by 1971, at which time more aggressive marketing and expansion made it a force in the United States. The formula of the Harlequin romance, which averaged 187 pages, was quickly set: "Harlequins are well-plotted, strong romances with a happy ending. They are told from the heroine's point of view and in the third person. There may be elements of mystery or adventure but these must be subordinate to the romance. The books are contemporary and settings can be anywhere in the world as long as they are authentic." Tania Modleski summarizes, "the formula rarely varies: a young, inexperienced, poor to moderately well-to-do woman encounters and becomes involved with a handsome, strong, experienced, wealthy man, older than herself by ten to fifteen years. The heroine is confused by the hero's behavior since, though he is obviously interested in her, he is mocking, cynical, contemptuous, often hostile, and even somewhat brutal. By the end, however, all misunderstandings are cleared away, and the hero reveals his love for the heroine, who reciprocates." The reader knows that the heroine has nothing to fear from the male and thus feels herself empowered by this knowledge. Romance fiction provided leisure, "what constitutes narrative pleasure for women," rather than serious reading.[33]

The rise of the romance novel was paralleled by the formulaic fiction of the "gothic" romance. In the United States, Phyllis Whitney's *Thunder Heights*, released in 1960 by Ace Books, along with Victoria Holt's *Mistress of Mellyn*, selling over a million copies for Doubleday, proved the popularity of the "gothic" romance as an alternative to the paperback mystery, sales of which had fallen off in the late fifties, especially among women readers. Appleton editor Patricia Myrer became literary agent for Whitney and the Englishwoman Holt, anticipating a great potential market for novels "whose plots centered about developing love relationships between wealthy, handsome men and 'spunky' but vulnerable women." First printings of these novels ranged from 800,000 to a million copies, making the gothic genre so successful that by the end of the decade many other publishers had entered into competition with variations on the formula—short books that could be read in one evening at bedtime or longer titles for weekend or vacation reading.

Modleski describes the formula for attracting the potential reader as initially signaled by a cover illustration of a young woman "wearing a long, flowing gown and standing in front of a large, menacing-looking castle or mansion. The atmosphere is dark and stormy, and the ethereal young girl appears to be frightened." Indeed, "in the typical Gothic plot, the heroine comes to a mysterious house, perhaps as a bride, perhaps in another capacity, and either starts to mistrust her husband or else finds herself in love with a mysterious man who appears to be some kind of criminal. She may suspect him of having killed his first wife . . . or of being out to kill someone else, most likely herself. She tries to convince herself that her suspicions are unfounded, that, since she loves him, he must be trustworthy, and that she will have failed as a woman if she does not implicitly believe in him. Often, but not always, the man is proven innocent of all wrongdoing by the end of the novel, and the real culprit is discovered and punished."[34]

The reader of the gothic novel feels as fearful and powerless as the heroine, identifying with a woman's traditional plight and perhaps experiencing the more contemporary yet deep strain of fearfulness among socially isolated women in their own suburban homes. Modleski concludes, "Gothics provide one kind of outlet for women's feelings of estrangement and the sense of disorientation consequent upon what is usually considered the most momentous change in their lives"—marriage and settling down to homemaking. "And so frequent a complaint of Gothic heroines is that environments which had in the past seemed so various and so beautiful are now menacing and ugly"—as perhaps the shiny new split-level that was the American woman's dream house had become for many a sinister place. Although Betty Friedan never drew this analogy, perhaps the Gothic novel's popularity stems from prevalence of "the problem that has no name"—the deep unease of middle-class, suburban American women. Joanna Russ calls gothics "a kind of justified paranoia: people are planning awful things about you; you can't trust your husband (lover, fiance); everybody's motives are devious and complex; only the most severe vigilance will enable you to snatch any happiness from the jaws of destruction."[35]

Gothic readership was so great that by the early seventies top gothic authors outsold equivalent writers in all other categories of paperback fiction. At a peak between 1969 and 1972, about 35 titles appeared a month and over four hundred a year, becoming "a true cultural phenomenon." Their profitability dispelled "the lingering vision of publishing as the province of literary gentlemen seriously devoted to the 'cause' of humane letters." Distributors marketed these books at supermarkets and drugstores, especially in suburbs, and then in bookstore chains like B. Dalton, founded in 1966.[36]

Mysteries and suspense novels were also a popular genre for women readers, although a more difficult field for women writers. Charlotte Armstrong (1905–1969), a.k.a. Jo Valentine, wrote a dozen mysteries from a particularly feminine perspective in the sixties. Mary Jean DeMarr writes, "Sometimes, terror is evoked when an innocent person is trapped in an enclosed space with several people, at least one of whom poses a threat"—distinctly a woman's fear. Armstrong's mysteries turn on children, elderly characters, and problems in family relationships—women's responsibilities. Patricia Highsmith (1921–), writing crime novels as Claire Morgan, won international awards for work that broke from the formula. In Highsmith's books, characters may be simultaneously innocent and guilty, crossing a fine line into criminality or insanity. Similarly, Margaret Millar (1915–) continued a well established career; and Helen McCloy (1904–), first woman president of the Mystery Writers of America, regularly produced detective and suspense novels and short stories, as she had since the forties.[37]

More women began writing fantasy and science fiction in the sixties. Leigh Brackett (1915–), who won the title "Queen of Space Opera," as one of the few women writing in that male-dominated field, produced sensuous, "rowdy, lush and exotic" stories set "on a colorful Mars, a luxuriant Venus with its Sea of Morning Opals and Mountains of White Cloud, and on a harsh, hellish Mercury." Brackett influenced younger writers like Marion Zimmer Bradley (1930–), whose "Darkover" series used primarily gay male characters. Bradley, mother of three, also wrote from a feminist/lesbian perspective shaped by her work on the *Ladder*, a lesbian magazine, publishing lesbian novels under the pseudonym Lee Chapman. Bradley, in turn, helped launch the mystery-writing career of Juanita Coulson (1933–). Breaking into the male field of science fiction was so difficult that Joan Carol Holly (1932–) used the pseudonym J. Hunter Holly to publish ten pulp novels with the recurring theme of alien invasion. Holly's work was curtailed from 1966 to 1970 by a brain tumor; but after its removal she continued writing and teaching creative writing under her own name.[38]

Only in the sixties did women sci-fi writers begin to flaunt their gender. Lillian Craig Reed (1932–) wrote as Kit Reed, a gender-neutral name. Her first sci-fi novel, *Armed Camps* (1969) created a female protagonist who retreats to a pacifist commune to avoid daily violence while her male counterpart becomes a military specialist. Margaret St. Clair used the male pseudonyms Idris Seabright and Wilton Hazzard from 1949 on, although for *Sign of the Labrys* (1963) she wrote in an unabashedly female voice. The cover blurb exclaimed: "Women are writing Science Fiction!!!!!" "Women are closer to the primitive than men. They are conscious of the moon-pulls, the earth-tides. They possess a buried memory of humankind's obscure and ancient past." Ironically, that novel had a male protagonist. *The Dolphins of Altair* (1967) reflects St. Clair's growing interest in environmentalism.[39]

Ursula Kroeber LeGuin (1929–), also mother of three, was the decade's major science-fiction writer, publishing her first story in 1962, then producing the novels *Rocannon's World* (1966), *Planet of Exile* (1966), and *City of Illusions* (1967) in the Hain series. *The Left Hand of Darkness* (1969), the fourth Hain novel, reflects LeGuin's interest in Taoism, a balance of opposites, by probing the planet Gethen/Winter, where "androgyne," humanoid hermaphrodites make love regularly a few days each month, involuntarily assuming the sexual functions of either gender. They avoid restrictive gender roles and live in peace but still face political tensions, betrayal, and disappointments. LeGuin emphasizes "the second half of the traditional quest, the return, culminating in rebirth." Influenced by her father, she has favored anthropology rather than futurist technology. In the Earthsea trilogy, beginning with *A*

Wizard of Earthsea (1967), LeGuin has probed serious human problems in a fairy-tale setting. A 1987 poll by *Locus* magazine ranked her fourth among the top twenty science-fiction novelists of all time, second only to Tolkien of top fantasy novelists. She has also won awards for her children's fiction.[40]

One of the most prolific and popular fantasy and science fiction writers was Alice Mary Norton, who used the male name André Norton to insure the popularity of over a hundred of her books—adventure stories, westerns, mysteries, and gothics. Often, Norton used the western genre with an outer-space setting. *Witch World* (1963) launched a nine-volume series, six written in the sixties, that featured strong female protagonists; and she was the first woman writer to win the coveted Gandalf award for lifetime achievement in fantasy. Other science-fiction novelists working in the sixties included Christine Brooke-Rose, Rosel George Brown (1926–1967), Diane Detzer, Zenna Henderson, Lee Hoffman, Cecelia Holland, and Evelyn E. Smith. Joan Aiken worked in the fantasy genre. Major science-fiction short story authors included Sonya Hess Dorman, Carol Fries Emshwiller, and Sydney Joyce Van Scyoc, the latter of whom offered a pantheistic environmental view from her first publication in 1962. Catherine Lucille Moore, whose sci-fi novels bore only her initials C.L. to conceal her gender, also wrote television scrips in the sixties after her husband's death. Joanna Russ published a dozen stories and one novel after her 1959 debut, launching a prominent but controversial science fiction career that did not fully reveal her lesbian-feminist perspective until the seventies. Kate Meredith Wilhelm married Damon Knight, science fiction writer and editor, in 1963 and started writing her own psychological science fiction stories and novels featuring female protagonists.[41]

Juvenile fiction was always more open to female authors. Harriet Stratemeyer Adams (1892–1982), who began writing popular juvenile literature series in 1930 under various pseudonyms, continued her prolific writing in the sixties, contributing to the Nancy Drew Mysteries and Dana Girls Series under the name Carolyn Keene, to the Hardy Boys Series as Franklin W. Dixon, to the Tom Swift Series as Victor Appleton II, and to the Bobbsey Twin Series as Laura Lee Hope. As Ann Sheldon, she wrote four books in the Linda Craig Series between 1960 and 1966. Mary Childs Jane (1910–1991) wrote the popular Mary Jane mysteries.

Some popular writers broke from formulas. Jacqueline Susann entered the *Guinness Book of World Records* in the fall of 1969 for selling

6.8 million copies of *Valley of the Dolls* in the first six months after publication. Susann immediately followed that success with another best-seller, *The Love Machine*, which she doggedly pushed on television talk-shows, becoming a celebrity. Perhaps Andrea Dworkin had Susann as well as many male authors in mind when she complained that sixties women were "traded, gang-banged, collected, collectivized, objectified, and turned into the hot stuff of pornography," largely through popular literature and the media.[42]

Music: Jazz and Country-Pop

In the heyday of jazz through the fifties, women confronted formidable odds, including the belief that women could and should not play most instruments. Critic Bill Cole describes "tremendous male chauvinism in jazz . . . too often women have been treated as mere sex objects or exploited . . . by members of the orchestra." Many women found increasing difficulties in the sixties as distinct categories of music blurred—blues, gospel, jazz, country, and rock—to become amalgams like "soul" or modern jazz. Women traditionally excelled as vocalists, but even classic jazz singers "were destroyed or diminished in the fast-moving scene" which fell on hard times in the sixties, competing with the popular music industry. Willene Barton (1913–), tenor saxophonist and head of a group (1959–60), remembers that "when the always precarious business of jazz nearly toppled under the onslaught of rock and soul," she "just dropped out. I got tired of leading a band, 'cause to afford a certain type of musician you have to be making a certain kind of money. So I couldn't afford the kind of musicians I needed, and . . . some of them had gotten out of the business."[43]

Lena Horne, Carmen McRae, Ella ("First Lady of Song") Fitzgerald, Anita O'Day, Chris Connor, June Christie, Nancy Wilson, Pearl Bailey, and Sarah Vaughan made the transition from the big band era of the forties to the solo performances of the sixties but found their careers less prosperous. Eartha Kitt moved to France where she found a bigger audience. Despite a few recordings and concerts, the once-prominent career of Helen Hume (1913–1981) "reached a nadir" in 1967, although she would later stage a comeback. Some younger vocalists persisted. Annie Ross, a white singer, joined Jon Hendricks and Dave Lambert in 1958 to form a trio and became popular for her ability as a lyricist to simulate instrumental sounds. She quit the group in 1962 because of poor health and opened Annie's Room, a London jazz club. Dinah

Washington (born Ruth Jones, 1924–1963), the most popular black female singer of the fifties, ranged from gospel to blues and jazz until her
death from alcohol and diet pills. Morgana King (1930–), Carol Sloane
(1937–), Irene Kral (1932–), Helen Milcetic Merrill (1930–), Teddi King
(1929–1977), and Shirley Horn (1934–) were other major jazz vocal
stylists in the sixties. Sheila Jordan (1928–) developed her singing talents after moving from Detroit to New York. Backed by composer
George Russell, she recorded *Portrait of Sheila*, her debut album in
1963; but because her vocal styling was difficult to classify, she found
jobs few and far between until the seventies. After Nancy Wilson
(1937–) released her first album, *Like in Love* (1960), she was called "the
singularly most important singer of the decade" or "the girl with a thousand beautiful faces," able to "lift a song off the printed page and groove
it to her own identity." In the sixties, Wilson expanded her creative
work to embrace acting for television and theatre.[44]

Singer, pianist, and composer Nina Simone (born Eunice Waymon
in 1933), brought "a gospel intensity to her brand of secular preaching."
From 1959 on, she used music to extend her civil rights activism with
songs like "Mississippi Goddamn" and set to music the poetry of many
black writers. Her own "Four Women" is "a starkly drawn portrait of
the stereotypical roles assigned to black women in America, a sharp
line-drawing of social realities."[45]

Abbey Lincoln (born Gaby Lee) left nightclub performing in the
early sixties to team up with Thelonious Monk, pianist Mal Waldron,
and her husband, percussionist Max Roach, and to write or perform
music for several albums, "searing statements of black reality and consciousness" like "We Insist! Freedom Now Suite" (1960), and "Straight
Ahead (. . . to Nowhere)" (1961). Her "rather grainy vocal texture, a
sweet-and-sour delivery and a broad emotional range, from scathing to
buoyantly joyful" accentuated the "bitterness and coiled-up, near-
claustrophobic rage" of these compositions.[46]

Development of "free" or "experimental" modern jazz provided some
opportunities for women. Jeanne Lee (1939–) built upon experience in
both classical song and spirituals in the early sixties when she signed
an RCA contract to record her "sound poems," which she describes as
"making your own words, making sounds, being a cloud, being a vi-
bration, being a voice, many voices. The [free-form] instrumentalists
are doing the same thing—finding new ways of working through their
horns." Jay Clayton performed both traditional and experimental jazz
song.[47]

Singers in the sixties broke down boundaries between gospel, blues, jazz, rhythm and blues, and pop music. Roberta Flack (1940–), trained in classical piano, shifted her interest to Afro-American music in 1965, blending musical styles. Other examples of this trend are Lorez Alexandria and Dakota Staton (1932–). The decade also witnessed a revival of interest in blues and rediscovery by some afficianados of "old-timers" like Big Maybelle Smith (1924–1972); but she would never achieve the star status of the likes of Janis Joplin, who drew heavily on the work of Big Mama Thornton (1925–) and Bessie Smith (d. 1937).

Female jazz pianists always found acclaim. Although Nellie Lutcher (1915–) retired to real estate and Hazel Scott (1920–) to roles on television series in the sixties, Rose Murphy (Matthews) (1913–) and Dorothy Donegan (1924–) continued long careers; and Patricia Brown (1931–) made the transition to R & B, recording with Aretha Franklin. Shirley Scott (1934–), "First Lady of the Organ," formed a trio with Stanley Turrentine (later her husband) in the early sixties and performed on several "definitive" recordings with the likes of Count Basie, Duke Ellington, Charlie Mingus, and John Coltrane.[48]

Mary Lou Williams (born Mary Elfreida Scruggs-Burley, 1910–1981), "The First Lady of Jazz" and "an unique, living repository of jazz history," continued major performances at clubs, campuses, and festivals, giving lecture-concerts at the Smithsonian and Whitney Museum and recording extensively. She initiated and produced the Pittsburgh Jazz Festival in 1964 and composed many works, including *Mary Lou Mass*, "an encyclopedia of black music . . . from spirituals to bop and rock," which premiered in 1971 with choreography by Alvin Ailey.[49]

Younger women also emerged as jazz keyboardists. Although pianist Joanne Brackeen (1938–) retired for a time, after her marriage to saxophonist Charles Brackeen, to "make sure my children had a mother during their younger years," she still played and wrote music, and that was enough. When they moved to New York in 1965, she began to appear in public again." By 1969, she won a prestigious position with Art Blakey and the Jazz Messengers.[50]

Toshiko Akiyoshi (1929–) immigrated from Japan to the United States in 1956 to study at Boston's Berklee College of Music and was immediately recognized as a talented keyboardist and composer; but she recalls, "I dealt with both racial and sexual prejudice. I played clubs and TV wearing a kimono, because people were amazed to see an Oriental woman playing jazz." Patti Brown (1931–), a classical pianist, switched to jazz and joined the Quincy Jones band in 1960, although she often performed solo and provided original compositions for other major jazz performers. Black pianist, organist, and composer Amina Claudine Myers, based in Chicago, was one of the few women involved in the influential collective, the Association for the Advancement of Creative Musicians (AACM). Critics described her music as "an eclectic mix—strong doses of gospel-barrelhouse-blues as well as the rumble and crash of modern atonality, stride piano meshing with spirituals, then yielding to avant-garde 'free' playing of a characteristic, nervous intensity."[51]

Alice McLeod Coltrane (1937–) returned to the U.S. in the early sixties after studying with expatriate pianist Bud Powell in Europe. Versatile on keyboards, vibraphone, and percussion, she teamed with different musicians, then met and married tenor saxophonist John Coltrane. Continuing her career while giving birth to three sons, she replaced McCoy Tyner in Coltrane's quartet from 1966 until her husband's death in 1967. Always drawn by "musical spiritualism and mysticism," she converted to Hinduism, took the name Turiya Apaina, and from 1968 on turned to the harp, tamboura, organ, and wind chimes to achieve "tranquilizing and meditative effects." She explained, "I would like to play music according to the ideals set forth by John and continue to let a cosmic principle of the aspect of spirituality be the underlying reality behind the music as he had."[52]

Vera Auer, a vibraphonist, immigrated from Austria in 1961, studied at John Lewis' School of Jazz in Lenox, Massachusetts, and formed her own jazz group. Carol Kaye, dubbed the "chick with a pick," became part of the Los Angeles jazz scene playing an electric bass guitar, but worked as a typist to support herself. Mary Osborne (1921–) was an early electric jazz guitarist, successful on the East Coast for three decades before moving to California in 1968, where she and her husband operated the Osborne Guitar Company, manufacturing guitars and amplifiers as well as teaching music, while she continued to perform. Guitars, pianos, and even vibraphones had always been thought permissible for female musicians, often coupled with their vocals; playing other instruments met with more resistance.[53]

Despite the persistent belief that "Girls who want to be musicians should stick to instruments . . . the playing of which doesn't detract from their feminine appeal," many women played wind and percussion instruments. Valve trombonist Maxine Sullivan (born Marietta Williams in 1911) was "lured back into show business" from retirement in

1968 to tour internationally with The World's Greatest Jazzband. El-
vira "Vi" Redd (1930–), acclaimed "the leading female saxophonist . . .
in the history of jazz," performed "in every major jazz festival in the
world" in the sixties with the likes of Count Basie and Dizzie Gillespie.
Liner notes for her recorded work in the 1970 Charlie Parker Memorial
concerts in Chicago describe her as "the beautiful lady-progenitor of
the Parker style . . . as creative and facile as any male counterpart."
Evelyn Young (1928–) was often the lone female in blues, jazz, and
R & B bands, especially in Memphis, and was noted for her talents on
saxophone, clarinet, and piano. Clora Bryant played the trumpet in a
number of distinguished bands but remembers, "Being a woman, and
being a black woman, and playing a trumpet—that's three things I consider against me. Now, if I played the piano, I don't think sex or race
would enter into it. With the wind instruments, though there's competition, period."[54]

By decade's end, more opportunities opened for younger musicians
with instruments once considered male. Barbara Donald (1942–) sang
as well as played the trumpet and saxophone, becoming a rare female
presence in the sixties avant-garde, "free," or "experimental" modern
jazz scene, although she felt in the seventies that she was "still struggling to become accepted as a woman artist, and fighting this planet's
low conception of music." The petite Janice Robinson (1951–), whose
"powerful personality surged forth when she spoke through the trombone," launched a career that spanned jazz, Broadway, the symphony,
and several television spots from 1967–70.[55]

Trombonist Melba Liston (1926–) developed jazz credentials that surpassed those of most male performers by the late fifties. A critic described her style: "her tone is warm, yet light and delicate; she brings
forth a soufflé of sound. No pyrotechnics, no dazzle—but she swings.
Better, she sings with her trombone (and on rare occasions with her
voice, in a manner evocative of Billie Holiday—as if something were
being broken, then put together in a new way)." She orchestrated the
album *Lonely and Sentimental* (1960) for singer Gloria Lynn, toured with
Quincy Jones's Orchestra, acted and played in the musical *Free and
Easy*. She composed and arranged music on a freelance basis for many
major commissions—by Count Basie, Duke Ellington, Diana Ross, and
other notables.[56]

Although many still discouraged women from percussion instruments as "unladylike" Pauline Braddy Williams (1922–) was called
"Queen of the Drums" and "a second Chick Webb." Dottie Giaimo

Dodgion (1929–) began playing the drums after marrying alto sax player Jerry Dodgion; her first husband had frowned on her drumming. Dodgion remarks, "I know several lady players who were really very, very good, but they didn't get support from their husbands and they gave it up. That would be competition: 'Who do you love? Me or your instrument?' . . . If they only realized that the happier a woman is with herself, the happier she could be with him." When the Dodgions moved to New York in 1961, her career took off, despite grueling male competition: "You had to prove yourself all the time, everyplace. A woman drummer—you think they were going to differentiate? But I . . . tried not to get an attitude, tried not to be bitter because of that. Bitterness wouldn't have helped me at all to improve myself." Her first break with Benny Goodman's band helped her find work with other notable musicians, keeping her busy through the sixties. Still, she remembers discrimination: "You have to be better than better. All the instruments are male-dominated. . . . [and] the drums are—pardon the expression—the balls of the band. When a guy turns around and sees a lady sitting there, it threatens his manhood some way. . . . It used to be piano players and singers—that's the only thing ladies were fit for. Guitar once in a while." Professional women drummers were rare.[57]

Few women were involved in the business of jazz, although Victoria Spivey established her own label, Spivey/Queen Vee Records, in the sixties. Helen Keane developed a prominent career as jazz manager and producer in the sixties from beginnings as a teen-aged secretary at MCA. It was the largest talent booking agency in the world in the forties, but had a definite rule against women becoming agents. Nevertheless, her first client was Harry Belafonte. After marriage and a baby, she transferred to CBS, buying television talent rather than selling musicians, and developing her natural executive abilities. After a second marriage and a second child, she opened her own management office in her apartment in 1962. She became manager for the great jazz pianist Bill Evans from 1967 on; but she also promoted dancer-choreographer Alvin Ailey and other musicians. She produced records for Evans and others and in 1968 co-produced the first Montreux Jazz Festival.[58]

One of the most successful women on both the creative and the business end of sixties jazz was Carla Borg Bley (1938–). She began as a pianist but was encouraged by her jazz pianist husband Paul, himself at the center of the sixties' California avant-garde jazz movement, to become a composer as a means of "keeping the royalties in the family."

After 1959, she specialized in "miniature" or "haiku-like" pieces, taking a "fresh and challenging approach to writing music, [and] at a time when many artists were reaching beyond chord changes, exploring the music of other continents and otherwise departing from established conventions." After divorcing Bley, she married Michael Mantler, a 1965 founder of the Jazz Composers Orchestra, which showcased the work of experimental composers. They developed the New Music Distribution Service to help get the music from two hundred small independent record companies out to the public. As a composer, Bley earned international stature with *Escalator over the Hill*, an opera produced from 1967 to 1972 and recorded on a three-record set. She describes it as a "chronotransduction," using an eclectic combination of musicians and singers and "multilingual and multicultural in its borrowings from musical sources around the world." Critics called it a tour de force, "an ironic, engaging and poetic reading of the sixties," resisting musical classification, "as stoned as the times it reflects" and as influenced by the Beatles as by jazz.[59]

Trends of the sixties led to a rediscovery of jazz roots as well as to modernism. The veteran pianist and vocalist Wilhelmina "Billie" Goodson Pierce (1907–) continued to work with her cornetist-husband De De to keep alive New Orleans Jazz at Preservation Hall. Another New Orleans traditionalist was pianist Dolly Douroux Adams (1904–), who formed the Dolly Adams Band with her three sons. Lady Charlotte's Men of Rhythm, organized by Olivia Charlotte Cook and the group formed by Emma Barrett performed traditional jazz. Accordionist Ida Guillory fronted for her otherwise all-male Queen Ida's Bon Ton Zydeco Band, with her son on percussion, playing "a heavily syncopated, ethnic, and danceable" music similar to reggae but tapping the roots of black music of the Bayou, the birthplace of blues and jazz.[60]

Despite the passing from prominence of fifties pop singers like Doris Day and Rosemary Clooney, and despite the rise of rock 'n' roll, a field remained for balladeers. Country music carried on the tradition of fifties pop music at the same time as it became more commercial, reinvigorated by honky-tonk and the saga song. The Country Music Association (CMA), founded in 1958, encouraged radio programming of music staged by the Grand Ole Opry and produced primarily in Nashville. The number of all-country stations rose from 81 in 1961 to 328 in 1966. Indeed, half of the records released in the sixties came from Nashville. Country music played to an audience limited primarily by class (working) and geography (southern and midwestern) as in the fifties. It still attracted older listeners. The average listener was 30 to 40, married with two children, a skilled or semi-skilled worker earning about $6,000 or a housewife, living in or near a metropolitan area. Although there were major female country singers throughout the sixties, only male performers were elected to the Country Music Hall of Fame and Museum, from its 1961 founding through 1967.[61]

Through folk festival appearances, "Mother" Maybelle Carter became a major influence on the early-sixties city folk revival, especially for Joan Baez. In 1927, the Carter Family had emerged from the Virginia-Tennessee Blue Ridge region and had "virtually invented country music as we now know it." The trio—Maybelle and Sara, cousins, and Maybelle's brother-in-law A. P.—had a close-harmony singing style accompanied by Maybelle's flat-picking guitar on classics like "Worried Man Blues," "Foggy Mountain Top," "Wildwood Flower," and "Can the Circle Be Unbroken."[62]

Following the example of Kitty Wells (born Muriel Deason), who opened up country music to women in the fifties, other singers vied for the title of "Queen of Country Music"—among them Jan Howard, Wanda Jackson, Jeannie Seely, Marion Worth, Jean Shepard, and Dottie West. Some, like pop singers Patti Page and Doris Day, crossed over from the characteristic country style to pop vocals and probed recurring themes of women's response to infidelity, divorce, and husbands' drinking. Theirs were songs of maudlin sentimentality, tales of love lost and a woman's subordination to "her man" in a working-class, if not actually rural America characterized as country. Melba Montgomery became an overnight sensation in 1963, her meteoric rise matched by that of Connie Smith with "Once a Day" in 1964. Skeeter Davis (born Mary Frances Penick) profited from the honky-tonk resurgence. Mary John Wilkin, teamed with Danny Dill, became a major country songwriter, authoring "The Long Black Veil," which was recorded by various country performers as well as Joan Baez.[63]

Tammy Wynette, a former Tupelo, Mississippi, hairdresser, became a leading country vocalist after her first recording in 1966. Like so many other country singers, her songs like "Your Good Girl's Gonna Go Bad" documented women's images and reality in working class America. She crossed over to pop charts with "D-I-V-O-R-C-E" (1968) and "Stand By Your Man" (1969). Loretta Lynn, a coal miner's daughter from Butcher Hollow, Kentucky, sang songs ranging from traditional country weepers to "tough-woman songs that are nearly female honky-tonk," like "You Ain't Woman Enough to Get My Man" and

"Before I'm Over You" to social commentary like "The Pill" and "One's on the Way"—"examples of instinctive working-class feminism." Her "Dear Uncle Sam" tells of a woman's sadness on losing her "sweetheart" in the war. Lynn was featured as "the nation's most popular country singer," on the Wilburn Brothers' syndicated television show.[64]

The new career of soprano Dolly Parton (1946–) was perhaps the major event in country music in the sixties, standing out in contrast to the persisting pattern. Moving to Nashville after graduating from high school in 1964, Dolly, fourth of a dozen children, married construction contractor Carl Dean and pursued a singing career. Her "big break" came in 1967 when she replaced "Miss Norma Jean" Beasler, "one of the most highly regarded and authentic-sounding female country entertainers in the nation," as co-host of Porter Wagoner's syndicated television show, which was carried by more than a hundred stations. Parton recorded eight Top-Ten hits with Wagoner until she went solo in 1973.[65]

Parton was "one of the few successful country singers who did not adopt the nasal whine that characterized country singing." Her pure, clear-as-a-bell voice recalled the folk tradition of the thirties that was alive still in her youth in the Blue Ridge region of East Tennessee. Also, "in contrast to the often tragic and always exhausting lives of so many female country singers," Parton "always retained an impression of being mistress of her own destiny, adapting, but never compromising, her style and material to suit demands made of her" in the business. Yet her prolific autobiographical lyrics embodied "the proper Southern virtues of fundamentalist religion, respect for the family, worship of one's parents, praise for the right husband/lover, and weepy, heartfelt laments over the wrongs suffered at the hands of a callous/drinking/running-around husband." She first hit the top of the country charts as a solo act in 1970, the year of her first album. Parton created her trademark image by caricaturing a "busty blonde" but never suggesting vulnerability.[66]

Nashville country music isolated itself from the new youth-oriented pop (discussed in chapter eight, "Youth Culture"). The pop audience of the sixties barely knew the country stars, even though many were young themselves. This split grew during the Vietnam War, which was regularly defended by country music artists. Rare crossovers occurred between country and pop charts—Brenda Lee succeeded on several occasions and Paul and Paula with "Hey Paula" (1962). In contrast, the Memphis sound, with recordings generally classed as rhythm and blues

(R&B), produced a few nationally known hits like "Angel of the Morning" (1968), by Merillee Rush and the Turnabouts. Linda Ronstadt, with the Stone Poneys in 1967 and later solo, returned to a more traditional pop music that defied classification as rock while making concessions to country and folk music.

Sports

Through the sixties, the institutions of organized academic, amateur, and professional sports became even more patriarchal and sexist than before, with few programs and areas fully open to women beyond traditional female fields—tennis, ice skating, swimming, field hockey, golf, track, gymnastics, volleyball; and in those, great discrepancies remained despite the decade's supposed movement toward equality. The "Female Athletic Revolution" did not make headway until the seventies. Through the sixties, women faced great opposition from both the public and the professionals, who perpetuated the myths of female masculinization, levying innuendoes of lesbianism, and criticizing the "unfeminine" aggressiveness of physical competition or muscular development. Fitness was not feminine, but suspect. From elementary school on, few girls were socialized to enjoy let alone to excel in sports. Lore continued to circulate that athletic girls risked damaging their reproductive systems if not their heterosexuality and marriage chances.

Rather, girls aspired to be the cheerleaders on the sidelines of the games, dressed in cute, sexy, scanty uniforms and performing non-taxing choreographed gymnastics. Selection to prestigious high school, college, or university cheerleading "squads" amounted to popularity or beauty contests rather than true measures of athletic ability. Other girls exhibited dexterity and even competitiveness as baton twirlers, performing as majorettes before high school and some college bands with the more proficient making their way to the National Baton Twirling Institute, called by its male director "the second largest girls' youth movement in America" and an individualistic sport.[67]

Female sports stars emerged, nonetheless. On 3 September 1960, U.S. sprinter Wilma "Skeeter" Rudolph (1940–) won in track and field an unprecedented third Olympic gold medal in Rome, winning the nicknames "Black Pearl," "Tennessee Tornado," "Chattanooga Choo-Choo," and the "Natural Gazelle." Rudolph had to fight racism as well as sexism. She remembers, "When I got back from the Olympics, my hometown [Clarkesville, Tennessee,] which had never been integrated, decided to have a parade for me. I told them I could not come to a parade that would be segregated. So, I sort of broke that barrier in my hometown. . . . it was to pave the way for other blacks in the town." Race was not Rudolph's only hurdle. Either she had to defend her femininity, protesting she was not a "tomboy," or she endured publicity that focused on her gender rather than ability. In 1960 the *New York Times* condescendingly described her "bright plaid skirt" and the "delicate gold buttons on her purple bodice," noting her apology for black flat "slippers," "my legs get too tired if I wear [high heels] before a race."[68]

Despite such odds, other American women excelled in track and field. The Mississippian Willye B. White, a five-time Olympian in track and field from the fifties through the seventies, ran her way out of a racist culture to international prominence and appointment to Johnson's President's Commission on Olympian Sports. Supported by a rare athletic scholarship at Tennessee State University, Rudolph's alma mater, Wyomia Tyus (1945–) from Griffin, Georgia, became the "world's fastest female" in the 1964 Olympics; and in 1968, she anchored the U.S. women's 400-meter relay team in victory. Madeline Manning Jackson won a gold medal and set a 2:0.9 world record in the 800-meter event in 1968.

Newsworthy accomplishments followed as more Olympic events opened for women—in 1960, the 800-meter track, Kayak pairs, foil fencing, and the 200-meter breaststroke; in 1964, the 400-meter individual track event, the Pentathlon, and the 400-meter medley; in 1968, the 200- and 800-meter freestyle swimming, 100-meter breaststroke, 200-meter backstroke, and 200-meter butterfly. As the Olympics opened up, so did wells of skepticism about female athletes' sexuality. In 1968, the Barr Sex Test was administered for the first time. Women of all nationalities lined up for doctors to determine their femininity and receive certification. Inherent was the notion that athletic women were so masculine that they might not be real women. The test revealed an intrinsic sexism that questioned any physically talented woman. Myths prevailed that athletics would make girls masculine or that athletic women might indeed be men.[69]

Figure skating always had public appeal as the most feminine Olympic event. In 1960, Carol Heiss (1940–) fulfilled her deathbed promise to her mother to win an Olympic gold medal, then chose retirement, proclaiming, "I want to get an education and marry and have a family. Skating is for now. Education and marriage are for always." Peggy

Fleming won even more media acclaim along with a gold medal in women's figure skating at the 1968 Olympics in Grenoble. Gymnastics also seemed an acceptably graceful feminine sport. Cathy Rigby was the first American woman to win a medal in international competition at the 1970 World Gymnastic Championships in Yugoslavia.[70]

One of the great symbolic events that opened sports to amateur women came in 1967 when Katherine "Kathy" Switzer "illegally" ran the Boston Marathon. John "Jock" Semple, "father" of the amateur event, was so infuriated when she "sneaked" in, registered only under a first initial, that he tried to run her down, and was blocked only by her boyfriend's interference. Roberta Gibb had tried to register in 1966, receiving a blunt refusal. The Amateur Athletic Union (AAU) and the Boston Athletic Association (BAA) did not formally sanction women as contestants until 1972.[71]

Tennis star Billie Jean Moffitt King, a fireman's daughter, was undoubtedly the decade's most famous sportswoman. Unseeded at age seventeen in 1961 and coached by Alice Marble, she doubled with Karen Hantze to make up the most precocious team to that date at Wimbledon, generally considered a "world championship." King won major events in 1962 and 1965 and emerged as a leading "amateur" international player in 1966 in singles, in doubles teamed with Rosemary "Rosie" Casals, and in mixed doubles—the first American sweep of the decade. The Associated Press declared her Female Athlete of the Year in 1967, as her successes continued; and in 1968, she won Wimbledon singles for the third straight year and doubles with Casals for the second. In 1968 King successfully pleaded for "open" tennis, integrating pros and amateurs in prize money tournaments; but that was a minor victory.[72]

King, Casals, the Englishwoman Ann Haydon Jones, and the Frenchwoman Françoise Durr pioneered in professionalizing women's tennis by helping Gladys Heldman organize sponsorship by the Philip Morris tobacco company, manufacturer of the new Virginia Slims cigarette, which was marketed to women. Winning the Italian tennis championship in 1970, King took home $600 compared to the male prize of $3,500. King and colleagues became the first professional women's troupe, boycotting Jack Kramer's Pacific Southwest Tournament when he refused to allot women more than 1/12th of prize money—$1,500 for women versus $12,500 for men. Thereafter, the Virginia Slims tournament, advertised as "Ballbusters," became an annual women's event. King, Casals, Nancy Richey, Heldman, and five other top tennis players formed a professional women's circuit in 1970 and were promptly expelled from the anachronistic United States Lawn Tennis Association (USLTA) which still held that women's tennis should be a vocation for those wealthy enough to support themselves on the competition circuit. King's victories continued to 1971, when she became the first woman athlete to win over $100,000 a year. She "retired." in 1975, having won 19 Wimbledon titles and having lent her celebrity to the burgeoning women's movement.[73]

Similarly, professional golf had long been popular for women but was so much less lucrative than for men that talented Carol Mann considered quitting in 1963 due to the time requirements and financial burden of touring with the Ladies' Professional Golfing Association (LPGA). Mary Kathryn "Mickey" Wright (1935–) left Stanford for the professional golfing tour in the mid-fifties and became the first major female "star" since Babe Didrikson. From 1960 to 1963, Wright won the Vare Trophy for the woman with the lowest average strokes per round (73,25), with an unprecedented grand slam in 1961—the U.S. Open, LPGA, and Title Holders, equivalent to the male Masters' championships. In her 1963 heyday, she broke records and dominated the women's tour, profiting from the recent increase in women's prize money to earn over $30,000. Wright campaigned for gender parity in golfing purse money, which came nowhere near matching the $1 million purse for male golfers. Still, she protested, "it's out of line for society to pay athletes that far out of proportion to what they pay really important people like scientists, teachers, and others who help preserve our civilization." Her efforts were unsuccessful. In 1967, Kathy Witworth became the top female prize winner of $32,937 compared to Jack Nicklaus's $188,998; and such discrepancies continued for years.[74]

Through the sixties, sports media increasingly discriminated against women behind and in front of the scenes. *Sports Illustrated* continued "both the symbolic annihilation and trivialization of women in sport." For the first time in 1967, not one sportswoman appeared on its cover. There were no female athletes' photographs in the magazine in 1961– 62 and 1965–70. When women's images appeared, they were in passive, not active poses. Few advertisements featured women, even as sex objects. On television, Ellie Riger worked in various jobs in ABC Sports, becoming associate producer of live coverage of the 1968 Olympics in Grenoble and Mexico City. Confined to low-level editing and sales tasks, she resigned discouraged in 1969 to free-lance. Her plight spurred NOW to campaign against media discrimination in 1972, winning her an appointment as the first female producer in television sports.[75]

Problems of discrimination in female college sports preoccupied delegates at the 1969 Women's Sports Conference in Denver, sponsored by the Division of Girls' and Women's Sports of the American Association of Health, Physical Education, and Recreation; still, development of athletics for women depended primarily on voluntarism under the Amateur Athletic Union (AAU). In the academic year 1970–71, only 294,015 girls (seven percent) were involved in interscholastic sports on the secondary school level; in 1971–72, only 31,000 women participated on the college level. Allen Guttman cites the Syracuse, New York, school system as representative in 1969 with $90,000 allotted for boys' sports versus $200 for girls; and the latter was cut when the budget was tight. Discrepancies were even greater on the college level.[76]

Female physical educators from 278 colleges and universities finally met in 1971 to replace the inactive Women's Division of the National Collegiate Athletics Association (NCAA) with the Association for Intercollegiate Athletics for Women (AIAW); but even then, factions emerged—those who would "masculinize" women's sports versus those for a feminist alternative without competition, scholarships, and championships. Female athletes had few opportunities in organized high school or college sports until implementation of Title IX of the Higher Education Act of 1972 that prohibited exclusion "on the basis of sex" from "any interscholastic, club, or intramural athletics"; and even then, implementation came slowly.[77]

Advances in professional women's sports surpassed advances in amateur athletics with many firsts in the sixties, but even these were minor compared to the expansion of professional men's sports. Some of the sixties' advances for sportswomen were merely token media events. In 1969, Diane Crump (1949–) became the first woman jockey to ride in a Hialeah Parimutuel Race; and Barbara J. Rubin became the first winning female jockey at an American thoroughbred track in Charles Town, West Virginia. As with other changes rooted in the sixties, real progress did not occur until the seventies or after. One historian describes conditions for women through the early seventies as "evolutionary" and only later "revolutionary."[78]

Still, increasingly visible advances made by sixties sportswomen offered new and immediate models for individualistic ambitions to surmount one's "personal best," to surpass qualified competitors, and to expand established limitations—models and metaphors for the rewards of hard work and proof of skills that had long been there for men. Women's areas of competition and striving before the sixties were more traditionally circumscribed to beauty pageants, cheerleading competitions, bake-offs, and culinary contests. Those continued, but increasing media focus on women's sports inspired many young women in all fields of endeavor to pursue goals that had not before been within their grasp or considered suitable to their sex, to hope for recognition similar to that of men based on ability and in areas that had been male monopolies. In sports as in other areas of American popular culture, women broke through previously set bounds. Media, that did so much to perpetuate the status quo, unwittingly paved the way for women changing the future and their place in it.

8

Youth Culture

Youth culture developed in the sixties to become more than synonymous with popular culture, indeed, to dominate it as lucrative new
industries arose to tap the market of baby boom teenagers. Women
were important both as producers and consumers, although often overshadowed by a dominant masculinity.[1]

Popular Music

Women shaped the popular music associated with youth; but as in
other areas of endeavor, they were often manipulated and exploited.
Behind the scenes, marriage, managers' greed, and lack of support from
record labels cut short many women's budding careers. Themes in the
music reinforced traditional gender roles. Women sang of girls' quests
to capture husbands through dating, while men boasted of having
women "under their thumbs."

Entrepreneurs of the growing popular music business realized that
baby-boom teen-aged girls constituted a major new market for male
"teen idols" from 1959 to 1963. Magazines like *Sixteen*, *Dig*, and *Teen*,
and television shows like Dick Clark's *American Bandstand* purveyed and
promoted popular music, appealing primarily to female fans. Film media relied on visual "cuteness" and "personality" more than musical ability or originality to sell songs by the likes of Paul Anka, Bobby Darin,
Frankie Avalon, and Ricky Nelson. Promoters hoped to surpass the

financial success of the male "heart-throb" Frank Sinatra with a previous generation of "bobby-soxers," believing that mothers would not object to their daughters' "swooning" over clean-cut young male stars of the sort they would not mind greeting at their doors as dates. Such performers were marketed as alternatives to the more sexually "dangerous" and "hoody" images of Elvis or Jerry Lee Lewis.

A few girl performers were promoted similarly—Brenda Lee (1944–), Connie Francis (born Concetta Franconero in 1938), and former Mouseketeer Annette Funicello. Lee made both pop and country charts with her Nashville recordings, her childlike voice reflecting the cadence of black rhythm and blues. Between 1959 and 1966, "Little Miss Dynamite" accumulated 19 hits on the Billboard top twenty list, including "Sweet Nothings," "I'm Sorry," and "I Want to Be Wanted." During her 1960 tour, her manager spread the rumor she was a 32-year-old midget. Lee, like Connie Francis, appealed both to adults and teens, continuing the age ambiguity of fifties music. Francis updated oldies like "Among My Souvenirs" (1960), "Together" (1961), and "If I Didn't Care"; and she remained popular throughout the decade in Italy and Spain.

ABC's *American Bandstand*, which had been broadcast five afternoons a week for an hour and a half since 1957 to millions of teen-aged viewers, was by 1961 one of the highest-rated daytime television shows ever. Regulars included Justine Carrelli, Arlene Sullivan, Arlene de Pietro, Barbara Levick, Pat Molittieri, and Frani Giordano—Philadelphia school girls, most from West Catholic High. As lead dancers to the week's *Billboard* hits, they became stars, receiving about 15,000 fan letters a week. Along with teen starlets like Annette Funicello, Connie Stevens, and Shelley Fabares, they made it fashionable to be Italian-American. Charlotte Greig judges that they "helped to provide the nation with a specifically feminine idea of the teenager, one . . . fairly close to reality. The Bandstand girl, ordinary yet fascinating, with her sprayed hair and her dance routines, proved herself to be at the heart of rock 'n' roll."[2]

Bandstand popularized Chubby Checker's record "The Twist" in the fall of 1960, launching a dance craze of swivelling hips that shocked television censors and led parents and moralists to condemn it. The Twist swept the nation—a craze into 1962. *Time* and *Newsweek* did feature stories. Celebrities like Judy Garland and ZsaZsa Gabor twisted at New York's Peppermint Lounge. It was the first of a series of liberating dances that would offend elders. Partners did not touch but moved wildly, improvising to the rock beat; men no longer "led" women through their steps. Watusi dancers, grooving to the song by Philadelphia's Orlons, kept the beat with hips not feet. The Swim was done like the Twist in the hips with swimming arm motions. The Hully Gully started as a game-like, shuffling, kicking dance of synchronized group movements punctuated by improvisation. Other dance crazes were the Frug, the Hump, the Bird, the Dog, the Boogaloo, the Funky Chicken, the Pony, and the Monkey, done at slick discothèques like Shepheard's and Trude Heller's in New York, the Whiskey à Go-Go in Los Angeles, as well as at high school gyms across the nation. Dee Dee Sharp from Philadelphia launched a hit and a dance with "Mashed Potato Time" (1962) but flopped with her "Gravy (For My Mashed Potato)"—the sudden end of a star and of a dance. Little Eva [Boyd] and the "Locomotion" were equally short lived. Finally, in 1965, the Jerk popularized free-style, individualistic, egalitarian dancing for the rest of the decade; all that mattered was that each dancer moved as "moved by" the beat.

Meanwhile, 1958 to 1966 marked the Girl Group era. Many singers were still in inner city high schools; some were as young as fourteen, from lower- to middle-class families, suddenly thrust into and out of the limelight. Prior to the Chantels (1957–1959), who established the girl-group sound with their strong rhythm & blues (R&B) vocal style tempered with gospel and black doo-wop, few female rock and roll vocal groups recorded, let alone had hits. The Girl Groups' sudden popularity was central to pop music's transformation, as they effected the mass crossover of black music into white pop. Through them, Tin Pan Alley tried "to co-opt and control rock 'n' roll; and because the songwriters and producers involved were so young . . . , their very attempt to sweeten up and sanitize the black sound to appeal to a teenage public brought with it something genuine: a new, female-centered pop sensibility that was wonderfully fresh."[3]

Performers usually got only a pittance of profits from producers and record companies. Often they only performed songs written by others, with the producer managing the recording process, the product beyond the singers' control. Producer Phil Spector was notorious for creating, exploiting, and discarding girl groups. Records by the Crystals, Bob B. Soxx and the Blue Jeans, Darlene Love, and the Ronettes "sparkled" because of Spector's "multilayered, multitextured Wall of Sound" studio techniques; but the "arrogant, reclusive, even ruthless" Spector owned his girl group names to insure that singers not escape his grasp.

He chose various vocalists to record hits like "Da Doo Ron Ron" and "Then He Kissed Me." The five-member Crystals had a hit for Spector with "There's No Other Like My Baby" (1961). Dee Dee Kennibrew, an original Crystal, remembers, "We were never allowed any say in what we did at all. We were very young . . . but we were teenagers making teenage music, and we would have liked . . . some input. But no way! There was nothing we could do; Phil Spector was our record company, our producer, our everything." As if to prove his powers, Spector made the Crystals record the sadomasochistic "He Hit Me (And It Felt Like A Kiss)" with a dull, plodding beat. He gave the Crystals one more hit—"He's a Rebel" (1962)—but with a new lead singer, Darlene Wright, whom he renamed Darlene Love. She received a paltry $1,500 and no royalties; the original Crystals got nothing.[4]

The Shirelles, a black quartet composed of Shirley Owens (Alston), Doris Coley (Kenner), Micki Harris, and Beverley Lee, began singing at high school dances in Passaic, New Jersey, in 1958 after hearing the Chantels. Florence Greenberg, a friend's mother, signed them to Tiara Records contracts; and they performed on *American Bandstand* in 1960. They became the first girl group with a number one hit, "Will You Love Me Tomorrow" (1961), and with "Dedicated to the One I Love" were the first to have two songs in the Top Ten simultaneously. Other hits followed in 1963—"Mama Said," "Baby It's You," "Soldier Boy," and "Foolish Little Girl." Greig praises their songs' frank discussion of sexuality and dating, calling them "go-betweens, emissaries between the sexes, summoning up their emotional courage on behalf of teenage boys and girls too shy and inarticulate to speak directly to each other." Although their records sold to a broad teenaged public, their live performances were largely limited to the so-called segregated "chitlin' circuit"—Harlem's Apollo, Brooklyn's Fox and Paramount, Philly's Uptown, Chicago's Regal, and Baltimore's Royal. If one of the Shirelles was sick, Dionne Warwick filled in.[5]

Despite two 1963 hits, "He's So Fine" and "One Fine Day," the potential of the Chiffons' "vibrant, peppy vocals and smooth delivery" was also controlled by managers and producers who "sought only to exploit the girls' singing talent." Without knowledge of the record business, groups like the Chiffons were "prime targets for eager managers looking to make a fast buck." Their last hit, "Sweet Talkin' Guy" (1966) featured Judy Craig's fine voice; but the group held together, recording as the Four Pennies and appearing on the rock and roll revival circuit.

The Ronettes recorded "Be My Baby" to surpass the Chiffons in 1963 as "the greatest of all the girl groups," although they had no Top Ten hits. After breaking into show-business as go-go dancers at New York's Peppermint Lounge during the Twist's popularity, the two sisters Veronica (Ronnie) and Estelle Bennett and their cousin Nedra Talley became Spector protegées. Ronnie was the lead singer with "the sexiest voice in rock & roll." Critics thought the Ronettes "looked like they sang rock & roll" with their slender bodies, high beehive hairdos, heavy eye make-up, and tight skirts slit up the leg. The group had several hit singles in 1963 and 1964. They toured as warm-up act with the Beatles and the Rolling Stones; but when Ronnie and Phil married in 1966, the Ronettes immediately fell into oblivion. Spector refused to let his wife, now "Veronica," appear on stage, locking her at home with only classical music, and threatening to put her in a glass coffin if she left him. They divorced in 1973.[7]

The first white girl group was the Angels, two sisters and a friend from Orange, New Jersey, who made the charts with "My Boyfriend's Back" (1963). Barbara Allbut, who wanted a music career, recalls their brief popularity: "My parents didn't try to stop us, . . . but inwardly I know my mother was cringing. . . . Actually, I think she was afraid that we weren't going to do well, and that we'd embarrass ourselves. . . . But my father was proud of us. . . . If he'd see our record on the jukebox he'd play it and tell all his friends, 'That's my daughters!'" Wearing prom dresses, they abandoned R&B for old-fashioned ballads, singing backgrounds for a time before turning to the motel lounge and supper club circuit, reliable "gigs" for "respectable" women.[8]

The Shangri-Las—the sisters Mary and Betty Weiss and the twins Marge and Mary Anne Ganser—projected a different image. Tough, white "greaser" street-girls from Queens, they began in skirts but turned to tight black leather and go-go boots. Popularity of their 1964 hit "Leader of the Pack," written by Ellie Greenwich and proclaiming female rebellion, grew when the song was banned in England. It, and songs like "Remember (Walking in the Sand)," were short stories of frustrated teenage love. Their last hit was "I Can Never Go Home Any More," followed by "Long Live Our Love," a bad but tearfully patriotic lament about a boyfriend's departure for Vietnam. Marge Ganser died in 1980—of a drug overdose or terminal illness, it was rumored.[9]

Other girl groups had just one hit or two, at best, before being abandoned by agents or producers. In 1964, the Ad-Libs ("The Boy from

New York City"), the Jaynetts ("Sally Go 'Round the Roses"), the Exciters ("Tell Him"), the Dixie Cups, and the Jelly Beans ("I Wanna Love
Him So Bad" and "Baby Be Mine") were trios and quartets of women
who fell back into ordinary life after fleeting fame. The Cookies (Dorothy Jones, Earl-Jean McCrae, and Margaret Ross) were more fortunate
than most. After placing on the charts with "Chains," "Don't Say
Nothin' Bad About My Baby," and "I'm Into Something Good," they
were relegated to background "doo-wah" accompaniment. Their hits
remain familiar through versions by the Beatles and Herman's Hermits.
In 1964, attention turned to the male British Invasion and away from
American Girl Groups.

By 1965, teens were spending $100 million annually just on 45 rpm
records and were beginning to buy LP albums. Teenage rock echoed
both sexual dilemmas and the standards of the day, especially as voiced
by single girl singers. The Cookies' "Will Power" expressed the teen-
aged woman's quandary as a date badgers her to stay out late and give
him more liberties. Linda Scott's "I Told Every Little Star" (1961),
Shelley Fabares' "Johnny Angel" (1962), Marcie Blaine's "I Wanna Be
Bobby's Girl" (1962), and Peggy March's "I Will Follow Him" (1963)
expressed a simpering, naive, myopic adoration of the boyfriend and
the willingness to surrender all ambition for him. Other pop lyrics like
Ronnie and the Hi-Lites' "I Wish That We Were Married" (1962) and
The Dixie Cups' (Barbara and Rosa Hawkins with Joan Johnson)
"Chapel of Love" (1964) reinforced traditionalism with ballads of de-
sexualized juvenile romance acceptable even to middle-class parents.
Their voices were stylized as airy, insipid, virginal, waiflike, or
"sweet," depending on one's perspective. Girls sang plaintive mini-
melodramas celebrating their submissive role in teenage romance—a
major theme in the first half of the decade.[10]

For these girls, fame was ephemeral, their names absent from most
discographies and pop music histories. Only Lesley Gore (1946–)
stands out with "It's My Party" (1963), "Judy's Turn to Cry," "She's
a Fool," and "You Don't Own Me" (1964), all indignant rather than
whining but still in the "weeper" genre. Gore wrote many of her own
songs, recording "Sunshine, Lollipops, and Rainbows" and "California
Nights" in 1967. One of the most fortunate of the girl singers, Gore
came from a wealthy family, graduated from Sarah Lawrence in 1968,
and has played minor roles in the pop music business since.

The women of Motown struck a different note. Barry Gordy, Jr.'s
Motown Records, or Hitsville USA, founded in Detroit (the Motor

City) in 1960, was urban and black; its music aimed to cross over to a white mass audience by avoiding the controversial themes of R&B. It gave new opportunities to young, talented black women to shape the direction of rock and roll and to reach a general, national audience in an unprecedented way, breaking from earlier segregated "race" recordings and the fifties "Negro market." Motown's "Sound of Young America" hits regularly appeared on both pop and R&B charts. Women figured prominently on Motown labels, but often took second place to male stars. Martha and the Vandellas sang: "Calling out, around the world. Are you ready for a brand new beat?" Tammi Terrell (1946–) sang duets with Marvin Gaye—"Ain't Nothing Like the Real Thing (Baby)" and "You're All I Need to Get By." She never achieved the renown of Gaye, the "prince" of Motown. Even Motown was not ideal for women. Raynoma Gordy, the founder's ex-wife, claims credit for much of the company's early success and complains that she has been left unacknowledged and uncompensated by her autocratic husband. Kim Weston remembers being told to "shut up and sing," when she protested conditions that left her without promised fame or royalties.[11]

Mary Wells (1943–1992) was one of Motown's first stars after she came to Gordy to sell a song she composed, "Bye Bye Baby," recorded for her 1960 debut. Wells teamed up with Smokey Robinson in 1962 to produce a string of hits on both the pop and R&B charts—"The One Who Really Loves You," "You Beat Me to the Punch," and "Two Lovers" in 1962 and "What's Easy for Two is So Hard for One" and other songs in 1963. Wells's solo single, "My Guy" (1964), was her biggest hit; and she sang two duets with Gaye before leaving Motown in 1965 for Twentieth Century Fox Records, hoping to become an actress. There and with other record companies, she could not duplicate her Motown successes and retired to raise a family.

The Shirelles' success inspired Gordy to sign the Marvelettes with Tamla Records, a Motown affiliate. Gladys Horton, Katherine Anderson, Georgenna Tillman, Juanita Cowart, and Wanda Young were all born in 1944 and classmates at the rural Inkster (Michigan) High School, where they won a talent contest and a Motown audition. Their friend Georgia Dobbins wrote their first single, "Please Mr. Postman" (1961), but did not join them because of caring for her sick mother. That recording reached Number One and was later covered by the Beatles. But Motown treated the Marvelettes badly. Cowart and Tillman could not take the stress and dropped out. Other hits by the trio, with Horton and Young taking turns as lead singer, include "Playboy" (written by Horton), "Beechwood 4-5789," and "I'll Keep Holding On," all placing high on both the pop and R&B charts. Gordy abandoned them in 1963 to cultivate Martha and the Vandellas and the Supremes; but the Marvelettes kept recording hits like "Too Many Fish in the Sea" (1964) and "Don't Mess with Bill" (1966) until Horton quit to marry and the group split up in 1969.[12]

Martha Reeves (1941–) teamed up with Annette Sterling, Gloria Williams, and Rosalind Ashford (1943–) as the Del-Phis while in high school; and they cut one record for Chess. Reeves worked as a secretary at Motown before Gordy tapped her and her friends to sing backup for Marvin Gaye. In 1963, Gordy decided to feature Reeves, Ashford, and Betty Kelly (1944–), as Martha and the Vandellas, with a more aggressive, soulful image than the Supremes. They produced some of the most popular dance songs of the decade—"Heat Wave," "Quicksand," "Nowhere to Run," "I'm Ready for Love," and their biggest hit, "Dancing in the Street" (1964). After Kelly left, replaced by Lois Reeves, Martha's younger sister, the group became Martha Reeves and the Vandellas, emulating the Supremes' sound with "Jimmy Mack" (1967); but Gordy abandoned them, even losing their name in a gambling game. Their farewell Detroit performance was in 1972. Motown girl groups like the Marvelettes, the Vandellas, and the Velvelettes could have done much better had Gordy supported and cultivated them as he did the Supremes.[13]

The trio of Florence Ballard (1943–1976), Mary Wilson (1944–), and Diana Ross (1944–) grew up together in Detroit's Brewster public housing project and in their early teens started singing with Betty McGlowan as the Primettes, paired with the male Primes (later the Temptations). Because of their local popularity, Gordy hired them fresh out of high school in 1961, sending them to singing, dance, and charm courses to polish their style; but the Supremes got no advances or salary and only small royalties, much of it withheld because Gordy claimed expenses exceeded profits. Ballard renamed the group the Supremes because it sounded more sophisticated, but success did not come until 1964 when their two-million-seller "Where Did Our Love Go" crossed over from black R&B to popular rock and roll charts. Twelve number one pop singles, many gold records, major television appearances, and sold-out concerts quickly followed. Fame from British tours in 1964, 1965, and 1967 helped popularize them through mainstream America as the female equivalent to the Beatles, especially among female fans. Their hits included "Baby Love," "Come See About

Me," "Stop! In the Name of Love," "Back in My Arms Again," "I Hear a Symphony," "You Can't Hurry Love," "You Keep Me Hangin' On," "Love is Here and Now You're Gone," and "The Happening." The Supremes seemed role models of upward mobility. Their "woman-oriented" themes and proto-feminist messages questioned the costs and consequences of the concurrent sexual revolution.[14]

In 1967 Ballard left the group she founded, feeling personally defeated as it was re-billed Diana Ross and the Supremes. She lost her Motown royalties and died of a heart attack precipitated by alcoholism in 1976 while living on welfare with her three children in Detroit. Cindy Birdsong (1939–) replaced Ballard to record "Love Child" and "I'm Gonna Make You Love Me" (with the Temptations). Ridiculous commercialism led the group to sponsor "Supremes' White Bread" and to play three nuns in a television episode of Tarzan; they dabbled in politics too, endorsing Humphrey for the Presidency. "I'll Try Something New" was prophetic and "Someday We'll Be Together" ironic as Ross went solo in 1969, seeking her own stardom, leaving the "group" to flounder for four years before folding. Ross's increasingly sophisticated image did not fit with the countercultural tenor of the times; but she built her own career by playing to Las Vegas style audiences and varying her repertoire with show tunes. Through the seventies, she pursued super-stardom in films and music, reaching a more mature, lucrative audience.[15]

Another success story rivaling that of Diana Ross began in 1961, when Aretha Franklin (1942–) launched a career that made her "Lady Soul." Crossing in 1960 from sacred to secular music, she fused "the unpredictable leaps and swoops of the gospel music she grew up on" as a Baptist minister's daughter "with the sensuality of R&B and the precision of pop," and inspiration from Dinah Washington (1924–63), "Queen of Blues" and a family friend. Franklin's first hit single, "I Never Loved a Man (the Way I Loved You)," followed by "Think," established her bold, belted-out style. Signed by Columbia Records and then by Atlantic, she set a record by winning every Best Female R&B Grammy from 1967 to 1974. In 1967 alone, she made over a dozen million-selling records, including "I Never Loved a Man (the Way I Love You)," "Baby I Love You," "Chain of Fools," "Since You've Been Gone," and "I Say a Little Prayer." "Respect" (1967) was one of the first feminist demands voiced in pop music. The Carole King-Gerry Goffin team wrote some of her songs, although Franklin did all her own vocal arrangements with gospel-style call-and-response choruses, often featuring the Sweet Inspirations with her sister Carolyn. In 1968, she received an award from Martin Luther King, Jr., as an epitome of black pride and appeared on *Time*'s cover. One of the most successful and enduring of sixties careers, Franklin continued to record and perform to major audiences into the nineties.[16]

Franklin met her goal of emulating the success of Dionne Warwick (1940–), who produced her own first two Top Ten hits in 1964. With a grounding in black gospel music, Warwick played to an older pop audience with a series of hits written by Burt Bacharach and Hal David, from "Don't Make Me Over" (1962) to "I'll Never Fall in Love Again" (1969). It was the decade's longest string of hits and "one of the most commercially successful recording careers" of the sixties. Spending most of 1963 in France, Warwick was dubbed "Paris's Black Pearl," but returned home to record pop classics like "Anyone Who Had a Heart" (1963), "Walk on By" (1964), "Message to Michael" (1966), "I Say a Little Prayer" (1967), and "Do You Know the Way to San José" (1968). After parting with Bacharach in 1972, her career retrenched to supper clubs for a time but persisted, as did critical and popular esteem for her talent.[17]

Gladys Knight (1944–), born in Atlanta to a musical family, also emerged from a grounding in gospel. At the age of four she was popular on the southeast gospel circuit, and at seven won national fame on Ted Mack's television amateur hour and made many television appearances. She formed the Pips in 1952 with sister Brenda, brother Merald, and cousins William and Eleanor Guest, touring on the national R&B circuit in the late fifties. Their record, "Every Beat of My Heart" (1961), became a Top Ten pop million-seller; but Gladys Knight and the Pips, with their polished dance routines, were known primarily to R&B audiences until signed to Motown's Soul label in 1967, recording "I Heard It Through the Grapevine" (1967), "The Nitty Gritty" (1969), and "If I Were Your Woman" (1971). Critics praised Knight as "a warm, intelligent woman who sang in a gritty but supple gospelish tenor with sharp, often ironic phrasing"; but her mass appeal escalated through the seventies only after she left Motown, frustrated by lack of support.[18]

Few performers emerged from and continued to draw upon the rich black musical roots of rock in bars and local honky-tonks to achieve pop stardom. Anna Mae Bullock (1938–), who called herself Tina, was a 16-year-old from Brownsville, Tennessee, when she met Ike Turner, founder of an East St. Louis group, the Kings of Rhythm. Tina's singing won the group their first hit, "A Fool in Love" (1960). Ike and Tina married in Tijuana in 1962. Other hits followed for the "First Couple of Soul"; and they ended the decade with "Proud Mary" (1969). Through it all, Tina Turner withstood extensive physical abuse from her husband, even performing once with a broken jaw Ike had inflected. Ike's extensive womanizing, as well as his proprietary attitude, led to the end of their marriage and joint career in the seventies; but the ever-young Tina Turner, exuding sexuality as in the sixties, staged a dramatic come-back to rock popularity in the eighties.

Songwriters

Many of the sixties' chart-topping pop songs, although usually performed by male singers or groups, were written by women, often in collaboration with a husband and usually based in New York's famous Brill Building. Carole King mass-produced melodies with lyricist husband Gerry Goffin, whom she met in 1958 at Queens College. Their hits included the Shirelles' "Will You Love (Still) Me Tomorrow?," the Chiffons' "One Fine Day," the Drifters' "Up on the Roof," the Cookies' "Don't Say Nothin' Bad (About My Baby)," Aretha Franklin's "Natural Woman" (King's and Jerry Wexler's), among others. "Little Eva" Boyd, King's babysitter, recorded their hit "Locomotion," marketed with its own dance. Even much of the so-called "British Invasion" and its imitators derived success from King's songs—"Chains" by the Beatles, "I'm Into Something Good" by Herman's Hermits, "Don't Bring Me Down" by the Animals, and many songs for the Monkees. The couple divorced in 1968. King had begun a singing career in 1962 with "It Might as Well Rain until September" but did not pursue performance until the release of her 1971 album *Tapestry*, which sold ten million copies and validated her talents as one of the era's greatest singers as well as songwriters.

Ellie Greenwich (1940–) began a prolific songwriting career in 1962, teamed with, then marrying Jeff Barry. Their songs include "Hanky Panky," "Leader of the Pack," and "River Deep, Mountain High." They produced "Da Doo Ron Ron," "Then He Kissed Me," "Be My Baby," and "Chapel of Love" for music publishers Leiber and Stoller and Spector's girl groups. Greenwich's "Doh Wah Diddy" was originally released by the Exciters, a New York girl group in 1963, but achieved hit status when recorded by the British Manfred Mann. Greenwich doubled as a producer, even lending her voice for several nonexistent, "dummy" groups such as the Raindrops for "What a Guy." She recalls, "We'd throw a few people together and have them go out and lip synch the record. There really wasn't a Raindrops." Greenwich also sang under the pseudonyms of Ellie Gaye, Ellie Gee, and Kellie Douglas, explaining, "I did want to perform in the sixties but Jeff didn't feel I should; we were very busy writing for all the groups and producing. I didn't mind saying no, but it always sat there, the thought, 'Gee, what if I had.' And then, as time went on, I got scared." Barry then demanded that Greenwich remove her name from records she equally co-wrote and co-produced so he could "build his name," expecting to become "the sole breadwinner" when she had children and stayed home. Unsurprisingly, their personal partnership, like the "naive, romantic optimism of the girl-group era" they had helped create, ended in divorce in 1965, although their professional collaboration lasted until 1967.[19]

Valerie Simpson (1948–) teamed with Nickolas Ashford after they met in 1964 at Harlem's White Rock Baptist Church. They wrote songs, initially sold for $75 each, until Ray Charles had a hit with their "Let's Go Get Stoned." Gordy hired them to write and produce some of Motown's greatest hits—"Ain't No Mountain High Enough," "You're All I Need to Get By," and "Reach Out (And Touch Somebody's Hand)." They married in 1974 and began to perform their own work, playing an important role in the rise of soul and soul-based rock in the seventies.[20]

Another rare female/male, personal/professional music industry relationship that endured through and after the sixties was that of wife/husband team Cynthia Weil and Barry Mann. Their songwriting collaboration extended in subject from teen romance to social commentary, from the Righteous Brothers' "You've Lost That Lovin' Feelin'" to the Crystals' "Uptown" about urban social inequalities and "We Gotta Get Out of This Place," another inner-city critique popularized by the British group, the Animals. Weil wrote the lyrics, more socially aware than the innocent optimism of King-Goffin songs; and Mann did all the production.

Folk Music

Folk music, suppressed by McCarthyism in the fifties, was resurgent in the sixties. The Weavers, including Ronnie Gilbert, staged a Carnegie Hall Reunion in 1963. Coffeehouses that had hosted the Beat jazz scene in the late fifties turned to folk music in the sixties. In Cambridge-Boston, the folk-music scene at first featured amateurs or students, who were paid a maximum of ten dollars a night at such clubs as Alhambra, Tulla's Coffee Grinder, the Golden Vanity, and the Salamander. Club 47 (Passim's in the 1990's), known for jazz, began folk nights on Tuesdays and Fridays and paid Joan Baez (1941–) the usual for her first professional appearance in 1958. It and the Unicorn also featured Judy Collins (1939–). Coffeehouses provided opportunities for folk musicians like Maria Muldaur (1943–). Tom Rush recalls that at first folkies "were vaguely embarrassed by the discrepancies between the music we had adopted . . . of the poor and illiterate, and our parents' swimming pools or our college courses"; but "attitudes started to change around 1960" with Baez's ascent to stardom. Comfortable backgrounds remained for those on both sides of the spotlights, but guilt diminished with involvement in and celebration of social causes.[21]

Songwriter and soprano Baez quickly rose to fame after the 1959 Newport Folk Festival. Daughter of a Quaker physics professor, she had grown up in various academic communities and had dropped out of Boston University to pursue a folk music career. Originally billing herself as "sister mystic," she was proclaimed "folk queen." She played again at the 1963 Newport Folk Festivals, winning a two-month, sold-out Carnegie Hall debut in 1962. Her first album from Vanguard in 1961 rivaled in popularity those of Harry Belafonte, the Kingston Trio, and the Weavers.

From the steps of the Lincoln Memorial, Baez led the crowd of two hundred thousand in singing the anthem "We Shall Overcome" during the 28 August 1963 Civil Rights March. She shared the podium with Martin Luther King, Jr., and veteran gospel singer Mahalia Jackson. Jackson (1911–1972), active in the civil rights movement since helping King in Montgomery in 1955 with the bus boycott, sang an old slave spiritual as a personal lament and testimonial: "I been 'buked and I been scorned / I'm gonna tell my Lord / When I get home, / Just how long you've been treating me wrong." Yet Baez, not Jackson, was in the spotlight. Baez sang for the Fall 1964 Free Speech student demonstrations at Berkeley and the Selma to Montgomery, Alabama, civil rights march in Spring 1965, becoming "the voice that meant protest" and "the madonna of the disaffected." She and other folksingers called public attention to songs of the true "folk"; but they, not the authentic voices reaped the lion's share of fame and fortune.[22]

Baez served as an important mentor for Bob Dylan, as did his less famous girlfriend Susan Rotolo, the black blues singer Victoria Spivey, and New York folk singer Carolyn Hester. Baez selflessly included him on concert bills, promoting his stardom. From 1963 to 1965, they were constantly together as friends, lovers, and performers, but it was Baez who preceded in talent and fame. The halcyon days did not last, and Dylan went his own way. Like Dylan, Baez disappointed folk purists in 1965 when she used electric guitar and bass in her *Farewell, Angelina* album.[23]

Yet, Baez proved repeatedly that her social consciousness was real. She could be counted on to give her time and voice to many causes. In 1965, she founded the Institute for the Study of Nonviolence in Carmel, California, focused more on the anti-war than the civil rights movement. She set a standard for other folkies like Judy Collins and Barbara Dane, who joined male singers to form the Mississippi Caravan of Music to work in Freedom Schools and register potential voters. In 1968, she released two albums, *Baptism* and *Any Day Now* and published her memoir, *Daybreak*, dedicated "with love, admiration, and gratefulness to the men who find themselves facing imprisonment for resisting the draft." That year, Baez withheld her taxes to protest the war and married David Harris just before they were both jailed for an Oakland antidraft demonstration. Although Baez bore Gabriel, his child, in 1969, their union was more symbolic of joint commitment than a close personal relationship. In July 1969 he began serving a three-year sentence for refusing induction into the Army. She sang her emotions for the anti-war cause on *David's Album* (1969) and *One Day at a Time* (1971). The couple divorced in 1973 shortly after his release.

Similarly, Buffy Saint-Marie (1941–), a Cree Indian with a haunting vibrato voice, launched her career in Cambridge coffeehouses, where she was discovered in 1964 by Vanguard Records, for which she recorded several LPs. Her antiwar song "Universal Soldier" became an anthem as the Vietnam conflict escalated, copied by the likes of Donovan and Glen Campbell. Although a prolific writer, her work is best known in performances by others, including Elvis Presley, who in 1972 recorded her "Until It's Time for You to Go."

Coffeehouse folk music, easily performed by amateurs, spread nationally in the early sixties, reaching even small college towns; but professionalization spelled the death of many of the coffeehouses themselves, curtailing opportunities for aspiring women. Commercialization of folk music began early in the decade. Gerdes' Folk City, opened in 1960, staging competitions of old and new "folkies"—the

Weavers, Jean Ritchie, Judy Collins. After 1965, because of commercialization, co-optation by popular music norms, or the hegemony of the new electronic rock associated with psychedelica, the "folk scene" declined.

The trend toward professionalization appeared in 1961 when Albert Grossman, a manager, united three singers—Peter Yarrow (1938–), Paul Stookey (1937–), and Mary Travers (1937–). After a debut at New York's Bitter End, Peter, Paul, and Mary signed with Warner Brothers Records to become the sixties' most popular acoustic folk group. The strikingly attractive Mary with straight, long blond hair encouraged the group to record children's songs, including "Puff the Magic Dragon" (1963), once mistaken for a pro-drug message. In 1969, they released an LP called *Peter, Paul, and Mommy.* The three proved their commitment to various causes, including civil rights and the anti-war movement, and appeared on the front lines from Selma-Montgomery to Berkeley and Washington with Baez. They broke up in 1970. Similarly, Grossman discovered Carly Simon (1945–) in 1965, hoping to turn her into "a female Bob Dylan"; but a recording of "Baby Let Me Follow You Down" flopped as did a short collaboration with sibling Lucy as The Simon Sisters. Not until 1970 did Carly Simon record her first album, simply bearing her name.

After training in classical piano, Colorado-born Judy Collins (1939–) launched her career in Chicago coffeehouses in 1960 and went national in 1961 with an album, *A Maid of Constant Sorrow.* She then expanded her repertoire of traditional Anglo-American folk songs and ballads with protest songs and works by the likes of Dylan. On her albums *In My Life* (1966) and *Wildflowers* (1967), she moved from folk rock to "art songs" by Jacques Brel and Brecht-Weill-Blitzstein, combining the political and the theatrical. Work on *Wildflowers* with Stephen Stills led to his song celebrating their affair, "Suite: Judy Blue Eyes" (1969). Some critics consider her gold album *Who Knows Where the Time Goes* (1968) her best with its combination of folk- and country-rock, marked by a hit single, "Both Sides Now." In the seventies, she produced eclectic anthologies of "artier" work that appealed to a smaller group of stalwart fans.

The folk movement spawned other enduring careers. In 1968, the Canadian Joni Mitchell (born Roberta Joan Anderson, 1943–), who had written songs for Judy Collins, Tom Rush, Buffy Sainte-Marie, and Dave Van Ronk, launched her own singing career with acoustic guitar pieces based on her personal life. Her first single, "I Had a King," tells the story of her marriage which failed in 1966: "I had a King dressed in drip-dry and paisley. / Lately he's taken to saying I'm crazy and blind." She called her style "sock-it-to-me-softly music"; and one critic observed, "she plays Yang to Bob Dylan's Yin, equaling him in richness and profusion of imagery and surpassing him in conciseness and direction." In 1969, "Clouds" became her first hit, better known in Judy Collins's later version, "Both Sides Now," and she wrote and recorded "Woodstock," called the "anthem of a generation." Her successes continued through the seventies as she experimented with avant-garde jazz.[24]

The sixties also revealed other folk music within and beyond the North American boundaries. Jean Ritchie of Viper, Kentucky, who popularized the mountain dulcimer in folk circles, was one of many "true" folk practitioners, many women, who informed the styles of the popular folk revival. Perhaps the greatest ambassador of imported folk was Miriam Makeba, who first toured the United States with Harry Belafonte, only to find herself exiled from the racist regime of her native South Africa. Makeba's popularity plunged dramatically and radio stations boycotted her music after her May 1968 revelation of her marriage to Black Power activist Stokely Carmichael.[25]

Largely forgotten, unfortunately, are the women behind the scenes—especially in the early-sixties halcyon days in Greenwich Village. Robbie Woliver, journalist and co-owner of Gerdes' Folk City, considers "It's more than coincidence that Dylan's genius emerged during his years with girlfriend Susan Rotolo," who was best known for their street embrace on the *Freewheelin'* album cover (1962). Rotolo was a 17-year-old Village resident from "a cultured, left-wing, political family." Woliver credits her influence on Dylan as "highly creative" when they lived together, inspiring songs like "Boots of Spanish Leather," "Tomorrow is a Long Time," "Restless Farewell," and "All I Really Want to Do." Many said she "politicized and intellectualized Dylan," urging him to write protest songs as well as love ballads. Through her job at the Circle in the Square Theatre, she introduced him to Brecht. But the fame of her image on that album cover overshadowed and shattered the relationship. Songwriter Carol Belsky remembers, "Suze was the epitome of everything that was hip. . . . That cover was a symbol of my generation, the free-spirited freedom." The "freewheelin" Dylan left Rotolo for Baez and his own fame.[26]

Feminist messages did not appear in pop music until 1971 when Australian singer Helen Reddy (1942–) released her debut album, featuring

"I Am Woman," which became a movement anthem and won the Grammy Best Song of 1972.

Alternative Lifestyles

Tom Wolfe presents a view of "surfer girls" in his study of "The Pump House Gang" (1965) at Windansea Beach in LaJolla, California: "Donna, a twenty-one-year-old and her eighteen-year-old boyfriend . . . killed themselves in a murder/suicide pact on the steps of the Pump House. The local explanation was that she couldn't see anything beyond surfing. Her life had come to an end because she was now twenty-one. Another girl, Jackie, who was fourteen, gave me a composition she'd written after surfing with her boyfriend on twelve-foot waves at dawn which was full of poetry about 'reverse stances' and 'fast-flowing suction.'" Surfers had their own vocabulary. Girls were "wahini," a Hawaiian term, or "beach bunnies." "Bitchin" meant very good. Wolfe observed, "There were some absolute knock-outs among the girls, many of whom had that pre-Raphaelite look of undone natural hair parted down the middle." Their styles became common "in the hip world" shortly thereafter.[27]

Across the nation at waterfront resorts like Seaside (Oregon), Ocean City (Maryland), and Hampton Beach (New Hampshire), in the summers from 1963 to 1965, especially on the Fourth of July and Labor Day, teenagers acted out this "free" lifestyle to the dismay of "town fathers." The sight of bikini clad girls tossed into the air from makeshift blanket trampolines, snakedancing on the beach, and throwing around undergarments suggested impending anarchy, indeed even Communist plots, to many middle-of-the-road Americans; and "mobs" of thousands of youth, many of them girls, turned out repeatedly ready for mischief. Police lashed back, often violently. Official reports concluded that "the gyrations of the young have always been subjected to raised eyebrows on the part of the adult generation," that "today's dancing is the sort of thing that ought not to be done in public," particularly on the beach by girls with few clothes on, clearly immoral if not actually inciting riots. Such beach highjinks, however, were tame compared to what would follow in post-1965 lifestyles.[28]

Even before the rise of the counterculture, such alternative youth lifestyles, even if just holiday behavior, rebelled against conventional middle-class suburban conformity, morality, and the work ethic, challenging norms of proper behavior and reveling in leisure with a seize-the-day mentality premised in a basic insecurity fostered by growing up with fear of the bomb. The naming of the bikini for the island where America tested its atom bomb was not just coincidental; but beach culture was also a product of a more pervasive American cult of youth and a harbinger of the sexual revolution played out in rhythm to rock and roll music.

Counterculture Music

In 1966, youth culture received a certain legitimacy when *Time* selected men and women 25 years or younger as its "Man of the Year." Exaltation of youth coincided with a time when baby boomers became affluent teenagers with money to spend on popular music and easy access to alcohol, then drugs. Despite myths about the sixties, baby boomers' youth often made them prone to seek pleasure rather than serious political commitment. Indeed, many wanted to escape from their political awareness, which could easily overwhelm them. Most white, middle-class teens simply were too young for it and sought escapism rather than ideology or commitment to a cause.

A major theme of rock in the decade's second half was misogyny. Mick Jagger of the Rolling Stones sang of male domination, "Under my thumb, the girl who once had me down / Under my thumb, the girl who once pushed me around." As if in response, Marianne Faithfull (1946–) one of the few women of the British Invasion, gained popularity through her first album, simply bearing her name in 1965, and through *Go Away from My World* and *Faithfull Forever* (1966); but based as it was on the haunting, hollow lament of her voice, her popularity could not be sustained as her suffering caught up with her image. She underwent a divorce, a torrid affair with Jagger, heroin addiction, and attempted suicide. The girl-group era and the timid "birds" of the British Invasion faded from fashion after 1966, but a new generation of gutsy women singers arose.

The pseudo-hippies of rock were less strident. The couple Sonny and Cher performed together, originally in folk-rock but quickly moving to a more pop profile. While taking acting lessons, Cherilyn La-Pierre Sarkasian (1946–) had met songwriter Salvatore Bono (1935–) when both worked for Phil Spector. They married in 1964 and capitalized on a mod image of togetherness from their 1965 debut with hit singles like "I Got You Babe" and "Baby Don't Go" in 1965 to "The Beat Goes On" (1967). Cher recorded several solo hits—"All I Really

Wanna Do" (1965), "Bang Bang (My Baby Shot Me Down)" (1966), and "You Better Sit Down Kids" (1967), projecting increasing independence. They made two movies: *Good Times* (1967) and *Chastity* (1969), the latter inspiring their daughter's name. Their marriage did not even last through their popular television series (1971–77); but they remained friends, in the spirit of the sixties.

The Mamas and the Papas, four West Coast veterans including Michelle Gilliam Phillips (1945–) and Mama Cass Elliott (1941–74) of the Greenwich Village folk scene, also specialized in polished folk rock from 1966 to 1968, the year Michelle and the group's songwriter/leader John Phillips divorced. Four of their albums made the Top Ten. They were best known for their hit "California Dreamin'" (1966). They helped organize the Monterey International Pop Festival of 1967, which brought the Jefferson Airplane and Janis Joplin to national fame. Mama Cass, the group's most visible member, went solo for the next few years until her sudden death in London in 1974, supposedly from choking.[29]

In 1966, mezzo-soprano Grace Wing Slick (1939–), former model and singer for the Great Society, formed by her first husband Jerry in 1965, replaced the pregnant Signe Tory Anderson, the original singer of the Jefferson Airplane, just as that group emerged as a major band in the folk-rock scene at San Francisco's Fillmore in Haight-Ashbury. All five band members helped write songs, anthems of the psychedelic. Described by *Time* in 1966 as "a cheerful synthesis of Beatles and blues, folk and country, liberally sprinkled with Indian raga," epitome of the San Francisco Sound, the group's popularity was assured by *Jefferson Airplane Takes Off* (1966). Slick contributed Great Society songs "Somebody to Love" and "White Rabbit" to *Surrealistic Pillow* (1967), the first of many gold-record albums and singles. Many contained bitter social commentary. Many towns banned "White Rabbit," charging it advocated drugs. Controversy escalated as RCA censored the word "shit" and other "obscene language" from "Spayre Change," a nine-minute psychedelic jam-collage on the *After Bathing at Baxter's* album (1967).[30]

On the cover of *Life* in 1968, Grace Slick visually dominates Jefferson Airplane males, befitting her name as "Queen of Rock," sitting barefooted in defiant, cross-legged pose, her long, straight hair hanging over a white Indian caftan, decorated in gold. In cubic spaces stacked below her, the male musicians, dressed in Western or drab hippie clothes, lounge anonymously. Media focus on Slick irritated bandfounder Marty Balin, creating a tension that fed the volatile vocals they both brought to songs on *Crown of Creation* (1968) and *Bless Its Pointed Little Head* (1969). *Volunteers* (1969), under their total "artistic control," addressed the era's political turmoil and generation gap with inflammatory lyrics like "Up against the wall, motherfuckers" repeated in the chorus of "We Can Be Together." The Airplane's success rose to a crescendo with performances at Woodstock and Altamont at decade's end. The original group broke up in 1970 as three members left; and Slick had a daughter, China, with Paul Kantner in 1971. Slick produced *Blows Against the Empire* (1970) with Kantner and guest musicians, billed as Jefferson Starship. Marty Balin, the last original band member, quit in 1971; and Slick and Kantner formally launched Jefferson Starship as a new era began, leaving behind sixties psychedelica for a slicker sound that persisted into the eighties.[31]

Life's cover article on "The New Rock" in 1968 introduced to the American public another unconventional young singer—"Sound. Loud and heavy. The voice raw and tortured."—describing Janis Joplin as "a female Leadbelly, a Texan, in and out of four colleges, a folk singer for something to do. . . . taken in by the rock-blues band, Big Brother and the Holding Company. There was no money, no instruments, no direction; and Janis didn't think she was going to be a singer. Now they play to 7,000 people at Winterland and feel honored to entertain at the Hell's Angels annual party. . . . Janis stomps. The band plays harder and faster. Faces twist. Janis screams. 'Come on, come on, come on and take it. Take another little piece of my heart, now, baby. Oh, yeah, now take it. . . .' Her hair thrashes, and she picks up the bottle she keeps with her and belts down more Southern Comfort." Janis was a shooting star, dramatically rising to fame with an unprecedented tough blues-mama style and image; but she was white.[32]

Before and independent of radical feminism, Janis Joplin (1943–1970) epitomized rebellion against traditional, genteel female roles. She ran away from home in Port Arthur, Texas, at 17 after graduating from high school in 1960, drifting to sing in Austin and Houston blues clubs. During brief studies at University of Texas, she had an unfortunate blind date with William Bennett (later Reagan's Secretary of Education and Bush's Drug Czar); and her classmates voted her "ugliest man on campus" in 1963. Singing with the bluegrass Waller Creek Boys, she saved money to move to San Francisco, drawn by the Beat poets. She remembered, "In Texas, I was a beatnik, a weirdo. Texas is O.K. if you want to settle down and do your thing quietly, but it's not for outrageous people, and I was always outrageous."[33]

By 1965, her move West was complete; and she joined the new Big Brother and the Holding Company in 1966. Her music was popular and unprecedented, although naive critics compare her to Billie Holiday. She stopped the show at the first Monterey International Pop Festival in 1967 by singing "Love Is Like a Ball and Chain"; and Columbia Records signed the group for the album *Cheap Thrills* (1968) with its million-selling single "Piece of My Heart." She wrote a number of her own songs, including "Down on Me." Joplin skyrocketed to stardom, appearing on Ed Sullivan, Tom Jones, and Dick Cavett television shows as well as at the 1968 Newport Folk Festival and major venues like the Fillmore East, London's Albert Hall, and Madison Square Garden. Earning $150,000 that year, she left behind her backup musicians and went solo on *I Got Dem Ol' Kozmic Blues Again, Mama.* She formed the Kozmic Blues Band for "Try (Just a Little Bit Harder)" in 1969 and then teamed with the Full Tilt Boogie Band in 1970.

A biographer dubbed Joplin the "Princess of Liberated Feelings": "It was as if she had been wound up, very tightly, and was unwinding very fast, spinning. All the released energy was flowing out to us and into us and back to her to be charged up again. . . . She came across as hot, temperamental, impulsive. . . . Liberation! Janis was at once lusty and sensual, bawdy and sexy." Joplin moaned, crooned, and shrieked the blues, much to the despair of her mother who asked, "Janis, why do you scream like that when you've got such a pretty voice?" Through style and movement, she also "turned the meaning of beauty counter-clockwise" as the quintessential countercultural woman. Like many rock performers of her generation, Joplin lived self-destructively. Her trade-mark was her open swigging of 100-proof Southern Comfort on stage. Her 1969 hit, "Me and Bobbie Magee," written by former lover Kris Kristofferson, celebrated the free but melancholy life of the open road—"Freedom's just another word for nothing left to lose." Janis died in Hollywood's Landmark Hotel in October 1970 of a heroin-morphine overdose. Her album *Pearl* (1971) was one of three posthumous albums.[34]

Despite major women's contributions to sixties rock 'n' roll, the pop music business remained male dominated. In assessing the spirit of the sixties from its music, one must focus on the denigrating images of women and macho perspective that were definitely "in the air," projected over radio, heard at parties, and increasingly elsewhere in public, typified by the lyrics of Jim Morrison of The Doors and Mick Jagger of The Rolling Stones, using "little girls" hedonistically if not brutally.

Jimi Hendrix's "foxy lady" was not a feminist. These voices, rather than those of women, dominated the decade, especially at its end.

One woman remembers her disillusionment at Woodstock in 1969, which she saw not as a romantic festival of peace, love, and rock 'n' roll but as a brutal experience, a kind of concentration camp mobbed by thousands of ill-fed people, requiring an arduous effort to slog through mud and over hundreds of half-clothed, writhing bodies to line up at a rare Port-a-Potty half a mile away. The profit-motivated mega-concert and superfestival of the Woodstock Music and Art Fair or Aquarian Exposition on the weekend of 15–18 August on Max Yasgur's 600-acre farm near Bethel and White Lake, New York, in the Catskills drew an estimated 300,000–400,000 and was touted as epitomizing the spirit of a generation. Despite stunning performances by Tina Turner, Janis Joplin, and Melanie, it was a male-dominated event. Only after the fact did Joni Mitchell write the festival "anthem," although she was not even there but appearing on *The Dick Cavett Show*, where she gushed about how wonderful it all was. The making of the myth of the sixties was well underway.

Counterculture Experiments

The quest for alternatives and escapism in the counterculture was not new, nor was it monopolized by the young. Indeed, the mecca for the sixties' esoteric philosophers and cultural radicals was nearly two decades old, a site perched midway on the California coast at Big Sur. The Esalen Institute, formally named in 1964, had attracted intellectuals, bohemians, and assorted seekers since the mid-forties. Many of them were notable women like Laura Huxley, wife of writer Aldous Huxley and herself a lecturer and seminar leader in the Human Potentialities movement she helped launch there in 1962. Esalen conferences and workshops brought in individuals like Charlotte Selver, who taught "sensory awareness" as a physical-training discipline, and Imogen Cunningham, who taught photography. There, Ida Rolf developed a procedure called Rolfing or "structural integration," combining techniques of hatha yoga, osteopathy, and physical re-education suggested by the Human Potentialities movement. Young experts came also: Joan Baez spoke at a seminar on "The New Folk Music" in 1964. Virginia Satir of the Palo Alto Mental Research Institute became a faculty member for a time in 1966 and conducting family therapy sessions. Esalen premised the New Age movement of the eighties.

But Esalen was overshadowed by San Francisco's Haight-Ashbury district as counterculture capital from 1965 into 1967, although the my-thologized Haight had only about 7,000 counterculture inhabitants at its peak. Women who tried the hippie lifestyle there were often sexually exploited under motto of "free love." The Communication Company, producer of posters and neighborhood news, recorded on 16 April 1967: "Pretty little 16-year-old middle-class chick comes to the Haight to see what it's all about & gets picked up by a 17-year-old street dealer who spends all day shooting her full of speed . . . then feeds her 3000 mikes [micrograms of LSD, 12 times the standard dose] & raffles off her temporarily unemployed body for the biggest Haight Street gang-bang since the night before last. The politics & ethics of ecstasy. Rape is as common as bullshit on Haight Street."[35]

Such was the general treatment of women on the infamous psyche-delic bus tour Ken Kesey led for a motley crew dubbed the Merry Pranksters, beginning in 1964. The stars were the macho Kesey, Neal Cassady, Hunter S. Thompson, Baba Ram Dass, and Paul Krassner. Kathy Casano went along for the ride. When she had a Bad Trip at Larry McMurtry's Texas ranch, wandering about in only a blanket, the Pranksters named her Stark Naked and abandoned her after phoning her old San Francisco boyfriend to come for her. More fortunate was Gretchin Fetchin, nicknamed the Slime Queen because of the glee with which she swam in green pond slime on a "Good Trip." These incidents pale when compared to one horrendous episode, remembered by Paul Perry, in which a "tripping" female fellow traveller "offered to have sex" with the Hell's Angels—four or five at a time "like a bunch of cats toying with a mouse" through the night at a Pranksters Party at Kesey's house. Women were accessories on the bus, entertainment at best if they remained "groovy," disposable commodities if they became "bum-mers" bringing the males "down."[36]

Culture critic Joan Didion anatomized "the District" of the Haight in a searing essay, "Slouching Towards Bethlehem" (1968), describing the tragic naïveté of the "flower children," including run-aways as young as 14, "sloughing off both the past and the future as snakes shed their skins," many of them escaping from broken homes or conventional parents who banned short skirts or long hair. Their lives were anes-thesized by diverse drugs—"tripping" on marijuana ("grass"), hash (a "luxury item"), LSD, peyote, amphetamines ("crystal"), or heroin ("smack")—while they experimented with yoga, meditation, macrobiotics, and free love to fill an inexorable void epitomized by their pre-sentistic platitudes. An outside investigator deemed old at 32, Didion pessimistically concludes, "We are seeing the desperate attempt of a handful of pathetically unequipped children to create a community in a social vacuum. . . . we could no longer overlook . . . , no longer pre-tend that society's atomization could be reversed. . . . At some point between 1945 and 1967 we had somehow neglected to tell these chil-dren the rules of the game we happened to be playing. Maybe we had stopped believing in the rules ourselves."[37]

Some women held leading positions in the Haight community, but their success was often due to dubious male motives. Charles Perry reports that KMPX-FM, billed as the first underground or hippie radio station, was "the only station in town with female sound engineers, because one of the DJs had fallen in love with a waitress at a North Beach vegetarian restaurant and cagily suggested to Donahue [the man-ager] that the station hire some female engineers rather than those ugly old male engineers. The waitress got her third-class license in May and on June 5 [1967] the station hired a second female engineer." Despite the station's slogans of "freedom and love," the staff grew discontented about meager wages and staged a walkout in 1968.[38]

A few women stood out in the counterculture. Bill Graham largely credits Bonnie MacLean with the success of his Fillmore Auditorium, the large hall where the best hippie bands performed: "if there was one person without whom the Fillmore wouldn't have happened, it was Bonnie. . . . she was such an integral part of the whole thing we went through—the difficulties with downtown, getting the permits, setting up the place right, making sure everything ran smoothly week to week. Bonnie was another critical eye for me. . . . and she was creative." She did "subtle, decorative, and amusing" chalk billboard art announcing current and coming acts and produced posters and smaller handbills in 1966. Graham married her. A few other women designed psychedelic rock posters in a field dominated by men—Gail Moscoso, Terri Tep-per, and Linda Nimmer.[39]

Luria Castell, a former student activist who had visited Castro's Cuba, and Ellen Harmon were two of four founders of the Family Dog, a group devoted to creating a "loose, expressive atmosphere with cos-tume and rock music and a sense of frontiers." They sponsored a dance and other events every other week at the International Longshoremen's and Warehousemen's Union Hall near Fishermen's Wharf, thanks to

Castell's labor connections, promoting alternative rock and groups like Frank Zappa's Mothers. Enduring only from 1965 into 1966, these events set much of the tone associated with the Haight.[40]

In January 1967 hippies staged the first "Human Be-In" in Golden Gate Park while rebellious youth flocked to New York's East Village or formed communities or colonies in downtrodden, cheap-rent neighborhoods in cities and college towns. Most "flower children" were from suburban, middle-class families, intent on rejecting their parents' conformity and materialism as well as commitment. A new sort of sexism permeated the youth culture. As Shulamith Firestone complained, "Liberated men needed groovy chicks who could swing with their new lifestyle." Living together—in heterosexual or homosexual couples or in larger groups—became increasingly the rule in the counterculture, a rejection of "uptight" or "straight" moral standards and a celebration of "free love." The slogan, "Make Love Not War," addressed to young men, had the counterpart, "Girls Say Yes to Guys Who Say No," both promising sexual favors to men.

Newsweek summarized in 1967: "For the hippies, sex is not a matter of great debate, because as far as they are concerned the sexual revolution is accomplished. There are no hippies who believe in chastity, or look askance at marital infidelity, or see even marriage itself as a virtue. Physical love is a delight—to be chewed upon as often and as freely as a handful of sesame seeds." *Newsweek* warned Middle America, "The old taboos are dead or dying. A new, more permissive society is taking shape. . . . The crucial question is where the new permissiveness is leading, whether the breakdown of the old order is going to lead to some new moral system, or whether it is simply going to lead to the progressive discarding of all social restraint." *Time* also found that pictures of 2,000 nude hippies in San Francisco's Golden Gate Park sold plenty of magazines to a middle-class that delighted in being shocked.[41]

Timothy Leary's call to "turn on, tune in, drop out" had minimal appeal to women. Until about 1966, drug use seemed more a political act of defiance, the mark of a fifties bohemian than merely a recreational escape. Lee H. Bowker claims that young women were exposed to drugs primarily through their boyfriends, who were more likely to interact socially with drug dealers, most of whom were male. "More females [were] threatened than attracted" by boyfriends' display of "newly-gained sophistication" about drugs, promoted to make men "socio-sexually desirable." Some young women succumbed to "drug seductions" because they were "socialized to please males." Also, boys had more money, enabling them to control drug distribution and hence to dominate girls sexually. Females rarely became drug dealers but often maintained a moderate level of recreational drug use tied to dating.[42]

Sara Davidson's cult autobiography *Loose Change* (1977) reinforces Bowker's analysis of women's recreational drug use. The book moves through Davidson's life when she was a UC-Berkeley undergraduate in the early sixties, moves on to her experiences in the radical youth movement, and to her work at the decade's end as a journalist with leftist sympathies. Davidson notes that college-aged and slightly older white middle-class women used drugs to make them feel good and provide temporary relief from or help with tenuous relationships. She used drugs after trying a joint passed at a 1965 dinner at a former sorority sister's home, and tried LSD with her husband at the Human Be-In at Golden Gate Park on 4 January 1967. Returning to Berkeley to cover Governor Ronald Reagan's firing of the University of California president, Davidson ran into the man who introduced her to pot; and he "turned her on" to acid (LSD). Stoned, listening to the Beatles and dancing nude to liquid light projections on the walls in a room lined with pink fur, she experienced the most fantastic party of her life. Despite these happy episodes, Davidson presents a negative view of drug and alcohol use by people trapped in unhappy marriages yet trying to be "hip." She believed a casual joint usually led to other drugs—illegal tranquilizers, LSD, psychedelics like MDA, and even angel dust, an equine tranquilizer.[43]

Grace Slick suggested a contemporary motive for drug use in a song she wrote, "White Rabbit," which recalled *Alice in Wonderland* and other stories her parents had read her. Such retreat to fantasy, aided by chemical ingestion, helped her and others accept realities like the bomb, war, and civil unrest. Joanne Stark, a former hippie, explains that psychedelic drugs helped her "to accept an idea of life that was not linear, not rational, full of surprises, full of jeopardy. . . . part of a sense of disintegration, that it was good for life to disintegrate, that ordinary life had been a trap, a one-way conveyor belt, and that these drugs would open you to the delights of experience."[44]

Others turned away from mainstream culture by joining a hippie commune or "family," alternatives to the nuclear family. Whether in a rambling Victorian house in a decaying urban neighborhood or on an old farm in the California or Vermont hills, communes often institutionalized sexual freedom and regular drug use; but like the streets of the Haight, they were rarely truly liberating for women. Many of these youths found gurus for their "up to the country" or "back to the land" movement in an older couple, Helen and Scott Nearing, whose *Living the Good Life* was based on their years in rural Maine. The book became so popular that it was reissued in 1970, including practical advice on hand-built houses and subsistence gardens.

In the name of the "natural" or "organic," women found a redefinition of the old phrase "anatomy is destiny," playing traditional earth-mothers and peasant women, making fresh bread, tending kitchen gardens, and plying their needles to create hippie fashions. Women continued to be sex objects, expected to participate impulsively in "free love" with any countercultural man. Such was the case of Genie Johnson (1950–), member of John Sinclair's Trans Love Energies Unlimited, a Detroit hippie community and "free store." In 1967 she worked unpaid making beads and sandals and printing poetry books to sell to support the commune and build a psychedelic dance hall, The Mystic Knights of the See Lodge. Likewise, Barbara, living in a two-couple open household in the Haight, told Joan Didion she "learned to find happiness in 'the woman thing'" while staying with Indians where women were "shunted off. . . . never to enter into any of the men's talk." Barbara "grooved" on this "woman's trip," ironically not unlike that of the suburban housewife's life that the hippies were supposedly rejecting.[45]

Some sixties films reflect the counterculture's casual sexuality and sexism and the undercurrent of violence and fear that accompanied it, demonstrating a disturbing nihilism. In *Petulia* (1968), set in San Francisco, British star Julie Christie (1941–) is battered by her impotent American husband (Richard Chamberlin). Director Richard Lester portrays them as "emotional eunuchs in a society so riddled with the cancer of its own failing that commitment is never made," indicting gender roles in both mainstream society and the counterculture in the 1967 Summer of Love. In Michaelangelo Antonioni's *Zabriskie Point* (1969), two young would-be radicals "meet in the southwestern desert where they sexually and ideologically connect." The characters bear the first names of the real actors—Daria Halprin and Mark Frechette; and the desert serves as a metaphor for American culture. In the film, women and men are sapped of personality and passion, rendered gender neutral. In *Easy Rider* (1969) by Peter Fonda and Dennis Hopper, women are either naive teenagers, earth-mothers, or whores; the film explores freedom exclusively in male terms.[46]

Many films pretending to represent the counterculture actually used styles and issues only as decor for scripts that timidly surveyed "revolutionary" issues before concluding in favor of mainstream culture. In *The Rain People* (1969), Francis Ford Coppola probed both the destruction of the American environment and female liberation; but the film fluctuates between admiring and admonishing Natalie (Shirley Knight) for her quest for self-identity. Coppola cleverly highlights Natalie's habit of referring to herself in the third person and dramatizes her indecision during a series of long-distance phone calls to her abandoned husband, simultaneously promoting and discrediting her liberation.[47]

Men in the counterculture as in the New Left often proved crass and heartless in their treatment of women. While Stokely Carmichael may have jested in his infamous remark, "The only position for women in SNCC is prone," it captured the spirit of many radical and countercultural males. Marge Piercy complained in 1969 that "Fucking a staff into existence is only the extreme form of what passes for common practice in many places. A man can bring a woman into an organization by sleeping with her and remove her by ceasing to do so. A man can purge a woman for no other reason than he has tired of her, knocked her up, or is after someone else; and that purge is accepted without a ripple. There are cases of a woman excluded from a group for no other reason than that one of its leaders proved impotent with her."[48]

As a writer for the New Left journal *Rat*, Robin Morgan knew many a revolutionary man "supposedly dedicated to building a new, free social order" who thought nothing of "absent-mindedly" ordering "his 'chick' to shut up and make supper or wash his socks." Countercultural males had not rejected the gender roles or power relationships of mainstream culture—indeed, many promoted a "gender caste system" that was even more exploitative, through the "sexual revolution." Morgan lamented at decade's end, "We have met the enemy and he's our friend. . . . It hurts to understand that at Woodstock or Altamount a woman could be declared uptight or a poor sport if she didn't want to be raped."[49]

9

The Arts

The Visual Arts

The arts and literature in the sixties took on increasingly public subjects and abandoned traditional forms. The struggle for expression and the impetus to experiment, born of a deep and growing sense of displacement, led artists to break rules and cross boundaries. The photographed grotesques of Diane Arbus and the frenetic happenings of the New York art scene, like the Living Theater of Judith Malina and Julian Beck, assaulted the viewer and denied a simple response of acceptance or rejection. Much art, like literature, became more political—sometimes blatantly so. Distinctions between high and low culture blurred or were swept away by rejection of what seemed to many a destructive establishment elitism of a cultural aristocracy who had controlled ethics, aesthetics, conventions, and presentation of the arts. Although the move to make major arts institutions and museums more socially relevant did not gain momentum until the mid-seventies, it had its roots in the sixties' radical re-definition of what constituted art. Women worked in all media, but, as had long been true, still found it more difficult to display their work and to reap the rewards of grants, patronage, and institutional recognition; and they were in the vanguard of those struggling to give artists more control over their work and its presentation.

Photography

Photography had been one exceptional art medium relatively open to women. As visual images became increasingly important in mass and high cultures, a generation of older women photographers culminated notable careers in the sixties. Dorothea Lange (1895–1965) had solo shows at the San Francisco Museum of Art and the Oakland Museum in 1960 and won a place on the Honor Roll of the American Society of Magazine Photographers in 1963. While fighting esophagus cancer, she designed her retrospective exhibition that was posthumously hung at the Museum of Modern Art (MoMA) in 1966. Her last book, *The American Country Woman* (1967), grew out of an exhibition that traveled internationally (1960–1967). The most popular show sponsored by the U.S. Information Agency, it was a celebration of the strength, pride, and endurance of average rural women; it reaffirmed Lange's reputation as one of the century's major documentary photographers.

Another was Margaret Bourke-White (1904–1971), a major photojournalist, forced into retirement by Parkinson's disease and only able to publish her autobiography *Portrait of Myself* (1963). Imogen Cunningham (1883–1976) continued an active career that dated from her turn-of-the-century Pictorialism, winning a Guggenheim Fellowship in 1970. Similarly, Lotte Jacobi (1896–1990) continued her studies at University of New Hampshire (1961–62) and at Atélier 7 in Paris in 1963. In the same year she opened her gallery, Lotte Jacobi Place, a New Hampshire base from which she continued to work. Barbara Morgan (1900–) still worked on various projects, including a 1964 *Aperture* monograph, and lectured nationally.

After 18 years of meticulous research and photography, Laura Gilpin (1891–1979), long known for her images of the Southwest, published *The Enduring Navaho* (1968), to win the Western Heritage Center's 1969 award for nonfiction. The Indian Arts and Crafts Board of the Interior Department awarded her an Appreciation Award in 1967; but tragically a major travelling exhibition to start a nationwide tour was lost in transit in 1969. Also, Helen Levitt (1918–), known for humanist documentaries of New York's street life, resumed work after a long illness, winning Guggenheim Fellowships (1959, 1960) to study techniques of color photography. Her color work, continuing her previous urban focus, was shown at the Museum of Modern Art (MoMA) in 1963 but was stolen and remains unrecovered. Discouraged, she ceased street photography until 1971.

While older photographers expanded the subject matter of women artists, the career and sensibility of Diane Nemerov Arbus (1923–71) was most notable in transforming photography in the sixties. Arbus, mother of two daughters, turned from fashion to art photography after the 1960 breakup of her marriage. *Life* rejected her work as not "upbeat" enough; but she produced photo essays for *Sports Illustrated*, *Harper's Bazaar*, *Glamour*, and *Saturday Evening Post*, over 250 images in more than 70 articles, often with her own text. Although Arbus made commissioned portraits of the rich and famous, she preferred those images of misfortune and adversity that she felt she had not experienced in the "unreality" of her privileged, protected childhood. Her rebellion against comfortable conformity was intensely personal; she experienced a "thrill" in confronting her fears and "obsessions." Her fascination with taboos and antitheses of beauty led to such shocking images that her blatantly direct, confrontational, front-lit photographs seemed new, although inspired by studies with Lisette Model (1955–57). Arbus photographed eccentrics or "freaks" at Coney Island, at Hubert's Freak Museum on 42nd-Street, and at circuses, calling them "aristocrats" for having "already passed their test in life," for having been "born with their trauma," which most people only could dread throughout their lives.[1]

In 1960, Arbus frequented the Bellevue morgue, brothels, flophouses, and a pet crematorium for "The Vertical Journey: Six Movements of a Moment within the Heart of the City," a photoessay for *Esquire*. In 1962, she started using a 2¼" Rolleiflex, held at elbow level; unlike her 35mm camera, it permitted her to look her subject in the eye while photographing. She labeled her work "contemporary anthropology." Guggenheim Fellowships in 1963 and 1966 encouraged work featured in the 1967 MoMA "New Documents" show, assuring both her international reputation as leader of the "new" documentary style and acclaim by major museums. Arbus was always there at avant garde events—gallery openings, happenings, events at the Judson Memorial Church, even Ethel Scull's trendy parties. Her last assignment was on Ozzie and Harriet, "The Happy, Happy, Happy Nelsons," for *Esquire*. Already a legend, she committed suicide on 26 July 1971 at age 48 by slitting her wrists in the bathtub. In 1972, she became the first American photographer represented at the famed Venice Biennale; and MoMA's retrospective show of her work was seen by 7.25 million people as it traveled across North America.[2]

Similarly, Alisa Wells (1929–) turned to photography after growing dissatisfied with her role as a housewife in the fifties, and the breakup of her marriage. A student of Ansel Adams in 1961, of Beaumont and Nancy Newhall, and later of Nathan Lyons, Wells moved from four-by-five view-camera studies of natural forms to experimental, manipulated images involving solarization (exposure of the unfixed print to light), staining, multiple exposures, old glass-plate negatives, and double-frame images illustrating time lag. Switching to a 35mm camera, she produced "poetic interpretations of the human condition." Although she became Associate Curator at the Eastman House in Rochester and her images were in great demand for publications and shows, she hesitated to go public until 1967; then she titled series of images "The Glass Menagerie" (1968) and "Found Moments Transformed" (1969), to express "her feelings of self-hate, self-destruction, and self-inquiry." Zen Buddhism helped her overcome a sense of dependence and inferiority. One critic notes that "Many cannot relate to her work because her photographs are too personal. Her work is so autobiographical that it is for many viewers too intimate an encounter."[3]

Using a four-by-five view camera in 1968, Judy Dater (1941–) began her specialization in conceptual portraits, especially of women, usually displaying their sexuality. She collaborated closely with Jack Welpott, whom she married in 1971. Together, they tried to capture the spirit of contemporary women, whose "heads are in a completely different place from those of their mothers." Dater sought out "the free spirits among women" and was a founding member of the Visual Dialogue Foundation in San Francisco, a support group and exhibition space for young photographers and photohistorians.[4]

Color photography, first introduced in 1936, was considered the stuff of advertising and ignored by those aspiring to produce art until the sixties. Marie Cosindas (1925–), who began creative work in black-and-white, led an aesthetic revolution from 1962 on through still-lifes produced with Polacolor instant sheet film as one the few photographers to whom Polaroid offered its new film, asking only for experimentation. Her mentor Ansel Adams encouraged her because she "thought in color." Through meticulous technical control—filters and varied exposures, lights and temperatures—Cosindas justified color for serious art; her work seemed "more painterly than photographic"; but for that reason and because of her images' content—as assemblages of artifacts, feathers, flowers, fabrics, fruits and vegetables—they were "often disparaged or dismissed." Some suggested she had sold out to the company; but her pioneering work won acclaim from MoMA photography curator John Szarkowski with a show in 1966—only the fourth color photography exhibition in that museum's history. It came at a time when Pop Art and Minimalism "called for an end to 'pretty' colors that played on the viewer's sentimental memories and associations." That year, Boston's Museum of Fine Arts honored her with the first one-person exhibition it had ever given a living photographer. One-woman shows followed at the Art Institute of Chicago, the Metropolitan Museum of Art, and internationally; and younger photographers learned from her in the seventies. Tom Wolfe judges that Cosindas "opened up the most startling and spectacular *terra incognita*," advancing "the state of the art in color photography to a plateau that only she has been able to occupy" with "the sort of fireproof reputation enjoyed by Weston and Adams."[5]

Experiments by other women photographers pushed the medium's limits. Eve Sonneman (1946–) began pairing photographs as "dyptyches" showing disjunctions in time in 1968 before moving to color work. Naomi Savage (1927–) combined color photoetchings and inked and intaglio relief prints. Joan Lyons (1937–) and Bea Nettles (1946–) were part of a school of American artists using photolithography and silkscreen, manipulated to create unusual effects. Such efforts furthered recognition of photography as a fine art.[6]

Grace M. Mayer continued to be influential in the world of photography as curator of MoMA's department of photographs, a position she assumed in 1959. In 1961, she organized a retrospective exhibit of her friend Edward Steichen's work and from 1962 to 1968 was in charge of his archive and began writing his biography.

The Arts Establishment

As sculptor and fine arts professor Joan Brigham observes, "there was a generation gap between women in the art world of the sixties." The older generation had a much harder time winning acceptance by the art establishment; and therefore they worked like men, producing finished objects that would stand up to critical scrutiny. Younger artists were more interested in concepts and worked with a diversity of new materials; they readily worked in groups, foregoing individual fame for the sake of collective projects that were often issue-oriented and controversial. They formed collaborative galleries and performance spaces and found other ways to by-pass the "system."[7]

According to art historian Whitney Chadwick, the sculptor Louise Nevelson (1899–1988), the Abstract Expressionist painter Lee Krasner (1908–1983), and other women of their generation, "worked steadily for many years before receiving the recognition given their male contemporaries at a much earlier date." In the fifties, artists like Krasner and Elaine De Kooning often tried to mask authorship of their work; but "the decision to erase gender as part of the creative process was less an attempt to hide their identities as women than to evade being labelled 'feminine' by becoming the man/woman whose creative efforts earned praise"—in other words, to counter the male-dominated arts establishment of critics and curators that could make but more frequently broke an aspiring artist's career. Only after the death of her husband, Jackson Pollock, did Krasner return to New York to embark upon her most productive period from 1964 to 1974, producing canvasses covered by swinging arcs of color. Krasner's first major show was in London in 1965, not in the United States.[8]

Georgia O'Keeffe (1887–1986), whose work had been neglected during fifties Abstract Expressionism, was rediscovered after being featured in the Metropolitan Museum's "Four American Masters" show in 1958. She was made a member of the American Academy of Arts and Letters in 1962 and of the American Academy of Arts and Sciences in 1966. That year, major retrospectives of her work appeared at Fort Worth's Amon Carter Museum and Houston's Museum of Fine Arts. Finally in 1970, she hung her own show at the Whitney Museum of American Art, with her agent Doris Bry as co-curator. O'Keeffe continued to paint and maintain her own rugged individualism at her New Mexico ranch, perhaps repulsed by critical comments like that of Willard Huntington Wright who charged, "All these pictures say is 'I want to have a baby'." O'Keeffe countered, "I am trying with all my skill to do a painting that is all of women, as well as all of me." Her biographer notes, "O'Keeffe had outlived her own aesthetic obsolescence to become classic." Although she resisted the label of feminist, new feminists adopted her as "an iconic figure" and "exemplar of feminist behavior."[9]

Chadwick observes that despite a lack of institutional support, the period from 1955–65 was "important in bringing recognition to a number of women sculptors," but many artists only achieved success by conforming to the arts establishment's male standards. Louise Nevelson had been exhibiting her assemblage sculpture for three decades and received acclaim abroad before she was recognized at home as a major American artist. Although Nevelson had her first major show at New York's Nierendorf Gallery in 1946, an early "blatantly sexist critical response" kept her out of galleries for a decade. One critic later admitted, "We learned the artist was a woman in time to check our enthusiasm. Had it been otherwise, we might have hailed these sculptural expressions as by surely a great figure among the moderns." Nevelson's first solo American museum exhibition did not occur until 1960. She represented the United States in the 1963 Venice Biennale and had her first one-person show at the Whitney in 1967. Her abstract wooden sculptures of monumental scale, assembled of recycled materials— crates, fragments of furniture, architectural elements, garbage, bric-à-brac, and modern materials like aluminum, Plexiglas, or Formica, all unified by a coat of either matt black, white, or gold paint—became prominent in American cityscapes by decade's end, installed in urban plazas with the support of new programs requiring that one percent of the costs of new construction be spent on public art. Nevelson's work combined Cubism and Constructivism, Dada ready-mades and Surrealist dream-objects.[10]

The sculpture of Louise Bourgeois (1911–) grew increasingly sexual in the sixties at the same time as the mature artist served as mentor and inspiration for a new generation of young feminist artists. Bourgeois was born near Paris and moved to the United States in 1938 when she married Robert Goldwater, an art historian. They had three sons. After her first show in 1948, she worked "in comfortable obscurity," known only to a few art-world insiders for years. In the sixties, Bourgeois abandoned wood in favor of papier-mâché, plaster, and latex, sculpted or cast, and shifted her style to Surrealism. Dore Ashton judges that "Few have been able to work in a traditional medium with such force and invention." Chadwick describes Bourgeois's production of abstract bulbous and penile forms as "sometimes merging organically into composite forms, often part phallic, part fecal. The primary, sensual world she evokes is undifferentiated and 'polymorphously perverse'." Others called her work "both aggressive and vulnerable." Critic Lucy Lippard adds, "On the one hand, Bourgeois' subject is power— or power and powerlessness—and on the other, it is growth and germination." A prime example is her "Fillette" (1968), a ambiguous name for a latex dildo with gonads, erect yet seeming in decay—sure to serve the modernist intent to "shock the bourgeoisie." Bourgeois was acclaimed as "the elder statesperson" of sixties Eccentric Abstractionists; but MoMA did not give her a retrospective until 1982.[11]

Although painting in the sixties shifted away from Abstract Expressionism, Helen Frankenthaler (1928–), the one woman prominent in the style, did not have her large one-person New York show at the Whitney until 1969, two decades after earning Clement Greenberg's critical approval. By then, male painters like Morris Louis and Kenneth Noland had emulated her stained canvas, "soak-stain," or "pour" techniques to win their own reputations. Like so many other women artists, Frankenthaler won recognition abroad before at home—winning first prize in the Paris Biennial of 1959 and representing the United States in the 1966 Venice Biennale. Meanwhile, Frankenthaler's work evolved as she switched to acrylics in 1963 and radically simplified her canvasses with more formal, designed structure and less fragile color. Some critics praised her "anti-establishment stance" and her contempt for "the slickness of the unslick"; but others saw her style as becoming more masculine, more about technique than content. The "macho enclave of Abstract Expressionism's inner circle" left little room for women like Frankenthaler, Lee Krasner, Yvonne Thomas, and Joan Mitchell, despite their talents. Because of this, Mitchell remained an expatriate in Paris.[12]

Unwilling to take on the men or conform to style, many other women artists like Jo Baer (1929–) and Miriam Schapiro (1923–) abandoned Abstract Expressionism and turned to the formalist abstraction and attention to surface color of Postpainterly Abstraction, to the immense industrial shapes of Minimal sculpture, or to Pop Art. Baer's paintings were single-color canvases, empty fields emphasizing the color line of the frame. A former Abstract Expressionist, Ethel Schwabacher (1903–1984), created controversial paintings of women "which specifically referred to a nature/culture dichotomy." Such oppositions and contrasts became a recurring theme for women artists in the sixties.[13]

The Geometric Abstractionist paintings of Agnes Martin (1912–), monochrome (white or off-white) canvases with barely perceptible lines and grids of great delicacy, were influential and innovative. Running "totally counter to the prevailing spirit of abstract expressionism," the "poetic and geometrical purist" Martin's paintings were minimalist, "patiently repetitive" grids with fanciful names like "Starlight" (1962), "Night Sea" (1963), "Drift of Summer" (1965), and "The Cliff" (1966). Some were huge squares of rich colors; others, simple pencil lines on bare canvas—all non-representational. Martin wrote extensively, often in verse, about her work's theoretical and philosophical underpinnings—basically a belief in innate ideas and classicism. She ceased to paint in 1967, having developed a "high if narrowly based reputation."[14]

Lippard observes that Martin and other women artists seemed particularly attracted to the grid. Loretta Dunkelman used modules or repetitive forms in her 1964 collages. Brenda Miller painted a basic grid structure or skeleton at that time, shifting to sculpture in boxes in 1967 but maintaining the grid. Michelle Stuart (1938–) began using "simple unadorned boxes as containers" or frames for her sculpture in 1963, making them modular units in 1965. She writes, "The grid was used as a framework or 'scaffolding' for inner experiences imposed upon it." Mary Miss (1944–) admits that since 1966 her sculptures "suggest extendable networks both indoors and outdoors." Paula Tavins explains use of the grid as her attempt "to establish a visual vocabulary that made reference to repetition, molecular structure, and energy." This testimony disproves Lawrence Alloway's allegation that women artists adopted the grid or "synonymous forms," as if in conspiracy, *because* of their common association in Lippard's Ad Hoc Women's Committee, formed to promote women's art at decade's end.[15]

Other women artists moved away from modernism toward Pop Art and other forms, challenging established styles. The Venezuelan/French-born sculptor Marisol Escobar (1930–), simply called Marisol, a New York resident since 1950, specialized in cubistic, life-sized figures. Her early small terra cotta figures inspired by folkart and surrealism and shown at New York's Stable Gallery in 1962 established her fame; but left-handed compliments by the likes of Andy Warhol, calling her "the first girl artist with glamour," only echoed arts establishment sexism. Marisol's talent and charismatic personal image made her a media celebrity rivaling Warhol in Pop Art. Indeed, one of her pieces in a 1964 show was "Andy Warhol"; and to counter his famous renditions of women as cartoons—"slick nudes, pin-ups, and sex objects" like Marilyn Monroe and Jackie Kennedy—she presented "John Wayne." Marisol's sculptures were often based upon her own face or other anatomical parts, augmented by real objects or props such as clothing. Many satirize urban society. Carter Ratcliff describes "The Party" (1965–66), fifteen life-sized wooden figures posed rigidly: "The meticulously decorated surfaced of the figures emphasize their obsession with apparel," while "blank eyes show inpenetrable inwardness." Portrait sculptures achieve "sharp, sometimes acidulous satirical comments on public figures and the world of fashion." Her "Self-Portrait" (1961–62) even suggests a proto-feminism, Chadwick suggests, presenting "women encased and imprisoned in wooden blocks and stultifying social roles, endlessly repeated figures, monstrous babies. . . . and her obsessive use of self-images, when combined with stereotypical presentations of women living out circumscribed roles, built a chilling picture of America middle-class life in the 1960s."[16]

Other women produced Pop Art. Elizabeth Murray (1940–) moved from Chicago to San Francisco to New York, developing what she considered "weird fantasy painting" like that of Warhol and Oldenburg, before shifting to Plain Painting abstractionism. Henri praised the young June Leaf (1929–), new in New York from Chicago in the late sixties, for her "expressionist and almost caricature-like manner." Leaf's "Dreams: The Ascent of the Pig Lady" (1969) was representative of the room/environments she created, posing stuffed dummies or life-sized cut outs to make statements of social and cultural criticism. May Stevens (1924–) used her experiences in civil rights as inspiration for her canvases like "Big Daddy, Paper Doll" (1968), in which, writes Chadwick, "fragmented but menacing male figures are used to explore the relationship between patriarchal power in the family and in social institutions like the American judicial system."[17]

Sculptor Lee Bontecou (1931–) won acclaim for her large constructions of old laundry conveyor belts sewed on steel frames, first exhibited in 1960 and "compared to everything from airplane engines to female sexual parts." Bontecou, Marisol, Sylvia Stone, and other artists provided female role models and inspiration for younger artists. Bontecou especially inspired other sculptors like Eva Hesse to use non-traditional industrial materials in their work.[18]

The career of sculptor Eva Hesse (1936–1970) exactly spanned the decade. She exhibited some drawings in group shows in 1961, the year she married Tom Doyle, a sculptor. Summering at Woodstock, they collaborated with others in the Park Place Group and organized the Ergo Suits Travelling Carnival—sculpture, dance, and happenings. Her first one-woman show of drawings was at the Allan Stone Gallery in 1963. In 1964, she went to Germany, where, commissioned by an industrialist, she developed her characteristic style, blending painting and sculpture, combining string, rope, latex, metal, clay, wire mesh, found objects, and industrial materials. Her palette was monochrome, ranging from black to gray to white, with occasional tan and copper.

With the end of her marriage in 1965, overcoming a sense of aban-donment and panic, Hesse entered a geometrical period in 1966, fash-ioning tightly bound black organic forms that some critics described as erotic—boxes with highly tactile surfaces like her "Accession II" (1967), drawings and sculptures based on a grid, perhaps inspired by Agnes Martin. In 1966, Hesse's sculpture appeared in gallery shows—"Ab-stract Inflationism and Stuffed Expressionism" and the "Eccentric Ab-straction," curated by Lucy Lippard (1937–). By then, Hesse's work reflected Minimal and Conceptual Art, labeled by one critic "Serial Surrealism." Her most famous work, "Hang-up" (1965–66), was a large, thin, empty frame pierced by a long loop of bent rod that extended eleven feet onto the floor. It attracted critical acclaim, sparking five years of fame and frantic creativity in which Hesse probed the absurd. She produced many "soft" sculptures.[19]

Hesse's work appeared in a number of Process group shows. Process Art was a highly conceptual school that made documentation like dia-ries and notes integral to artistic creation. Hesse's work was highly au-tobiographical and psychological, difficult to separate from her life, as she often explained, full of her sense of absurdity and humor. Much was sexually or anatomically suggestive. The terms "strong and vul-nerable, tentative and expansive" describe both Hesse and her work. A January 1964 entry reflects a personal feminism, "I cannot be so many things. I cannot be something for everyone. . . . Woman, beautiful, artist, wife, housekeeper, cook, saleslady, all these things. I cannot even be myself or know who I am." Elsewhere, Hesse observed, "For me . . . art and life are inseparable." Hesse "came to realize that the self she was finding through her work was really worth something," wrote Lippard. "In her emphasis on absurdity, however, she remained an ex-istentialist artist." Tragically, Hesse died in 1970 at age thirty-four of a brain tumor.[20]

Acclaim came posthumously with a 1972 show curated by Linda Shearer at the Guggenheim, which travelled nationally. Lippard judges, "The critical neglect of Hesse's achievements and refusal to take her as seriously as other artists," during her life, "can probably be as-cribed to the fact that as a woman, she couldn't *be* the 'new Pollock.'" Her friend Sol LeWitt remembers, "She was very hurt," in 1968 by her "first confrontation with art politics and anti-feminism." Posthumous reviews treated her as "a tragic female stereotype," often misquoting from her diaries, rather than as the influential artist she was. Hesse became "a myth, the art world's answer to Sylvia Plath and Diane Arbus," writes Lippard. "That she did not commit suicide and had, on the contrary, an immensely strong will to live and to work, was ignored." Kasha Linville Gula also observes, "The American public finds it necessary to turn its great women artists into tragic figures and then to forget about their work—as if their deaths, with the emphasis on suicide, somehow explain their artistic output. . . . By implication, any woman who carries her art to heights that subordinate her personal life is bound to die tragically, probably by her own hand." Hesse, however, believed to the end that "the way to beat discrimination in art is by art. Excellence has no sex."[21]

Lynda Bengalis (1941–) received some establishment recognition after moving to New York from New Orleans in 1964, declaring her intention "to make something very tactile, something that related to the body" and winning rapid recognition because of her espousal of "process" or what critics considered abstract expressionism transposed into an actual environmental enterprise. Her sculpture suggested participation and hinted at the aftermath of a happening. Her flat, triangular rubber piece "Bounce"—inevitably judged Pollock-like—was selected for the Whitney Museum's 1969 "Anti-Illusion: Procedures/Materials" show; but it was not included because curators insisted she hang the work she meant for the floor. Complying, she designed subsequent work to be displayed on walls.[22]

Other women artists won acclaim for innovative work using various new materials. Ruth Vollmer (1899–1982) based her three-dimensional plastic and acrylic shapes on mathematical models, some of them biomorphic. [Varda] Chryssa (1933–) created Light Art compositions of curvilinear or rectilinear neon mounted in Plexiglas boxes mirroring repetitious patterns. Leonore Tawney (1925–), a weaver, transcended her craft to create sculpture after moving to New York from Chicago in 1957, inventing new sorts of looms to produce large, elongated, anthropomorphic works of linen and wood with names like *The Queen*, *The Virgin*, and *The Bride*. Sheila Hicks (1934–) drew upon Bauhaus and pre-Columbian inspirations to develop textile weaving and tapestry as art, not craft, winning major prizes and competitions. Anne Truitt (1921–) created minimal structures of painted wood. Beverly Pepper (1924–) fashioned steel sculptures placed to be framed by sky.

After 1963, a number of politically engaged black women artists attacked racism in various media; but they did not receive adequate critical recognition until the seventies. Emma Amos and others instilled Pop Art with social consciousness, exploring "the connections between patriarchy, racism, and imperialism" and epitomizing a reform spirit. Print-maker Elizabeth Catlett (1919–) worked from a sensibility shaped by personal involvement in civil rights. Faith Ringgold (1930–) was the most influential, inspired by African art and the writings of Leroi Jones (later Amiri Baraka) and James Baldwin. This mother of two emphasized the violence in black-white relations in her twelve-foot-long mural "Die" (1967), part of her "American People Series" (1963–67). In 1967, when controversy over misuses of the flag was a conservative cause, she did a series of political paintings incorporating American flags, explaining that this was "the only truly subversive and revolutionary abstraction one can paint." "The Flag is Bleeding" (1967), "a bittersweet plea for racial harmony," shows a white woman, white man, and black man with a knife behind a superimposed bloodied flag. When it became the centerpiece in the People's Flag Show at the Judson Memorial Church in November 1970, Ringgold and two others, the "Judson Three," were arrested and prosecuted for "flag desecration."[23]

The rise of such talented black artists revived the spirit of the Harlem Renaissance. Ringgold's "Black Light Series" (1967–69) probed the optical possibilities of the color black, as well as the problems of blackness in American culture, to create an affirmative black aesthetic. In 1966, Ringgold and others mounted the first art exhibition in Harlem in over three decades, showcasing the work of the painter Lois Mailou Jones (1905–) and the sculptor Augusta Savage (1892–1962). It stimulated formation of the Smokehouse Associates to decorate the inner city with murals on building walls and the Black Emergency Cultural Coalition (BECC). In 1970, the Whitney finally included works by black women artists Betye Saar (1926–) and Barbara Chase-Riboud (1935–) in its Sculpture Biennial after a protest led by Ringgold in 1968.

Barbara Chase (1939–), graduated from Yale in 1960, married French journalist Marc Riboud, had two sons, and traveled widely before settling down in 1967 to produce masks and vestments of silk, wool, hemp rope, bronze, and wood. She dedicated her first one-woman show in 1970 at the Bertha Schaefer Gallery to the assassinated Malcolm X, although her sculptures were "abstract, totemic works," and not obviously political. Else Honig Fine defines Chase-Riboud's work as dealing "with opposites, feeling the need to join opposing forces, male/female, black/white."[24]

In California, Betye Saar, a black mother of three, specialized in Pop Art, multi-media collages of racial stereotypes. "The Liberation of

Aunt Jemima" (1972) epitomized her focus on white stereotypes of blacks with a "mammy" doll holding a rifle and revolver along with her broom, a cartoon of a black nursemaid with a white baby, and a backdrop of multiple images of the smiling Aunt Jemima logo. Other works played upon the stereotypes of Uncle Toms and Little Black Sambos, toy guns, and occult and political images.

By the sixties' end, Super Realism or Artificial Realism grew out of Pop Art and Dada to transform American painting and sculpture. Audrey Flack (1931–), trained in Abstract Expressionism, was one of the first artists to react against that style with her painting "Kennedy Motorcade—Nov. 22, 1963," based on a newspaper photograph. Flack painted a series of photo-realistic portraits of public figures and canvases of garishly colored religious images and jewelry. Sylvia Sleigh and Dotty Attie were also Photo-Realist painters; but women were more dominant in this movement in Europe than in the United States.[25]

Bridget Riley was part of the school of kinetic or Op Art emerging in 1965. Her black and white "Optical" paintings seemed to be three-dimensional and kinetic—giving an illusion of pulsing, flickering, vibrating, or bending. Riley based her work on theories of perception, of the inseparability of neuro-physiological and psychological responses, to achieve "a poetic balance between order and disorder." Critics like Lucy Lippard and Barbara Rose, however, tended to devalue Op Art, especially when the fashion industry and the youth culture adapted it to "mod" clothing and decoration. Although Riley and others insisted their work had a "social orientation," referring to technology, mass production, and social consciousness, critics dismissed Op Art as a simple celebration of technique, "conformist," or even kitsch.[26]

Despite the struggles and marginality of women artists, a few women were part of the arts establishment—the curators, critics, and collectors who could make or break aspiring artists' careers. They encountered their own difficulties in finding niches in the highly competitive, male-dominated art world. An achiever as well as a survivor, Dorothy C. Miller was an influential MoMA curator, organizing a series of shows beginning with *Sixteen Americans* in 1959, setting parameters for sixties modernism by focusing on Neo-Dada and Post-Painterly Abstraction. Her show, *Americans 1963*, marked MoMA's official acceptance of Pop Art. Fine arts academics were sometimes able to influence and validate trends, as when Linda Nochlin (1931–) and her students mounted the exhibit, "Realism Now," in 1968 at the Vassar College Art Museum. Nochlin contributed her writing to catalogues for other exhibitions of works of New Perceptual Realism and Photo-Realism. Raising the question in order to deny its premise, Nochlin's article, "Why Are There No Great Women Artists?" (1971) was very influential in demonstrating the need for art history to look differently at its subject and thus to see women's work.[27]

A few women had always shaped art trends through galleries, although they had far to go to rival powerful male dealers, gallery owners, and curators. Edith Gregor Halpert (1900–1970) was an influential art dealer and collector of American contemporary art since the forties. Her international reputation was assured by her appointment as curator of the 1959 National Art Exhibition sponsored by the State Department and sent to Moscow, despite the objections of the House Un-American Activities Committee. Halpert moved her Downtown Gallery to the Ritz Towers in 1965 whence she continued to defend modernism and other progressive art. Eleanor Ward shaped policy at the Stable Gallery, giving Warhol his first show in 1962. Virginia Dwan and Betty Parsons included a number of younger women in the "stables" of artists shown at their galleries. Paula Cooper (1938–) opened her gallery at 98–100 Prince Street in 1968, combining two lofts to become one of the first art dealers in New York's SoHo district, launching a movement that drew other dealers and the avant garde to transform that area. Cooper provided a place to show the work of young, striving woman artists.[28]

The sixties witnessed the rise to prominence of the female art critic. Barbara Rose (1937–), an art historian and critic married to Abstract Expressionist Frank Stella, wrote for *Art International*, *Art Forum*, and *Art in America*—all influential publications. Dore Ashton was a leading antiformalist who rejected the idea of evolutionary progress in art along with the importance of history and empiricism. Art historian Lucy Lippard, starting from MoMA's library, turned to criticism in 1964 to become an authoritative voice, reviewing and explaining the avant garde as a free-lancer for *Art in America* and the *Village Voice*. She produced the regular "New York Letter" for *Art International* as well as several monographs. Disillusioned by the art world's "competitive careerism," she became an activist who "identified with artists," not with other critics and curators. Lippard joined artists issuing the "Statement of January 5, 1969," to demand pluralization by race and gender of art shown by the museums and to protest the Vietnam war. Promulgating the activist spirit of the sixties avant garde and feminists, she cofounded *Heresies*, *Printed Matter*, and Political Art Documentation/ Distribution (PADD). Other prominent women critics included Jill Johnston of the *Village Voice*, Corrine Robins of *Arts Magazine*, and Grace Glueck of the *New York Times*. All these made the sixties the age of the woman critic at a time when art magazines served the dual functions of trade journals and information/entertainment for an increasingly sophisticated museum-going public.[29]

Collectors were important in shaping New York's sixties art "scene," socially and aesthetically. The most influential neophiliac collectors, Ethel (Spike) and Robert Scull, were forces to be reckoned with, especially in Pop Art. Spike was the "hostess with the mostess," celebrated by Tom Wolfe as one of New York's great and fashionable success stories. Spike commented, "My philosophy is, Enjoy." Warhol called the Sculls "models and heroes" for most "swinging mod couples in the city." Burton and Emily Tremaine tried to rival their parties as did Dominique de Menil and Lita Hornick.[30]

Women in this rarified social milieu were often treated more as "performance pieces" or collectibles, created by the likes of Warhol, than as creative agents in their own right. Warhol's regulars competing for "Superstardom" included Baby Jane Holzer, blond, miniskirted wife of a wealthy broker; Brigid "Polk" Berlin, a runaway, often topless, "druggy" daughter of the Hearst Corporation President; Susan Bottomly, called International Velvet, beautiful daughter of a Boston attorney general; and the German singer Nico, whose melancholy, monotone voice was a trademark of the Velvet Underground. Warhol made them famous for more than just 15 minutes with experimental "underground" films like *Chelsea Girls*, *Beauty*, *Bitch*, *Poor Little Rich Girl*, *Kitchen*, and *Tub Girls* from 1963 on. By 1965, New York's social arbiter Eugenia Sheppard ranked Warhol's group—often including Diana Vreeland, Liza Minnelli, Elizabeth Taylor, Lee Radziwill, and Bianca Jagger—just below Jackie Kennedy's coterie as the city's most fashionable. Many women aspired to be part of it—Viva, Claris Rivers, Geraldine Smith, Ingrid Superstar, even Valerie Solanas, Warhol's would-be assassin. Isabelle Collin Dufresne (1935–), introduced to Warhol by her "companion" Salvador Dali in 1963, equated the avant-garde eccentric with Mozart and manipulated him to become a "celebrity," changing her name to Ultra Violet (not Warhol's suggested Poly Ester and Notre Dame), enjoying years of his highly publicized parties, and profiting by publishing her memoirs.[31]

More famous but tragic was Edith (Edie) Minturn Sedgwick (1943–1971), eccentric member of one of New England's oldest and distinguished families, named "Girl of the Year" in 1965 by *Life, Time, Esquire,* and *Vogue.* Ultra Violet remembers Edie as "Andy's counterpart, more boyish than he—his gestures girlish, her motion muscular." She was all Andy ever wanted to be—gregarious and "bubbly." "Now that Marilyn is dead, here is Edie"; but by 1967, the self-destructive drug cycle between barbiturates and amphetamines consumed her life. She dealt drugs, stole to feed her habit, and turned into an anorexic, dying, a total wreck, in 1971.[32]

Warhol's loft, the "Factory," a 24-hour "happening," was the scene of all sorts of exploitation of women in the name of the avant-garde. In 1969 newspapers reported that Warhol and his "assistant" Brigid Polk agreed "on a mutually satisfactory division of labor." For at least two years "Miss Polk," had been doing all of Warhol's art work, even signing his name. As his part of the bargain, Warhol "graciously agreed to let her keep up the good work," omitting reference to her work in his memoirs but calling her "incredibly hostile" and other derogatory things. The women he manipulated were no more individuals than were his multiple images of Marilyn.[33]

Warhol was not the only artist collecting female followers and coordinating others' work. Coteries were important in establishing status—professionally for artists and socially for collectors and hangers-on. None focused on women as in the twenties; and women played decidedly secondary roles. Helen Frankenthaler was one of the few women, along with critic Rosalind Krauss and curator Jane Harrison Cone, in a famous group formed by critic Clement Greenberg, called the Green Mountain Boys, a play on his name and the Vermont location of Bennington College, where many of the "Boys" taught. Lippard belonged for awhile to a younger circle, the Bowery Boys, which perhaps included more prominent women than other coteries—Nancy Holt, Eva Hesse, the dealer Virginia Dwan. Critic Barbara Rose, married to painter Frank Stella, travelled between groups with increasing influence. Artists had less social mobility. Dorothea Rockburne and Eva Hesse were in Carl André's coterie. Name dropping and having one's name listed in a group's media coverage was crucial to a system that ravenously fed on new styles and names. Still, the art world gradually became a bit more democratic, giving more opportunities to women than existed in the fifties, especially after mid-decade as the number of galleries, aspiring artists, critics, and others associated with the arts proliferated.[34]

The Performing Arts

The Avant-Garde

As before, women found more creative opportunities in the avant-garde on the fringe of the arts establishment in New York and California. As British artist and critic Adrian Henri argues, avant-garde trends were multidisciplinary, collaborative, and international. Perhaps the most noteworthy avant-garde innovation of the sixties was the "happening," the most discussed, visible, and notorious of new developments in the arts, one in which women excelled. Happenings blended experimental theatre, dance, music, and other arts, inspirated by Dada, Surrealist, Bauhaus, and Futurist experiments.

Allan Kaprow and colleagues at the New School for Social Research and the Pratt Institute arranged the first happenings in 1958; but many others pioneered in these multi-media performance pieces. Unpredictable because they democratically involved performers and audience in semi-spontaneous events, some were well-planned, scripted, and choreographed, bearing the name of a single author, artist or "creator," and a title. Others were just ad hoc, untitled, fun events with shared innovation. Audiences were small, and most came for entertainment rather than to participate in art. Happenings were staged in public or private places, indoors or out, in community centers or bars in arts districts. New York's avant-garde center was the Judson Church, which defined as its mission to "go out to the community around it, rather than expect the community to come to it." As focus for the arts, civil rights, and reform politics, Judson provided a stage and creative haven for artists, its programs dealing with housing, alcoholism, and drug addiction. It hosted the Judson Poets' Theater, films, Pop and political art shows, and various happenings, most free of charge.[35]

In 1962 Yvonne Rainer (1934–) and Steve Paxton organized the Judson Dance Workshop in the church's basement, launching what would later be called post-modern dance, the first new avant-garde dance since the thirties. Collaboration between Merce Cunningham and John Cage created "Events" and a course taught first in 1960–61 by John Dunn to students including Rainer, Paxton, Marni Mahaffay, Simone

Forti, Ruth Allphon, Ruth Emerson, Trisha Brown, Elaine Summers, and Dunn's wife Judith, a Cunningham dancer. Many studied with Doris Humphrey (1895–1958) at Connecticut College and drew inspiration from Ann Halprin, a choreographer who interpreted the philosophy and aesthetics of her own teacher Margret H'Doubler, who was at the University of Wisconsin in the forties.[36]

Halprin, teaching in San Francisco from 1955 on, emphasized improvisation based upon intuition or concepts of the "natural"—including both nature itself and the more metaphysical/spiritual nature within. She believed movement should not fight against the body's natural tendencies, and criticized the tense movements of ballet and modern dance. She schooled students in Gestalt therapy, Zen, Taoism, existentialism, scientism, body alignment work, and altered states of consciousness. Halprin's Dancers' Workshop continued through the sixties to work with ordinary people and community groups to "create a common language through movement experiences" and "collectively create rituals and ceremonies out of life situations."[37]

Simone Forti (1935–), an Italian-Jewish refugee raised in Los Angeles, was a major force in the Judson Dance Theatre after 1959. She convinced Rainier to return with her to San Francisco for several months of study in 1960 with Halprin, her former teacher. Forti and Rainer lured fellow student Trisha Brown and composer La Monte Young back to New York to work in the Judson Dance Theatre, melding Halprin's dance philosophy with a belief in democracy, collectivity, and other contemporary avant-garde ideas to create the "Judson aesthetic." Forti's movement style mimicked animals and children, drawing on her experience teaching nursery school. Citing Piaget's psychology, she modeled happenings on games with set rules but no exactly prescribed "steps" or gestures. Divorcing Abstract Expressionist painter Robert Morris, Forti married happenings creator Robert Whitman in 1962 and devoted herself to his work. In 1966, she administered and documented "Nine Evenings: Theater and Engineering," at the 69th Regiment Armory for Experiments in Art and Technology (EAT). In 1967, she resumed choreography.[38]

Forti was a major new choreographer and the first member of the Judson Dance Theatre to gain a national reputation. Judson choreographers favored dancers with little previous training, wanting an unpolished, spontaneous, "natural," look. They made decisions based on "total-consensus," breaking down the traditional choreographer-dancer hierarchy. The Judson Dance Workshop also gave aesthetic inspiration to artists like Deborah Hay, Ruth Emerson, and Frances Barth, whose interests included music, movement, poetry, painting, and sculpture. Jennifer Tipton did lighting design. During summers in the early sixties Elizabeth Keen, Laura de Freitas, June Ekman, and Sally Gross joined them in the informal rural arts colony near Woodstock, New York. Jill Johnston, in her *Village Voice* column and *Art News* reviews, spread Judson's fame and even participated herself, performing and choreographing.[39]

Although many original Judson members left by 1963, newcomers Meredith Monk and Phoebe Neville helped form a "second Judson generation" by 1965, directing their attention to happenings. John Herbert McDowell described the meeting of artists, performing and in the audience, "as important historically as Paris in the 1920s . . . the explosion of interacting ideas from a variety of fields . . . opened up new attitudes about what dance could be." Dubbed Miss Merrie or Miss Danger to describe her performance spirit, Monk, an experienced dancer, worked at New York's Café au Go Go in its landmark 1964 season. Alfred Hansen recalled, "She approaches happenings in a completely anarchistic way and invariably comes very close to putting out eyes, hurting herself badly or destroying expensive machinery. But her performances are not to be missed." Neville, an older, "more committed" dancer than Monk, shared such risk-taking, approaching performances "so filled with danger and joie" and "uninhibited" that she might carelessly hurt herself; and in a legendary event, Hansen's "Hall Street Happening," dancer Cynthia Mailman fell through a skylight to the floor twelve feet below, incurring injuries but not stopping the performance.[40]

The actress Lillian Levy played a central role in many early happenings—sometimes simply sitting silently enmeshed in a polyethylene column. Florence Tarlow, who worked at the New York City Public Library, was acclaimed by happening artists as "the mother of us all" for central roles played in many early performance pieces. Hansen described Betty Thomson as "a cowgirl from out West. . . . making giant pop art jig saw puzzle paintings" at rooftop happenings "with a fashion show feeling," with costume as important as script. Happenings attracted veteran performers and art world habituées—Anita Baker, Lucinda Childs, Lette Eisenhauer, Grace Glueck, Camille Gordon, Baby Jane Holzer, Alison Knowles, Judy Nathanson, Pat Oldenburg, Lil Picard, and Mimi Stark. Many willingly participated nude or nearly so.[41]

Some male insiders insisted on referring to women performers simply and anonymously as "girls"; and their accounts of the movement contain few womens' names. Happenings creator Michael Kirby, in particular, writes, "If I call for a single female in a work, whether it be a twist dancer or the dream girl. . . . she is usually the embodiment of a number of old, archetypal symbols. . . . the nature goddess (Mother Nature). . . . either benign, yielding nature or devouring, cruel nature." He scripted the "girl" in "The Courtyard" to be "Aphrodite (Miss America) as well—a goddess of Beauty, which is another subdivision of the large, benign nature image: a further refinement of it into the realm of love, the realm of beauty and art." Many happenings and their creators continued to stereotype women in simplistic, sexist ways, considering them only as images, often nude, rather than as individuals.[42]

Still, women like Rainer and Carole Schneeman engineered their own happenings, blending experimental theatre, dance, and Concept Art. Rainer manipulated objects. In one piece, she moved a pile of mattresses, one by one, from one gallery corner to another. In "The Bells," she repeated seven simple movements for eight minutes. The dancer Lucinda Childs did similar work informed by Zen and Dada. Among the most controversial happenings was Schneemann's "Meat Joy," performed at the Judson in 1964. The author/performer took off her clothing and displayed dead animals, chickens, and fish while male and female friends paraded around in bikinis with dead chicken heads in their mouths, writhed on the floor together, and "voluptuous, scantily clad girls play[ed] provocatively with the decaying carcasses." Henri praised Schneeman's work that "promotes the cause of sexual liberation and frequently uses her own body as an intrinsic part of her environment." Lippard called it "proto-feminist," full of strategies "to free women from the bonds of male-defined pornography, to give women their own natural eroticism . . . suppressed in America's puritan culture by disapproval at one extreme and witch-hunting at the other."[43]

One of the few avant garde films produced by a woman was Schneemann's *Fuses* (1967). Three years in the making, *Fuses* was meant "to disentangle a specifically feminist use of the woman's body, a specifically feminist female sexuality, not only from mass media appropriation, but also from the misogyny of the male underground." Explicitly and graphically depicting intercourse between the artist and her male lover, *Fuses* was called pornography, although presenting an egalitarian, non-phallocentric perspective; few saw it.[44]

Interdisciplinary happenings, often with more rehearsed collaboration of several artists and/or performers and mixed media, stretched definitions of the "fine arts." At the Second Annual New York Avant-Garde Festival, organized by Charlotte Moorman, Nam June Paik combined his experiments in art and technology with her cello music. Moorman and Paik blended sexuality, humor, and irreverence in their collaborations. In "TV Bra for Living Sculpture" (1969), she played his cello composition wearing a brassiere of two three-inch television sets. Pictures on the "boob-tubes" changed with the musical tones. That year, vice police arrested both for indecent exposure for performing "Opera Sextronique" with Moorman dressed differently for each of four acts: in a bikini studded by battery-powered lightbulbs, in a topless evening gown, in a football helmet and shirt but nothing below the waist, and finally in nothing but with a large bomb in lieu of cello. After a notorious trial, Paik was acquitted but Moorman convicted with a suspended sentence.[45]

San Francisco had an equivalent of the Judson Theatre when Rain Jacopetti and her husband Ben dropped out of the Berkeley Drama Department in 1965 to found the Open Theater, presenting cabaret pieces, multimedia experimental performances, and light shows. Their most notorious event involved a Scott Paper educational filmstrip on menstruation, re-edited and played backwards. Charles Perry remembers, "Rain had stood up into the projector beam and the result was an animated diagram of menstrual processes projected on her body. She stripped off her clothes to heighten the effect," thus launching a vogue for projections on nude bodies at happenings.[46]

Rain argued in the theater's prospectus "for more experimentation with ritual, although it might have to be self-conscious, fragmented or even sham ritual in order to overcome the problem of how art is related to its audience." Different from New York's "happenings," these events were "Revelations." She paraphrased the newly reprinted *I Ching*, the ancient Chinese book of oracles: "A time has come for man again . . . to exalt in fellowship with men—we call it God, all pervading spirit, state of enlightenment, what you will. . . . The hangup is that we each call it after our own vision. . . . The words are old, worn and misused . . . which have gathered unacceptable connotations to those who choose others. . . . Believe it, and it will exist."[47]

Yoko Ono, a member of Fluxus, a group that invented instruments, was well-established in New York's avant garde before her highly publicized marriage to Beatle John Lennon. Ono's performance pieces used random environmental sounds, staged mixed-media performances, and involved other talented women like Laurie Anderson (1947–). Ono worked in various arts—painting, sculpture, performance, poetry, music, and especially in "thought-pieces," creative ideas that might or might not be realized. Taking delight in "shocking the bourgeoisie," Ono's greatest "performance" was the media event she made of her relationship with Lennon. She encouraged her new husband to hold a press conference from their honeymoon bed and collaborated with him on a 1968 album, *Two Virgins*, with a cover jacket showing the two nude—front and back. By 1969, the two were directing their energies toward shared projects—films, art events, experimental music, and business. In September 1969, John jammed with Yoko, Eric Clapton, and other musicians at a Toronto rock festival, thus creating the Plastic Ono Band and hastening the split of the "Fab Four." Yoko contributed cuts to other Plastic Ono Band albums by yodeling and shrieking, as in Primal Scream Therapy. Journalists and fans accused her of breaking up the Beatles. The real cause of the group's demise was not Yoko but the band's complex business dealings, for which they were not prepared, and their growing male egos.[48]

One of the most notorious happenings of the decade occurred in June 1968 when the aggrieved writer, Valerie Solanas tried to assassinate Andy Warhol with a .32 caliber gun. In 1967 Solanas had issued the manifesto for her Society for Cutting Up Men (SCUM): "There remains to civic-minded, responsible, thrill-seeking females only to overthrow the government, eliminate the money system, institute complete automation, and destroy the male sex. . . . It is now technically possible to reproduce without the aid of males (or, for that matter females) and to produce only females. We must begin immediately to do so. The male is a biological accident. . . . an incomplete female, a walking abortion, aborted at the gene state." Olympia Press bought the manuscript for a pittance, then sold movie rights to Warhol, impelling the attack. Solanas was sentenced to three years in prison and was in and out of mental institutions thereafter. Warhol was hospitalized for two months. Her act ended an era. Warhol returned to the Factory; but he and his work were never the same.[49]

The avant-garde arts community was not exclusively social and/or decadent. Many artists displayed a social consciousness and probed political themes. Yvonne Rainer performed her "Convalescent Dance" as an anti-war protest during Angry Arts Week in 1967. Lucy Lippard became increasingly politicized after 1968. On 10 April 1969, 300 art-

ists came together at the New York School of Visual Arts to form the
Art Workers' Coalition (AWC) to channel dissent and coordinate public
protest for civil rights and against the war, especially angry that museums stayed open on Vietnam Moratorium Day. Faith Ringgold was
in a militant wing, the Guerilla Art Action Group (GAAG), that staged
confrontational, protest-oriented happenings. Poppy Johnson helped
coordinate protest by GAAG, DIAS, and AWC against the My Lai
(Song My) massacre. On 3 January 1970, they brought a photo poster
of dead babies to Picasso's "Guernica" in MoMA and held a memorial
service as Joyce Kozloff displayed her own 8-month-old Nikolas to dra-
matize the tragedy. The protest ended with reading of a Denise Levertov poem. The informal AWC met that May in Rainer's loft to
consider action to close down New York museums following the Cambodia invasion and the Kent State and Jackson State killings; and Rainer choreographed "M-Walk," a mass march through Soho for that
occasion. Johnson and Robert Morris led the New York Art Strike
Against War, Racism, Fascism, Sexism, and Repression—about five
hundred demonstrators peacefully blocking the entrance to the Metropolitan Museum and infiltrating the Whitney and Guggenheim.[50]

Protests led by women artists against racism and sexism resulted in
organized efforts. When Robert Morris assembled a show at New
York's School of Visual Arts attacking American racism, sexism, and
militarism, but devoid of any women's art, Ringgold organized a protest so effective that additional works were hastily added to correct if
not balance the presentation. She also formed Women Students and
Artists for Black Art Liberation (WSABAL). When the Whitney Museum Annual opened in December 1969 with only eight women (15
percent) out of 143 artists exhibited, feminists called media attention to
the travesty, organized Women Artists in Revolution (WAR), and submitted formal protests to museums. WAR retaliated with a feminist
show, "Mod Donn," at the Lafayette Street Public Theatre that May.
Collaborating with WSABAL, Lippard formed an Ad Hoc Committee
of AWC in September 1970 to pressure the Whitney. As a result, 22
percent of works in the 1970 Whitney Annual were by women; and the
museum mounted retrospectives of Georgia O'Keeffe and Louise
Nevelson.[51]

Social protest was most evident in Concept Art. A "piece" hung by
Adrian Piper in 1970 consisted solely of a statement: "The work originally intended for this space has been withdrawn. The decision to
withdraw has been taken as a protective measure against the increas-

ingly pervasive conditions of fear. Rather than submit the work to the deadly and poisoning influence of these conditions, I submit its absence as evidence of the inability of art expression to have meaningful existence under conditions other than those of peace, equality, truth, trust and freedom."[52]

AWC died at the end of 1971 when women artists, the core of its activists, directed their energies to feminism. In 1970, a promising young artist posted a declaration at her first one-person show of paintings and sculpture at California State University-Fullerton: "Judy Gerowitz hereby divests herself of all names imposed upon her through male social dominance and freely chooses her own name, Judy Chicago." A self-avowed feminist, Chicago (1939–) adopted as her icon the "personal/universal" butterfly, "ancient symbol of female transformation and sexuality, of the goddess' epiphany." She created the first women-only, feminist art course at Fresno State College in 1970 and invited Miriam Schapiro to speak. In 1971, the two created a feminist art program at the California Institute of the Arts in Los Angeles. Together, wrote Lippard, they "made the transition from geometric abstractions in sculpture and painting to works specific to women's experiences of themselves and their bodies in which open, central forms predominated." Their imagery celebrated "sexual difference and affirm[ed] woman's otherness by replacing connotations of women's inferiority with those of pride in the female body and spirit."[53]

The primitivism of Louise Bourgeois' sculpture and Carolee Schneemann's performances pointed the way toward the environmental art movement in which women were prominent in the seventies, when many were particularly attracted to the feminist and countercultural aspects of "primitivizing art." In her 1963 performance, "Eye Body," Schneemann posed nude with live snakes crawling on her body. For Lippard, this was "a graphic reflection of the goddess' dominion over the serpent—a universal symbol of rebirth and fertility connected with woman, water, and healing." Lippard explains, "With the rise of the new feminism in the late 1960s, women's longing for a history and mythology of our own found an outlet in a revisionist view of prehistoric matriarchies. . . . we began to find out that women had once been seen as the omnipotent deity, source of all things." A major shift dates from 1970, when Lippard "looked at the work of virtually thousands of women artists" and could no longer deny "that there is a uniquely female expression, although whether this is 'innate' or the result of social conditioning is still a controversial question."[54]

The new quest for a women's art found a particular outlet in environmental art, which was tempered by "the realization of how men's domination of nature has often led to ecological disaster." Environmental art played upon ancient symbolism and ritual, sharing elements with some of the early-sixties happenings, melding archaeological and geological perspectives with new ecological concerns. Early works like Anne Healy's immense cloth banners "Two to One" (1968) were for urban sites. Michelle Stuart began doing drawings of earth sculptures inspired by the moon's surface in 1968; and Nancy Holt, married to earthworks pioneer Robert Smithson in 1963, collaborated with him on major works before making her own "Views Through a Sand Dune" (1972) on a Rhode Island beach. Poppy Johnson celebrated Earth Day in 1970 by clearing a vacant urban lot in the Village and planting sunflowers. In 1971, Grace Bakst Wapner installed monoliths painted to resemble stone at Woodstock, New York; but it was not until the seventies that many American and British women artists distinguished themselves as forces in this movement.[55]

Music and Dance

Despite growing emphasis on popular music, traditional symphony and opera expanded its audience in the sixties as did classical ballet. Women forged inroads into male-dominated classical music; but their struggle was as hard as in other professions and arts. Few won chairs in major orchestras. Not until 1972 when the San Francisco Symphony promoted timpanist Elayne Jones did a black woman occupy an orchestra's first chair.

Operatic singers fared slightly better. The soprano (Mary) Leontyne Price (1927–), the first black woman to earn worldwide acclaim as "prima donna assoluta," made a transition from Broadway in the fifties to her Metropolitan Opera debut in 1961, receiving an unprecedented 42-minute ovation. She was best known for her portrayal of *Aïda*. By the mid-sixties, her fame was international, supplanting that of Marian Anderson, who retired in 1965.

Sarah Caldwell (1928–) used a base at Boston University and $5,000 to found her Opera Group (later Company) of Boston in 1957. Through the sixties, with only about four productions a season, it earned the reputation as "one of the most innovative companies in the

United States." Caldwell was the driving force, the Company's primary fund-raiser, producer, occasional conductor, and person responsible for a litany of "firsts"—the first American production of Schoenberg's *Moses und Aron* (1966), the first of Rossini's *Semiramide*, the first of Moussorgsky's *Boris Godunov* (1966), and the first American appearance of Australian soprano Joan Sutherland.[56]

Success came more slowly for Eve Rabin Queler (1936–), who worked part-time and studied while raising her two children in the early sixties. Queler founded her own Opera Orchestra in New York in 1967 to present unstaged operas in concert form. Like Caldwell, who often denied having difficulties because of her sex, Queler tried to ignore gender discrimination but admitted, "I know that some orchestra managers, when approached to engage me, turned me down because 'we already have hired our woman guest conductor for the season.'" She did not call herself a conductor in her résumé until 1970. The Opera Orchestra worked its way up from public school performances to its debut at Carnegie Hall in 1972.[57]

The New York City Opera hired Judith Somogi (1943–) in 1966 as a rehearsal pianist without title. Gradually, she rose through the ranks, conducting backstage, filling-in with the orchestra until her 1971 conducting debut. The American Symphony Orchestra type-cast her to conduct three dozen children's concerts like *Amahl and the Night Visitors* and *Help! Help! The Globolinks*. The rank of assistant conductor finally came in 1974 when she became the first woman to lead Gilbert and Sullivan's *The Mikado*. Somogi, like Caldwell and Queler, insistently denied experiencing discrimination, perhaps so as not to alienate the "powers-that-be" who finally let her display her talent. The Metropolitan Opera did not even have a backstage restroom for women in the early sixties and often used that as an excuse to by-pass women.[58]

The Metropolitan and New York City Operas remained reluctant to perform works by women composers. Peggy Glanville-Hicks (1912–) moved to Greece to have her opera *Nausica* (1961) produced before it was recorded and broadcast in America. The San Francisco Opera commissioned her *Sappho* (1963); but she left for Australia because of establishment blocks to deserved fame. No major New York company performed an opera by a woman composer until 1974 when the Met staged Thea Musgrave's *Voice of Ariadne*. Women won some acclaim through orchestral composition. Louise Juliette Talma (1906–) wrote *All the Days of My Life* (1965), a cantata for tenor, clarinet, cello, piano, and percussion commissioned by the Koussevitsky Music Foundation, followed by another twelve-tone construction, *The Tolling Bell* (1969).[59]

With major commissions, Elinor Remick Warren (1906–) was one of the sixties' most prolific woman composers, building on a three-decade reputation for orchestral and choral works. *Genesis* and the recently discovered Dead Sea Scrolls inspired her *Abram in Egypt* for baritone solo, chorus, and orchestra, performed at the Los Angeles International Music Festival on 7 June 1961. *The Crystal Lake* (1958), "inspired by the High Sierras landscape," was one of a half-dozen women's works performed by the New York Philharmonic from 1965 to 1975. Warren wrote a Requiem Mass, in Latin and English, for orchestra, mixed chorus, mezzo soprano and baritone solos—it premiered in Los Angeles in 1966. Stanford University commissioned her *Symphony in One Movement* (1971). Warren received first prize in every biennial contest of the National League of American Pen-Women from 1964 through the decade.[60]

Other notable women composers favored contemporary idioms and experimental techniques. Marga Richter (1926–) composed a three-movement piano sonata in 1953 displaying "wide-ranging pitches, free use of tone clusters and other dissonances, and . . . a strong rhythmic drive, in which chordal passages alternate with running passages"; but it was not performed until 1964. Richter's *Abyss*, also an orchestral suite, was staged as a ballet in 1965. Compositions of Ursula Mamlock (1928–) ranged from the flute solo *Variations* (1961) to *Haiku Settings* (1967) for flute and soprano. Hindu poetry inspired her *Stray Birds* (1963) for flute, cello, and soprano, dedicated to the assassinated President Kennedy. From 1964 to 1970, Joyce Mekeel (1931–) taught at the New England Conservatory; she wrote *The Shape of Silence* (1969) for a solo flutist who would walk and whisper, as well as play the instrument in unusual ways.[61]

Some works by Barbara Kolb (1939–) resembled performance art. Her *Three Place Settings* (1968) used texts about food and wine written for narrator and chamber music. Other Kolb works blended simultaneous live and taped performances.[62] Composers Joan Tower (1938–) and Shulamit Ran (1949–) also had unconventional styles. In 1969, Jean Eichelberger Ivey (1923–) founded the Electronic Music Studio at Baltimore's Peabody Conservatory to develop works like *Pinball* (1965), an impressionistic collage of taped real-life sounds in the genre called musique concrète. Ivey's *Continuous Form* (1967), combined with nonsynchronized film excerpts, was often aired between educational television station programs.

Californian Pauline Oliveros (1932–) combined taped music and electronic improvisation after 1961. Her *In Memoriam Nicola Tesla, Cosmic*

Engineer (1968), commissioned by the Merce Cunningham Dance Company, was "sound sculpture." She pioneered in "astro-bio-geo-physical applications of electronic music," inventing equipment to record unusual sounds and lights for musical use in the likes of *Valentine* (1968), which featured heartbeats of four cardplayers and narrative on the history of playing card manufacture.[63]

Other compositions tapped traditions in the American musical idiom. Radie Britain's (1903–) *Cosmic Mist Symphony* (1962), dedicated to Ted Morton, whom she married in 1959, was inspired by the American Spanish Southwest and won a 1964 National League of American Pen-Women award. Alice Parker (1925–) used traditional songs, spirituals, folkmusic, and carols for her acclaimed vocal arrangements. *Martin Luther King: A Sermon from the Mountain* (1969) was a cantata based on King's writings and favorite Biblical texts. She based her first opera, *The Martyrs' Mirror* (1971), on Mennonite hymns.[64]

As elsewhere, black women faced double odds. Margaret Bonds (1913–1972) continued to compose, perform, and teach her work—art and popular songs, choral works, piano pieces, orchestral compositions, and two ballets—inspired by black traditions, blues, jazz, and the spirituals she learned as a child in Chicago. She based her *Three Dream Portraits* (1959) on Langston Hughes's writings. Bonds worked with the Chamber Society bearing her name and performed as a solo pianist with the Chicago Symphony, Chicago Woman's Symphony, New York Symphony, and other orchestras. She taught and directed at the American Theater Wing, the Stage for Youth, East Side Settlement House, and White Barn Theater, and was minister of music at her Harlem church and Cultural Community Center. Her work won an award from the American Society of Composers, Authors, and Publishers (ASCAP). The Northwestern University Alumni Medal (1967) was particularly dear after the discrimination she had felt there as a student in the thirties. From 1967 until her death, she taught music to inner-city children in Los Angeles, and wrote *Credo* for chorus and orchestra, performed in 1972.[65]

Although trained in Europe, Julia Amanda Perry (1924–) tapped many of the same inspirational sources as Bonds. In 1965, the New York Philharmonic performed her *Short Piece for Orchestra* (1962), with its syncopation and percussion. *The Sympleqades*, a three-act opera about the Salem witchcraft hysteria, took over a decade to complete. Other black composers working in the sixties included Evelyn LaRue Pittman (1910–) and Lena Johnson McLin (1929–).[66]

Women musicians of all races encountered difficulties winning seats on orchestras. Formation of several all-black, mainly black, or "integration concerned" orchestras and "elite art" instrumental ensembles in the late-fifties and sixties created opportunities for women, particularly those playing instruments often considered unfeminine. An exception in breaking into the establishment was the internationally acclaimed, award-winning black timpanist Elayne Jones Kaufman (1929), who worked with the American Symphony Orchestra from its 1962 founding, with the Dimitri Mitropoulos Conducting Competition Orchestra from 1961–71, and as an "extra" for the New York Philharmonic, Metropolitan Opera Orchestra, and various theatres, ballets, and operas. In 1960 alone, she made over 300 solo appearances, when not teaching at colleges and conservatories across the country; but she led an early-sixties campaign for an antidiscriminatory clause in the American Federation of Musicians bylaws. National Educational Television focused on her outstanding career in a 1965 special, "A Day in the Life of a Musician." Arthur Fiedler chose her among the "select three" American blacks, all women, for his World Symphony Orchestra in 1971; and Leopold Stokowski praised her genius. In 1972, the San Francisco Symphony selected her from forty competitors as its timpanist and the first black employed in a major American symphony orchestra.[67]

Classical or art dance grew in popularity through the sixties with major performances by the American Ballet Theatre and other companies. Choreographer George Balanchine, whose enormous influence on American ballet was well established by the sixties, glorified a particularly feminine ideal for the ballerinas of his New York City Ballet; typically, they were "young, long-legged, fast-moving, technically brilliant, but usually rather lacking in personality." The autobiography of Suzanne Farrell, Balanchine's favorite from the time she joined the company in 1960, is both admiring and bluntly critical of the tumultuous challenges experienced under his tutelage. Another, younger Balanchine dancer, Gelsey Kirkland, is much more scathing in her account of the ballerina's experience. Lucia Chase, cofounder-director of the American Ballet Theatre, received the 1968 Capezio Dance Award. Martha Graham (1894–1991) continued to innovate in American dance through the company bearing her name, although her work was denied federal aid through the sixties as "obscene" or because she was "too old." She ceased performing in 1969 but continued to choreograph until her death. Her biographer credits her with having "emancipated both women and the dance—the most militant feminist who ever lived."

Similarly, Twyla Tharp developed in 1964 a major modern dance company bearing her name and was "noted for her melding of contemporary and classical ballet dance forms." She also developed works for major ballet companies internationally.[68]

Choreographers and composers increasingly looked to folk dance for creative inspiration. Katherine Dunham continued to pioneer in modern dance by melding elements from Caribbean and African folk tradition, dividing her time between her Children's Workshop in East St. Louis, Illinois, and her Haiti home. She explained that the two places have more in common than social problems: "Both places have their structure. The family is very strong. I like that because it's probably the only salvation for young people. Our program is socialization through the arts. I see it as taking the rough edges off their lives and trying to channel them into ways of thinking and behaving that will help them in other parts of the world."[69]

Performing Arts

The world of commercial theatre, especially in New York, remained generally closed to women other than actresses. In regional and off- and off-off Broadway theatre, however, women played significant roles, as actors, playwrights, directors, and producers. In the tradition of Margo Jones (1912–1955), whose Theatre '47 in Dallas had been the location of many important premieres of American dramatists, Ellen Stewart in New York, Zelda Fichandler at the Arena Stage in Washington, D.C., and Nina Vance at Houston's Alley Theatre enriched the cultural life of their cities and introduced new plays and playwrights to the American stage. Women playwrights like Megan Terry, Maria Irene Fornes, and others enlarged the subject matter of drama in the sixties and, ever inventive, created new dramatic techniques and a renewed emphasis on theatre's communal nature.[70]

Theatre: On Broadway

Overshadowed by film, Broadway declined through the sixties, with only 33 theatres operating in 1969 (compared to a high of 80 in 1925) with an average of 50 productions each season, compared to a record 280 in the twenties. Nonetheless, New York's theatre district offered many opportunities for women singers and actresses. Fifties Broadway hits continued with Julie Andrews's creation of the role of Eliza Doolittle in *My Fair Lady*, one of the most spectacular hits in Broadway history. Barbra Streisand made her Broadway debut as Yetta Tessye Marmelstein in *I Can Get It For You Wholesale* (1962), for which she won the New York Critics Award. Catapulted to stardom, she made the transition to film versions of Broadway musicals as Fanny Brice in *Funny Girl*, a major box office draw of 1968–69, for which she won an Academy Award (tied with Katharine Hepburn). Streisand again took Broadway to Hollywood with *Hello! Dolly* (1969) and *On A Clear Day You Can See Forever* (1970); in 1970 she received a special Broadway Tony Award as "Actress of the Decade."

For most women playwrights, directors, and producers, the chance of such success was slight. Lillian Hellman (1905–1984) was an exception. Her last major play, *Toys in the Attic*, appeared on Broadway to critical acclaim in 1960 but she remained a significant figure in the arts during the decade and beyond, and her plays received many productions across the country. The first volume of her much-debated provocative series of memoirs, *An Unfinished Woman* (1969), brings Hellman from childhood into her early career in film. It recounts her introduction to left-wing politics and her relationship with Dashiell Hammett, mingling fiction and fact.

The career of one of the most promising women playwrights was cut short by early death. Lorraine Hansberry (1930–1965) gained instant fame with *Raisin in the Sun* (1959), about the struggle of a black family to move into a white neighborhood. Successfully counteracting the distorted, exotic, or minstrel stereotypes of blacks on the American stage, while also suggesting the cost to black women of society's humiliation of black men, the play ran for 530 New York performances. The first play by a black woman to receive a Broadway production, it won the New York Drama Critics' Best Play of the Year Circle Award for 1959. Hansberry was the youngest American recipient, the fifth woman and the first black to receive that honor. The 1960 film version won the 1961 Cannes Film Festival Award.[71]

Active in the civil rights movement in the fifties, Hansberry became increasingly militant and outspoken as the movement gained strength. Despite the disappointing rejection of her controversial docudrama *The Drinking Gourd* (1960), commissioned by NBC for the Civil War Centennial, the early sixties were a strikingly prolific period for Hansberry. She published an account of fifties civil rights struggles in *The Move-*

ment: Documentary of a Struggle for Equality (1964), and wrote many essays, poems, and short plays.

In October 1964, Hansberry's second play, *The Sign in Sydney Brustein's Window*, opened in New York. By then she was seriously ill with cancer, and the play suffered from her inability to make revisions during rehearsal. Although the theatre owners wanted to close it almost immediately, the play ran for 101 performances, kept in production by donations from people who cared for Hansberry and for the "politics of caring" reflected in the play's story of a disaffected liberal who learns the importance of involving himself in others' causes.[72]

After Hansberry's death, her husband, Robert Nemiroff (from whom she was divorced in 1964), collected her work in two volumes. *To Be Young, Gifted, and Black* (1969) brings together pieces in a variety of genres; it was also produced as a theatre piece in 1968–69. *Les Blancs: The Collected Last Plays of Lorraine Hansberry* (1972) includes the title play, a critique of the imperialist mentality that had assumed the right to colonize Africa and impose European standards of "civilization" upon its inhabitants, and *Toussaint*, an unfinished play that Hansberry had intended as scenario for an opera about the Haitian liberator.[73]

Off and Off Off Broadway: Theatre Experiments

In small experimental theatres off Broadway and outside New York an impressive number of women expanded definitions of theatre and of women's roles in it. Playwright Rochelle Owens remembers the sixties as "a unique time politically and artistically," when women, "for complex sociological reasons began to get a little share of the pie." Many women playwrights were "groundbreakers for . . . other factions defined later as pop culture. We were all fairly young and it was a time of creative consciousness." In the "late fifties, early sixties," many playwrights had come to New York who "weren't welcome in the existing Broadway theatre," Megan Terry remembers. Young energetic, and idealistic people like Terry, Maria Irene Fornes, Lanford Wilson, and Joe Chaikin, "democratized the theatre" and moved away from the imitative model that had kept American theatre a copy of the European.[74]

In New York, what Helene Keyssar calls a "network of playwrights" developed around such experimental centers as the Judson Poets' Theatre, the Open Theatre, and, especially fruitful for women playwrights, the Café LaMama Experimental Theatre, founded in 1961 by Ellen Stewart. Stewart had come to New York in 1950 to attend design school; in Chicago, where she had grown up, no design school would admit blacks. She began the coffeehouse theatre on East Ninth Street because her brother and a playwright friend "wanted to do theatre." From casual beginnings, Café LaMama became the launching ground for a remarkable number of playwrights and composers, more than any other contemporary theater in the United States. Working always under financial constraints, Stewart produced Rochelle Owens and Megan Terry and presented early work by Elizabeth Swados. Director Tom O'Horgan began at LaMama, where he developed methods for teaching actors that culminated in his staging of *Hair*, "LaMama's all-time success." In 1969, the year that LaMama moved into larger quarters, Stewart won the Margo Jones award for producing new playwrights.[75]

In drama as in other art forms, women expanded the range of their subject matter and turned to social and political criticism. The Vietnam war and then the emergence of feminism provided the experience of conflict which women such as Barbara Garson, Megan Terry, and others transformed into drama. By the end of the sixties, the new feminism influenced avant-garde performance art on both coasts. Joan Holden, working for the San Francisco Mime Troup, wrote and produced radical political plays inspired by popular culture and the commedia dell'arte. Her best known work is *Independent Female* (1970), with the happy ending of two lovers each going their own way—a handsome young sexist man and an independent woman.

Barbara Garson's *MacBird*, a parody of *Macbeth*, questioned the conclusions of the Warren Commission regarding the death of President Kennedy and satirized Lyndon Johnson's lust for power—and proved a phenomenon of political theatre. The play had its roots in a 1965 antiwar rally. By the 15–16 October 1965, International Days of Protest, Garson's idea had expanded to a brief playlet; within a year it became a full-length commentary on contemporary politics. *MacBird* had its first professional production at New York's Village Gate Theatre in January 1967; subsequently the Berkeley Free Press, a leaflet factory begun by Garson and her husband during the 1964 Free Speech Movement, printed and distributed thousands of copies, and the play had a number of productions.[76]

The most prolific social and political playwright was Megan Terry, whom Helene Keyssar calls "the mother of feminist drama." Coming to New York from Seattle in the early sixties, she collaborated with Joseph Chaikin to establish the experimental non-hierarchical Open

Theatre where "the actors would be cocreators with the writer and the director and . . . have equal status as human beings." Through her Open Theatre playwright's workshop, Terry developed both her radical transformational drama, challenging "the hegemony of the consciousness of the intractable individual that had so dominated American drama in the fifties," and a collaborative and feminist playwriting style. Her earliest New York plays, *Hothouse* (not produced until the seventies) and *Ex-Miss Copper Queen on a Set of Pills* (1963), were written to "redress the balance" of a theatre dominated by male characters. At a time when "there were no parts for women," *Calm Down, Mother: A Transformation for Three Women* (1965) used three women, named generically (Woman One, Woman Two, Women Three), to represent a multitude. The characters shift sex, age, class, temperament, even from human being to object in some cases.[77]

Terry's best known work in the sixties was *Viet Rock* (1966), "the first rock musical" and a powerful anti-war statement. Not political in any simple sense, the play uses what critic Richard Schechner calls a "conglomeration of styles, sources, and effects" to present a complex reflection on war. A group of characters transform through such figures as General Curtis LeMay (commander of United States forces in Vietnam), Eleanor Roosevelt, boxer Cassius Clay, Christ and the Virgin Mary. *Viet Rock* also reflects Terry's feminist perspective: she calls attention to the derogatory language used for women and for female attributes, and suggests the complex relation of race and gender by having South Vietnamese soldiers played by women. The collaborative nature of both the writing and the performance meant that *Viet Rock* was different each time it was performed—at Ellen Stewart's Café LaMama, where it opened; at Yale; and elsewhere. The initial critical reception was hostile, and the Directors Guild picketed the play. Eventually, however, as the crisis over the Vietnam war grew, the play's significance became apparent and it was translated into many languages and widely performed.[78]

Terry's other plays in the sixties include *Keep Tightly Closed in a Cool Dry Place* (1965), a play for three male actors that drew on the famous Sheppard murder case, and *Comings and Goings* (1966), which explores male-female relationships and questions the relation between power and gender. *Approaching Simone* (1970), Terry's first critical success and the winner of an Obie (Off-Broadway) award for best play, is a dramatic treatment of the life of French writer, philosopher, and Jewish

martyr Simone Weil. Uncharacteristic of Terry in its focus on a single
character, the play uses the ensemble of actors to embody ideas and
characters from Weil's life. Terry wanted to place her subject's "heroic
spirit, her enormous will, in front of other women. 'Then, people
will say, "My God, it *is* possible; women are free to do this and
can.'"[79]

Although there were exceptions, it remained difficult throughout the
sixties for women to negotiate professional productions of their plays
or to find work themselves as directors or producers. The struggle was
particularly difficult for black women, and more yet for other marginalized groups. Alice Childress, whose theatrical career had begun with
the American Negro Theatre in 1941, had been the first black woman
to have a play professionally produced in the United States (*Gold
Through Trees*, 1952); she was also the first woman to win an Obie for
playwriting, for *Trouble in Mind* (1955). But in the sixties Childress encountered resistance to her new play about an interracial love affair;
Wedding Band: A Love/Hate Story in Black and White premiered at the
University of Michigan in 1966, after several rejections. In *Wine in the
Wilderness* (1969), Childress confronts political pieties: the play tells
the story of Tommy, a factory worker in her early thirties who asserts
her independence both against other blacks who judge her by white
middle-class values and against her own longings for companionship.[80]

By the time her first play was produced, Adrienne Kennedy had
been writing for ten years, mostly fiction. *Funnyhouse of a Negro*, first
produced at Edward Albee's New York theatre workshop at Circle in
the Square, was a radical departure. The play marked a "total change"
in Kennedy's writing, a change she attributes to a long period of travel
abroad, especially to several months residency in newly liberated
Ghana. "Almost every image in *Funnyhouse* took form while I was in
West Africa where I became aware of masks." It also created a change
in her life: "I couldn't cling to what I'd been writing—it changed me
also. . . . I think the main thing was that I discovered a strength in
being a black person and a connection to West Africa." Although *Funnyhouse* was a box office failure, it won an Obie (1964) and drew attention to Kennedy as a new voice in the theatre.[81]

Funnyhouse draws on expressionist techniques to embody the interior
conflicts of a woman alienated from her culture by both race and gender, conflicted by the fact of her birth as daughter of a black man and
a white woman. Kennedy's other plays in the sixties similarly embody

the pain and anxiety of racial identity, and the difficulty of establishing identity; they employ powerful, often violent imagery and an ongoing exploration of taboo subjects. *The Owl Answers*, staged in 1963 and published in *Cities in Bezique* (1969), portrays Clara Passmore's movement through time and space in search of self-recognition; she receives knowledge that renders her incapable of speaking in a human voice. *A Lesson in Dead Language* (1964) focuses on menstruation and the fear of the bleeding woman. *A Rat's Mass*, staged in 1965, deals with the difficult subject of incest, set in the grotesquerie of the transformation of human beings into rats. Kennedy spent the end of the sixties in London, supported by Guggenheim and Rockefeller fellowships, and wrote plays about two very different counterculture heroes: *The Lennon Play: In His Own Write* and *Sun*, a play about Malcolm X, staged in 1967 and 1968 respectively.[82]

Nor surprisingly, women in the Asian-American and Latina communities did not write for the theatre in the sixties, nor for some time to come. Amy Ling's bibliography of the writings of Chinese-American women lists no plays. Yolanda Broyles Gonzalez, reviewing the history of El Teatro Campesino, the workers' theatre of the United Farm Workers' organization, points out that the collaborative work of the company, which included several women, has been subsumed under the name of its director, Luis Valdez. Roles available to women were limited to "one-dimensional stereotypes"; "women are also divided into one of two sexual categories: whores or virgins." The women in the company did not initially resist these categorizations: the importance of "larger" political issues, of addressing the *raza*, the Chicano people, made women's issues seem unimportant or divisive. Their dissatisfaction grew, however, and "led to one of the longest and deepest struggles in the development of El Teatro Campesino."[83]

Responding to the difficulties women continued to encounter, in the early seventies six women playwrights—Megan Terry, Julie Bovasso, Adrienne Kennedy, Maria Irene Fornes, Rosalyn Drexler, and Rochelle Owens—banded together to form the Women's Theatre Council. The Council included several playwrights who had been involved in an earlier collective, the New York Theatre Strategy, also a women's group with Fornes as president and Drexler as treasurer. The impetus came from the sense of new energy in the theatre. As an all-women's group, they "couldn't raise any money," so the Theatre Strategy eventually brought in men.[84]

The Council's aim was specifically feminist; it would "escape the reductions [they] perceived in the 'masculine-oriented theatre'; gone would be 'the bitch, the goddess and the whore with a heart of gold.' . . . Ours are feminine dreams. Now we can say yes, we are women," Fornes told a reporter. The organization was short-lived but reflected women's recognition of the need for collective action. Council members had already broken new ground with their work. Bovasso (1930–1992), well known as an avant-garde dramatic actress, had founded the experimental Tempo Playhouse while she was still in her twenties. She wrote her first play, *The Moon Dreamers*, in the mid-sixties; it had its first professional production in 1967. For the 1968 season she won triple Obies for writing, directing, and acting in a "mock epic," *Gloria and Esperanza*.[85]

Maria Irene Fornes, who had emigrated to New York from Cuba at fifteen, originally intended to be a painter. In mid-fifties Paris she saw the original production of Samuel Beckett's *Waiting for Godot;* and it changed her life: "something in me understood that I was to dedicate my life to the theatre." She finished *Tango Palace* (1963) in nineteen days, "obsessed with the idea of writing a play." Active in off-off-Broadway theatre through the decade, she worked with both the Judson Poets' Theatre and the Open Theatre. In 1965 she won two Obie awards, for *Successful Life of 3* and *Promenade*. Both "dazzling, inventive fantasies," they combine Fornes's search for a new language for theater with a sensibility that is both comic and ironic.[86]

As the Vietnam war took over the imaginative and affective life of the country in the latter half of the decade, Fornes, like many other artists, turned to political subjects: both *Vietnamese Wedding* (1967) and a musical, *Red Burning Light* (produced in 1968) are protest plays. *Molly's Dream*, first staged in 1968, combines Fornes's interest in female protagonists with her wryly tender, linguistically and theatrically inventive reflections on the vagaries of human nature. Like her other plays, it is concerned less with plot than with the process of theatre.[87]

Rosalyn Drexler also intended initially to be an artist, and she continued to paint and sculpt during the sixties. (Her work from this period was shown in a retrospective in 1986.) A novelist as well as a dramatist, she had been writing for fifteen years before winning recognition as a playwright, an Obie Award in 1964 for *Home Movies*, first produced at Judson Church. In her plays Drexler examines the absurdities of traditional gender roles; in the spirit of the evolving feminist theatre, she mixes a range of forms and sources of language as well as transformational techniques to produce results that are far from the traditional well-made play and often shocking. *The Investigation* (1966) was her "first café play." *The Line of Least Existence* (1968), first produced in England, assaulted its audience with loud rock music as a way to insist on its theme. Like Megan Terry, Drexler benefited from the assistance of Ellen Stewart and Café LaMama in making possible the production of her plays.[88]

Rochelle Owens, one of the early creators of what became known as off off Broadway, began as a poet. Her first collection of poems, *Not Be Essence that Cannot Be*, appeared in 1961; like her plays, the poems are unconventional in the theatricality of their language and deliberately experimental. Owens had her first success as a playwright in 1965 with the production of *Futz*, a play about a man who consummates his love affair with his sow, Amanda. The play had originally been scheduled for production in 1963 by Julian Beck and Judith Malina's Living Theatre, but circumstances intervened.[89]

Like most of Owens's plays, *Futz* has a deliberate element of the shocking, but that was not its only goal; rather, it uses her fascination with the grotesque to raise questions about social hypocrisy and to reflect her concern with the "mysteries of the intangible" Gender issues dominated her work in the late sixties: *Beclch* (1967) is the theatrical embodiment of "feminist rage incarnate"; *He Wants Shih!* (1968) concerns itself with the "psyche of men who hate women." The critical response was frequently negative; one male critic called *Beclch* the "work of a housewife who writes plays." Another dismissed *He Wants Shih!* as written by a "dirty-mouthed poet." In Owens's view, women playwrights' work in the sixties helped to transform the possibilities of theatre.[90]

In the theatre as elsewhere the sixties did not witness a revolution of opportunity for women, but the decade did see bursts of theatrical energy and inventiveness in which women played major parts. As playwrights and producers, women artists transformed new understandings of social justice into art; and they defied the conventions of a staid establishment.

10

Literature

The sixties brought new subjects and new ways of treating them to American poetry and fiction. It was a time, Ted Solotaroff observed, "in which the literary consensus, like the political and social ones, broke apart and began to fly off in various directions." While writers continued to produce novels of manners and traditional poetry, new forms from other discourses—journalism, popular culture—entered and intersected with the traditional forms of serious literature to produce work that reflected the uncertainty of the times. The personal voice frequently predominated, unmediated by academic literary controls or by conventions of form: the "autobiographical impulse was as catching as a virus," perhaps because the "faith in common, objective experience . . . [had] reached an all-time low." The discoveries Americans made about themselves and their country, through both internal and external struggles, and the new voices raised in interpretation—from urban ghettos and Delta towns, from women discovering their marginality—altered subject matter and form and transformed American literature in permanent ways.[1]

Women Writers and Social Movements

While it was possible to be a writer in the sixties without direct involvement in the social movements that characterized the decade, it was almost impossible to ignore them. As writers struggled with the question of how adequately to respond to the demands of the times, many women moved away from traditional forms and subjects. Women's writing became increasingly public, claiming voice and space that women had not before occupied.

The work of poet Adrienne Rich (1929–) is both reflection and guide to that transformation in women's consciousness. Rich remembers the late fifties and early sixties as times of "rapid revelations: the sit-ins and marches in the South, the Bay of Pigs, the early antiwar movement." The "masculine world of the academy" offered to provide "expert and fluent answers" to the large questions raised by these events. But Rich wanted "to think for myself—about pacifism and dissent and violence, about poetry and society, and about my own relationship to all these things." Her meditations led to a transformation of her work, from the early rather derivative poems praised by W. H. Auden for being "neatly and modestly dressed," to the prophetic poetry of the late sixties which at once reflected and charted the change occurring in women's consciousness.[2]

Rich published her first volume of poetry, *A Change of World* (1951) the year she graduated from Radcliffe College. Married in 1953, she had three sons and published a second volume, *The Diamond Cutters* (1955), before she was thirty. While juggling conflicting responsibilities, Rich began in 1954 to date her poems: she had "come to the end of the kind of poetry" she had been writing and "felt embarked on a process that was tentative and exploratory, both as to form and materials." Beginning with "Snapshots of a Daughter-in-Law," written between 1958 and 1960, Rich turned to a "longer, looser mode than I'd ever trusted myself with before," a liberating of her poetic voice that reflected the freedom to identify herself for the first time as a "female poet," celebrating woman's emergence into the freedom of the word: "her mind full to the wind . . . her cargo no promise then:/delivered/ palpable/ours."[3]

During the late sixties, Rich taught disadvantaged urban students in the SEEK (Search for Education, Elevation and Knowledge) program at the City College of New York and in several other universities. This work, her involvement in anti-war demonstrations, and her growing awareness of the need to understand the connections between political and personal experience inform the four volumes of poetry she published in these years: *Necessities of Life* (1966); *Selected Poems* (1967); *Leaflets* (1969); and *The Will to Change* (1971). The intersections of the multiple forms of violence and oppression come together in the latter volume: there are poems on the ghetto, on the war, on personal loss, on the destruction of ideas by fear, on the discovery of the problems of communicating in "the oppressor's language," and, in such poems as "Planetarium," on the discovery in history of models for understanding women's oppression and ways to overcome it.[4]

For many women writers, the need to respond to the multiple tragedies of the sixties—war and violence in Vietnam and at home, in the South and the cities—precluded a full imaginative acceptance of the message of the new women's movement. Rich's work evolved uniquely in its recognition of the interrelationships among the forms of oppression. Centered in a self-reflective integrity and social imagination that allow the poems to be almost always political without being polemical, the body of her poetry offers a path through the decade. Powerful in its formal accomplishment, it imagines for American women the experience of her generation and of those that follow.

War, Peace, and Revolution

In poetry especially, but also in fiction, women writers joined the national anguish over the war in Vietnam, mourning the loss of the young and resisting the continuation of the violence. The powerful antiwar poems of Denise Levertov (1923–) articulate this anguish: "The same war/continues./We have breathed the guts of it in, all our lives,/ our lungs are pocked with it,/the mucous membrane of our dreams/ coated with it, the imagination/filmed over with the gray filth of it." Seeking to do the poet's work, she found her vision clouded by the flames and violence of Vietnam: "because of this my strong sight/my clear caressive sight, my poet's sight I was given/that it might stir me to song,/is blurred."[5]

At their darkest, when Levertov is almost overwhelmed by the war's ceaseless violence, some of her poems are angry and despairing; but the despair is uncharacteristic. All of her work is characterized by the lucidity and clarity of one who acknowledges the primacy of the spiritual. Never simply or conventionally "religious," the poems reflect the poet's belief "that there is a form in all things (and in our experience) which the poet can discover and reveal." Levertov was deeply influenced by the work of William Carlos Williams, whom she discovered after coming to the United States from England in 1948. His insistence on clarity and directness of language and image and on poetic attention to the significance of the commonplace accorded with her skills and temperament. Responding to the stimulus of American culture and language, she became, as Richard Howard commented, "not merely an agent but an origin of that language."[6]

Levertov's commitment to clarity and order was severely challenged by the violence of the sixties: with a long history of political activism, she began to focus on political themes out of a sense of "social obligation." In the late fifties and early sixties in New York City she had demonstrated against compulsory air-raid drills and against nuclear proliferation; work against the war in Vietnam followed logically. She and poet Muriel Rukeyser (1913–1980), with whom she later traveled to North Vietnam, were among the founders of the Writers and Artists Protest Against the War in Vietnam, and Levertov took part in many demonstrations in Berkeley, Boston, and elsewhere. Arrested more than once, she became deeply committed to resistance. "There comes a moment when only anger is love," she came to believe, when tolerance becomes criminal, and the only choice is "revolution or death. . . . Of course I choose/revolution."[7]

That anger inhabits "Staying Alive," a collage of poems, reflections, and letters occasioned by the arrest and trial of Levertov's husband, Mitchell Goodman, who was indicted with Dr. Benjamin Spock and others on conspiracy charges for their draft resistance work. There is also sadness in those poems, however, and a great longing for peace. Levertov has been criticized for her political poems, but true always to her values, she has continued throughout her distinguished career to find ways to locate her poetry in the struggle for justice.[8]

Many other writers joined in the protests against the war. Muriel Rukeyser, long concerned with issues of justice (she had reported on the Scottsboro Trials in the thirties and worked on behalf of Spanish Civil War Loyalists) joined protests, was arrested and jailed, and inspired younger women writers with the generosity and richness of her personality and her always complex poetry. The title sequence of her last volume, *Breaking Open* (1973), is a series of reflections on political imprisonment; it concludes with affirmation of a community of transformation. She celebrates openness: praising the work of artist Kathe Kollwitz, Rukeyser asks, "What would happen if one woman told the truth about her life?/The world would split open." In "The Poem as Mask (1969)" she urged women to a new directness: "No more masks! No more mythologies!," but rather "myself, split open."[9]

For Grace Paley (1922–), who began as a poet but achieved fame as a writer of remarkable short stories, opposition to the war in Vietnam was a clear and direct moral imperative. She gave most of her efforts to that cause in the sixties: always a writer whose work appeared slowly and sparely, she published only brief sections of a (never finished) novel and a few short stories and occasional pieces during the decade. Paley founded the Greenwich Village Peace Center in 1961, and she was also a founder and indefatigable supporter of the antidraft organization, Resist. Frequently arrested for civil disobedience, she spent six days in jail in 1966 for a sit-down protest against the Armed Forces Parade.[10]

Paley travelled to Hanoi with a peace delegation in 1969, returning to report on devastation by United States bombing that bordered on genocide. The experience affirmed her commitment to resistance, and her belief that women's role in peacemaking was crucial. "Our experience in counseling resisters was that the mothers would stand by their sons and support their positions. But the fathers would be embarrassed. I believe women could have ended the war if they'd had a sense of their own power."[11]

Even artists whose work was not so closely allied with political concerns involved themselves in the movements against the war. Physician and writer Han Suyin (1917–), best known for her 1952 novel *Love Is A Many Splendored Thing*, turned to politics in the sixties. Giving up her medical practice in 1965, she wrote and spoke in the United States on behalf of the political and social reforms of the government of the People's Republic of China, and against the American prosecution of the war in Vietnam. Levertov, Rukeyser, and Paley were not alone in travelling to Vietnam as peace seekers. Novelist and critic Mary McCarthy (1912–1989) went to Vietnam twice, to Saigon in 1967 and to Hanoi in 1968. She was working on the novel *Birds of America*: "I said to myself, How can I be writing about a 19-year-old boy, draft-bait, and this war is going on and I'm not doing anything!"[12]

Critic Susan Sontag (1933–) travelled to Hanoi in 1968. The result, "Trip to Hanoi" (1969), is a moving example of the New Journalism, a powerful personal response to the ravages of war from a sensibility which resists but recognizes its identity as an American. Like the work of Joan Didion (1934–), whose journalistic essays about social upheaval at home (especially "Slouching Toward Bethlehem") are the work of a moralist forced by circumstances into cynicism, Sontag's political journalism reflects her internal struggle. She went to Vietnam full of doubt about the validity of political protest and about herself as a political activist: she could not see that anything she wrote could add to the "already eloquent opposition to the war." The experience proved too

powerful for skepticism, however, challenging her criteria of moral and
social value as she struggled to rationalize her presence, defying her
need to retain her authenticity in the face of such difference. Sontag
later rejected "Trip to Hanoi" as too self-revealing: the "model of writing as self-expression is much too crude," she later told an interviewer.[13]

A graduate of the University of Chicago at eighteen, Sontag had also
studied at Harvard, Oxford, and the University of Paris. Much of her
work was concerned with transmitting to America the ideas of such
French philosophers and critics as Sartre, Artaud, and Barthes. She
published two philosophically speculative novels, both with male protagonists, *Death Kit* (1963) and *The Benefactor* (1967). An enthusiastically
received and much discussed collection of essays, *Against Interpretation*
(1966), included "Notes on Camp," an assessment of the modern sensibility as revealed in its marginal expressions.[14]

Speaking Out of Silence

The other great social movements of the decade had a profound and
lasting impact on women's writing. Feminist ideas more directly inform
the work of the seventies than of the decade before, but in the work of
such writers as Tillie Olsen (1913–) and Marge Piercy (1936–) in fiction, as of Adrienne Rich in poetry, the understanding of the need for
women to break silence is powerful. The southern civil rights movement gave voice, as the women's movement later would, to many who
had been silenced. Its vocabulary of struggle and triumph over oppression, and the validation given by the civil rights movement to the history and experience of black people in the United States, transformed
the work of older black writers and enabled the coming into voice of
many new writers, a great number of them young women. Writers like
Alice Walker (1944–), Toni Cade (1939–), Toni Morrison (1931–), Nikki
Giovanni (1943–), and Sonia Sanchez (1934–) built on the strength of
black language and experience, and on the model of such writers as
Gwendolyn Brooks, to forge a new literary aesthetic, one in which the
experience of empowerment was central. They spoke of their anger at
the past, and offered a clear analysis of the errors of the present, but
above all black writers celebrated the rediscovery of a rich history and
artistic tradition.[15]

The sixties provided a crucible for this new art. Critic Cheryl Wall
lists the major works by black women writers published in 1970: they
included the first novels of Alice Walker and Toni Morrison, and the

ground-breaking anthology, *The Black Woman*, edited by Toni Cade. Like the feminist anthology *Sisterhood is Powerful*, also published that year, Cade's book declared the existence of a generation who looked at the conditions of American life and women's lives differently and would not look back. *I Know Why the Caged Bird Sings*, the first volume of Maya Angelou's remarkable memoirs, was also a 1970 publication. Angelou (1928–), an actress and poet, had been encouraged to tell the story of her life by novelist Paule Marshall (1929–), whose semi-autobiographical *Brown Girl, Brownstones* (1959) so brilliantly told the story of a young girl attempting to find her way between cultures. Marshall's work in the sixties included a collection of stories, *Soul Clap and Hands and Sing* (1961), and an epic novel, *The Chosen Place, The Timeless People* (1969), set in the Barbados.[16]

Younger black women writers also had models in the work of Margaret Walker (1915–) and Gwendolyn Brooks (1917–). Walker's path-breaking historical novel, *Jubilee* (1966), the story of her grandmother's life from slavery to Reconstruction, had been thirty years in the making. Walker's account of the process, *How I Wrote Jubilee* (1972), details the journeying and searching that went into the book, written while she sustained heavy family responsibilities and teaching duties. It was a "consuming ambition, driving me relentlessly. Whenever I took a job, whether in Chicago in the thirties, in West Virginia and North Carolina between 1942 and 1945, or in Jackson, Mississippi, where I began teaching in 1949, I would hound the librarians to help me find books and materials relating to my story." After many years of a difficult teaching career that left little time to write, Walker returned to Iowa (1961–62), where she studied for the doctorate in English and began the final phase of writing her novel, now also her dissertation. "On the morning of April 9, 1965, at ten o'clock, I was typing the last words, 'Come biddy, biddy, biddy, Come chick, chick, chick.' And I was grateful to God and everybody who had seen me through to that moment."[17]

Brooks was the first black poet to win a Pulitzer Prize, receiving the award in 1949 for *Annie Allen*, her mock-epic poem of a young black girl coming of age and coming to terms with her blackness and her chances in the world. Warmly compassionate and wise, the poetry has the linguistic and formal complexity and inventiveness that characterized Brooks's early writing, which she later described as "Negro" writing. The shift in Brooks's perception of her audience and her mission as a writer came, as she reports in her autobiography, *Report from Part One*, from her exposure to radical young black writers and the Black

Arts Movement at the Second Black Writers Conference at Fisk University in 1967. Listening to Amiri Baraka, John Oliver Killens, and others articulate the "black aesthetic," she experienced an "awakening." "Until 1967," she recalled later, "I had sturdy ideas about writing and about writers which I enunciated sturdily. . . . Until 1967 my own blackness did not confront me with a shrill spelling of itself."[18]

From the beginning, however, Brooks's poems are full of individual black voices, confronting the large and small tragedies of life and reflecting the realities of the black urban experience—Mrs. Small and the insurance salesman, the "real cool" young men whose sad fate Brooks prophesies, "chocolate" Mabbie who suffers from her darkness in a world that values light skin. *The Bean Eaters* (1960) uses contemporary events much more directly than the earlier poems and is much more directly critical of the failures of white society. "A Bronzeville Mother" reflects bitterly on lynchings in Mississippi. "Lovers of the Poor" satirically describes white middle-class women visiting the homes of Chicago's black poor:

> Sleek, tender-clad, fit, fiftyish, a-glow, all
> Sweetly abortive, hinting at fat fruit,
> Judge it high time that fiftyish fingers felt
> Beneath the lovelier planes of enterprise . . .
>   Their guild is giving money to the poor.[19]

The impact of the civil rights movement echoes throughout the volume, prompting critics to accuse Brooks of having "forsak[en] lyricism for politics." She responded that "to be Black is political." A volume of *Selected Poems* appeared in 1963, including some new work reflecting Brooks's increasingly critical view of American race relations. The most striking change came with *In the Mecca* (1968) and the small Broadside volumes *Riot* (1969) and *Family Pictures* (1970), which take a different stance toward the audience, speaking to and for blacks, especially urban residents who suffer from deprivation and violence. *In the Mecca* appeared in the midst of political chaos; and Brooks assumes the role of "Watchful Eye," "Tuned Ear," and "Super-Reporter" to tell the stories of inhabitants of Chicago's Mecca apartment building, long past the glory that gave it its name. Brooks's intention was "to present a large variety of personalities against a mosaic of daily affairs, recognizing that the *grimmest* of these is likely to have a streak or two streaks of sun. In the Mecca were murders, loves, lonelinesses, hates, jealousies.

Hope occurred, and charity, sainthood, glory, shame, despair, fear, altruism."[20]

Throughout her early career, Brooks's work was presented by white mainstream publishers. After *In the Mecca*, she began to publish with Broadside, a small black press located in Detroit. *Riot* and *Family Pictures* reflect her adoption of the black aesthetic and her increasing concern and anger at the pain and violence of ghetto life. In the title poem of *Riot*, she mocks the fear of "John Cabot, out of Wilma, once a Wycliffe,/all whiteblue rose below his golden hair," as he confronts "the Negroes coming down the street." The poem ends in violence, Cabot dead and the riot born of desperation moving on beyond him.[21]

Following the 1967 Fisk meeting, Brooks also began a poetry workshop at her house in Chicago for the members of a youth gang, the Blackstone Rangers, along with the youth organizers who worked with them: they included Don L. Lee and Carolyn Rodgers. In 1971, which was also the year of an "epiphanic" first trip to Africa, Brooks edited an anthology, *Jump Bed*, composed of poetry by the group. Her admirers responded with a volume of poetry and tributes, *To Gwen with Love*, recognizing her role as mentor to the Chicago Black Arts Movement.[22]

In the late sixties young black women writers "proclaimed 'a new day.'" They created a poetry that drew on the blues tradition to "celebrate their collective and individual dark-skinned selves" and fiction that featured strong young female characters who, as Cheryl Wall points out, were "survivors rather than victims" and "trenchant social critics." Some, like June Jordan and Alice Walker, were active in the civil rights movement in the South and elsewhere, while others became involved in political and social action through their college experiences or through reading the work of activist black writers.[23]

Jordan (1936–) was in New York in the sixties, where her activism found expression in her work on the film of Warren Miller's novel, *The Cool World*, the story of the killing of a black youth by New York police. Her plan to redesign Harlem, drawn up in 1964 with Buckminster Fuller after the Harlem Riot of 1964, later (1970–71) won a Prix de Rome in Environmental Design. The riot had both radicalized her and confirmed her decision to be a writer. In the week after, "I realized I was now filled with hatred for everything and everyone white. Almost simultaneously it came to me that this condition, if it lasted, would mean I had lost the point: not to resemble my enemies, not to dwarf my world, not to lose my willingness and ability to love. . . . So, back in 1964, I resolved . . . to use what I loved, words, for the sake of the people I loved." From 1967 to 1969 Jordan directed the experimental SEEK program, an open enrollment plan designed to allow disadvantaged young people to attend the City College of New York. Jordan's first book of poetry, *Who Look at Me*, appeared in 1969; her first novel, *His Own Where* in 1971.[24]

Alice Walker, born in Georgia to sharecropper parents, was the youngest of eight children. Her mother, Minnie Grant Walker, was a powerful influence, the source of Walker's tribute to black women in *In Search of Our Mother's Gardens* (1983). It was to her that Walker "went in search of the secret of what has fed that muzzled and often mutilated, but vibrant, creative spirit that the black woman has inherited, and that pops out in wild and unlikely places to this day."[25]

Walker attended Spelman College in Atlanta, and later transferred to Sarah Lawrence, graduating in 1965. There she met Muriel Rukeyser, who sent her student's poems to a publisher. *Once: Poems*, published in 1968, draws on her experiences of East Africa, where she lived for a time, and her involvement in the southern civil rights movement. The long title poem, "Once," provides wry observations on the violence and sadness of the southern struggle through a series of sometimes funny, more often poignant vignettes.

Walker's first novel, *The Third Life of Grange Copeland* (1970) was published while she was a doctoral candidate at Russell Sage and teaching at Jackson State University in Mississippi. It tells a generational story of the long effects of racism, the failures of relationships between black men and women and women's strength; Grange Copeland can be redeemed only when he realizes his responsibility for his actions and reaches out to the child Ruth. The novel was intended to be realistic: "I wanted the reader to be able to . . . see a little of Georgia from the early twenties through the sixties . . . to feel the pain and the struggle of the family, and the growth of the little girl Ruth. . . . I didn't want there to be any evasion on the part of the reader . . . I wanted him or her to say, 'She has to mean this. This is a mean man: she *meant* him to be a mean man.'" Walker also wrote some of the short stories that appeared in *In Love and Trouble* (1973) during the sixties. Her second novel, *Meridian* (1976), drew extensively on her movement experiences. It "started when I became aware that the very brave and amazing people I knew in the civil rights movement were often incredibly flawed, and in a way, it was these flaws that both propelled them and 'struck' them." She was concerned to show the cost of the control and heroism that was the public face of movement activists and also to create a novel that would move away from the realistic; its form, she says, is like a "crazy quilt" or, alternatively, like a Romare Bearden collage.[26]

Of the new generation of black women poets, the work of Nikki Giovanni is most characteristic in theme and content and most inventive in language and form. Erlene Stetson notes that she speaks "primarily to black audiences," fusing "English with black elements. Her poetry relies heavily on distinctively black ideas, jazz, the blues, African drumming rhythms, chants, and symbols and images from black culture and ritual. At the same time it ignores traditional rules of versification, punctuation, grammar, and even spelling. Chanting rhythms give an aura of ritual to her work." Through the combination of these devices, she developed a "supple language" attractive to her black audience and respectful of African and African-American oral traditions.[27]

In her early autobiography, *Gemini* (originally published in 1971), Giovanni offers a family history to explain her determination: "My family on my grandmother's side are fighters. My family on my father's side are survivors. I'm a revolutionist. . . . I was trained intellectually and spiritually to respect myself and the people who respected me. I was emotionally trained to love those who love me. . . . My life is not all it will be. There is a real possibility that I can be the first person in my family to be free." Giovanni worked with the Student Nonviolent Coordinating Committee (SNCC) in the late sixties and transposed SNCC's by then revolutionary rhetoric into her poems. The first two volumes, *Black Feeling Black Talk* and *Black Judgement* are strong and often angry, using evocative, often deliberately antipoetic language to create a community and to urge political activism. Some ponder violence: one poem asks the question with which Meridian was faced, "Nigger/Can you kill?" But her themes are not only revolutionary. She writes love poems, and poems which celebrate her family and her childhood: "Nikki-Rosa," an autobiographical poem ends with a hope that "no white person ever has cause to write about me/because they never understand Black love is Black wealth and they'll/probably talk about my hard childhood and never understand that/all the while I was quite happy."[28]

Like Giovanni, Sonia Sanchez moves across a rhetorical range to celebrate the lives of her black subjects and to deplore the violence against them in language which reimagines the sound and power of that violence. A revolutionary spirit in her demand for black rights and black consciousness, she also named and deplored the oppression of women.

A graduate of Hunter College (1955), Sanchez first became involved in activism in the tumultuous atmosphere of San Francisco State University where in 1966 she helped introduce the first Black Studies program in the United States. She later worked to organize Black Studies programs at other colleges. *Homecoming* (1969), her first book of poems, draws on the life of the streets in sadness and anger; it memorializes Malcolm X, celebrates sex, and holds up for examination the failures of white America. "lead/ers of free/a/mer/ica/say. give us your/hungry/ illiterates/criminals/dropouts/(in other words)/your blacks/and we will/ let them fight/in Vietnam/defending America's honor."[29]

In the introduction to Sanchez's second volume of poetry, *We A BaddDDD People* (1970), Dudley Randall describes her as a "revolutionary" who "wants to make a better world." Praising the political directness and the powerful orality of her work, he notes that "she hurls obscenities at things that are obscene. She writes directly, ignoring metaphors, similes, ambiguity, and other poetic devices." The poems in this volume use blues rhythms and the speech rhythms of the street to call for a revolution away from violence and drugs, away from capitalism and an obsession with "white america." Responding to a speech during the student strike at San Francisco State, Sanchez writes, "no mo meetings/where u talk bout/whitey. the cracker/who done u wrong." She also wrote plays on similar themes during the sixties. "The Bronx Is Next Door" described life in Harlem while the autobiographical "Sister Son/ji" traces the growth of a black woman's radical female consciousness."[30]

That consciousness is also the center of the work of Audre Lorde (1934–) who, through most of the sixties, "had been 'the librarian who wrote.'" Her autobiographical "biomythography," *Zami: A New Spelling of My Name* (1982) tells a compelling story, rich in powerful and poetic images, of growing up black in New York City in the 1940s and 1950s, and growing into her lesbian identity. In the summer of 1960, library school complete, she turned to a "new job, new house, new living the old in a new way. Recreating in words the women who helped give me substance." In 1968, the year of publication of her first book of poems, *The First Cities*, she left her job as a librarian at Columbia to become a teacher of creative writing. Later that year she became poet-in-residence at Tougaloo College: the position was "pivotal for me. . . . I came to realize that this was my work. That teaching and writing were inextricably combined, and it was there that I knew what I wanted to do for the rest of my life."[31]

As a "black lesbian feminist warrior poet," Lorde has always defied the easy classifications that make a poet "socially acceptable and not too disturbing, too discordant." In speaking for herself, she also speaks for others: "when I say myself, I mean not only the Audre who inhabits my body but all those feisty, incorrigible black women who insist on standing up and saying 'I *am* and you cannot wipe me out, no matter how irritating I am, how much you fear what I might represent.'" She experienced the sixties through multiple consciousnesses: woman, black, lesbian, and remembers that "in the sixties, many black people who spoke from a complex black identity suffered because of it, and were silenced in many ways." A political insistence on black unity was especially difficult for lesbians and gay men, who had "played active and important roles on many fronts in that decade's struggle for black liberation," but had been cautioned against revealing their sexual identity. Twenty years later, Lorde told Claudia Tate, she realized that "when I said we needed to understand each other I had not really perfected a consciousness concerning how important differences are in our lives. . . . I have become more powerful because I have refused to settle for the myth of sorry sameness, that myth of easy sameness."[32]

Story-Telling: Women's Fiction

In fiction as in poetry, the sixties was a watershed time, as new and often revolutionary voices intersected with the work of writers who continued to work within traditional forms. Few women writers made the fiction best-seller lists; typically throughout the decade the annual list includes only one woman novelist's name. Jacqueline Susann (1921–1974) had two best-sellers, as did romantic mystery writer Mary Stewart (1916–). *To Kill a Mockingbird* (1960) by Harper Lee was a 1961 bestseller and winner of the Pulitzer Prize for fiction for that year. It is a story of racial intolerance and injustice in a small Alabama town, told from the perspective of a young girl, and also a novel of female acculturation. In 1963 Mary McCarthy had her only bestseller with *The Group*. This sexually explicit novel about nine Vassar graduates of the class of 1933 depicts the distance between the expectations of educated women and the limited options available to them; it brought McCarthy considerable notoriety. She hoped its fame would assure her of a large audience for her condemnation in *Vietnam* of an "immoral American military presence" there, but that transference did not occur.[33]

Two prolific novelists began their careers in the sixties. Anne Tyler (1941–) published two novels, *If Morning Ever Comes* (1964) and *The Tin Can Tree* (1965). Critics saw both as having promise, though lacking in development. Joyce Carol Oates (1938–) published her first collection of stories, *By the North Gate*, in 1963, and her first novel, *With Shuddering Fall*, in 1964. By 1970, Oates had published two more story collections and three more novels. *A Garden of Earthly Delights* (1967), *Expensive People* (1967), and *them* (1969) form a loose trilogy about rural, suburban, and urban America, probing themes of alienation and autonomy.[34]

As black women poets were redefining the language and subject matter appropriate to their art, black women also brought new energies to fiction. The stories of Toni Cade, written in the sixties and published in 1972 in *Gorilla, My Love*, and the early novels of Alice Walker insist on the importance of the individual woman's voice: the sassy, bright, yet vulnerable adolescent on the city streets of Cade's stories, or the idiosyncratic determined Meridian, whose survival is prophetic. Toni Morrison (1931–) began her distinguished career in fiction with *The Bluest Eye* (1970). A book of terrible sadness, it tells the story of Pecola Breedlove, who desperately needs love and believes that the only way to find it is to look like Shirley Temple, blond and blue-eyed. The brutality that she suffers and her retreat into madness and, ultimately, death are balanced by the strength of Claudia, who tells Pecola's story. The act of speech (writing) is an act of survival and triumph here, and in others of Morrison's novels.

The work of Alice Walker and Toni Morrison redefined the meaning of "southern fiction." Generally taken to mean the work of white writers—William Faulkner's and Eudora Welty's Mississippi, Flannery O'Connor's tragicomic portraits of rural Georgia, the grotesques of Carson McCullers and Tennessee Williams—with the work of Walker and Morrison, southern writing took on a new dimension. Walker acknowledged her forebears: as a college student in the sixties, she had read eagerly in the work of Flannery O'Connor (1925–1964). Coming to realize that "she would never be satisfied with a segregated literature," she shut out the white author to concentrate on the black women writers she had not been allowed to know. Ultimately, she understood that she would "have to read Zora Hurston *and* Flannery O'Connor, Nella Larsen *and* Carson McCullers, Jean Toomer *and* William Faulkner" before she "could feel well read at all." O'Connor remained particularly important to her: for Walker, she had "destroyed the last vestiges of sentimentality in white Southern writing; she caused white women to look ridiculous on pedestals, and she approached her black characters—as a mature artist—with unusual humility and restraint."

Flannery O'Connor died in 1964 at the age of thirty-nine from lupus erythematosus, ending a startling literary career. Hers was a truly distinctive voice, bringing together the forms of the southern grotesque, with its blend of humor and tragedy, with the substance of a fiercely lived Catholicism. Her mission was to shock readers into the awareness that they live at odds with their human nature. She explained: "When you can assume that your audience holds the same beliefs you do, you can relax a little and use more normal means of talking to it; when you have to assume that it does not, then you have to make your vision apparent by shock." O'Connor published two novels; both are unsentimental, seriocomic visions of a "Christ-haunted South," their protagonists driven by a violent faith. The novels and two short story collections, *A Good Man Is Hard to Find* (1955) and the posthumous *Everything That Rises Must Converge* (1965), comprise a unique body of fiction, original in voice and structure, profoundly aware of the work of grace in the most unlikely places.[36]

Another major Southern voice, that of Carson McCullers (1917–1967), also fell silent in the sixties. She published her last novel, *Clock Without Hands*, in 1961. She had worked on the book for twenty years, returning to its theme "of how much responsibility a person may take on himself" through the years of publication of such well-known works as *The Member of the Wedding* (1946) and *Ballad of the Sad Cafe* (1952). Her final work, a trilogy of stories written in 1966 and 1967, is, like *Clock Without Hands*, an attempt to deal with the subject of race relations and the "unfulfilled promises, gross unemployment, and shameful living conditions" of black Americans.[37]

Eudora Welty (1909–) published three novels and four collections of short stories before 1960; her only novel of the period, *Losing Battles* (1970) is a comic novel focusing, as all her novels do, on family life, in this case on the release of a family member from prison. Her work is deeply imbued with the sense of place of a Mississippi which evolves but remains the same. Although Welty's stories are seldom topical, she did publish in the sixties a story about the murderer of civil rights leader Medgar Evers: "That hot August night when Medgar Evers . . . was shot down from behind in Jackson, I thought, with overwhelming directness: Whoever the murderer is, I know him: not his identity, but his coming about, in this time and place. . . . I wrote his story—my fiction—in the first person: about the character's point of view, I felt, through shock and revolt, I could make no mistake."[38]

The South also provided inspiration and setting for a number of other women writers. While the best of Katherine Anne Porter's (1890–1980) work, exquisite short fiction often with Southern settings, was written long before the sixties, she produced her best-selling long novel, *Ship of Fools*, in 1962. Shirley Ann Grau (1929–), whose fiction is set in her hometown of New Orleans, published two novels in the sixties, *The House on Coliseum Street* (1961) and *The Keepers of the House* (1964). The latter, a novel about miscegenation, the ruin of a politician's career and the break up of his family, won a Pulitzer Prize. Hortense Calisher (1911–), daughter of a first generation German Jewish mother and a second generation southern and Jewish father, inherited her father's pride in his roots. Writing with the voice of a male narrator until *Textures of Life* (1963), she consciously tried to make that novel as "female" as she could. She published two other collections of short stories in the sixties, a pair of novellas, and *Journal from Ellipsia* (1965), a science fiction novel in the mode of *Erewhon*. Although it was not intended to be a feminist novel, one critic surprised Calisher by calling it "the first feminist novel of the decade and the new era." A 1969 novel, *The New Yorkers*, dedicated to her mother, considers the "interlocking themes of Jewishness, class, sexuality, and gender."[39]

Writing of the emergence of black literature in the sixties, critic Jules Chametzky notes that "among so-called white ethnics, the rediscovery of the pluralistic nature of American culture produced similarly self-conscious and assertive ethnic identification." While male writers like Saul Bellow, Bernard Malamud, and Philip Roth received the bulk of critical attention, for Jewish American women writers, "the struggle to confront and resolve conflicts between Jewish heritage and female identity" became a dominant theme. As Joyce Antler points out, "their work provides a new mapping of the Jewish female self, a self connected, though often in ambiguous ways, to Jewish tradition."[40]

Among older Jewish women writers, Jo Sinclair [pseudonym for Ruth Seid] (1913–) had written pioneering fictions of sexual and ethnic tensions and differences in the forties. Sinclair published her fourth novel, *Anna Teller*, in 1960; more old-fashioned than her earlier books, it tells the story of a Hungarian refugee in the United States. Edna Ferber (1885–1968) published her last novel, *A Kind of Magic*, in 1963, the conclusion of a remarkably successful career.[41]

The new clear voice of feminism spoke in the novels of two women of different generations, both Jewish, both determined to break stereotypes. Very influential among younger women writers for her analysis of the forces arrayed against women's expression, Tillie (Lerner) Olsen (1913–) wrote her first novel when she was nineteen. *Yonnondio*, which reflects Olsen's political sense of the social inequities of American life, was not published in its entirety until 1974. Active as a young woman in the Young People's Socialist League and the Young Communist League, Olsen worked—as a pork trimmer, mayonnaise canner, and tie presser—married, and raised four daughters in the thirties and forties. They were decades of silence during which "the simplest circumstances for creation did not exist." When her youngest child started school, "beginnings struggled toward endings." She stole time, on the bus, moments at work, "the deep night hours for as long as I could stay awake, after the kids were in bed, after the household tasks were done. . . . It is no accident that the first work I considered publishable began: 'I stand here ironing, . . .'" Olsen did not return to her writing until the mid-fifties. In 1962, she gave a very influential talk at the Radcliffe Institute where she was one of the early fellows. Called "Silences," it traced the "unnatural" silences, the "thwarting of what struggles to come into being, but cannot" in a number of writers, and stressed particularly women's struggles to write under the burden of domestic responsibilities.[42]

"I Stand Here Ironing" appeared in the collection *Tell Me A Riddle* (1961). It is the internal monologue of a fatigued, guilt-ridden, and loving mother who fears that she has irreparably damaged her daughter because she has had to raise her alone and work in the years since her husband deserted her. Marveling at her daughter's comic acting talent, and hoping she will have the freedom to develop it, she concludes: "Let her be. So all that is in her will not bloom—but in how many does it? There is still enough left to live by. Only help her to know . . . that she is more than this dress on the ironing board, helpless before the iron."[43]

As Antler points out, Olsen's strong feminist vision is also at its core a Jewish vision, drawn from her background in Jewish socialism. This background "taught her 'knowledge and experience of injustice, of discrimination, of oppression, of genocide and of the need to act against them forever and whenever they appear,' as well as 'an absolute belief in the potentiality of human beings'. . . . What is Yiddish in me. . .

is inextricable from what is woman in me, from woman who is mother.'"[44]

Marge Piercy (1936–) has carried on both Olsen's political commitment and her sense of the significance of Judaism, although not in its traditional forms, to her work as writer and feminist. She is "passionately interested in the female lunar side of Judaism," she told an interviewer. A 1958 graduate of Northwestern University, Piercy became deeply involved in the antiwar and student movements of the sixties. In "Grand Coolee Damn," reprinted in Robin Morgan's groundbreaking feminist anthology, *Sisterhood Is Powerful* (1970), Piercy devastatingly anatomizes the misogyny of male activists in the movement and explains her turn toward the women's movement. Her first volumes of poetry, *Breaking Camp* (1968) and *Hard Loving* (1969), document her burgeoning feminist consciousness. She speaks with rage of "Rape [which] fattens on the fantasies of the normal male/like a maggot in garbage" and satirically of the exploitative submission of woman by man: "We sat across the table./he said, cut off your hands. . . ./they might touch me./I said yes." Her early novels *Going Down Fast* (1969), set in the midst of the travesty of "urban renewal" in the crumbling inner city, and *Dance the Eagle to Sleep* (1970), a dystopian vision of the breakdown of post-movement society, reflect her ongoing commitment to the hope for social change. They also reflect, however, her realism about the struggle and about the destructive conflicts that arise among individuals despite their dedication to a common cause. *Small Changes* (1973) documents the communitarian and political struggles of urban radicals and vividly recreates the transformation of a woman's consciousness. A later novel, *Vida* (1980), focusing on an activist who has had to go underground, draws on Piercy's experience of political activism in the sixties and seventies, and details the toll it took on individuals as political fervor faded.[45]

Cynthia Ozick (1928–) represents a very different, markedly Jewish literary sensibility: her short stories and novels have from the beginning probed and explored Judaism in a scholarly and Talmudic fashion. As orthodoxly Jewish as Flannery O'Connor is Catholic, she shares also with O'Connor a resistance to identifying writers by gender. "To be responsible as a writer is to be responsible solely to the seizures of language and a dream." In 1965, however, Ozick published a frequently quoted satirical essay, "Provisions of the Demise of the Dancing Dog," which recalls her encounter through a teaching experience with what she calls the Ovarian Theory of Literature and attacks Norman Mailer for his "Testicular Theory." He "has attributed his own gift, and the literary gift in general, solely and directly to the possession of a specific pair of organs. One writes with these, Mailer has said . . . and I have always wondered with what shade of ink he manages to do it."[46]

Feminism went too far for Ozick, however: since "literature universalizes . . . a writer with an ambitious imagination needs an appetite beyond the self. For writers who are women, the 'new truth' of self-regard, of biologically based self-confinement, is the Great Multiple Lie freshly got up in drag." Ozick's first novel, *Trust*, focusing on the intellectual journey of a young "bookish" woman, appeared in 1966; she had worked on it for more than six years. In 1971, she published a collection of short stories, *The Pagan Rabbi and Other Stories*, which won prizes from B'nai Brith and the Jewish Council.[47]

For some women, the resurgence of feminism affirmed their view of the world. Poet, playwright, fiction writer, and prolific children's book author Eve Merriam (1916–1992) combined wit, a love of language, and a sharp feminist analysis in her work starting in the 1950s. The *Double Bed from the Feminine Side* appeared in 1958, and she published a groundbreaking children's book, *Mommies at Work* in 1961. In *After Nora Slammed the Door: American Women in the 1960s, the Unfinished Revolution* (1964), Merriam interprets women's lives from a point of view that is much more aware of class issues than *The Feminine Mystique;* the book received less attention than it deserved because of the magnitude of the response to Friedan's book. Best known for her writings for children, Merriam's work in the 1960s and 1970s for both children and adults reflected her passion for social justice as well as her love for language. *Epaminondas* (1968) is a rewrite of a traditional folktale to alter its sexist and racist language. *The Inner City Mother Goose* (1969), an adult book written in the wake of the violence and assassinations of 1968, powerfully sets off the reality of urban life for black children against the expectations set up by the nursery rhyme form; the book became a Broadway play, *Inner City* (1971). Poems like *A Husband's Notes About Her* (1976), and *The Club* (1976), a devastating satirical theatrical revue, continued her feminist readings of male-female relations.[48]

The women's movement of the late sixties and early seventies brought a significant turn to the career of novelist and poet May Sarton (1912–). She had been writing and publishing since the age of seventeen, and by the sixties had published novels, plays, and poetry, often concerned with relationships among women and with understanding the woman artist. In *The Small Room* (1961) Sarton provided a remarkable anatomy of the passions and personalities at a private women's college in New England. More pathbreaking, however, was *Mrs. Stevens Hears the Mermaids Singing* (1965), which openly treats the lesbian experience.

There was very little serious lesbian literature available before the seventies: of some 1,600 titles in the bibliography *The Lesbian in Literature*, prepared by Gene Damon and Lee Stuart and published in 1967 by the Daughters of Bilitis, the great majority were earmarked as "trash." The paperback book market, which peaked in the fifties and early sixties, provided numbers of "lesbian stories for the masses," but these typically portrayed "sadistic and inexplicably evil lesbians, often spouting feminist philosophy and corrupting the innocent; or confused and sick lesbians, torturing themselves and being tortured by others because of their terrible passions, made inescapable by nature or nurture." The intended audience was male, although Bonnie Zimmerman points out that the novels were read by lesbians "because they offered proof of lesbian existence," an existence denied by the mainstream culture. Thus Sarton's affirmative novel of lesbian relationships was a positive step.[49]

The novel was a singular phenomenon, however, and serious lesbian fiction remained virtually nonexistent until the 1969 publication of *A Place for Us* (reprinted as *Patience and Sarah*) by Alma Routsong (1924–), writing as Isabel Miller. This historical novel tells the story of the lives of a nineteenth-century painter and her companion: "any stone from their hill is a crystal ball," the author concludes, foretelling a future in which such stories can be openly told. The novel "came into the world quietly and would not have had its current significance" if it had not been for the social transformations of the late sixties, Zimmerman comments. "Lesbian life and literature was never the same after this time."[50]

Poetry: Women's Expression of Self

Adrienne Rich and Denise Levertov, and young black poets like Nikki Giovanni and Sonia Sanchez provide vivid illustrations of the new modes of public poetry that women explored in the sixties. That public poetry does not represent the whole of women's poetic writings, however, nor the whole of the work of those poets. Women continued to write in traditional modes, and two, Sylvia Plath and Anne Sexton, redefined the confessional mode.

Among poets who spanned generations, Marianne Moore (1887–1972) continued into the sixties to revise and add sparingly to the exquisite body of her poetry. Increasingly, she became a subject of public adulation, "the kind . . . that led her to being asked at one point to throw out the ball" at the first Brooklyn Dodgers game. Unmistakable in her cape and tricorne hat, this poet of complex verbal arabesques was also well known as a baseball fan. *Helen of Egypt*, a powerful evocation by H.D. (Hilda Doolittle) (1886–1961) of the spiritual power of women to regenerate a world destroyed by male violence, appeared in 1961, the year of the poet's death. Poet Louise Bogan (1897–1970) published her final volume, *The Blue Estuaries*, in 1968.[51]

The work of Elizabeth Bishop (1911–1979), characteristically spare in output, remained of great significance. Bishop was raised in Nova Scotia and New England, and graduated from Vassar (1934), where she founded a literary magazine with, among others, Mary McCarthy. Soon after graduation she began the travel that became trope and metaphor for her work. From 1951 to 1966 Bishop lived in Brazil, where she shared her life with her female lover; the fact of that relationship is not overtly a subject for her poems, however. Although she told an interviewer that she had "always considered myself a strong feminist," her work avoids the personal or the obviously political. Some poems, notably "In the Waiting Room," do draw on memories of her childhood; in that poem, as Gertrude Reif Hughes observes, she "rejects the sexual politics that assign passivity and self-denial to women."[52]

Questions of Travel, published in 1965, contains poems about Brazil and "Elsewhere." Among them, "The Armadillo" is a superb example of Bishop's ability to move meditatively inward, while maintaining the observed integrity of her subject. The volume also contains the wonderfully observed "Filling Station," a quietly meditative portrait of a world of men oddly decorated with a "hirsute begonia" and a "big dim doily." Why, the poet asks, this touch of domesticity? Her answer becomes a "celebration of custodianship": "Somebody embroidered the doily./Somebody waters the plant,/or oils it, maybe. Somebody/arranges the rows of cans/so that they softly say:/ESSO—so—so—so/to high strung automobiles./Somebody loves us all."[53]

Sylvia Plath (1932–63) died a suicide at the age of thirty-one; she was living in London with her two children, recently and unhappily separated from her husband, the poet Ted Hughes. Plath's first volume of poetry, *The Colossus*, appeared in 1960. The title poem is one of the first drawn from Plath's ongoing mythologizing of her father, who had died when she was eight. He appears again in the poems on bee-keeping and, finally, in the viciously angry "Daddy" with its ritual killing of husband and father. Her marriage began to crumble in 1962, because of Hughes's infidelity; by then they had two children. Its dissolution and her rage and despair led her to vow that she would become "a rich, active woman, not a servant-shadow as I have been," and led to the remarkable outpouring of poetry of the last eight months of her life.[54]

Plath's novel, *The Bell Jar*, was published in England in 1963 under the pseudonym of Victoria Lucas; its story of a young American woman coming of age in the fifties and seeking death contributed greatly to the legend that Plath became after her suicide. It ranks with Friedan's *Feminine Mystique* as a scathing, personal analysis of the roles and images to which women had to conform. Critic Gayle Green includes *The Bell Jar* as the best of a group of sixties novels written by women encountering madness. In the eight months before her death, she was working at a remarkable pace, and the poems for which she is best known were written mainly during that time. Publication of *Ariel* (in England in 1965, in the United States in 1966) assured her reputation as a major poet, but also made her virtually a cult figure.[55]

Poems such as "Lady Lazarus," "Daddy," and "The Applicant," each defying female stereotypes or resisting predictable female feelings, have led to a too simple identification of Plath as a proto-feminist; the struggle to define herself against her own experience and the myth she created in the process are phenomena too complex to be neatly defined. Her letters home reveal a powerful determination to maintain the face of success, and the pressure that always remained to live up to the image—successful young writer/wife/mother—that she had created for herself. Her poems, even, perhaps especially those "fiercely innovative" and "ferociously vituperative" ones written in the frenzy of the last months, show spectacular poetic control.[56]

When Anne Sexton (1928–1974) heard of the death of Sylvia Plath, whom she had known through poetry seminars at Boston University, she wrote that "I know at the news of your death,/a terrible taste for it, like salt." Sexton, like Plath, had made many suicide attempts before her final successful one in 1974. Like Plath, too, although not so successfully, Sexton took the details of her life as her material: "I am the only confessional poet," she told an interviewer in 1972. Sexton had a long struggle with mental illness, and was hospitalized on several occasions from 1954 on. She began to write as therapy, and then discovered that she had a genuine talent which was nurtured through her study with poet John Holmes and, later and most importantly, in the writing seminar given by Robert Lowell at Boston University.[57]

To Bedlam and Part Way Back (1960), Sexton's first book of poetry, is a darkly autobiographical account of the poet's experience of madness. It also exemplifies Sexton's statement that she "could leave nothing out": almost defiantly, its subjects include drugs, incest, masturbation, and menstruation. *All My Pretty Ones* (1963), which contains poignant poems about the loss of her parents and her separations because of illness from her daughters, was nominated for a National Book Award. Her third volume, *Live or Die* (1966), which posed the question Sexton constantly asked herself, received a Pulitzer Prize. Although never political in any full sense, Sexton spoke out against the war in Vietnam in public readings in the late sixties; she also received an honorary Phi Beta Kappa from Harvard in 1968 and won a Guggenheim fellowship in 1969. Honors and success did not provide peace, however, and the control she sought in her life and her art became more elusive. After 1968, as Jane McCabe comments, she turned out poetry "at an increasingly rapid and distressingly uncontrollable rate."[58]

Through poetry classes, Sexton also met Maxine Kumin (1925–), who became her closest friend and confidante; they shared a private telephone line, discussed revisions of their poems together, and collaborated on three children's books. Very different from Sexton in personal and poetic style, Kumin's directness of language and her acceptance of the daily realities as a means to survival led to a series of distinguished books of poetry, as well as several novels. Her first volume, *Halfway*, appeared in 1961. *The Privilege* (1965) celebrates the poet's Jewish background while *The Nightmare Factory* (1970) is a more overtly political book, the title poem a response to the terror of an endless war. It is also personal however, written according to Kumin, to exorcise "a series of bad dreams about my recently dead father."[59]

Many other women poets gave new energy and direction to poetry in the sixties. Diane DiPrima (1939–) added her voice to the call for revolution. She had achieved fame in the fifties as the woman writer among the Beats; her early poetry reflects the rejection of bourgeois ordinariness characteristic of that movement. In the sixties, she coedited a journal, *Floating Bear* (1961–69), an amalgam of poetry, news, and hints for surviving hard times; she and coeditor Leroi Jones [Amiri Baraka] were arrested for distributing obscene material through the mails. Inevitably, DiPrima protested the obscenity of the war in Vietnam, publishing an anthology, *War Poems*, in 1968. It includes poems by Gregory Corso, Allen Ginsberg, and other male poets of the Beat generation; DiPrima is the only woman poet represented in the volume. In the same year she began the publication of *Revolutionary Letters*, a series of short poems that became a popular underground press publication. The poems indict a failed America, destroying its natural beauty by greed; offer survival hints for those going underground ("know in advance/the person/places you can go to/means to get there"); urge revolution and praise revolutionaries ("SMASH THE MEDIA, I said,/AND BURN THE SCHOOLS/so people can meet, can sit/and talk to each other, warm and close.")[60]

Through the decade, Diane Wakoski (1937–) taught junior high school while publishing such idiosyncratic volumes as *Coins and Coffins* (1962), *The George Washington Poems* (1967), and, responding to the violence of America and the war, *Inside the Blood Factory* (1968). Transforming women's new permission for autobiography, Wakoski's poems present the self in a variety of disguises, from George Washington to the "King of Spain." Louise Gluck (1943–) published her first volume, *Firstborn*, in 1968. Carolyn Kizer (1925–) noted wryly in 1963 that it was "unwomanly" to discuss the "fate of women;" the first of her volumes of poetry that do that so well also appeared in the sixties: *The Ungrateful Garden* in 1961 and *Knock Upon Silence* in 1965. From the sixties on, the poetry of American women has been a feast of remarkable richness.

In 1970 feminist, poet, and editor Robin Morgan published the anthology that announced *Sisterhood Is Powerful;* it marked the coming into existence of a movement that was confident of its reason for being. That same year saw publication of Toni Cade's *The Black Woman* and the origins of feminist literary criticism in Kate Millett's *Sexual Politics*. The explosion of writing authored by women in 1970 reflects at least in part a recognition on the part of mainstream publishers that there was a new audience, seeking a new kind of reading; but it also represents a great coming into voice for women, an experience prepared for by the rich range of sixties women's literary expression. In literature, as elsewhere, it was a decade of preparation for the voice of feminism. Recognition by so many prominent writers of the necessity to turn their attention to social and political issues, however anti-literary the direction might seem, broke a path on which other women could walk.[61]

11

Dress and Presentation of Self

Rapidly changing dress styles through the sixties provide a measure of the transformation of attitudes of and about women; but changes often were more "cosmetic" than real indices of social and economic status. Media focus on women's presentation of self trivialized or glamorized but rarely reflected or instigated real life changes. Still, when women were questioned about the greatest changes they experienced in the sixties, one response almost unanimously identified dress.

As first lady, Jacqueline Kennedy established an ideal of youthful fashion sophistication, inaugurating a new era by wearing Oleg Cassini's designer clothes—over 300 outfits from 1960 to 1963. Her image of modern female beauty contrasted dramatically with the dowdiness of her predecessor, Mamie Eisenhower. The carefully scripted "Jackie Look" was young, poised, cosmopolitan, elegant, yet simple—calculated to convey the impression of "Camelot," although Cassini interpreted the linear, architectural, A-line silhouette of an "Egyptian princess" for this woman with a Nefertiti head and "sphinxlike quality." Cassini intended the "Jackie Look" to be "simple, charmingly young and innocent. It was unpretentious, well-cut, and implied, 'I am not going to use fashion as a weapon to impress.'"[1]

The Jackie Look, echoed and reinforced by Audrey Hepburn, influenced the way stylish American women dressed. Box-jacketed suits and dresses with sheath and A-line skirts replaced the crinolined, hourglass figures of the fifties and endured through the decade. A single large button or two closed a jacket or coat. Kneecaps discreetly showed below hems, more leg than since World War II. Fashion critic Jean Krueger Neal noted that knee-length skirts were marketed as "part of contemporary life, a 'necessity' in the fast-moving world of modern women."[2]

Through the first half of the decade, genteel and middle-class ladies' fashions worn by young and old included hats, "crisply" starched white collars, and gloves. Young women going to New York jobs as late as 1966 knew it was necessary and proper to wear gloves in public, even on the subway. Jackie Kennedy's signature pillbox hat, created by Cassini for her bouffant hairdo, was widely imitated. The First Lady made news in 1962 when she wore a wide, flat hairbow instead of a hat at a Washington luncheon, signalling rejection of the hat as a necessity for the well-dressed lady. By 1964, fashion leaders like Betty Furness made headbands a way to be "classy looking" and "dressy" without wearing a hat.

Both teenagers and matrons emulated Jackie's bouffant hair, "teasing" or "ratting" under layers of hair to give it height and fullness. The long, thin handle of the rat-tail comb helped puff up the "do." Teenagers often carried the style to extremes, particularly in the helmet-like "bubble" or the "beehive" style. Short "bubbles" ended on the cheek with curls called "guiches" affixed to the face by hair spray or even clear nail polish. Longer "bubbles" ended in a perky bottom "flip" around the head. The "beehive" had longer hair teased and mounded in a conical form, a huge chignon atop the head. Preparation for the bubble and the beehive required uncomfortable sleeping in jumbo rollers, curlers, and pincurls. For those who wanted to avoid intensive hair care, development of synthetic Dynel in 1965 produced inexpensive, easy to clean wigs. The young experimented with different styles, lengths, and colors. Long falls or swatches permitted those with short cuts to seem to have long hair, either as flowing tresses or braided chignons.

While the "Jackie Look" had an enormous influence, the Ivy-League or "collegiate look" persisted into the sixties. It included matching pastel tweed or flannel, A-line or "slim" skirts and delicate wool cardigan or pullover sweaters—"Villager" or "Bobbie Brooks" clothes, the former more prestigious. More informal dress or "sports wear," associated with the collegiate look, featured straight, plaid "guaranteed to bleed" [to fade and blend when washed] Indian madras cotton skirts, bermuda shorts, or plaid woolen kilts—an updated anglophilia. As Ellen Melinkoff observes, "There was a minor but continuing conservative strain all through the sixties, although it never made the front pages."[3]

Over the course of the sixties many young women rejected the poise, posture, and proper ladylike behavior and dress inculcated through the middle class; but evidence of nonconformity in dress appeared among some teens as early as in the fifties. Secondary school administrations frowned at the rise of teen culture, especially among girls, and reacted to fads and fashions with codified dress regulations, which had formerly been a matter of unwritten custom. Girls were forbidden to appear in high school wearing slacks, let alone "dungarees." Many schools banned make-up or placed limits on excessively styled hair—both to regulate appearance and to limit the time girls spent grooming themselves in the "ladies' room." Even before the rise of the new feminism, young women organized to expand their rights to vary dress options. At Battle Creek Central High School in Michigan in 1963, a petition drive successfully won for girls a monthly "Slacks Day," when dressy pants were permitted, but not the tighter, shorter-legged capris or Jax pants that replaced fifties "pedal pushers." In most sororities at the University of Michigan until 1968, girls could only wear pants to lunch if they were art students with studio courses.

Through the decade, even after the appearance of the first bellbottoms in 1961, most women's pants fit snugly at the top, fastened by a flat zipper in the back or side, but not with fly fronts, considered too "mannish"; sleek-look stretch pants with stirrup foot were popular. In 1962 British designer Mary Quant presented the first designs for a "trouser suit." The tailored but feminine and mod pantsuit inspired by Yves St. Laurent that could be worn on dressy occasions did not catch on until the fall of 1967. Often trouser suits included tunics, like minidresses over bellbottom pants. Pants were worn primarily by the young, however; and it was not until the decade's end and later that mature women made them part of their wardrobe.

Time warned in 1966 that pantsuits were not "as yet right for all places and occasions." Dress codes still banned them in many schools and businesses; and etiquette expert Amy Vanderbilt discouraged them for *Ladies Home Journal* readers. Some priests and ministers told women not to wear them to church. Even rich and fashionable women wearing pantsuits were turned away from expensive restaurants, a trend that inspired *Laugh-In*'s Judy Carne to stage a publicity stunt at New York's fashionable "21." After the management refused to seat her, Carne took off her bottoms, turning her outfit into a mini dress and getting a table. Press coverage resulted in an immediate change in restaurant policy; but most employers continued to ban women in pants through the sixties. The outspoken Flo Kennedy complained, "Here I am a woman attorney being told I can't practice law in slacks by a judge dressed in drag [in robes]." Not until the mid-seventies did women's pants become generally accepted.[4]

Popular trends increasingly fixed the image of casual, youthful energy as the dominant female ideal; and production of "sports" clothes dominated the ready-to-wear market. Ellen Melinkoff remembers, "Junior styles were a new concept. The same baby boomers that brought about the subteen and teen fashions of the fifties were responsible for this attention to young women as a separate fashion entity from their mothers. . . . We had money to spend, so manufacturers were there to serve us. . . . Fun clothes were something your mother would never wear." Fashion writer Brigid Keenan recalls as a teenager in the mid-fifties wearing clothes like her mother's: "There was no real style for girl of my age. . . . clothes that were available made a teenager look either years older . . . or years younger. Then along came Mary Quant."[5]

Beginning in 1955, British designer Quant, a former art student and proponent of the ultra-modern or "mod," created a youth market in fashion. With her boyfriend Alexander Plunket Greene, she produced her own short, skinny pinafores and tunics, simple jackets, scanty underwear, and outrageous accessories—a new "swinger" style that quickly swept America. Quant saw her customers as liberated sexually and socially, representatives "of a whole new spirit." In 1960 a few cosmopolitan Americans discovered Quant's knee-length jumpers, intended to have "the look of the precocious child." *Seventeen* featured her spring fashions in 1961; and in 1962, her straight, short, box-like dresses of huge, checkered fabric squares sparked American interest in the "shift" dress, actively marketed by J. C. Penney in an attempt to give its stores a new youthful, fashionable image. The loose, light, waistless "shift" or "sack" dress was popular in the summer of 1963. Melinkoff remembers feeling "the first tremors of the youthquake." Quant introduced American women "to the fashion-is-fun, life-as-the-ater" way of living.[6]

Quant revolutionized women's fashions in 1965 with her miniskirt, four to seven inches above the knee, not to be worn by the inhibited because of the way it limited movement for those who did not choose to "show all." Her message was: "You'll see the world differently from inside a mod minidress than in a shirtwaist and girdle." One critic observed, "we looked like . . . dolls. . . . Twenty-year-olds no longer looked thirty; they now looked ten." Another explained, "Quant invented the girl." She hoped to make dress transcend conventional propriety and status: "Sex is taken for granted. They talk candidly about everything from puberty to homosexuality. The girls are curiously feminine but their femininity lies in their attitude rather than in their appearance" whether dukes', doctors', or dockers' daughters. "They are not interested in status symbols. They don't worry about accents or class. . . . Snobbery has gone out of fashion, and in our shops you will find duchesses jostling with typists to buy the same dresses. . . . They represent the whole new spirit . . . a classless spirit that has grown out of the Second World War." Melinkoff argues that the miniskirt was both liberating and feminist: "We were being overtly sexy yet able to maintain control. . . . Before the mini-mod look, we dressed in feminine styles. . . . We couldn't reveal too much cleavage, too much leg, or surely we would be ravished. . . . We had given up the . . . chaperone, so our clothes would have to help us keep order. . . . Our clothes were meant to heighten the fantasy, to keep us from being attacked. Minis were so sexy that we could never have worn them in public without thinking, 'I can handle it.' . . . We could not feel like putty in men's hands. They had to be putty in ours. . . . To wear a mini was to work from a position of strength. It still made us sex objects, but we were sex objects with a sense of our own power." Yet what sort of power was projected by the Big Baby Mod Look of 1965—minis, puffed sleeves, ruffles at the throat and wrists, and tiny, flat shoes?[7]

Quant's black tights and boots with the mini-skirt eventually gave way in America to the vogue for fishnet stockings and Go-Go boots, often in white—the signature color of Paris designer André Corrèges, who accessorized his finely cut, futuristic, vinyl microminis with head-hugging helmet hats and boots, suggestive of the space age. Go-Go Girls, wearing short shorts called "hot pants," danced in cages on television shows like *Laugh-In* and *Hootenanny* and in bar clubs in major cities. The term "à go-go" originated in the first years of the sixties, meaning "As much as you like; to your heart's content; galore," according to the *Random House Dictionary of the English Language*—a feminine version of the culture of abundance, the optimistic belief in the modern to replace the traditional.[8]

Quant also dictated a new look in make-up—a cosmetological revolution. Pale pink, pearlescent lipstick, nearly white, or nude lip gloss replaced mothers' bright red. Sheer, colorless powder and a light, powder blush replaced the thick liquid or pancake foundation and rouge of the older generation. Eye make-up became heavier than ever before with black eyeliner on bottom and top lids for a wide-eyed appearance. Long false eyelashes became standard for many young women. In *How to Get a Teenage Boy and What to Do with Him When You Get Him*, Ellen Peck deemed false eyelashes "the number one weapon in the arsenal of female flirtation"; and Laura Cunningham explained in *Cosmopolitan* in 1965, "Why I Wear My False Eyelashes to Bed."[9]

Popularization of Quant's girlish, or even boyish, styles launched the careers of several models who achieved star status. The best known were the British model Lesley Hornby, nicknamed "Twiggy," and Penelope Tree. The press dubbed the sixteen-year-old, 5'6" Twiggy, weighing 90 pounds and measuring 31"-23"-32", "lean and bendy, like a tree in winter," the "Face of '66." She took her unisex look to America, modifying her straight skull-hugging cap of hair only occasionally with a long, false braid to achieve the "Lolita look." Twiggy endured through the decade but her popularity gradually faded. Penelope Tree was nearly as thin as Twiggy, and Grace Coddington emulated that look. Another celebrity model, Jean Shrimpton, modeling since 1960, became famous for her tousled hair, huge eyes, long hair, and huge white lips—the quintessential sixties look. Veruschka, a six-foot-tall German countess, achieved fame in *Vogue*, posing in various sorts of body paint that virtually became her trademark, especially after her role in Antonioni's film *Blow Up* (1966), about male manipulation of the female model. Fashion photographers like Sarah Moon interpreted the minimal look of fashion on models' extremely thin bodies—considered an ideal long before the term "anorexia" gained currency and remaining unchallenged by the feminists into the seventies.[10]

Another London designer, Barbara ("Biba") Hulanicki, had launched her own influential neo-romantic or "hippie" line in 1964, popularizing "French cut" tee-shirts with narrow little shoulders or cut-away armholes, maintaining that "if you looked narrow across the top then you looked narrow all over, and these designs suited the new Twiggy shape of girl to perfection." The new feminine ideal became a "waiflike body with thin shoulders and hollow chest, a pale face with huge, elaborately made-up eyes"—later to be termed anorexic. A version of this look appeared in the controversial film *Bonnie and Clyde* (1967) as Faye Dunaway revived thirties styles—the wearing of berets, slinky dresses cut on a bias, and tiny, rib-hugging, short-sleeved sweaters. These tight "Poor Boys," introduced in America in 1965, were part of the new "prêt-à-porter" trend, ready-to-wear clothing copied from designer styles in London and Paris. In 1965, American designer Sandy Horwitz started going abroad regularly to copy styles for marketing through department stores and better boutiques.[11]

Even before Quant, an avant garde sensibility—the desire to shock the bourgeoisie—had taken hold in fashion, sparked by the Vienna-born, California designer Rudi Gernreich. In 1964 Gernreich designed a high-waisted but topless bathing suit, held up by suspenders. When *Women's Wear Daily* published the official photograph of the suit modeled by Peggy Moffatt, the edition completely sold out and the editor's own copy was stolen. *Life* published a photo of Moffatt with arms discreetly covering bare breasts. Gernreich proclaimed nipples "this year's most important fashion accessory" and predicted that clothes were disappearing. He sold over 3,000 topless suits, which were condemned by the Vatican and by American moralists who picketed department stores selling them. That July, arrests were made for indecent exposure on Chicago and Los Angeles beaches. Gernreich followed the swimsuit with a topless cocktail dress, quickly copied by Mary Quant.[12]

Gernreich's "no-bra bra," a flimsy, transparent garment providing minimal support, spurred competitors to devise backless bras, sideless bras, and even frontless bras. Warner's lingerie marketed a skin-tight, flesh-colored, nylon body stocking in summer of 1964. In April 1965 *Playboy* proclaimed "an age of limitless revelation. . . . Today's woman, to the delight of males who suffered through the femme-concealing fashions of the fifties, has rediscovered that sex and style can be synonymous." In January 1968, before radical feminists in America dumped (but did not burn!) their bras in protest at the Miss America Pageant, Yves Saint-Laurent showed a model in bra-less transparent blouse in his spring collection. Young American feminists might be said to have co-opted bralessness, albeit with ordinary tee-shirts as covering, from high fashion. Many who enjoyed the freedom of bralessness still remained discreet by wearing two bandaids to conceal nipples through thin shirt fabric. Some women would only go braless if they passed the "test" of placing a pencil underneath each breast. If pencils dropped, the bust was judged firm and upright enough for the fashion.[13]

By 1969, given the trend towards exposure, Quant predicted that "body cosmetics and certainly pubic hair—which we can now view in the cinema and on the stage—will become a fashion emphasis, although not necessarily blatant." Newspapers named the summer of 1970 "the nudest ever." Keenan called it "the grand finale of a long, slow strip-tease" going on all through the sixties. "It started at the very beginning of the decade when we stepped out of our corsets and roll-ons, and the rigmarole of stockings and suspenders was replaced by flesh-colored tights." Seventies fashions did not go any further.[14]

After 1965, the young who questioned authority rejected mainstream ideals of appearance. Susan Gill, a New York designer since 1966, describes the second half of the decade as unprecedented—fashion changed "so fast, as never before and never since." The last years of the decade saw a diversity of styles come and go, new and then obsolete in a single season, every six months—wide-legged, mannish "buffalo" pants worn with "Poor Boys"; gaucho suits with mid-calf, skirt-like legs; long "maxi" coats worn over mini skirts; common men's jeans tucked into boots; real, tall, leather boots for women for winter instead of the old, dainty, high-heeled, dressy boots ringed with fur around the ankle. Young women began shopping at Army-Navy surplus stores. Faded and tattered denim, bell-bottom jeans—called "dungarees" by the older generation—became universal among those rejecting middle-class fashions. Gill considered each "another sort of rebellion . . . once we women got the freedom." In the winter of 1967, fashion arbiters called for ankle-length coats over mini-skirts; and in 1968, they pushed mid-ankle-length "midi" skirts. But many women rebelled. A writer for *Harper's Bazaar*, observed, "Fashion was stripped of its dictatorial powers in 1968 by a revolutionary assertion of individuality. Stylish women throughout the world put the catch phrase 'do your own thing' into practice by replacing the safe couture-approved dress with costumey, role-playing clothes that were outward projections of their inner selves."[15]

Repeated innovations diversified clothing; and with the appearance of the midcalf-length "midi" and ankle-length "maxi" skirts in 1968, women had new freedom to customize their own personal look. Long skirts appeared on counterculture women before designers attempted to popularize the midi and the maxi skirt, and they persisted well into the seventies. Those on limited budgets discovered they could quickly and cheaply create an outfit by hemming and putting elastic for the waist in a double panel of fabric. The young also liked the bare midriff look, accentuated in the last years of the decade by hip-hugger pants, low slung at navel rather than waist level. As Ellen Melinkoff remembers, "To show off the midriff was a statement of freedom." Even hippy inspired clothes—loosely crocheted tops, vests, and dresses—revealed considerable skin.[16]

The popular peasant look favored kaftans, ponchos, gauzy blouses, and rustic beads imported from third world countries like India, Peru, Bali, and Morocco. By the end of the decade, wearing such clothes suggested sympathy with those peoples, even by those not committed enough to join the Peace Corps. Rejecting dressy, dainty costume jewelry, the young bought and mixed long strings of beads of wood, ceramics, feathers, papier-mâché, or other natural materials, suggestive of Indians, Africans, or other native peoples. Others were of gaudy lucite, deliberately "fake," "cheap," and "fun" looking. New ethnic boutiques and "head shops" in college towns and cities sold imports. In the second half of the decade, young women began piercing their ears; often performing the task themselves in dorm rooms using ice cubes, corks, common needles, and alcohol—a do-it-yourself, countercultural ritual for many.

Black women broke the color barrier in modeling even before the slogan "Black is Beautiful" was coined by civil rights advocates. In 1964 *Harper's Bazaar* presented a six-page feature that catapulted Donyale Luna to stardom. Although the *New York Herald Tribune* condemned the article's description of Luna's "grace and strength of a Masai warrior" as racist, other journalists heralded the feature as first glimpse of the tip of an iceberg—"the completely new image of Negro women . . . the Fashion Negress." But too frequently, fashion media depicted Luna and other black models as exotic if not primitive and savage—crouching, clawing, and growling like wild animals. Nevertheless, they helped redefine beauty to include and even feature the African-American.[17]

More than ever before, women in the sixties displayed their ideology, philosophy, politics, or anti-hierarchical style through choice of clothing and presentation of self. According to Joan Cassell, one could immediately distinguish a women's-rights feminist, a member of a group like NOW, from an advocate of women's liberation by the "uniform" worn.[18]

Despite—or perhaps because of—all these breakthroughs and challenges to fashion norms, dress codes persisted. At the end of the decade at the Buckingham, Browne, and Nichols School in Cambridge, Massachusetts, skirt length was measured by ruler as girls knelt on the floor. Hippie chic was equally discouraged, and girls were sent home for wearing floor-length "granny" dresses just as quickly as for miniskirts.

No one epitomized that radical eclecticism of late-sixties women dress better than Janis Joplin, whose custom-made hippie garb came from seamstresses and designers like Lydall Erb of New York. The folk-rock and hippie vogues in music were matched by a taste for "funky" or old-fashioned clothes or styles recycled as new counter-cultural dress. Hippie women reverted to the crafts of their grandmothers or more distant female ancestors—elaborately embroidering old, worn denim pants or patchwork skirts with intricate, idiosyncratic designs; crocheting vests and shawls; quilting used fabric scraps in gaudy patterns inspired by a psychedelic sensibility; tie-dying T-shirts in clashing, "electric" colors. What they could not make, they bought. The counter-culture created a new sort of folk art of dress that was anti-modern, favoring the styles and crafts of a mythological, idealized, pre-industrial frontier past, where women broke away from genteel rules to live a more simple, authentic, and cruder existence while still retaining their old domestic skills with needle and thread.

Joplin shunned make-up and seldom washed her long brown hair. Her clothes, often vests and pants of embroidered velvet and denim, were hand-made. She wore granny glasses, gaudy beads, bracelets, rings, and feathers from second-hand stores. Joplin told one reporter, "Like man, I really don't give a damn about clothes. Basically, clothes are a facade, nothing more. I groove on my clothes now because I have to." Fashion was for comfort and freedom, she exclaimed, "Anything that interferes with my thing, baby, forget it." She insisted, "The secret is freedom, and that means no bras or girdles. You got to do what you want to do and wear what you want to wear. Everybody is so hung up on the matching game—the shoes have to match the bag which matches the coat and dress. But the big question is, is it matching your soul?"[19]

In a decade of hair symbolism, women's styles changed from the bouffants of the Kennedy era to styles influenced by British minimalism. Quant popularized short, straight, geometric hair with bangs, the trade-mark cut of Vidal Sassoon—an easy-to-maintain style that eliminated the need for setting hair in curlers. Many women with naturally curly hair resorted to chemical straighteners or even to ironing it to achieve a look like Twiggy or *Laugh-In*'s Goldie Hawn. Blond hair was also ideal, easily achieved at home with products like Summer Blond, less harsh than fifties' peroxides and touted with promises like "Blonds have more fun!" After 1965, long, free-flowing, blunt-edged straight hair appealed to young women who liked its low maintenance and symbolism of sensuousness and freedom. They abandoned curlers as objects of repression, oppression, or the gear of the older generation.

Shampoo and brushing were all that distinguished this style from the hippy's. A young woman who let her hair grow long could experiment with the counterculture on weekends or vacations simply by foregoing regular grooming. Hair, as the rock musical of that name underlined, became a significant symbol of rebellion for both sexes. A certain "natural," unisex, androgynous, and anti-fashion standard in dress and hair became part of the countercultural uniform for women as well as men by the end of the decade.

Black lesbian-feminist Audre Lorde was one of the first to assert the sort of racial pride that would underlie the "Black is Beautiful" movement at the end of the decade. In her 1962 poem "Coal," Lorde sings, "I am Black because I come from the earth's inside/now take my word for jewel in the open light." Yet the decade left her more perplexed than positive. In her poem "Who Said It Was Simple" (1970), Lorde ponders the spectacle of white women at a lunch counter before a political march discussing their black maids, "problematic girls," and concludes: "But I sho' am bound by my mirror/as well as my bed/see causes in color/as well as sex/and sit here wondering/which me will survive all these liberations."[20]

By 1968, entertainers like Miriam Makeba and Cicely Tyson popularized an "authentic" African look—hairdos that framed the face with a halo of hair made bouffant by natural frizziness, and called the "Afro," or tiny braids of hair intricately sculpted across the scalp called "cornrows," sometimes allowed to swing long, adorned by beads. Fashionable black women abandoned old attempts to emulate white ideals by straightening or "conking" their hair or by wearing wigs, as the Supremes and other Motown girl groups had done. *Women's Wear Daily* took note in 1968: "Suddenly it has become fashionable to be black. Now everybody wants to be a soul sister." Some young white women with straight hair got tight permanents in order to emulate the Afro; and Nancy Wilson had a hit song, "Black is Beautiful." In 1969, *Life* featured the twenty-year-old Black model Naomi Sims on its cover with the headline, "Top Model" and her observation, "Black women have captured the limelight and we are here to stay. The world is looking at us. Being a black female should be considered an asset."[21]

Ordinary women wore fewer and briefer undergarments by the end of the sixties than in previous decades. Development of new synthetic fibers like spandex and Lycra permitted manufacture of girdles considered absolutely "scanty" by fifties standards, when zippers, bones, and stays made girdles reminiscent of the Victorian era. Since garter belts were still considered slightly naughty, women contended until the spread of "panty" girdles in the early sixties with the discomfort and unsightly gap between girdle and stockings. Even after development of pantyhose early in the decade, it took a while for the young to discard their "panty" girdles because the new, one-piece garment, so easy to slip into and out of and so unrestricting, was considered too sexy if not outright improper and immoral. Mothers cautioned daughters that jiggling rears and rounded bellies unrestrained by girdles looked "sluttish." A particularly female generation gap appeared when daughters in their early teens begin resisting their mothers' insistence that they wear girdles. Mothers usually bought daughters their first girdle at puberty, in junior high school, or for their first mixed-gender party or dance. Wearing a girdle, even if it had the cute, girlish name of "frillykin," was a rite of passage not always welcome. Indeed, most of the items of women's "oppression" thrown into the Freedom Trash Cans at the Miss America protests of 1968 and 1969 were not objects imposed upon women by men but artifacts of a time-honored women's culture to which mothers initiated daughters.

Sixties women chose softer bras than the highly structured, wirey, pointed breast supports of the past; and the Twiggy look ended the fifties' popularity of padded bras. Women experimented with new sorts of underwear—bra slips short enough to fit under miniskirts, bikini underpants, or pettipants that were a cross between a short slip and culotte pants and facilitated discreet movement even in minis. Wild colors and prints replaced the formerly standard white for underwear.

If "girls" rejected traditional undergarments, they found other ways to confine their bodies. During the sixties, thin was "in" as American girls attempted to emulate the skin-and-bones, flat as an ironing board, androgynous "birds" like Twiggy. To achieve the popular look of a "bird," British slang term for a girl, a woman had to eat like one. Gloria Steinem recalls being a "scrupulous dieter, sometimes insisting on nothing but hot water and lemon for both breakfast and lunch, keeping practically nothing in her refrigerator, and bingeing on Sara Lee cakes." Fat had yet to be redefined as a feminist issue. An estimated 80 percent of habitual female drug-users either had a poor image of their physical body or enjoyed the "high" produced by diet pills, although in large doses they caused toxic psychosis, psychic dependence, or addiction. Most diet pill users were far from obese.[22]

Publishers and manufacturers capitalized on the renewed vogue for dieting. Best-sellers included *The Overweight Society* (1965) by Peter Wyden (editor of the *Ladies Home Journal*), Dr. Irwin Stillman's *Doctor's Quick Weight Loss Diet* (1967), and Naura Hayden's *The Hip, High-Protein, Low-Calorie Easy Does It Cookbook* (1972). Between 1968 and 1970, 600,000 Jack Feather Sauna Belts were sold. Diet food sales rose ten percent annually through the sixties. In 1961, Metrecal, a 900-calorie complete-food diet drink, had $100 million in sales and a growing market, spawning many competitors. Pet Milk's Sego ads featured actress Tippi Hedren modeling Catalina swimsuits. Sales of Sego and Metrecal alone totalled $450 million in 1965. The National Obesity Society was renamed the American Society of Bariatrics in 1961; and by 1972, 400 bariatrician physicians specialized in treating obesity with prescription drugs. Despite this trend, cyclamates, approved by the FDA since 1951 as low-calorie artificial sweeteners, were banned on 1 February 1970 as a carcinogen.[23]

Despite the sixties' fashion vagaries and a growing feminist consciousness, the popularity of beauty pageants still promulgated a mainstream, traditional ideal of female beauty. Beauty contests, large and small, took place over five thousand times a year on the international, national, state, and local level. Titles included the mainstream Miss Universe, Miss USA, Mrs. America, Miss Teen International, Junior Miss, Miss American Secretary, and National College Queen as well as the more esoteric, like Miss Gum Spirits of Turpentine, Miss Frankfurter, Maid of Cotton, Miss Connecticut Sweater Girl, and Miss Junior Achievement. The 1962 National College Queen Pageant idealized "the well-rounded average," chosen after competition in blouse-ironing, hamburger cooking, serving judges coffee, decorating sandals, and debating the "right and wrong hairstyles." Little Miss America was chosen from girls aged four to eight based on "beauty of face, figure, charm, poise, and personality." Most contests asked for talent but emphasized a slim, well-groomed look in swimsuit and evening dress. All emulated Miss America, chosen annually since 1921. The "beauty queen" inevitably promoted many products during her year's "reign," with most proceeds going to the competition organizers. Girls trained intensively for beauty pageants, like budding athletes, from an early age.[24]

Young girls also received training in older ideals of fashionable, feminine dress and presentation of self from the Barbie doll, first marketed by Mattel in 1959 and named after the daughter of company founders Ruth and Eliot Handler. With blond hair, pointed breasts, and long legs, Barbie presented a stereotyped, exaggerated ideal of the perpetually teenaged prom queen or fashion model. In 1961, a boyfriend/companion doll, Ken, was introduced and then girlfriends Stacey, Casey, and Midge as well as little sister Skipper. Girls could collect outfits and accessories for miniature role playing, such as the "Barbie Goes to College" set with a three-dimensional cardboard soda fountain rather than a library or the "Slumber Party" kit complete with a book entitled *How to Lose Weight*. Children even learned lessons of female competitiveness, pitting Barbie with her fifties hour-glass figure against a mod younger-cousin doll, Francie, who appeared in 1965 with a more boyish figure like Twiggy. Career clothes for Barbie were limited to stewardess, nurse, and nightclub singer, except for the futuristic astronaut. Finally in 1967 Mattel created the British Stacey, an actual Twiggy doll, by adding Casey's head to Francie's body and providing fashions like miniskirts and hippy granny gowns. New editions of Barbie kept up with the latest hairstyles—changing from the ponytail of 1959, to the bubble of 1961, to the flip in 1964, and finally long, straight hair in 1967. Mattel even gave Barbie a black friend, Christie, more in an attempt to tap a larger market of blacks than as a nod to integration.

One of the best summaries of the status quo, the growing tyranny through the sixties of feminine fashion despite the apparent liberalization of traditional norms of women's dress, came from radical feminist Dana Densmore in her essay, "On the Temptation to Be a Beautiful Object" (1968):

We are constantly bombarded . . . by images of feminine beauty . . . used extensively in advertising. . . . The image sells everything, not just beauty products. . . . Inevitably it penetrates the subconscious in an insidious and permanent way. . . . Many of us are scarred by attempts as teenagers to win the promised glamor from cosmetics. Somehow it always just looked painted, harsh, worse than ever, and yet real life fell so far short of the ideals already burned into our consciousness that the defeat was bitter too. . . .

How often the date sat impatiently below while the girl in anguish and despair tinged with self-loathing applied and wiped away the magical products that despite their magic were helpless against her horrifying plainness. She would never be a woman, mysteriously beautiful. Then, as we grow older and better looking, our faces more mature and our handling of cosmetics more expert, there are times when nature and artifice combine to make us unquestionably beautiful, for a moment, an hour, an evening. . . . We do succeed, we make ourselves objects, outside ourselves, something we expect others to admire because we admire, and which we admire through others' admiration. . . .

The more beautiful we are, the more admired our appearance, the closer we approach the dream . . . the less reality our personality and intellect or will have. It is unthinkable that this work of art has a will, especially one which is not as totally soft and agreeable as the face it presents. You cannot be taken seriously, people will not hear what you say. (If they did they would be shocked and displeased—but since they do not take it seriously they say "You are too pretty to be so smart"—by which they mean, you are an object, do not presume to complicate the image with an intellect. . . . Do not dare to spoil my pleasure in your beauty by showing it to be only the face of a real person; . . . you will only succeed in marring your beauty).

How can anyone take a manikin seriously?[25]

12

Our Bodies, Ourselves

Through the sixties, women began to take increasing control of their own bodies, especially their reproductive capabilities. Many became less willing to rely on the dictates of professionals, although they relied even more on doctors' prescriptions, especially of the new birth control pill. Independent of feminist demands, professional discussion of abortion and development of new reproductive technologies arose; but the model of the Boston Women's Health Collective—its health care center and comprehensive advice manual, *Our Bodies, Ourselves* (1971)—sparked a revolutionary re-examination of women's health issues and invigorated women's quest to understand and control their own bodies.

Contraception

When birth control pioneer Margaret Higgins Sanger (1879–1966) and philanthropist Katharine Dexter McCormick (1875–1967) died in 1966 and 1967, a major era in the history of women's search for control over their bodies ended. In 1951, McCormick had responded to Sanger's appeal for funds to develop an anovulant pill, giving two million dollars to support the research of Dr. Gregory Pincus, biochemist at the Worcester, Massachusetts Foundation for Experimental Biology and his assistant, Harvard Medical School obstetrician-gynecologist Dr. John Rock. Sanger biographer Ellen Chesler speculates that her quest for a better birth control than the diaphragm compensated for her being pushed out of the Planned Parenthood Federation of America and the related international federation she founded, both of which became increasingly conservative and bureaucratic through the fifties.[1]

One of the first women to graduate from the Massachusetts Institute of Technology (1904), McCormick met Sanger during World War I. Both had been active in suffrage, and McCormick also had a long interest in medical research into hormones because of her husband's fatal mental illness. McCormick became actively involved with Sanger's birth control movement, smuggling diaphragms from Europe in defiance of the Comstock laws criminalizing contraceptives. McCormick's support helped keep Sanger's Clinical Research Bureau open and operating. Their efforts won moral support in 1961 when the National Council of Churches endorsed birth control for family limitation.[2]

Until development of Enovid—trade name for "The Pill"—the diaphragm, perfected in Holland, with spermicidal jelly, had been the preferred contraceptive, the chief form of birth control fitted at Planned Parenthood and other public health clinics. The results of Pincus's research, the first successful use of synthetic steroids as a women's oral contraceptive, were announced at the 1955 Planned Parenthood Conference in Tokyo and in *Science* in 1956. Before the product could be marketed, the researchers required a "population of fertile women in a clearly overpopulated area" for testing. A new housing project in a suburb of San Juan, Puerto Rico, became recruiting grounds for "nontransient medically indigent women" on whom the drug could be tested. Researchers were only interested in whether the pill would prevent pregnancy, not in possible side effects. Participating women were not even given physical examinations. The original subjects were poor, uneducated Puerto Ricans who "drifted in and out of the program." In one group of 811 women, 556 dropped out in the first year, with 100 percent turnover by the third year. They were treated as expendable guinea pigs; in one study limited to 718, five died before taking the pill for a full year. No autopsies were performed, although three had symptoms of blood clots. Still, in 1960, the United States Food and Drug Administration (FDA) approved sale of the pill, basing its decision only on these minimal studies.[3]

The Pill was the first medication authorized for a social rather than a medical purpose (although it also regulated menstruation), and was the first method separating contraception from the sex act. Its revolutionary potential for redirecting women's lives was apparent from the outset. Its relative cheapness and ease of administration made birth control available to more of the American population and proved a boon to poorer women who could not afford multiple children, the expenses of private physicians, or illegal abortions. Availability of the Pill through a physician's prescription also helped justify the legality of birth control. Still, enthusiasm was not universal, in the medical community and elsewhere, and opposition persisted from the Roman Catholic and fundamentalist churches.[4]

In the wake of initial positive response to Enovid's marketing, concerns about its safety grew. Searle Pharmaceuticals, the manufacturers, called a conference of thirty physicians in Chicago in 1962 to discuss findings on 132 Enovid users who had suffered severe blood clots; eleven had died. Physicians spent a day arguing over figures that were mere guesses and estimates manipulated to prove various death rates per million. Nonetheless, doctors reassured manufacturer and users that to that date there was "no evidence to suggest a causal relationship" between the Pill and thromboembolism (clotting disorder). They recommended no further studies.[5]

The FDA appointed its own advisory committee, led by Dr. Irving S. Wright, to "eliminate persistent pockets of [public] uneasiness." The Wright Committee drew the same conclusion in its 1963 report, although it noted a "statistically significant hazard of fatal thromboembolism in women over thirty-five." By July 1963 there had been 400 cases of Enovid-associated thromboembolism, with forty deaths. Professionals knew that women taking the Pill faced greater dangers from thromboembolism, stroke, and arterial dysfunction and even from liver tumors, gall bladder disease, diabetes, heart attack, and miscellaneous cancers than women who did not take oral contraceptives. One physician testified during FDA hearings that many abnormal metabolic changes could be observed in Pill users, and many physicians warned wives and family members against it.[6]

Writer Barbara Seaman responded to her physician husband's concern over the reported hazards of Enovid. Doing her own research in international medical journals, she became alarmed that prolonged use of synthetic estrogen was linked to a litany of problems—blood clotting, strokes, sterility, decreased sexual responsiveness, cancer, heart disease, diabetes, weight gain, arthritis, depression. Seaman, like other critics, worried most about blood clotting. Responding to the evidence, Searle reduced both progestin and estrogen levels in the Pill beginning in 1961 and several times thereafter, trying to minimize dangers without diluting efficiency.[7]

The media sensationalized the Pill's problems. In 1967 the *Ladies' Home Journal* ran a cautionary tale as if addressing children: "Once upon a time some scientists found a Pill that would keep women from having babies when they didn't want them." The authors warned of "emotional illness and future pregnancy problems," and that "most women can take them without dropping dead, but many women can't." They blamed women for whatever befell them for using for such a product: "Women are getting the Pill because their demand for it is so strong that their own doctors, the medical profession . . . and possibly even the Federal Government do not dare to try to forbid the medication." They noted that the FDA had lifted the four-year limit, considered the longest a woman could safely take the Pill, rather than create a black market in the drug.[8]

While concern over the Pill's safety persisted, feminists called it safer than pregnancy. The Boston Women's Health Collective, formed in 1969, pointed out that the ratio of regular maternal deaths was eight times that of deaths related to the Pill. Twenty-five of each 100,000 women died giving birth or during pregnancy, while only three of that number died from complications from the Pill. Despite increasingly open discussion about sex and the wide popularity of oral contraceptives, the Boston Women's Health Collective emphasized that the evidence of Senate hearings on the Pill made it more necessary than ever for women to know their bodies. Health Collective members pointed out that the "Pill is no different from any other drug in that the main interest of the drug companies is first and foremost to make a profit." Doctors received support from manufacturers for writing favorable reports on the Pill. Doctors, demographers, and pharmaceutical companies were motivated to hush up its dangers. Feminists called Harvard's Dr. Robert Kistner "one of the most ardent defenders of the Pill at the Congressional hearings," and identified him as a physician who did not warn his patients about the Pill's dangers because compelled to maintain "a kind of MD-priesthood mystique." Although the Pill seemed to be medicine's greatest gift to womanhood, feminists restrained jubilation.[9]

Others promoted it. In *The Baby Trap* (1970), the best known of many anti-natal books and articles of this period, Ellen Peck provides her reader, assumed to be a young woman, with practical information to prevent pregnancy. Arguing for voluntary childlessness for both ecological reasons—in light of the population explosion—and to support women's desire for "wide personal experiences," Peck strongly advocates the Pill. Defending women against the idea that sex without risk would lead to promiscuity, she points out that: "Moralists might look at it this way: the Pill doesn't have to imply that a girl plans on a wild sex life any more than car insurance has to indicate that a driver is planning on a lot of auto wrecks." Peck hints, however, that women may become promiscuous because the Pill will let them enjoy sex with impunity—like men.[10]

Central to the debate were not merely issues of women's health but of morality and social stratification based on gender. The Pill was the most effective and popular contraceptive. For pharmaceutical companies, it was lucrative. Total sales were over $120 million per year by 1969 when an estimated eight to fifteen million women were using it, half of them American; and 83 percent of these used the Pill to prevent conception altogether, to manage the timing of pregnancies, or to avoid other methods that may have already failed them at least once. Others took it on prescription to relieve menstrual discomforts, to regulate the ovulatory cycle, or even as part of a long-term plan to promote conception. The typical American consumer was a young, educated, non-Catholic Westerner, childless but intending to have two children, no more. Of the married, half were under twenty-five.[11]

Although the most vocal opposition to artificial birth control came from the Roman Catholic Church, at least 11 percent of married Catholic women under 45 were using the Pill in 1964, only slightly less than the 18 percent of non-Catholic married women; but Catholics usually insisted use was for medical reasons only. Despite Pope Paul VI's papal encyclical, *Humanae Vitae* (1968), condemning artificial contraception, by 1969 over 37 percent of a group of fertile Catholic women, subjects in a 1965 study and married four years or more, reported that they still took the Pill. The encyclical, much more absolute in its proscriptions than the committee advising the Pope on it had hoped, caused turmoil among Catholics. A Gallup poll shortly after the encyclical showed that 54 percent opposed its condemnation of artificial birth control. Among young Catholic adults, 80 percent of those in their twenties disagreed with the Church's position and insisted that Catholics be allowed to follow their own consciences in family planning.[12]

Dr. John Rock, a Catholic and a co-developer of the Pill, expressed his disappointment at the Pope's rigidity: "Given the requirements of mankind, one hardly expected the avowed leader of Christianity to abdicate so completely responsibility for the ultimate welfare of all." Rock, the father of five and a pronatalist, came to believe that since men and women could not live happily together without frequent coitus, "human fertility would have to be controlled if the family were to remain a strong institution."[13]

Opposition or at least skepticism regarding the Pill also came from some black activists, who saw it at worst as genocidal and at best as a case of the government "promoting family planning for the poor at the expense of maternal and child health services." The issue was deeply political, linked by black male activists to the cause of black revolution. In 1967 Imamu Amiri Baraka (formerly Leroi Jones) organized a Black Power Conference in Newark that unanimously passed an anti-birth control resolution. "For us to speak in favor of birth control for Afro-Americans," Daniel Watts wrote in the *Liberator* (May 1969), "would be comparable to speaking in favor of genocide." Many black women refused the roles that men suggested, however: Linda LaRue, Frances Beal, and Sonia Pressman saw black men's call for black women to bear many black children for the revolution as another form of sexism.[14]

Toni Cade expressed black women's concerns as women and revolutionaries: "It is a noble thing, the rearing of warriors for the revolution. I can find no fault in the idea" but "with the notion that dumping the Pill is the way to do it. You don't prepare yourself for the raising of super-people by making yourself vulnerable—chance fertilization, chance support, chance tomorrow—nor by being celibate until you stumble across the right stock to breed with. You prepare yourself by being healthy and confident, by having options that give you confidence, by getting yourself together, by being together enough to attract a together cat whose notions of fatherhood rise above the Disney caliber of man-in-the-world and woman-in-the-home, by being committed to the new consciousness by being intellectually and spiritually and financially self-sufficient to do the right thing. You prepare yourself by being in control of yourself. The Pill gives the woman, as well as the man more control." Black women used the Pill but often started using it later in their marriages to end fertility rather than to time births.[15]

Despite the millions using the Pill by 1965, over half of all women of reproductive age never used it and never intended to. Through the first half of the decade, the Pill's dropout rate ranged from 32 to 47 percent per year. The 1965 National Fertility Survey showed that 20 percent dropped it for nonmedical reasons—wanting pregnancy, separation from a sexual partner, or menopause. Another 15 percent stopped for subjective reasons—fear that they might forget to take it regularly and become pregnant, fear that it might not work for them, or simple annoyance with daily Pill-taking. Almost two-thirds stopped because of pregnancy-like side effects—weight gain, fluid retention, tender breasts, nausea, tension, and the like. The first three months were crucial for most women; if they persisted longer they were apt to continue.[16]

The American birthrate fell during the sixties, but the Pill cannot be solely credited with a trend that began in 1957—three years before its marketing—and that has much more to do with the rapid increase in the number of women entering the workforce and marrying later than with availability of new birth control. Except among the religiously orthodox, attitudes toward birth control were changing. In 1961 the National Council of Churches of Christ approved use of birth control devices as moral. Beginning in the late fifties, non-orthodox Protestants and Jews moved "from uncompromising hostility" to contraception "to fervid endorsement of its use, even making it a moral obligation to control family size." The Pill did, however, give women a sense of freedom from the consequences of active sexuality. Polls found that Pill users had intercourse 39 percent more often each month than the non-users.[17]

Use of other forms of birth control also increased as anxiety over the population explosion, mounting pressures on women trying to combine responsibilities of home and paid work, and a rising resistance to traditional definitions of women's roles shaped a growing antinatalism. Over 20 percent of women relied on male condom use and 13 to 16 percent used the diaphragm, spermicidal jelly or foam, or a combination. In 1967 physicians inserted one to two million intrauterine devices (IUDs). It was not known exactly how this small device in the shape of a spiral, bow, or ring worked; but it was inexpensive, simple, and reversible. Effectiveness ranged from 1.6 to 11.3 pregnancies per year per hundred users. Of the one to two million IUDs inserted in 1967, about 10 percent were spontaneously expelled within a year, with many pregnancies. In 40 percent of these cases, a second IUD was successfully retained. Heavy bleeding, severe cramps, and infections were drawbacks for some; but those who tolerated the IUD could supposedly remain carefree for three years. The device worked better for those who had already borne a child.[18]

Vasectomies and tubal ligations, types of sterilization for men as well as women, prevented pregnancy and spread responsibility for birth control but were not particularly popular choices. In 1965 about 8 percent of white women under age forty reported that either they or their husbands had undergone a sterilizing operation for contraception—an increase from the 1960 estimate of 5.6 percent. Beatrice McClintock, her sister Dr. Helen Edey, Ellen Brush, and Louise Mills formed the Association for Voluntary Sterilization to spread information on the procedure. Characteristically, women took on more responsibility for this type of procedure, with five wives undergoing the more difficult tubal ligation for every three husbands submitting to vasectomy. Most were mothers over age 26 with two to three children.[19]

Various governmental programs used sterilization to control certain populations, raising justifiable concerns of racial discrimination if not genocide: doctors occasionally recommended sterilization for women "in lower educational classes" who seemed unable to control fertility any other way or for women who were judged "deviant." One study reported that one-third of all Puerto Rican mothers in their twenties and thirties had been sterilized by 1965.[20]

The rhythm method, based on identifying times of lower fertility in the menstrual cycle before and after ovulation when women could have intercourse without too much fear of becoming pregnant, was introduced in the United States in 1932; and the World Health Organization described a revised version called natural family planning (NFP) in 1967. In 1951, Pope Pius XII told Catholic couples they could use rhythm as the only "natural" method of birth control for reasons including "economic needs aside from serious poverty and social motives which included population questions." Pope Paul VI endorsed it in 1968, failing to note any inconsistency in approving the separation of intercourse from procreation while condemning use of mechanical means for the same end. Critics like Lucy Freibert noted that use of rhythm made the woman a kind of machine with so many usable days in each cycle and that intercourse became "so highly stressed that the total sexual relationship is thrown out of proportion." Confused lay Catholics often followed their own consciences in directions other than those of the Vatican.[21]

Despite the dangers of oral contraceptives, the anovulant Pill was the newest, cheapest, safest, most efficient, and most aesthetic means of birth control known, widely credited as an important factor in the sixties "sexual revolution." For this reason and for the new personal control that it gave to women, the Pill profoundly worried some Americans. In "The Pill and Morality" in the *New York Times Magazine* in 1965, Andrew Hacker wondered "whether national character will be weakened." While some social analysts erroneously called the Pill "the entire cause of the women's revolution," Barbara Ehrenreich in *Re-Making Love: The Feminization of Sex* argues that it "contributed . . . but by no means caused it." Social and cultural change, not the Pill, reshaped some women's sexual mores: "Without a concentration of young, single women in cities, there would have been no sexual revolution. But without the Pill, there would still have been the diaphragm."[22]

Writer Nora Ephron, who graduated from Wellesley and moved to New York in 1962, tells of her first birth control choice. Having read *The Group*, she knew that the Margaret Sanger clinic provided it. There, she was greeted by "a very austere nurse type who did not look like the kind of person who wanted to know you were single—which was ridiculous . . . because you would've said you were a hooker and they would have given you a package of Pills." Ephron lied that she was engaged. With about eight other women, she waited in a little room until "a nurse came in, carrying a very dignified-looking attaché case . . . filled with this insane rubber relief of the inside of a lady." With such an absurd demonstrative model, the nurse explained the clinic's four prescribed birth control methods: "First, she shot a little contraceptive cream into the attaché case. Next she inserted a diaphragm. . . . Finally, she inserted a coil. . . . So I chose birth-control pills." But Ephron stopped using the Pill everytime she broke up with someone and then had to postpone sex with another man until she could reactivate the Pill's cycle, recalling, "I had a problem making a commitment to sex; I guess it was a hangover from the whole Fifties virgin thing. The first man I went to bed with, I was in love with and wanted to marry. The second one I was in love with, but I didn't have to marry him. With the third one, I thought I might fall in love. It was impossible for me to think that I might be a person who 'had sex'. . . . It was awful."[23]

Ephron's naïveté and ambivalence were typical. Through the sixties, most women and their doctors rarely discussed sex and birth control. They knew little about orgasms, about feminism, or about Helen Gurley Brown's *Sex and the Single Girl* (1962), which set out an ideal of female sexual liberation; they had not read Barbara Seaman's *The Doctors' Case Against the Pill* (1969). Amazingly, in 1964 a Cleveland mother was arrested for giving birth control information to her teen-aged daughter. Not until 1965, when polls showed American couples were using diverse birth control methods, did the Supreme Court through the *Griswold v. Connecticut* decision finally give physicians the right to prescribe contraceptives in states that had banned them. At the sixties' end, Wisconsin laws still restricted access to birth control information, devices, and medication; in Massachusetts, an anti-birth control law remained in force until 1972.[24]

Thalidomide

In 1960, Dr. Frances Oldham Kelsey, a Food and Drug Administration (FDA) medical officer, prevented the birth of thousands of deformed babies in the United States by blocking licensing of the tranquilizer and sleeping pill thalidomide for general use. She rejected the new-drug application of the William S. Merrell Company for Kevadon, its brand name, because it was not proven effective in inducing sleep in research animals. Yet thalidomide had been a popular over-the-counter drug in about twenty countries, especially England and West Germany, since 1958. Merrell reapplied unsuccessfully with data that Dr. Kelsey's pharmacologist husband described as "an interesting collection of meaningless pseudoscientific jargon . . . intended to impress chemically unsophisticated readers."[25]

Under continued pressure from Merrell, in 1961 Kelsey found British medical evidence that the drug was toxic and linked to peripheral neuropathy, inflammation of the nerves producing numbness and itching of the hands and feet. Merrell formally complained to Kelsey's FDA superiors about her "somewhat libelous" claim that the company had known of this; and she prepared for a fight, hiring a lawyer. Later that year, a West German pediatrician linked thalidomide to the births of "seal-like, limbless babies." Fifteen weeks later, Merrell informed its clinical investigators, 1,267 American doctors given samples of the pill for testing on their patients, of these dangers and told them to destroy or return the pills. The FDA found that ten American women who obtained thalidomide from domestic sources and took it in the first trimester of pregnancy gave birth to deformed babies. Seven more cases resulted from the drug obtained abroad.[26]

Thalidomide came to public attention through the case of Sherri Chessen Finkbine, already famous as Miss Sherri on the fifties children's television show *Romper Room*. She had four children under age seven and was expecting her fifth in 1962. Her husband had brought the "Sleeping Pill of the Century" back from Europe, and Sherri Finkbine, who had taken it often, became frightened after reading of deformities. Her doctor believed she had "a clear and unambiguous case for abortion," although her state of Arizona permitted the procedure only when the mother's life was threatened. She could have had her abortion at a local hospital had she maintained discreet silence; but she wanted to warn wives of National Guardsmen, recently home from Germany after the Berlin Wall crisis. Her front-page article, "Baby-Deforming Drug May Cost Woman Her Child Here," caused abrupt cancellation of her abortion. The Finkbines were deluged with reactions, positive and negative. Denied a visa to Japan, Sherri Finkbine flew in her fourth month to Sweden where an obstetrician performed the procedure and confirmed fears that the embryo was so seriously deformed it would not have survived. Back home, she lost her job but became a household name nationally. In 1965, she gave birth to her fifth child.[27]

While Sherri Finkbine received more notoriety than sympathy, Dr. Kelsey, who had prevented thalidomide from becoming a national disaster, received due acclaim. She received the President's gold medal Award for Distinguished Federal Civilian Service, the highest honor for a government worker, in 1962. Dr. Helen B. Taussig's behind the scenes work earned less publicity, but this Johns Hopkins pediatric cardiologist, co-discoverer of the blue-baby operation, and winner of the Presidential Medal of Freedom, devoted herself to research on the European dimensions of the thalidomide tragedy. Writing in the *New England Journal of Medicine* in July 1963, Taussig reported difficulty in tracing the effects of thalidomide due to the drug's many trade names but found a direct correlation between deformities and the sedative. *The Journal of the American Medical Association* refused to print her warning, perhaps because the mass circulation *Time* had already featured the story. Undaunted, Taussig published other articles, made speeches, and testified before Congress. Largely because of the combined efforts of Drs. Kelsey and Taussig, the FDA banned thalidomide's sale in the United States.[28]

Abortion

In the early sixties abortion was a medical issue, discussed primarily by doctors. Americans still wanted children, according to sociologist Alice Rossi; as late as 1966 "an average of 3.4 children was considered ideal by white women age 21 and over." Rossi found that "college graduates had a desired family size mean of 3.2; 38 percent wanted four or more children." Not wanting children was thought unnatural; the fifties identification of large families with affirmation of the future continued.[29]

Films offered examples of "girls" persisting through unwanted pregnancies: Sandra Dee in *A Summer Place* (1959); Natalie Wood in *All the Fine Young Cannibals* (1960); Rita Tushingham in *A Taste of Honey* (1961); Connie Stevens in *Parrish* (1961); and Leslie Caron in *The L-Shaped Room* (1962). If a middle-class girl "got herself in trouble," found herself in the "family way," and could not or would not marry the father (or vice versa), she was expected to go away surreptitiously to have the baby at a Home for Unwed Mothers, give it up for adoption, and return home as from an extended visit to a long-lost aunt, knowing all the while that the gossip mills were working overtime. Matters were far more complex for poor women.

At the beginning of the decade, all of the states had anti-abortion statutes that dated from as early as the 1870s. Many banned abortion even for women with grave diseases, although exceptions were sometimes made for cancer, heart diseases, severe hypertension, or kidney disease. With movement for reform coming slowly, an estimated million women chose the dangerous, secret underground alternative of illegal or "criminal" abortions. Information often came through a grapevine of friends who provided names only—no credentials, no guarantees. Complex underworld "black market" abortion rings existed in many cities, involving druggists, taxi drivers, hotel employees. One matronly nurse required that patients be brought blindfolded to her modest apartment in Philadelphia's Market District, where she administered a saline injection into the uterus, while the patient lay on her bed, covered with a challis spread, in view of a crucifix on the wall. Dismissed with only a few tranquilizers, one patient nearly bled to death of an incomplete abortion, and was saved by a D & C (Dilation and Curettage, or scraping of the uterus) in a large New York public hospital. Other women tried even more dangerous self-induction. Annually, about 350,000 women were admitted to hospitals with complications, of which 5,000–10,000 proved fatal.[30]

Abortion law reform, first proposed in the late 1950s, was essentially conservative. It did not take into account a woman's possible desire not to have children, an almost unthinkable idea then in mainstream professional rhetoric and in mass culture. The American Law Institute (ALI), a national nonprofit organization dedicated to "rationalizing" the law, drafted a Model Penal Code in 1959. Section 230.3 states bluntly that "a licensed physician is justified in terminating a pregnancy if he believes there is substantial risk that continuance of the pregnancy would gravely impair the physical or mental health of the mother, or that the child would be born with grave physical or mental defect, or that the pregnancy resulted from rape, incest, or other felonious intercourse. All illicit intercourse with a girl below the age of sixteen shall be deemed felonious." The code stipulates that justifiable abortions be performed only in licensed hospitals, except in emergencies. Approved in 1962, the code became a blueprint for abortion law reform.[31]

A movement to enact the reform of state statutes followed, although it was not until 1967 that Colorado became the first state to change its laws. Attempts at reform based on the Model Code failed in Illinois, Kansas, New York, and Minnesota between 1963 and 1965. In California in 1963, state assemblyman Anthony Beilenson proposed a Therapeutic Abortion Act. The bill languished, blocked by vocal opposition from Catholics, one quarter of the state's population, and by fundamentalists; but in unprecedented public hearings, assemblymen also heard moving pro-reform plaints from individuals as well as groups like the Junior Chamber of Commerce and the American Association of University Women. One woman testified, "I was raped by two men that forced my car over to the side of the road in 1960. I had to have the baby because no doctor would help me with an abortion. *Please* help other unfortunate women." Through efforts of the California Committee on Therapeutic Abortion (CCTA), one of the first formal abortion reform organizations, the Beilenson Bill finally passed the senate 48 to 30 in 1967 and was signed by Governor Ronald Reagan after removal of the provision for abortion in cases of fetal deformity. North Carolina enacted similar reform shortly thereafter.[32]

Between 1967 and 1970, 15 other states modified their laws: all allowed abortion by a licensed physician for maternal health or in cases of rape or incest, while nine of them also permitted abortions for suspected fetal deformity. Most of the revised laws included residency requirements and stipulated that abortions could not be performed after a certain point in the pregnancy. Residency requirements ranging from 30 to 180 days were intended to deter "abortion tourism." In 1970, Hawaii, Alaska, New York, and Washington passed broader reforms, but prolegalization forces lost in Arizona, Maryland, and Vermont. Alaska and Hawaii dropped the requirement for cause and permitted abortions for any reason when provided by a licensed physician in an accredited hospital on a "nonviable fetus" (defined as before quickening, at about four to five months). An estimated 8,000 legal abortions were performed between 1963 and 1965, with the number rising to 20,000 in 1969. Many hospitals set maximum quotas that could not be exceeded for any reason, while elite teaching hospitals performed abortions more readily than those that served the poor.[33]

Sociologist Nancy Howell Lee found in 1969 that most women seeking abortion were previously married, with children, often living on alimony or other support from previous husbands. Others were unmarried career women, single or previously married, supporting themselves, or unmarried women who had conceived by a man they could not or did not want to marry, or women contemplating divorce. Most were in stable or exclusive relationships, had had two to four previous longterm relationships, took their love affairs seriously and were not promiscuous. Still, they were not using contraceptives or used them carelessly.

With landmark legislation in many states, the abortion debate, formerly confined to professionals or to women's desperate private discussions, became public, furthered by the availability of the Pill, reassessment of the relationship between sexuality and reproduction, and changing attitudes toward sexuality and sex roles. In addition, demographer Paul Ehrlich's best-seller *The Population Bomb* (1960) had focused concern on the "population explosion" and on the morality of having large numbers of children. His book led to the idea of "zero population growth," individuals reproducing only themselves and to formation of the organization ZPG.[35]

In many reform states, insurance programs like Blue Cross began to cover therapeutic abortions. Even with reform, poor women were still discriminated against because they could not pay for hospital stays and surgical fees, let alone the psychiatric consultations some states required. The National Medical Committee for Human Rights passed a resolution, "Approximately 1,200,000 women per year obtain illegal abortions. . . . There must be medical freedom to help panicky women make rational choices and, if need be, have safe, early, and inexpensive abortions."[36]

The movement for abortion law reform and, subsequently, for legalization, received support from professional organizations, from individuals banding together to bring about change and from some churches. It was also assisted by increased public awareness in the wake of the thalidomide scare. The 1962 Finkbine case forced people to think about abortion and its morality, revealing fundamental disagreement about whether or not an embryo was a "real" or merely a potential person and raising questions of the "moral meaning of 'handicap,'" the role of intervention and control in human life, and the larger question of what qualities individuals . . . must have to be considered 'fully' human." Over half of those in a 1962 Gallup poll believed that Finkbine had made the right decision, that fetal deformity justified abortion; 32 percent opposed it and 16 percent had no opinion.[37]

Fetal deformity as grounds for abortion remained in the public mind during the 1964–65 national epidemic of rubella or German measles, cause of 30 percent of major infant deformities from blindness to severe mental retardation. Through the fifties, rubella caused 10 to 20 percent of legal abortions; but many boards of health were unwilling to certify the disease with its ephemeral rash as justifying abortion. Dr. Virginia Apgar of the National Foundation—March of Dimes estimated that 15,000–20,000 defective measles babies were born annually, yet only ten California hospitals granted abortions for rubella in 1960. In 1966, the San Francisco Nine (obstetricians) were indicted for performing abortions on measles-infected mothers without legal permission, an event that mobilized national professional support for them. These events accelerated professional debate and accentuated differences between "strict constructionists" who wanted to enforce their moral views through the law and "broad constructionists" who favored more lenient laws and enforcement.[38]

Reform proposals received support from 1964 to 1967 from professional organizations like the American Medical Association, American Bar Association, American Academy of Pediatrics, California Medical Association, and California Bar Association. The American Medical Women's Association called for legalization of abortion as did the National Association for Mental Health and the American Public Health Association. It was an idea whose time had come. A subgroup of the American Psychiatric Association declared that a woman "has as much right to decide whether or not to abort as she has to decide whether or not to marry," and *Modern Medicine* reported in 1969 that 51 percent of physicians favored abortion on demand. Many early physician-activists wanted to legalize "what they were already doing." A number of reputable doctors specialized in abortion, often because of their commitment to caring for women. The luckiest women found physicians like Dr. Robert Douglas Spense of Ashland, Pennsylvania, or Dr. Milan Vuitch, a District of Columbia surgeon who was arrested in 1968. Vuitch charged patients $100 to $300, less than the $1000 that could be commanded by qualified practitioners.[39]

Debate on legislation in various states led in 1964 to the formation of the Association for the Study of Abortion (ASA), an organization of doctors, lawyers, theologians, and social workers who came together to study abortion reform and educate the public. The ASA believed that public apathy on the abortion issue was due to lack of information. When a 1965 National Fertility study of 5,600 married women found that only five percent favored abortion on demand, the California Committee on Therapeutic Abortion (CCTA) formed to launch an educational campaign.

Patricia Maginnis, a former WAC medical technician in her thirties, was an early activist for abortion on demand. She founded the tax-exempt research and educational Society for Humane Abortion (SHA) in California in 1961, aided by Lana Phelan. Drawing on information furnished by Dr. Helen Taussig and civil liberties lawyer Harriet Pilpel, SHA, composed primarily of women, became the first group to call for free access to abortion as a matter of women's "rights." They organized leafletting, lectures, and petitions to make "the 'unspeakable' speakable," to open the issue of repeal, not simply reform, to public dialogue. Meanwhile, SHA made referrals to Mexican abortionists "inspected for cleanliness and respectability."

In 1966, Maginnis created the Association to Repeal Abortion Laws (ARAL), a California political action group. Like SHA, ARAL organized civil disobedience by dispensing lists of abortionists, thus advertising this service. Beginning in 1966, they offered free public classes to teach self-abortion techniques across the nation. Despite pickets like the Catholic Mothers Outraged at the Murder of Innocents (MOMIS), classes usually drew at least 100. ARAL leaders were arrested in San Mateo County but were successfully defended by the ACLU on First Amendment grounds. Lawrence Lader describes ARAL's sense of mission as stemming from the members' "marginal backgrounds," social and economic, which led them to rebel against the "law for the rich." Luker notes, "these tactics transformed the debate. Now women who wanted abortions were no longer victims, a less-than-legitimate group of rule breakers who wanted the rules changed," but individuals "crusading for a basic civic right." Elsewhere, Edith Rein organized the Wisconsin Committee to Legalize Abortion, and Ruth Steel, a Planned Parenthood officer, was so active for reform in Colorado that the press dubbed her the "Carrie Nation of the Bedroom."[40]

Lader himself helped launch the movement for repeal rather than reform as chairman of the National Association for Repeal of Abortion Laws (NARAL). In his influential book *Abortion* (1966), he argued that marital privacy was guaranteed by the Constitution, quoting Pilpel:

"Does it not constitutionally deny a woman's life, liberty, and pursuit of happiness if, despite her wishes and the opinions of concurring doctors, she is forced to bear a child she doesn't want, and objectively, shouldn't have."[41]

A network of abortion referral services conducted by "gentle lawbreakers" sprang up across the country. Organizers of such services knew that after passage of England's 1967 Abortion Act, they could send women who could afford it there; between 5,000 and 35,000 went annually prior to legalization of abortion in the United States. Bill Baird created his Parents' Aid Society to assist women seeking abortion and birth control in Boston in 1967. Many clergymen became activists in abortion reform following the May 1967 founding of the New York Clergy Consultation Service on Abortion by Rev. Howard Moody at Judson Memorial Church. In 1968 the Episcopal Church, United Methodist Church, and United Church of Christ issued resolutions in favor of women's rights to abortion. Such referral services also galvanized support for ALI bills in various states from the American Lutheran Church, the New York City Protestant Council of Churches, the New York State Council of Churches, and the Episcopal Diocese of New York.[42]

"Abortion tourism" did not guarantee safety or sanitation. Susan Brownmiller had her first abortion while in Cuba "to observe the Castro Revolution." Hemorrhaging followed that continued from the Havana clinic back to New York. For her second abortion, she flew to a private clinic in Puerto Rico. In *The Search for an Abortionist* (1969), Nancy Howell Lee documented the difficulties women experienced inside and outside the legal and medical system. She concluded, however, that despite immense procedural difficulties and the common warnings of psychological consequences, few women suffered enduring stress, depression, or guilt.[43]

Dr. Harold Rosen, author of *Therapeutic Abortion* (1954), added a new conclusion to a second edition, significantly retitled *Abortion in America* (1967), noting that the abortion debate had become a woman's issue: "Women in our society are no longer chattels. Our abortion laws have long . . . served to keep them so. Mature legal consideration of mother, family, children, and society should lead legislatures not to pass more liberal abortion laws but to abolish such laws altogether." The extralegal abortion rate proved that the decision to abort, "right or wrong," already belonged to women. Rosen urged legislators and jurists to legalize these decisions. Rosen himself and other New York doctors had banded together to perform abortions "openly but illegally for $75," a rare demonstration of individual doctors acting on behalf of women.[44]

With the 1967 legislation in California and elsewhere, anti-abortion forces also mobilized, their rhetoric becoming steadily more militant. There had always been religious controversy about the moment when life begins and its implication for abortion. Opposition to abortion came primarily from the Catholic Church, which believes that life begins at conception. The Second Vatican Council (1962–1965) stated in "The Church in the Modern World" that abortion is infamy: "From the moment of its conception, life must be guarded with the greatest care, while abortion and infanticide are unspeakable crimes." Still, in a 1965 nationwide poll conducted by the Association for Abortion Reform, Catholics and Protestants differed only slightly—64 percent of Catholics accepted abortion to protect the mother's health as compared to 73 percent of Protestants; 47 percent of Catholics and 57 percent of Protestants favored abortion in cases of rape; and the numbers were almost identical regarding cases of fetal deformity.[45]

Early anti-abortion activists consisted primarily (but not exclusively) of Catholic male professionals mobilized on the state level to block reform legislation but acting primarily as individuals from belief that "an embryo is a child from conception onward and that abortion ends the life of an innocent child." As Kristen Luker points out, however, these anti-abortion activists "did not understand that for many people abortion was 'unspeakable' not because it represented the death of a child but because it represented 'getting caught' in the consequences of sexuality. Sex, not abortion, was what people didn't talk about."[46]

In New York, the Catholic Church helped defeat reform bills in 1967 and 1968, although a state survey showed that 72 percent of Catholics favored liberalization of abortion laws. Elizabeth Elkind, Abortion Reform Society Executive Secretary, calls 1967 the "year of the holy war." Priests read pastoral letters at Sunday masses condemning abortion, denounced specific legislators as pro-reform or wavering, and distributed preprinted postcards for parishioners to mail to their representatives. Opponents countered pro-reform demonstrators' images of bloody coat hangers with pictures of destroyed fetuses and signs reading "Thanks, Mom, you didn't flush me down the toilet." But a mass anti-abortion movement of ordinary citizens, mainly women driven by principle, did not form until the seventies. For many legislators, as for many Catholics, it was excruciatingly difficult to balance personal moral principles against demands for "rights" by those who did not share their beliefs.

In September 1967 the Joseph P. Kennedy, Jr., Foundation and the Harvard Divinity School cosponsored the First International Conference on Abortion in Washington, but women had little voice. Only three of 59 panelists and less than ten percent of delegates were women. Most were anti-abortion and from the health and legal professions. Conference recommendations were conservative. Maginnis and Phelan picketed, their signs reading "End Butchery" and decorated with coat-hangers and knitting needles. The *Washington Post* ran the headline, "Conference Termed 'Stacked'." Maginnis gave one of her famous do-it-yourself abortion classes as an alternative event, then embarked on a national speaking tour.[47]

Abortion reformers received unexpected support in the 1968 report submitted by Johnson's Presidential Advisory Council on the Status of Women. Its chairwoman, former U. S. Senator Maurine Neuberger of Oregon, recommended repeal of all abortion laws, the first time that such a position was taken under federal auspices. Court cases and oral and written testimony also promoted pro-choice attitudes. In one of the most famous cases, *People v. Belous*, on 5 September 1969, the California Supreme Court reversed the conviction of Leon P. Belous, a Beverly Hills physician who referred a woman to another doctor for abortion. The U. S. Supreme Court refused to hear an appeal.[48]

Public opinion had changed rapidly. A 1967 Gallup poll showed 21 percent of women supported abortion on demand in the first trimester. Legislators began to see women as a new constituency, especially as the idea of the "right" to abortion was articulated by professionals, echoing patients' needs and the rhetoric of the new feminism. A 1969 Gallup poll showed 40 percent approved of abortion in the first trimester. Charles and Leslie Aldridge Westoff surveyed the trend in *From Now to Zero: Fertility, Contraception and Abortion in America* (1968 and 1971). In the late 1960s the women's movement recast the abortion issue from a feminist perspective, expanded the public debate with a new rhetoric, and voiced demands for easier access to abortion. Natalie Shainess claimed that a woman was denied abortion on demand because she "is regarded as nothing more than an encapsulating amniotic sac." But neither the issue of a woman's right to govern her own body and control the quality of her life nor the issue of the personhood and "right to life" of a fetus had been resolved by decade's end.[49]

Feminists entered the abortion reform movement late. Two months after the September 1969 Washington Conference abortion became a major issue at the second national convention of NOW. After long emotional debate involving members who wanted to keep the organization from appearing radical, NOW ratified a Bill of Rights for Women including a clause asserting "The right of women to control their reproductive lives by removing from the penal code laws limiting access to contraceptive information and devices and by repealing penal laws governing abortion"—"the first 'official' involvement of the women's movement with the abortion issue." Jean Faust remembers first being blocked "by traditional labels. We were afraid of being called 'loose women' if we included abortion in our platform." Betty Friedan retained her conviction that NOW should avoid issues "that got into the private side of life"; and a number of conservative feminists quit NOW over the issue to form the Women's Equity Action League (WEAL).[50]

Radical feminists, worried about NOW's cautiousness, met with Lader to affiliate with his National Association for Repeal of Abortion Laws (NARAL) in New York in August 1968, enlisting Ruth P. Smith of ASA, Dr. Lonny Myers, and others. It sponsored the First National Conference on Abortion Laws in Chicago in February 1969 and named Shirley Chisholm Honorary President and former Senator Maurine Neuberger Vice President. NARAL drew an array of radicals, professionals, sociologists, legislators, and women from such organizations as the YWCA, and even persuaded Friedan to speak. Chisholm declared: "We consider it a national disgrace that referral services have been forced to operate in a twilight zone."[51]

In January 1969, the Abortion Committee of NOW's radical New York chapter founded an independent statewide organization, New Yorkers for Abortion Law Repeal (NYALR). NYALR members picketed and invaded hearings on abortion reform in the state legislature, demanding that "the meeting be turned over to them since women are the only 'real experts' on abortion." Many NYALR members joined Redstockings, which in March held counter-hearings at the Washington Square Methodist Church and disrupted state legislative hearings on legal reform.[52]

Nationally, public feminist pro-choice activities escalated in 1968 and 1969. In Chicago, feminists staged guerilla theater plays depicting the brutalities of illegal abortions for surprised members of the American Medical Association convention. The Detroit Women's Liberation Coalition stormed the office of a county attorney known for prosecuting abortionists. Radical feminists, in a series of local actions from 1967 on, focused more attention on abortion than NOW did and radicalized rhetoric about the subject. Lana Phelan told the CCTA in February 1968: "The compulsory breeding of women by church and state is nothing more than ecclesiastical and legislative pimpery in which the bodies of all women are utilized for state profit and pleasure." In 1968 a District of Columbia group published a pamphlet, "It's All Right, Ma (I'm Only Bleeding)." Kathy Amatniek led radicals to break up hearings of the Joint Legislative Committee on the Problems of Public Health, hearing witnesses—14 men and one nun—on 13 February 1969. Los Angeles NOW picketed the District Attorney's office. Demonstrators invaded an AMA convention in New York in 1969, led by Dr. Lonny Myers dressed in a white lab coat, her hands tied by red tape symbolic of the law. NARAL called a national demonstration on 8 May 1969, Mother's Day, and on other "days of anger," with sit-ins in a dozen cities. Their signs read: "Illegal Abortions Support the Mafia" and "No More Lysol, Soap, Arsenic, or Coat Hangers." That year, Redstockings sponsored a public "speakout" in which women like Gloria Steinem recounted horror stories of their abortions; Seattle Radical Women and Female Liberation in Boston repeated the program. Feminists also organized their own referral services.[53]

A few isolated crusaders, like Boston's Bill Baird, forged a coalition with radical feminists like New York's Ti-Grace Atkinson to use civil disobedience as a technique to test laws in court. Atkinson, former president of the New York NOW chapter, lambasted the Catholic Church in a lecture at Catholic University in March 1971, charging it "with murder in the first degree, premeditated and willful, . . . with conspiracy to imprison and enslave women . . . into marriage and the family, . . . with forcing many . . . into prostitution, . . . with inciting rape . . . by degrading and sadistic propaganda." She concluded, "Mutherfuckers! . . . The struggle between the liberation of women and the Catholic Church is a struggle to the death. So be it!" When Atkinson declared that Mary, mother of Christ, was "knocked up," Patricia Buckley Bozell, co-editor with her husband of the conservative *National Review* and sister of columnist William F. Buckley and Senator James L. Buckley, leaped to the stage and swung at Atkinson, who later explained that her diatribe provoked violence because it was "the first time in two thousand years that a woman had stood up to the Church."[54]

A month after Atkinson's controversial appearance, feminist lawyers Florynce Kennedy and Diane Schulder convened a coalition of organizations and individual women "to bring formal suit against the Catholic Church for using its tax exempt funds for lobbying purposes." A year later, the Supreme Court decided in favor of "privacy" in *Eisenstadt v. Baird*.[55]

In some large cities, feminists found support from "radical medical groups" that dispensed inexpensive, sympathetic medical aid to "the growing number of hippies, 'street people' or radicals, for drug use, riot injuries, venereal disease, and unwanted pregnancies." In Chicago, the Jane Collective, initially an abortion referral service, grew from the work of a single University of Chicago graduate student using the pseudonym "Jane." As more women became involved, a collective developed, nonhierarchical in structure, and volunteers started to perform abortions themselves, empowering women by showing them their capabilities. The Jane Collective developed a women-centered analysis of sociopolitical problems.[56]

The most famous and enduring group was the Boston Women's Health Collective, inspired in 1969 by a workshop on "Women and their Bodies" at Emmanuel College. Members of the Bread and Roses women's liberation group determined to develop a "laywoman's course on health" after discovering from a questionnaire that "there were no 'good' doctors and we had to learn from ourselves." Gleaning information from medical books or medically trained people, they wrote papers individually or communally on topics decided upon collectively— Patient as Victim, Sexuality, Anatomy, Birth Control, Pregnancy, Prepared Childbirth, Postpartum and Childcare, Medical Institutions, Medical Laws, and Organizing for Change—compiled in the landmark publication, *Our Bodies, Ourselves* (1971).[57]

The chapter on abortion is informative rather than prescriptive and includes statistics, history, and information on woman's anatomy. It describes equipment needed for vacuum suction or dilation and curettage and compares abortions performed by doctors, unskilled abortionists, or the pregnant women themselves. An addition to the 1973 edition includes personal accounts of abortion experiences. These women rejected an authoritarian stance and shared their knowledge as they were learning, reflected by use of the pronouns "we" and "our" instead of "you" and "your." They proclaim, "Abortion is our right— our right as women to control our bodies."[58]

The feminist *Everywoman's Guide to Abortion* (1971) aimed to curtail illegal and dangerous abortions by informing women how and where they could go to avoid "compulsory motherhood" safely and cheaply given the limitations and "unprecedented opportunity" of the "recent liberalization of abortion laws in several states." It listed referral services and doctors performing "medically sound, albeit (in most cases) illegal abortions for reasonable fees." Most abortions then cost from $100 to $750, excluding travel and related expenses. Doctors profited, charging $300 for a therapeutic abortion using the standard D & C that usually cost only $200, raising the fee to $1000 if performed illegally. Feminist referral services exercised "a certain degree of bargaining power . . . to force doctors to lower their fees considerably." They listed physicians in America and abroad "who treat women humanely, who do not themselves make sexual advances (an apparently common practice) and who refrain from including a 'morality lecture' with the operation." That advice was clearly not for poor women who could not afford fees or travel. Authors concluded that "Only in America has a vast profit-making industry grown up around abortion."[59]

Many lay Catholics continued to disagree with or disobey Church rulings on birth control and abortion. Catholics' approval of abortion to preserve the mother's health or avoid fetal deformity grew even after Pope Paul VI issued his encyclical *Humanae Vitae* (1968) declaring that "directly willed and procured abortions, even if for therapeutic reasons, are to be absolutely excluded as licit means of regulating birth." Based on a 1969 Gallup Poll on abortion, Judith Blake, a reform activist, found Catholic disapproval of abortion for economic reasons only ten percent greater than non-Catholic—74 versus 64 percent with 79 percent of non-Catholic women and 76 percent of non-Catholic men disapproving. Although 62 percent of Catholic women knew the Church banned all abortions, 25 percent of them believed the Church would allow abortion to save the mother and felt the Church would allow abortion in cases of fetal deformity.[60]

Greatest support for abortion reform was in the far west and east while the south was "the bastion of conservative attitudes toward abortion." Disapproval of elective abortion was higher among largely fundamentalist southern non-Catholics than among Catholics. The general public continued to oppose elective abortion for economic reasons or as a means of birth control. The uneducated opposed abortion more than the educated, and women opposed abortion more than men. College-educated, non-Catholic women also opposed elective abortion and were just as likely as poorly educated women to disapprove of contraceptives for unmarried "girls." Upper-class women considered motherhood women's principal career and hence experienced "ambivalence and uncertainty when confronted by major changes in the conditions of this career"—the possibility of alternative choices. Abortion to preserve the mother's health or prevent child deformity was publicly accepted, while abortion "on demand" for discretionary or "selfish" reasons received minimal, yet rapidly growing support.[61]

The profile of late-sixties activists indicates that the abortion debate had "become a debate among women" about the "place and meaning of motherhood." A war between feminists and traditionalists erupted when the focus of the debate shifted from the "medical profession's right to make life-and-death decisions" to the "moral status of the embryo" and, thereby, to the "relative rights of women and embryos." Kristen Luker characterizes "the average pro-choice activist" as "a forty-four-year-old married woman who grew up in a large metropolitan area" in a middle-class, educated family. She "married at age twenty-two, has one or two children, and has had some graduate or professional training. . . . She is married to a professional man, is herself employed in a regular job, and her family income is more than $50,000 a year. She is not religiously active, feels that religion is not important to her, and attends church very rarely if at all." In contrast, "the average pro-life woman is also a forty-four-year-old married woman who grew up in a large metropolitan area. She married at age seventeen and has three children or more. . . . she has some college education or may have a B.A. degree. She is not employed in the paid labor force and is married to a small businessman or a lower-level white collar worker; her family income is $30,000 a year. She is Catholic (and may have converted), and her religion is one of the most important aspects of her life; she attends church at least once a week and occasionally more often." The pro-life activist obviously made a career of her family and "supporting abortion (and believing that the embryo is not a person)" was against her vested interest. Pro-choice activists perceived "any situation that both practically and symbolically affirms the primacy of women's reproductive roles as a real loss to them." Luker found that "insofar as abortion allows a woman to get a job, to get training for a job, or to advance in a job, it does more than provide social support for working women over homemakers; it also seems to support the value of economic considerations over moral ones." Thus it was only natural that the debate had become so emotional; no matter which side won, "one group of women would see the very real devaluation of their lives and life resources."[62]

Opposition to legalization of abortion also came from some blacks, often because of their evangelical Christian heritage. Although some black women leaders such as Shirley Chisholm and Florence Rice of the Harlem Consumer Education Council supported reform, many black women displayed little interest in abortion, which, at best, they considered a white "women's lib" issue. According to estimates, blacks in the sixties had only 10 percent of illegal abortions, perhaps because of expense, perhaps because of religious fundamentalism. At the Black Power Conference in Newark, New Jersey, in 1967, consensus declared both birth control and abortion forms of "Black genocide." Brenda Hyson echoed views of various Black groups in an article in the *Black Panther* (1970): "Perhaps it is a victory for the white middle-class mother who wants to have a smaller family, thus enabling her to have more material goods or more time to participate in whatever fancies her at the moment. But most of all it is a victory for the oppressive ruling class who will use this law to kill off Black and other oppressed people before they are born."[63]

Sociologist Alice Rossi conceded that pressure on Congress for family planning legislation was indeed a "poorly concealed mandate from the well-to-do" wishing "to see fewer and smaller families on welfare and a halt to any increase in the proportion of blacks in the American population." Many Blacks felt that abortion was a "relatively rare crisis as contrasted to such problems as unemployment, racism, poverty, bad housing, police rioting, and war." They distrusted the "white women's movement, a natural consequence of the D and C (divide and conquer) techniques of the oppressive establishment," as they distrusted the establishment's systems and institutions, especially the courts. Many blacks associated more lenient abortion laws with compulsory sterilization and few feminists were sensitive enough to realize that "the white women's movement must be careful not to use Black women's plight to make their case for them." In *Abortion Rap*, Diane Schulder and Florynce Kennedy warned that "White women must let the Black movement formulate its own ideas and strategies in its own time and way."[64]

Changes were immense by decade's end. States broke "radically with a century-old tradition of harshly punitive treatment of abortion." Historian Rosalind Petchesky adds, "The activity was so sudden, so sweeping, that it caught even proabortion organizers by surprise." One feminist recalls, "We rode the crest of something I still can't define—but that something was clearly changing attitudes on the part of the American public." Voices for women's choice included feminists intent on giving women control over their own bodies as well as scientists and social scientists urging population limitation. Organizations like NOW called for "abortion on demand." And *Newsweek* acknowledged that the majority of Americans supported that position.[65]

The Supreme Court decisions in *Roe v. Wade* and *Doe v. Bolton* on 22 January 1973 legalized abortion on demand during the first trimester of pregnancy, made second-trimester abortions more easily available, and repealed previous laws, stunning some Americans into action. Both women had sought abortions despite state restrictions. In both cases, the Court affirmed the woman's right to privacy, concluding that the Fourteenth Amendment is "broad enough to encompass a woman's decision whether or not to terminate her pregnancy." The decisions vacated the restricted reasons for abortion listed in the ALI code, allowed the state the right to require certain facilities for abortion in the second trimester (but not in the first), but no longer allowed the state a voice in the woman's decision.[66]

Despite the wave of abortion reform legislation in 16 states from 1967 on, few abortion activists on either side had anticipated such liberalization. *Roe* and *Doe* did not cause rising abortion rates but accommodated social changes "rooted in the same cluster of interacting conditions that produced the overall fertility decline among U.S. women that began in the early sixties," ending the post-war "baby boom." Women increased their college attendance, married later, entered and kept jobs after marriage to cope with the Great Inflation of the Vietnam era if not to develop their own careers, and postponed childbearing through birth control and abortion. After the peak fertility years of 1955 to 1959, childbirth rates plummeted through the decade among all population groups.

Childbirth

Through the sixties, most American women had their babies in hospitals, and obstetric practice continued a "servitude to mechanization and the materialization of childbirth." Physicians reigned supreme, "controlling" the process with the "whole arsenal of contemporary technology and pain relievers" such as barbiturates, amnesics, narcotics, muscle relaxants, forceps, and scalpels, many used merely to make the process quicker and less troublesome for the staff. Cesarean delivery became increasingly common. Women were maternity patients, with no control or voice, few choices about place and procedure; birth was pathological. Most went through labor and delivery in starkly institutional semiprivate rooms or wards, crowded because of the baby boom. They were suspended in stirrups, surrounded by staff rotations of "experts" that brought in an array strangers to intervene through childbirth's various stages. Drugs obliterated the sensation and memory of giving birth. Husbands, family, and friends were relegated to pacing in the proverbial waiting room. Critics called hospitals more prepared for war casualties than for maternity. Still, physicians wondered why women displayed "pregnophobia" and fears about delivery.[68]

Psychiatrist Ernst Simmell called the obstetrician-gynecologist "custodian of the female reproductive system, the normality of which guarantees normal wives," otherwise "beset" with "psychobiological" problems; only the physician's intervention could prevent "frigid wives" and "postpartum cripples," psychosomatic problems if not full-blown mental illness resulting from childbirth. Late fifties' obstetrician training urged psychiatric evaluation of all maternity patients, and medical literature warned against problems of women engaging in "bridge-table obstetrics," gossiping about childbirth experiences and exchanging horror stories. Historian and nurse Margarete Sandelowski found that childbearing women were "psychosexually threatening to some physicians" and were "also suspect because they were perceived as undermining physicians' claims to expertise in obstetrics." Professional defensiveness grew through the fifties and sixties along with discussion of natural childbirth like the Lamaze method, increasingly used in Europe after 1951. Some doctors even alleged Soviet origins of Lamaze and suggested that "the motivations and general emotional stability of American women" attracted to it were suspect.[69]

The sixties witnessed the first stirrings of women's attempts to seize control of their own reproductive systems, and, as in ancient times, to turn to other lay women rather than professional physicians in time of need. Lila Karp's first novel, *The Queen Is in the Garbage* (1969), tells of a woman who lived through miscarriages, blood poisoning, and hideous abortions. As she goes into labor and gives birth, Harriet's pains and fears blur with those of her past, of her abuse by parents, estranged husband, and lover. Suicidal thoughts and nightmarish dreams dominate her. Eight hours after birth, her daughter dies. Her only support comes from two women friends who remain by her side and coach her.

Even her male physician acknowledges, condescendingly, the women's competence and care: "You ladies are certainly making my job easy tonight. There isn't much for me to do here with you two around."[70]

Between 1963 and 1973, the number of trained, practicing midwives grew from 400 to 1,400; but midwives accounted for delivery of less than one percent of American babies in contrast to 80 percent worldwide. Nurse-midwives were not permitted to practice in New York City's municipal hospitals until 1961; and they could only assist physicians in deliveries until 1971, when they received a certain degree of autonomy in some maternity wards. Most of the nation was even slower to change. The movement favoring lay midwives practicing in patients' homes or operating home birth centers would not flourish until the seventies.[71]

Although based in the counter-cultural spirit of the sixties, natural childbirth did not become a trend until the seventies. One of the nation's first birth centers was established in 1971 in California to create "a sisterhood concerned with birth and its process. . . . We are finding out about the natural capabilities of women . . . and have taken our birthright, freedom, and decided for ourselves what our rituals of birth will be." Doris Hair emerged as a leader in the International Childbirth Education Association, and many proclaimed her book *The Cultural Warping of Childbirth* (1972) as a manifesto and turning point. The women leading the new movement declared, "Doctors are always enemies of women." They targeted male obstetricians "who elect to play the role of the Father and God to their patients, forcing women into the role of helpless, stupid, ridiculous little girls." Lamaze classes and Leboyer delivery in a birthing chair, warms tubs of water for mother and baby, and use of midwives for home delivery were all practices inspired by the "sixties spirit," giving more control over childbirth to the mother and removing it from the patriarchal obstetrician.[72]

Reproductive Technologies

Scientists escalated research and development regarding reproductive technologies in the sixties, making breakthroughs that had both positive and negative consequences for women. An increasing number of women turned to artificial insemination to have children. The preferred practice used fresh donor semen (AID), with the identity of the donors, most of whom were physicians or medical students, usually kept secret. About two-thirds of those choosing the still rare procedure were single, and many were lesbians. Others were married and "motivated by their husbands' infertility." By 1960, an estimated 5,000–7,000 AID children were born annually. The Roman Catholic Church and the Church of England condemned the process.[73]

Gena Corea observed that "most men greeted AID with alarm, for it threatened the very basis of patriarchal descent. While they eagerly used artificial insemination in animals, they were in no rush to set up banks for human sperm." Advances in artificial insemination followed introduction by Dr. Jerome K. Sherman of liquid nitrogen for deep-freezing human sperm and made possible the founding of sperm banks. By 1965, only about a dozen babies born in the United States and Japan had been conceived from thawed sperm. A leading British eugenicist, Sir Julian Huxley, proposed a system of "EID—eugenic insemination by deliberately preferred donors," urging that "AID, then under a legal and moral cloud, must be made fully respectable," and that donor anonymity be abolished, permitting the prospective mother to choose the eugenic make-up of the child she would bear. Sherman agreed, proposing in 1964 a nation-wide system with "Cross-matched cataloguing of characteristics of mind and body of the donors," and "transport of frozen human semen from selected donors, available from all over the country and world in designated centers, and establishment of a clearing house with all pertinent information on stored semen, functioning in association with consultants in medicine, genetics, psychology and social work in such programs as germinal choice."[74]

Dr. S. J. Behrman spoke to the American College of Obstetricians and Gynecologists in 1968, advocating "semen banks as a mechanism of positive eugenics." Behrman saw the advances as part of a century-old effort to control fertility but interpreted control from a male perspective, lauding the new ability of a man to "engender a child a continent away even after his own death" through use of frozen sperm, while having the advantage of a vasectomy during life. The first American commercial human sperm cryobank opened in 1970, followed in 1971 by New York City's Idant, which became the largest. The Hermann J. Muller Repository for Germinal Choice in California, was not set up until 1976—by an entrepreneur, Robert K. Graham, not a physician. Ironically, Muller, who died in 1967, had opposed Graham's project because of support from "reactionary people" like the "racially biased" Dr. William Shockley, a believer in "biological determinism."[75]

Such ideas were common among genetic scientists like Francis Crick, co-discoverer of DNA, who declared at his 1963 symposium, "Man and

His Future," with only one woman on the program, "I think that if we can get across to people the idea that their children are not entirely their own business and that it is not a private matter, it would be an enormous step forward." Crick proposed that women be "licensed to bear children," that the government "put sterilants in the food or water supply," and that taxes be levied on children to discourage the poor from having them. Shockley urged "temporary sterilization by means of time-capsule contraceptives, of all young women and of every woman after each delivery," reversible only with government approval. Nobel-Prize winning geneticist Joshua Lederberg and Crick also proposed plans "simply to encourage by financial means those people who are more socially desirable to have children." They viewed women, Corea says, as "mother machines" to be manipulated and "run" by male experts in science and government.[76]

Even more frightening to the future of women, discoveries in 1969 and 1970 permitted scientists for the first time to count gynosperm (XX cells, those creating females) and androsperm (XY, those producing males) and to stain chromosomes to locate the Y chromosome. The research permitted doctors to identify androsperm quickly, simply, and cheaply, opening up the possibility of insuring birth of a male child.[77]

Other advances would prove mixed blessings for women. Many scientists experimented in the sixties with making various sorts of apparatuses to take the place of the uterus or placenta. Scientists at the Vanderbilt University Medical Center performed basic research on in vitro fertilization of laboratory animals—mice and hamsters; but the British team of reproductive physiologist Dr. Robert G. Edwards and obstetrician-gynecologist Dr. Patrick Steptoe made major breakthroughs that would permit birth of the world's first human test-tube baby late in the seventies. Advances were made with laboratory animals in techniques that would later result in the possibility of surrogate motherhood. In 1963, scientists transported fertilized sheep eggs via a rabbit and then successfully implanted the embryos into two ewes which then delivered healthy lambs. Corea reports that the experiment even led to "speculation on the possibility of using animals as incubators for human embryos."[78]

Over-the-Counter and Prescription Drug Use

The availability of drugs, both legal—as in the use of thalidomide—and illegal, and their use by women posed many problems. Millions of pregnant women had taken drugs, including meclizine and cyclizine, promoted to counteract pregnancy nausea, as well as chlorocyclizine for allergies, hay fever, insect bites, and colds. In May 1963 the FDA's Bureau of Medicine recommended these be taken off the market or labeled with a warning that they might not be safe during pregnancy. The Bureau had evidence of at least forty cases of meclizine-related birth defects. In 1965, the FDA recommended that manufacturers send a warning letter to physicians but withdrew the cautionary advice because of secret pressures. According to a critic, "the mental attitude was indistinguishable from that of the thalidomide case," giving the benefit of the doubt to manufacturers, not to the pregnant woman and her embryo. Since drugs were being prescribed primarily to women, and drugs affected the female reproductive system, the crux of the issue became gender rather than class, the rights of the female consumer contrasted to those of the physician or pharmaceutical company.[79]

Ladies' Home Journal reported in 1971 that the typical female drug user was the average middle-class woman next door. Carl Chambers and Dodi Schultz found that women used less marijuana, heroin, cocaine, LSD, and other illicit drugs than men but were "distinctly over-represented among those using tranquilizers, antidepressants, strong sedatives, dangerous diet pills, and powerful analgesics." More frequently than men, women used the "crutches" of barbiturates, major and minor tranquilizers, pep pills, noncontrolled narcotics (drugs not legally classified as narcotics because normal dosages are not potentially addictive), nonbarbiturate sedatives, antidepressants, controlled narcotics, and diet pills. In 1963, pharmacists filled about 95 million prescriptions for psychotherapeutic drugs for some 30 million Americans trying to cope with anxiety, depression, tension, and other psychic disturbances. Valium, developed in 1967, quickly became the most frequently prescribed drug in the United States. Advances in research on antipsychotic drugs led to the development of drugs such as lithium which reduced mental hospital populations from 550,000 in 1955 to 190,000 in 1977.[80]

Sometimes a doctor advised alcohol instead of referring a "bored, lonely or depressed" housewife to a counselor, thus dismissing her problem as trivial. A national study in 1968 confirmed that "women were more likely to have used psychotherapeutic drugs than men, Jews more likely than Catholics or Protestants, and whites more likely than blacks" with no significant differences in education, occupation, and income group. A 1968 California study found that women were "almost twice as likely to be frequent drug users than [sic] men, age was related to the type of psychotherapeutic drug used, persons separated or divorced were more likely to have reported frequent use than married or single persons, but that neither income nor education was related to use." Most of the 45 percent of the women using mood-altering drugs had had them prescribed by physicians, who were twice as likely to prescribe them for women as for men.[81]

Ruth Cooperstock reports that 78 percent of physicians interviewed "wrote more mood-modifying prescriptions for their female than for their male patients" because they saw women as biologically more vulnerable and more self-indulgent. Women, according to physicians and pharmaceutical companies, expressed different life stresses and were less reluctant than men to seek help. Such stereotypes dominated drug ads in physicians' journals. While young men dominated the illegal drug culture, and 21 percent were ranked as heavy drinkers versus five percent of women, more than 50 percent of mood-modifying prescriptions to women consisted of only eight drugs: "two minor tranquilizers (Librium and Valium), one major tranquilizer (Stelazine), and five sedative and hypnotic drugs (Phenobarbital, Sodium Amytal, Tuinal, Seconal Sodium, and Butisol Sodium). Mood-altering drugs were convenient for the doctor to prescribe. A few experts pointed to "an underlying sexual basis for this prejudice" since "illogical, persistent, and damaging beliefs constitute prejudice" and "all these [physiological] conditions affect women, whereas the majority of specialists and textbook authors are men." Despite the popular myth of the suburban housewife syndrome, Ruth Cooperstock reports that city rather than suburban residents received the larger share of the prescriptions for mood-modifiers.[82]

Despite lack of evidence, physicians readily believed that primary dysmenorrhea, nausea during pregnancy, and labor pains had psychogenic origins. They conventionally prescribed barbiturates and sedatives for early labor despite their "lack of analgesic effect" and proclivity to cause excitement or delirium, not sedation. The prime example of the medical belief in the inherent pathology of women was presented by Brooklyn gynecologist Dr. Robert A. Wilson, who in his best-selling book *Feminine Forever* (1966) claimed that "menopause is a curable, preventable deficiency disease," which merely requires an understanding physician and administration of estrogen. Wilson called menopause "a serious, painful, and often crippling disease" and the age of forty a dividing line that can break a woman's line in half. He claimed that "only fifteen percent of women are so fortunate as to avoid serious suffering during menopause and to retain most of their vitality." Wilson cloaked his misogyny in his male professional voice, his terms reminiscent of courtly love, and his concept of "waning womanhood": "A man always marries Helen of Troy or Aphrodite—an angelic, ethereal creature whose beauty was sung by poets of the past. And through the daily round of shopping for groceries, drying dishes, or tending babies, he stubbornly clings to the image of his wife as a mysterious, dreamlike incarnation of some superb fantasy. Men are incredibly loyal this way, providing they get a little cooperation from their wives in supporting this gallant fantasy . . . a truly feminine woman is the idol that inspires his own capacity to lift himself beyond his ordinary limits. Desire, to be sure, is part of this drive. But the femininity of a woman also evokes in man the capacity for adoration . . . [Romance] remains the common man's only path beyond his commonness, and the uncommon man's impetus toward whatever heights he may reach." Wilson expected, as did Dr. David Reuben, author of the popular *Everything You Always Wanted to Know About Sex*, that women were prone to emotional breakdown because their vaginas shriveled up to neuter them. He played on women's worst fears and sense of guilt in aging—themes echoed through popular culture; but he offered a "magic bullet" to counteract the inevitable, a pill equivalent to a fountain of youth.[83]

Urged on by drug companies' financial incentives, Wilson popularized estrogen replacement therapy (ERT) to begin years before menopause to prevent its symptoms—memory loss, hot flashes, nervousness, neurosis, headaches, indigestion, painful sex, backaches, and hot flashes, evidence of a peculiarly female "living decay." Wilson's promotional efforts succeeded beyond the wildest expectations of his sponsor Ayerst, producer of Premarin, a conjugated equine estrogen derived from horse urine. ERT became a sixties vogue among women approaching middle age. By 1975, when medical studies began to link the drug with cancers, only three other drugs were more widely prescribed than Premarin in the United States. Dr. William J. Sweeney, author of *Woman's Doctor*, claims that only a quarter to a third of women experience unpleasant menopausal symptoms and do need help, "but many doctors respond with overkill treatments. The enemy is old age and doctors attack it with estrogen, the 'youth pill'." Women readily acquiesced because menopausal myths directly touched on sexual and gender roles as well as the female ideal of youthfulness—an image contributing to stress between generations of grandmothers, mothers, and daughters.[84]

Many women obtained drugs from sources other than their physicians or used them in ways not prescribed. One in 25 regular users of antidepressants and major tranquilizers did not follow her doctor's orders, and one in ten regular users of minor tranquilizers (Librium, Miltown, and Valium) got the drug from other sources. Coeds (15 percent) and working women (30 percent) ranked highest in non-prescribed use of relaxants and barbiturates (Nembutal and Seconal). Housewives led in self-medication with diet pills, with one in four regular users taking them illegally, a third choosing their own dosages. The dimensions of the problem were reflected in popular culture in such forms as the Rolling Stones' song, "Mother's Little Helper."[85]

Physicians and pharmaceutical companies knew that women were a potential growth market for products that promised to make them feel or look better, younger, thinner, or more sexy. With the exception of the ban on thalidomide, the FDA was too willing to approve them without adequate testing. Such was the case of silicone for breast enlargement. Use of the semi-inorganic polymer produced by Dow Chemicals expanded from burn therapy to elective plastic surgery in the sixties. It was popularized by Carol Doda, a topless dancer who made news in 1964 by having her bust expanded from 36 to 44DD through a "novel operation" of 20 weekly injections costing $3000. By the sixties' end, silicone breast implants, internal "falsies," were being used increasingly for cosmetic "improvement."[86]

The sixties were thus a paradoxical decade for women in the area of health, as in so many other ways. Aided by new birth control technologies and the increasing availability of safe and legal abortion, women had greater opportunity to control their bodies and their futures. At the same time, increasingly sophisticated and manipulative marketing techniques identified and played to women's fears of physical unattractiveness and provided substances that controlled, rather than liberated their users.

13

Private Lives

As in most aspects of women's lives, traditional assumptions and practices regarding women's health and sexuality generally remained the social norm through the sixties, although some profound changes began. A 1966 poll showed that 35 percent of Americans still believed the ideal family had four or more children, just as they had in 1945 and 1957. Not until a 1971 poll did this percentage drop to 23. In 1969, 68 percent believed premarital sex was wrong; a figure that dropped to 48 percent in 1973. Even at the decade's end, according to the *New York Times*, the number of unmarried couples living together, and practicing "cohabitation," was only a "tiny minority" limited to "the dissident youth subculture—the intellectual, politically liberal to radical, from middle- and upper-middle-class backgrounds, anti-materialistic and anti-Establishment."[1]

Change escalated after 1965. Surveying Americans at the end of the sixties, one reporter concluded that they were "rejecting the rigid moral positions of the past, whether on abortion or extramarital affairs or 'aberrant' sexual behavior." Margaret Mead anticipated that trends toward "a new morality," unprecedented since the twenties, would "put a seal of approval on premarital sex." In *Future Shock* (1970), Alvin Toffler predicted that an accelerating pace of change would unsettle all aspects of life: "As conventional marriage proves itself less and less capable of delivering on its promise of lifelong love . . . we can anticipate public acceptance of temporary marriages." There was a striking and steady drop in the birthrate after 1964, after an era of dramatic fertility, as the age of marriage began to rise. New ideas and language about women's relation to their bodies and their right to control them entered public awareness, and transformed the way in which women would henceforth think of themselves.[2]

Sexuality

In the sixties, sex and sexuality became a public subject. As historians John D'Emilio and Estelle Freedman argue "the dominant meaning of sexuality" in America continued to change "from a primary association with reproduction within families to a primary association with emotional intimacy and physical pleasure for individuals." The advent of new birth control methods, the separation of sex from procreation, the existence of a uniquely large cohort of young people together in colleges and universities, the questioning of all traditional authority and institutions in the wake of powerful social movements—these and other causes led to a renewed openness in discussion of sex. Some proclaimed a "sexual revolution," but it was unclear that it benefitted women as much as men. Women heard that the only way to prove that they were truly "liberated" was to "put out," to be sexually available. Older women heard husbands announce the end of long marriages because of their newly discovered "love" for someone else, more desirable and younger. Those who chose homosexuality were still left out.[3]

A major sixties event was the debunking of the primacy of the vaginal orgasm. Freudianism perpetuated the myth that the vagina rather than the clitoris was the prime organ of female erotic sensation. Women were told that vaginal not clitoral orgasm was the ultimate goal of sexuality. Conservative writer Midge Decter summarized that view in *The New Chastity*, dismissing the clitoral orgasm as "unfunctional, gratuitous, [and] masturbatory," since it "required no penis and led to no possibility of conception." She stereotyped women who preferred or knew only clitoral orgasm as immature, masculine, and neurotic. Those who achieved vaginal orgasm were thought mature, feminine, maternal—in a word, normal. Many "experts" defined frigidity as inability to experience vaginal orgasm. These notions persisted and even permeated popular culture, although only a quarter of adult women ordinarily had vaginal orgasm.[4]

In *Human Sexual Response* (1966), Dr. William Howell Masters and Virginia E. Johnson, sexologists from Washington University in St. Louis, proved this belief wrong. Although the book described in detailed, dry, clinical terms the physiological changes in the male and female bodies during sex, it sold 250,000 copies in four years and sparked many summary articles and fictionalized books. From studies in the private clinic and Reproductive Biology Foundation they established in 1964, Masters and Johnson concluded that there was no basic difference between clitoral and vaginal orgasms nor between the personalities of those who had one or the other. They showed that, anatomically, female orgasm originates in stimulating the clitoris or other erogenous zones, and that the vagina has few nerves. While many women, particularly feminists, welcomed this news, many moralists and others criticized their clinical approach as dehumanizing sexuality, condemned their use of "partner surrogates" as akin to prostitution, and called their work amoral, at best.[5]

The media spread Masters's and Johnson's messages: America's 45 million married couples were sexually incompatible to some degree. "The great cause of divorce" was "human sexual inadequacy," they argued in a 1970 book by that name. They redefined frigidity as mere "orgasmic dysfunction" because "women are victims of the double standard" grounded in patriarchy. A *Time* cover article in May 1970 summarized the impact of Masters's and Johnson's views: "Whatever the 'sexual revolution' may mean, it certainly has freed modern women of the Victorian notion that females do not enjoy sex: the modern woman knows what she is missing erotically speaking," while "the American male has succumbed to the widely advertised notion that he should be the super-performer in what has been called the decade of orgasmic preoccupation—a preoccupation that could be enhanced by Masters's and Johnson's emphasis on sex as a form of salvation." The therapists recommended the "female superior" position in coitus to "offer the woman a better chance of achieving orgasm" and to relieve male inadequacies, "since it allows the woman partner more freedom of movement and, hence, more control." One historian concludes that Masters and Johnson did "more to advance the cause of women's sexual rights than anything else" in the previous quarter century and reflected an "explicit feminism" in "their opposition to any concept or practice that would portray the sexuality of women as a pale replica of that of men" and in their argument that "the woman's right to orgasm is just as absolute as the men's."[6]

Less known but equally important was the work of Dr. Sophia Josephine Kleegman (1901–1971), an obstetrician-gynecologist. Her pioneering book, *Infertility in Women* (1966), stressed that the usual practice of blaming a couple's infertility on the woman was wrong. She also extended the diagnostic value of the Papanicolau (Pap) smear test for cervical cancer by adding the endometrial aspiration test and through development of instrumentation techniques. As director of the New York University-Bellevue Medical Center Infertility Clinic from 1958 until her death, Kleegman turned her attention to women's sexual dysfunctions and urged serious, non-sexist consideration of their physical and psychological causes—repressive upbringing, fear of pregnancy, stress, and other emotional factors. She encouraged development of sex education and marriage counseling and the education of physicians in sexuality. After twelve years of crusading as president of the American Association of Marriage Counselors, beginning in 1960, she convinced the NYU Medical Center to include one lecture on the subject of the pre-marital interview in its curriculum.[7]

Also important in both professional and lay education in sexuality was Lena Levine (1903–1965), a gynecologist and psychiatrist who wrote many books and pamphlets on women's medical and psychological problems. Long involved with the birth control movement, she lectured widely on sexuality, sex education, and planned parenthood. Her purpose was to counter repressive Victorian and misogynist myths, especially those surrounding menstruation, virginity, menopause, and female sexual arousal. Levine published *The Frigid Wife: Her Way to Sexual Fulfillment* (1962) and *The Emotional Sex: Why Women Are the Way They Are Today* (1964).[8]

"Paradoxically, the first major challenge to the marriage-oriented ethic of sexual liberalism came neither from political nor cultural radicals but rather from entrepreneurs who extended the logic of consumer capitalism to the realm of sex." Medical analyses occupied less public attention than advertisements exploiting the "sexual revolution" in the popular media. Hugh Hefner's *Playboy*, founded in 1953, continued with its female nude centerfold to win a circulation of over one million by 1962, rising to six million in the seventies. He declared his crusade against "our ferocious antisexuality, our dark antieroticism in America" and called his nude photos "a symbol of disobedience . . . an end of Puritanism." The "Playmate of the Month" rivaled the relatively purer Miss America in promoting good causes as well as themselves and Hefner's growing corporation. Hefner portrayed Playmates as girls-next-door: "Actually, potential Playmates are all around you," he told *Look* in 1967. Hefner also opened Playboy clubs, staffed by "bunnies," scantily dressed young women expected to follow a very rigid code of sexy behavior. One of them, for a time, was Gloria Steinem, later a major spokesperson for the new women's movement, who infiltrated the Chicago Club to write a magazine story about bunnies' lives.[9]

Knowing that surveys showed a large female readership of *Playboy*, Helen Gurley Brown promoted hedonism and libertinism for young women in her best-selling *Sex and the Single Girl* (1962). The happily married Brown offered advice to striving career women on "Squirming, Worming, Inching, and Pinching Your Way to the Top." Brown urged "girls" to "play the field," to "reconsider the idea that sex without marriage is dirty." Contesting the age-old idea that only men were sexually aggressive with active libidos, she called on readers to admit that they too had a "proclivity for it." She argued that sex could be a "powerful weapon" as well as fun for the ambitious woman. Long before the women's movement expressed doubts about marriage, Brown told young women that marriage was only "insurance for the worst years of your life." For their best years, they did "not need a husband." Capitalizing on the first book's success, Brown offered *Sex and the Office* (1964) with practical advice on office decoration as well as tips on using sexuality for job advancement.[10]

Brown delivered a revolutionary message in urging single girls to overcome inhibitions, to disregard mothers' advice and the traditional female ambition to marry well and soon, to discard virginity as a useless trump card not to be held back to win the marriage game; but she preached to the converted or the ready-to-be, to the "new woman" described by Joan Didion in "The Great Reprieve" in *Mademoiselle* in 1961: "Girls who come to New York are above all uncommitted. They seem to . . . want to prolong the period when they can experiment, mess around, make mistakes. In New York there is no gentle pressure to marry. . . . no need, as one girl put it, 'to parry silly questions about what everyone at home refers to delicately as my plans.' New York is full . . . of people with a feeling for the tangential adventure . . . the interlude that's not likely to end in a double-ring ceremony."[11]

Brown created a regular forum for her libertine sexual philosophy by transforming the dying *Cosmopolitan* after 1965 into a female equal of *Playboy*, albeit without centerfold or male nudity. Like *Playboy*, "Cosmo" featured fine writers like Nora Ephron, Jeannie Sakol, Jill Robinson, and Gael Greene. While it continued to publish articles on fashion, hygiene, interior design, and food like other women's magazines, its tone and purpose changed radically from a focus on pleasing husbands or prospective males to an emphasis on pleasing men in general and hence oneself as a sexual woman. Media analyst Kathryn Weibel finds that "Like the housewifely reader of *McCall's* . . . the Cosmo reader is also a great entertainer and clever at interior decorating. . . . also just as passive in her relationships to men." Brown's new editorial policy doubled advertising revenue in three years and attracted a large readership. By the decade's end, circulation approached two million.[12]

Another sixties sensation capitalized on the new-found freedom for women to talk about sex. Joan Terry Garrity, writing as "J," proclaimed oral sex "delicious" in her manual *The Sensuous Woman* (1969), which quickly sold nine million copies. Although revolutionary in its frankness and use of slang, "J's" approach to sex was phallocentric, not feminist. She urged women to fake orgasms, believing that they were essentially non-orgasmic. Garrity's main worry in publishing her book was what her mother would say on discovering her identity; she did not consider that much of what she suggested remained illegal in many states. This book joined a growing list of bestsellers capitalizing on sex, particularly after the 1969 Supreme Court decision legalizing private consumption of materials previously defined as pornographic.[13]

A younger, college-age cohort found its "sex manifesto of the free love generation" in Robert Rimmer's 1966 novel, *The Harrad Experiment*, which had over 20 paperback printings in a year. Rimmer postulated a collegiate "program designed to achieve sexual sanity" by "teaching a new sexual ethic and moral code." He imagined a collegiate utopia of 400 handpicked and computer-matched young men and women who "live, learn, and love together in a unique atmosphere of sexual freedom—Harrad College." The novel warned of the dangers in American society it intended to counteract: "Social pressure for prolonged continence often creates fear, anxiety, and actual repulsion between the sexes. The results: too early marriage ending in divorce, unwanted children born out of wedlock, sexual frustration before and continuing into marriage, and a sex-obsessed society with little or no knowledge of what dynamic love is. A society that deeply frustrates human interrelationships creates fear, hate, anxiety, and a feeling of loss of identity which are the keynotes of modern life." To bolster his utopian social arguments, Rimmer ended his book with a five page bibliography of sociological and psychological works, but also cites Hefner.[14]

Rimmer's major audience was made up of the college-age, baby-boomers he fictionalized. Reflecting on the upheavals of recent years,

Time warned: "First it was free speech, then filthy speech. Now it is free love, as students, former students and non-students continue to test the limits of the permissible. . . . Student committees promoting sexual freedom have been organized at Stanford, the University of Texas, and U.C.L.A." The Syracuse University *Daily Orange* commented: "In this fictional world real and dramatic things are happening . . . ground is being broken for a new society of men and women." At the University of Michigan, boyfriends recommended the book to their dates to bolster private debates on expanding sexual liberties.[15]

Universities, with unprecedentedly large numbers of youth crowded together, were almost inevitable testing grounds for the new mores of the "sexual revolution." Sophisticated undergraduates scorned the naive innocence of traditional "panty raids," crowds of male students chanting beneath windows of locked women's dorms in hopes that coeds would throw down some underwear. Rather, college women crusaded to end paternalistic, in loco parentis rules that they sign in and out of dormitories, observe restrictive hours, and not have privacy with the opposite sex in their rooms. At the University of Michigan, South Quad dorm residents demonstrated in 1965 against parietal rules. Other students targeted university health services for refusing to prescribe birth control pills to unmarried students. Many women students moved in with their boyfriends, despite institutional bans, risking expulsion. By the sixties' end, many progressive institutions converted some residence halls into "coed" dorms, although men and women often remained segregated on separate floors or building wings.

In SDS cell meetings, remembers a former female Harvard student, women "pondered the best way to lose our virginity. 'Should you do it with someone you love or just friends?' There was a lot of emphasis on not associating sex with love in order not to get these two things confused." She saw the changing mores as temporarily positive: "Our sexual freedom meant something until coldness and manipulation got transmuted into it," until it was transformed to the casual "your place or mine" of strangers meeting in seventies singles bars or new singles apartment complexes.[16]

Hippies went nude at Be-Ins and at Woodstock for free and to be free. *Newsweek* proclaimed in 1967: "For the hippies, sex is not a matter of great debate. . . . The sexual revolution is accomplished. There are no hippies who believe in chastity or look askance at marital infidelity, or see even marriage itself as a virtue. Physical love is a delight—to be chewed upon as often and as freely as a handful of sesame seeds."

Flower children wore buttons: "Make Love Not War," "I'm Willing If You Are," and "Take It Off." Free love or sexual permissiveness was institutionalized in some communes.[17]

Other retreats like the 15-acre "Sandstone," a "destination resort" created by engineer John Williamson in the Santa Monica mountains, provided sexual holidays for upper-middle-class tourists for a price. There, they experimented with "swinging," swapping spouses, and casual group sex. For quicker titillation, many went to new bars with topless and scantily clad "go-go" dancers that spread across the nation following the success of the first—San Francisco's Condor Club—in 1964. Such promotion of sexuality resulted in the seventies in a series of self-help books like Alex Comfort's *The Joy of Sex: A Gourmet Guide to Love Making* (1972). Advertisers knew that singles had enormous discretionary buying power, making up a $60 billion annual market by mid-decade that could be enticed by the "sexual sell" if not sexual products. Young, prosperous singles "embodied the unspoken fantasies of a consumer society extended to the sphere of sex." So ran the "erotic revolution."[18]

Many feminists decried the outmoded sexuality of the double standard "defined by men to benefit men," pointing out that the new sexual trends often served to place women in more demanding, less individually controlled sexual situations. In a 1968 speech at Cornell, Kate Millett declared that "sexual freedom has been partially attained," but "is now being subverted beyond freedom into exploitative license for patriarchal and reactionary ends." The "truly liberated" woman was expected to be free with her body. Yet feminists rejected the persistent division of women into "good girls" and "bad girls" based on sexuality. Shulamith Firestone and Anne Koedt of New York Radical Women (NYRW) urged women "to dare to be bad" in that group's *Notes from the Second Year* (1970). Ellen Willis recalls that "radical feminists attacked both traditional morality and the sexism that had distorted a so-called sexual revolution envisioning women's sexual freedom mainly as women's right-cum-obligation to have sex on men's often exploitative terms. Most of us wanted the sexual revolution extended to women: we demanded an end to the double standard of morality that still lingered despite men's lip service to women's emancipation; equal consideration for women's sexual pleasure and emotional needs; the right to actively pursue sexual relationships as men have always done—and without forfeiting our right to refuse sex; the social acceptance of lesbianism; and, of course, reproductive freedom."[19]

Firestone went even further, calling pregnancy "barbaric" in her revolutionary tract, *The Dialectic of Sex* (1970). In a brave new world approach, she argues for separation of sex from procreation and, like others, speaks out against motherhood as enslaving for women. Her genuine feminist revolution would ensure a return to "natural polymorphous sexuality" with "all forms of sexuality . . . allowed and indulged."[20]

Anne Koedt was the most influential in articulating the radical realization of sexuality as a feminist issue. Based on research by Masters and Johnson, Koedt wrote "The Myth of the Vaginal Orgasm" for NYRW's *Notes for the First Year* (1969), an article widely reprinted and quoted. She explained that women had been "defined sexually in terms of what pleases men." Koedt questioned defining women as "frigid" because they did not achieve orgasm only by vaginal penetration and pointed out that women often felt forced to fake orgasms and remain unsatisfied. "Recognition of clitoral orgasm would threaten the heterosexual institution," Koedt observed, "for it would indicate that sexual pleasure was obtainable from either men or women, thus making heterosexuality not an absolute but an option." Koedt's explanation opened up "the whole question of human sexual relationships beyond the confines of the present male-female role system."[21]

Despite the persistence of strong moralistic, anti-sexual taboos in American culture, historians D'Emilio and Freedman conclude that late-sixties America had become a "sexualized society," permeated by the "belief in sex as the source of personal meaning" but also frequently by a male search for sex as gratification. The President's Commission on Obscenity and Pornography found in 1970 that the sexual content of mass media was growing "progressively stronger" after a series of court decisions from 1957 to 1967 that redefined obscenity and ended a century of Comstockery. Hollywood largely abandoned its self-censoring Production Code, in place since 1930. FBI statistics showed a 61 percent increase in arrests of prostitutes (not of their partners) between 1960 and 1969 with a 120 percent increase for juveniles (under age 18), the increase correlated with the growth of the drug culture. Incidence of venereal disease (syphilis and gonorrhea) doubled from 1965 to 1970, rising elevenfold among teen-agers. Responses to more visible prostitution ranged from a 1969 reprint of traditionalist William Acton's description of the prostitute as "a social pest, carrying contamination and foulness" to feminist Ti-Grace Atkinson's assertion that she was "the only honest woman left in America." New ideas about prostitution led to calls for legalization and formation of the first "unions" in the seventies.[22]

By the sixties' end, write D'Emilio and Freedman, "the expectation that marriage would fulfill the quest [for sexual fulfillment] could no longer be sustained. Aided by the values of a consumer culture and encouraged by the growing visibility of sex in the public realm, many Americans came to accept sexual pleasure as a legitimate, necessary component of their lives, unbound by older ideals of marital fidelity and permanence." Still, despite the airing of new ideas, the status quo persisted for most women in and beyond the decade. Powerful moral conservatives, backed by the John Birch Society, targeted even moderate sex educators like the veteran Mary Steichen Calderone, whose Sex Information and Education Council of the United States (SIECUS) aimed to expand the basic school curriculum. SIECUS estimated that there were over 300 organizations mobilizing to block sex education by the decade's end.[23]

Lesbians

Society's growing sexuality was not just heterosexual. Gay liberationists made progress based on "the persistent, plodding work of the activists" in the fifties, sustained by and continuing the spirit of the civil rights movement. As the civil rights struggle had provided impetus and analysis to the women's movement, the women's movement enabled some lesbians to champion lesbian-feminist issues by the sixties' end. The women's movement "offered the psychic space for many women to come to a self-definition as a lesbian"; and young homosexuals, male and female, had new alternatives to internalizing the self-hatred fostered by medicine, law, and society. Not only did homosexual women and men become visible in proclaiming that gay is good, but lesbian feminists even became women's movement leaders, although many "egalitarian" feminists still rejected them.[24]

Lesbianism had been taboo, and Freud's hypothesis that homosexuality was the result of "childhood trauma and arrested development" was still accepted well into the sixties. Dr. Frank S. Caprio, the fifties "expert" on lesbians, called them neurotic, unable to make a heterosexual adjustment, and willing to use congenital excuses for homoeroticism to evade responsibilities of being wives and mothers. Cold Wariors labeled homosexuals "a threat to national security." The FBI initiated a surveillance system to keep them off the federal payroll while the military "stepped up its purges of homosexual men and women." Historians conclude that "for lesbians especially, who faced the constricted employment opportunities that all women confronted, the workplace discrimination of Cold War America imposed serious hardship."[25]

Countering such hostility, homosexual women and men formed support organizations. The male Mattachine Society dates from 1950. In September 1955, Del Martin and Phyllis Lyon, with three other lesbian couples, formed the Daughters of Bilitis (DOB), the first lesbian organization and an alternative to the homosexual bar scene, providing a safe place for women to meet and dance. There were broader concerns as well: DOB aimed "to teach the Lesbian a mode of behavior and dress acceptable to society"; too many lesbian activities were restricted because "they wouldn't wear skirts."[26]

DOB's first annual convention met in San Francisco in 1960, but the group did not receive media attention until 1966. Rita Laporte was elected national president in 1968. From 1956 to 1972, DOB published a journal, the *Ladder*, to reach the lonely, isolated lesbian who lived away from big cities, to educate the "variant" (a term that gave way to "lesbian" around 1967), to increase public knowledge about homosexuality, and to find ways to bring about justice for this minority group. Barbara Grier, editor from 1968 to 1972, more ambitiously determined to turn the journal "into, at least the *Atlantic Monthly* of Lesbian thought."[27]

In 1967, DOB published a survey by Gene Damon and Lee Stuart on *The Lesbian in Literature*, finding that most books about lesbians were "trash," chiefly written by men to titillate male readers. *The Fox* (1968) and *X, Y, and Zee* (1972), like so many novels, depicted lesbians negatively to appeal to a male point of view. A rare exception was May Sarton's *The Small Room* (1961). In films *The Killing of Sister George* (1969) depicted a lesbian relationship more frankly than any other films of the sixties about homosexuality, such as *The Children's Hour, Advise and Consent*, and *Walk on the Wild Side*. These more positive works, write D'Emilio and Freedman, "served as mapping expeditions that made exploration and discovery easier for countless numbers of gay men and lesbians."[28]

In 1967, changes in the *Ladder* reflected the editors' and DOB's awareness that "lesbians were women," not "members of the third sex" to be grouped with male gays. Editors Barbara Giddings, Helen Sanders, and Gene Damon added a new goal for the journal: "to provide the lesbian a forum for the interchange of ideas within her own group," and "to raise all women to full human status, with all of the rights and responsibilities this entails; to include ALL women, whether Lesbian or heterosexual." The fall 1970 issue carried a new editorial statement asserting a more feminist stance while maintaining "a firm distinction between lesbians and heterosexual women," a sentiment "with roots in lesbian-feminist consciousness, whose expression the growing women's movement encouraged"; but the journal folded because younger lesbians associated it with "the politics of adjustment," a conservatism of an older, less militant, middle-class generation. One historian summarizes, "Initially the *Ladder's* goal was limited to achieving the rights accorded to heterosexual women, that is, full second-class citizenship. In the fifties, women as a whole were as yet unaware of their oppression. The Lesbian knew. And she wondered silently when her sisters would realize that they too share many of the Lesbian's handicaps, those that pertained to being a woman."[29]

Barbara Giddings of Philadelphia began to work quietly in the mid-sixties with lesbian and gay male activists in the "homophile movement," seeking to enlarge definitions of equality in public policy to include sexual preference, enlisting aid from the American Civil Liberties Union and lobbying the medical profession to remove homosexuality from the category of mental disorders, and bolstering their argument with evidence drawn from Kinsey and Masters and Johnson. Kinsey declared in his discussion of lesbianism and masturbation that a male was not necessary for female sexual fulfillment. Masters and Johnson added data about female orgasms and the importance of the clitoris. Gays continued to draw some support from the DOB but went far beyond the few who had previously dared to "come out." Still, their movement remained small.[30]

A breakthrough for lesbians in organized religion occurred in 1964 when a Methodist minister discovered how alienated young homosexuals were by and from his church. Five DOB members participated in a three-day "Live-In" and established the Council on Religion and the Homosexual (CRH). Problems at a New Year's Ball to benefit the new CRH and mark the start of 1965 precipitated a press conference by seven clergymen expressing "anger and dismay at the way the police had 'broken faith' with the Council and for the 'deliberate harassment' and intimidation" of guests. About 500 homosexuals had crossed a picket line of fifty police officers (and one policewoman) to be greeted by waiting CRH clergymen in the hall. All were shocked by the police use of intimidating tactics, for no apparent reason except harassment, motivated by anti-homosexual laws. As a result, Councils on Religion and the Homosexual sprang up elsewhere. After that event, the Young Democrats of California and Wisconsin passed resolutions advocating revision of laws that criminalized homosexual behavior.[31]

The sexual revolution among "straights" also eased the way for lesbians. During the 1967 Summer of Love, "flower children" or "hippies" made bisexuality public since many "grooved on" each person as a person, regardless of race, gender, or other characteristics—and "grooving" could lead them to sex.[32]

A feminist theory emerging after 1968 declared that "the personal is political," and demonstrated that the dilemmas women encountered came from a socially constructed and enforced gender role system consigning them to socially inferior positions. Some looked back to Alfred Adler, Freud's contemporary, who called lesbianism "a means of protest over being accorded an inferior position in society"; others cited de Beauvoir's sympathy for those women unwilling to undertake the difficult task of "reconciliation between the active personality and the [passive] sexual role." By broadening lesbianism to mean women-oriented women, not defined simply by an erotic orientation but by reinforcing the personal as political, more women-loving women dared to "come out," to find support in communities of women, and to seek political power. Colette Reid, a Washington, D.C., feminist, remembers the changes she realized by the late sixties: "Almost everything I was reading . . . led me toward lesbianism." Reid concludes, "If 'The Myth of the Vaginal Orgasm' was true, then intercourse was not necessary or even relevant to my sexual satisfaction. If [Millett's] *Sexual Politics* was right that male sexuality was an expression of power and dominance, then I was choosing my own oppression to stay in a relationship with a man. If sex roles were an invention of society, then women—not just men—were possible people to love, in the fullest sense of that word. If I could hug and kiss a woman I loved, why couldn't I touch all of her body? Since my husband really thought men were superior, then wasn't my needing to be in a relationship with someone superior to me, self-hating and woman-hating? The conclusion seemed inescapable."[33]

Many lesbians, like Reid, were influenced as much by feminism as by lesbian sexuality. Taking their struggle public shaped the course of the women's movement through the activism of Ti-Grace Atkinson, Rita Mae Brown, Millett, and others, despite resistance by Betty Friedan and moderate feminists. But most lesbians continued to live quiet lives, whether "in the closet" or "out," not making the personal political even if they did not hide their sexual preference. Many remained silent because anti-homosexual laws remained on the books in most cities and states; and police used them to harass gays and lesbians. A major catalyst for the Gay Liberation Movement occurred on Friday, 27 June 1969. New York police started what to them seemed a routine raid on a gay bar, Greenwich Village's Stonewall Inn. Male and female patrons' resistance turned to riot and the torching of the club. Homosexuals immediately organized the Gay Liberation Front (GLF), styled after New Left organizations, declaring: "We are a revolutionary homosexual group of men and women formed with the realization that complete sexual liberation for all people cannot come about unless existing social institutions are abolished. We reject society's attempt to impose sexual roles and definitions of our nature." Martha Shelley of GLF declared, "We are women and men who, from the time of our earliest memories, have been in revolt against the sex-role structure and nuclear family structure." "Gay Power" graffiti spread across the city, then the nation.[34]

Shirley Willer, national DOB president attending the North American Conference of Homophile Organizations (NACHO), had announced in 1966, "the Lesbian has agreed (with reservations) to join in common cause with the male homosexual, but her role in the homophile movement to date has largely been one of mediator between the male homosexual and society." Her challenge went unanswered until the 1970 NACHO Conference in San Francisco, when on 26 August, Women's National Strike Day, seven lesbians from DOB, NOVA, and Gay Women's Liberation again disrupted the meeting to spotlight the homophile movement's irrelevance to women's needs. Although DOB leaders knew that lesbians were not any more welcome in the women's movement than in the homophile movement, they redirected their attention toward feminist groups because lesbians as life-long breadwinners were particularly concerned with "equal pay for equal work," with being taxed at the highest rates as singles, and with the need for child care since many were working mothers. The coalition helped bring about the December 1973 American Psychiatric Association ruling that homosexuality should no longer be considered a "mental disorder," and the resolution that homosexuals should be accorded full civil rights.[35]

Psychology and Mental Health

Widespread use by doctors of drug therapy for women reflected a belief that most women's problems were psychological in origin. Women were subjected to definitions of psychological dysfunction rooted in sociocultural expectations that were often at odds with the real complexity of their lives. Marynia Farnham and Ferdinand Lundberg in *Modern Woman: The Lost Sex* (1947) gave scientific credence to the popular belief that woman's ambition to be more than a wife and mother was "the desire for the impossible, a desire to be a man" and thus pathological.[36]

Betty Friedan's *The Feminine Mystique* (1963) challenged this premise. After studying Gestalt psychology at Smith, Friedan began graduate work in psychology at Berkeley in 1942 but gave up school for marriage. As an occasional journalist through the fifties, she contributed antifeminist propaganda to the "mystique" with articles in *McCall's*, *Mademoiselle*, and the old *Cosmopolitan* bearing titles like "I Was Afraid to Have a Baby." She knew from dual perspectives how women could be manipulated psychologically to remain passive consumers. Her book began with her personal uneasiness, "I sensed it first as a question mark in my own life, as a wife and mother of three small children, half-guiltily and therefore half-heartedly, almost in spite of myself, using my abilities and education in work that took me away from home." Friedan, compensating for her own deteriorating marriage of fifteen years, began her research in 1957 by interviewing members of her 1942 Smith class. The task was more complex than she or her publisher anticipated. What should have been a book for the fifties appeared four years late.[37]

All but six of the 189 women who returned Friedan's questionnaire had been married and 179 still were. Only 11 were childless. They averaged 2.9 children, and 52 had four children or more. Most were full-time mothers and homemakers. Only 12 held full-time jobs; and only one pursued a profession. Still, Friedan perceived "a strange discrepancy between the reality of our lives as women and the image to which we were trying to conform." Friedan dubbed the women's problem a new neurosis, that hitherto "had no name," a malaise affecting educated middle-class women, frustrated and bored, kept in suburban homes in a false round of busyness, and denied the place in the world for which their education had prepared them.[38]

As Friedan finished each chapter, she wondered if she were crazy for analyzing the "schizophrenic split" between the reality of women's lives and the attempt to conform to an ideal image. Unlike Farnham and Lundberg, Friedan considered this split or "identity crisis" a problem of acculturation shaped by Freudianism, not by personal pathologies. She attacked Freud's "sexual solipsism," an idea "hardened into apparent fact, that has trapped so many American women today." Friedan dismissed simplistic answers that the problem that has no name was merely a "matter of loss of femininity or too much education, or the demands of domesticity."[39]

The "problem that has no name" had "burst like a boil through the image of the happy American housewife" by 1960, Friedan noted; and "by 1962 the plight of the trapped American housewife had become a national parlor game." She dismissed the popular response that the problem was merely one of a "loss of femininity or too much education or the demands of domesticity." She argued for women's self-realization, outside family and home, urging women to become active, to formulate a "new life plan" involving "creative work" and "professional achievement" as well as marriage and motherhood. Friedan proposed individual not social solutions; she was not urging the creation of a new women's movement. Nor was she the first to call attention to suburban housewives' frustrations—*Redbook* had run an article in 1960 on the subject and had received 10,000 responses. But Friedan's book struck a chord; it was an immediate best seller of over 300,000 copies in its first year. Hundreds of women wrote to Friedan to affirm her message and exclaim in relief, "I thought I was the only one who felt that way."[40]

The future of the nation depended on throwing light on the feminine stereotypes, Friedan argued. American women who adjust to being just a housewife are in as much danger "as the millions who walked to their own death in the concentration camps." They "have learned to 'adjust' to their biological role. They have become dependent, passive, childlike; they have given up their adult frame of reference to live at the lower human level of food and things. The work they do does not require adult capabilities; it is endless, monotonous, unrewarding. American women are not, of course, being readied for mass extermination, but they are suffering a slow death of mind and spirit."[41]

Mental health professionals held to a different standard. In a significant and often-cited 1969 study of concepts of "healthy" or "mature" gender roles held by 79 clinical social workers, psychologists, and psychiatrists, Inge Broverman found clear consensus. Professionals agreed that "normal" women were submissive, dependent, emotional, illogical, indecisive, sneaky, easily offended, and lacking self-confidence, while "normal" men were aggressive, independent, unemotional, logical, objective, not easily influenced, and self-confident. American culture valued stereotypically masculine traits, such as independence and self-confidence, more highly than stereotypically feminine traits—gentleness and sensitivity. For a woman to be healthy, she had to "adjust to and accept the behavioral norms for her sex, even though these behaviors are generally less socially desirable and considered to be less healthy for the generalized competent, mature adult." Broverman noted the message that clinicians gave their patients: "Adjust yourself to the stereotypes; only thus can you be normal and healthy."[42]

The Freudian notion that "anatomy is destiny" thus persisted; and Friedan had little influence on most self-proclaimed objective, professional social scientists who continued to cling to and proclaim biological bases of gender differences. As late as 1969 in *Men in Groups*, the Canadian anthropologist Lionel Tiger stressed evolutionary biology as determining behavioral differences such as male aggressiveness, bonding in groups, occupational preference, and leadership ability, concluding it would be hazardous "with numerous latent consequences should women ever enter politics in great numbers" and even dangerous "at times of war and national crisis. . . . for women to have high political office." Men, explained the diminutive media star, were "stronger and tougher, both physically and in terms of social action." He warned that "even a but partly female-dominated policy may go beyond the parameters of 'healthy' possibility, given the basic conservatism of the species."[43]

Freudianism influenced even Erik Erikson who rephrased the psychology of women in more positive terms, speaking of "productive inner-bodily space" and the resulting "biological psychological, and ethical commitment to take care of human infancy." Erikson updated the Victorian notion of "separate spheres" through the testing with blocks of 300 children, divided equally for gender, finding that girls constructed interior rooms while boys recreated the "public" spaces of building exteriors. Ignoring the cultural factors at work in the experiment in his quest to validate and renew traditional assumptions, Erikson concluded that "real" women's "natural dispositions" were essentially maternal and noncompetitive.[44]

Even Judith Bardwick's text, *Psychology of Women* (1971), intended to be definitive, accepted the "anatomy is destiny" idea, emphasizing anatomical, hormonal, and chromosomal differences as primary determining factors in shaping women's character. Although Bardwick considers socialization as secondary, she notes that after puberty conditioning discourages female competition except in interpersonal relationships. Thereafter, "dependency, affiliation, passivity and conformity versus independence, achievement, activity and aggression are the important variables. The origin of the differences lies in early constitutional proclivities which the culture enhances by reward and punishment along sex-specific lines."[45]

In "The Politics of Sickness," feminists Barbara Ehrenreich and Deirdre English point out that the task of controlling women shifted from gynecology to psychiatry. Many psychologists clung to Freudian ideas about women's "penis envy," satisfied only by bearing a baby—preferably male. As many observers noted, rebellion against the female role—that is, the multiple roles of wife, mother, and housewife—was often defined as mental illness. A desire not to have children, choosing an abortion, post-partum depression, promiscuity, and frigidity could all be signs of mental illness because interpreted as rebellion against female roles. Mild post-partum depression received little clinical attention because it was "so common as to be unworthy of mention." To want an abortion was unnatural; to commit suicide for not being able to obtain one was doubly so. Professionals generally believed that abortions caused great mental anguish, yet in 1970 the Johns Hopkins Hospital Center for Social Studies in Human Reproduction conducted research showing that abortions are no more traumatic than births, a finding verified by Nancy Howell Lee. Doctors also assumed that menopausal women were subject to grave emotional disturbances, but such an assumption merely provided another rationale "for excluding women from desirable jobs."[46]

Even issues concerning women's reproductive system received psychoanalytical explanations. Gynecologist Thomas H. Green asserted in *Gynecology: Essentials of Clinical Practice* that painful menstruation was sometimes caused by "rejection and misunderstanding of the feminine role," curable with marriage and childbearing. Dysmenorrhea was cured not by physiological change, but by the maturity a woman displayed in establishing a "normal" relationship with a man.[47]

Dr. Frank S. Caprio's *The Sexually Adequate Female* (1953) perpetuated the Freudian theory that clitoral orgasm was pathological in the adult: "Whenever a woman is incapable of achieving an orgasm via coitus, provided the husband is an adequate partner, and prefers clitoral stimulation to any other form of sexual activity, she can be regarded as suffering from frigidity and requires psychiatric assistance." This notion prevailed until Masters and Johnson clinically disproved the vaginal orgasm in *Human Sexual Response* (1966), articulating some of the most "revolutionary" ideas of the decade and permitting women—heterosexual and lesbian—to claim their own sexuality. Their research gave physiological proof to the skepticism about Freud's libido theory expressed by the German psychoanalyst, Dr. Karen Horney, who founded the New York Psychoanalytic Institute in 1941 and published *Feminine Psychology* (1967). Here was one of the major breakthroughs for women in the sixties. Inspired by Anne Koedt's "The Myth of the Vaginal Orgasm" (1968), feminists used such new scientific data to attack sexism by psychologists, physicians, and society in general and to demand sexual satisfaction formerly denied them by the "experts." Feminists rejected the old lore that masturbation could cause insanity.[48]

Change came more gradually for mentally ill women. Responding to recurring stereotypes of women as psychologically dysfunctional, Phyllis Chesler noted in her study, *Women and Madness* (1972), that there were "very few genuinely (or purely) mad women in our culture," even though female and male psychiatric symptoms differed. Women displayed "depression, frigidity, paranoia, psychoneurosis, suicide attempts, and anxiety" whereas men displayed "alcoholism, drug addiction, personality disorders, and brain diseases," Chesler wrote. "Typically female symptoms all share a 'dread of happiness'—a phrase coined by Thomas Szasz to describe the 'indirect forms of communication' that characterize 'slave psychology'." She decried a 1963 report by a male clinician who bragged how he "managed" a group of "paranoid" women back to "feminine" health—all too typical of medical professionals in the sixties.[49]

Treating women for mental illness was not only lucrative, it also reinforced patriarchal power. Sex-based discrimination was evident in the admission, treatment, and release of patients incarcerated for mental illness. Women more vulnerable to commitment than men included runaway adolescent females, sexually active females whose parents or husbands objected, women involved in custody suits, and single mothers receiving financial state aid. Unhappy creative or intellectual women like Sylvia Plath and Kate Millett were also candidates. Since fewer women than men worked and fewer held positions of authority or were the sole support of their families, economic status also became a sex-related factor in commitment. Lesbians were committed at the youngest age of any group because "what is perceived (and experienced) as an extreme rejection of one's 'feminine' role is the most stressful and dramatically punished of all female offenses in our society."[50]

Women's institutional treatment often involved conditioning in and enforcing sexual stereotypes. It could be mild, including use of cosmetics and clothing as therapy or requiring female inmates to do domestic chores in the institution or even in doctors' homes; or it could be harsh—a patient who had forgotten how to cook "remembered like magic" after a few electroshock treatments. Repression of sexual feelings and behavior was particularly strict for women in mental institutions, where "patients are made to inhabit an eternal American adolescence, where sexuality and aggression are as feared, mocked, and punished as they are within the Family." Since "women have already been bitterly and totally repressed sexually," the effect of such institutional control was more negative for them. Chesler thought that some female patients might "be reacting to or trying to escape from just such repression, and the powerlessness it signifies, by 'going mad'." Clinicians punished women for mildly aggressive behavior that was tolerated as natural in men; aggression was not part of the behavior of "normal" women. Even Chesler believed that "'depression' rather than 'aggression' is the female response to disappointment or loss. . . . Women are in a continual state of mourning—for what they never had—or had too briefly, and for what they can't have in the present, be it Prince Charming or direct worldly power. . . . 'depressed' women are (like women in general) only verbally hostile."[51]

Close supervision did not "protect the female as patient-child from rape, prostitution, pregnancy, and the blame for all three." From 1968 to 1970, there were many newspaper accounts of the prostitution, rape, and impregnation of female mental patients by professional as well as non-professional staff and by male inmates. Furthermore, institutions would not prescribe contraceptives or perform abortions for patients.[52]

The most drastic treatment was psychosurgery. The first lobotomies (removal of all or part of the brain's frontal lobe) in the fifties disabled about 50,000 Americans. In 1964, 72 percent of psychotics and 80 percent of neurotics operated on were women, many in middle age. Between 400 and 600 such operations were performed annually, primarily on women, children, homosexuals, prisoners, and the old—"the 'leftovers' of society, who must pay for their loneliness by being robbed of their minds." One doctor contended that "women respond 'better' to lobotomies" due to "their passive conditioning." It was more socially acceptable to lobotomize women because "creativity, which the operation totally destroys, is, to this society, an expendable quality in women." Opponents saw that older women were particularly victimized by psychosurgeons like a Dr. Freeman, "'dean of lobotomists,' [who] openly stated that lobotomized women make good housekeep-ers." Dr. Barbara Roberts summarized: "Unlike burning at the stake, psychosurgery can silence rebellion while preserving the useful work women do with their hands, their backs, and their uteruses." Despite electroshock therapy and new psychoactive drugs (including LSD used therapeutically), psychosurgery continued in the early seventies on women, most of whom were "relatively well-functioning" but labeled "neurotic."[53]

Chesler notes that "experimental or traditional medication, surgery, shock, and insulin coma treatment, isolation, physical and sexual violence, medical neglect, and slave labor are routinely enforced" in the mental asylum, which "closely approximates the female rather than the male experience within the family." Women "embark and re-embark on 'psychiatric careers' more than men do . . . because they feel, quite horribly, at 'home' within them." As patients, they received "substitute mothering."[54]

Radical feminists increasingly challenged the bedrock of modern psychology—linking male chauvinism and psychological oppression. The New York feminist group Redstockings pointed toward the new direction in thinking about mental illness in women and women's need to take control of their own lives. In the summer of 1969 "The Redstocking Manifesto" proposed a "pro-woman" line that "held that the criticism of women—even any one woman—was a case of 'blaming the victim.'" Redstockings proclaimed: "Women are an oppressed class. . . . We are exploited as sex objects, breeders, domestic servants, and cheap labor. We are considered inferior beings whose only purpose is to enhance men's lives. . . . We reject the idea that women consent to or are to blame for their own oppression. Women's submission is not the result of brainwashing, stupidity or mental illness but of continual, daily pressure from men. We do not need to change ourselves, but to change men."[55]

Inspired by Simone de Beauvoir, Kate Millett in *Sexual Politics* and Shulamith Firestone in *The Dialectic of Sex*, both published in 1970, attribute cultural problems to Freudianism. Firestone acknowledges that "Freudianism is so charged, so impossible to repudiate because Freud grasped the crucial problem of modern life: Sexuality." She criticizes "feminine neurosis about personal appearance" created by the contradiction in the "demands of Sex Privatization" and the "demands of the Beauty Ideal," as contributing to women's sense of inferiority. Feminists rejected Freudian theories, especially penis envy, castration, Oedipal and Electra complexes, narcissism, and masochism, indeed all the modern psychological constructs based on a male "nature" as norm.

They rejected even more liberal psychologists like Erikson. Millett complains that he simply replaced the theory of penis envy with "uterine glorification . . . a gentler form of persuasion."[56]

Voices challenging Freud's misogyny became a chorus, one of the earliest being Philip Rieff's chapter on "Sexuality and Domination" in *Freud: The Mind of the Moralist* (1961). By the sixties' end, a new group of psychologists emerged with social-learning theories of gender differences conditioned by parental rewards and punishments. William Simon and John Gagnon declared, "We see sexual behavior . . . as scripted behavior, not the masked expression of a primordial drive." Walter Mischel taught that characteristics of female dependence and male aggression were learned at home and in school, and were not genetic. Anthropological studies like those of Margaret Mead documented that what Americans consider innate sex-appropriate characteristics are not universal. Mead concludes: "Many, if not all, of the personality traits which we have called masculine or feminine are as lightly linked to sex as are the clothing, the manners, and the form of headdress that a society at a given period assigned to either sex." Such theories challenged the conventional wisdom, still actively promulgated by influential child psychologists like Haim Ginott, whose best-selling manual *Between Parent and Child* (1965) urged parents to raise boys to be "he-men" and breadwinners and girls to be "shy maidens" and homebodies.[57]

New trends in humanistic psychology began to counteract the paternalistic, pathological view of the psychology of women. Charlotte Bertha Bühler (1893–1974) with Abraham H. Maslow, Carl Rogers, and Viktor Frankl organized the Old Saybrook Conference in 1964 that gave birth to a movement emphasizing the importance of individual growth and self-fulfillment as motives in human behavior, based on the belief that sexual attitudes were, in Maslow's words, more "functions of personality and social and cultural relationships than of sheer biological endowment." Maslow felt that psychology took over where religion left off and that the self, female or male, was inherently healthy and "self-actualizing." Bühler became first president of the new Association for Humanistic Psychology from 1965–66. Her religious and holistic interests are evident in *The Course of Human Life* (1968) written with Fred Massarik and in *An Introduction to Humanistic Psychology* (1972) with Melanie Allen.[58]

Perhaps psychologist Naomi Weisstein had the last word in 1969, summarizing how both academic theories and clinical practice discriminated against women by ignoring social and cultural context: "Psychology has nothing to say about what women are really like, what they need and what they want, essentially, because psychology does not know." She wondered about the past fifty years of so-called psychoanalytic experience: "Did their psychiatrist cow them into reporting something that was not true? . . . Did psychiatrists ever learn anything different than their theories had led them to believe?" The decade's attack on Freudianism formed a basis for the later development of a new psychology of women.[59]

Marriage, Family, and Home

In the first half of the sixties as before, 40 percent of all brides were teenagers. Half of all women married before age twenty. One Iowa study showed that 39 percent of girls marrying before finishing high school did so because of pregnancy; but illegitimacy rose rapidly, even before the so-called sexual revolution. Still, one of the greatest demographic trends from 1957 on was the growing tendency of women to postpone marriage and hence lower their fertility. The number of single women in their twenties skyrocketed. Through the sixties, the percentage of 18- and 19-year-olds never married rose from 67.7 to 75.4 percent; those between 20 and 24, from 28.4 to 35.8 percent. By 1970, only 63 percent of adult American women were married.[60]

Rosalind Petchesky thinks it foolish to try to trace simple causes and effects of complex demographic change: "We cannot untangle whether women postpone marriage and childbearing because of the greater availability of jobs and educational possibilities or seek jobs and education because they are less encumbered with marriage and motherhood, for the simple reason that the two processes are mutually reinforcing. Yet the totality of these conditions adds up to a situation in which more women are spending more years of their lives outside marriage and without direct dependence on men, focused on activities other than domesticity and childrearing."[61]

Increasingly through the sixties, the image of the efficient housewife and her plentiful leisure time came under attack. Friedan explained that *The Feminine Mystique* aimed to debunk "the image of the happy American housewife," because "by 1962 the plight of the trapped American housewife had become a national parlor game." Women socialized during the day because, as sociologist Herbert Gans discovered, they believed that in the evenings and on weekends "a husband has first call on his wife's companionship."[62]

Editors of *Ladies' Home Journal* received a barrage of complaints from both women and men about their story on 34-year-old Janice Crabtree, who lived "in a handsome pink brick ranch house on the best and newest street in Grapevine, Texas." By 9:00 A.M. "she is wearing rouge, powder and lipstick, and her summer dress is immaculately fresh." Husband Billie said she finished all her housework "like greased lightning" in her first hour awake: "Hurrying through the house in her pajamas and robe, she makes four beds in quick, stepsaving motions and hangs up night clothes. She wipes the bathtubs and washbowls and straightens the towels. Then she may run a dustcloth over the grand piano or pick up some crumbs with the vacuum." Her system left her with the entire day for bridge: "During winter months she may play as often as four days a week from 9:30 A.M. to 3 P.M."; but she was "careful always to be home before her sons return from school." Janice admitted, "Sometimes I feel I'm too passive, too content. But I'm grateful for my blessings . . . for my good health, faith in God and such material possessions as two cars, two TVs and two fireplaces. . . . I feel just like Queen Elizabeth" sleeping in a four-poster bed with pink taffeta canopy, in a room apart from her snoring husband. Janice had a personal utopia, a woman's sphere in suburbia with all the latest consumers' goods; but readers' responses to the picture were overwhelmingly negative. Betty Friedan observed in 1963 that the idea of such "feminine millstones hanging around their necks" repelled many men.[63]

Esther Peterson, Kennedy's Women's Bureau head, asserted, "Certainly today's homemaking chores are no great challenge" to the middleclass woman. "Her sense of frustration is likely to heighten as her children go to school and there is even less need for her in the home." The Women's Bureau reported in 1971 that "homemaking is no longer a full-time job," that even women with children who did not work while their children were young still faced a period of twenty-five years or more of working life expectancy between ages forty and sixty-five. Echoing Friedan's understanding of "the problem that has no name," sociologist Jessie Bernard judged that "the housewife syndrome might be viewed as public health problem number one."[64]

Yet many American women delighted in their roles as homemakers. They read and shared "Hints from Heloise," syndicated by Heloise Cruse in 512 newspapers, offering advice on how to do-it-yourself in all domestic areas; but her hints were rarely time-saving. She reinforced the compulsive cleaner with advice on what solvents to use on curtain rods for special cleaning. Yet she pretended permissiveness, reassuring women they did not have to dust under the bed weekly. Her instructions for homemade dog food, finger paints, or gift wrap were often "make work" projects consuming vast quantities of time and effort with minimal savings. For those who failed to clip and save the columns, *Heloise All Around the House* (1967) summarized them.

The flourishing industry in crafts products encouraged creative domesticity, urging women to make their own holiday decorations or macramé wall hangings and plant holders to display their handicraft talents and personalize their homes. Instructions for projects—making birdhouses out of empty bleach bottles or bathroom wallpaper with cutouts—filled women's magazines and newspapers and shaped home decor that can only be called kitsch. As Maxine Margolis observes, these efforts "are difficult to justify on the basis of the money they save unless the time spent by the person doing them has no value." They led "to conspicuous changes in the home's decor," while proving "that the housewife really *is* working."[65]

Other women in the sixties diversified American food tastes, launching a gourmet revolution. In 1961 the *New York Times* predicted that the future housewife, aided by home computers, would "spend half her day preparing an exotic meal at which many foods would be tasted and consumed over a three hour period." Although the trend ran counter to the simultaneous rise of fast-food franchises, sophisticated tastes spread to Middle America largely because of Julia McWilliams Child (1912–) and her cookbooks. Child was trained at the famous Cordon Bleu cooking school and opened her own cooking school, "L'Ecole des Trois Gourmandes"; but it was through 119 episodes of her television program, *The French Chef,* that she earned national fame and taught the public to appreciate the complexity of sauces, soufflés, crêpes—exotic fare for the conventional American palate. The series originated on 26 July 1962 from Boston's educational public television station WGBH-TV. By 1966 a *Time* cover story boasted that the show had "made her a cult from coast to coast and put her on a first-name basis with her fans." She promoted epicureanism, although Edith De Rham cautioned, "To bake one's own bread in this day and age makes about as much sense as taking a covered wagon to California."[66]

For the younger, aspiring housewife, Jinx Kragen and Judy Perry guaranteed that their *Saucepans and the Single Girl* (1965), with recipes for casual, slightly exotic food, would "do more for a bachelor girl's social life than long lash mascara or a new discothèque dress." Included in their menu named "Food Fit for a Man in a Brooks Brothers Suit" were Flawless Fondue and Strawberries with Kirsch. All he had to do was furnish the Mateus. The fondue vogue swept the nation, spawning cookbooks like Anita Prichard's *Fondue Magic*. New brides received fondue pots and utensils in lieu of toasters. Fondue got the woman out of the kitchen's isolation, making preparation at the table a performance and eating a communal experience. Other cookbook authors capitalized on the idea that food was sensual, even part of sexual foreplay. Such was the tone of Kathryn Popper's *Honorable Hibachi* and Mimi Sheraton's *The Seducer's Cookbook* both encouraging men to cook. Liberation of the kitchen may not have been new, but it did introduce men to the idea that they could and should become more active in food preparation.[67]

For women who wanted to "take it easy" rather than be ambitious in the kitchen, Peg Bracken's popular books offered time-saving advice: *The I Hate to Cook Book* (1960), *The I Hate to Housekeep Book* (1962), and *Peg Bracken's Appendix to the I Hate to Cook Book* (1966). Bracken simplified and humanized the old etiquette of white gloves and calling cards with a new "informal, adaptable code based on good intentions and good character," integrating a new etiquette into everyday, middle-class, suburban life. Her books *I Try to Behave Myself* (1964) and *I Didn't Come Here to Argue* (1969) were witty alternatives to the traditional rules of Emily Post, who died in 1960.[68]

For those intent on controlling, not expanding, their tastes, there was the eccentric nutritional advice of Adelle Davis (1904–1974), with degrees in "household science" and biochemistry, who had held public attention since the forties for her criticisms of pasteurized milk, advocacy of fertile over infertile eggs, and recommendation of hazardously large daily doses of vitamins A, D, and E. After *Exploring Inner Space* (1961) about her LSD experiments (under the pseudonym of Jane Dunlap), she authored *Let's Get Well* (1964). By decade's end and the growing health food movement, it sold over ten million copies along with her previous three advice manuals. She attributed social problems like divorce, alcoholism, impotency, and crime to bad eating. In 1969 the White House Conference of Food, Nutrition, and Health called the diet guru the nation's most harmful source of false nutrition information; but *Time* proclaimed her in 1972 "the high priestess of a new nutrition religion." She remained a popular figure until her 1974 death of bone marrow cancer.[69]

Anthropologist Margaret Mead correctly complained in 1969 that commercial media presented a tyrannical ideal, unprecedented in human history, against which each American woman self-consciously measured her own life and home, "not good enough to the extent that it deviates from the national, artificial standard. Against such measures of status, no woman—no matter how fortunate or beautiful or loved, no matter how well-read or trusted by her children and adored by her husband—can ever vote herself a complete success or completely happy." This side of the "feminine mystique" led sixties women, as in the fifties, to strive to professionalize their work in the home, to perfect skills in the arts and crafts of decorating, to purchase the proper products for economy and usefulness, to provide meals that would rival those in the best restaurants. Mead characterized the modern homemaker's whole life, with "little or no domestic help," even for the "wealthiest and busiest," as "managerial" and full of unprecedented consumptive choices: "She needs a knowledge of foods and their nutritive values, of clothing, of drugs, of cosmetics, and of household equipment. Some 20 percent of American families move every year, which can mean long distances between herself and her relatives and former neighbors, who might help her make the myriad choices she has to make every day. For such help, she relies chiefly on the mass media—especially television."[70]

Through the sixties, most American women maintained their homes without domestic help. Mead noted, "It has taken only one servantless generation for an educated and affluent woman to think she prefers doing all the work herself, using her college-trained mind on the pots and pans, rather than taking the trouble to first train and then put up with a helper. The habit of doing her own housework and spending money on other things parallels the present emphasis on raising one's own children rather than turning them over to servants to be reared. It is largely because most American women have rejected help, plus the fact that being a servant is considered degrading, that there are few trained servants and few nursemaids to be found by those American women who want them."[71]

Mead criticized media for depicting ideal homes as "filled with equipment for domestic tasks, which the mother-wife-hostess is pictured as whipping her way through with great efficiency in between social, philanthropic, or professional activities. An efficiency based on a tremendous capital investment in equipment, a very high degree of education and experience, and a high family income thus has become the standard against which every woman can judge herself as fortunate or unfortunate, a success or a failure. And even as women judge themselves against this standard of managerial efficiency, husbands and children also judge their performance against the same expectations. It is a setting in which the kitchen is a white-tiled palace, mother's hands are soft, her hair is immaculately done, and the television set is working perfectly."[72]

This domestic utopia could become a woman's prison or an asylum, as feminists increasingly pointed out at decade's end. In a radical essay, "The Politics of Housework" (1969), Pat Mainardi challenged the rationalizations of domestic self-sacrifice and "women's work" in the home; but the feminist critique of domesticity became so strident that it alienated many women and intensified a generation gap between daughters intent on making it in the "public sphere" and mothers who had invested their entire sense of self in their homes and families.[73]

Mead nonetheless explained the major social change shaping interpersonal family relationships of women: "Freedom to work has meant that any woman without a husband to support her is expected to work; fathers and brothers and sons no longer feel it is their duty to support daughters and sisters and mothers. Spare female relatives—extra hands to hold the baby, . . . someone to stay at home for the delivery man, someone else to share the long hours of nursing a sick child—have thus disappeared from the home." Socialization furthered the trend: "Today's American girl has been reared in a home in which there were only two adults of opposite sex. She leaves that home as soon after puberty as she can get away, for marriage or for college. For the most part, she is unprepared, for reasons having to do with her own upbringing and independence, to share her home with another woman."[74]

By the sixties' end, due to long-term trends, Mead observed that "husbands are taking over many of the responsibilities once performed by female relatives or servants among the well-to-do—helping with heavy household work, taking care of the children, carrying the laundry to the laundromat, and even attending prenatal classes with their pregnant wives and staying with them through delivery—an age-old prerogative of the wife's mother. Probably no other aspect of the lives of American women is so isolating as the lack of ability to cooperate closely, within the same four walls, with other women." Suburbanization isolated many young wives from a support network of older kin; but it also, as Mead points out, led to an informal but noticeable pattern in which husbands began to share more household maintenance than ever before, a trend predating feminist demands.[75]

Children

The birth rate, far higher than in other modern nations, peaked in 1955–58 at 25.3 per thousand people; in 1960, even college-educated women had similar fertility statistics. Still, the percentage of childless white women aged 25 and 30 began to climb after an all-time low in 1964–65. Although, or perhaps because, motherhood and childcare occupied the attention of most married women, increasingly young married women made the conscious decision to remain childless or to postpone having children indefinitely. After the peak "baby boom" years, American women's fertility began to decline dramatically, particularly the first-birth rates for those under age 24. By 1965, the average American woman had her last child at age twenty-eight. At the decade's end, 13 million households contained a married couple without children, often with both spouses working.[76]

To further this demographic trend, Dr. Paul Ehrlich founded Zero Population Growth (ZPG) at Yale in 1968. Its popularity supported by Ehrlich's best-selling book, *The Population Bomb*, ZPG claimed over a hundred chapters in thirty states by 1970. It stressed the need to stem population growth in the name of limited resources and environmental problems and urged married people to have no more than two children, reproducing only themselves.

Many advice givers and child raising experts, whose influence over women's lives increased markedly after post-World War II, preached that the mother was the primary parent and should stay home with her children. Popular magazines of the sixties continued to extol a cult of motherhood. Anthropologist Ashley Montagu declared, "I put it down as an axiom that no woman with a husband and small children can hold a full-time job and be a good homemaker at one and the same time." Many social scientists, like psychoanalyst René Spitz, still blamed mothers for an array of children's psychosocial, mental, and even physical disorders and ailments, the "psycho-toxic diseases of infancy." Haim Ginott emphasized in *Between Parent and Child* (1965) the mother's role and warned against the father's over-involvement even in basic child care, lest "the baby end up with two mothers." As late as 1970, some psychiatrists still argued that mothering behavior was regulated by a pituitary hormone, that to become a mother a woman would have to experience "biologic regression," undoing any "active, extroverted ego-ideal" developed before marriage. All emphasized keeping children, not women, happy.[77]

As late as 1968, when 40 percent of women with children were in the labor force, Dr. Benjamin Spock still insisted in his very popular *Baby and Child Care* that children needed mothers' full time care. The pediatrician was sure that mothers would see that "good mother care during early childhood" was the surest way to produce "useful, well-adjusted citizens," and would realize that "the extra money she might earn, or the satisfaction she might receive from an outside job" was "not so important after all." Such advice ignored "a dysfunction between what most of the experts were saying and what growing numbers of middle-class women were doing," writes historian Maxine Margolis.[78]

Change occurred by the mid-sixties: the popular government pamphlet *Infant Care*, revised in 1963, recommended that "wise mothers" make fathers "part of the picture" for baby care. Dr. Margaret Ribble's widely read *Rights of Infants* revised her 1943 suggestion that mothers give full, undivided attention to their children, that the children have "the understanding care of one consistent individual—his mother," and that fathers should have little to do with babies until three months of age. In 1965 Ribble restored the rights of fathers and described the child's "deepest need" as "the understanding and consistent care of his parents," announcing to the mother "that her husband is capable and interested in assuming his father role *from the start in this joint venture*" and recommending paternal care "because it lessens considerably the chance of an exaggerated mother attachment." The shift to advising shared parenting is seen between T. Berry Brazelton's *Infants and Mothers* (1969) and his *Toddlers and Parents* (1974).[79]

Yet when Edith De Rham declared in 1965 that "without a doubt, a totally balanced, heterosexual approach to parenthood is vastly superior to the matriarchal system imposed . . . on children today," she placed tacit blame on traditional mothers. If the "parasitic relationship" between mothers and children did not harm the children, "the psychological interdependence of mother and child threatens to change the mother's personality. . . . at best, she will become childlike herself; at worst, she will be transformed into the despised and voracious MOM." The antidote was increased paternal involvement.[80]

Bruno Bettelheim adopted a pro-woman, if not feminist, tone in 1962 by acknowledging that "The children of women who are doing interesting work on their own during the day will often find more sensible and sympathetic mothers." Working mothers provided useful models for daughters in particular: "The mother who urges her girl toward intellectual achievement while staying at home herself poses a contradiction which probably is not lost on the girl." F. Ivan Nye and Lois Wladis Hoffman echoed this tone in *The Employed Mother in America* (1963), arguing that the mother working outside the home produced independent children. Margaret Mead added in 1962 that the ideal of American motherhood was based on ethnocentrism: "Actually, such an exclusive and continuous relationship is only possible under highly artificial urban conditions, which combine the production of food outside the home with the practice of contraception." Feminists like Betty Friedan and sociologist Alice Rossi expanded upon this perspective.[81]

Among these experts, Dr. Spock offered the most practical advice to mothers; but manufacturers made baby care quicker and easier. Development of disposable diapers, first test marketed by Proctor and Gamble in Peoria, Illinois, in 1961, made obsolete the washing or sending out of dirty cloth diapers. They minimized diaper rash, and tape tabs eliminated safety pins that could open and hurt the child. Originally priced at an expensive ten cents apiece, the diapers did not sell until perfected, repriced at six cents each, and renamed Pampers in 1966. One of the new conveniences of modern American disposable culture, they seemed a boon. No one considered the environmental consequences of the waste. Also, disposable hygienic plastic bags for nursers eliminated the need for time-consuming boiling to sterilize baby bottles; and canned concentrated infant formula and pureed baby foods shortened mothers' kitchen preparation time.

By 1969, Margaret Mead found that for the first time in history, children of both sexes were cared for by both sexes. She asked, "Will this circumstance iron out the differences traceable to the fact that children throughout history have been reared by women? We are in fact in the midst of tremendous revolution in the biological and social roles of men and women. The only prediction that can be made with certainty is that enormous and continuous readjustment must be made by, and new learning will be demanded of, both sexes." Other cultural critics, however, worried about "why young mothers feel trapped" and why anti-natalism was growing. Again, the phenomenon preceded feminists' demands.[82]

Mothers and Daughters: The Generation Gap

Although Connie Francis began the decade with the plaintive, filially pietistic pop ballad hit "Mama" (1960), cultural changes in the sixties created a so-called "generation gap" with different manifestations among women than among men. When Bob Dylan sang, "Your sons and your daughters are beyond your command" and "The Times They Are a 'Changin'," he referred to young people's new and different concerns with public, political, and social issues—creating a gap that was particularly acute when sons rejected traditional male goals and styles. The "generation gap" for women began with the development of teenage culture in the fifties, even before it became a buzz-word in the press. Usually it involved subtle rebellion of the baby boom age-cohort against expectations imposed by mothers and grandmothers. Often its manifestations were more personal and private than those of men, although also concerned with dress and lifestyle.[83]

Parents of baby boomers were children of the Depression. Having learned patterns of frugality based on a sense of economic insecurity, many reacted with ambivalence to their children's privileges at a time of unprecedented materialism and opportunity. One father, although a professional, meticulously measured the amount of hot water his teen-aged daughter used in her weekly bath in the early sixties, driven by a parsimony instilled in his own youth. The generation gap pitted members of two distinct age cohorts against each other, with interactive cognitive dissonance based on separate belief systems grounded in the cultural climates in which they had come or were coming of age.[84]

Young girls growing up in the sixties as in the fifties constantly received reminders about being "girlish" and acquiring "ladylike" behavior. Different mothers drew the line of propriety in various ways. One forbade the hula-hoop and the Twist. Another refused to buy Barbie dolls because they were too "risqué." Another banned singing questionable songs like "Son of a Gun, We'll Have Big Fun on the Bayou." Acculturation of a "young lady" was far more complex in contrast to trends in popular culture and behavioral change than simply instilling a sense of etiquette and proper dress.[85]

Mothers warned daughters about the dangers of losing their virginity, of getting into situations beyond their control. Virginity remained the trump card to be guarded to win a husband. Girls repeated truisms like "Why would a man buy a cow if he can get the milk for free." One mid-sixties University of Michigan coed, invited to a party by her "wild" roommate, wore two Tampaxes in addition to her girdle as a makeshift chastity belt, a final line of defense in case someone slipped "something funny" in her drink. The well-instilled fear of being thought a "bad girl" led those who tried sex to keep it a secret even

from their best female friends. Nevertheless, many young women se-
cretly behaved much differently from the traditional ideal, and the resulting cognitive dissonance was one component of the generation
gap.[86]

Others rebelled more visibly. By 1968 many young white women,
even if not actual hippies, shocked their mothers by discarding make-
up, abandoning the permanents, hair sets, and hair-spray of the beauty
parlor to let their hair grow long, straight, and scraggly or to copy the
"Afro" of Blacks. To the horror of mothers and grandmothers, many
young women began to do other "unladylike" things, like sitting cross-
legged on the floor, even when wearing skirts, going out in public with
bare legs uncovered by nylons, and going barefoot whenever possible—
even if they did not become "hippies." Some of the more rebellious
stopped shaving legs and underarms.

But the generation gap involved more than differences of behavior
and dress. An education gap separated mothers and grandmothers from
young baby boomers, often the first women in their families to go to
college. Older women had not anticipated the consequences as their
daughters developed interests and ambitions quite different than their
own and enjoyed unprecedented, although still limited opportunities
and choices. They could not understand why increasingly their daughters postponed marriage and children, seemingly rejecting the roles in
which they took pride. The very sense of self—worth, values, beliefs,
expectations—of an older generation was challenged within their own
families even more than by feminism. Political differences only compounded this far more fundamental alienation. Yet in 1970, Margaret
Mead published her *Culture and Commitment: A Study of the Generation
Gap*, expressing an optimistic belief that constructive, positive thinking
could bridge generational differences, despite the irreversible evolutionary changes impelled by modern technology, a population explosion, and destruction of the natural environment.

Although a women's generation gap primarily pitted those in their
teens and twenties against older sisters, mothers, and grandmothers,
evidence exists that connections between older generations of women
were far from ideal. A 1962 study found that a quarter of a sample of
recently divorced, middle-aged women had never discussed their marital problems with their mothers. One fifty-year-old was so fearful of
maternal disapproval that she did not "confess" her divorce until a year
after it was final. For many women in the sixties, there was no generation gap; for other, it was acute.[87]

Divorce

On 4 May 1960, Lucile Ball divorced Desi Arnaz; and the happy American family so popular with sit-com viewers in ten million American homes from 1951 to 1957 came to an end. In May 1961, the storybook romance of Marilyn Monroe and Arthur Miller ended in a Mexican divorce. In March 1964, Elizabeth Taylor married Richard Burton ten days after divorcing Eddie Fisher, who had divorced Debbie Reynolds to marry Taylor—all shocking the nation. Reynolds (1932–), on the screen as in real life, despite her pure image, portrayed unhappy wives if not actual divorcees in films including *The Second Time Around* (1961), *My Six Loves* (1963), *Goodbye Charlie* (1964), and *Divorce American Style* (1967). Similarly, Deborah Kerr (1921–) starred in *Marriage on the Rocks* (1965). "D-I-V-O-R-C-E" was a hit country song.

This theme pervaded the mass media in the sixties while divorce became an increasing reality in everyday American life. Continuing a national trend escalating since the fifties, the divorce rate climbed significantly in the sixties, doubling between 1965 and 1975 and coinciding with the end of the baby boom, the increased participation of women in the work force, and the "sexual revolution." Sociologists warned that "the state of marriage is a calamity" and "the total institution of marriage in American society is gravely ill" with monogamy "enveloped by deterioration and decay," especially on the West Coast where "mate swapping" became a vogue in some circles. By the decade's end, 25 percent of all U.S. marriages ended in divorce. What was the cause; what was the effect? Many worried.[88]

Many argued that the so-called "sexual revolution" objectified women as sex objects as never before and glorified the cult of youth, permeating even middle-class, suburban America. It enticed middle-aged men, psychologically upset because of what would later be labeled "mid-life crisis," to seek younger women in extramarital affairs, in the process breaking up longtime marriages. The rise of adultery was a trend difficult to quantify but one that got extensive literary treatment. Within three weeks, John Updike's *Couples* (1968) became a bestseller; and Hollywood paid half a million dollars for movie rights.[89]

Divorce statistics had been growing steadily for half a century, and the institution of marriage was weaker than ever before. The divorce rate rose from 9.2 per thousand in 1960 to 16.9 in 1970. From 1963–69, divorces of couples married for fewer than five years increased 62 percent; the number of those divorcing after longer marriages increased

37 percent, and termination of marriages of 20–30 years doubled. Divorce varied by class. One sociologist observed, "An astonishing proportion of marriages . . . are not particularly happy. The average citizen is more tied by marriage vows than classes above him. Decorum, religion, and the high cost of divorce keep him bonded to disagreeable marriages. Even the poor can more casually get out of unhappy marriages" than the working class. One quarter of black marriages ended in divorce, and non-white female-headed families rose to 29 percent in 1971.[90]

Female-Headed Households

In a substantially growing number of households, because of "illegitimacy" (as it was still called), divorce, and widowhood, the mother was the single head and solely responsible for child support, as well as care. Lee claims that since "Negro women, who make up only about 12 percent of the population, have more than half of all illegitimate births that occur each year . . . an individual woman may accept the possibility of raising a fatherless child with little difficulty." The popular singer Aretha Franklin, for example, has been described as a restless girl who had two children by the time she turned seventeen. But contrary to beliefs, this problem had no racial limits. Most single women heads of family put in the "double day" or bore the "double burden,'" still responsible for most household maintenance and childcare in addition to putting in a workday of eight hours or more. Most of these families fell below the poverty level.[91]

Aid to Families with Dependent Children (AFDC), expanded in 1961 for women not living with husbands, helped some of these women escape total destitution; but it rarely lifted them above poverty. AFDC even discouraged two-parent families among the needy. Until a 1968 court decision, laws in 19 states and the District of Columbia permitted withholding federal aid under Social Security from dependent children if their mothers engaged in extramarital affairs with men who were thus deemed "substitute fathers," even though they had no legal duty and usually no inclination to support the children. In essence, the law exercised arbitrary control over many women's private lives. Due to the increase in female-headed households and liberalized eligibility guidelines, AFDC case loads grew from 3 million recipients in 1960 to 11.4 million in 1975; still many families living in poverty applied for no benefits. Dr. Frances Piven, a Columbia political scientist, criticized civil rights leaders like Urban League Director Whitney Young who thought it "more important to get one black woman into a job as an airline stewardess than it was to get fifty poor families onto welfare."[92]

Such poor women of all races formed the National Welfare Rights Organization (NWRO) in 1967 "to educate those eligible persons not receiving aid and to win for recipients additional benefits to which they were entitled." This most visible of many welfare rights groups, aiming to coordinate activism nationally, had 800 affiliates in all 50 states by 1971 with a leadership of paid professionals, many of them, like Executive Director George Wiley, male. Wiley formed the National Coordinating Committee of Welfare Rights Groups, with one welfare recipient from each of eleven states, to promote grassroots activism through pickets, sit-ins, school boycotts, hearings, court actions, and national conferences. At its peak in 1969, the NWRO had 22,500 dues-paying members, most in northern industrial states. But as one participant recalls, there was chronic tension between the professionals "with very precise ideas about what they wanted to do" and welfare mothers "who were not going to get into something where the case worker types told them what to do."[93]

A major ally for ghetto women on the Executive Committee was Johnnie Tillmon, black mother of six, who began organizing mothers from Watts in Los Angeles in 1963, claiming that the federal bureaucracy "nurtured female dependency." She wrote "Welfare is a Women's Issue" because bureaucrats "tried to control recipients' sex lives, economic resources, consumer purchases, childcare provisions, and choice of housing," subjecting them to a "humiliating and frustrating" maze of red tape, interviews, and visits. In turn, welfare gave them only a pittance, "barely enough for food and clothing." Tillmon criticized the mean-spirited suggestion that the poor were making money off the system: "Having babies for profit is a lie that only men could make up, and only men could believe." Historian Jacqueline Jones judges that "the group initially held great promise as a vehicle for grassroots ghetto organizing, but gradually dissolved in the face of external pressures as well as internal." Perhaps because of the gap between leadership and constituents, it "attracted only nominal support (and in some cases open hostility) from middle-class groups like the NAACP, the National Urban League, and NOW, which found the slogan 'Welfare is a Right' embarrassing or irrelevant to their own programs."[94]

Trying to decrease AFDC rolls, LBJ's administration began the Work Incentive Program (WIN) in 1967, requiring all recipients except those caring for preschool children at home to register for job training and placement. Persons most likely to be employable received priority, and many black women didn't get off welfare because the unskilled or low-skilled jobs they were given paid so little. Jones concludes, "In effect, WIN helped to subsidize low-wage jobs for women; many turned eagerly to work, at least partly because AFDC payments were so meager, but they also had to fall back on AFDC when their jobs paid so little." WIN was flawed by a catch-22 that took support away from women just when they were beginning to find jobs and skills.[95]

Late-sixties public policy was informed by flawed and even racist social theory. One fourth of black families were headed by women in 1965; and by 1974 the percentage increased to one third. In a study, "The Negro Family: The Case for National Action," released in March 1965, Harvard sociologist Daniel Patrick Moynihan, then LBJ's Assistant Secretary of Labor, popularized "the idea that Black women were matriarchs, i.e. all-powerful, domineering, sexually permissive, and aggressive women." The "Moynihan Report" gave "scholarly respectability" to the idea that black women, especially those gainfully employed, "had deprived [black] males of all ages of their self-respect," creating a "tightening tangle of pathology" resulting in female-headed black households. Single mothers, he wrote, disseminated a female culture to their children, thus lessening sons' chances of healthy sex-role development. Thus, black men needed to get away to an "utterly masculine world . . . a world away from women, a world run by strong men of unquestioned authority, where discipline, if harsh, is nonetheless orderly and predictable." Moynihan saw a solution in the U.S. Army, where "you get to know what it means to feel like a man."[96]

Black and white male scholars seized upon these ideas, attacking "momism" and blaming the "church-going, overworked, . . . harassed, cranky, frustrated" mother for the general "disorganization" of the black family and the antisocial tendencies of ghetto youth in particular; but Angela Davis challenged this theory in the *Black Scholar* in December 1971. Attorney Pauli Murray said "delicately" that the report "censured" black mothers "for their efforts to overcome a handicap not of their own making and for trying to meet the standards of the country as a whole." Others were not so restrained. One woman noted that she had "heard a lot of women wish they were men, but . . . never heard no man wish he was a woman." Black women social scientists set to work gathering statistical and demographic evidence to debunk the idea of black women's "privileged status."[97]

Black Power advocates countered that the Moynihan Report was a ploy to get blacks to fight a white man's war. Stokely Carmichael lashed back: "The reason we are in the bag we are in isn't because of my mama, it's because of what they did to my mama." The Report did long-term damage, expanding upon the general criticism throughout the fifties of "momism" as giving rise to all sorts of social and psychological pathologies; but it did so in a racist way, far more damaging than the criticism of the "Jewish mother" in Philip Roth's *Portnoy's Complaint* (1969). It gave many black men some new words with which they could criticize black women, and it spread the stereotype of the black woman as domineering matriarch, making many women's lives harder.[98]

Black women experienced a triple burden by the decade's end, wrote Maya Angelou, the "crossfire of masculine prejudice, white illogical hatred, and Black lack of power." Angelou described the terrible conjunction of stereotypes and reality, "The Black woman embodied a contradiction that makes her a living legend. She has nursed a nation of strangers, yet she's supposed to be mean and vicious, and given to violent, revengeful acts. She's supposed to be obsessive about the desire to have children out of wedlock, and yet she's supposed to castrate them and be cold and indifferent to them. By day she is supposed to be black and beautiful, by night she is alone. Because she has for over a hundred years been such a mainstay and such a breadwinner, she's worked herself into the position of a man-loser. The more she copes, the more she's asked to cope. So the more she copes. . . . Suddenly we are in the position of matriarchal ogres. That way no one has to deal with this living, breathing, needful person who wants a family, who wants a man, who wants a Christmas." Angelou concludes, "The fact that the adult American Negro female emerges as a formidable character is often met with amazement, distaste, and even belligerence. It is seldom accepted as an inevitable outcome of the struggle won by survivors and deserves respect if not enthusiastic acceptance."[99]

Older Women

Demographers realized that American women lived much longer lives than men; and social scientists studied the social and cultural consequences of the phenomenon. Impelled by reports of a greater sex differential in mortality than ever, the University of California's San Francisco Medical Center sponsored a symposium, "The Potential of

Women," in 1963. Males succumbed to heart disease, cancers, diabetes, and even accidents at a far higher rate and at earlier ages than women. Male physicians, writes historian Eugenia Kaledin, were "unnerved" by the statistics. Gynecologist Edmund W. Overstreet dared exclaim, "When you come right down to it, perhaps women just live too long! Maybe when they get through having babies they have outlived their usefulness." Overstreet claimed to express his colleagues' concern: "Is a woman's post-menopausal status a normal physiologic condition, or is it actually a pathologic disease state?" Yet through the sixties, older women played increasingly active roles in the public sphere. By 1970, over half of women aged 45 to 55 worked. They and others lived active lives, devoting considerable energies to volunteerism, associations, and reform causes.[100]

In 1963, fewer than a quarter of Americans over 45 had a surviving parent; but the trend toward living longer impelled real estate developers as well as reform-oriented organization founders to act. The first community for senior citizens was opened at Sun City, Arizona, in January 1960. Based on a suburban aesthetic and shaped by the increased female life expectancy, such developments were even more women's places than the suburbs of young families; and like the suburbs from which they were often indistinguishable, these communities institutionalized a ghettoization of age that reflected and contributed to a weakening of relationships between the generations. But they were not available to many older women, particularly widows, who remained marginalized, often living in poverty in older, disintegrating urban neighborhoods. Many older widows found support networks, as always, in clubs, church groups, and other voluntary associations; but these organizations did little to meet their real and increasing needs in rapidly changing times.[101]

Ethel Percy Andrus (1884–1967), an educator, launched her second career in 1958 by founding the American Association of Retired Persons (AARP) for people over age 55 and developing it aggressively through the sixties. AARP aims "to better the lives of older Americans through service, advocacy, education, and voluntary efforts" and provides insurance, discounts, and other benefits along with retirement-readiness programs. In 1961 President Kennedy appointed her to the advisory committee of the White House Conference on the Aging. Andrus urged the elderly to start second careers or engage in volunteerism; in 1963, she established the Institute for Life Long Learning, sponsoring classes at first in Washington, D.C., and then in Florida and California. Before her death at age 83, Andrus saw AARP expand to numerous chapters, engage in lobbying and voter education, champion health care and quality of life issues, and tackle other issues of elderly rights—issues publicized through AARP educational broadcasts on over 500 radio stations and in *Modern Maturity*, the monthly magazine she edited. A few more radical women formed Older Women's Liberation (OWL), but the Gray Panthers were not founded until the seventies. These efforts filled an important gap, since the women's movement largely ignored the problems of older women.[102]

14

The Women's Movement

The resurgence of feminism in the sixties has complex origins that have barely been traced to date and that frequently are oversimplified. A myth prevails that Betty Friedan's *The Feminine Mystique* (1963) sparked the women's movement and the feminist sensibility of the latter part of the decade. Friedan did urge women to "stop giving lip service to the idea that there are no battles left to be fought for women in America"; but her message was generally directed at the white middle-class suburban women about whom she wrote, not at women marginalized by class or race nor at those women who revived feminism as a call for "liberation."[1]

The impact of *The Second Sex* (1949) by Simone de Beauvoir (1908–1986), translated into English in 1952, was substantial, although the extent of American reader response remains unassessed. The book greatly influenced Kate Millett and shaped her *Sexual Politics* (1970); and it struck a chord with sculptor Eva Hesse, who read it in 1965 and quoted it in her diary, "What woman essentially lacks today for doing great things is forgetfulness of herself; but to forget oneself it is first of all necessary to be firmly assured that now and for the future one has found oneself." Hesse wrote Ethelyn Honig, another aspiring artist: "I wonder if we are unique, I mean the minority we exemplify. The female struggle, not in generalities, but our specific struggles. . . . A singleness of purpose, no obstructions allowed, seems a man's prerogative. His domain. A woman is side-tracked by all her feminine roles from menstrual periods to cleaning house to remaining pretty and 'young' and having babies. . . . She also lacks conviction that she has the 'right' to achievement. . . . Therefore she has not the steadfastness necessary to carry ideas to the full developments. There are handfuls that succeeded, but less when one separates the women from the women that assumed the masculine role. A fantastic strength is necessary and courage. . . . My determination and will is strong but I am lacking so in self esteem." Hesse recommended that Honig read de Beauvoir as a corrective.[2]

Another force in shaping a new American feminist consciousness was *The Golden Notebook* (1962) by Doris Lessing (1919–), a fictional account of a woman's struggle for identity and freedom in contemporary London. Eleanor Flexner's *Century of Struggle* (1959) gave the new feminists a sense of history upon which to build. A new intellectual basis growing through the first half of the sixties premised a resurgence of feminism. Still, from 1930 on, as Millett points out, feminism was eclipsed by a patriarchal counter-revolution; and much of the new feminism associated with the sixties did not fully develop until the seventies.[3]

Egalitarian Feminist Organizations

Members of State Commissions on the Status of Women, many of whom were women and far more activist than officials of Kennedy's Presidential Commission on the Status of Women, met annually at a national convention from 1963 on. At the July 1966 meeting, many rallied around Betty Friedan, New York representative, determined to require the Equal Employment Opportunities Commission (EEOC) to enforce provisions in the 1964 Civil Rights Act against gender discrimination. Meeting in Friedan's hotel room, women including Kathryn Clarenbach, Mary Eastwood, and Pauli Murray organized to force EEOC action on sex discrimination complaints filed under Title VII— first, segregation of Male/Female want ads. The group's intention soon expanded "to take action to bring women into full participation in the mainstream of American society now, exercising all the privileges and responsibilities thereof in truly equal partnership with men."[4]

Dorothy Haener of the UAW Women's Department credits black trade unionist Dollie Lowther Robinson, working in the Labor Department Women's Bureau in 1965, with first suggesting formation of "an NAACP for women." Haener attributes the bitter frustration encountered by women unionists with laying the groundwork for the rise of the women's movement. Certainly, state protective labor legislation had traditionally been used as a shield by male unionists and politicians, as well as some women, against egalitarian feminists' demands, particularly concerning an ERA.[5]

These and other forces led to the 1966 founding of the National Organization for Women (NOW). Men were included from the start; and Richard Graham, a rare sympathizer at the EEOC, joined Friedan and Betty Furness in launching NOW. Marlene Sanders, a television news reporter, and Muriel Fox, a public relations pioneer, helped Furness advise Friedan on NOW's image. At a 21 November press conference, Friedan wore a ruffled red blouse and sat on a Victorian loveseat in her apartment to announce NOW as "a civil rights organization. Discrimination against women in this modern world is as evil and wasteful as any other form of discrimination."[6]

Three hundred charter members elected Friedan as President and Dr. Kathryn (Kay) F. Clarenbach of the University of Wisconsin as Board Chair of the "private, voluntary, self-selected group." Graham and Aileen Hernandez were vice-presidents; Caroline Davis, UAW Women's Department Director, was Secretary/Treasurer. Minority members included Addie May Hunter and Hernandez, who succeeded Friedan as President. Other founders included Catherine East of the Women's Bureau and Mary Eastwood of the Justice Department. Dorothy Haener and Caroline Davis persuaded the UAW to provide clerical services for NOW; although, under pressure from the AFL-CIO, the UAW withdrew support in 1968. National officers as well as those of state and local chapters came from academe, the professions, government service, unions, and existing women's organizations.[7]

At its 29 October organizational meeting, planners framed NOW's Statement of Purpose, the most comprehensive call for women's rights since the 1848 Seneca Falls Declaration of Sentiments: "We believe that a true partnership between the sexes demands a different concept of marriage, an equitable sharing of the responsibilities of home and children and of the economic burdens of their support. We believe that proper recognition should be given to the economic and social values of homemaking and child care." NOW's founders promised, "We will protest and endeavor to change the false image of women now prevalent in the mass media and in the texts, ceremonies, laws and practices of our major social institutions . . . church, state, college, factory or office which in the guise of protectiveness . . . foster in women self denigration, dependence, and evasion of responsibility, undermine their confidence in their own abilities and foster contempt for women." NOW members, paying $5 dues each, increased to 1,200 in 1967 and to over 48,000 in 1974 with over 700 chapters in the United States and nine other nations.[8]

NOW's tactics were reformist, not revolutionary, aiming to achieve change by working within the political system and the "establishment" institutions. It petitioned EEOC to end gender-segregated help wanted ads; and members picketed regional EEOC offices, dumping red tape symbolic of the agency's slowness in tackling sex discrimination. Through a lawsuit, NOW successfully ended airline policies that forced retirement of stewardesses who married or reached their early thirties. Congresswoman Martha Griffiths lectured airline executives, "If you are trying to run a whorehouse in the sky, then get a license." NOW formed task forces on marriage and divorce, employment, textbooks, images of women on television, and women in sports. Both on the local and national level, it set up speakers bureaus, subcommittees to scrutinize legislation, and lobbying mechanisms to run letter-writing and phone-calling campaigns.[9]

From the perspective of many ordinary women, NOW was far too liberal. The resolution adopted as part of its Bill of Rights at the 1967 national convention called for "the right of women to control their own reproductive lives," and the goals of liberalizing abortion laws and expanding access to contraception proved controversial even among some NOW members who feared the issue would "damage the image" of women's rights. Some resigned. Other demands included paid maternity leave, educational aid, job training, and tax deductions for child care.[10]

To provide an alternative to such "radicalism," Arvonne Fraser, wife of a Minnesota Congressman, convened about two dozen women who were reluctant to associate their feminist political activism with their husbands' careers. They considered NOW too radical, especially over issues like abortion. Originally dubbed "the Nameless Sisterhood," the group became the Women's Equity Action League (WEAL) early in 1969. By 1970, Fraser, Dr. Bernice Sandler, the Ohio lawyer Elizabeth Boyer, and others chartered WEAL in Ohio as a moderate national organization, an alternative to NOW, smaller and more focused on promoting female participation in political parties and government as well as on correcting administrative, educational, and legal inequalities through a measured, "conservative" approach. WEAL "was to exercise a positive influence on legislation and practices" regarding women's work and education, and to "gain access to the planning and implementation levels of government and industry to press for our interests." WEAL assisted NOW's lobbying with welcome news on Congressional bills concerning women through its *Washington Report*. Occasionally, WEAL also took direct action. In 1970, it intervened in a suit to eliminate sex-segregated employment want ads; and it filed sex discrimination complaints for not hiring or promoting more women against more than 250 colleges and universities receiving federal funds—over ten percent of the nation's higher education institutions. NOW similarly targeted over 1,300 corporations.[11]

Several smaller women's pressure groups formed to tackle specific problems. Federally Employed Women (FEW), created in 1968, fought discrimination by the federal government, a major employer of women. Human Rights for Women began in 1968 to do research and provide legal services for anti-discrimination campaigns on the state level. Existing groups like the National Federation of Business and Professional Women's Clubs, the National Council of Negro Women, the American Association of University Women, and the Young Women's Christian Association—whose national hierarchical organizational structures and middle-class constituencies had been models for NOW, WEAL, and other egalitarian groups—began to address women's rights and problems.

These organizations saw few legislative successes until the seventies. Only on the issue of the ERA did there seem to be unanimity on NOW's National Board and in its state and local groups. Other women's issues like abortion, day care, and lesbian rights proved controversial and divisive. Power struggles and philosophical differences were counter-productive from the first; but NOW took over the task of the National Women's Party (NWP) in promoting the ERA and in working for equal rights in many areas—education, employment, society, and culture. NOW was not prepared to accept even the modified conclusion of the PCSW that an ERA was "not NOW necessary." Through the seventies, egalitarian women's organizations devoted most of their energies to the ERA and reproductive rights. Secondary concerns included equal educational opportunities, electing women to political office, and women's access to credit.

Women's Liberation

The Women's Liberation movement began quietly, spontaneously, and on the grassroots level in various locations across the nation from

1967 on as small groups of ten to thirty members began to meet regularly to discuss common concerns. By the late sixties, many young women had had enough of sexism in the counterculture as well as in mainstream culture and called for more sweeping changes than the liberals of the egalitarian movement dared contemplate. They dropped out of male-dominated organizations and into radical feminism. Many others still identified with the New Left and retained their Marxism, decrying members of NOW and WEAL as "bourgeois feminists." In contrast to NOW liberals, these others defined themselves as radical or cultural feminists, socialist feminists, or politicos—categories that described the fragmentation of the "movement" in various ways in various places virtually from the moment it began. Others, like Ti-Grace Atkinson and Florynce Kennedy, dropped out of NOW when it proved too structured and moderate for them.[12]

Radical feminists tended to be a generation younger than many egalitarians. Their philosophy repudiated the nineteenth-century feminist idea that women were essentially different from men, inherently more chaste, sexually passionless, and moral yet more vulnerable to exploitation and abuses if not "protected" by laws governing marriage and the workplace. The radicals categorically rejected the old feminism premised on the "cult of true womanhood." Cultural feminists, however, an offshoot of the radicals, were closer to their nineteenth-century sisters in emphasizing gender differences and cautioning against the oppressiveness of the "sexual revolution." Socialist feminists and even more radical politicos remained in the New Left even after many of their sisters had become disillusioned by male hegemony, still subscribing to the SDS credo of "The Port Huron Statement," that "late capitalist society creates mechanisms of psychological and cultural domination over everyone," yet failing to target the men in that society who controlled those mechanisms.[13]

A gap of ideology and style, and even a certain animosity separated and fragmented the women's movement from the late sixties on. Egalitarians failed to address the problems of poor and minority women. Radicals rejected egalitarians' liberalism and gradualism and their belief in the "system"; and egalitarians, in turn, with Friedan as chief spokesperson, decried efforts by these new feminists as waging a "bedroom war" which would only "turn off" mainstream American women and sabotage attempts to improve the status of women in the public sphere. Major differences over basic assumptions on women's nature, their cultural roles, and the efficacy of the political process belied proclamations of "sisterhood" and undermined the goals of all. Rejection of the "establishment" and the "system" by liberationists, in the "spirit" of the decade, included a counterproductive disregard for or rejection of organizational efficiency, for manipulative structures of management and techniques of political lobbying—as male ways to perpetuate control. Yet liberationists' grassroots, democratic philosophy produced various self-help programs and "counter-institutions" on the community level that became self-perpetuating and persist to the present.[14]

Politicos

New Left "politicos" like Marilyn Webb and Bernardine Dohrn called for a general socialist revolution rather than women's liberation. A Marxist victory, they argued, would wipe away women's oppression ingrained in the class system. They retained ties to such Old Left groups as the Socialist Workers' Party (SWP), the Progressive Labor Party (PL), and the Young Socialist Alliance (YSA), and to newer groups like the SDS and Weathermen; and they used women's issues as part of their organizing strategies. They held contempt for egalitarian feminists as "personalists" or self-absorbed elitists interested only in "making it" like men in "the system."[15]

Some radical feminists criticized "politicos" for seeking the approval of an "invisible audience" of male "lefties." Barbara Epstein, member of both SDS and the Communist Party in the early sixties, recalls "'Male chauvinism' was a phrase that one did not utter unless one was ready to be laughed at. . . . I found the only way to deal with sexist behavior in SDS, if it was on the part of another [Communist] Party member, was to bring it up in the Party. In SDS I would not be listened to."[16]

Feminists experienced considerable hostility in the New Left. In 1965, a feminist speaker urging discussion of women's issues at the SDS national convention faced jeers and shouts of "She just needs a good screw." The first informal, independent radical women's group met around Heather Booth at the 1965 SDS national conference. Another group, the Women's Radical Action Project (WRAP) formed in Chicago in the summer of 1967, drew up a list of demands to be presented to the National Conference for New Politics (NCNP), a New Left meeting that fall. The Chicago women, led by Joreen Freeman and Booth, won support from other radical women like New York's Shulamith Firestone but were astonished to hear their male "comrades" denigrate their plank as "trivial." One patronizing male dared pat the enraged Firestone on the head, urging, "Calm down, little girl." The women responded by issuing a formal call "to the Women of the Left" to launch a women's liberation movement to break down "the solid wall of male chauvinism . . . a social problem of national significance not at all confined to our struggle for personal liberation within the Movement."[17]

The 1967 SDS Convention for New Politics generated women's groups in New York and Chicago. Some SDS chapters already had women's caucuses with varying degrees of autonomy. University of Chicago SDS women formed their own independent group, the Women's Radical Action Project, gaining public visibility for a sit-in to protest the 1968 firing of sociology professor Marlene Dixon due to "her radical politics and her gender." Dixon and Loyola University professor Naomi Weisstein formed a caucus at the New University Conference. Another group, the Gallstones, retained ties with the men of the New Left and the underground press.[18]

The rapidity of the phenomenon of women organizing within the New Left stirred male animosity. Some women were hissed and thrown out of the June 1968 SDS Convention. A debate on whether sexism or capitalism was the greater problem resulted in that winter's SDS Resolution on Women, reluctantly supported by the men: "Women are not oppressed as a class but they are oppressed as women within each class." It admitted that "male supremacy persists in the movement today" and that "a socialist revolution could take place which maintains the secondary position of women in society. Therefore, the liberation of women must become a conscious part of our struggle for people's liberation." SDS explained women's oppression in material terms: "Women form a reserve army of labor to bring down wages; they save the economy enormous costs by performing free services such as housekeeping; and they help obscure the class nature of society." Male authors of the position paper explained away their sexism with self-serving excuses couched in leftist rhetoric: "The nature of women's material conditions places them in a relationship which acts as a lightning rod for men's justified frustration, anger, and shame in their inability to control their natural and social environment. This means . . . that the original forces of their exploitation and oppression are transformed and diverted into oppressive violence towards those who have even less power than they do (e.g. women)." In this document, as in SDS itself, women were parenthetical.[19]

SDS activists Kathy McAfee and Myrna Wood responded by urging a new movement for working-class women. At the same time, they developed a feminist rhetoric that transcended class: "Male chauvinism—the attitude that women are the passive and inferior servants of society and of men—sets women apart from the rest of the working class." Roxanne Dunbar complained in 1969 "that women have had a separate historical development from men" and "have developed separately as a caste. The original division of labor in all societies was by sex. . . . A caste system is a *social system*, which is economically based. It is not a set of attitudes or just some mistaken ideas which must be understood and dispensed with. . . . [It] does not exist just in the mind. Caste is deeply rooted in human history, dates to the division of labor by sex, and is the very basis of the present social system in the United States."[20]

These women were inspired by Juliet Mitchell's widely circulated essay, "Women: The Longest Revolution," first published in the *New Left Review* (November/December 1966). Mitchell found socialist theory as well as feminism not comprehensive enough to explain the complex ideological underpinnings of women's oppression. Both socialist and feminist reform plans were piecemeal and doomed to failure. Until changes occurred in all four aspects of women's status—production (work and earnings), reproduction, socialization of children, and sexuality—the liberation of women would not be complete. Similarly, New Left sociologist Marlene Dixon called for radical change in the name of "the whole soft underbelly of this society"—women as well as other oppressed minorities. Acceptance of theories like Mitchell's as well as reaction against sexism within the New Left impelled many politicos to break away into feminism. Jane Alpert made the transition from politicos to radical feminism through participation in New York City Consciousness Raising groups where she met Ellen Willis and Robin Morgan, a veteran writer from the New Left magazine *Rat*.[21]

Alpert engineered the January 1970 women's take over of the *Rat* with other staff women, intending to publish a women's issue of the paper, retaliating for the "sex-and-porn special" produced by the male staff. Morgan brought in reinforcements of about thirty women and wrote an essay, "Good-Bye to All That," a bitter indictment of male radicals and call for a women's revolution, signaling a schism in the New Left. Under the banner of the Women's Liberation Front (WLF), women considered their own interests and decried the male chauvinism inherent in leftist politics. Alpert with others published the *Rat* for two more years as a feminist periodical before she fled "underground" to avoid prosecution for previous Weatherman activities.[22]

Radical Feminists

The first radical feminists had roots in the New Left. Shulamith Firestone returned home from the 1967 National Conference for New Politics (NCNP) so disgusted that she and Pam Allen founded New York Radical Women (NYRW), an organization which participated in anti-war and other activities. They declared, "We ask not if something is 'reformist,' 'radical,' 'revolutionary,' or 'normal.' We ask: is it good for women or bad for women?" They were "critical of all past ideology."[23]

At a large Washington anti-war demonstration in January 1968, the New York radicals joined with about five thousand women of the Jeannette Rankin Peace Brigade, a coalition of more moderate pacifists. The younger women had a larger agenda, however. A NYRW faction attracted several hundred women to a torchlight march to Arlington Cemetery to stage the "Burial of Traditional Womanhood." There, Kathy Amatniek spoke, drawing upon her experience in the civil rights movement and coining the slogan "Sisterhood is Powerful," a rallying cry justifying coalitions of radical women with egalitarian feminists and with any other women based on common concerns of gender.[24]

Radical feminist fervor impelled Ti-Grace Atkinson, once a Republican and head of New York's NOW chapter, to walk out of NOW with several other dissidents, including Florynce Kennedy, on 17 October 1968 because of "irreconcilable ideological conflicts" between those who "want women to have the opportunity to be oppressors, too, and those who want to destroy oppression itself." New by-laws retained a hierarchy of offices and official committees; and Atkinson wished to set up a radical system of collectivism and anonymity. While Betty Friedan aimed "to get women into positions of power," Atkinson felt that women should "get rid of positions of power." She also charged that NOW was not truly "feminist," especially concerning sex roles, marriage, family, abortion, and class. The charismatic Atkinson, a Columbia graduate student in political philosophy, modeled her October 17th Movement after a revolutionary cadre, renaming it The Feminists. Atkinson embarrassed mainstream feminists, as when she shared the stage with Eunice Kennedy Shriver at Catholic University and publicly mocked Shriver's belief in the Catholic doctrine of the immaculate conception of Jesus.[25]

Between 1967 and 1968, the term "women's liberation" remained under debate. Many preferred simply to call themselves "radical women."

Atkinson claims to have used the term "radical feminism" first in a 13 June 1968 press statement urging the release of Valerie Solanas, Andy Warhol's would-be assassin. Some felt that the term "feminist" was too general and did not distinguish them from liberal NOW members, while others argued that all feminists were inherently radical. These nascent, diverse groups came together in November 1968 at the first national women's liberation conference in Chicago. There, Amatniek announced that she would henceforth be known by a "matrilineal name form"—Sarachild. Variations on radical feminism quickly appeared across the country. In the UCLA Women's Liberation Front, SDS member and co-founder Devra Weber recalls, "the radical feminists were opposed to patriarchy, but not necessarily to capitalism. In our group at least, they opposed so-called male dominated national liberation struggles."[26]

Many radical women became disillusioned with the macho tactics of leftist colleagues. Shulamith Firestone remained in the New Left until an incident at a Counter-Inaugural demonstration in January 1969, when her mention from the podium of women's "oppression" provoked catcalls like "take her off the stage and fuck her!" Ellen Willis, *Village Voice* writer, marked radical feminist secession from the "patriarchal" New Left with an article in the *Guardian* (February 1969): "We have come to see women's liberation as an independent revolutionary movement, potentially representing half the population. We intend to make our own analysis of the system and put our interests first, whether or not it is convenient for the Left." Willis and friends began to refer to "sex-class" rather than simply class concerns, while still criticizing egalitarian feminists for striving for "formal equality within a racist, class-stratified system."[27]

In 1969 Willis and Firestone founded the Redstockings, modeled on the radical black power organizations. The "Redstocking Manifesto" urged the "pro-woman line" developed by the collaboration of Kathie Sarachild and Carol Hamisch of New York and Judith Brown and Carol Giardina of Gainesville, Florida. They insisted "that criticism of women—even any one woman—was a case of 'blaming the victim'." Redstockings proclaimed: "We are an oppressed class. . . . exploited as sex objects, breeders, domestic servants, and cheap labor. . . . considered inferior beings whose only purpose is to enhance men's lives. . . . We reject the idea that women consent to or are to blame for their own oppression. . . . We take the woman's side in everything."[28]

The Manifesto demanded that men stop oppressing women in personal relationships as well as in larger social and cultural terms, explaining "Because we have lived so intimately with our oppressors, in isolation from each other, we have been kept from seeing our personal suffering as a political condition." Redstockings used blunt anti-male rhetoric: "All men receive economic, sexual, and psychological benefits from male supremacy. All men have oppressed women" and were "male chauvinist pigs." They explained, "Women's submission is not the result of brainwashing, stupidity or mental illness but of continual, daily pressure from men. We do not need to change ourselves, but to change men." This would also lessen exploitation of racism, capitalism, and imperialism, "extensions of male supremacy . . . the oldest, most basic form of domination," they believed.[29]

Redstockings developed cooperative, collective, or communal strategies and structures through smaller, informal groups called phalanxes, later developed into Brigades. They emphasized sisterhood, spoke positively of everything women did, and developed a new feminist language and psychology. They made the personal political, opting for "life-style revolutions" as individuals, fostered through the process of "consciousness raising." Redstockings organized abortion rights marches and two Congresses to Unite Women. By 1970, Redstockings existed in places like Ann Arbor and San Francisco.[30]

On 5 December 1969 the New York Radical Women became the New York Radical Feminists (NYRF). Diane Crowthers and Cellestine Ware joined Firestone and Koedt to form the Stanton-Anthony Brigade. Ware was one of the few black women to join the radicals. That December, NYRF also issued a manifesto, "The Politics of Ego," drafted by Firestone and Koedt, protesting the leftist feminist view that oppression was rooted in class and capitalism and asserting that male chauvinism had more to do with a psychology of power that required oppression of women to reinforce male "ego satisfaction," machismo, or "male chauvinism," and was manifested only secondarily in economic relationships. Activists like Firestone saw the liberationists as truly revolutionary—the beginning of a new era. Like French Revolutionaries who marked a watershed in history by renumbering years, she named the New York journal *Notes from the First Year*. According to Kathie Sarachild, she was "asserting immediate consciousness of present history, daring to take herself . . . and the present generation seriously."[31]

Willis explains that radical feminists coined the terms "sexism" and "sexual politics" to make the point "that sexuality, family life, and the relations between men and women were not simply matters of individual choice, or even of social custom, but involved the exercise of personal and institutional power and raised vital questions of public policy." Sexism was "a social system . . . whose intent and effect was to give men power over women . . . [It] enforced women's prescribed behavior with a wide range of sanctions that included social condemnation, ridicule, ostracism, sexual rejection and harassment, the withholding of birth control and abortion, economic deprivation, and male violence condoned by the state."[32]

Willis remembers, "more than any other issue, abortion embodied and symbolized our fundamental demand—not merely formal equality for women but genuine self-determination." Feminists aimed at nothing less than "women cut loose from their anatomical destiny; women putting their needs and desires before their age-old obligation to create and nurture new life; women having sex on their own terms and without fear; women becoming players on the world stage instead of providing the backdrop—and the safety net—for men."[33]

Some radical feminists believed the only solution was rejection of all men, calling on women "to isolate themselves from men in order to come to terms with what it means to be female." Heterosexual relations, they argued, were inherently power related. The New York based group The Feminists set up a quota in 1969 whereby no more than a third of members could be married or living with a man. They emphasized "sisterhood" or "female solidarity, respect for women as women, support for all women by women." "Sisterhood is Powerful" became a slogan on buttons, T-shirts, and banners at rallies; but positive bonding soon gave way to an exclusivity rejecting even sympathetic male participation in events. The Furies in Washington, D.C., was the leading voice of "political lesbianism," arguing that all women should become lesbians regardless of erotic inclination. This lesbian/separatist faction attracted considerable media attention to the dismay of conservatives like Friedan who disliked the "lavender menace"; and anti-feminists tried to convince the public that all feminists were of this persuasion. Inside the movement, the "gay-straight split" proved divisive and destructive, especially on a local level.[34]

Many of the liberationists rejected formal organizational structures and tried to make group meetings as democratic as possible. The Feminists devised a "disc system" to guarantee equal participation and keep individuals from dominating meetings. Every woman received the same number of discs at the meeting's start, surrendered one each time she spoke, and could no longer speak when she ran out of discs; but the system did not limit the length of the contribution which sometimes turned into monologue or speech.

By the end of 1969, women's liberation organizations existed from Florida to Canada, from Miami to Seattle and in countless cities and towns in between. Some counted 35 groups in the San Francisco and Berkeley-Oakland East Bay area, 30 in Chicago, and at least 50 in New York City. One of 25 in the Boston area was Bread and Roses, a self-proclaimed "socialist women's liberation" group; another, Cell 16, a closed, nearly secret group listed Abby Aldrich Rockefeller as a member. Formed by Roxanne Dunbar (1939–), Dana Densmore, and others, Cell 16 did not recruit new members but urged interested women to form their own "groups." Dunbar and friends left for New Orleans in 1970 to found the Southern Female Rights Union for the poor. By 1970, about 10,000 women or more were involved in groups. Communication between groups was informal. Despite a conclave of twenty women from seven states at Sandy Spring, Maryland, in August 1968 and a larger meeting of 200 in Chicago that November, no efforts were made to form a national confederation, let alone an authoritarian, hierarchical, structured organization.[35]

These women used various tactics to spread their message. Demonstrations were often small in scale, but gained media attention—which was often negative, focused on outrageousness. LBJ ordered FBI surveillance. In September 1968, women stormed the Miss America pageant in Atlantic City. Although the winner usually received a monetary prize including scholarship money, feminists criticized the exploitative ideals of beauty with which they believed most American women could not or should not compete. Charging that the winner was actually selling her body along with consumers' goods, they carried signs proclaiming: "Cattle Parades Are Degrading to Human Beings," "Can Make-Up Cover Up the Wounds of Our Oppression?" "Miss America Is Alive and Angry—in Harlem," "Girls Crowned—Boys Killed," "No More Beauty Standards—Everyone Is Beautiful." The protest received ten times more coverage in the *New York Times* and other newspapers than that year's winner—Judith Ann Ford, Miss Illinois. Television cameras panning the auditorium focused on an immense banner proclaiming

"WOMEN'S LIBERATION." Organizer Carol Hamisch judged that the protest might have been a mistake because of the "antiwoman-ism . . . presented to the public to the detriment of the action."[36]

Contrary to journalists' reports, however, feminists did not burn their bras in the 1968 and 1969 Miss America protests. Using "street theater" tactics, they dumped bras along with other everyday symbols of women's "oppression," sexual objectification, and "enslavement"—girdles, high-heeled shoes, curlers, make-up, false eyelashes, dish-cloths, steno pads, and magazines like *Family Circle*, *Vogue*, *Ladies' Home Journal*, *Cosmopolitan*, and *Playboy*—into a "freedom trash can." They crowned a live sheep, bedecked in yellow and blue ribbons, singing "Ain't she sweet, making profits off her meat" and "There she is, Miss America!" They proclaimed the human winner a "degraded mindless-boob girlie symbol." Hecklers challenged them with jeers: "Lesbians!" "Screwy, frustrated women."[37]

On 12 February 1969, birthday of Abraham Lincoln, "the Great Emancipator," feminist picketers—both NOW members and radicals—and media turned out in blizzard conditions to picket and sit in at the Plaza Hotel's Oak Room, which excluded women daily from noon to three, thus banning female executives from one of New York's power centers—a policy that had been in place for sixty years. Betty Friedan was reluctant to participate, although she herself had once been turned away there.

Founders of the Women's International Terrorist Conspiracy from Hell (WITCH), a NYRW offshoot, wanted to "raise the consciousness" of American women across the political spectrum. WITCH enlisted other radical feminists for specific actions at the Counter-Inaugural in January of 1969, including a public burning of voter registration cards. Barbara Mehrhof and Shulamith Firestone received an understandably angry rejection to their invitation to the aged veteran feminist Alice Paul that she join them in repudiating suffrage as an agent for change.[38]

These tactics, "zap" actions, and guerrilla street theater events staged to attract media attention, backfired by playing into the hands of anti-feminist journalists intent on discrediting the women's liberation move-ment. Members appeared, dressed as witches, in public places like the American Telephone and Telegraph Company or the New York Stock Exchange, "hexing" the male establishment. Rayna Rapp (1946–) or-ganized University of Michigan SDS women into a WITCH chapter that invaded the state legislature to lobby for abortion law reform: "We hexed these old men with a chant about how they were going to die because they were all men and they were controlling women's bodies." In 1969, New York WITCH invaded a bridal fashion show singing "Here come the slaves, off to their graves," following the example set the previous year by radical feminists in San Francisco. That year, The Feminists picketed the New York City Hall marriage license bureau, proclaiming that marriage enslaved women. Actions by such "hard core" radical feminist groups were often limited in scale, organized by a dozen or so individuals on the local level. Such was the "nude-in" staged at Iowa's Grinnell College to protest a *Playboy* journalist on campus.[39]

At the sixties' end, many feminists rightly believed their movement had barely begun. The Women's Strike for Equality declared for 26 August 1970, fiftieth anniversary of ratification of the women's suffrage amendment, was to mark the official new beginning, the start of the revolution; and it united NOW with radical feminists, at least for the occasion. It was much more successful than organizers had envisioned. Kate Millett optimistically declared at a march of about 10,000 on New York's Fifth Avenue, "Today is the beginning of a new movement. Today is the end of millenniums of oppression."[40]

Thousands of women went out "on strike" in other cities as well, protesting inequities, demanding legal abortions, day care, and equal educational and employment opportunities. Miami feminists staged a "liberation garden party," smashing dishware. Karate instructors gave self-defense lessons to women in Philadelphia's Rittenhouse Square. Housewives in Los Angeles marched with their pots and pans. Two thousand marched in San Francisco. A small girl bore a sign, "I Am Not a Barbie Doll." Placards revealed rage, determination, and even humor: "Don't Cook Dinner Tonight—Starve a Rat." Or, "Repent, Male Chauvinists, Your World is Coming to an End." In several cities, small groups of women "liberated" male-only restaurants, bars, and clubs. Others invaded corporate offices protesting advertisements portraying women as "servants and sex objects."

The day was devoted to real issues as well as street theatre—demands for child care, safe and legal abortions, and equal opportunities in education and employment. The secretaries who marched in Boston with their typewriters, along with a thousand other demonstrators, would be among the founders of the nation's first clerical union, Nine to Five. NBC's *Today* show focused on women's rights with an all-female cast. Brandishing signs reading "Storks Fly. Why Can't Mothers?," stewardesses picketed airlines, protesting policies not to employ married women, let alone mothers with children, the start of a labor movement which transformed the job description to the non-gender-specific "flight attendant," which men as well as mothers and middle-aged women could fill.

While some radical feminists took to the streets, took over magazines like the *Ladies' Home Journal*, or formed small organizations characterized by outrageous rhetoric, others took to their studies and wrote tracts and feminist theory that would energize the women's movement in the seventies. The movement proselytized and became cohesive through a growing number of informal newsletters and other publications. Between 1968 and 1972, the number of regular periodicals increased from two to over sixty, some with national circulation. The first was Chicago's *The Voice of the Women's Liberation Movement* (1967 to March 1969), formed by former SDS member Joreen Freeman. An example and model for others was *Notes from the First Year*, a mimeographed journal first published in June 1968 by the New York Radical Women, issued in three consecutive years and primarily distributed locally.

Other publications were *No More Fun and Games: A Journal of Female Liberation* and *The Second Wave* out of Boston, *Everywoman* in Los Angeles, *Off the Pedestal* in San Francisco's Bay Area, New York's *Up from Under* and *Majority Report*, *Women's Liberation* in Kansas City, *The Female Liberation Newsletter* in Minneapolis-St. Paul, and *Women: A Journal of Liberation*, from Baltimore but covering national events. Editors Roxanne Dunbar and Dana Densmore stated that *No More Fun* "reflects our intense rage, isolation and fear." Washington, D.C., produced three periodicals—*Quest*, *off our backs*, and *The Furies*. Numbers and titles, as well as sporadic publications—*Aphra*, *Liberation, Inc.*, *Majority Report*, *Women*, and Berkeley's *It Ain't Me Babe*—proliferated as groups also took advantage of the relatively new, do-it-yourself printing technology marketed by Xerox in 1960, an improvement over the older mimeograph. In 1969 Marlene Dixon judged that "the papers and manifestoes written and circulated would surely comprise two very large volumes if published, but this literature is almost unknown outside of women's liberation."[41]

Notes contained news items as well as essays that became central movement documents—Anne Koedt's "The Myth of the Vaginal Orgasm" and Pat Mainardi's "The Politics of Housework." Topics ranged from "the enslavement of beauty, the temptation of becoming a beautiful 'object,' admonitions against shaving your legs or under your arms, polemics on the politics of housework, essays on sexist language, and . . . use of the term 'lesbian' to condemn any woman who acted independently." The November 1968 *No More Fun* focused "On the Temptation to be a Beautiful Object" with contributions by Dana Densmore, Roxanne Dunbar, Jayne West, Jeanne Lafferty, Betsy Warrior, and Lisa Leghorn.[42]

Other radical publications printed articles on the new movement. Sociologist Marlene Dixon wrote "Why Women's Liberation?" in *Ramparts* (December 1969). Although she recognized the commonality of psychological oppression experienced by women, she attacked "the mysticism of sisterhood" and urged movement avoidance of "female chauvinism," "racism," and "liberal guilt." The *Village Voice*, more established as a countercultural periodical, gave liberationists positive press. *Voice* editors sent Vivian Gornick in 1969 to cover the "libbers." She remembers, "I came back converted." Her article proclaimed, "The Next Great Moment in History is Theirs." She recognized parallels between feminism and civil rights, recognizing her own "'nigger mentality,' the terrible inertia of spirit that accompanies the perhaps irrational but deeply felt conviction that no matter what one does, one is going to end up a thirty-five-year-old busboy." Later Gornick waxed poetic about the heady atmosphere of those years, "bliss was it in that dawn to be alive. Not an I-love-you in the world could touch it. There was no other place to be, except with each other. We lived then, all of us, inside the loose embrace of feminism. It was as though we'd been released from a collective lifetime of silence."[43]

Perhaps the most radical and influential publication was Shulamith Firestone's *Dialectic of Sex* (1970), blending Marxism with feminism, calling for elimination of sexual class by a revolutionary seizure of control of reproduction analogous to the need for proletarian revolt and seizure of means of production. She called radical feminism intrinsically revolutionary, even if not directly informed by leftist ideology. In Firestone's utopian plan, artificial reproduction techniques would enable women to monopolize control of their own bodies and child care would be provided by small groups of professional adults rather than by mothers confined to the home. These solutions would end all social domination based in the "tyranny of the biological family" but would also make traditional motherhood obsolete.

Firestone identified "an oppressive 'culture of romance,' fetishized eroticism ('the displacement of other social/affective needs onto sex') and sexual privatization of women ('the process whereby women are blinded to their generality as a class which renders them invisible as individuals to the male eye')." She attacked the male belief that "all women are basically alike—they all like compliments about physical attributes and like to be classified as 'blonds, redheads, or brunettes," a practice that "dupes women into confusing their individuality with their sexuality . . . dependent on men for ultimate realization and evaluation."[44]

Also early and influential was Kate Millett's *Sexual Politics* (1970), developed from a 1968 speech to Cornell feminists into her Columbia dissertation, awarded distinction and immediately published. Millett provided a new approach to cultural criticism drawing upon history, psychology, anthropology, and sociology and specifically targeting male literary giants—D. H. Lawrence, Henry Miller, and Norman Mailer among others. She drew connections between literature, criticism, other cultural agents, and reactionary politics of which sexism was one manifestation but the only one she discussed, omitting consideration of racism or imperialism and barely addressing class. She insisted on the long unused capability of criticism "of seizing upon the larger insights which literature affords into the life it describes, or interprets, or even distorts." Going against the critical trends persisting in the sixties—New Criticism and literary history—she took "into account the larger cultural context in which literature is conceived and produced." She won acclaim as a pioneer, one of the first to formulate serious feminist criticism.[45]

Millett decried patriarchy or "power-structured relationships" as "the most pervasive ideology of our culture" used by one group, essentially male, to govern others, to create "vast gray stockades of sexual reaction" or the last caste system, a remnant of feudalism. She attacked chivalry as etiquette's token substitute for true respect and equal rights for women. Although she admitted that chivalry was better than "machismo" or "oriental behavior," she realized "how much of a concession traditional chivalrous behavior represents—a sporting kind of reparation to allow the subordinate female certain means of saving face. While a palliative to the injustice of woman's social position, chivalry is also a technique for disguising it." Such was the kindness of master for servant, a palliative behavior to please in the shortrun and in the longrun to keep women in their place. This idea reverberated through a generation of women, no longer pleased when men gestured to open doors or help them be seated; and it revolutionized social formalities. Millett asserted that cultural forms effect as well as reflect reality, arguing that artistic violence presages violence in real life. The impact of *Sexual Politics* on the general public, feminists, and scholars was immediate: it sold 80,000 copies in its first six months.[46]

Although *Sexual Politics* was acclaimed as pioneering, it was not produced in an intellectual vacuum. Millett drew inspiration from the literary analysis in Simone de Beauvoir's *The Second Sex* (1949); but *Sexual Politics* was the first major work of literary criticism of the new feminism and of great "ovular" importance in development of subsequent feminist literary and cultural criticism. This major literary event helped launch the "women's renaissance" of the seventies; but feminist literary analysis was not unprecedented. Mary McCarthy collected critical essays on literature and the arts written between 1946 and 1961 in *On the Contrary: Articles of Belief* (1962); and the difficult-to-read *Thinking About Women* (1968) by Mary Ellmann criticized the sexism pervading literary culture, focusing on women's voices in literature and the negative male response to it—"phallic criticism." Ellmann wrote that men "produced and legitimated society's reservoir of knowledge" in which "men were central, positive, various, active, admirable, while women were sex-objects, seen only in relation to men; women were 'other,' where they were deemed to exist at all." Chapters covered "Feminine Stereotypes," gender-based "Differences in Tone," "Phallic Criticism," and "Responses" of women writers to personal experience. She blamed academe, especially graduate literature departments, for systematically excluding women from admission and hence making the professional teaching, creation, and criticism of literature a male domain. Ellmann charged, "Books by women are treated as though they themselves were women, and criticism embarks, at its happiest, upon an intellectual measuring of busts and hips."[47]

Like Firestone, Millett linked literature to larger trends in society, politics, and culture. Both attacked Freudianism; but Millett extended her criticism to Erik Erikson who replaced the theory of penis envy with "uterine glorification . . . a gentler form of persuasion." She decried the pattern in which science had systematically rationalized male power in biological-physiological terms, thus giving "patriarchy logical as well as historical origin." She had no patience for "liberals" like Erikson who favored women in the public realm only because of innate virtues—"realism of householding, responsibility of upbringing, resourcefulness of peacekeeping, and devotion to healing" traditionally exercised in the private sphere. "One cannot but note," she observed, "that the force of this recommendation is to urge that women participate in political power not because such is their human right, but because an extension of their proper feminine sphere into the public domain would be a social good." Millett called this an argument "from expediency rather than justice." But Erikson echoed earlier social feminists—from Jane Addams to Eleanor Roosevelt. Discarding their ideas represented a radical rejection of a main current in earlier feminism and of basic concepts of the nature of women deeply embedded in American culture.[48]

Sexual Politics struck painful nerves among male critics. In a lengthy diatribe against "The Middle Class Mind of Kate Millett" in the December 1970 *Harper's*, Irving Howe called Millett names—a "feckless," "morally shameful," "squalid" "female impersonator," yet "brilliant in an unserious way." He finds "that such a farrago of blunders, distortions, vulgarities, and plain nonsense could be passed by the English Department of Columbia University for the doctoral degree is an interesting fact." George Stade, one of Millett's thesis advisors, told *Time*, "Reading the book is like sitting with your testicles in a nutcracker." Mailer got even more personal, in an extended review, "The Prisoner of Sex," combining confession and exhibitionism, and published in *Harper's* in March 1971. Mailer complained that "his ghost-phallus was apparently being chewed half to death by a squadron of enraged Amazons, an honor guard of revolutionary vaginas." Gore Vidal was only slightly gentler in the *New York Review of Books*, charging that Millett had opened up more than a Pandora's box of feminist rage. *Time* dubbed Millett "the Mao-Tse-Tung of Women's Liberation," noting that "she and her sisters" would despise such a description "for the movement rejects the notion of leaders and heroines as creations of the media— and mimicry of the ways that men use to organize their world."[49]

Sexual Politics and the author's starring role in the new movement drew attention to Millett's private life and made her controversial, even notorious. Millett raised sexual preference as an issue for discussion. At a forum sponsored by Gay People at Columbia University, Teresa Juarez, a Radicalesbians member, forced Millett to admit publicly that, despite being happily married, she was a lesbian. This was not news for those in the movement, since Millett had participated in a "zap action" takeover of the second annual Congress to Unite Women that May by forty lesbians who presented their position paper, "The Woman-Identified Woman," which redefined lesbianism as "the quintessential act of political solidarity with other women."[50]

Time sent a reporter with a tape recorder to confirm the revelation; and its cover story, "Women's Lib: A Second Look," proclaimed that until *Sexual Politics* "the movement had no coherent theory to buttress its intuitive passions, no ideologue to provide chapter and verse for its assault on patriarchy." *Time* belittled the 35-year-old author as "a sometime sculptor and longtime brilliant misfit in a man's world." It used her for a "lesbian-baiting," media exploitation of diversity of choice as a means of discrediting all feminists and predicted, "Kate Millett herself contributed to the growing skepticism about the movement by acknowledging at a recent meeting that she is bisexual. The disclosure is bound to discredit her as a spokeswoman for her cause, cast further doubt on her theories, and reinforce the views of those skeptics who routinely dismiss all liberationists as lesbians." Millett felt *Time* used her "as a club to beat the movement."[51]

Negative publicity forced even conservative feminists to come to terms with lesbians' social and cultural dilemma and precipitated an emergency strategy meeting in Dolores Alexander's New York apartment. Although Friedan lived in that building, she absented herself. Realizing that the media was ready to use Millett's book to discredit even moderate feminists, she was determined not to associate herself with it. But Ivy Bottini, New York NOW President, declared that the "real test of sisterhood" had begun: "Lesbianism as an issue had never before surfaced [publicly] in any earlier phase of feminism."[52]

At a rally a few days before the conference, some women distributed lavender armbands to marchers for abortion and child-care centers. Their leaflets read: "It is not one woman's sexual experience that is under attack. . . . It is the freedom of all women to openly state values that fundamentally challenge the basic structure of patriarchy. If they succeed in scaring us with words like 'dyke' or 'lesbian' or 'bisexual,' they'll have won. AGAIN. They'll have divided us. AGAIN. Sexism will have triumphed. AGAIN. . . . They can call us all lesbians until such time as there is no stigma attached to women loving women. SISTERHOOD IS POWERFUL!!!" Friedan, presented with an armband, "let the piece of purple cloth fall through her fingers to the floor of the flatbed truck" serving as speakers' stand.[53]

In response, radical feminists led by Ti-Grace Atkinson, Susan Brownmiller, and Florynce Kennedy staged the "Kate Is Great" press conference on 18 December 1970 at New York's Square Methodist Church, decorated with banners reading "We Stand Together as

Women, Regardless of Sexual Preference" and "Is the Statue of Liberty a Lesbian, Too?" Gloria Steinem sat next to Millett, supportively holding her hand. Millett declared, "Women's liberation and homosexual liberation are both struggling towards a common goal: a society free from defining and categorizing people by virtue of gender and/or sexual preference. 'Lesbian' is a label used as a psychic weapon to keep women locked into their male-defined 'feminine role'. . . . A woman is called a lesbian when she functions autonomously. . . . [this is] what women's liberation is all about."[54]

In "The Woman-Identified Woman" in the *Ladder*, Rita Mae Brown identified homophobia as a means used to oppress all women: "Lesbian is a label invented by the Man to throw at any woman who dares to be his equal, who dares to challenge his prerogatives, . . . who dares to assert the primacy of her own needs. . . . in this sexist society, for a woman to be independent means she can't be a woman—she must be a dyke. That in itself should tell us where women are at. It says clearly: woman and person are contradictory terms."[55]

Ti-Grace Atkinson agreed, claiming that "from the conservative beginnings of this [feminist] movement, men have been countering all accusations of injustice toward women with the charge that these accusations were being made by 'just a bunch of lesbians.'" Such lesbian-baiting was exactly what Friedan feared the most because "dyke" (a derogatory term then in most circles) alienated both women and men, and men felt threatened by women who thought them superfluous, at best. Friedan loathed the man-hating rhetoric of the women she felt were going through a stage of "pseudo-radical infantilism." It disturbed many women in the movement and kept others out of it.[56]

As a link between lesbianism and feminism became acknowledged, many forces came together which led to a powerful lesbian-feminist vanguard of the movement. Brown led many lesbians from the older Daughters of Bilitis into radical feminism in 1970. Lesbians like Brown began to play more visible roles even in mainstream women's organizations like the New York City chapter of NOW. Middle-of-the-road feminists were so taken aback by the lesbian positions on issues, however, that some tried to purge them from NOW. Brown resigned, explaining: "Lesbian is the one word that can cause the Executive Committee a collective heart attack." Friedan called lesbians a "lavender menace," while Susan Brownmiller suggested a "lavender herring," not considering them threats to the movement. Even some radical feminists were "skittish if not hostile toward lesbianism." They saw it as "sexual rather than political." Roxanne Dunbar of Boston's Cell 16 argued that "the task of feminism was to get women out of bed rather than change the gender of their partners."[57]

By 1970, some feminist writers declared lesbianism a logical extension of feminism. Older lesbians, whose feminism had until then been "buried under the rubbish of society's views, were able to re-examine in daylight what it was in the first place that made them decide to commit themselves to making women prime in their lives." Millett and others inspired many radical feminists to consider lesbianism as a political statement—the epitome of "the personal is political." The bi-sexual Millett called coitus "a charged microcosm" of "sexual politics"; but her ideas were an articulation, not the cause, of a trend. Women became feminists first and then chose to become lesbians, "not hampered by the weight of all the old images." The New Women found "strength and solidarity in their examination during consciousness-raising of their choice to be lesbians."[58]

Most of them knew nothing of Freudianism and had not internalized the feeling of being sick. Not that such knowledge would have mattered much because these women were coming out in "a society that had far less respect for authority," unlike the fifties, "an era when respect for 'experts' was at a height." New feminist journals and publishing houses provided an antidote against literary images of lesbians from "cheap paperbacks that promised tales of lurid passion." Finally, new lesbians did not come out in isolation. Either they had a support group of women to "help them validate their choice, or—if they had no physical support—they had lesbian-feminist literature, which by 1970 was being published all over the United States in the form of newspapers, newsletters, magazines, pamphlets, and books."[59]

Friedan threatened NOW colleagues with a suit, writes Marcia Cohen, because "this coalition—her coalition—had never asked her permission to make the pro-lesbian statement"; but she did not stop the momentum of feminist indignation. At its 1971 convention, NOW passed a resolution to support lesbians "legally and morally," heeding Millett's plea that the organization acknowledge "the oppression of lesbians as a legitimate concern for feminism." Lesbian-Feminists came out of the closet and out of existing women's organizations, forming groups like "Those Women" (later the Furies Collective) in Washington, D.C. As D'Emilio and Freedman observe, "Throughout the period from 1969 to 1971, women's organizations across the country were wracked by a 'gay-straight' split, as tensions reached the boiling point."[60]

For some, lesbianism was a political imperative for realizing feminist goals. As Charlotte Bunch observed, "Lesbianism threatens male supremacy at its core. . . . Feminists must become lesbians if they hope to end male supremacy." Bunch was a married feminist, organizing women's liberation groups, when she discovered "that lesbians had a certain kind of energy and sense of identity about women that embodied much of what the women's movement was all about. . . . lesbianism provides a positive, very strong, woman-oriented selfhood. Every woman should have that self-identity. . . . I saw that this was a very powerful force for the women's movement, and for the philosophy that feminism was trying to create." These ideas, however, let alone the suggestion of an ultimatum, was not one that even many radical feminists were willing to accept—let alone the average American woman. It would not be until the mid-seventies that NOW and other women's organizations would make major concessions to lesbian issues.[61]

Originally, Ti-Grace Atkinson regarded lesbianism as a "sexual" position and feminism as a "political" one. When she claimed that "lesbianism is based ideologically on the very premise of male oppression, the dynamic of sexual intercourse," she committed the fallacy that Lillian Faderman and Del Martin and Phyllis Lyon tried to counteract, an identification of lesbianism with sexual behavior. For Faderman "'lesbian' describes a relationship in which two women's strongest emotions and affections are directed toward each other. Sexual contact may be a part of the relationship to a greater or lesser degree, or it may be entirely absent." Martin and Lyon open *Lesbian/Woman* with a definition: "A lesbian is a woman whose primary erotic, psychological, emotional, and social interest is in a member of her own sex." Atkinson's initial response to lesbians, in fact to all women, was seen as misogynist because she claimed that "all sex is reactionary and that feminism is revolutionary."[62]

Atkinson also complained that "lesbianism . . . is based on the primary assumption of male oppression, that is, sex. Lesbianism reinforces the sex class system." Yet she came to regard lesbianism as "a kind of code word for female resistance" and "symbolic of feminism as a political movement." Her change in attitude reflects an increasing trend of lesbians coming to terms with themselves in society and the alteration of the women's movement by lesbian-feminists. Martin and Lyon observed, "Both Radicalesbians on the East Coast and Gay Women's Liberation in the West have identified almost wholly with the women's movement and have only an indirect alliance with the homophile movement. Gay Women's Liberation is not an organization, but a state of mind—a group of women who are for 'liberation' in every sense of the word." Lesbianism was no more erotic at its core than was heterosexuality, but lesbians showed themselves to be a powerful political force by the decade's end.[63]

The most powerful definition was formulated by the Radicalesbians in their position paper, "The Woman-Identified Woman" (1970): "A lesbian is the rage of all women condensed to the point of explosion. She is the woman who, often beginning at an extremely early age, acts in accordance with her inner compulsion to be a more complete and freer human being than her society—perhaps then, but certainly later—cares to allow her."[64]

Although Ellen Willis suggests that some feminists "also gave voice to a strong strain of sexual conservatism that viewed sexual freedom— or even sex itself—entirely in terms of male irresponsibility, misogyny, and violence," D'Emilio and Freedman conclude that "despite the negative sexual epithets that were often thrown at them—frigid, castrating, dyke, frustrated, or simply, ugly—women's liberation was not 'antisexual.'" Rather, the movement was attacking the sexual objectification of women, the reduction of women by the media and by men to little more than their sex appeal or their reproductive organs. Feminists disputed the possibility of equality in marriage or in other sexual relationships when women were economically dependent on men or had internalized values that made them doubt their self-worth. To them, the oppression of women had contaminated the sex itself, while the sexual ideology of modern America reinforced female inequality. . . . When women achieved full autonomy, then and only then would 'sexual freedom' have real meaning."[65]

In 1970 Robin Morgan compiled and edited *Sisterhood is Powerful*, the major anthology of readings from the women's movement. With a wide range of voices calling for change, it validated the movement as such and provided texts for further interpretation and development. It recounts how liberationists split from the New Left after realizing that "we were doing the same work in the Movement as out of it: typing the speeches men delivered, making coffee but not policy, being accessories to the men whose politics would supposedly replace the Old Order." Other early overviews were Leslie B. Tanner's *Voices from Women's Liberation* (1970) and William L. O'Neill's *The Woman Movement: Feminism in the United States and England* (1969).[66]

Books by writers outside the United States contributed to American feminism. In *Woman's Estate* (1971), British socialist-feminist Juliet Mitchell describes the tendency of married mothers to display "small-minded, petty jealousy, irrational emotionality and random violence, dependency, competitive selfishness and possessiveness, passivity, a lack of vision and conservatism." She argued for a new interpretation of production to take women's traditional work into account. Australian Germaine Greer cut a swath through the American media by bluntly attacking the oppression of women in *The Female Eunuch* (1970). Publication of these and other feminist books by mainstream, commercial publishers was also a sign of the changing times, signaling recognition of burgeoning public interest in feminism.[67]

Many feminists like Millett realized sexism was deeply ingrained in language as well as culture. Linguist Ethel Strainchamps wrote, "The word man originally meant human being, but males appropriated it." English usage of the word in compounds descriptive of occupations of skill or power—such as chairman, foreman, handyman—traditionally monopolized by males or defined as "men's work," embedded discrimination in society. Feminists wanted to reform language in a sex-neutral way. Many went beyond changing their own names; Varda One suggested new words like girlcott, sheroes, and herstory. Feminists also adapted their own epithets: "male chauvinism," "male chauvinist pigs," "machismo," and "sexism." They coined the term of address "Ms." as a new equivalent to "Mr.," to treat a woman's marital status as irrelevant; the term gained relatively wide acceptance by the end of the 1970s.[68]

Even radical feminists, however, failed to recruit many women of color into their movements, only occasionally addressing issues of meaning for minority women. There was the Free Our Sisters/Free Ourselves demonstration in support of Black Panther women in New Haven; the successful Free Joan Bird Campaign (Bird had defended herself against an attack by a guard, killing him) resulting in her release in July 1970 from a Women's House of Detention after fourteen months; and the successful support for striking telephone workers by women's groups, the Gay Liberation Front, and the Conference for Women in May 1970; but little more. A rapprochement between feminists and black women in the name of Sisterhood did not occur.

Meanwhile, "libbers" or "libbies" became derogatory terms applied to radical feminists by those who considered them un-American in the most clichéd, fundamental way—against Motherhood, if not Apple

Pie. The backlash against radical feminism began even before the sixties' end. Alice Echols reports that "by 1969, the FBI began to spy upon
and infiltrate" the movement, trying to exacerbate factionalism and
"conflicts around class, elitism, and sexual preference" with tactics like
those used against the student and civil rights movements.[69]

Hard-hats, male construction workers, infamous for harassing attractive women passing their urban work sites with wolf whistles, appeared at many feminist demonstrations, taunting women as bra-less
"traitors to their sex." So many opponents engaged in "dyke-baiting,"
accusing activists of sexual deviance. Conservative journalist George
Gilder growled in 1973, "Women's liberation wants to liberate us from
the very institution that is most indispensable to overcoming our present social crisis: the family. They want to make marriage more open,
more flexible, revocable at a time when it is already opening up all over
the country and spewing forth swarms of delinquents and neurotics."
Gilder claimed that women with money demoralize men and weaken
ties to family and community.[70]

Even though the women's movement had barely gotten off the
ground by the sixties' end, a reactionary element began to organize.
Members of New York's Pussycat League, Inc., believed that "the lamb
chop is mightier than the karate chop" and rallied round the slogan,
"Purr, Baby, Purr." Such a message would later make the fame of Mar-
abel Morgan, whose books instructed women in how to be successfully
sexy. The mainstream press, dependent on revenue from advertisers
intent on preserving the buying habits of the traditionalist female consumer, tried to undermine feminist trends through jeremiads against
the social doom liberation would bring. Typical of this approach was
the piece, "Is a Women's Revolution Really Possible?" addressed to the
largely female readership of *McCall's* in 1969. The male authors warned
that if women became truly liberated, all aspects of society—family,
sex, and work—would radically change in ways for which no one was
prepared.[71]

This opinion and tone echoed through the seventies and eighties as
antifeminists, some of them conservative women like Phyllis Schlafly,
made careers out of reactionary polemics. They blamed feminists for a
myriad of social ills and called for a return to traditional "family" values
and gender roles. Although anti-feminists claimed that liberation feminists were anti-motherhood, in fact many radicals decried the "double
burden" of "working" mothers and created the slogan, "Every mother

is a working mother." But even some liberal feminists like Betty Friedan revealed a deep-seated antagonism to radical feminism, denouncing "sexual politics" as promoting man-hating and sex warfare.[72]

Yet the radical feminist critique of sexuality's role in culture did have some concrete effects in the seventies in the reform of penal codes for rape, eliminating in some places questions about the victim's sexual history and raising the notion that rape is not a crime of sexual passion but an act of deranged violence. Twenty-five states completely rewrote their laws in response to feminist ideas about the crime, and almost all states made some changes. New terms such as "sexual harassment," "date rape," and even "marital rape," drawn from radical feminist critiques entered the vernacular language and even the law—either legislated by states or adjudicated internally by corporations and colleges.[73]

Through the seventies and eighties, feminism's gains repelled some veteran feminists no longer in control of the movement. Feeling bypassed, some media stars modified their original stances, especially over sexuality, in a spirit of conservative revisionism. Germaine Greer tempered her call for extreme sexual emancipation from her best-selling *The Female Eunuch* (1970) and proclamations made on many television talk shows. She proclaimed her reactionary *Sex and Destiny* (1984) an "attack upon the ideology of sexual freedom," even touting chastity, abstinence, arranged marriages—asexuality as liberating. Friedan reacted against what she called feminist "extremism" in *The Second Stage* (1981) and numerous public appearances. To this day, she criticizes feminists working against rape and sexual violence, let alone lesser injustices, as "wallowing in that victim-state." Indeed, the mercurial Friedan lashes back angrily when asked why the term "feminism" has taken on negative connotations in the public mind, perhaps aware that with her growing conservatism she, as well as the media and reactionaries, not just the outrageousness of some radicals, has played a role in that process in the wake of the sixties.[74]

Consciousness Raising

Consciousness Raising (CR) groups developed all over the nation in the late sixties to politicize individual women through informal, confessional discussions with friends about experiences of discrimination in their personal lives. The Redstockings organized some of the first cell group "bitch sessions," and each meeting attempted to spawn another group. Other groups were formed on a grassroots, informal, local level, often called simply "our group." Some of the first developed from other reform movements. Formation of the first "women's groups" were announced in the Boston area at day-long anti-war conferences at M.I.T. and attended by women active in the anti-draft movement. The group that attracted Sue Thrasher, first Executive Secretary of the Southern Student Organizing Committee (SSOC) and only female officer, met weekly with women staff members of *The Great Speckled Bird*, an Atlanta underground newspaper, who complained about discrimination within the movement. Cathy Cade's group grew out of Civil Rights in New Orleans when "everybody started talking about the ridicule that they had to go through from the men in their lives to come to this one meeting." They concluded that they, as women, had something important to discuss.[75]

Based on her experience with the prototypical Redstockings' Consciousness Awakening Women's Liberation Group, Kathie Sarachild predicted in 1968 that Consciousness Raising would be a "radical weapon." It was based on the Chinese practice of "speaking bitterness" but was also influenced by similar gatherings among civil rights workers. Sarachild was mistaken, however, about the radicalism; the CR movement, like women's liberation in general, involved primarily educated, white, middle-class women who rallied together under the slogan "The personal is political" to tackle the problems of their everyday lives, issues involving relationships, sexuality, marriage, motherhood, and work, and to learn what it meant to be feminist. It was not a "youth" movement, since many early CR members were in their late twenties or thirties.[76]

At best, CR encouraged realization, wrote one participant, that "married or not, our bodies had ownership by many: men, doctors, clothes and cosmetic manufacturers, advertisers, churches, schools—everyone but ourselves." A major conversation topic was sexuality, the so-called "sexual revolution," and objectification of women as "sexual objects." In Boston, Dana Densmore and friends in the Bread and Roses Collective conceived of a "declaration of independence" from the tyranny of sexuality. She explains, "Under the banner of 'not denying our sexuality' and pointing to repression in the past . . . many of us now embrace sexuality and its expression completely uncritically. . . . Sexual relations in the world today are oppressive. . . . Sex is everywhere. It's forced down our throats. It's the great sop. . . . It makes us look as if we're free and active . . . and people seem to believe that sexual freedom is freedom." Meredith Tax, also in Bread and Roses, agreed, "Any man has this power as man, the dominant sex, to dehumanize women, even to herself. No woman can have an autonomous self unaffected by such encounters," such as the whistles and catcalls of construction workers or the leering strangers who "make her a participant in their fantasies" against her will.[77]

Criticism of CR began early, especially in San Francisco's *Women's Page*, a 1969 newsletter. Ti-Grace Atkinson and The Feminists recognized the possible benefits in alerting women to sources of personal oppression; but they warned that new sources of oppression might result in the form of "prison guards," women within the groups like those outside, who dictated standards of behavior and exercised dictatorial leadership. Groups urged gender separatism. One man remembers how threatened he felt, returning home in the evenings when his wife's CR group met in their Brooklyn apartment. He had to quietly bypass the living room where the group stood in a circle, arms outstretched with clenched fists like Black Panthers, singing Helen Reddy's "I Am Woman" (1971); divorce followed shortly thereafter.[78]

CR participant and revisionist Sylvia Ann Hewlett observes, "the focus was on individual redemption, not on promoting societal change." CR "prompted emotional and behavioral changes without mobilizing energy for political action." Like new trends in psychological "group therapy," CR permitted catharsis, frank expression of discontentment and rage, rewarding individual soul-searching testimony with peer support. Ironically, despite the feminist caveat that "there are no personal solutions," CR took women off the streets and thrust them back into their homes. Female friends lounging cross-legged on ochre-colored shag rugs in suburban recreation rooms or oriental rugs on urban living room floors, may have been a source of personal empowerment for some; but for others the groups were similar to the literary and sewing circles of the 1890s or the bridge clubs of the 1950s. Depending on the participants, the quality of discussions ranged widely from intense social and psychological analysis to practical sharing of advice on health, child-rearing, relationships, job strategies, fashions, and finances.[79]

Women sometimes victimized each other in the movement. Elinor Langer knew from New York radical women's groups that "we tyrannized ourselves with ideas that could only destroy us . . . to be working class or gay was to be in the most revolutionary, therefore correct position. . . . [It] was like a permanent purge in which we always identified with those who confessed. . . . No one could be smarter than anyone else, or prettier, or more talented, or make more money, or do anything significant on her own." Langer discovered that "even though the governing idea of the women's movement of the time was that our-politics-grows-out-of-our-experience, it really couldn't. Our politics made it difficult to be honest about our experience, and sometimes the two were contradictory." Langer's experience is an example of how women could and did terrorize and tyrannize each other with guilt over political issues.[80]

Both mainstream women's organizations and women's liberation groups generally failed to attract the participation of minority women, most of whom felt they had to devote their energies to civil rights. Many black women looked upon the new feminism as an upper-middle-class, white woman's movement that did not address their needs. Nor did CR raise the social consciousness of white, middle-class feminists about the plight of "sisters" of other classes or races; few groups were pluralistic in membership.

Cumulative societal and cultural results of the CR movement are hard to assess. Psychologist Phyllis Chesler observed some immediate results: "Some women started living together; some began living alone for the first time. . . . Some women left their husbands; others began to live with a man. . . . Women stopped giggling and competing with each other for male attention. . . . Some women stopped going to beauty parlors and began to value their time; they needed fewer adornments to 'make up' for being female. . . . consciousness raising was the single activity most universally associated with women's liberation," and "for many women, their weekly 'rap' sessions constituted their only feminist activity. But. . . . there is little evidence to show that the experience mobilized women to push for public policy change." CR was "an approach that deemphasizes broad-based social action in favor of personal redemption." Personal redemption or the narcissistic concern for self differentiated the "me decade" of the seventies from the spirit of the sixties; and thus CR was transitional.[81]

Epilogue: When Did the Sixties End?

As early as August 1966, *Esquire* pronounced it "time to call an end to the sixties," evincing an ideological discontent, a dislike of new styles, and a weariness with a decade marked by a litany of violence, war, and sudden deaths: "Medgar Evers, Marilyn Monroe, Sylvia Plath, four black girls in a Birmingham church, JFK, civil rights workers, Malcolm X, soldiers in Vietnam, Eva Hesse. More would follow—Martin Luther King, Jr., RFK, Diane Arbus, Janis Joplin, people in urban riots, Black Panther leaders, students protesting the war, youth at a rock concert, on and on. Each death seemed to signal the passing of an important aspect of an era characterized by idealism and change in so many facets of American life; each left public mourners who feared that some of the promise of change, articulated by so many, had died along with these exemplars. A crescendo of tragedies, many of them including women either as victims or perpetrator-victims, capped the decade and signaled its spiritual as well as chronological demise in a way and with an intensity unprecedented for the end of other decades.[1]

The most notorious event to cap the sixties was the Tate-LaBianca murders. In 1967, the psychotic, self-proclaimed patriarch Charles Manson established his commune "family" focused on drugs, sex, and violence at a ranch near Los Angeles. The first member was Mary Theresa "Mother Mary" Brunner, a University of California librarian, mother of his son Pooh Bear; more "all-American girls" followed. Leslie "Lulu" Van Houton had been a Girl Scout, A-student, and Homecoming Queen. Patricia "Katie" Krenwinkel, a former Sunday school teacher, once wanted to be a nun. Lynette "Squeaky" Fromme, once a psychology major interested in social work, called Manson "Daddie." Nancy "Brenda" Pittman ran away from home at 16 "because there was nothing to keep me there," echoing the rebelliousness of so many other teen girls who "dropped out" for the counterculture. Manson, like Andy Warhol with his avant garde entourage or Phil Spector with his singers, renamed his women and had them perform for him. They wove their own hair into a ceremonial vest intricately embroidered for Charlie; and they got pregnant, delivering their babies at parties then involving the children in orgies.

Manson's women did whatever he asked, even mass murder, to convince him of their fidelity. On two consecutive August 1969 nights they killed Sharon Tate, eight-months-pregnant wife of Roman Polanski and star of the film, *Valley of the Dolls,* and Abigail Folger, coffee-fortune heiress who did volunteer work in Watts. Adding to the toll of five people collectively stabbed 169 times and shot seven times were neighbors Leon and Rosemary LaBianca the next night. Manson bragged, "In the end, the girls would be just dying to do something for me. . . . They'll work twenty-four hours a day if you give them something to do. I can get along with girls, they give up easier. I can make love to them. Man has this ego thing. . . . With a girl, you can make love with her until she's exhausted. You can make love with her until she gives up her mind." The Manson saga remains an extreme perversion of the sexism women endured within society but especially on its countercultural fringes. Conservative voices capitalized on the story, wrongly calling it a product of the new freedoms of the decade rather than recognizing it as the extreme work of a mad fascist patriarch.[2]

Again, the bloody sixties seemed to finish in a crescendo on 4 May 1970, when Alison Kraus and Sandra Scheurer and two other students were shot to death by the Ohio National Guard at Kent State University in Ohio during protests against Nixon's bombing of Cambodia. Followed by the less publicized killing of students at Jackson State University a few days later, these events seemed to mark the end of the sixties' innocence and the optimism that students could protest to move the "system." The well-known photograph of another young girl kneeling over one of the dead, arms outstretched in horror and grief represents the despair of the generation; she was only a high school student passing by the campus. Universities across the nation precipitously closed for the duration of the semester to avoid further unrest, and student activism was never the same again. Disillusionment and cynicism became the legacy of the decade for many.

Participants, pundits, and critics seized upon each new event to proclaim the turbulent decade's end. Many dated the demise of radicalism with the breakup of SDS, punctuated by the violent end of its offshoot, the Weathermen, as survivors like Bernardine Dohrn, on the FBI ten-most-wanted list, went underground on the first of January 1970. After the deadly explosion of their bomb factory in a Greenwich Village townhouse on 6 March, Kathy Boudin, Cathy Wilkerson, and Jane Alpert joined the ranks of "Weather Sisters" in hiding. By August, radical black activist Angela Davis was also among "the nation's most wanted fugitives," implicated in a hostage taking at the Marin County, California, courthouse resulting in four dead. Voices of those who equated the sixties simply with radicalism and its excesses welcomed these incidents as harbingers of the end of all that.[3]

For women, a powerful legacy of hope for change remained despite divisiveness and controversy in movements fraught with factionalism and animosities. Robin Morgan marked the transition between decades when she split from New Left male organizations in favor of the new feminism, firing "the shot heard round the Left" in January of 1970 with her polemical essay "Good-bye to All That." Morgan chants, "Goodbye, goodbye forever, counterfeit Left, counterleft, male-dominated cracked-glass-mirror reflection of the Amerikan Nightmare. Women are the real Left. We are rising . . . in our unclean bodies; bright glowing mad in our inferior brains." Thousands of ordinary women greeted the seventies as the start of a new feminist era; they marched in cities across the nation on 26 August 1970 to celebrate their political potential on the fiftieth anniversary of receiving suffrage, to proclaim a host of demands, and to display a newly empowered sense of sisterhood. But Alice Echols and Ellen Willis argue that even the new feminism, just launched in 1966 with formation of NOW, went through "explosive rise, wrenching schism," and, by 1973, "abrupt decline."[4]

Some of the defiant euphoria of the sixties faded under economic and social pressures as well as an anti-feminist backlash and a growing conservative spirit. Media helped make "liberation" and "feminism" negatively loaded words, if not epithets in many circles. Many agreed these were extinct by 1976—the Bicentennial. Betty Ford remained a rare "establishment" voice urging ratification of the Equal Rights Amendment, an issue that lost political momentum under Carter's Democratic administration. Phyllis Schlafly successfully mobilized reactionaries against the ERA through her Eagle Forum. As Susan Faludi argues, the "backlash" was underway. The seventies proved that it was difficult to determine intentions toward women based on party affiliation; while the eighties, unfortunately, made "which side you were on politically" all too clear, particularly in terms of women's issues.[5]

The domestic ideology and complacency of the fifties persisted and even had a resurgence. But a sense remained that it was possible for women to imagine living their lives other ways than their mothers had known, especially as more and more women moved into the workplace and demanded greater educational and professional opportunities. Many women, especially those born during and after the 1946–1964 baby boom, began to think and behave in ways that diverged from prescribed gender roles and traditional images. They continued to do so in subsequent decades. They developed new expectations about their places outside as well as inside the family, many aspiring to "have it all." These socioeconomic and attitudinal changes became factors in the "generation gap," as younger women found themselves separated in lifestyle and ideology from the generations before them. Increasing numbers of young women who came of age in the sixties and after postponed marriage to pursue education and careers. This demographic phenomenon as well as growing use of new methods of birth control introduced in the sixties made 1972 the low point in the birth rate, a "baby bust." The real legacy of the sixties was the internalization of feminism and other social ideals by many who did not join NOW or other movements, let alone identify with radicalism.

Predictions and proclamations of the death of the sixties, then and since, were premature, reactions to a growing groundswell in favor of change in American society and culture. From the beginning, the very term "sixties" was used as much as an adjective as a noun, connoting a mindset willing to redefine not only images and styles but also reality, often in radically new ways. That is particularly the case for American women. Many sixties changes were merely cosmetic, matters of style and dress reform. Although sixties revolutionary fashions, the miniskirt and the topless look, quickly passed from vogue, the long quest for women to wear pants for proper occasions in public places, periodically pushed since the mid-nineteenth century, met with success. By 1972, even middle-aged, middle-class women in the Middle America were regularly wearing pastel polyester pants suits and that generation continues to do so today.

Still, the driving spirit of the sixties "We Decade" seemed to be eclipsed by the "Me Decade" of the seventies. These labels describe a shift in the cultural climate and in the dominant mentality of two different eras towards and then away from engagement with large social problems. When researchers followed up on a 1952 Cornell Study of women in 1968–69 and again in 1974 and 1979, they found a striking contrast between the decades. Like fifties students, those of the seventies espoused "privatism." Focused on personal concerns, family, leisure, and career, they were generally "oblivious to broader social or ideological interests" and responsibility, showing "no sign of much moral obligation for the environment or for overpopulation and no sign of new commitment to work for social betterment," especially contrasted to sixties students. Though to a lesser degree than in 1952, in the seventies undergraduates returned to "faith in government and the military," "support for free enterprise," and religious belief (though not to formal practice). In 1969, only 45 percent of entering undergraduates reported "an essential or very important objective" of being prosperous in life, in contrast to 63 percent in 1979. While the exemplar of the sixties was the hippie, that of the seventies and eighties was the yuppie; but unlike in the fifties, more women after the sixties were striving for individualistic success.[6]

New doors had been opened for women in many areas of public endeavor closed to them before and during the sixties. For instance, in 1973, believing that the ERA would be ratified as a constitutional amendment, the Pentagon opened up diverse job categories in the military to women, expanding their roles in the armed services to an unprecedented degree, a legacy of the sixties revealed during the Gulf War of 1991. Similar dramatic changes in numbers and notables have appeared in corporations, the professions, media, the arts, and popular culture. But discussion of such advances in the wake of the sixties begins with Winifred Wandersee's study of women in the seventies and merits at least a book on the eighties.[7]

The intense conservative reaction that mobilized in the seventies and gained a political foothold in the eighties is one clear index of the impact the sixties had in changing the future for women. Reaganism and right-wing efforts in the nineties promoted a New Traditionalism and used the banner of amorphous, undefined "family values" to undo some sixties' advances, particularly as they applied to women and their lives, private and public. In the 1988 presidential campaign, George Bush's campaign euphemism, "a thousand points of light," was a nostalgic plea for voluntarism, the free work performed primarily by women until financial necessity and their quest for equal access to work and careers rechanneled their energies. As this book goes to press, in the academy efforts to thwart curriculum expansion through study of race, class, and gender reflect a similar desire to negate the longterm impact of the change of vision dating from the sixties, and many Women's Studies programs, conceived in the sixties and expanded dramatically since, are endangered and being cut in the name of academic financial exigency.[8]

Still, the legacy of change remains in the status of American women in all aspects of life. From a women's perspective, it is difficult to talk about the end of the sixties, since the effects of the women's movement have continued to reshape society and culture, albeit gradually and unsteadily. Equity and equality remain to be achieved in most areas of life, public and private; but now women students take about half of the places in law and medical schools. 1992 has been proclaimed the "year of the woman" in politics. Yet through the eighties, the "feminization of poverty" became a national phenomenon that continues to expand. News stories abound about battered women, sexual harassment in the workplace, and eating disorders among women trying to conform to the tyranny of an unreasonably idealized body type. Madonna updates and plays upon the image of Marilyn Monroe, but with a twist that even some scholars argue owes much to feminism.[9]

In many areas of life, the old adage holds true—"the more things change, the more they remain the same." Nineties female undergraduates pursue majors that their sixties mothers would have learned were "unfit for girls"; but women at elite colleges still find prestige in formal dances with particularly eligible dates and in showing off their diamond engagement rings senior year. Women who choose a different lifestyle—lesbianism, postponing marriage for career, or the single life—are still under enormous pressure from older, traditionalist relatives to make a match with a good man and settle down to marriage and children.

Through the eighties the mass phenomenon of replacing an understanding of the history of American women in the sixties with nostalgia and myth has amounted to a selective, collective amnesia; this book aims to be a corrective. With the mini-skirt, sixties graphics, and retrorock musical styles back in vogue, simplification and selectivity of memory characterizes our present era, a perversion of recycling. Eighties journalists wonder, "Will We Ever Get Over the '60s?"; or they warn, "Look Out! Here Come the Sixties!" Media seizes upon every opportunity to celebrate thirtieth, twenty-fifth, and twentieth anniversaries of everything from assassinations to Woodstock. Youth today wonders whether they will be able to produce their own, original culture in the face of this onslaught. Still, even many of the most educated youth of the eighties and nineties forget or never learned what really happened; and, as usual, a balanced, objective understanding of the place of women in the sixties is absent in most books on that era.[10]

But in 1992 as this book nears completion, news media has rediscovered how pertinent were women's experiences in the sixties to contemporary issues and events. The escalating debate about abortion has refocused interest on the case of Sherri Finkbine. The AIDS epidemic is cited as ending the "sexual revolution." Mary Wells, a Motown classic, dies of cancer at age 49, her treatment paid for by friends' donations because she had no health insurance and could not meet the bills. Wells was deprived of her deserved royalties, after signing exploitative record contracts in the sixties. Francie Larrieu Smith, 39-year-old marathoner in the 1992 Olympics, remembers growing up in the "dark ages of athletics for women" and marvels at the distances women have come with so many new routes for display of ability opened to them since the sixties.[11]

There remains, now as then, hope among many for changing the future—hope that stems from the sixties and from lessons learned during that tumultuous decade. The sixties did not die, they just became history that for many, particularly women, can serve as a "usable past." Much work remains undone, although great strides have been made. We have met the future, two decades later, that had preoccupied that future-oriented era; but it is not as then conceived. It is us, however changed.

NOTES

Introduction

1. "America Today," *Look* 23:1 (4 January 1960), 44.

2. Wright, Building 258–60; Kaplan, *Dream*, 2.

3. Woloch, *Women*, 498–99; Clarence J. Enzler, "Future Homemakers of America," *The World Book Year Book* (1963), 308.

4. "The Roots of Home," *Time* (20 June 1960), 15.

5. Carol Ames, "Shirley Hardie Jackson," in *Notable American Women: The Modern Period*, Barbara Sicherman and Carol Hurd Green, eds. (Cambridge: Harvard University Press, 1980), 373–74 (hereafter cited as *NAW:MP*).

6. Betty Friedan, *Mystique;* Gans, *Levittowners;* Komarovsky, *Blue-Collar Marriage.*

7. Woloch, *Women*, 501; in Kessler-Harris, *Out to Work*, 302.

8. Lopata, *Occupation Housewife*, 183.

9. Benjamin F. Miller and Zelma B. Miller, "Young Mothers Are the Beat Generation," *Parents' Magazine* 35 (March 1960), 43; Hymowitz and Weissman, *History of Women*, 327.

10. "Crypto-Feminism," *Harper's* (October 1962), 44.

11. For the influence of the Great Inflation, see Harris, *America Now.*

12. Kaledin, *Mothers and More*, 105.

13. Hole and Levine, *Rebirth of Feminism*, ix–x.

14. On cultural change in the fifties, see Dickstein, *Gates of Eden*, Part I, Ch. 2 and 3.

15. Marshall McLuhan, *Understanding Media: The Extensions of Man* (New York: New American Library, 1965), 44. See also Peck, *Uncovering the Sixties.*

16. See William Chafe, *Women and Equality.*

17. Richard Flacks, *Making History: The Radical Tradition in American Life* (New York: Columbia University Press, 1988); Dickstein, *Gates of Eden;* Muriel Rukeyser, *Breaking Open* (New York: Random House, 1973), 133–34.

18. See Kirkpatrick Sale, *SDS*, p. 344.

19. See Friedan, *Mystique*, 44 et passim.

20. See Brandwein, Brown, and Fox, "Women and Children," 498–514, for divorce statistics.

21. Hugh Carter and Paul C. Glick, *Marriage and Divorce: an Economic and Social Study.* Rev. ed. (Cambridge: Harvard Univ. Press, 1976), 244–247.

22. Moynihan, *Negro Family*, known as the Moynihan Report.

23. "Personalities of 1969," *1970 World Book Year Book*, 451.

Chapter One

1. Proponents included the National Federation of Business and Professional Women, the American Association of University Women, the General Federation of Women's Clubs, the American Association of Women Ministers, the American Medical Women's Association, the American Society of Women Accountants, and the National Association of Colored Women. Mrs. Anna Kelton Wiley to Mrs. Ralph Smith, 27 April 1960, *National Women's Party Papers*, film A236, reel 106. See Linden–Ward, "The ERA," *John F. Kennedy*, ed. Harper and Krieg, 237–249.

2. Anti-ERA groups included the Amalgamated Clothing Workers, Americans for Democratic Action, the American Federation of Teachers, the American Nurses Association, the Communications Workers of America, the International Ladies' Garment Workers, the National Council of Negro Women, the National Federation of Settlements and Neighborhood Centers, the Retail Clerks International, the Textile Workers Union, and the National Board of the YWCA.

3. "Budget Message," manuscript, box 1, folder 7, Esther Peterson Papers, Schlesinger Library, Cambridge (hereafter cited Peterson Papers).

4. Peterson, "Statement . . . by 24 National Organizations on the So–Called ERA" and "Proposal for the Democratic Party Platform with Respect to Legal Status of Women," delivered at the Advance Platform Hearings of the D.N.C. (27 June 1960), ERA 60–62 file, Peterson Papers. Also see Allen Morris, ed., *Official Report of the Proceedings of the Democratic National Convention and Committee*, JFK Memorial ed. (Washington: National Document Publisher, 1964), 67.

5. Republican Platform, 1960, quoted in "ERA 'Special' NWP" file, Peterson Papers.

6. Katherine Pollak Ellickson, "The President's Commission on the Status of Women: Its Formation, Functioning, and Contribution," typescript, January 1976, Schlesinger Library.

7. In one interview conducted in 1971, Peterson claimed credit for inception of the commission. Interview conducted by John Harmon Florer in Florer, "NOW: The Formative Years" (Ph.D. diss., Syracuse University, 1972), 30. One example of Peterson's views on NWP feminists is in Peterson letter to Calvin W. Rawlings, Democratic National Committeeman for Utah,

23 February 1963, Peterson. Memo, "The Nuisance ERA," Peterson to Mike Feldman, Presidential Counsel, 12 May 1961, ERA 60–61 file, Peterson Papers.

8. Alvin Shuster, "President Names Panel on Women: Group Will Press for an End to Discrimination of Sex," *New York Times* (15 December 1961). During the thirties, Mrs. Roosevelt had opposed the ERA, proposing as alternative a study commission to evaluate women's economic, civil, social, and political status and to recommend legislation and litigation. Through the fifties she still believed preservation of protective legislation for women was more valuable than what she considered assertion of the abstract principle of legal rights. See Chafe, *American Woman:* 188; Lash, *Eleanor*, 317, 353.

9. Ellickson, "The President's Commission," 4. See President's Commission on the Status of Women (PCSW), document 18 (12 and 13 February 1962, minutes), 7, PCSW Files, John F. Kennedy Presidential Library.

10. "Goals for Community Services," 18 January 1963, PCSW Papers, file 1 (29 July–19 November 1963).

11. Caroline Farrar Ware, "Women Today: Trends and Issues: A Background Memorandum Prepared at the Request of the PCSW," 2 July 1962, typescript, PCSW Papers, Kennedy Library; Margaret Mead and Frances Bagley Kaplan, eds., *American Women: The Report of the President's Commission on the Status of Women and Other Publications of the Commission* (New York: Scribner's, 1965), 18; Memo to Members of the PCSW, Commission Committees, and Friends from Esther Peterson, June 1963, Subject: "Background Information on the PCSW," film A236, reel 108, NWP Papers; Transcript, February 1962, typescript, ERA File, Peterson Papers.

12. "Confidential Background Paper on the PCSW," December 1961, document 4, 2, PCSW Papers; Katherine Brownell Oettinger, "Role of Women in Government," typescript, PCSW Papers, Kennedy Library; "Statement of Basic Principles," 9 April 1962, typescript, box 1, file 3, PCSW Papers, Schlesinger Library. Also see "Statement in Explanation of a Bill to Provide Equal Pay Without Discrimination on Account of Sex in Enterprises Engaged in Interstate Commerce," February 1963, typescript, "ERA" File, Peterson Papers.

13. "Goals for Community Services," 18 January 1963, file 1 (29 July–19 November 1963), PCSW Papers, Kennedy.

14. [Peterson,] "Statement of Basic Principles," 9 April 1962, file 3, box 1, PCSW Papers, Kennedy Library; Peterson, "The Proposal," 2 June 1961, ERA 60–61 file, Peterson Papers. Mead and Kaplan, *American Women*, 6.

15. "Statement of Basic Principles"; "Statement by the President from the Office of the White House Press Secretary," 14 December 1961, Box 1, File 2, PCSW Papers, Schlesinger Library; Peterson, "Confidential Background Paper on the PCSW," December 1961, document 4, box 1, PCSW Papers, Kennedy Library; Ware, 23; Subcommittee on Implementation," Minutes of the Sixth Meeting," 1–2 March 1963, File B-26, Box 1, PCSW Papers, Kennedy Library. See Barbara Welter, "The Cult of True Womanhood," originally pub-

lished in 1966, reprinted in Welter, *Dimity Convictions: The American Woman in the Nineteenth Century* (Athens: Ohio University Press, 1976).

16. "American Women: Report of the President's Commission on the Status of Women," October 1963, typescript, 79, 34, PCSW Papers, Kennedy Library; "Goals for Community Services."

17. John Kennedy, "Statement," 14 December 1961, typescript, file 1, PCSW Papers, Kennedy Library; "Goals for Community Services"; Mead and Kaplan, 32.

18. Mead and Kaplan, 19; "American Women," typescript, 26.

19. Subcommittee on Implementation, transcript of meeting, file B-26, box 1, 17, Kennedy.

20. Peterson interview conducted by Geri Calkins, in "The ERA in America: A History," radio documentary produced by National Public Radio, Washington, 1981.

21. Mead and Kaplan, 4, 7, 17, 21, 27; Friedan, *Mystique*, 361.

22. Catherine East, "Newer Commissions," in Irene Tinker, *Women in Washington: Advocates for Social Policy* (Beverly Hills: Sage, 1963), 35; Griffith quoted in *Congressional Record*, 89th Cong., 2nd sess., 20 June 1966, 13691; Hole and Levine, 39–40, 42. See *Pittsburgh Press Co. v. Pittsburgh Commission on Human Relations*, 413 U.S. 376 (1973). The last states to add commissions were Alaska, Connecticut, New Mexico, Ohio, and Texas.

23. Goldstein, *Constitutional Rights of Women*, 112. See Kessler–Harris, *Women's Wage*, 106–12, 155–57.

24. Hole and Levine, 31; Gabin, *Feminism in the Labor Movement*, 191. On 18 May 1970 the Supreme Court extended the law to cover "substantially equal" but not identical work at the Wheaton Glass Company of New Jersey. See Moran, "Reducing Discrimination," 32–33.

25. *U.S. v. Libbey-Owens-Ford, United Glass and Ceramic Workers of North America, AFL-CIO, Local No. 9*; *New York Times* 8 December 1970, 53; Hole and Levine, 31, 34, 39; Gabin, 192.

26. Hole and Levine, 34–35. In 1968, Griffiths framed H.R. 14297 to add "sex" to the 1957 Civil Rights Act as well.

27. Gabin, 191; Bird, *Born Female*, 15. See Murray and Eastwood, "Jane Crow," 232–56.

28. Hole and Levine, 42.

29. Editorial, *New York Times*, 31 August 1965.

30. Hole and Levine, 106; Gabin, 191.

31. Hole and Levine, 39.

32. Hole and Levine, 44, 47–48; Evelyn Harrison, "Talent Search for Womanpower," *AAUW Journal* (March 1965):100. The term "affirmative action" was first coined in the Kennedy Administration. Most of the 600,000 women, 25 percent of all federal employees, had clerical jobs and women held less than 10 percent of professional and administrative positions, but during the Johnson years, women entered new fields as letter carriers; customs, im-

migration, and naturalization inspectors; data-processing programmers; bank examiners; medical officers; and Internal Revenue agents.

33. Takaki, *Strangers from a Different Shore:* 419–47; Daniel, *American Women*, 250. See Reimers, *Golden Door*, 95–96; and Daniels, *Coming to America*.

34. Hole and Levine, 45, 48–49.

35. President's Task Force on Women's Rights and Responsibilities, *A Matter of Simple Justice* (Washington: GPO, 1970); Hole and Levine, 49–50.

36. *Simple Justice* quoted in Hole and Levine, 50–51. See [Koontz] Department of Labor, *To Benefit Women*.

37. "NOW News Release," 25 June 1970; *New York Times*, 26 July 1970 and 31 July 1970. Previous anti–ERA groups like the ACLU and organizations of professional women reversed their stance.

38. Hole and Levine, 106, 55–58. Senator Carl Hayden (D-Arizona) first attached this rider in 1950.

39. Cary and Willert Peratis, *Women and the Law*, xi.

40. Goldstein, *Constitutional Rights of Women*, 90–91.

41. Goldstein, 109; Kanowitz, *Women and the Law*, 23–25.

42. Kanowitz, 23–25.

43. Goldstein, 310–11, 322–23.

44. *Weeks v. Southern Telephone and Telegraph Co.*, 408 F.2d, Rev. and rem., S.D. Ga. 277F. Supp. 117 (1969). Wording cited in Dothard *v.* Rawlinson, 1977, quoted in Goldstein, 507; Hole and Levine, 36–37. In *Bowe et al v. Colgate–Palmolive Co. et al.* (1969) the court rejected limiting rules within companies.

45. Cary and Peratis, 56–58.

46. Cary and Peratis, 25–26; Goldstein, 111–12.

47. Leuchtenburg, *In the Shadow of FDR*, 88, 93, 99.

48. Ibid., 101–103.

49. Quoted in Leuchtenburg, 103. "Jackie," *Time* 77:4, 20 January 1961, 25.

50. Gould, xii; Leuchtenburg, 135; "The Land: America the More Beautiful," *Time* 88, 30 September 1966, 53.

51. Leuchtenburg, 144.

52. Mary McGrory, "A Lady Looks at the First Lady," *America* 112 (20 February 1965), 242; Kearns, *Lyndon Johnson*, 218.

53. "Mrs. Lyndon B. Johnson's Challenge to Women," *Saturday Evening Post* 237, 27 June 1964, 88–89, adapted from an address at the American Home Economics Association in Detroit, 24 June.

54. Ibid., 89; Harrison, "Talent Search," 99. LBJ also placed women in high posts in Civil Defense, Consumer Affairs, the United Nations, Public Housing, and Welfare; and during his administration 56 woman scientists and engineers worked at the Goddard Space Flight Center.

55. "Personalities," *The World Book Year Book* (Chicago: Field Enterprises, 1970), 452–53; "Elizabeth Duncan Koontz," in Lynn Gilbert and Gaylen

Moore, eds., *Particular Passions: Talks with Women Who Have Shaped Our Times* (New York: C. N. Potter, 1981), 129–133.

56. Karen DeCrow, "Women and Politics," *Mademoiselle*, February 1970, 34.

57. Ibid., 34. See Lamson, *Few Were Chosen*. Other Congresswomen were Frances Payne Bolton (R–Ohio), Florence P. Dwyer (R–New Jersey), Edith Green (D–Oregon), Julia B. Hansen (D–Washington), Catherine May (R–Washington), Charlotte T. Reid (R–Illinois), and Leonor K. Sullivan (D–Missouri). See Costanti and Craik, "Women as Politicians," 217–236; Werner, "Women in Congress," 16–30.

58. DeCrow, 34. See Werner, "Women in State Legislatures," 40–50.

59. "Bella for Congress! A New Development in WSP Political Action," [Women's Strike for Peace] *Memo* (April 1970):21.

60. See Chisholm, *Unbought and Unbossed;* "The Negro Woman in Politics," *Ebony*, August 1966, 94–100.

61. Morello, *Invisible Bar*, 169.

62. "Democrats Weigh '68 Rights Pledge," *New York Times*, 14 February 1967, 1. Jeffrey's eight–person committee included Helen T. Gunsett of Ohio and Mary E. Fantasia of Massachusetts.

63. Shafer, *Quiet Revolution*, ch. 4, 5, 17; Helen B. Shaffer, "Status of Women," 5 August 1970, in *Editorial Research Reports on the Women's Movement* (Washington: Congressional Quarterly, 1973), 58–59. See Amundsen, *The Silenced Majority*, 144.

64. Wandersee, *On the Move*, 33–34; Cohen, *The Sisterhood*, 171.

65. Wandersee, 26, 29–30.

Chapter Two

1. Reagon, in Cluster, *They Should Have Served*, 35; Morris, *Origins of the Civil Rights Movement*, 156. In 1961, Bernice Johnson was a student and NAACP Youth Council member at Albany State College in Georgia.

2. For an account of women's central role in the Montgomery bus boycott, see Jo Ann Gibson Robinson, *The Montgomery Bus Boycott and the Women Who Started It*, ed. David Garrow (Knoxville: Univ. of Tennessee Press, 1987); Reagon, "My Black Mothers and Sisters," 95.

3. Denise McNair, aged 11, and 14–year–olds Cynthis Wesley, Carole Robertson, and Addie Mae Collins died.

4. Robinson, 23, 45–46. See Blumberg, *Civil Rights*, 40–41.

5. Morris, 49–50.

6. Highlander, founded by Myles Horton, had long been a center for development of community leadership and for strategic planning for the civil rights movement. On the Highlander School as a civil rights movement "halfway house," see Morris, *Origins*, 139–57. See also Horton, *We Make the Road*. Septima Clark, quoted by Morris, 149; Clark, "Literacy and Liberation." *Freedomways* 4 (First Quarter, 1964), 116.

7. See Durr, *Outside the Magic Circle*, ed. Barnard; and interview with Tom Gardner in *Wellesley Alumnae Bulletin*, 1983.

8. Giddings, *When and Where*, 269. Particularly heroic was the teenaged Elizabeth Eckford who came to school alone, not in the company of the other blacks (including Carlotta Walls, Gloria Ray, Thelma Mothershed, Melba Pattillo, and Minniejean Brown). Less publicized was the case of black honor student Josephine Boyd, who braved harassment to attend the all–white Greensboro (North Carolina) High School. On the Central High School students, see Audrey Edwards and Craig K. Polite, *Children of the Dream: The Psychology of Black Success* (Garden City: Doubleday, 1992).

9. See Bates, *The Long Shadow of Little Rock*. Also, see her interview by Morris, *Origins*, 201.

10. Quoted in Forman, *Black Revolutionaries*, 215.

11. Giddings, 267.

12. Quoted in Cantarow et al., *Moving the Mountain*, 53, 84.

13. Memo, Ella J. Baker to Committee on Administration [SCLC], re S.C.L.C. as a Crusade, 23 October 1959, SC628, Ella Baker folder, Social Action Collection, SHSW.

14. For a full discussion of the four students and the events in Greensboro, see Chafe, *Civilities and Civil Rights*, Morris, 195, 204–209. Raines, *My Soul Is Rested*, 104. Blumberg, 71; Lynd, ed., *Nonviolence in America*, xli.

15. Forman, 216.

16. Baker, in Cantarow, *Moving*, 84. Baker, reflections on the April 1960 conference in the *Southern Patriot*, May 1960; that was the journal of the Southern Conference Educational Fund, a pioneering civil rights organization directed by longtime activists Ann and Carl Braden.

17. Clayborne Carson, *In Struggle*, 18.

18. Evans, *Personal Politics*, 48.

19. See Zinn, *SNCC*, 51. Nash and others in the Nashville group also feared that a voter registration emphasis would give the federal government too much power over SNCC. Forman, 221; Morris, 234–6.

20. Baker in Cantarow, *Moving*, 84.

21. Watters, *Down to Now*, 51; Connie Curry, quoted in Raines, 107.

22. SNCC report on the southwest Georgia project, January 1962–December 1963, quoted in Forman, 274; Zinn, 135.

23. Moody, *Coming of Age*, 264–67.

24. Ibid., 328.

25. Woloch, *Women*, 482.

26. Charles Sherrod, "On Crackers, Cucumbers, and Collards," a SNCC Field Report, (20 September 1962), in Forman, 276. "Night Riders Shoot Worker," *Student Voice*, vol. 4, no. 7 (9 December 1963), in *Student Voice*, ed. C. Carson.

27. Sherrod, in Forman, 276. Also see comments in letters from northern white volunteers in Sutherland, ed., *Letters from Mississippi*, 34–63, passim.

28. Sutherland, 61.

29. Garland, "Builders," 32–33. Daisy Elizabeth Adams Lampkin, an NAACP founder, remained in the movement until her death in 1965 at age 82. See Elizabeth Fitzgerald Howard, "Daily Elizabeth Adams Lampkin," Sicherman and Green, *NAW:MP*, 406–08.

30. Quoted in Garland, 32–33. Virginia Foster Durr noted many years later that the situation was similar in the white community: "Except for a few men like Cliff[ord] Durr and Aubrey Williams, the women were much braver than the men, because of their economic position. The men were terrified that if they took the side of the blacks, they would lose their business, or job . . . or be ostracized in some way that would make it impossible for them to earn a living. But the women, white and black, in Montgomery, went ahead and formed an interracial prayer group for the first time and integrated Church Women United and the League of Women Voters, which were tremendous battles. Tom Gardner, "Virginia Foster Durr '25: Human Rights Activist," *Wellesley Alumnae Bulletin* (1983) 513.

31. Charles Cobb and Charles McLaurin, "Memorandum Re: Preliminary Survey on the condition of the Negro farmers in Ruleville, Mississippi, at the close of the cotton season," 19 November 1962. In Grant, *Black Protest*, 472–73. See "From Sharecropper to Lobbyist: The Political Awakening of Fannie Lou Hamer," in Williams, *Eyes on the Prize*, 245–47, 249; excerpt from Hamer, *To Praise Our Bridges*.

32. Hamer to Anne Romaine and Howard Romaine, 1966. SC1069, Social Action Collection, SHSW. Carson, *In Struggle*, 74–75, 125–26.

33. Cobb and McLaurin, "Memorandum," 473–474.

34. "Life in Mississippi: An Interview with Fannie Lou Hamer," *Freedomways* (Spring 1965): 231–242. For other details of her life see also the interview with Hamer in Raines, 249–255. Perry Hamer was unemployed until Headstart came to Ruleville, through Fannie Lou Hamer's efforts; and he became a school bus driver for the program.

35. Reagon, liner notes for Fannie Lou Hamer, *Songs My Mother Taught Me*, a cassette of songs and speeches by Hamer produced by Reagon. Reagon was one of the original members of the Freedom Singers, a touring group who raised money for the movement by concerts. She received her Ph.D. in history from Howard University and went on to work at the Smithsonian; she is also a founding member of the women's singing group "Sweet Honey in the Rock."

36. See, for example, "Mass meeting speech," in Hamer; King, *Freedom Song*, 351–53.

37. Hamer in Haines, 252–54.

38. Quoted in Nan Robertson, "Mississippian Relates Struggle of Negro in Voter Registration," *New York Times*, 24 August 1964; Williams, 241–42. Rita Schwerner, widow of CORE worker Michael, murdered in Philadelphia, Mississippi, that June, was to have been second to testify.

39. Among the few whites organizing the MFDP was Rita Schwerner; the MFDP delegation had 64 blacks and four whites.

40. Baker, interview with Anne Romaine, SHSW; Hamer to Anne Romaine, SHSW; quoted in Robertson, *New York Times,* 24 August 1964, 17.

41. Annie Devine to Anne Romaine, 1966: SC1069, SHSW; Garland, "Builders," p. 33. The three witnessed the House of Representatives reject the appeal, 228 to 143, on 17 September 1965; they were the first black women to sit on the House floor. For stories on the MFDP campaigns and candidates, see *The Student Voice,* vol. 5. no. 9 (28 April 1964) and vol. 5, no. 13 (2 June 1964) in Carson, ed. On Gray's work with SCLC, see Romaine interview with Sandy Leigh, asst. director of MFDP Washington office, November 1966, SC1069, SHSW.

42. "Statement to the Committee by Mrs. Fannie Lou Hamer, Ruleville, Miss., Vice–Chairman, Mississippi Freedom Democratic Party, 22 May 1969, Jackson, Miss." In Hamer Collection, Bethune Archives, National Council of Negro Women, Washington, D.C.

43. Paule Marshall, "Hunger Has No Color Line," in Stanford, ed., 250–51. Ill with cancer from 1975 on, Hamer worked through that winter and the following year to try to ensure an integrated Mississippi delegation for the 1976 convention. She died in 1977 at age sixty.

44. Lanker, *I Dream a World,* 223. Unita Blackwell interview, The Civil Rights Documentation Project (Moorland–Spingarn Collection, Howard University), quoted in Giddings, *When and Where,* 287.

45. Rubye Doris Smith Robinson interview (as "Sarah"), in Josephine Carson, *Silent Voices,* 82; Reagon, "Rubye Doris Smith Robinson," *NAW:MP,* 585.

46. *Student Voice,* vol. 2, no. 2 (February 1961) and vol. 2, no. 3 (March 1961), in C. Carson, ed., *Student Voice, 1960–1965,* 33, 39. Diane Nash in Henry Hampton and Steve Fayer, *Voices of Freedom: An Oral History of the Civil Rights Movement* (New York: Bantam, 1990), 82–83.

47. See "Lucretia Collins, The 'Spirit of Nashville'", in Forman, 145–157. The crowd also beat television cameramen filming the event. For an account of the Parchman experience, see Reagon, "Songs of the Civil Rights Movement, 1955–1965: A Study in Cultural History" (Ph.D. diss., Howard University, 1975).

48. Reagon, "Robinson," in *NAW:MP,* 586.

49. Evans, *Personal Politics,* 184.

50. Forman, 475.

51. Nash, "Inside the Sit–Ins," *The New Negro,* 45, 49.

52. Evans, 40; In C. Carson, *Student Voice,* vol. 3, no. 2, 53–56. The judge refused to allow her to abandon her appeal and delayed proceedings to a date beyond the time of her child's birth. She did serve a 10–day sentence for contempt of court. DeBenedetti, *An American Ordeal,* 169. Nash declined to run for election as SNCC's first chairwoman. She travelled to North Vietnam with Deming and the wife of one of the Fort Hood Three (G. I. protestors) at the invitation of the Vietnamese Women's Union. On their return to the United States the women reported widespread civilian casualties in North Vietnam;

the federal government tried to seize their passports. DeBenedetti, 170. Diane Nash Bevel, "Journey to North Vietnam," *Freedomways* (Second Quarter 1967), 118–19.

53. See Gitlin and Hollander, *Uptown*. ERAP is discussed in the section on Student Movements.

54. See Rothschild, *A Case of Black and White*, on the origins of participants. The National Council of Churches ran a volunteer training camp at Western College for Women in Oxford, Ohio, in the spring of 1964.

55. See Cowan's autobiography, *An Orphan in History*, for an account of his mother's life and her involvement in civil rights. Polly Cowan was heir to the Spiegel merchandising fortune; she put both her money and her efforts into the civil rights movement until her death in 1976. Materials on the Wednesdays in Mississippi (WIMS) project are in the Bethune Archives, NCNW.

56. See also Kate Wilkinson, "A Sociological Analysis of an Action Group: "Wednesdays in Mississippi." (Master's thesis, University of Mississippi, 1966); "Wednesdays in Mississippi," *Sarah Lawrence Alumnae Magazine* (Fall 1964). Ruth Batson, report of WIMS-Boston Team, 14–16 July 1964, in WIMS papers, Bethune Archives, NCNW.

57. Evans, 33–34. Mary King involved Hayden in the discussion of the memo on women presented to SNCC in 1964, although Hayden said later that she was not a coauthor, (SNCC Reunion conference, Trinity College, Hartford, Conn., 1989). King and Hayden coauthored "Sex and Caste: A Kind of Memo", which appeared in *Liberation* in 1966 and is a very significant early document of the new women's movement of the 1960s. It is reprinted in M. King, *Freedom Song*, 571–74.

58. Smith, *Our Faces, Our Words*. Robinson, 654. Thrasher in Lukas, *Don't Shoot*, 135.

59. Thrasher, 157–8.

60. Anne Braden, speech at "The Sixties Speak to the Eighties: a Conference on Activism and Social Change," University of Massachusetts–Amherst, 22 October 1983; Carson, *In Struggle*, 162. Senator James Eastland called SCEF the leading voice of Communism in the South for its school desegregation work. Through the SCEF newspaper, the *Southern Patriot*, the Bradens created a link between black and white activists and got out news of violent reactions unreported in mass media.

61. Evans, 51.

62. Deming, *We Are All Part of One Another*, 108.

63. Belfrage, *Freedom Summer*, 24.

64. Rothschild, "White Women," 470–73.

65. Helen Yglesias, interview with Carol Hurd Green, August 1986. Cole's brother was a leader of the 1968 Columbia University strike.

66. Ilene Strelitz Melish, "Memoir," quoted in Rothschild, 475; Elizabeth Sutherland, ed., *Letters from Mississippi* (New York: McGraw-Hill, 1965), 22–23.

67. Rothschild, "White Women," 474.

68. Belfrage, *Freedom Summer*, 151; Sutherland, *Letters*, 199–200. Sutherland uses pseudonyms for the letter writers, hence the names in quotation marks.

69. Sutherland, 95–97. See the special issue on Mississippi Freedom Schools of *Radical Teacher* 40 (Fall 1991).

70. "Jo" to "John" and "Cleo," in Sutherland, *Letters*, 202.

71. Cynthia Washington, "We Started from Different Ends of the Spectrum," in Evans, *Personal Politics*, 238–9.

72. Sutherland, 163.

73. Washington, 239; Walker, *Meridian*, 106–7, 110.

74. Report of the Waveland Conference, in the Civil Rights Collection, SHSW, November 1964.

75. Sutherland, 172.

76. The history of response to this comment is interesting: early accounts take it seriously and see it as representative. Cynthia Washington says that she and Muriel Tillinghast overheard it and that they were "not pleased." Washington, 239. Recent accounts, and a speech at the Trinity College reunion of SNCC by Mary King emphasize its context, a comment at the end of a long and tiring day of reviewing the complex events of the summer, and see it as evidence of Carmichael's brand of humor, not to be taken as evidence of his attitudes; others disagreed. King, 454. Also see Echols, *Daring to Be Bad*, 31–32, 310; C. Carson, 325n; Morgan, *Sisterhood*, xxi.

77. "Jo," unpublished diary, Civil Rights Collection, SHSW, n.p..

78. Minutes of SNCC conference, Holly Springs, Miss., April 1965, Civil Rights Collection, SHSW. Also see King, 484–9, and Sellers, 30–31. Minutes of SNCC conference. President Lyndon Johnson submitted the Voting Rights bill to Congress in March 1965.

79. Ibid.

80. Susan (Lorenzi) Sojourner, interview with CHG, Washington, April 1986.

81. By 1967, Sue Thrasher and SSOC moved on to labor organizing, campus protest, and antiwar work.

82. Hampton and Fayer, *Voices of Freedom*, 451–53, 481.

83. Blumberg, *Civil Rights*, 149–50.

84. Hampton and Fayer, 350, 359–60. The Watts riot encompassed 46.5 square miles, one and a half times the area of Manhattan, killed 34, injured over a thousand, and damaged or destroyed over a thousand buildings.

85. Ibid., 363, 371, 513–14. See articles by Bonita Dawkins on Free Health Centers, by Rosemari Mealy on police violence in the Philadelphia ghetto, and by Sharla Woods, "Bussing Doesn't Mean Education," in *Black Panther* 4:21 (25 April 1970), 6, 13, 14. Other women wrote regularly for that weekly national newspaper.

86. *Black Panther* 4:21 (25 April 1970), 375, 381, 388–89.

87. Ibid., 427–29.

88. Ibid., 429, 431–32.

89. Ibid., 433–35, 440–43.

90. Ibid., 446–47.

91. "Jackson State," *The Report of the President's Commission on Campus Unrest* (Washington: GPO, 1970), 411–59.

92. Hampton and Fayer, 485–89. See Diane Ravitch, *The Great School Wars: New York City, 1805–1973: A History of the Public Schools as Battlefield of Social Change* (New York: Basic Books, 1974), 316–28.

93. Hampton and Fayer, 490–98.

94. Ibid., 498–500, 504–05, 509.

95. Toni Cade, "The Pill: Genocide or Liberation?" in *The Black Woman*, 164; Brenda Hyson, "Black Mothers," *Black Panther* 4:21 (25 April 1970), reprinted in Schulder and Kennedy, *Abortion Rap*. This position is discussed more fully in the chapter "Our Bodies, Our Selves."

96. Hampton and Fayer, 511–12; Elaine Brown, "The Most Crucial Question Facing Black People Today Is To Be or Not To Be," *Black Panther* 4:21 (25 April 1970), 2–3.

97. Hampton and Fayer, 521, 526, 530, 533–37. Johnson and the others sued; and in 1982, after "the longest civil rights trial in U.S. history," they received a settlement of $1.85 million from the federal, county, and city governments.

98. Hampton and Fayer, 539–40; Bettina Aptheker, "The Surveillance and Imprisonment of Women Activists in the Sixties," unpublished paper, 5th Berkshire Conference on the History of Women, June 1981, in the collection of Schlesinger Library.

99. Cleaver and Davis quoted in Marcelyn Dallis, "Black Women, Black Protest: The Impact of Black Women in the Civil Rights Movement," proposal to the Massachusetts Foundation for the Humanities and Public Policy, January 1988.

100. Andrew L. Newman, "American Indians," *The 1974 World Book Year Book*, 356; Crow Dog, *Lakota Woman*, 75–76.

101. Crow Dog, 80, 124, 189.

102. Ibid., 189, 119–21, 4.

103. Ibid., 137, 162.

104. Ibid., 131, 78, 249.

Chapter Three

1. Sandler, *Equal Rights*, 263–72.

2. Friedan, *Mystique*, 75.

3. Also see Frisof, "Textbooks and Channeling," 26–28, for analysis of presentation of women in five social studies textbooks. Dr. Sandler, *Equal*

Rights for Men and Women, 263–72; Howe, "Sexual Stereotypes," 197; Solomon, *In the Company of Educated Women*, 198. See Rossi, "Women in Science," 1196–1202.

4. See Newcomer, *A Century of Higher Education*. The overall number of students in college rose 142.6 percent between 1960 and 1969. In 1960, 1.8 bachelors degrees went to a man for each to a woman.

5. Patricia Bell Scott, "Education for Self-Empowerment: A Priority for Women of Color," in Eleanor M. Bender, Bobbie Burk, and Nancy Walker, eds., *All of Us Are Present: The Stephens College Symposium: Women's Education: The Future* (Columbia, Mo.: James Madison Wood Research Institute, 1984), 62.

6. Echols, *Daring to be Bad*, xiv; Freeman, "Women's Liberation," 468–78.

7. Female colleges included Connecticut, Mount Holyoke, Smith, Vassar, and Wheaton; male institutions, Dartmouth, Amherst, Wesleyan, Williams, and Bowdoin. Boston College and California Institute of Technology became coeducational before 1973.

8. Ingalls, "Women's Colleges," 18–19. Quoted in Bird, "Women's Colleges," 64. Simpson was one of three men to replace women presidents in prestigious women's colleges in the sixties. The others were at Sarah Lawrence and Bryn Mawr. Millett, "Libbies," 42–50.

9. Trent with Golds, *Catholics in College*, 45–46. Ruether, "Women's Colleges," 63.

10. Trent, *Catholics*, 262; Ruether, "Women's Colleges," 63–64.

11. Ruether, "Women's Colleges," 63–64.

12. James Davis 1961 study cited in Solomon, 199–200; *Newsweek* 55, 7 March 1960, 57–60. See Albjerg, "Bright Girls," 141–44; Ademeck and Goudy, "Identification"; Ademeck, "College Major," 97–112; Almquist and Angrist, "Career Salience," 242–49; Almquist and Angrist, "Role Model Influences," 263–79; Anderson, ed., *Sex Differences*.

13. *Newsweek* 55, 7 March 1960, 57–60; Bender, "College Girl Sees No Future," quoted in Bender, Burk, and Walker, 19.

14. Florence Howe, "The Education of Women, 1970," in Martin, ed., *American Sisterhood*, 274, 279, 280. Reprinted from *Liberation* (August–September 1969).

15. "The Span of a Woman's Life and Learning," reprinted in *National Business Woman*, June 1960, 13; Fitzgerald and Lantz, "Adult Coed," 8.

16. Fitzgerald and Lantz, "Adult Coed," 9.

17. Gleazer, "Growth and Status," Harlacher, "Community Services," in Lee C. Deighton, ed. *Encyclopedia of Education*, 321–29; Cremin, "Focus on Education (1964)," 39–40; Cremin, "Focus on Education (1965)," 40–41; Stern, "Automation (1965)," 224. Another source reported 627,806 enrolled in junior colleges in 1963, or 13.8 percent of students in higher education. See Hechinger, "Education," 317. See Blocker, Plummer, and Richardson, Jr., *The Two–Year College*; Leonard F. Robertson, "An Explanatory Study of the Effects of

the Cooperative Education Program in Beginning Occupations on Selected Employment Factors," *Journal of Business Education* 42:3 (1966):121; Diener, *Growth of an American Invention;* Shoulders, *Junior College.*

18. Fitzgerald and Lantz, 9; North, "The New Education," 28.

19. For a brief biographical article on Bunting see Rayner, *Wise Women,* 59–68.

20. Bunting, "The Radcliffe Institute," 279–86; "The Radcliffe Institute . . . After Birth?" 13.

21. Rice, "Continuing Education," 241–42; North, 48.

22. Dolan, "QED," 136; "My Lady Fair," *Adult Leadership* (May 1969):32; Berry, "Effects," 10.

23. Joy Rice, "Continuing Education," 240, 242–46.

24. Graham, "Status Transitions," *Academic Women,* 20; Solomon, *Educated Women,* 199–200.

25. National Institute of Health, *Special Report on Women and Graduate Study: Resources for Medical Research, Report No. 13* (Bethesda, MD: NIH, U.S. Department of Health, Education, and Welfare, 1968), vii–ff; Cless, "A Modest Proposal," 621–22, 627.

26. Florynce Kennedy, *Color Me Flo,* 39.

27. L. Morrow, "Women in Medicine," a Report to the Conference of Professional and Academic Women, NYU Law School, 11 April 1970. Mimeographed. Walsh, *Doctors Wanted,* 242–43. Jacqueline Seaver, "Women Doctors in Spite of Everything," *New York Times Magazine,* 31 March 1961, 67, quoted in Walsh, 242–43.

28. Lopate, *Women in Medicine,* 22; See Schwartz, "Medicine as a Vocational Choice," 7–12.

29. Corea, *The Hidden Malpractice,* 15, 32; Lopate, vi–vii, 28, 170, 187; Walsh, *Doctors Wanted,* 244. Linden–Ward holds a 1972 PHT degree, a certificate from the medical school of Loyola University of Chicago.

30. Howell [Campbell], *Why Would a Girl,* 30–35, 65–66, 74; Ruzek, 84. See also Howell, "Why Would a Girl Go Into Medicine?," *Monograph* (November 1973); Cartwright, "Conscious Factors," 210–25.

31. Joni Magee, interview in Morantz, Pomerleau, and Fenichel, *In Her Own Words,* 212.

32. Lopate, *Women in Medicine,* 88–95, 100–101.

33. Ibid., 135–37.

34. Walsh, 268–69; Sandler, *Equal Rights,* 263–72.

35. "Objectives and program of the AMA Committee on Nursing," *Journal of the American Medical Association* 181 (4 August 1962), 430, cited in Woods, 164; Melosh, *The Physician's Hand,* 207; Woods, 165; Melosh, 208.

36. Hine, *Black Women in White,* 191–92; Gloria R. Smith, "From Invisibility to Blackness: The Story of the National Black Nurses' Association," in Hine, *Black Women,* 157–58.

37. Cynthia Woods, 165–66.

38. Melosh, 208–209.

39. Kramer, "Discrimination" in *Women on Campus*, 39–41; Epstein, *Woman's Place*, 66.

40. Fox, "Woman Graduate Student," 33–35; Stokes, "Women Graduate Students" in *Women on Campus*, 36; Grace E. Mack, "Black Woman Graduate" in *Women on Campus*, 42–45.

41. Wohl, 83–84; "Women at the Top," *Newsweek*, 27 June 1966, 77.

42. Rossi quoted in Lopate, 36. For another view, see Meier, "Mother–Centeredness," 115–21.

43. Beatrice Hyslop, "Letter to the Editor," *American Historical Review* 62 (1956):288–89. Also see Rossi and Calderwood, *Academic Women;* Sandler, *Equal Rights*, 263–72. See Bernard, *Academic Women*. Simon, "The Woman Ph.D," 221–36; Clinas, "Women on College Faculties," 917–18; Scully, "Women in Higher Education," 2–5.

44. Ellman, *Thinking About Women* 29; Mattfeld and Van Aken, *Women and the Scientific Professions*, 47–48.

45. Sandler, *Equal Rights*, 270; Sherman, *Women as Interpreters*, 439. See Wilbur Zelinsky, "The Strange Case of the Missing Female Geographer," *Journal of American Geography* 25:2 (1973), 101–05; Tyler, "University Administration," 6–12.

46. Scott, *Gender*, 186; Higham gives Mary Beard two footnotes, and AHA President Nellie Neilson is not even mentioned.

47. See Kay Klotzberger, "Political Action by Academic Women," in Rossi and Calderwood, 359–91; Scott, *Gender*, 193.

48. Helen Taussig, "The Evils of Camouflage as Illustrated by Thalidomide." *New England Journal of Medicine* (11 July 1963), 92–94.

49. Elisabeth Young-Bruehl, "Hannah Arendt," *NAW:MP*, 33–37. See Stephen Whitfield, *Into the Dark: Hannah Arendt and Totalitarianism* (Philadelphia: Temple University Press, 1980).

50. For early historiography, see David M. Potter, "American Women and the American Character," *Stetson University Bulletin* 62 (January 1962):1–22, reprinted in *American Character and Culture*, John A. Hague, ed. (DeLand, FLA.: Everett Edwards Press, 1974), 67–69; Lerner, "New Approaches," 333–56; Gordon, Buhle, and Schrom, "Women in American Society," 11. In Page Smith's *Daughters of the Promised Land* (Boston: Little Brown, 1970), the male author emphasizes importance of fathers to notable daughters.

51. Rossi, "Sex Equality," 3–6, 16.

52. Evans, *Personal Politics*, 183, 185–86; Marilyn J. Boxer, "For and About Women: The Theory and Practice of Women's Studies in the United States," in Minnich, O'Barr, and Rosenfeld, *Reconstructing the Academy*, 70–71; "Feminism and Women's Studies: Survival in the Seventies," in *Report on the West Coast Women's Studies Conference*, edited by [Joan Hoff Wilson and] Women's Studies Board at California State University, Sacramento (Pittsburgh: Know, Inc., 1974), 19–20; "Women's Studies," *Newsweek*, 25 October 1970, 61;

Trecker, "Women's Place," 83–86, 92. See also Rossi and Calderwood, *Academic Women*, 139–61.

53. Sheila Tobias, "Female Studies—An Immodest Proposal" (Ithaca: Cornell University Press, 20 July 1970 Mimeographed); Florence G. Howe, ed., *Female Studies II* (Pittsburgh: Know, Inc., 1970). See Stimpson, "The New Feminism" in *Women on Campus*, 37–39.

54. Martha Weinman Lear, "The Second Feminist Wave," *New York Times Magazine* (March 10, 1968); Linden-Ward, "Kate Millett," 419.

55. Barber, Women's Revolt, in *Women on Campus*, 85–86.

56. Spender, *Women of Ideas*, 726.

57. Sandler, 44.

58. Woloch, *Women*, 500.

59. Gornick, "Who Says" *New York Times Magazine*, 53.

60. "Female Equality, Not Pills Causing Sexual Revolution," *Michigan Daily*, 6 January 1967, 2; Peck, *Uncovering the Sixties*, 207. See also Collins and Sedlacek, "Counselor Perceptions," 13–16.

61. Hechlinger, "College Morals" *New York Times Magazine*, 120; "Students Fight a Dress Code from the 60s," *New York Times*, 16 December 1990.

Chapter Four

1. Oppenheimer, *Female Labor Force*, 30. See Robert Bibb, "Blue–Collar Women in Low–Wage Industries: A Dual–Market Interpretation," *The American Working Class: Prospects for the 1980s*, eds. Irving Lewis Horowitz et al. (New Brunswick: Transaction Books, 1979), 125–49; Keniston and Keniston, "American Anachronism," 355–75; Stimpson, Preface to, and Benería, Introduction to *Women, Households*, ix, xiii, 6, 16, 18–19. For statistics, see U.S. Bureau of the Census, *Statistical Abstracts of the United States: 1973* (Washington: GPO, 1973), 219, 221–22; U.S. Department of Labor, *U.S. Working Women: A Databook* (1977); and U.S. Department of Labor, Employment Standards Administration, *Handbook on Women Workers*, Bulletin 297.

2. Ruth E. Hartley, "Women's Roles," 214; Blau, "Women in the Labor Force," 37. Kessler–Harris, *Out to Work*, 302, 312; Kreps, *Sex in the Marketplace*, 2.

3. Maxine Margolis, *Mothers and Such*, 225; Billy Graham, "Jesus and the Liberated Woman," *Ladies Home Journal* 87 (December 1970), 42. See pamphlet, "Who Are the Working Mothers," published regularly by the Women's Bureau, U.S. Department of Labor, *Employment in Perspective: Working Women* (Washington: GPO, 1982); Degler, "Revolution Without Ideology," 163–210. Even in 1968, 53 percent of women opposed a married woman's contribution to family income, although that percentage had been declining steadily from 1964 on.

4. Gannon, "Temporary Help Industry," 44–49.

5. Sally L. Hacker, "Sex Stratification, Technology, and Organizational Change: A Longitudinal Study of A.T. & T.," in *Women and Work*, 249, 256.

See Hoos, *Automation;* Faunce, Hardin, and Jacobson, "Automation," 340; Jean A. Wells, "Women's Job Prospects," *AAUW Journal* (October 1964):20; Shepherd, *Automation.*

6. Mueller, "American Women," 122; Margolis, 225–26; Kennedy, *If All We Did Was Weep,* 205. See Davies, "Women's Place," 1–37; Glenn and Feldberg, "Degraded and Deskilled," in *Women and Work,* 202–17; Benét, *Secretarial Ghetto* and *Secretary;* and Jackall, *Workers in a Labyrinth.*

7. Rivlin, "American Women," 123; Koontz, Foreword to "Day Care Facts," iii–v; Strasser, *Housework,* 283. See Waldman and McEaddy, "Where Women Work," 3–23. A suburban Chicago high school teacher earned $6000 in 1968–69.

8. Kennedy, *If All We Did,* 204–05; Oppenheimer, *Female Labor Force,* 30; Yates, 88; Smuts, *Women and Work.* Full–time was defined as 35 hours or more per week for 50–52 weeks.

9. Mead, "American Woman" (1969), 460.

10. Margolis, *Mothers & Such,* 226. Harris, *America Now,* 228.

11. Ibid.; Margolis, 204; Kennedy, *If All We Did,* 202–4; Mueller, "Women and Their Work," 122; Sexton, *Blue Collars,* 63–65. Also see Miller, *Rich Man, Poor Man;* and Levitan, ed., *Blue–Collar Workers,* 36–37.

12. Benería and Stimpson, *Women, Households,* 121; Sexton, *Blue Collars,* 69; Koontz: Foreword to "Day Care Facts." Of female household heads, 70 percent worked, 38 part–time; 75 percent of those who did not work were in poverty.

13. Kennedy, 105.

14. Adams, "Room at the Top," 9–10.

15. Stern and Stern, *Sixties People,* 25–27.

16. Buber, "Women Who Work," in Woloch, 506; Agassi, 234–35; Bibb, "Blue-Collar Women," 133, 138–39; U.S. Department of Labor, "The Economic Role of Women," reprinted in *Economic Report of the President* (GPO, 1973), 157–58.

17. See Marigean Suelzle; "Women in Labor," in *Women's Liberation.*

18. Cook, "Women and the American Trade Unions." 124–32.

19. Barbara Mikulski, introduction to Seifer, *Absent from the Majority,* viii–x. Mikulski's comments reflect both the class and the religious backgrounds of her neighbors: predominantly Polish and German Catholic, they experienced both the secular upheavals of demonstrations and new lifestyles, and questions raised by the Second Vatican Council. Quoted in Stanley H. Rutenberg, "The Union Member Speaks," in Levitan, ed, 160.

20. Kreps, *Sex in the Marketplace,* 9–11; Table 8–1 in U.S. Department of Commerce, Bureau of the Census, "A Statistical Portrait of Women in the United States," *Current Population Reports,* Series 23:58 (GPO, 1974), 35. See "Work, Education and the Chicana," in Lopez, 119–124. 48 percent of Cuban women worked compared to 31 percent of Puerto Ricans.

21. Giddings, *When and Where,* 299.

22. Stebbings, "Underestimated."

23. Woloch, *Women*, 505; Koontz, v. For another view, see Gross, "Plus sa [sic] change."

24. Mead, "American Woman Today," *World Book Year Book* (1969), 86.

25. Mikulski, ix.

26. See Cook, "Women," 124–32; Raphael, "Working Women," 27–33. For a male unionist view on working women, see Stanley H. Rutenberg, "The Union Member Speaks," in Levitan, 160; Bibb, "Blue–Collar Women," 125–49; Virginia A. Bergquist, "Women's Participation in Labor Organizations," *Monthly Labor Review* (October 1974), 3–9. For an exception, see Margaret M. Troxell, "It's Equal Pay for Women Linotype Operators, Members of ITU— The First Union to Provide Equality on the Job," *Indianapolis Star and News* (September 1960).

27. Bessie Hillman, "Gifted Women in the Trade Union," in Cassara, *American Women*, 99; Foner, *Labor Movement*, 478.

28. Gabin, *Feminism*, 164, 185, 203–04.

29. Gabin, 211, 213.

30. Ibid., 218–19, 222.

31. Ibid., 189, 192, 197, 204, 209, 222–24.

32. Foner, *Labor Movement*, 417–19; Baxandall et al., *American Working Women*, 368, 371.

33. Foner, 420, 424.

34. Cantarow et al., *Moving the Mountain*, 97; Baxandall et al., *American Working Women*, 368–371.

35. Cantarow et al., 99.

36. Baxandall et al., 369; Foner, *Labor Movement*, 421.

37. Foner, 426.

38. Lerner, *Majority Finds Its Past*, 236; Foner, 439. See Green, "ILGWU in Texas," 144–69.

39. Alfred Vogel, "Clerical Workers Are Ripe." More women began to enter the skilled trades by the decade's end. See Hedges and Bemis, "Sex Stereotyping," 14–22.

40. "For Women: A Difficult Climb to the Top," *Business Week* (2 August 1969), 42, 46. The 1960 census showed that of 1.2 million persons listed as "managers, officials, and proprietors" and earning $10,000 a year, only 2 percent were women.

41. Gatlin, *American Women*, 208; "Petticoats Rustle on Executive Ladder," *Business Week* (September 1962), 53; D. L. Graham, "Double Life," 8–9, 29.

42. Bowman et al., "Women Executives," 15; "Petticoats," 53; "Women at the Top," *Newsweek* (27 June 1966), 77.

43. "For Women," *Business Week*, 46.

44. "Women at the Top," *Newsweek*, 77; U.S. Civil Service Commission, Statistics Section, *Study of Employment of Women in the Federal Government, 1967* cited in Epstein, *Woman's Place*, 96.

45. "Black Capitalism: The Rarest Breed of Woman," *Time* (8 November 1971), 102.

46. Roslyn S. Willett, "Working in 'A Man's World': The Woman Executive," in Gornick and Moran, 518–19.

47. "Women at the Top," 76. The well–worn ladies' room excuse also appeared in the New York Bar Association for keeping women out of the legal profession.

48. Adams and Briscoe, 9–10. See EEOC, *A Unique Competence: A Study of Equal Employment Opportunity in the Bell System* (GPO, 1971), quoted by Sally Hacker in Kahn–Hut et al. *Women and Work*, 291.

49. "For Women," 43.

50. "Lawrence: 'Love Is the Key'," *The Good Housekeeping Woman's Almanac* (New York: Newspaper Enterprise Associates, Inc., 1977), 209.

51. Longcope, "Cosmetic Family," 39, 42.

52. A 1964 article notes a Bureau of Labor study of twenty offices where electronic data processing equipment had been installed. Most new jobs went to young college–educated men rather than to women already there. The effect of modernization as elsewhere was a "decrease in new employment opportunities for women." Wells, "Women's Job Prospects," 18–24; "For Women," 43, 46.

53. "For Women," 44; Wohl, "What's So Rare," 128.

54. "Black Capitalism," *Time*, 102.

55. "For Women," 42, 46.

56. "For Women," 42, 46; Epstein, 46.

57. "Day Care For Children of Working Mothers," *National Business Woman* (April 1960), 12.

58. Bremner, *Children and Youth*, II, 704, Spock, 13.

59. Woloch, 507. Rossi, "Equality Between the Sexes," in Lifton, ed., *Woman*, 110–111.

60. Mudd, "Impact," 123. Mueller, "American Women," 122.

61. Rothman, *Woman's Proper Place*, 268–74.

62. Ibid., 268–69.

63. Bremner, 718–9; Hazlett, 125, 130, 279–80.

64. Lopate, *Women in Medicine*, 163–65, 167–68. Lopate quotes Elizabeth Fowler, "Personal Finance: Working Wife Finds that Her Pay Doesn't Double the Family's Income," *New York Times* (29 December 1966).

65. Friedan, *Second Stage*, 203.

66. Mead, "American Woman Today," 87.

67. Hole and Levine, 82. See Babchuk and Booth, "Voluntary Association Memberships," 32–45.

68. Mead, "American Woman Today," 87.

69. Hole and Levine, 103–04.

70. Margaret Moore, "Crime–Fighting."

71. Rachlin, "Urban Institutions," 22–23; "WOW: A Model for Encouraging Women's Potential," *AAUW Journal* (January 1970); Koontz, "Voluntar-

ism." WICS membership was drawn from the National Council of Negro Women, the National Council of Jewish Women, the National Council of Catholic Women, and Church Women United.

72. *The 1963 World Book Year Book*, 405; 1969, 445.

73. Lanker and Angelou, "I Dream," 218.

Chapter Five

1. Cohen, *The Sisterhood*, 171; Cole, *"Tipi to Skyscraper,"* 119; U.S. Dept. of Labor, "Underutilization," iv. See Epstein, *Woman's Place*, 66; Theodore, *Professional Women*.

2. Etzioni, *"Semi–Professions,"* v–vii, xv; Grimm and Stern, "Sex Roles," 694. See Toren, *Social Work*.

3. Epstein, *Woman's Place*, 66. See Theodore, *Professional Woman;* Horner, "Fail," 36; Gornick, "Fear Success," 50–53.

4. According to table from Debra Renee Kaufman, "Professional Women: How Real Are the Recent Gains?", in Freeman, *Women*, 330. See Stricker, "Cookbooks and Law Books," 1–19.

5. Doris L. Sassower, Report to the Conference of Professional and Academic Women, New York University Law School, 11 April 1970. Mimeographed, in author's collection.

6. Quoted in Morello, *Invisible Bar*, 209.

7. "Abortion Reform Urged in Albany," *New York Times* (8 March 1966); *Who's Who of American Women* (1974–75).

8. Gilbert and Moore, "Ruth Bader Ginsburg," *Particular Passions*, 153–59. Elizabeth Dole, a Cabinet member in the Reagan and Bush administrations, recounts the joke she often heard at Harvard Law School: "What's the difference between a female law student and garbage? At least garbage gets taken out."

9. Morello, *Invisible Bar*, 172.

10. Kennedy, *Color Me Flo;* Morello, 162; Morello, 163–64; Kennedy and Schulder, *Abortion Rap;* "Diane Schulder" in Acton et al., *Mugshots*, 198.

11. Quoted in Morello, 167.

12. Doris Sassower, "Women in the Law: The Second Hundred Years," *ABA Journal* 57 (April 1971), 330.

13. Morello, 209–212.

14. "Eleanor Holmes Norton," in Gilbert and Moore, *Particular Passions*, 143–45; Caroline Mahoney, "Constitutional Lawyer: Eleanor Holmes Norton," in Stanford, *On Being Female*, 266–69.

15. Morello, *The Invisible Bar*, 44.

16. Sassower, "Report," 11 April 1970.

17. *Biographical Dictionary of the Federal Judiciary*, 132–33; Obituary, *New York Times* (25 April 1985), 27. Johnson's other appointees were Jane Green and Shirley Hufstedler. "Constance Baker Motley," in Gilbert and Moore, *Particular Passions*, 135–141. See also Rayner, *Wise Women*, 147–57.

18. Lopate, *Women in Medicine*, 120–23; Wertz, 218. See also Bowers, "Women in Medicine," 362–65.

19. Lopate, "Women in Medicine," 120–23. See Scher, "Women Psychiatrists" (1973), 1118–22.

20. Lopate, 127–28, 185; Mary Roth Walsh, *Doctors Wanted*, 264.

21. Lopate, 182–83.

22. Morrow, "Women in Medicine," n.p.; Lopate, 147–48, 153.

23. Lopate, 159–60.

24. Walsh, *Doctors Wanted*, 265; Morantz–Sanchez, *Sympathy and Science*, 344–46. For an account of medical education at WMC in the mid-sixties see interviews with Joni Magee and Susan Benes in Morantz et al., *Her Own Words*.

25. See chapter 13 in this book. See also Lopate, 173–74.

26. Robert J. Waldinger, "Virginia Apgar" in *NAW:MP*, 27–28.

27. Gallagher, "Women's Entry into Pharmacy," 4–9; "Can Women Aid Rx Manpower Shortage? Deans, Druggists Say Yes in Survey," *American Druggist* (9 February 1959), 5; Ohvall and Sehgal, "Practice Continuity and Longevity of . . . Women Pharmacists," 518–20; "Report of the Committee on Future Enrollment Problems," *American Journal of Pharmaceutical Education* 34 (1970), 403; Austin and Smith, "Women in Hospital Pharmacy: A Study in Eight States," *American Journal of Hospital Pharmacy* 28 (January 1971); *Employment Impacts of Health Policy Developments*, Special Report No. 11 (Washington, D.C.: National Commission for Manpower Policy, October 1976). Recruitment brochures are in the Kremers Reference Files of the American Institute of the History of Pharmacy, Madison, Wisconsin.

28. Lyle Saunders, "The Changing Role of Nurses," *American Journal of Nursing* 54:9 (September 1954), 1094–5, also cited by Woods, "Individual Dedication" in Maggs, *Nursing History*, 163; Kenneth Benne and Warren Bennis, "Role Confusion and Role Conflict in Nursing," *American Journal of Nursing* 59:2 (March 1959), 196–8, cited in C. Woods, "Individual Dedication," 164.

29. Corea, *Hidden Malpractice*, 60–61, 63; Goldstein, 289, a pattern that would be challenged as reverse discrimination in *Mississippi University for Women v. Joe Hogan* in 1982. See L. I. Stein, "Male and Female," in Spradley and McLundy, *Conformity*.

30. Lopate, 114; Corea, 62–63.

31. Cited in Woods, 156; Melosh, *"The Physician's Hand,"* 46; Brown, *Nursing for the Future*, quoted by Woods, 162. See Pohl, "Baccalaureate for Nursing," 180–83.

32. "Objectives and program of the AMA Committee on Nursing," *Journal of the American Medical Association* 181 (4 August 1962), 430, cited in Woods, 164–65; Melosh, *"Physician's Hand"*, 207–08, 214; Fred Katz, "Nurses," in Etzioni, *Semi–Professions*, 54; Lopate, 114; Corea, 62–63.

33. Nancy Milio, "Margaret Arnstein," *NAW:MP*; *Mademoiselle* 64 (January 1967), 47.

34. Corea, 63. Melosh, 159–205; Hine, *Black Women in White*, 188.

35. See Kobrin, "American Midwife," 350–63; Litoff, *American Midwives*, Wertz and Wertz, *Lying–In*, 218. Also, see below, section on "Pregnancy and Childbirth," pp.   .

36. Lanker, *I Dream a World*, 215.

37. Rogan, *Mixed Company*, 272, 275.

38. Ibid.

39. Rogan, *Mixed Company*, 276; Marling and Wetenhall, "Sexual Politics of Memory," 341–72; *1969 World Book*, 448.

40. Rogan, 273, 275.

41. Rogan, 60–61; VanDevanter, *Home By Morning*, 290, and interview with CHG, April 1986. This information was confirmed in an interview with Frances Shea Buckley by Blanche Linden–Ward in April 1990.

42. Pete Earley, "Forgotten Women," *Washington Post* (25 March 1981), A13; Kane, "Inside the Death Factory."

43. Maurer, *Strange Ground*, 55; Kathy Kafer, "Vietnam Aftershock," *Baltimore News-American* (26 January 1981), 1–2B; Logan, "Fighting Loneliness." Also see Hardy, et al., *Words of War*. MacPherson, *Long Time Passing*, 525–26, 528.

44. VanDevanter, *Home*, 24; Rogan, 274; BLW, interview with Frances Shea Buckley, 10–31–90. See Norman, *Women at War;* Jean Holm, *Women in the Military: An Unfinished Revolution*. See Buckley and Furey, *Visions of War*, an anthology of poetry of women in the Vietnam War.

45. Kane, "Inside the Death Factory," 1981; MacPherson, *Long Time Passing*, 530–31.

46. Jhan Robbins, "The Woman Who Stayed," *McCalls* 92 (September 1965), 96–97; MacPherson, 532–33.

47. "Good Samaritan in Vietnam," *Ebony* 23 (October 1968), 179–84; Norma Meyer, "Actress Confronts Post–Vietnam Syndrome," *Daily Breeze* (12 November 1980).

48. Whitbread, "Servicemen's Marriages," 94, 146; Whitbread, "Families of the Men," 53–55, 113–115.

49. MacPherson, *Long Time Passing*, 314.

50. Sheehan, *Bright, Shining Lie*, 438–39.

51. "Waiting Out the War—Wife or Widow?" *Life* 67 (7 November 1969), 75; Leonore Hershey, "Echo of Heroes," *McCalls* 91 (July 1964); "The Family: Second Life for War Widows," *Time* 94 (25 July 1969).

52. Sapiro, *Women in American Society*, 180–81. Marzolf, *Up From the Footnote*, 59; Abe Peck, *Uncovering the Sixties*, 208.

53. Kay Mills, *Place*, 58, 66, 69, 71, 73.

54. Marzolf, *Up From the Footnote*, 86. See Lublin, "Discrimination Against Women," 357–61.

55. Mills, *Place*, 83–4, 179–183. Mills notes that the sixties made choice possible with more women graduating from college, marrying later, using birth control, and changing expectations.

56. Quoted in Mills, *Place*, 183. Mills notes that the Gannett newspaper

chain was an exception to the rule of limited access for blacks. By the mid–sixties, under the direction of Al Neuharth, Gannett was doing aggressive recruiting of both women and minority journalists. See 300–306.

57. Susan Brownmiller, "Report on the Status of Women in Communications," New York University Law School conference, 11 April 1970, mimeographed; Lucy Komisar, "Report on the Status of Women in the Media," New York University Law School conference, 11 April 1970, mimeographed; Marion Marzolf, *Footnote*, 96–97.

58. See Marion Marzolf, "Marguerite Higgins," *NAW:MP*, 340–41.

59. Emerson, *Winners and Losers*, ix.

60. McCarthy, *Vietnam;* also see McCarthy, *Seventeenth Degree.*

61. Mary McGrory, "Doris Fleeson," *NAW:MP*, 239–241.

62. "McGrory, Mary," in *Contemporary Authors* 106 (1982), 342–45; Mills, *Place*, 141–43.

63. Tuchman et al., 20, 23.

64. Brownmiller, "Status of Women."

65. *Time* (1968), 95; Loudon Wainwright, *The Great American Magazine: An Inside History of LIFE* (New York: Knopf, 1986), 337.

66. Diamonstein, *Open Secrets.*

67. See Steinem, *Outrageous Acts.*

68. Mills, *Place*, 104. See her chapter, "The Girls in the Balcony," for a full account of the Press Club struggle.

69. Hunter, "New Concept," 583–602; Brownmiller, Report to NYU conference, mimeo, n.p.

70. *Newsweek* proclaimed "Women Join Revolt, Cite Sex Bias"; "Newswomen Hit Men Only Gridiron Club," *The Guild Reporter* (27 March 1970). Hunter, "New Concept," 583–602 passim. Hunter points out that there were several studies of the depiction of women in the mass media in general and in women's magazines in particular beginning in the mid-sixties and increasing in number in the early seventies. See her list, 584. The basis for *The Feminine Mystique* was, of course, such a study. Marzolf, *Footnote*, 86; quoted in Mills, 83–84.

71. Komisar, "Report." See Smith and Harwood, "Women in Broadcasting," 339–56.

72. Margaret Supplee Smith, "Aline Milton Bernstein Saarinen," *NAW: MP*, 614.

73. Weibel, *Mirror*, p. 51; Gelfman, *"Television News"*; Komisar, "Report." OCLC has a spoken recording by Komisar, *Women in the Arts* (St. Paul: Minnesota Public Radio, 1973).

74. Gent, "Women Filmmakers."

75. Cole, *Tipi*, ix–x; Mary Otis Stevens, "Struggle for Place: Women in Architecture, 1920–60," in Torre, 96.

76. Torre, *Architecture*, 102.

77. DeBlois designed the Pepsi–Cola/Olivetti building (1959) and the Union Carbide building (1960) in New York and the Emhart Manufacturing

Company building (1962) in Bloomfield, Connecticut. Torre, *Architecture*, 112–114.

78. Ibid., 188.

79. Ibid., 118–19.

80. Ibid., 123–26.

81. Ibid., 126.

82. Ibid., 128–29.

83. Torre, 140–41; Masotti and Hadden, *Suburbia*, 187.

84. Torre, 138–39; Jane Jacobs, *The Death and Life of Great American Cities* (New York: Random House, 1961), 372–73.

85. Cole, *Tipi*, 118, 124; "Rights Between the Sexes," *Architectural Forum* (Apr 1973), 71.

86. Rossi, "Women in Science," 1196–1202. Conferences were held at Marymount College in 1963 and MIT in 1964. Similar conclusions appear in M. Ostrofsky, "Women Mathematicians in Industry: The Road to Success is Difficult," *AAUW Journal* (March 1964), 114–18; and Motz, "Married Woman in Science," 374–76.

87. See David, *Career Patterns;* S. S. Robin, "The Female in Engineering," in Perucci and Gerstl, *Engineers*, 203–218.

88. Cohen, *Sisterhood*, 171; Morgan, *Sisterhood*, 41.

89. Judy Cooper, "It Could Have Happened 20 Years Ago," *Equal Times* [Boston] (31 July 1983), 6.

90. Ibid.

Chapter Six

1. "Port Huron," in Jacobs and Landau, *New Radicals*, 150–55. James Miller, *Democracy*, 44.

2. MacPherson, *Long Time*, 186.

3. Breines, *Community*, 96; MacPherson, *Long Time*, 187, 206; Zaroulis and Sullivan, *Who Spoke Up?*, 30–32.

4. Breines, *Community*, 96; MacPherson, *Long Time*, 206.

5. MacPherson, 200.

6. Evans, *Personal Politics*, 130, 141; MacPherson, 216.

7. Fruchter, "SDS."; Breines, *Community*, 79, 82.

8. Alpert, *Underground*, 44.

9. MacPherson, 539–40, 543.

10. *Worklist* (7 April 1965), quoted in Breines, 84.

11. See Hoffman, "Coeds," 168. The documentary film *Berkeley in the 60s*, directed by Mark Kitchell (San Francisco: Resolution, Inc./California Newsreel, 1990) presents a thorough overview of that student movement, emphasizing the voices of female participants beyond the scope of their original leadership.

12. Evans, *Personal Politics*, 116; Breines, 14.

13. MacPherson, 552. See also the documentary, "The War at Home."

14. Powers, *Diana*. Frankfort, *Kathy Boudin*.

15. Stern, *With the Weathermen*, 39, 65, 72, 143–44.

16. Breines, 38–39; MacPherson, 552–54; Gallup Poll quoted in *New York Times* (15 May 1969), p. 68, col. 3.

17. Decter, "Peace Ladies," 49. See the Helen Lamont and Mary Dwyer collections at the Schlesinger Library and Adams, *Peacework*. SANE had women on its national board in the fifties. Stephanie May designed the bronze plaque, first awarded to Steve Allen. The Student Peace Union (SPU), started at University of Chicago in 1958 by young Quakers Ele and Kenneth Calkins, had chapters through the Midwest and became national in 1962.

18. WSP, "Commemorative Issue;" Eleanor Garst, "Women: Middle–Class Masses," WSP *"Memo"* (April 1970) 5–6 (both in the WSP Papers, Sophia Smith Collection, Smith College); Decter, "Peace," 49, 52–53; Adams, *Peacework*, 11, 198, 217. Garst later moved to the Santa Barbara Center for Study of Democratic Institutions and remained active in WSP. See Zaroulis and Sullivan, *Who Spoke Up?*, 10–11, 103–05.

19. Gervis, "Women Speak Out," 523–6. Ethel Taylor, "A Personal Reaction to the Urbana Conference," in "Issues for Discussion #1," 8 July 1963, WSP Papers, box 2, folder 6, Sophia Smith Collection.

20. Kuhn, "Lysistratas," 24.

21. Memo to All WISPers and Friends from the Washington Steering Committee, 1962, box 2, folder 6, WSP Papers. *New York Times* (16 January 1962), 1, 18.

22. Frances Herring, "To End the Arms Race—Not the Human Race," [WSP] *Memo* (April 1970), 3–4; Jeanne Webber, "You've Come a Long Way!" [WSP] *Memo* (April 1970), 13–14.

23. Coretta Scott King added international peace to the civil rights concerns of her husband, enlisting his voice at times. See Gill, "Maternal Pacifism."

24. Adams, *Peacework*, 13–14; Herring, *Memo*, 3. Swerdlow, "Ladies' Day," 492–520.

25. Evans, *Born*, 263–64.

26. Webber, "You've Come," *Memo*, 15; Viorst, "Javits Scolds," 7; Kuhn, "Lysistratas," 24; "The Right of Petition," *Nation* 196, 25 May 1963, 435; Adams, *Peacework*, 13.

27. *Washington Evening Star* (30 December 1964). Deming, "Prison Notes," parts 1–6, in *Prisons That Could Not Hold* (San Francisco: Spinsters Ink, 1985), 1–185. Deming had participated in walks for peace and civil rights in 1961 and 1962.

28. "Ten American Women Join Vietnam Group in Denouncing U.S.," *New York Times* (19 July 1965).

29. Barbara Deming, "Prison Notes"; Barbara Bick, "Women and the Vietnam War," *Memo* (April 1970), 9–11.

30. Zaroulis and Sullivan, *Who Spoke Up?* 103–05. See Gellhorn, "Little Children."

31. Irma Zigas, "Hell, No! We Don't Let Them Go!" *Memo*, 19. Lenore Marshall of the American Friends Service Committee, Josephine Pomerance of the Committee on World Development and Disarmament, and Catherine Cory, West Coast organizer of the Friends' Committee on National Legislation were particularly active.

32. Zigas, Hell, No, 19–20; Adams, *Peacework*, 15.

33. Joan Hoff Wilson, "Jeannette Rankin," *NAW:MP*, 568.

34. Cathy Wilkerson, letter "To WSP from SDS," 1968, in WSP Papers, Sophia Smith Collection. Mimeographed.

35. Zaroulis and Sullivan, *Who Spoke?* 51, 90, 103, 211, 337, et passim.

36. See *Harper's* (May 1969).

37. *Memo*, 8.

38. Mary Clarke, "Let's Keep on 'Keeping On,'" *Memo*, 22.

39. Stimpson, "Literature as Radical Statement," in Elliot, 1066–67. Rachel Carson's *The Sea Around Us* (New York: Oxford University Press, 1951) made the National Park Service add major parcels of seashore to its holdings for preservation and public use. Carson's testimony is in the *Congressional Record* (June 4, 6, 1963). Also see Paul Brooks, *The House of Life: Rachel Carson at Work* (Boston: Houghton Mifflin, 1972), 305, 308–9, and passim.

40. See Frank Graham, Jr., *Since Silent Spring* (Boston: Houghton Mifflin, 1970).

41. For a contemporary analysis of the changes in the directions of the churches and the impact of these changes, see Cox, "New Breed" in McLoughlin and Bellah, *Religion in America*, 368–383.

42. Italics are in the original. Joanne Cooke, "Editorial: Here's To You, Mrs. Robinson," *Motive* 29:6 & 7 (March–April 1969), 4. Guest editors for the issue were, in addition to Cooke, Robin Morgan and Charlotte Bunch Weeks.

43. Mormon elder N. Eldon Tanner, quoted in Derr, "Strength in Our Union," in Beecher and Anderson, *Sisters in Spirit*, 194; *Dialogue: a Journal of Mormon Thought*, edited by Claudia Buchanan (Summer 1971).

44. See chapter 2 on the Civil Rights Movement. Reagon, "My Black Mothers," 95. Cheryl Gilkes defines the Sanctified Church as "those independent denominations and congregations formed by black people in the post–Reconstruction South and their direct organizational descendants. Gilkes, "'Together and in Harness,'" 679; Magary Hussain, "Muhammad Speaks," quoted in Lincoln, *Black Muslims in America*, 34.

45. Richie, "Church," 73–74. Letters in response to the article appeared in the 11 March 1970 issue.

46. *Christian Century* (3 November 1965); Shaw, "Nevertheless," 110–112; 168–171.

47. Kenneally, "A Question," 147; Elizabeth Farians, "Phallic Worship: The Ultimate Idolatry," in Plaskow and Arnold, *Women and Religion*, 81; Carroll et al., *Women of the Cloth*, 42–43ff., 77. This book provides a study of women's

motivation for seeking ordination and an account of their experiences in the seminary, on the job market, and in pastorates. On this subject, see also Lehman, *Women Clergy.*

48. Norene Carter, "The Episcopalian Story," in Ruether and McLaughlin, *Spirit,* 361. The ordination of women received formal church approval in 1976. For a history of the debate over ordination in the Episcopal church, see Hewitt and Hiatt, *Women Priests.*

49. Hewitt and Hiatt, *Priests,* 12; Carter, 357.

50. Carter, "Episcopalian," 358–59.

51. Ermarth, *Adam's Fractured Rib,* 54.

52. Arnold Shankman, "Dorothy Rogers Tilly," in *NAW:MP,* 691–2. Also see Shankman, "Civil Rights, 1920–1970: Three Southern Methodist Women," in Keller et al., 211–233.

53. "Resolution–American Baptist Convention," in Doely, *Liberation,* 105–06.

54. Verdesi, *In But Still Out,* 133–34, 26–28, 30.

55. Quoted in ibid., 97; ibid., 96, 99; Ermath, *Rib,* 105.

56. Ermath, *Rib,* 105.

57. Statement of the women's caucus of the National Council of Churches of Christ, in Doely, 98–102. The statement notes the small number of women with active roles in the churches and discrepancies in salary between men and women church workers.

58. From an interview with Friedan in the first issue of *Lilith* (Fall 1976), quoted in Schneider, *Jewish and Female,* 504.

59. Heschel, Intro. to *Jewish Feminist,* 4; Gibson and Wyden, *Jewish Wife,* cited in Mimi Scarf, "Marriages Made in Heaven?" in Heschel, 63. The study was based on in–depth interviews of 200 Jewish women and 200 non-Jewish women selected from a national sample. On the consequences of women's exclusion from public prayer, see also Schneider, 60ff; Saul Berman, "The Status of Women in Halakhic Judaism," in Kiltun, *Jewish Woman,* 121–22.

60. Berman, 121–22; Gail Shulman, "A Feminist Path to Judaism," in Heschel, 106.

61. Paula Hyman, "The Other Half: Women in the Jewish Tradition," in Koltun, 105; Schneider, 46–47.

62. Preisand, *Judaism,* 62, xiv–xvi, 38–39.

63. Heschel, xxx; Ruether and McLaughlin, *Women of Spirit,* 342–43.

64. CJF included the Jewish Family Service, Jewish Centers Association, and Jewish Education Bureau; in most communities it also raised funds for the United Jewish Appeal. Deborah E. Listadt, "Women and Power in the Federation," in Heschel, 152–53; Sochen, *Consecrate Every Day,* 46, 76–78; Lipardt quoted in Preisand, 82.

65. Sochen, *Consecrate,* 76–78.

66. Sister Marie Augusta Neal, "Catholicism in America," in McLoughlin and Bellah, *Religion,* 312–13.

67. Callahan, *Illusion of Eve,* 204; Cunneen, *Sex: Female,* 40. Cunneen's

book is particularly interesting for its discussion of Catholic attitudes toward birth control.

68. Few women had access to formal training in theology; seminaries had generally been inhospitable to women, and there was little opportunity for women to study theology in universities. An exception was the School for Sacred Theology at Saint Mary's College (Indiana), founded in 1943 by its president, Sister Madeleva Wolff. The program closed in 1969 having awarded 76 doctorates and more than 300 master's degrees in theology to women. See Karen Kennelly, C.S.J., "Sister Madeleva Wolff," *NAW:MP*, 741–2. The chair was named for famed theologian Georgia Harkness, who had been passed over for a chair at Garrett after a long teaching career. That chair went to a young male theologian. See Dorothy C. Bass, "Georgia Elma Harkness," in *NAW:MP*, 311; Joan Chamberlain Engelsman, "The Legacy of Georgia Harkness," in Keller et al., 338–358.

69. "Rosemary Radford Ruether" in Gilbert and Moore, *Particular Passions*, 114; Ruether, preface to *Religion and Sexism*, 9; Rosemary Rader, O.S.B., "Catholic Feminism: Its Impact on U. S. Catholic Women," Kennelly, *Catholic Women*, 193–94.

70. Daly, *Church and the Second Sex*, 12, 179.

71. Daly, "The Women's Movement: An Exodus Community," in Clark and Richardson, *Women and Religion*, 265–71.

72. The Grail, a lay institute of women founded in the Netherlands in the 1920s and brought to the United States in 1940, modified its direction in the sixties away from focus on the lay apostolate and its link to liturgical reform and toward an increasing emphasis on ecumenism and on social justice issues. As the decade progressed, Grail became identified with the burgeoning feminist movement. It was a risky move, and Grail lost some of the popularity it had accrued during the fifties when Grail centers had opened in many cities and hundreds came to the movement's headquarters in Loveland, Ohio, to explore the "vital link between involvement in the liturgy and the lay apostolate to the world." Brown, *Grail Movement*, 15–16.

73. For biographical material on Day, see her autobiography, *The Long Loneliness* (New York: Harper and Row, 1952); and Miller, *Dorothy Day*.

74. Day, *On Pilgrimage*, 100–01.

75. Ibid., 299. For an overall account of Church involvement with Chavez and the UFW see Mosqueda, *Chicanos, Catholicism*.

76. The only book–length study of the Catholic Left is Charles Meconis, *Clumsy Grace*. The other woman was Mary Moylan, who went underground in 1970 as the Catonsville Nine were to go to prison. She remained underground until June 1979. Meconis, 67, 162. For an account of their years in Guatemala and the Catonsville Nine action see Melville and Melville, *Whose Heaven*. On the Catonsville Nine see also Meconis, chapters 1 and 2; *Delivered Into Resistance:* comp. by the Catonsville Nine–Milwaukee 14 Defense Committee (New Haven: Advocate Press, 1969); and Berrigan, *Catonsville Nine*. For a review of the Maryknoll order's commitment to social justice and the controversy sur-

rounding it, see Colman McCarthy, "The Maryknoll Order," *The Washington Post* (19 April 1981), G1, G4–5. Cook, "Uneasy World," 48.

77. Meconis, *Clumsy*, 54–56, 70–74, 76–78, 104, et passim.

78. Daly, *Second Sex*, 94. See Turk, *Buried Life*; Henderson, *Curtained World*; and Griffin, *Courage to Choose*. Also, more recently, Wong, *Nun*. Sister Borromeo, *The New Nuns*, 201.

79. Stern and Michael Stern, *Sixties People*, 28–29.

80. Bernstein, *The Nuns*, 227; Jay P. Dolan, et al., *Transforming Parish Ministry*, 156; Sister Katharine Hanrahan, quoted in Dolan et al., *Transforming*, 155.

81. Tobin, *Hope*, 18–20. Tobin had been elected president of the Conference of Major Superiors of Women in August 1964 and was being sent to Rome by that organization when the official invitation came. Hers was the first American order to undertaken renewal. In 1967 Sister Jacqueline Grennan, S.L., president of the order's Webster College, announced that it would become a lay institution because "the nature of higher education is opposed to juridical control by the Church." See "Webster College," *Commonweal* 85:16 (27 January 1967), 442; Trent with Golds, *Catholics in College*, 262–63; "A Candid Educator–Nun: Sister Jacquelin Grennan," *New York Times* (12 January 1967), 43.

82. For a description of the planning and organization of a chapter, see Sister Valentine, *Nun*, 110–14 and Sister Reidy, in Borromeo, *Nuns*. See discussion by Valentine, 125ff; Sister Maria Reilly, O. P., interview with Carol Hurd Green (7 July 1981).

83. Bernstein, *Nuns*, 163; Dolan et al., *Transforming*, 164. Tobin, *Hope*, 60; Mother Patricia Barrett, R.S.C.J., "Nuns in the Inner City," in Borromeo, 102–05.

84. "Finding Identity, Black Nuns Putting 'Soul' Into Religious Life," *New York Times* (15 August 1970), 27, 41.

85. "Archbishop Curbs Glenmary Sisters," *National Catholic Reporter* 2:46 (21 September 1964), 11. See also "Shackling the Sisters," *Commonweal* 85:1 (7 October 1966), 5–6, and O'Gara, "The Archbishop," 47; Mary Beth Dakoske Duffey, "Fidelity to a Promise of Service," *Catholic Rural Life* 31:4, 16–18; "Glenmarys Down to 15; 50 Leave for Lay Work," *National Catholic Reporter* 3–39: 1, 12.

86. Documents from the Chapter of Renewal are reprinted in Doely, *Liberation*, 70–76; Turk, *Buried Life*, 149–155; "Nuns, Cardinal McIntyre clash," *Boston Globe* (19 January 1970), 3.

87. "The Nun: A Joyous Revolution," *Newsweek* (25 December 1967), 45; Samuel Eisenstein, "Communications Primer," in Kent, 21; Turk, *Buried Life*, 93–94.

88. Turk, 12; Rader, "Catholic Feminism," in Kennelly, 186–89. The 1966 report was reviewed and extended in 1982; Neal published the results in *Catholic Sisters*. Quiñonez and Turner, *Transformation*, 17–23, 142.

89. Sister Elena Malits quoted in Ebaugh, *Out of the Cloister*, 82; Rader, "Feminism," 188–89.

90. Dolan et al., *Transforming*, 173–74; Ebaugh, "Leaving Catholic Convents: Toward a Theory of Disengagement," in Bromley, *Falling from the Faith*, 100; Ebaugh, *Out of the Cloister*, 82.

91. Dolan et al., *Transforming*, 168–69; Kristin Morrison, interview with CHG, September 1987; Muckenhirn, quoted in "Nuns, Cardinal McIntyre Clash," *Boston Evening Globe* (19 January 1970), 3.

Chapter Seven

1. Joseph Boskin, "Rebellious Laughter: People's Humor in American Culture, 1950s to 1990s," book manuscript in progress. See also Nancy A. Walker, *A Very Serious Thing: Women's Humor and American Culture* (Minneapolis: University of Minnesota Press, 1988).

2. Robert Sklar in Sicherman and Green, *NAW: MP*, 489–90; Lee Strasberg, "Miss Monroe," in Obst, *The Sixties*, 68.

3. Alloway, article and book, 140–44. The eulogaic formula worked so well that Warhol began a "Liz" series when Elizabeth Taylor became so sick some thought she was dying. When she recovered, Warhol added bright colors to salvage the work. Calas, 117.

4. Haskell, *Reverence*, 324–25; Mordden, *Movie Star*, 229.

5. Weibel, *Mirror*, 127.

6. Haskell, 323.

7. Rosen, *Popcorn*, 311.

8. *Teen*, May 1963, 14–15; Stern and Stern, *Sixties*, 7–9.

9. Stern and Stern, 86.

10. Weibel, *Mirror*, 64–65.

11. Macdonald, *Movies*, 137; Haskell, *Reverence;* Weibel, *Mirror*, 126–28; Rosen, *Popcorn*, 322; Mordden, *Star*, 249.

12. Weibel, 129.

13. Mordden, 277–80. Ephraim Katz, "Raquel Welch," in *The Film Encyclopedia* (New York: Thomas Crowell, 1979), 1218. Welch made most of her films in Italy, France, Germany, and Britain.

14. Mordden, 277–80.

15. Weibel, 128; Haskell, 328.

16. Stern and Stern, 28–29.

17. Haskell, 327–29.

18. Haskell, 331–32. Keenan, *Women We Wanted*, 88. Rosen, 328–29. Haskell, "French Lesson." *Lears* 3:5 (July 1990), 71–72.

19. Weibel, 48; Tuchman et al., *Hearth and Home*, 9, 228, 47.

20. Tuchman, "The Symbolic Annihilation of Women by the Mass Media," *Hearth*, 9–13.

21. Review in (Riverside, California) *Press Enterprise* (31 May 1973).

22. Weibel, 54.

23. Ibid., 54–55.

24. Allen, *Speaking of Soap Operas*, 125–27. Modleski, *Loving with a Vengeance*, 85.

25. Allen, *Speaking*, 4, 14, 127, 138. Weibel, 56. Modleski, *Loving*, 87–89.

26. Edmondson and Rounds, *Mary Noble to Mary Hartman*, 40; Allen, 171; Evelyn C. Shakir, "Irma Phillips," *NAW:MP*, 542–43.

27. Weibel, 66–67.

28. Weibel, 64.

29. Weibel, 68–69. Stern and Stern, 18. The prime–time cartoon *The Flintstones* was aimed at an adult audience and attempted to capitalize on the format created by *I Love Lucy;* but Wilma and Betty were less engaging female characters than Lucy and Ethel.

30. Stern and Stern, 8, 11.

31. Weibel, 86. Whoopi Goldberg cites Nichols as a role model.

32. Ibid., 86–87.

33. Radway, *Reading the Romance*, 39–40; Modleski, *Loving*, 32, 35–36, 60.

34. Modleski, 59.

35. Modleski, 60–63; Russ, "Somebody Is Trying," 667.

36. Radway, *Reading*, 31–35.

37. Mary Jean DeMarr, "Charlotte Armstrong," *American Women Writers* (New York: Frederick Ungar, 1983), 28–29.

38. Yntema, *100 Women*, 12, 36, 62–63.

39. Yntema, 109, 116–17.

40. Yntema, *100 Women*, 70–71. Spivack, *Merlin's Daughters*, 9; LH 223, 234 quoted in Rosinsky, 30.

41. Spivack, *Daughters*, 9. See Joanna Russ, *Picnic in Paradise* (New York: Ace Books, 1968).

42. Dworkin, *Right–Wing Women*, 91.

43. Dahl, *Stormy Weather*, 92–93, 119, 201; Bill Cole, *John Coltrane* (New York: Schirmer, 1976), 192; Dan Morgenstern, *Jazz People* 261–62, 166. Barton moved to Australia in 1964 where her talents were more appreciated; many jazz greats found greater recognition and appreciation abroad from the sixties on. Except for a few "stars," mainly vocalists, most female jazz musicians are omitted from standard histories of the genre or given short shift.

44. Dahl, *Stormy*, 147–49, 152, 232, 241; Dempsey J. Travis, *An Autobiography of Black Jazz* (Chicago: Urban Research Institute, 1983), 191–94, 477–85.

45. Dahl, 155–56.

46. Ibid., 156; Morgenstern, *Jazz People*, 201.

47. Dahl, 180.

48. D. Antoinette Hardy, *Black Women in American Bands and Orchestras* (Metuchen, NJ: Scarecrow Press, 1981), 179, 181, 184–85, 189, 197; "Dorothy Donegan," in Travis, *Autobiography of Black Jazz*, 299–309.

49. Hardy, *Black Women*, 176–78; "The Spirit of Mary Lou," *Newsweek* (20 December 1971), 67. Kansas City named a street in her honor in 1973, and she received many honorary degrees.

50. Dahl, 171.

51. Dahl, 165, 170.

52. Ibid., 169; Handy, *Women*, 192–93; "Alice Coltrane Interviewed by Pauline Rivelli," in Rivelli and Levin, *Black Genius*, 122.

53. Dahl, 173, 175, 259–60.

54. Lorraine [Mrs. Xavier] Cugat, "Mrs. Cugat Can't See Gals as Tooters: Kills Glamor," *Down Beat* (4 May 1959), 13; "Maxine Sullivan," in Travis, *Autobiography of Black Jazz*, 451–55; Dahl, 217; Handy, 124, 137, 139.

55. Dahl, 178; Handy, 145.

56. Dahl, 251; Handy, 136–37; "What Happened to Melba Liston?" *Ebony* (June 1977).

57. Handy, 150; Dahl, 219–20.

58. Dahl, 189, 244–47.

59. Dahl, 205–06, 207.

60. Handy, 53, 64, 170–71.

61. Bill C. Malone, *Country Music U.S.A.: A Fifty–Year History* (Austin: University of Texas Press, 1968), 265.

62. Chet Flippo, "The Carter Family," in Dave Marsh and John Swenson, eds., *The New Rolling Stone Record Guide* (New York: Random House/Rolling Stone Press, 1983), 84.

63. Malone, *Country Music*, 287–88, 303. For a content analysis of country music, see Karen A. Saucier, "Healers and Heartbreakers: Images of Women and Men in Country Music," *Journal of Popular Culture* 20:3 (Winter 1986), 147–166.

64. Malone, 284.

65. Malone, 283.

66. Charlie Gillett, *The Sound of the City: The Rise of Rock and Roll* (New York: Pantheon, 1983), 365.

67. Kurman, "Girls' Cheerleading," 57–63; Terry Southern, "Twirling at Ole Miss," in *Smiling Through the Apocalypse: Esquire's History of the Sixties* (New York: Esquire, 1987), 147–58 (originally in *Esquire* in February 1963). Through the sixties, some major institutions like the University of Michigan continued to ban female cheerleaders and majorettes.

68. Lanker, *I Dream a World*, 213; Mangan and Park, *From 'Fair Sex' to Feminism*, 295.

69. Boutilier and San Giovanni, *Sporting*, 37; For the 1968 Olympic Boycott Movement, see Lynda Huey. *A Running Start* (New York: Quadrangle/New York Times Book, 1976).

70. Heiss, *New York World Telegram and Sun* (21 March 1960).

71. See John Semple, *Call Me Jock* (Waterford, CT: Waterford Publishing, 1981).

72. See Billy Jean King and Kim Chapin, *Billy Jean* (New York: Harper and Row, 1974).

73. Ellen W. Gerber, "A Chronicle of Participation," in Gerber, ed., *The American Women in Sport* (Lexington, MA: Addison-Wesley, 1974), 130; Allen

Guttman, *Women's Sports: A History* (New York: Columbia Univ. Press, 1991), 209. Awards at the United States Lawn Tennis Association's (USLTA) U.S. Open were not gender equalized at $25,000 until 1973.

74. Boutilier and San Giovanni, 40; *New York Post* (20 July 1964); Reet Howell, ed. *Her Story in Sport: A Historical Anthology of Women in Sports.* (West Point, NY: Leisure Press, 1982). The trend continued. In 1968, top female earner Whitworth received $48,380 compared to Billy Casper's $121,944; in 1970, $30,255 versus the $157,037 of Lee Trevino; in 1971, $41,182 versus $244,490 of Jack Nicklaus.

75. Boutilier and San Giovanni, 194, 209–11.

76. Guttmann, 221.

77. Barbara Gimla Shortridge, *Atlas of American Women* (New York: Macmillan, 1987), 69; Guttmann, 212–13.

78. See Guttmann.

Chapter Eight

1. For a discussion of the rise of "youth culture" in the sixties, see Gans, *Popular Culture*, 94–100.

2. Greig, *Will You Still Love Me*, 29.

3. Robert Santelli, *Sixties Rock: A Listener's Guide* (Chicago: Contemporary Books, 1985), 52; Greig, *Love Me*, 38.

4. Santelli, *Sixties Rock*, 49–50, 55–56; Greig, *Love Me*, 48–52. 50: Ironically, he commissioned "He Hit Me" from King–Goffin. Kennibrew sued and retrieved the Crystals name.

5. Greig, 31, 43.

6. Santelli, 56–57.

7. Santelli, 58; Greig, 58.

8. Greig, 71–72.

9. Greig, 80.

10. Leuchtenburg, *A Troubled Feast*, 65; see Greig.

11. Nelson George, *Where Did Our Love Go?* The Rise and Fall of the Motown Sound (New York: St. Martin's Press, 1985), 193–200. *See also* "Motown 25: Yesterday, Today, and Tomorrow," broadcast by NBC, May 1983.

12. An oral history of Gladys Horton is in Greig, 104–08. See Wilson, *Dreamgirl*.

13. The name Vandellas either came from a combination of names of Detroit's Van Dyke Street and Della Reese, Reeves's favorite singer, or from a feminization of "vandal," since they stole the spotlight from anyone they backed. Greig, 112–115.

14. In 1961, the Primettes lost two previous members to marriage—McGlowan and then her replacement Barbara Martin. In the seventies, Jean Terrell replaced Ross and the Supremes carried on for a time. See also Wilson, *Dreamgirl*.

15. Greig, 124–130.

16. Pareles and Romanowski, *Rolling Stone Encyclopedia*, 202–203. See Bego, *Aretha Franklin;* Connie Johnson, "Aretha Back to Her Soul," *Los Angeles Times* (16 December 1981), pt. 4: 1, 3.

17. Bego, *Aretha*, 117, 181.

18. Ward et al., *Rock of Ages*, 500. Eleanor Guest and Brenda Knight left the Pips to get married before 1960.

19. Greig, 44–45. See Stephen Holden, "Ellie Greenwich: Her Life and Her Songs at the Bottom Line," *New York Times* (20 January 1984), sec. Y, 12.

20. Stambler, *Encyclopedia of Pop*, 18.

21. Tom Rush, "How Success Spoiled the Folkies," in Obst, *The Sixties*, 123.

22. See Baez, *A Voice*, Joan Didion, "Where the Kissing Never Stops," in *Slouching Towards Bethlehem*, 45–60.

23. See *Don't Look Back*, a 1967 film directed by D. A. Pennebaker about Baez and Dylan on tour in England in 1965.

24. Stambler, *Encyclopedia of Pop*, 467. For an assessment of Mitchell's early career, see "Into the Pain of the Heart," *Time* (April 1970).

25. See Makeba, *My Story.*

26. Robbie Woliver, *Bringing*, 73–76.

27. Tom Wolfe, "The Pump–House Gang," in Obst, *The Sixties*, 143–44.

28. See Kathleen Corcoran, "Youth in Turmoil: Hampton Beach, New Hampshire, in the Sixties," Emerson College senior thesis, 1969; "FBI Reports on Summer Riots, *The Christian Century* (14 October 1964), 1261; *Report of the Hampton Beach Project*, Office of Juvenile Delinquency and Youth Development, Department of Health, Education, and Welfare (GPO, 1965), 154, 159. For photographic images of the West Coast counterculture, see Dennis Stock, *California Trip* (New York: Grossman, 1970).

29. See Michelle Phillips, *California Dreamin': The True Story of the Mamas and the Papas* (New York: Warner Books, 1986).

30. Jon Pareles, "On–Again Off–Again Jefferson Airplane Is On Again," *New York Times* (September 1989, C10 and 12.)

31. "The New Rock," *Life* (28 June 1968).

32. Ibid.

33. See Megan Terry, "Janis Joplin," *NAW:MP*, 385–87; "Janis Joplin," *Village Voice* (22 February 1968); "Passionate and Sloppy," *Time* (9 August 1968), 71. Janis Joplin reveals her early and recurring rejection by her conformist high school peers in poignant testimony in the film *Janis*, directed by Howard Alk and Easton Findlay (Universal, 1974).

34. Landau, *Janis Joplin*, 7–9. See Friedman, *Buried Alive.*

35. Perry, *Haight–Ashbury*, 181; Didion, "Slouching Towards Bethlehem," 84–128.

36. Perry, *On the Bus*. The book itself is a document of the macho sensibility that dominated the counterculture. Ken Kesey and Tom Wolfe tell versions of these stories elsewhere. See English, "Strange Trip," 3, 41.

37. Didion, "Slouching," 84, 122–23.

38. Perry, *On the Bus*, 200.

39. Paul D. Gruschkin, *The Art of Rock: Posters from Presley to Punk* (New York: Abbeville Press, 1987).

40. Charles Perry, *Bus*, 28.

41. *Newsweek* (6 February 1967), 92; *Newsweek* (13 November 1967), 74, 78; *Time* (4 January 1968), 96.

42. Bowker, *Drug Use*, 64–66.

43. Davidson, *Loose Change*, 85–6, 108, 127–29. See also Cooperstock, "Sex Differences," 238–44.

44. Fraser, ed., *1968: Generation in Revolt*, 117.

45. Fraser, *1968*, 117; Didion, "Slouching," 112–113.

46. David Sanjek, "Apocalypse Then: Apocalyptic Imagery and Documentary Reality in Films of the 1960s," 10–11, paper presented at "Out of the Sixties," May 1990 conference of the New England American Studies Association, in Tischler, *Sights on the Sixties*, 13–14.

47. Ibid.

48. Piercy, "Grand Coolie Damn," in Morgan, *Sisterhood is Powerful*, 483. Also see Breines, *Community and Organization* for a discussion of Carmichael.

49. Robin Morgan, "Take a Memo, Mr. Smith," in Morgan, *Going Too Far*, 69; Morgan, "Goodbye to All That," in *Going Too Far*, 122–28.

Chapter Nine

1. Arbus, *Diane Arbus*, 3; Bosworth, *Diana Arbus*, 187, 196, 198.

2. Bosworth, *Arbus*, 187, 196, 198, 262.

3. Tucker, ed., *The Woman's Eye*, 127–28.

4. Welpott quoted in Tucker, *Woman's Eye*, 141.

5. Sally Eauclaire, *The New Color Photography* (New York: Abbeville Press, 1981), 12–13; Tom Wolfe in *Marie Cosindas: Color Photographs* (Boston: New York Graphic Society, 1978), 8, 10, 12–15. Cosindas used a Linhof box camera.

6. Eve Sonneman, *Real Time: 1968–1974* (New York: Printed Matter, 1976); Eauclaire, 106–110, 271–72, et passim; Anne Tucker, *The Woman's Eye* (New York: Knopf, 1976), 155–169.

7. Interview with Joan Brigham by Blanche Linden–Ward, Boston, April 1990.

8. Whitney Chadwick, *Women, Art, and Society* (New York: Thames and Hudson, 1990), 306, 308. Munro, *Originals*, 116, 118.

9. Lippard, *Overlay*, 50; Robinson, *Georgia O'Keeffe: A Life*, 498–99, 507–09. For an account of the institutionalized sexism of the arts establishment during the fifties and sixties, see Cindy Nemser, *Art Talk* (New York: Scribner, 1975).

10. Chadwick, *Women, Art*, 306, 308.

11. Lippard, *Overlay*, 63; Joseph Treen, "Discreet Charm of Louise Bourgeois: After Years of Obscurity, She Emerges as Grande Dame of the Art

World," *Boston Globe* (13 August 1990), 35; Dore Ashton, "Louise Bourgeois," in *Encyclopedia of American Art*, 79; Chadwick, 315; Sandler, *American Art*, 304–305.

12. I. Sandler, *American Art*, 3, 9, 29; Nancy Stapen, "Abstract Expressionism of the 60s Revisited," *Boston Globe* (18 February 1991), 69. Frankenthaler's 1969 show at the Whitney was co–sponsored by the International Committee of MoMA.

13. Chadwick, *Women, Art*, 307–09.

14. Eugene C. Goossen, "Agnes Martin," in *Encyclopedia of American Art*, 364; Alloway, *Topics*, 100, 102, 106, 108.

15. Lippard, "Top to Bottom, Left to Right," *Grids* (Philadelphia: University of Pennsylvania Institute of Contemporary Art, 1972).

16. Carter Ratcliff, "Marisol Escobar," in *Encyclopedia of American Art*, 362; Chadwick, *Women*, 310–11.

17. Robins, *The Pluralist Era*, 190; Henri, *Total Art*, 56; Chadwick, 318.

18. Chadwick, 310; Lippard, *Eva Hesse*, 67.

19. Sandler, *American Art*, 309.

20. Chadwick, 314–15; I. Sandler, *Art*, 306–309; Lippard, *Hesse*, 5–6, 24–25, 56.

21. Lippard, *Hesse*, 137, 180, 205; Gula in Lippard, *Hesse*, 182, originally *Ms* (April 1973). The most notorious reviews included Joyce Purnick's "Tortured and Talented" in the *New York Post* (13 December 1972); and Douglas Davis's "Cockroach or Queen," in *Newsweek* (15 January 1973), 73.

22. Robins, *Pluralistic Era*, 8, 20–21.

23. Chadwick, 316; Robins, *Pluralist*, 49.

24. Robins, 46; Fine, *Afro–American Artist*, 158, 233.

25. Calas and Calas, *Icons and Images*, 159.

26. I. Sandler, 226, 228, 231.

27. Ibid., 138.

28. Avis Berman, "Edith Gregor Halpert," in *NAW:MP*, 301–303.

29. Lippard, *Get The Message?: A Decade of Art for Social Change* (New York: E.P. Dutton, 1984), 3; also see Lippard, *A Different War: Vietnam in Art* (Bellingham, WA: Whatcom Museum of Art, 1991).

30. Warhol and Hackett, *POPism*, 86.

31. I. Sandler, 92; Sheppard, "Inside Fashion with Eugenia Sheppard," *New York Herald Tribune* 17 (October 1965), sec. 2, p. 2.; "Personalities," *The 1966 World Book Year Book*, 456; Ultra Violet, *Famous for Fifteen Minutes*, 4, 29, 80.

32. Ultra Violet, *Famous*, 204–213; Warhol and Hackett, *POPism*, 95–96, 121–24, 127, 147. See Stein, *Edie*.

33. Warhol and Hackett, *POPism*, 245.

34. See Alan Solomon, "The Green Mountain Boys," *Vogue* (1 August 1966); Gablik, *Has Modernism Failed?*, 61.

35. Hansen, *A Primer of Happenings*, 20, 24, 72; Kirby, *Happenings*, 9.

36. See Banes, *Democracy's Body;* and Johnston, *Marmalade Me.*

37. Banes, *Terpsichore in Sneakers*, 9, 24.

38. Ibid., 24–30.

39. Robins, 187.

40. Banes, 13–14; Hansen, *Primer,* 12, 73, 75–76, et passim.

41. Hansen, 12, 73, 75–76, et passim.

42. Kirby, *Happenings,* 49–50, et passim.

43. Hansen, 24–29; Henri, *Total Art,* 68; Lippard, *Overlay,* 67.

44. David James, "Carolee Schneemann's *Fuses,*" *Cinematograph* 3 (1988), 314–320; S. MacDonald, "Carolee Schneemann: Autobiographical Trilogy," *Film Quarterly* 34 (1980); C. Lovelace, "Gender and the Case of Carolee Schneemann," *Millenium* (fall/winter 1986–87); Carolee Schneemann, "A Feminist Pornographer in Moscow," *Independent* (March 1992).

45. Sandler, 238–39.

46. Charles Perry, 22–23.

47. Perry, 22–24. Rain and her husband later joined the Subud faith and changed their names to Alexandra and Roland Jacopetti.

48. Henri, 69. Yoko Ono's *Grapefruit* (London: Sphere, 1970) explains her aesthetic philosophy as of 1966.

49. SCUM Manifesto in Robin Morgan, *Sisterhood Is Powerful: An Anthology of Writings from the Women's Liberation Movement* (New York: Vintage, 1970), 577, and in Judith Clavir Albert and Stuart Edward Albert, *The Sixties Papers* (New York: Praeger, 1984), 462–66; Ultra Violet, 167–178, 183–189; Warhol and Hackett, 271–74, 286.

50. Banes, *Terpsichore in Sneakers,* 15. See Lippard, *A Different War.*

51. Chadwick, 320–21; Grace Glueck, "Women Artists Demonstrate at Whitney," *New York Times* (12 December 1970); Lippard, *Get The Message,* 24, 96. The first WAR show was "X12" in January 1970.

52. I. Sandler, 299; Lippard, *Six Years,* 168.

53. Chadwick, 321; Lippard, *Six Years,* 67–68. Chicago's landmark work, the "Dinner Party," appeared, piecemeal, between 1973 and 1979.

54. Lippard, *Overlay,* 6, 41–42, 66–67.

55. Lippard, *Overlay,* 41–42.

56. Christine Ammer, *Unsung,* 170–71.

57. Ibid., 171–72.

58. Ibid., 173–75.

59. Ibid., 175–77, 138–39.

60. Ibid., 142–43.

61. Ibid., 182–83.

62. Ibid., 184–88.

63. Ibid., 189–91.

64. Ibid., 149.

65. Ibid., 154–55.

66. Ibid., 156–58.

67. Handy, *Black Women*, 128, 149–53. Denial of Kaufman's tenure by the orchestra in 1974 resulted in a national outcry and a much publicized court case charging discrimination; she lost. Another black woman chosen by Fiedler was Patricia Prattis Jennings (1941–), a pianist for the Pittsburgh Symphony from 1964 (Handy, 193–95).

68. Arnold Lionel Haskell, "Ballet," *Encyclopaedia Britannica* macropaedia 2 (15th ed., Chicago: Encyclopaedia Britannica, 1981), 652; Robert Tracy with Sharon DeLano, *Balanchine's Ballerinas: Conversations with the Muses* (New York: Linden/Simon and Schuster, 1983), 99, 102, 111–12, 129–30, 142, 149–54; See Suzanne Farrell, with Tom Bentley, *Holding On to the Air: An Autobiography* (New York: Sunset Books, 1990) and Gelsey Kirkland with Greg Lawrence, *Dancing on My Grave: An Autobiography* (New York: Doubleday, 1986); McDonagh, *Martha Graham*, 12, 297; Ingalls, "Ohio State 'Breathless'," B5.

69. Lanker, *I Dream a World*, 21.

70. For a contemporary account of the development of Arena Stage see "Career in the Round," *National Business Woman* (June 1963), 4–7.

71. Doris Abramson, "Lorraine Hansberry," 310–311. See also Keyssar, *The Curtain and the Veil*, on Hansberry's "ambivalent intentions" in the play and her "Rites and Responsibilities: the Drama of Black American Women," in Brater, *Feminine Focus*, 228–231, for a feminist reading of *Raisin in the Sun*.

72. Abramson, "Hansberry," 311.

73. For a discussion of the latter two plays see Margaret B. Wilkerson, "Music as Metaphor: New Plays of Black Women," in Hart, ed., *Making a Spectacle*, 64–65.

74. Interviews with Rochelle Owens and Megan Terry in Betsko and Koenig, eds., *Interviews*, 345, 380–81.

75. Helene Keyssar, *Feminist Theatre* (New York: Grove Press, 1985), 22. *Hair*, which toured twenty-five countries and was translated into 14 languages, presented a controlled orgy of pop music and counterculturalism and featured such women as Donna Summer and Joan Armatrading; it did nothing, however, to address women's concerns. "Ellen Stewart," in Gilbert and Moore, *Particular Passions*, 33–37. See also Acton and Hodges, *Mugshots*, 216.

76. Barbara Garson, *MacBird* (New York: Grove Press, 1967), ix–xi.

77. Keyssar, *Feminist Theatre*, 62. Terry, in David Savran, *In Their Own Words: Contemporary American Playwrights* (New York: Theatre Communications Group, 1988), 241, 244, 253. Interview with Terry in Betsko and Koenig, eds., *Interviews*, 377–401.

78. Keyssar, *Feminist Theatre*, 67; Richard Schechner, introduction to Megan Terry, *Viet Rock* (New York: Bobbs-Merrill, 1967), 8–9, 17.

79. Terry in Keyssar, *Theater*, 61. From a 1972 interview with Terry, quoted in Keyssar, p. 70. See also the interview by Dinah Leavitt with Megan Terry in Chinoy and Jenkins, *Women in American Theatre*, 285–292.

80. Childress interview in Betsko and Koenig, *Interviews*, 63; "Alice Childress," in Blain et al., *Feminist Companion to Literature*. 205.

81. Adrienne Kennedy interview in Betsko and Koenig, *Interviews,* 248–49.

82. Kennedy, "Funnyhouse of a Negro," in Brasner and Consolo, *Black Drama;* Keyssar, *Theater,* 111. See also Jeanne–Marie A. Miller, "Black Women in Plays by Black Playwrights" in Chinoy and Jenkins, 254–60.

83. Ling, *Between Worlds;* Yolanda Broyles Gonzalez, "Toward a Re–Vision of Chicano Theatre History: The Women of El Teatro Campesino," in Hart, ed., *Making A Spectacle,* 209–238.

84. Betsko and Koenig, 128–29, 385.

85. Keyssar, 20–21.

86. Maria Irene Fornes, in Savan, *Our Words,* 54, 51; interview with Fornes in Betsko and Koenig, 155. The first of her plays to be produced, *The Widow,* was published in Cuba in 1961.

87. W. B. Worthen, "Still Playing Games: Ideology and Performance in the Theater of Maria Irene Fornes," in Brater, *Feminine Focus,* 168. Fornes also began her directing career with *Molly's Dream,* with its first production at New York's New Dramatists. Betsko and Koenig, 161.

88. Keyssar, 116; Betsko and Koenig, 132. Six of Drexler's early plays were published in *The Line of Least Existence and Other Plays* (New York: Random House, 1967).

89. A second collection, *I am the Babe of Joseph Stalin's Daughter: Poems 1961–1971,* appeared in 1972. The Living Theatre of Julian Beck and Judith Malina, the quintessential political and theatrical experiment, survived through political and financial storms from its beginning in their living room in 1951. Just as "Futz" was about to go into rehearsal in 1963, the Internal Revenue Service seized the Living Theatre building for tax arrears of $20,000. The troupe protested and staged a sit–in and a "play–in" in protest. All were arrested, and Malina and Beck served prison sentences in the winter of 1964 for "impeding federal officers in the pursuit of their duties." By then, the troupe was in Europe, where it remained until 1968. That year, the Living Theatre returned to the United States where it performed for about six months before returning again to Europe for an indefinite stay. During its brief return, the group, under Malina and Beck's direction and inspiration, stirred up controversy with such productions as *Paradise Now,* which included an invitation to the audience to shed their clothes and join the actors nude on stage in an expression of radical dismissal of the constraints on the human spirit. See "The Living Theatre: A Great Life in Brief," in Rostagno, *We, The Living Theatre,* 11–12.

90. Keyssar, 113. Interview with Owens, in Betsko and Koenig, 346–57.

Chapter Ten

1. Solotaroff, introduction to *Red Hot Vacuum* (New York: Atheneum, 1970), viii; "Autobiography in Art," Solotaroff, *Vacuum,* 284.

2. Adrienne Rich, "When We Dead Awaken: Writing as Re–Vision," *On Lies,* 44; W. H. Auden, introduction to *A Change of World* (New York: W. W.

Norton, 1951). Auden praised the poems because they "speak quietly but do not mumble, respect their elders but are not cowed by them, and do not tell fibs."

3. Rich, foreword to *Poems: Selected and New, 1950–1974* (New York: W. W. Norton, 1975), xv; "When We Dead Awaken," 44.

4. Rich, "The Burning of Paper Instead of Children," *The Will to Change*, 15–18.

5. Denise Levertov, "Life at War," in *Poems 1960–1967* (New York: New Directions, 1983), 229; Levertov, "Advent 1966," in *Relearning the Alphabet* (New York: New Directions, 1970), 4.

6. Levertov, "Some Notes on Organic Form," in *The Poet in the World*, 7. See also Mersmann, *Out of the Vortex*.

7. Levertov interview with Deborah Digges, 92nd Street Poetry Center, New York City, 22 April 1991. Her sixties poems are included in *The Sorrow Dance* (1967); *Relearning the Alphabet* (1970); and *To Stay Alive* (1971), all published by New Directions in New York. They went in 1972 at the invitation of a women's committee in North Vietnam, accompanied by Jane Hart, wife of then Senator Philip Hart. "From a Notebook: October '68–May '69," in *Alphabet* (1970), 92; also included as Part I of "To Stay Alive" in the volume of that name.

8. They later divorced.

9. Muriel Rukeyser, *Breaking Open* (New York: Random House, 1973), 25; Rukeyser, "The Poem as Mask" (1969), in Sandra M. Gilbert and Susan Gubar, *The Norton Anthology of Literature by Women: The Tradition in English* (New York: Norton, 1985), 1782.

10. "I just lost interest in the characters," she told an interviewer. Harriet Shapiro, "Grace Paley: 'Art Is On the Side of the Underdog,'" *Ms* 2:11 (May 1974), 43; Ivan Gold, "On Having Grace Paley Once More Among Us," *Commonweal* 89 (25 October 1968), 111–12. Paley's 1959 story collection, *The Little Disturbances of Man*, was reprinted in 1968. Critic Ivan Gold welcomed the return to print of these "quirky, anguished, funny, loving, deep and antic glimpses into the hearts and lives" of characters of all ages and sorts. He asked Paley what brought her to these fictions. Her answer was characteristic: "I felt bad about men and women." Gold, 40.

11. Paley in Shapiro, 45.

12. Amy Ling, *Between Worlds: Women Writers of Chinese Ancestry* (New York: Pergamon Press), xi; Mary McCarthy, in Carol Brightman, "Mary, Still Contrary," *The Nation* (19 May 1984), 613.

13. "Trip to Hanoi" appeared first in *Esquire* magazine and was reprinted in Susan Sontag, *Styles of Radical Will* (New York: Farrar, Straus and Giroux, 1969). She does not reprint any part of *Trip to Hanoi* in the 1983 *Susan Sontag Reader* and has in effect repudiated the piece and the moment in her career that it represents. Sontag interview with Geoffrey Movius, quoted in Clare D. Kinsman, ed., *Contemporary Authors*, vol. 17–20 (Detroit: Gail Research, 1976), 695. Didion is discussed in chapter 8 in the section on the counterculture.

14. At the age of seventeen she married sociologist Philip Rieff; their son was born when she was nineteen. She divorced Rieff in 1958.

15. Later Toni Cade Bambara.

16. Introduction to Cheryl Wall, ed., *Changing Our Own Words: Essays on Criticism, Theory, and Writing by Black Women* (New Brunswick: Rutgers Univ. Press, 1989), 2–3. Other books by black women writers published that year were Nikki Giovanni, *Re:Creation;* Louise Meriwether, *Daddy Was a Number Runner;* Sonia Sanchez, *We a BaddDDD People* (Detroit: Broadside Press, 1970); and Margaret Walker, *Prophets for a New Day* (Detroit: Broadside Press, 1970). See Cade, *Black Woman;* Morgan, *Sisterhood.*

17. In a section of her autobiography which Walker read to Claudia Tate, she says "my teaching career has been fraught with conflict, insults, humiliations and disappointments. In every case where I have attempted to make a creative contribution and succeeded, I have been immediately replaced by a man." Tate, *Black Women Writers,* 189; Margaret Walker, *How I Wrote Jubilee,* ed. Maryemma Graham (New York: Feminist Press, 1990), 14–23 passim.

18. Brooks, *Report from Part One* (Detroit: Broadside Press, 1972), *Report from Part One,* 73, 84, quoted by Melhem, *Gwendolyn Brooks,* 12.

19. "Lovers of the Poor," in Brooks, *Selected Poems* (New York: Harper and Row, 1963), 44.

20. Gayl Jones, "Community and Voice: Gwendolyn Brooks's 'In the Mecca,'" in Mootry and Smith, *A Life Distilled,* 193; Brooks, *Report from Part One,* quoted in Mootry and Smith, 165, 193; D. M. Melhem, *Heroism,* 15–16.

21. *A Street in Bronzeville* (1945), *Annie Allen* (1949), *The Bean Eaters* (1960), *Selected Poems* (1963), and *In the Mecca* (1968) were published by Harper and Row, as was a later anthology, *The World of Gwendolyn Brooks* (1971). Atlantic Press in Boston published *Maud Martha* (1953).

22. Brown et al., *To Gwen with Love;* Mootry and Smith, *Life,* 284.

23. Erlene Stetson, preface to *Black Sister,* xiv; Wall, *Changing Our Own Words,* 3.

24. Jordan, *Civil Wars,* x–xi. Virginia Blain et al., *Feminist Companion,* 590–91. Adrienne Rich taught in the SEEK program during these years.

25. Alice Walker, "In Search of Our Mothers' Gardens," *In Search of Our Mothers' Gardens* (New York: Harcourt, Brace and Jovanovich, 1983), 239.

26. Walker in Tate, 176–79.

27. Stetson, introduction to *Black Sister,* 33, 51–52.

28. Giovanni, *Gemini,* 33. The two volumes were published together by Broadside Press in 1968 and by William Morrow (New York) in 1970. "Nikki–Rosa," from *Black Judgement* (Detroit: Broadside Press, 1968), reprinted in Stetson, 233–34.

29. Sonia Sanchez is a pseudonym: her birth name was Wilsonia Driver; Sanchez, "the final solution" in *Homecoming* (Detroit: Broadside Press, 1969), 18. See Melhem, "Sonia Sanchez" in *Heroism,* 133–47.

30. Dudley Randall, Introduction to Sonia Sanchez, *We a BaddDDD People* (Detroit: Broadside Press, 1970). As anyone who has had the fortune to hear

them knows, Sanchez's own readings of her poetry are moving and powerful. "listenen to big black at s. f. state," from *We a BaddDDD People*, 48. "Sister Son/ ji" appeared in Ed Bullins, ed., *New Plays from the Black Theatre* and was produced in 1971. "The Bronx Is Next Door" was published in *Drama Review* in Summer 1968 and first produced in 1970. See Blaine, ed., *The Feminist Companion*, 942. The strong oral and chant quality of her poetry becomes even more strikingly impressive in light of the fact that she had to overcome a bad stutter. See Melhem, *Heroism*, 148–50.

31. Audre Lorde, in Tate, 100, 110. Lorde, *Zami: A New Spelling of My Name* (Freedom, CA: Crossing Press, 1982), 255. Zami is "a Carriacou name for women who work together as friends and lovers." Ibid.

32. Lorde, in Tate, 104, 114.

33. Hackett and Burke, *80 Years of Best Sellers;* Jacqueline Susann, *Valley of the Dolls* (New York: Geis, 1966) and *The Love Machine* (New York: Simon and Schuster, 1969).

34. The article on Tyler in *Contemporary Authors* (NRS, vol. 11), 511, says that Tyler now repudiates both of these early efforts.

35. Walker, *In Search*, 43, 59.

36. Flannery O'Connor, in Sally and Robert Fitzgerald, eds., *Mystery and Manners: Occasional Prose* (New York: Farrar, Strauss & Giroux, 1957), 33–34. Quoted by Fitzgerald, "Flannery O'Connor," *NAW:MP*, 515.

37. Carr, *The Lonely Hunter*, 203, 521.

38. Eudora Welty, preface to *The Collected Stories*, xi.

39. Calisher, *Herself*, 59, 37, 245; Antler, introduction to *America and I*, 11.

40. Chametzky, *Our Decentralized Literature*, 9; Antler, *America and I*, 1.

41. Antler, 10.

42. Ibid., 37–38; "Silences, 1962" in Tillie Olsen, *Silences* (New York: Laurel, 1983), 23–40. The essay was first printed in *Harper's Magazine* (1965), then included in a book by the same title (1978), including essays on various writers.

43. Olsen, "I Stand Here Ironing," in *Tell Me a Riddle* (New York: Laurel/ Seymour Lawrence, 1979), 21. The title story, first published in *Partisan Review* in 1956, won the O. Henry award as the best American story of that year.

44. Quoted by Antler in *America and I*, 12. Antler's source is an Olsen interview with Naomi Rubin, quoted in Bonnie Lyon, "Tillie Olsen: the Writer as a Jewish Woman," *Studies in American Jewish Literature* 5 (1986), 91.

45. Quoted in Blain et al., *Feminist Companion*, 853.

46. Cynthia Ozick, *Art and Ardor: Essays* (New York: Knopf, 1983), 245; Ozick, "Provisions of the Demise of the Dancing Dog," in *Art and Ardor*, 266.

47. Ozick, "Literature and Politics of Sex: A Dissent," in *Art and Ardor*, 285, 290; Blain et al., *Feminist Companion*, 822.

48. See Lydia Shaikin, "Eve Merriam, *Dictionary of Literary Biography* 61 (Detroit: Gale Research, 1987), 223–234. The article includes a complete list of Merriam's works through 1986.

49. Faderman, *Surpassing the Love of Men*, 355; Zimmerman, *The Safe Sea of Women*, 9. *A Place for Us* was published by Bleecker Street Press in 1969 and reissued that year by McGraw-Hill with the title *Patience and Sarah*.

50. Zimmerman, *Safe Sea*, 10.

51. Gilbert and Gubar, *Norton Anthology*, 1489.

52. Spires, "The Art of Poetry XXVII"; Gertrude Reif Hughes, "'Somebody Loves Us All': Elizabeth Bishop's Feminism," unpublished paper in possession of Carol Hurd Green.

53. Hughes, "Somebody Loves," 6; "Filling Station," in *Complete Poems*, 127–28.

54. Quoted by Judith Kroll, "Sylvia Plath," *NAW:MP*, 550. See also Alexander, *Rough Magic*; Stevenson, *Bitter Fame*.

55. *The Bell Jar* was published in the United States in 1971 to great popular success. Gayle Greene, "Mad Housewives and Closed Circles: Mad Housewife Fiction of the Sixties and Seventies," in Greene, *Changing the Story: Feminist Fiction and the Tradition* (Bloomington: University of Indiana Press, 1991), 58–85.

56. Kroll, "Sylvia Plath," 550. See Plath, *Letters Home*. The volume of letters, which also includes remarkably self–justifying or self–deluding commentary by Plath's mother, is also illustrated by many photographs. Gilbert and Gubar, "Sylvia Plath," *Norton Anthology*, 2193.

57. Sexton, "Sylvia's Death," *Norton Anthology*, 1996–98. Sexton interview with Carol Hurd Green, June 1972. For a biographical and critical study of Sexton see Middlebrook, *Anne Sexton*.

58. Jane McCabe, "Anne Sexton," *NAW:MP*, 643.

59. Carol Hurd Green, "The Writer Is a Spy," *Boston Review of the Arts* (August 1972), 24. Blain et al., *Feminist Companion*, 620.

60. V. Blain et al., *Companion*, 297. DiPrima, ed., *War Poems* (New York: Poets Press, 1968); DiPrima, *Revolutionary Letters Etc.*, *1966–1973* (San Francisco: City Lights, 1979), 31, 49, 23.

61. See Cade, *Black Woman*; Millett, *Sexual Politics*. See below 426ff.

Chapter Eleven

1. Suzy Menkes, "Oleg Cassini and the Value of Jackie Kennedy," *International Herald Tribune*, 5 June 1990, 8.

2. Neal in *1963 World Book Year Book*, 299.

3. Melinkoff, *What We Wore*, 133.

4. Melinkoff, *What*, 128–29; Abbott and Love, *Sappho*, 176.

5. Melinkoff, *What*, 117–18; Keenan, *Women We Wanted*, 97–98.

6. Melinkoff, 118; Keenan, 97–98.

7. Quant received the Order of the British Empire (O.B.E.) in 1966 for rejuvenating the London fashion industry. Melinkoff, 119; Keenan, 97; *Newsweek* (13 November 1967), 67; Quant in Greig, *Still Love Me*, 95.

8. Melinkoff, 119–20. The definition is from the *Random House Dictionary of the English Language*.

9. Stern and Stern, *Sixties People*, 17, 21. Cartoon eyes.

10. Shrimpton was so famous by 1964 that she published her memoirs; but she continued modeling into the early seventies. Keenan, *Women*, 100, 124, 127, 133, 149–51, 153–54.

11. Keenan, *Women*, 164.

12. Keenan, 164; Stern and Stern, *Sixties*, 54–55.

13. Stern and Stern, *Sixties*, 54.

14. Quant in David Bailey, *Goodbye Baby and Amen*, in Keenan, 169, 163.

15. Susan Gill interview by Blanche Linden–Ward, August 1990. Kathryn Zahony, "Fashion," in *1969 World Book*, 339.

16. Melinkoff, 125.

17. Keenan, 173–74.

18. Cassell, *A Group Called Women*, 34.

19. Quoted in Landau, *Janis Joplin*, 12.

20. Catharine R. Stimpson, "Literature as Radical Statement," in Emory Elliott, ed., *Columbia Literary History of the United States* (New York: Columbia Univ. Press, 1988), 1067.

21. Keenan, 174–78.

22. Steinem quoted in Cohen, *The Sisterhood*, 44.

23. See Schwartz, *Never Satisfied*, 67.

24. Javna and Javna, *60s! A Catalog*, 42. See Deford, *There She Is;* and Griffin, *Pageant Winner*.

25. Dana Densmore, "On the Temptation to Be a Beautiful Object" from *No More Fun and Games: A Journal of Female Liberation* (November 1968), reprinted in Salper, *Female Liberation*, 203–08.

Chapter Twelve

1. See David M. Kennedy, *Birth Control in America: The Career of Margaret Sanger* (New Haven: Yale University Press, 1970); Ellen Chesler, *Margaret Sanger and the Birth Control Movement in America* (New York: Simon and Schuster, 1992).

2. James Reed, "Katharine Dexter McCormick," in *NAW:MP*, 441–42; Reed, *From Private Vice*, 344. McCormick established the Harvard Neuroendocrine Research Foundation and subsidized the journal *Endocrinology*.

3. Reed, *From Private Vice*, 344; Chevalier and Cohen, "Terrible Trouble," *Ladies' Home Journal* 84:7 (July 1967), 44; Corea, *Hidden Malpractice*, 139.

4. Editorial, *Boston Globe* (10 May 1990).

5. Reed, 344.

6. Mintz, *By Prescription Only*, 273–74.

7. Barbara Seaman, *The Doctors' Case* (New York: P. H. Wyden, 1969); Chevalier and Cohen, 43–48; Reed, *From Private Vice*, 364.

8. Chevalier and Cohen, 43–48.

9. Reed, *From Private Vice*, 364.

10. Peck, *The Baby Trap*, 8–146.

11. Westoff and Westoff, *From Now to Zero*, 103–06.

12. Ibid., 188–89.

13. Reed, *From Private Vice*, 353. See Loretta McLaughlin, *The Pill, John Rock, and the Church: The Biography of a Revolution* (Boston: Little, Brown, 1982).

14. Toni Cade, "The Pill: Genocide or Liberation?" in *The Black Woman*, 164.

15. Ibid.

16. Westoff and Westoff, *Now to Zero*, 10.

17. "Birth Control—Or Not?" *Newsweek* 4 (August 1958), 48–49. May, *Homeward Bound*, 151.

18. Westoff and Westoff, *Now to Zero*, 53–54.

19. Ibid., 56–57.

20. Ibid.

21. Lucy Freibert, "American Catholics and the Rhythm Method from the 1930s to the 1960s," unpublished paper delivered at the Third Berkshire Conference on the History of Women (9–11 August 1976, session V, no. 3), 12, at the Schlesinger Library.

22. Andrew Hacker, "The Pill and Morality," *New York Times Magazine* (4 July 1965); Ehrenreich, Hess, and Jacobs, *Re–Making Love, Feminization of Sex* 146.

23. Obst, *The Sixties*, 71–72.

24. Editorial, *Boston Globe* (10 May 1990).

25. Mintz, *Prescription*, 249.

26. Ibid., 261. In Germany, where the drug was readily available, there were over 6000 cases of deformities.

27. "The Thalidomide Disaster," *Time* 80 (10 August 1962), 32; Kristen Luker, *Abortion*, 64.

28. Helen B. Taussig, "The Evils of Camouflage"; Mintz, 255.

29. Rossi, "Abortion and Social Change," 341.

30. Westoff and Westoff, 110; Lader, *Abortion*, 11, 13. For a selection of horror stories, see Luker, Abortion, 101–7. Also see Rossi, "Abortion and Social Change," 344.

31. Lader, *Abortion II*, 48–50, 62; Rosen, *Abortion in America*, 310.

32. Lader, *Abortion*, 5–6; Luker, 68–72, 82–91, 122; Editorial Research Reports, "Abortion Law Reform," 548. John Knox, a freshman assemblyman, first introduced the reform bill in 1961, but Beilenson took it over, shepherding it to passage to overturn California Penal Code sec. 274, in place since 1872, which provided for imprisonment of two to five years for women who had abortions.

33. The states were Arkansas, California, Delaware, Louisiana, Kansas, Maryland, New Mexico, North Carolina, Oregon, South Carolina, and Virginia. Glendon, *Abortion and Divorce*, 11–13.

34. Lee, *The Search*, 149, 43–44.

35. Hole and Levine, *Rebirth*, 284; Glendon, 11–13.

36. Lader, *Abortion*, 3.

37. Luker, *Abortion*, 65, 78–82; Gallup, *The Gallup Poll* 1:3 [1959–1971] (Wilmington: Scholarly Resources, 1972), 1784.

38. Luker, 38, 80–81, 86–87.

39. Luker, 88; Natalie Shainess, "Abortion Is No Man's Business," in Martin, *The American Sisterhood*, 167–69 (originally in *Today*, May 1970); Lader, *Abortion II*, 114.

40. Lader, *Abortion II*, 31, 62; Hole and Levine, 295; Luker, 90.

41. Lader, *Abortion II*, 12.

42. Ibid., 48–50, 62; Corea, *The Hidden*, 100–101; New York Clergy Consultation Service, "Statement of Purpose" (1968), quoted in Luker, 123.

43. Cohen, *The Sisterhood*, 176–77; Lee, *The Search*, 105.

44. Rosen, *Abortion in America*, 198; Westoff and Westoff, 118.

45. Schulder and Kennedy, *Abortion Rap*, 219.

46. Daniel Callahan, *Abortion: Law, Choice, and Morality* (London: Collier—Macmillan, 1978), 415; Luker, 128–30, 5; Schulder and Kennedy, 219–224.

47. Lader, *Abortion II*, 33.

48. Lader, *Abortion II*, 68.

49. Westoff and Westoff, 118, 149; Hole and Levine, 278, 284; "Abortion Law Reform," 545; Glendon, 13; Luker, 92–95, 193. See E. C. Moore, *Abortion and Public Policy: What Are the Issues?* (Washington: Population Association of America, 1971).

50. Cohen, *Sisterhood*, 141–2; Hole and Levine, 279; Lader, *Abortion II*, 36.

51. Lader, *Abortion II*, 62.

52. Hole and Levine, 296–98; Cohen, *Sisterhood*, 225.

53. Lader, 11, 81–82.

54. Cohen, 201–03.

55. Hole and Levine, 292. See above [section on "Litigation and Women], on Eisenstadt *v.* Baird.

56. Hole and Levine, 300; Wandersee, *On the Move*, 82–84. Also see Pauline Bart and Melinda Bart Schlesinger, "Collective Work and Self–Identity: The Effect of Working in a Feminist Illegal Abortion Collective," in Lindenfeld and Rothschild-Whitt, *Workplace Democracy*, 139–153.

57. *Our Bodies, Ourselves*, republished commercially in 1973.

58. Ibid., 1, 61–62.

59. Ebon, ed., *Everywoman's Guide to Abortion*, 1–3, 13–14; Hole and Levine, 299–300.

60. Blake, "Abortion and Public Opinion," 546–47.

61. Blake, "Abortion," 540–48.

62. Luker, 193, 197, 201, 206, 215.

63. Brenda Hyson, "Black Genocide," *The Black Panther* 4 (1970), 4.

64. Rossi, "Abortion" 342; Schulder and Kennedy, *Abortion Rap*, 146.

65. Alexander, "Politics of Abortion;" Petchesky, 103; Goldstein, 335.

66. Luker, 126.

67. Petchesky, *Abortion*, 103; Luker, 126.

68. Margarete Sandelowski, *Pain, Pleasure, and American Childbirth: From the Twilight Sleep to the Read Method, 1914–1960* (Westport, Conn.: Greenwood Press, 1984), 93–96, 108–109, 127.

69. Ibid., 95, 117–19. See Waldo Fielding and L. Benjamin, *The Childbirth Challenge: Commonsense Versus "Natural" Methods* (New York: Viking, 1962).

70. Karp, *The Queen is in the Garbage*, 54.

71. Corea, 227.

72. Dally, *Inventing Motherhood*, 174–75; Davis, *Moving*, 229–30.

73. Hewlett, *A Lesser Life*, 179.

74. Corea, *The Mother Machine*, 20–22.

75. Ibid., 23–24, 36.

76. Ibid., 28–29.

77. Ibid., 329.

78. Ibid., 328–29.

79. Mintz, *Prescription Only*, 264.

80. Chambers and Schultz, "Women and Drugs," 131; Kaledin, *Mothers and More*, 9.

81. Corea, *The Hidden*, 80; Lawrence S. Linn and Milton S. Davis, "The Use of Psychotherapeutic Drugs by Middle-Aged Women," *Journal of Health and Social Behavior* 12 (Dec. 1971), 331.

82. Cooperstock, "Sex Differences," 239–43. K. Jean Lennane and R. John Lennane, "Alleged Psychogenic Disorders in Women: A Possible Manifestation of Sexual Prejudice," *The New England Journal of Medicine* 288 (3 February 1973), 288–92.

83. Wilson, *Feminine Forever*, 18, 22, 31, 34, 37–38. See Delaney, Jupton, and Toth, *The Curse*, 167–68, 171–72.

84. Seaman, *Women and Crisis*.

85. Chambers and Scultz, "Women and Drugs," 192; Cooperstock, "Sex Differences," 243; Warhol and Hackett, *POPism*, 69.

86. Stern and Stern, *Sixties People*, 55. In 1966, the first case of cancer related to DES, a form of estrogen prescribed to about three million women, was discovered. Davis, *Moving*, 237–39.

Chapter Thirteen

1. May, *Homeward Bound*, 220–22.

2. Haynes Johnson, *Washington Post* (4 July 1971); "Margaret Mead Answers Questions," *Redbook* (March 1968), 10; Toffler, *Future Shock*, 25–26.

3. D'Emilio and Freedman, *Intimate Matters*, 303. See Cannon and Long, "Premarital Sex," 39–40; Bell and Chaskes, "Premarital Sexual Experience," 84.

4. Decter, *The New Chastity*, 78.

5. Masters and Johnson, *Human Sexual Response*. "Sex Education for Adults: Researchers Masters and Johnson," *Time* (25 May 1970). See "William Masters and Virginia Johnson," in Robinson, *Modernization of Sex*, 120–90.

6. *Time* (15 May 1970); Robinson, *Modernization*, 151–52, 122, 157.

7. Deborah Dwork, "Sophia Josephine Kleegman," in *NAW:MP*, 399–400.

8. Linda Gordon, "Lena Levine," in *NAW:MP*, 419–20.

9. D'Emilio and Freedman, *Intimate Matters*, 303; Weibel, *Mirror*, 139; *Look* (10 January 1967), 56; Steinem, *Outrageous Acts*,

10. Brown, *Sex and the Single Girl*, 4, 28, 34, 89, 94, 226, 257.

11. Ibid., 244–45, 247, 249; Joan Didion, "The Great Reprieve."

12. Weibel, 139.

13. J[oan Terry Garrity,] *The Sensuous Woman* (New York: Dell, 1969). Similar bestsellers were Terry Southern's and Mason Hoffenberg's *Candy* and Trudy Baker's and Rachel Jones's *Coffee, Tea, or Me*. A group of 21 *Newsday* writers, including two women, each contributed chapters to the deliberately "trashy," "unremittingly sexy" and "bad" bestseller, *Naked Came the Stranger*, by "Penelope Ashe" in 1969.

14. Rimmer, *Harrad Experiment*, 1–2.

15. Rimmer. The cover notes quote 1966 comments in *Time* and the Syracuse University *Daily Orange*.

16. MacPherson, *Long Time Passing: Vietnam and the Haunted Generation* (New York: N.A.L., 1984), 542–543.

17. *Newsweek* (6 February 1967), 92.

18. D'Emilio and Freedman, 326–27.

19. Kate Millett, "Sexual Politics; A Manifesto for Revolution," in Firestone and Koedt, *Notes from the Second Year*; Ellen Willis, Introduction to Echols, *Daring to be Bad*, xii.

20. Firestone, *The Dialectic of Sex*, 198, quoted in Echols, 211.

21. Koedt, "Myth of the Vaginal Orgasm," *Notes from the First Year*, reprinted in Koedt et al., *Radical Feminism*, 199, 206.

22. D'Emilio and Freedman, 326–27; William Acton, *Prostitution* (1969 reprint of 1851 book), 118; Gail Sheehy, "New Breed," 22; 10; Costello, "Legalization of Prostitution," 127–142; *Report* President's Commission on Obscenity and Pornography (GPO, 1970), 112. Also see "Sex: How to Read All About It," *Newsweek* (14 August 1970), 38–43; "Sex and the Arts: Explosive Scene," *Newsweek* 73 (14 April 1969), 67–70; Gilman, "Wave of Pornography," 36–37, 39–82; Scott and Franklin, "Changing Nature," 80–86. Although references to sex in media increased relatively faster in the fifties than in the sixties, the sense of an "erotic revolution" grew through the sixties. Still traditional taboos appeared repeatedly as in the call by Congresswoman Iris Blitch that Attorney General Robert Kennedy deny Elizabeth Taylor and Richard Burton re-entry into the country for their extramarital affair while filming *Cleopatra*. See "Georgia Legislator Scores Miss Taylor and Burton," *New York Times* (23 May 1962), 38.

23. D'Emilio and Freedman, 326–27.

24. D'Emilio, *Sexual Politics*, 235–36, 240, 244–45, 247, 249; D'Emilio and Freedman, 311.

25. Faderman, *Surpassing*, 203, 315, 359; D'Emilio and Freedman, 289, 292–94; Ehrenreich et al., *Re-Making Love*, 63–4; Gatlin, *American Women Since 1945* (Jackson: University Press of Mississippi, 1987), 20.

26. The name came from an erotic poem by Pierre Louys, "Songs of Bilitis," having meaning for lesbians and also masking their identity. Martin and Lyon, *Lesbian/Woman*, 72, 210–11, 222–25; Ehrenreich et al., *Re-Making Love*, 2; D'Emilio, *Politics*, 98, 101–2. In 1963, DOB listed only 30 lesbian bars in the entire nation.

27. D'Emilio, 102–4; Faderman, *Surpassing*, 379; Martin and Lyon, *Lesbian*, 225–41; Grier quoted in "Review: *The Ladder Anthologies*," in *Chrysalis* no. 2 (1977), 103.

28. D'Emilio and Freedman, 319–20; Rosen, *Popcorn Venus*, 354–55; Martin & Lyon, 13.

29. Faderman, 379–82; Martin and Lyon, 243.

30. D'Emilio and Freedman, 320; Gatlin, 20.

31. Martin and Lyon, 230–33.

32. Martin and Lyon, 73.

33. Faderman, 386; de Beauvoir, *The Second Sex*, 459; D'Emilio, 236; D'Emilio and Freedman, 311; Atkinson, *Amazon*, 83; Myron and Bunch, *Lesbianism*, 93.

34. Marotta, 72, 235; Martin and Lyon, 245; D'Emilio and Freedman, 317, 319, 321; Echols, 345. (See chapter 14 on the Women's Movement.)

35. Martin and Lyon, 247–49.

36. Robert Lundberg and Marynia Farnham, *Modern Woman: The Lost Sex* (New York: Grosset and Dunlap, 1947), 142.

37. Friedan, *Mystique*, 4, 7, 17, 21, 27.

38. Ibid.

39. Ibid.

40. Woloch, *Women*, 502; The Friedan collection in the Schlesinger Library contains letters from women of all ages and backgrounds, acclaiming Friedan's work.

41. Friedan, *Mystique*, 280, 294, 296.

42. Broverman et al., "Sex–Role Stereotypes," 1, 3, 6. See Weisstein, "Psychology Constructs" in Gornick and B. K. Moran.

43. Tiger, *Men in Groups*, 208.

44. Erik Erikson, "Inner and Outer Space," in Lifton, ed., *Woman*.

45. Bardwick, *Psychology of Women*.

46. Ehrenreich and English, *For Her Own Good*; Boston Collective, *Our Bodies, Our Selves*, 113; Corea, *Hidden Malpractice*, 100–101.

47. Corea, 95, 99.

48. Caprio's *Adequate Female*; Masters and Johnson, *Response*, 64; Hole and Levine, 178–9.

49. Chesler, *Women and Madness*, 26, 40, 246.

50. Robert T. Roth and Judith Lerner, "Sex–Based Discrimination in the Mental Institutionalization of Women," *California Law Review* 63 (753) 796, 798–801; Chesler, *Women*, 128. See also Kate Millett, *The Loony Bin Trip* (New York: Simon and Schuster, 1990).

51. Roth and Lerner, *Discrimination*," 801–05; Chesler, 36–37, 44–45.

52. Roth and Lerner, 801–05; Chesler, 36–37, 44–45.

53. Ruzek, *The Women's Health Movement*, 75–76; Barbara Roberts, "Psychosurgery: The 'Final Solution' to the 'Woman Problem'?" *Second Wave* 2, 14, 43.

54. Roberts, "Psychosurgery," 14–15; Ruzek, *Women's Health*, 75–76; Chesler, 35.

55. "The Redstocking Manifesto," in Papachristou, *Women Together*, 234; Cohen, 169. The concept of blaming the victim had been developed by psychologist William Ryan in response to the criticism of black women which had followed sociologist Daniel Patrick Moynihan's characterization of them as emasculating matriarchs in *The Negro Family: The Case for National Action*. See Ryan, *Blaming the Victim*. See Horner, "Fail: Bright Woman"; *Discrimination Against Women*, 91st Cong., 2nd sess. (Washington, D.C.: GPO, 1970), also in *Psychology Today* 3 (Nov. 1969), 36.

56. Marlene Dixon, "The Rise," 57; Firestone, *Dialectic*, 172; Hole and Levine, 176–78; Millett, *Sexual Politics*, 213.

57. Philip Rieff, *Freud: The Mind of the Moralist* (New York: Anchor Books, 1961), 191–204; Simon and Gagnon, "Psychosexual Development," 9–17; Ginnott, *Between Parent*, ch. 10.

58. See Bühler and Massarik, *The Course of Human Life* (1968) and Bühler and Melanie Allen, *An Introduction to Humanistic Psychology* (1972). Maslow pioneered in this area with his article, "Self-Esteem (Dominance-Feeling) and Sexuality in Women," in *Journal of Social Psychology* 16 (1942), reprinted in Ruitenbeek, ed., *Psychoanalysis*, 161–97 and with Abraham H. Maslow, H. Rand, and S. Newman, "Some Parallels Between Sexual and Dominant Behavior of Infra-Human Primates and the Fantasies of Patients in Psychotherapy," *Journal of Nervous and Mental Disease* 131 (1960), 202–212. See the *Journal of Humanistic Psychology*, founded by Maslow in 1961.

59. Hole and Levine, 180–81; Naomi Weisstein, "'Kinder, Küche, Kirche'," paper read at the American Studies Association, 1968, reprinted in Morgan, ed., *Sisterhood*, 228–245; *Motive* (Mar.–Apr. 1969), 78–85. See Weisstein, "Psychology Constructs the Female," in Altbach, ed., *From Feminism*.

60. Rosen, 335; U.S. Department of Commerce, *Marital Status*, Table B; U.S. Center for Health Statistics, "Marriage." Luker, *Abortion*, 116; Mead, "The American Woman Today," *The 1969 World Book Year Book*, 83–84.

61. Petchesky, *Abortion and Woman's Choice*, 111.

62. Friedan, 4, 7, 17, 21, 27; Gans, *The Levittowners*, 162.

63. Hoffman, "Through All My Housework," 184–90; Friedan, 261. See Tornabee, "The Bored Housewife," 97–99, 115.

64. Woloch, 506; Jesse Bernard quoted in Radl, *Mother's Day Is Over*, 86; and Ehrenreich and English, *For Her Own Good*, 282. For a class analysis, see Komarovsky, "The Homemaker," 226–29. Komarovsky found the "average" homemaker was a 28-year-old WASP with three children and an annual family income of $4300.

65. Margolis, *Mothers and Such*, 171, 173; See Margolis, "In Hartford, Hannibal, and (New) Hampshire, Heloise is Hardly Helpful," *Ms* 9 (June 1976), 28–36.

66. *Time* (25 November 1966); Edith De Rham in Margolis, *Mother*, 176. See Julia Child, Simone Beck, and Louisette Bertholle, *Mastering the Art of French Cooking* (New York: Knopf, 1961); Child, *The French Chef Cookbook* (New York: Knopf, 1968); and Child and Beck, *Mastering* vol. 2 (New York: Knopf, 1970).

67. Stern and Stern, 24.

68. "Peg Bracken," Lina Maniero, *American Women Writers*, v. I, A–E (New York: Unger, 1979), 212.

69. "Adelle Davis," *Time* (March 1972).

70. Mead, "American Woman Today," 83–84.

71. Ibid., 86.

72. Ibid.

73. Pat Mainardi, "The Politics of Housework" in Morgan, *Sisterhood*, 501–510; Dolores Hayden, "Catharine Beecher and the Politics of Housework," in Torre, *Architecture*, 49.

74. Mead, "American Woman Today," 86–87.

75. Ibid., 87. See Alice Kessler–Harris and Karen Brodkin Sachs, "The Demise of Domesticity in America," in Benería and Stimpson, 66–67, 81. Sociologists observed even blue–collar husbands helping with housework: see Rubin, *Worlds of Pain*, 103.

76. Woloch, 496; Petchesky, 111; Mead, 84. See Veevers, "Voluntarily Childless," 356–66.

77. Spock, *Baby and Child Care*, 155; Spitz, *The First Year of Life*, 106; Bowlby quoted in Margolis, *Mothers and Such*, 84–85; Ginnott, *Between Parent and Child*, 169; Anthony and Benedek, *Parenthood*, 179, discussed in Ehrenreich and English, 219–22. See Lois Wladis Hoffman, "Effects on Children: Summary and Discussion," in Nye and Hoffman, *The Employed Mother*, and Christina Haryman, *Dream Babies*, 228.

78. Spock, *Baby*, 155; Margolis, *Mothers*, 81. Spock did not advocate paternal involvement until the 1976 revised edition of his classic book.

79. Ribble, *Rights of Infants*, 101, 141–43. See Margolis, 83–85.

80. De Rham. *The Love Fraud*, 132, 158, 160–61; Hardyman, 288.

81. Bruno Bettelheim, "Growing Up Female," 124; Nye and Hoffman, *Employed Mother;* Margaret Mead, "A Cultural Anthropologist's Approach to

Maternal Deprivation," in Ainsworth, *Deprivation of Maternal Care*, 55–56. Critics were quick to criticize Bettelheim's "permissiveness," his suggestion that "good mothers" fed children "goodies."

82. Mead, "American Woman," 95; "Why Young Mothers Feel Trapped," *Redbook* (September 1960). See Peck and Senderowitz, *Pronatalism*.

83. See Kernan, "Her Mother's Daughter?" 343–50.

84. Sennett and Cobb, *Hidden Injuries*, 132–34.

85. Freeman, "Growing Up Girlish," *Transaction* 8:1–2 (November–December 1970).

86. See Walsh, "The Generation Gap," 4–11.

87. Rosalind Barnett in McCain, "As Daughters Grow Up."

88. Mead, 84; Lederer and Jackson, *The Mirages of Marriage*, 13; Rustum Roy and Della Roy, *Honest Sex* (New York: N.A.L., 1969); Roy, "Is Monogamy Outdated?" 19; Ehrenreich and English, 282.

89. See Callwood, "Infidelity," 76–77, 132–34; Hunt, *The Affair;* "What Women Really Think About Their Marriages," *Family Circle* (February 1968), 34, 94.

90. Sexton, *Blue Collars and Hard Hats*, 198; "The Divorced Woman," *Newsweek* 69 (13 February 1967), 64; U.S. Bureau of the Census, *Statistical Abstracts*, 67.

91. Lee, 151; "Aretha Franklin: Queen of Soul," *American Masters* (25 July 1989), WGBH–TV. See Billingsley, *Children of the Storm*.

92. Welfare payments for a family of four in 1966 averaged $146 a month nationally, $32 in Mississippi, far less than the $270 official poverty line. Kotz and Kotz, *A Passion for Equality*, 183, 199; Davis, *Moving*, 347–51.

93. Jones, *Labor of Love*, 306–307. See Piven and Cloward, *Poor People's Movements*, 292–305. Piven and Cloward, a professor of social work, influenced Wiley by suggesting a welfare rights organization in 1965 to work to establish a national minimum income. Kotz and Kotz, 198.

94. Jones, 306–08.

95. Ibid., 308.

96. Daniel Patrick Moynihan quoted in Ibid., 312.

97. Ibid., 312, 315. Aptheker, "The Matriarchal Mirage," 129; Murray quoted in Yancey and Rainwater, *The Moynihan Report*, 60. Quoted from Ladner, *Tomorrow's Tomorrow*, 41.

98. See Rainwater and Yancey, *The Moynihan Report;* and Paula Giddings, *When and Where*, 325–35.

99. Angelou, *I Know Why the Caged Bird Sings*, 231.

100. Kaledin, *Mothers and More*, 173–74.

101. See Lopata, "Living Arrangements," 41–61; Lopata, "Social Involvement," 41–58. Also see Frances Fitzgerald, *Cities on a Hill: A Journey Through Contemporary American Cultures* (New York: Simon and Schuster, 1986).

102. Mary McCay, "Ethel Percy Andrus," *NAW:MP*, 25–27. In 1991, the AARP was the nation's largest and most powerful lobbying group with the

second largest Washington office to the Pentagon. See Lewis and Butler, "Why Is Women's Lib Ignoring Old Women?," 223–31.

Chapter Fourteen

1. Betty Roszak was one of the first to call Friedan the catalyst in "The Human Continuum," in Roszak and Roszak, *Masculine/Feminine*, 297.

2. Lippard, *Eva Hesse*, 26–27, 205.

3. Lessing, *The Golden Notebook;* Merriam, *After Nora Slammed the Door;* Flexner, *Century of Struggle*. See Millett, *Sexual Politics*, on counterrevolution.

4. Cohen, *The Sisterhood*, 132–37.

5. Cohen, *Sisterhood*, 132, 134, 138.

6. Gabin, *Feminism in the Labor Movement*, 188.

7. Papachristou, *Women Together*, 220.

8. NOW's 1967 Statement of Purpose, in Hole and Levine, 85–86; Papachristou, *Women Together*, 220–21. Another founder was Anna Arnold Hedgman.

9. Cohen, 139.

10. Hole and Levine, 95; Cohen, 140–41.

11. Hole and Levine, 95–98; Papachristou, 221–22.

12. Freeman, *Politics of Women's Liberation*.

13. Echols, *Daring to Be Bad*, 16–17; see Breines, *Community*.

14. Echols, 13–14, 24.

15. Politico–criticism of mainstream feminists.

16. Marlene Dixon, "On Women's Liberation," 28; Echols, 26; See also Breines, *Community*.

17. Fraser, *1968*, 344. Wandersee, *On the Move*, 3. "Chicago Women Form Liberation Group: To the Women of the Left," *New Left Notes* (13 November 1967). Salper, *Female Liberation: History and Current Politics* (New York: Knopf, 1972).

18. Echols, 317, n87.

19. Salper, 174.

20. McAfee and Wood, "Bread and Roses"; Salper, 175.

21. Mitchell, "Longest Revolution," 11–37; Dixon, "The Rise of Women's Liberation," 57–64.

22. Alpert, 122–24, 242–44. See also Morgan, *Going Too Far*.

23. Salper, 173.

24. Firestone, "The Jeannette Rankin Brigade: Woman Power?" in *Notes from the First Year*. See Cathy Wilkerson's memoir to Women Strike for Peace (WSP) explaining why there is antagonism between the groups, photocopy in the collection of Carol Hurd Green.

25. Atkinson, *Amazon*, 14; Fraser, *1968*, 347; Cohen, 164–65; Morgan, *Going*.

26. "Women's Group Splits over Meaning of Feminism," *Washington Post* (18 October 1968). "The Feminists: A Political Organization to Annihilate Sex Roles," in Koedt et al., *Radical Feminism*, 368–69; Bosworth, *Diane Arbus*, 346; Cohen, 166.

27. Hole and Levine, 112, 134; Ellen Willis, "Women and the Left," in Firestone and Koedt, *Notes from the Second Year*, 55; Willis, "Sister Under the Skin?" *VLS* 8, June 1982, quoted in Echols, 3; Marge Piercy, "Grand Coolie Damn," *Leviathan* (1969), reprinted in Morgan, *Sisterhood*, 473–92.

28. Cohen, *The Sisterhood*, 169; "Redstockings Manifesto," 7 July 1969; Complete text in Tanner, *Voices* and in Morgan, *Sisterhood*, 533–36, 598; Echols, 332; also see Koedt.

29. Ibid., Salper, 176–77.

30. Salper, 177.

31. Kathie Sarachild, "The Power of History," 1975. Redstockings, eds. *Feminist Revolution* (New Paltz: Redstockings, 1975), 18; Echols, 187–89.

32. Echols, ix–x.

33. Echols, vii–viii.

34. Echols, 21; Yates, 77, 102.

35. Carden, *The New Feminist Movement*, 64, estimates that there were small women's groups in at least forty cities by the end of 1969. Quoted in Papachristou, 265.

36. Curtis, "Miss America Pageant"; Duffett, "Atlantic City is a Town with Class"; Deford, *There She Is*, 5, 256; Cohen, 149–50; Salper, 173; "White House Had Ears at Early Feminist Rally," *Boston Globe* (15 September 1991), 16.

37. Cohen, 151.

38. Echols, 12.

39. D'Emilio and Freedman, 313; Ron Fraser, *1968*, 300; Echols, Cohen, 170.

40. Hewlett, *A Lesser Life*, 141–2.

41. Dixon, "The Rise of Women's Liberation," 57. Salper, 152.

42. Cohen, 168–69.

43. Gornick, "The Next Great Moment in History is Theirs," and "Who Says," 24, 27.

44. Salper, 179; Firestone, 166, 168.

45. Millett, *Sexual Politics*, xii. The Cornell talk was reprinted in *Notes from the Second Year*, ed. Firestone and Koedt.

46. Millett, 37.

47. Millett, 29; Spender, *Women of Ideas*, 726.

48. Millett, 213, 27, 210.

49. Howe, "Middle Class Mind," 124, 129; *Time* (31 August 1970), 20–21; Mailer, "Prisoner of Sex," and *The Prisoner of Sex*, 15; Gore Vidal, *New York Review of Books* (22 July 1971), 11.

50. Echols, 241–17.

51. "Women's Lib: A Second Look," *Time* (14 December 1970), 50.

52. Cohen, 236, 242–43, 249–50; Echols, 219.

53. Faderman, 476.

54. Faderman, 476; Abbott and Love, *Sappho Was a Right-On Woman*, 119–34.

55. *The Alyson Almanac*, 21; Cohen, 247–51; Millett, *Sexual Politics*, 174; Salper, 182.

56. Faderman, 386; De Beauvoir, 459; Atkinson, *Amazon Odyssey*, 83; Friedan, 375.

57. Faderman, 382–84, 476; Echols, 212, 215–16; Cohen, 188, 211, 249–50; Davis, *Moving*, 264–67. *See also* Susan Brownmiller, "Sister Is Powerful," *New York Magazine* (15 March, 1970).

58. Morgan, xx.

59. Cohen, 247–51; Echols, 211, 228. *The Furies* appeared in January 1972.

60. D'Emilio and Freedman, 317.

61. Myron and Bunch, 29, 31–32; Charlotte Bunch, "Personal Statements," in Bird, *What Women Want*, 33–34.

62. Echols, 345; Marotta, *Politics of Homosexuality*, 235; D'Emilio and Freedman, 317. *Time* (14 December 1970). See Martin and Lyon, in Joanne Cooke et al., *The New Woman*, 78–88; Robin Morgan, "Lesbianism and Feminism," *Second Wave* 14–23.

63. Myron and Bunch, 29, 31–32; Bunch, "Personal Statements," 33–34.

64. Atkinson, 83–86, 131–32; Faderman, 17–18; Martin and Lyon, ix, 261; Hoagland and Penelope, *For Lesbians Only*, 17.

65. Willis, Introduction to Echols, xii; D'Emilio and Freedman, 244.

66. Morgan, ed., *Sisterhood*.

67. Mitchell, *Woman's Estate*, 162. Also see the increasing list of articles on women's issues in the *New York Times Index* or *Facts on File* from 1965 to 1970.

68. Strainchamps, *Rooms with No View*; Yates, *What Women Want*, 132–40. See Varda One, "Manglish," *Everywoman* (23 October 1970), 14.

69. Echols, 8.

70. Echols, 212; Gilder, "The Suicide of the Sexes," 42–54; Gilder, *Sexual Suicide*, 6. See Howard, "Is Women's Lib a Dirty Word? 46–51.

71. "Who's Come a Long Way, Baby?" *Time*, 31 August 1970, 21; Gagnon and Simon, "Women's Revolution?" 76.

72. Morgan, *Going Too Far*, 175; Ellis in Echols, xiv; Echols, 305.

73. D'Emilio and Freedman, 314.

74. Susan Faludi, *Backlash: The Undeclared War Against American Women* (New York: Crown, 1991), 320–22; Friedan interview by Linden-Ward, 24 September 1992.

75. Fraser, 343. For theories, see Peggy White and Starr Goode, "The Small Group in Women's Liberation," *Women: A Journal of Liberation* (Fall 1969), 56–57; Sarachild, "Feminist Consciousness-Raising" in Leslie B. Tanner, 154–57; "For Continuing Formation of Consciousness–Raising Groups," *Female Liberation Newsletter* (March 1970).

76. Sarachild, "Consciousness–Raising" in Redstockings, *Feminist Revolution*, 132–136; Echols, 320–56.

77. D'Emilio and Freedman, 312.

78. Jeanne Arrow, "Danger in the Pro-Woman Line and Consciousness Raising" (1970), Quoted in Ware, *Woman Power*, 111, and in Shaffer, "Women's Consciousness Raising" 14; in Hewlett, *Lesser Life*, 157–158; Echols, *Daring*, 61, 81–91; Davis, *Moving*, 98–100; Jeffrey Grossel interview by Linden-Ward, August 1989. The feminists mentioned "prison guards."

79. Hewlett, *A Lesser Life*, 153–157. See Shreve, *Women Together*.

80. Langer, "Notes," 79–81; Lazarre, "Feminists and Freudians" in West, 69.

81. Hewlett, 153–157, Chesler, *Women and Madness*, 243–44.

Epilogue

1. Warhol and Hackett, *POPism*, 194.

2. Los Angeles *Times* reprinted as *The Killing of Sharon Tate* (New American Library, Time-Mirror); Wenner, *Twenty Years of Rolling Stone*, 68–69.

3. Cohen, *The Sisterhood*, 187; Hampton and Fayer, *Voices of Freedom*, 539–40. The story of Angela Davis is told at the end of the section on Civil Rights.

4. Wandersee, *On the Move*, 1; Echols, *Daring to Be Bad*, introduction by Ellen Willis, vii. See Friedan, "Strike Day," in *It Changed*, 184–91.

5. See Faludi, *Backlash*.

6. Hoge, et al., "Trends," 266, 273; Levine, *When Dreams and Heroines Died*, 105, 111–12; Horowitz, *Campus Life*, 251. See Faludi, *Backlash*.

7. See Wandersee, *On the Move*.

8. "New Traditionalism" was the slogan of a new editorial policy and marketing strategy of *Good Housekeeping* in 1988 and 1989, promoted with full-page ads in the *New York Times*. See Faludi, 93–95.

9. For a discussion of Madonna as feminist, see Daniel Harris, "Make My Rainy Day," *The Nation* (8 June 1992), 790–93.

10. See, for example, the cover stories: "Look Out! Here Come the Sixties!" *New England Monthly* 5:3 (March 1988); "Will We Ever Get Over the '60s?" *Newsweek* (5 September 1988); "Woodstock: Where Are They Now?: 20th Anniversary Special," *Life* (August 1989); Louis Menand, "Bummer: The Grasping, Bourgeois, Uptight Soul of the 1960s," *The New Republic* (7 & 14 January 1991).

11. Obituary, "Mary Wells, 49, the Pop Singer Who Made 'My Guy' a 60's Hit," *New York Times* (27 July 1992); Francie Larrieu Smith interviewed by

Katie Couric on NBC's *Today Show* (31 July 1992). HBO (Home Box Office, cable television) released a feature-length docudrama about the life of Finkbine in June 1992 that sparked a series of articles of the where-is-she-now variety in magazines such as *People*.

BIBLIOGRAPHY

Manuscript Sources and Documents

The John F. Kennedy Presidential Library. Boston, Mass.: records of the Presidential Commission on the Status of Women.

State Historical Society of Wisconsin, Madison: Social Action Collection, civil rights and SDS papers.

Mary McLeod Bethune Archives, National Council of Negro Women, Washington, D.C.: NCNW papers and papers on the Wednesdays in Mississippi project.

The Schlesinger Library. Radcliffe College, Cambridge, Mass.: papers of Mary Eastwood, Betty Friedan, Pauli Murray, Esther Peterson, Kennedy's Presidential Commission on the Status of Women, and the National Organization for Women.

Sophia Smith Collection, Smith College, Northampton, Mass.: Women Strike for Peace papers.

Reference Works

Acton, Alan LeMond, and Parker Hodges. *Mugshots: Who's Who in the New Earth.* New York: World Publishing, 1972.

Albert, Judith Clavir, and Steward Edward Albert. *The Sixties Papers: Documents of a Rebellious Decade.* New York: Praeger, 1984.

The Alyson Almanac: A Treasury of Information for the Gay and Lesbian Community. Boston: Alyson, 1989.

Barlow, Judith E., ed. *Plays by American Women.* New York: Avon, 1981.

Betsko, Kathleen, and Rachel Koenig, eds. *Interviews with Contemporary Women Playwrights.* New York: Beech Tree Books, 1987.

Biographical Dictionary of the Federal Judiciary, comp. Harold Chase. Detroit: Gale Research, 1976.

Blain, Virginia, Isobel Grundy, and Patricia Clements, eds. *The Feminist Companion to Literature in English*. New Haven: Yale University Press, 1990.

Bremner, Robert H., ed. *Children and Youth in America: A Documentary History, vol. 3, 1933–1973*. Cambridge: Harvard University Press, 1974.

Bronson, Fred. *The Billboard Book of Number One Hits: The Inside Story Behind the Top of the Charts*. New York: Billboard, 1985.

Editorial Research Reports on the Women's Movement. Washington: *Congressional Quarterly*, 1973.

Elliot, Emory, ed. *The Columbia Literary History of the United States*. New York: Columbia University Press, 1988.

Encyclopedia of American Art. New York: E. P. Dutton, 1981.

Gallup, George H. *The Gallup Poll, Public Opinion 1935–1971*. vol. 3 (1948–1971). New York: Random House, 1972.

Gilbert, Sandra M., and Susan Guber. *The Norton Anthology of Literature by Women: The Tradition in English*. New York: Norton, 1985.

The Good Housekeeping Woman's Almanac. New York: Newspaper Enterprise Associates, 1977.

Howe, Florence and Ellen Bass, eds. *No More Masks! An Anthology of Poems by Women*. Garden City: Doubleday Anchor, 1973.

Kinsman, Clare D., ed. *Contemporary Authors: A Bio–Bibliographical Guide to Current Authors and Their Works*. vols. 17–20. Detroit: Gail Research, 1976.

[Koontz, Elizabeth.] *To Benefit Women at Work*. Department of Labor, Wage, and Labor Standards. Washington: GPO, Apr. 1969.

———. *Day Care Facts*. U.S. Department of Labor, Women's Bureau. Washington: Government Printing Office, 1970.

Mainiero, Lina, ed. *American Women Writers: From Colonial Times to the Present*. New York: Ungar, 1979.

Nite, Norm N. *Rock On: The Illustrated Encyclopedia of Rock n' Roll: Vol. 2: The Years of Change 1964–1978*. rev. ed. 1984; New York: Harper and Row, 1978.

Pareles, Jon, and Patricia Romanowski, eds. *The Rolling Stone Encyclopedia of Rock and Roll*. New York: Rolling Stone, 1983.

Santelli, Robert. *Sixties Rock: A Listener's Guide*. Chicago: Contemporary, 1985.

Sicherman, Barbara and Carol Hurd Green, *Notable American Women: The Modern Period*. (NAW:MP.) Cambridge: The Belknap Press of Harvard University, 1980.

Shortridge, Barbara Gimla. *Atlas of American Women*. New York: Macmillan, 1987.

Stambler, Irwin. *The Encyclopedia of Pop, Rock, and Soul*. rev. ed., 1989; New York: St. Martin's Press, 1974.

U.S. Center for Health Statistics. "Marriages Per One Thousand Single Women Fourteen Years of Age and Over." In *Vital Statistics of the Untied States*. Washington: GPO, 1980.

U.S. Department of Commerce, Bureau of the Census. *Historical Statistics of the United States, Colonial Times to 1970.* Washington: GPO, 1975.

——. "Marital Status and Living Arrangements: March 1978." *Current population reports,* series P-20, no. 338. Washington: GPO, May 1979.

——. "Poverty in the United States, 1959–1968." *Current population reports,* series P-60, no. 68. Washington: GPO, 31 December 1969.

——. "A Statistical Portrait of Women in the United States." *Current population reports,* Special Studies Series 23:58. Washington: GPO, 1974.

——. *Statistical Abstracts of the United States 1973.* Washington: GPO, 1973. 96th ed., 1975.

U.S. Department of Labor. *Employment in Perspective: Working Women.* Washington: GPO, 1982.

——. Bureau of Labor Statistics. *U.S. Working Women: A Databook.* Washington: GPO, 1977.

——. Employment Standards Administration. *Handbook on Women Workers.* Bulletin 297. Washington: GPO, 1975.

——. Women's Bureau. *Background Facts on Women Workers in the United States.* Washington: GPO, 1970.

——. *Fact Sheet on the Earning Gap.* Washington: GPO, 1971.

——. *Fact Sheet on Women in Professional and Technical Positions.* Washington: GPO, 1968.

——. *The Myth and the Reality.* Washington: GPO, 1971.

——. *Underutilization of Women Workers.* Washington: GPO, 1971.

——. *Women Workers Today.* Washington: GPO, 1970.

Who's Who of American Women, 1974–75.

The 1970 World Book Year Book: The Annual Supplement to the World Book Encyclopedia. Chicago: Field Enterprises, 1970.

The 1974 World Book Year Book. Chicago: Field Enterprises, 1974.

Books

Abbott, Sidney and Barbara Love. *Sappho Was a Right-On Woman: A Liberated View of Lesbianism.* New York: Stein and Day, 1972.

Abzug, Bella, S. *Bella! Ms. Abzug Goes to Washington.* New York: Saturday Review Press, 1972.

Acuña, Rudy. *A Mexican–American Struggle.* New York: American Book Co., 1971.

Adams, Elsie, and Mary Louise Briscoe, eds. *Up Against the Wall, Mother. . . .* Beverly Hills: Glencoe, 1971.

Adams, Judith Porter. *Peacework: Oral Histories of Women Peace Activities.* Boston: Twayne/G. K. Hall, 1991.

Adelstein, Michael E., and Jen G. Pival, eds. *Women's Liberation.* New York: St. Martin's, 1972.

Ahmann, Matthew, ed. *The New Negro*. Notre Dame: Fides, 1961.

Ainsworth, Mary D., ed. *Deprivation of Maternal Care: A Reassessment of its Effects*. Geneva: World Health Organization (WHO), 1962.

Alexander, Paul. *Rough Magic: A Biography of Sylvia Plath*. New York: Viking, 1991.

Allen, Pamela. *Free Space: A Perspective on the Small Group in Women's Liberation*. New York: Times Change, 1970.

Allen, Robert C. *Speaking of Soap Operas*. Chapel Hill: University of North Carolina Press, 1985.

Alloway, Lawrence. *Topics in American Art Since 1945*. New York: W. W. Norton, 1975.

Alpert, Jane. *Growing Up Underground*. New York: William Morrow, 1981.

Altback, Edith Hoshino, ed. *From Feminism to Liberation*. Cambridge: Schenkman, 1971.

American Historical Association. *Report of the Committee on the Status of Women*. 9 November 1970.

Ammer, Christine. *Unsung: A History of Women in American Music*. Westport: Greenwood, 1980.

Amundsen, Kirsten. *The Silenced Majority: Women and American Democracy*. Englewood Cliffs: Prentice Hall, 1971.

Anderson, S., ed. *Sex Differences and Discrimination in Education*. Worthington, OH: Charles A. Jones, 1972.

Angelou, Maya. *I Know Why the Caged Bird Sings*. New York: Bantam, 1971.

Anthony, E. James, and Therese Benedek. *Parenthood: Its Psychology and Psychopathology*. Boston: Little, Brown, 1970

Antler, Joyce, ed. *America and I: Short Stories by American Jewish Women Writers*. Boston: Beacon, 1990.

Aquila, Richard. *That Old Time Rock & Roll: A Chronicle of an Era. 1954–1963*. New York: Schirmer Books, 1989.

Arbus, Diane. *Diane Arbus*. Millerton, N.Y.: Aperture Monograph, 1972.

Atkinson, Ti–Grace. *Amazon Odyssey*. New York: Links Books, 1974.

Austin, Helen. *The Women Doctorate in America: Origins, Career, and Family*. New York: Russell Sage, 1969.

Baez, Joan. *And a Voice to Sing With: A Memoir*. New York: Summit, 1987.

Bailey, David, and Peter Evans. *Goodbye Baby and Amen*. New York: Coward McCann, 1969.

Banes, Sally. *Democracy's Body: Judson Dance Theater, 1962–1964*. Ann Arbor: UMI Research, 1983.

Banes, Sally. *Terpsichore in Sneakers: Post–Modern Dance*. Boston: Houghton Mifflin, 1980.

Barbour, Floyd, ed. *The Black Power Revolt*. Boston: Porter Sargent, 1968.

Bardwick, Judith M. *The Psychology of Women*. New York: Harper and Row, 1971.

Bardwick, Judith M., ed. *Readings on the Psychology of Women*. New York: Harper and Row, 1972.

Bates, Daisy. *The Long Shadow of Little Rock: A Memoir*. New York: David McKay, 1962.

Baxandall, Rosalyn, Linda Gordon, and Susan Reverby, eds. *American Working Women: A Documentary History, 1600 to the Present*. New York: Vintage, 1976.

Beauvoir, Simone de. *The Second Sex*. Translated by H. M. Parshley. New York: Alfred Knopf, 1952.

Beecher, Maureen Ursenbach, and Lavinia Fielding Anderson, eds. *Sisters in Spirit: Mormon Women in Historical and Cultural Perspective*. Urbana: University of Illinois Press, 1987.

Bego, Mark. *Aretha Franklin: The Queen of Soul*. New York: St. Martin's, 1989.

Belfrage, Sally. *Freedom Summer*. New York: Viking, 1965.

Bell, Robert R. *Premarital Sex in a Changing Society*. Englewood Cliffs: Prentice–Hall, 1966.

Bender, Eleanor M., Bobbie Burk, and Nancy Walker, eds. *All of Us Are Present: The Stephens College Symposium: Women's Education: The Future*. Columbia, MO: James Madison Wood Research Institute, 1984.

Benería, Lourdes, and Catharine R. Stimpson, eds. *Women, Households, and the Economy*. New Brunswick: Rutgers University Press, 1987.

Benét, Mary Kathleen. *The Secretarial Ghetto*. New York: McGraw–Hill, 1972.

———. *Secretary: An Enquiry into the Female Ghetto*. London: Sidgewich and Jackson, 1972.

Bequaert, Lucia. *Single Women: Alone and Together*. Boston: Beacon, 1976.

Bernard, Jessie. *Academic Women*. University Park: Pennsylvania State University Press, 1964.

Bernstein, Marcia. *The Nuns*. London: Collins, 1976.

Berrigan, Daniel. *The Trial of the Catonsville Nine*. Boston: Beacon, 1970

Berry, Mary Frances, and John W. Blassingame. *Long Memory: The Black Experience in America*. New York: Oxford University Press, 1982.

Betrock, Alan. *Girl Groups: The Story of a Sound*. New York: Delilah, 1982.

Billingsley, A. *Children of the Storm: Black Children and American Child Welfare*. New York: Harcourt Brace Jovanovich, 1972.

Bird, Caroline, with Sara Welles Briller. *Born Female: The High Cost of Keeping Women Down*. New York: David McKay, 1968.

Bird, Caroline. *What Women Want: From the Official Report to the President, the Congress and the People of the United States*. New York: Simon and Schuster, 1979.

Blocker, Clyde Edward, Robert H. Plummer, and Richard C. Richardson, Jr. *The Two–Year College: A Social Synthesis*. Englewood Cliffs: Prentice Hall, 1965.

Blumberg, Rhoda Lois. *Civil Rights: The 1960s Freedom Struggle*. rev. ed. 1991; Boston: Twayne/G. K. Hall, 1984.

Borromeo, Sister M. Charles [Maryellen Muckenhirn], ed. *The New Nuns*. New York: New American Library, 1967.

Boston Women's Health Collective. *Our Bodies, Ourselves: A Book By and For Women*. New York: Simon and Schuster, 1973.

Bosworth, Patricia. *Diane Arbus: A Biography*. New York: Knopf, 1984.

Bourke-White, Margaret. *Portrait of Myself*. New York: Simon and Schuster, 1963.

Boutilier, Mary A. and Lucinda San Giovanni. *The Sporting Woman*. Champaign: Human Kinetics, 1983.

Bowker, Lee H. *Drug Use Among American Women, Old and Young: Sexual Oppression and Other Themes*. San Francisco: Editorial Research Reports, 1977.

Brandt, Allan M. *No Magic Bullet: A Social History of Venereal Disease in the United States Since 1880*. New York: Oxford University Press, 1985.

Brasner, William, and Dominick Consolo, eds. *Black Drama*. Columbus, OH: Merrill, 1970.

Brater, Enoch, ed. *Feminine Focus: The New Women Playwrights*. New York: Oxford University Press, 1989.

Brazelton, T. Berry. *Infants and Mothers: Differences in Development*. New York: Delacorte, 1969.

Breasted, Mary. *Oh! Sex Education!* New York: Praeger, 1970.

Breines, Winifred. *Community and Organization in the New Left, 1962–1968: The Great Refusal*. New York: Praeger, 1982.

Bromley, David, ed. *Falling from the Faith: Causes and Consequences of Religious Apostasy*. Newbury Park: Sage, 1988.

Brooks, Paul. *The House of Life: Rachel Carson at Work; with Selections from Her Writings Published and Unpublished*. Boston: Houghton Mifflin, 1972.

Brown, Alden V. *The Grail Movement and American Catholicism, 1940–1975*. Notre Dame: University of Notre Dame Press, 1989.

Brown, Charles T. *The Art of Rock and Roll*. Englewood Cliffs: Prentice–Hall, 1983.

Brown, Helen Gurley. *Sex and the Single Girl*. New York: Bernard Geis, 1962.

Brownmiller, Susan. *Against Our Will: Men, Women, and Rape*. New YorK: Simon and Schuster, 1975.

Buckley, Lynda Van Deranter, and Joan Furey, eds. *Visions of War, Dreams of Peace*. New York: Time Warner, 1991.

Bühler, Charlotte Bertha, and Fred Massarik. *The Course of Human Life*. New York: Springer, 1968.

Cable, Mary. *American Manners and Morals*. New York: American Heritage, 1969.

Cade, Toni, ed. *The Black Woman: An Anthology*. New York: Bantam, 1970.

Calas, Nicholas and Elena Calas. *Icons and Images of the Sixties*. New York: E. P. Dutton, 1971.

Callahan, Daniel. *Abortion: Law, Choice and Morality*. London: Collier–Macmillan, 1970.

Callahan, Sidney Cornelia. *The Illusion of Eve: Modern Woman's Quest for Identity.* New York: Sheed and Ward, 1965.

Campbell, Margaret A., M. D. [Mary Howell, pseud.] *Why Would a Girl Go Into Medicine? Medical Education in the U.S.: A Guide for Women.* Old Westbury, N.Y.: Feminist Press, 1973.

Cantarow, Ellen, with Susan O'Malley and Sharon Strom. *Moving the Mountain: Women Working for Social Change.* Old Westbury: Feminist Press, 1980.

Cantor, Muriel and Suzanne Pingree. *The Soap Opera.* Beverly Hills: Sage, 1983.

Caprio, Frank S. *The Sexually Adequate Female.* Greenwich: Fawcett, 1953.

Carden, Maren Lockwood. *The New Feminist Movement.* New York: Russell Sage, 1974.

Carr, Virginia Spencer. *The Lonely Hunter: A Biography of Carson McCullers.* New York: Anchor, 1976.

Carroll, Jackson W., Barbara Hargrove, and Adair T. Lummis. *Women of the Cloth: A New Opportunity for the Churches.* San Francisco: Harper and Row, 1981.

Carson, Clayborne. *In Struggle: SNCC and the Black Awakening of the 1960s.* Cambridge: Harvard University Press, 1981.

Carson, Clayborne, ed. *The Student Voice: 1960–1965.* Compiled by the staff of the Martin Luther King, Jr. Papers Project. Westport: Meckler, 1990.

Carson, Josephine. *Silent Voices: The Southern Negro Woman Today.* New York: Dell, 1971.

Carter, Hugh and Paul C. Glick. *Marriage and Divorce: a Social and Economic Study.* Cambridge: Harvard University Press, 1976.

Cary, Eve, and Kathleen Willert Peratis. *Women and the Law.* Chicago: National Textbook Co., 1977.

Cassara, Beverly Benner, ed. *American Women: The Changing Image.* Boston: Beacon, 1962.

Cassata, Mary, and Thomas Skill, eds. *Life on Daytime Television: Tuning In American Serial Drama.* Norwood, N.J.: Ablex, 1983.

Cassell, Joan. *A Group Called Women: Sisterhood and Symbolism in the Feminist Movement.* New York: David McKay, 1977.

Cawelti, John G. *Adventure, Mystery, and Romance: Formula Stories as Art and Popular Culture.* Chicago: University of Chicago Press, 1976.

Chadwick, Whitney. *Women, Art and Society.* New York: Thames and Hudson, 1990.

Chafe, William H. *The American Woman: Her Changing Social, Economic and Political Roles, 1920–1970.* New York: Oxford, 1972.

———. *Civilities and Civil Rights.* New York: Oxford University Press, 1980.

———. *Women and Equality: Changing Patterns in American Culture.* New York: Oxford University Press, 1977.

Chametzky, Jules. *Our Decentralized Literature: Cultural Mediations in Selected Jewish and Southern Writers.* Amherst: University of Massachusetts Press, 1986.

Cherlin, Andrew. *Marriage, Divorce, Remarriage.* Cambridge: Harvard University Press, 1981.

Chesler, Phyllis. *Women and Madness.* New York: Doubleday, 1972.

Chester, Laura, and Sharon Barba, eds. *Rising Tides: Twentieth Century American Women Poets.* New York: Washington Square, 1973.

Chicago, Judy. *Through the Flower: My Struggle as a Woman Artist.* Garden City: Doubleday, 1975.

Chilman, Catherine S. *Adolescent Sexuality in a Changing American Society: Social and Psychological Perspectives.* Washington: U.S. Public Health Service, January 1980.

Chinoy, Helen Krich, and Linda Walsh Jenkins, eds. *Women in American Theatre: Careers, Images, Movements.* New York: Crown, 1981.

Chisholm, Shirley. *The Good Fight.* New York: Harper and Row, 1973.

———. *Unbought and Unbossed.* Boston: Houghton Mifflin, 1970.

Clark, Elizabeth, and Herbert Richardson, eds. *Women and Religion: A Feminist Sourcebook of Christian Thought.* New York: Harper and Row, 1977.

Cleaver, Eldridge. *Soul on Ice.* New York: Dell, 1968.

Cluster, Dick, ed. *They Should Have Served That Cup of Coffee.* Boston: South End, 1979.

Cohen, Marcia. *The Sisterhood: The Inside Story of the Women's Movement and the Leaders Who Made It Happen.* New York: Fawcett Columbine, 1988.

Cole, Doris. *From Tipi to Skyscraper: A History of Women in Architecture.* New York: George Braziller, 1973.

Cooper, David. *The Death of the Family.* New York: Random House, 1970.

Corea, Gena. *The Hidden Malpractice: How American Medicine Treats Women as Patients and Professionals.* New York: William Morrow, 1977.

———. *The Mother Machine: Reproductive Technologies from Artificial Insemination to Artificial Wombs.* New York: Harper and Row, 1985.

Cott, Nancy, ed. *The Roots of Bitterness: Documents of the Social History of American Women.* New York: Dutton, 1972.

Cowan, Paul. *An Orphan in History: Retrieving a Jewish Legacy.* New York: Doubleday, 1982.

Crow Dog, Mary, with Richard Erdoes. *Lakota Woman.* New York: HarperCollins, 1990.

Culver, Elsie, T. *Women in the World of Religion.* Garden City: Doubleday, 1967.

Cummings, Bernice, and Victoria Schuck, eds. *Women Organizing: An Anthology.* Metuchen: Scarecrow, 1979.

Cummings, Tony. *The Sound of Philadelphia.* New York: Methuen, 1975.

Cunneen, Sally. *Sex: Female; Religion: Catholic.* New York: Holt Rinehart and Winston, 1968.

Cunningham, Imogen. *After Ninety.* Seattle: University of Washington Press, 1977.

Dahl, Linda. *Stormy Weather: The Music and Lives of a Century of Jazzwomen.* New York: Limelight Editions, 1984.

Dally, Anne G. *Inventing Motherhood: The Consequences of an Ideal.* New York: Schocken, 1983.

Daly, Mary. *Beyond God the Father: Toward a Philosophy of Women's Liberation.* Boston: Beacon, 1973.

———. *The Church and the Second Sex.* New York: Harper and Row, 1968.

Dater, Judy. *Imogen Cunningham: A Portrait.* New York: New York Graphic Society, 1979.

Daniel, Robert L. *American Women in the 20th Century: The Festival of Life.* New York: Harcourt Brace Jovanovich, 1987.

Daniels, Roger. *Coming to America: A History of Immigration and Ethnicity in American Life.* New York: HarperCollins, 1990.

David, D. *Career Patterns and Values: A Study of Men and Women in Science and Engineering.* New York: Columbia University, Bureau of Applied Social Research, 1971.

Davidson, Sara. *Loose Change: Three Women of the Sixties.* New York: Doubleday, 1977.

Davis, Angela Yvonne. *Autobiography.* New York: Random House, 1974.

Davis, Angela Yvonne and Bettina Aptheker, eds. *If They Come in the Morning: Voices of Resistance.* New York: New American Library, 1971.

Davis, Elizabeth Gould. *The First Sex.* New York: G. P. Putnam, 1971.

Day, Dorothy. *On Pilgrimage: The Sixties.* New York: Curtis, 1972.

DeBenedetti, Charles. *An American Ordeal: The Antiwar Movement of the Vietnam Era.* Syracuse: Syracuse University Press, 1990.

Deckard, Barbara Sinclair. *The Women's Movement: Political, Socioeconomic and Psychological Issues.* New York: Harper and Row, 1983.

Decter, Midge. *The New Chastity.* New York: Berkeley, 1972.

Deford, Frank. *There She Is: The Life and Times of Miss America.* New York: Viking, 1971.

Degler, Carl N. *At Odds: Women and Family in America from the Revolution to the Present.* New York: Oxford University Press, 1980.

Delaney, Janice, Mary Jane Jupton, and Emily Toth. *The Curse: A Cultural History of Menstruation.* New York: Mentor, 1976.

D'Emilio, John, and Estelle B. Freedman. *Intimate Matters: A History of Sexuality in America.* New York: Harper and Row, 1988.

D'Emilio, John. *Sexual Politics, Sexual Communities: The Making of the Homosexual Minority in the United States, 1940–1970.* Chicago: University of Chicago Press, 1983.

Deming, Barbara. *We Are All a Part of One Another: A Barbara Deming Reader.*

Edited by June Meyerding. Philadelphia: New Society, 1984.

————. *Prisons That Could Not Hold.* San Francisco: Spinsters Ink, 1985.

DeRham, Edith. *The Love Fraud: Why the Structure of the American Family is Changing and What Women Must Do to Make It Work.* New York: Clarkson N. Potter, 1965.

Deutsch, Helene. *The Psychology of Women: A Psychoanalytic Interpretation.* London: Research Books, 1947; New York: Bantam, 1973.

Diamonstein, Barbaralee. *Open Secrets: 94 Women in Touch with Our Time.* New York: Viking, 1972.

Dickstein, Morris. *The Gates of Eden: American Culture in the Sixties.* New York: Basic, 1977.

Didion, Joan. *Slouching Towards Bethlehem.* New York: Farrar Straus and Giroux, 1968.

Diener, Thomas. *Growth of an American Invention: A Documentary History of the Junior and Community College Movement.* Westport: Greenwood, 1985.

Dienes, C. Thomas. *Law, Politics, and Birth Control.* Urbana: University of Illinois Press, 1972.

Diner, Helen. *Mothers and Amazons,* trans. and ed. by John Philip Ludin. New York: Julian, 1965.

Doely, Sarah Bentley, ed. *Women's Liberation and the Church.* New York: Association Press, 1970.

Dolan, Jay P., R. Scott Appleby, Patricia Byrne, and Debra Campbell. *Transforming Parish Ministry: The Changing Roles of Catholic Clergy, Laity, and Women Religious.* New York: Crossroad, 1989.

Donaldson, Scott. *The Suburban Myth.* New York: Columbia University Press, 1969.

Duberman, Martin. *Black Mountain: An Exploration in Community.* New York: Dutton, 1972.

Durr, Virginia Foster. In *Outside the Magic Circle.* Hollinger F. Bernard, ed. University: University of Alabama Press, 1985.

Dworkin, Andrea. *Right–Wing Women.* New York: Perigee, 1983.

Ebaugh, Helen Rose Fuchs. *Out of the Cloister: A Study of Organizational Dilemmas.* Austin: University of Texas Press, 1977.

Ebon, Martin, ed. *Everywoman's Guide to Abortion.* New York: Pocket Books, 1971.

Echols, Alice. *Daring to Be Bad: Radical Feminism in America, 1967–1975.* Minneapolis: University of Minnesota Press, 1989.

Edmondson, Madeleine, and David Rounds. *From Mary Noble to Mary Hartman: The Complete Soap Opera Book.* New York: Stein and Day, 1976.

Edwards, Audrey and Craig Polite. *Children of the Dream: The Psychology of Black Success.* Garden City: Doubleday, 1992.

Ehrenreich, Barbara. *The Hearts of Men: American Dreams and the Flight from Commitment.* Garden City: Doubleday, 1983.

Ehrenreich, Barbara and Deirdre English. *For Her Own Good: 150 Years of Experts' Advice to Women.* Garden City: Anchor/Doubleday, 1978.

Ehrenreich, Barbara, Elizabeth Hess, and Gloria Jacobs. *Re-Making Love: The Feminization of Sex.* Garden City: Doubleday, 1986.

Eisenstein, Zillah, ed. *Capitalist Patriarchy and the Case for Socialist Feminism.* New York: Monthly Review Press, 1979.

Elder, Glen, Jr. *Children of the Great Depression: Social Change in Life Experience.* Chicago: University of Chicago Press, 1974.

Ellmann, Mary. *Thinking about Women.* New York: Harvest, 1968.

Emerson, Gloria. *Winners and Losers.* New York: Harcourt Brace Jovanovich, 1976.

Epstein, Cynthia Fuchs. *Woman's Place: Options and Limits in Professional Careers.* Berkeley: University of California Press, 1970.

Equal Employment Opportunities Commission (EEOC). *A Unique Competence: A Study of Equal Employment Opportunity in the Bell System.* Washington: GPO, 1971.

Erens, Patricia, ed. *Sexual Strategems: The World of Women in Film.* New York: Horizon Press, 1979.

Ermarth, Margaret. *Adam's Fractured Rib.* Philadelphia: Fortress, 1970.

Etzioni, Amitai. *The Semi–Professions and Their Organization.* New York: Free Press, 1969.

Evans, Sara M. *Liberty's Daughters: A History of Women in America.* New York: Free Press, 1989.

———. *Personal Politics: The Roots of Women's Liberation in the Civil Rights Movement and the New Left.* New York: Knopf, 1979.

Faderman, Lillian. *Odd Girls and Twilight Lovers: A History of Lesbian Life in Twentieth Century America.* New York: Columbia University Press, 1992.

———. *Surpassing the Love of Men: Romantic Friendship and Love Between Women, From the Renaissance to the Present.* New York: William Morrow, 1981.

Faludi, Susan. *Backlash: The Undeclared War Against American Women.* New York: Crown, 1991.

Farrell, Suzanne, with Toni Bentley. *Holding On to the Air: an Autobiography.* New York: Sunset Books, 1990.

Ferman, Louis, et al. *Poverty in America.* Ann Arbor: University of Michigan Press, 1968.

Ferree, Myra Marx, and Beth B. Hess. *Controversy and Coalition: The New Feminist Movement.* Boston: Twayne, 1985.

Figes, Eva. *Patriarchal Attitudes.* Greenwich: Fawcett, 1970.

Filene, Peter. *Him/Her/Self: Sex Roles in Modern America.* Baltimore: Johns Hopkins University Press, 1986.

Fine, Elsa Honig. *The Afro-American Artist.* New York: Holt, Rinehart and Winston, 1973.

Finnis, Rob. *The Phil Spector Story*. London: Rockon, 1975.

Firestone, Shulamith. *The Dialectic of Sex: The Case for a Feminist Revolution*. New York: William Morrow, 1970.

Firestone, Shulamith and Anne Koedt, eds. *Notes from the Second Year: Women's Liberation*. New York: Radical Feminists, 1970.

Fishburn, Katherine. *Women in Popular Culture: A Reference Guide*. Westport: Greenwood, 1982.

Flacks, Richard. *Youth and Social Change*. Chicago: Markham, 1971.

Flexner, Eleanor. *Century of Struggle*. New York: Atheneum, 1971.

Foner, Philip S. *Women and the American Labor Movement from World War II to the Present*. New York: 1980.

Forman, James. *The Making of Black Revolutionaries*. New York: Macmillan, 1972.

Francoeur, Robert T. *Utopian Motherhood: New Trends in Human Reproduction*. Cranbury: A. S. Barnes, 1973.

Frankfort, Ellen. *Kathy Boudin and the Dance of Death*. Briarcliff: Stein and Day, 1983.

———. *Vaginal Politics*. New York: Quadrangle, 1972.

Fraser, Ron, ed. *1968: A Study Generation in Revolt: An International Oral History*. New York: Pantheon, 1988.

Freeman, Jo. *The Politics of Women's Liberation: A Case Study of an Emerging Social Movement and Its Relation to the Policy Process*. New York: David McKay, 1975.

Friedan, Betty. *It Changed My Life: Writings on the Women's Movement*. New York: Dell, 1976.

———. *The Feminine Mystique*. New York: W. W. Norton, 1963.

———. *The Second Stage*. New York: Summit, 1981.

Friedman, Myra. *Buried Alive: The Biography of Janis Joplin*. New York: William Morrow, 1973.

Frith, Simon. *Sound Effects: Youth, Leisure and the Politics of Rock 'N' Roll*. New York: Pantheon, 1981.

Fritz, Leah. *Dreamers and Dealers: An Intimate Appraisal of the Women's Movement*. Boston: Beacon, 1979.

Fusco, P., and G. Horwitz. *La Causa: The California Grape Strike*. New York: Macmillan, 1970.

Gabin, Nancy F. *Feminism in the Labor Movement: Women and the United Auto Workers 1935–1975*. Ithaca: Cornell University Press, 1990.

Gablik, Suzi. *Has Modernism Failed?* London: Thames and Hudson, 1984.

Gans, Herbert J. *The Levittowners: Ways of Life and Politics in a New Suburban Community*. New York: Pantheon, 1967.

———. *Popular Culture and High Culture: An Analysis and Evaluation of Taste*. New York: Harper, 1974.

[Garrity,] J[oan Terry.] *The Sensuous Woman*. New York: Dell, 1969.

Garskof, Michele Hoffnung, ed. *Roles Women Play*. Belmont: Brooks/Cole, 1971.

Gatlin, Rochelle. *American Women Since 1945*. Jackson: University Press of Mississippi, 1987.

Gelb, Joyce, and Marian Lief Palley. *Women and Public Policies*. Princeton: Princeton University Press, 1982.

Gelfman, Judith S. *Women in Television News*. New York: Columbia University Press, 1976.

George, Nelson. *Where Did Our Love Go? The Rise and Fall of the Motown Sound*. London: Omnibus, 1985.

Gerber, Ellen. W. *The American Women in Sport*. Lexington: Addison–Wesley, 1974.

Gibson, Gwen, and Barbara Wyden. *The Jewish Wife*. New York: Peter H. Wyden, 1969.

Giddings, Paula. *When and Where I Enter The Impact of Black Women on Race and Sex in America*. New York: William Morrow, 1984.

Gilbert, Lynn, and Gaylen Moore, eds. *Particular Passions: Talks with Women Who Have Shaped Our Times*. New York: C. N. Potter, 1981.

Gilder, George. *Sexual Suicide*. New York: Quadrangle, 1973.

Ginnott, Hain. *Between Parent and Child*. New York: Macmillan, 1965.

Giovanni, Nikki. *Gemini: An Extended Autobiographical Statement on My First Twenty Five Years of Being a Black Poet in America*. New York: Bobbs–Merrill, 1971.

Gitlin, Todd, and Nanci Hollander. *Uptown: Poor Whites in Chicago*. New York: Harper and Row, 1970.

Glendon, Mary Ann. *Abortion and Divorce in Western Law: American Failures, European Challenges*. Cambridge: Harvard University Press, 1987.

Golds, Jenette. *Catholics in College: Religious Commitment and the Intellectual Life*. Chicago: University of Chicago Press, 1967.

Goldstein, Leslie Friedman. *The Constitutional Rights of Women: Cases in Law and Social Change*. Madison: University of Wisconsin Press, 1988.

Gordon, Linda. *Woman's Body, Woman's Right: A Social History of Birth Control in America*. New York: Grossman, 1976.

Gornick, Vivian, and Barbara K. Moran, eds. *Woman in Sexist Society: Studies in Power and Powerlessness*. New York: New American Library, 1972.

Gould, Lewis L. *Lady Bird Johnson and the Environment*. Lawrence: University Press of Kansas, 1988.

Grant, Joanne, ed. *Black Protest: History, Documents, and Analyses 1619–Present*. New York: Fawcett World Library, 1968.

Grebler, Leo, Joan Moore, and Ralph Guzman. *The Mexican–American People: The Nation's Second Largest Minority*. New York: Free Press, 1971.

Greer, Germaine. *The Female Eunuch*. London: Gibbon and McKee, 1970; New York: McGraw-Hill, 1971.

———. *Sex and Destiny*. New York: Harper and Row, 1984.

Greig, Charlotte. *Will You Still Love Me Tomorrow?: Girl Groups from the 50s On.* London: Virago, 1989.

Griffin, Marie Fenton. *How to Be a Beauty Pageant Winner.* New York: Fireside, 1981.

Griffin, Mary. *The Courage to Choose: An American Nun's Story.* Boston: Little, Brown, 1975.

Gruberg, Martin. *Women in American Politics.* Oshkosh: Academia, 1968.

Gruschkin, Paul D. *The Art of Rock: Posters from Presley to Punk.* New York: Abbeville Press, 1987.

Guttmann, Allen. *Women's Sports: A History.* New York: Columbia University Press, 1991.

Haber, Joan, ed. *Changing Women in a Changing Society.* Chicago: University of Chicago Press, 1973.

Hackett, Alice Payne, and James Henry Burke. *80 Years of Best Sellers, 1895–1975.* New York: R. R. Bowker, 1977.

Hamer, Fannie Lou. *To Praise Our Bridges: An Autobiography.* Jackson, Miss.: KIPCO, 1967.

Hampton, Henry, and Steven Fayer. *Voices of Freedom: An Oral History of the Civil Rights Movement from the 1950s through the 1980s.* New York: Bantam, 1990.

Handy, D. Antoinette. *Black Women in American Bands and Orchestras.* Metuchen: Scarecrow, 1981.

Hansen, Al[fred] E[arl]. *A Primer of Happenings and Time/Space Art.* New York: Something Else, 1965.

Hardy, Gordon, et al., comps. *Words of War: An Anthology of Vietnam War Literature.* Boston: Boston Publishing, 1988.

Harper, Paul, and Joann P. Krieg, eds. *John F. Kennedy: The Promise Revisited.* New York: Greenwood, 1988.

Harris, Marvin. *America Now: The Anthropology of a Changing Culture.* New York: Simon and Schuster, 1981.

Hart, Lynda, ed. *Making a Spectacle: Feminist Essays on Contemporary Women's Theatre.* Ann Arbor: University of Michigan Press, 1989.

Hartmann, Susan M. *From Margin to Mainstream: American Women and Politics since 1960.* Philadelphia: Temple University Press, 1989.

Haryman, Christina. *Dream Babies: Three Centuries of Good Advice on Child Care.* New York: Harper and Row, 1983.

Haskell, Molly. *From Reverence to Rape: The Treatment of Women in the Movies.* New York: Holt, Rinehart and Winston, 1974.

Hays, H. R. *The Dangerous Sex: The Myth of Feminine Evil.* New York: Putnam, 1964.

Hayward, Carter. *A Priest Forever.* New York: Harper and Row, 1976.

Hechinger, Grace and Fred M. *Teen-Age Tyranny.* New York: Crest, 1963.

Henderson, Nancy. *Out of the Curtained World: The Story of an American Nun Who Left the Convent.* Garden City: Doubleday, 1972.

Henri, Adrian. *Total Art: Environments, Happenings, and Performance.* New York: Praeger, 1974.

Heschel, Susannah, ed. *On Being a Jewish Feminist.* New York: Schocken, 1983.

Hewitt, Emily, and Suzanne Hiatt. *Women Priests: Yes or No?* New York: Seabury, 1973.

Hewlett, Sylvia Ann. *A Lesser Life: The Myth of Women's Liberation in America.* New York: William Morrow, 1986.

Hine, Darlene Clark. *Black Women in White: Racial Conflict and Cooperation in the Nursing Profession.* Bloomington: University of Indiana Press, 1989.

Hine, Darlene Clark, ed. *Black Women in the Nursing Profession.* New York: Garland, 1985.

Hoagland, Sarah Lucia, and Julia Penelope, eds. *For Lesbians Only: A Separatist Anthology.* London: Onlywomen, 1988.

Hodgson, Godfrey. *America in Our Time, from World War II to Nixon: What Happened and Why.* New York: Vintage, 1978.

Hole, Judith and Ellen Levine. *Rebirth of Feminism.* New York: Quadrangle, 1971.

Holm, Jean. *Women in the Military: An Unfinished Revolution.* San Francisco: Presidio, 1982.

Hoos, Ida. *Automation in the Office.* Washington: Public Affairs Press, 1961.

Horowitz, Helen Lefkowitz. *Campus Life: Undergraduate Cultures from the End of the Eighteenth Century to the Present.* Chicago: University of Chicago Press, 1987.

Horton, Myles. *We Make the Road by Walking: Conversations on Education and Social Change.* Philadelphia: Temple University Press, 1990.

Howe, Florence, and Paul Lauter. *The Conspiracy of the Young.* New York: World Publishing, 1970.

Howe, Florence. *Myths of Coeducation: Selected Essays 1964–1983.* Bloomington: Indiana University Press, 1984.

Howell, Reet, ed. *Her Story in Sport: A Historical Anthology of Women in Sports.* West Point, N.Y.: Leisure, 1982.

Huber, Joan, ed. *Changing Women in a Changing Society.* Chicago: University of Chicago Press, 1973.

Huey, Lynda. *A Running Start.* New York: Quadrangle, 1976.

Humphrey, Muriel, ed. *Women in the U.S. Labor Force.* New York: Praeger, 1979.

Hunt, Morton. *The Affair: A Portrait of Extra-Marital Love in Contemporary America.* New York: World Publishing, 1969.

Hymowitz, Carol and Michaele Weissman. *A History of Women in America.* New York: Bantam, 1978.

Isserman, Maurice. *If I Had a Hammer: The Death of the Old Left and the Birth of the New Left.* New York: Basic Books, 1987.

Jackall, Robert. *Workers in a Labyrinth: Job and Survival in a Bank Bureaucracy.* Montclair: Universe Books, 1978.

Jackson, Kenneth T. *Crabgrass Frontier: The Suburbanization of the United States.* New York: Oxford University Press, 1985.

Jacobs, Harold., ed. *Weatherman.* Palo Alto: Ramparts Press, 1970.

Janeway, Elizabeth. *Man's World, Woman's Place: A Study in Social Mythology.* New York: Morrow, 1971.

Javna, John, and Gordon Javna. *60s!: A Catalog of Memories and Artifacts.* New York: St. Martin's, 1988.

Jenness, Linda, ed. *Feminism and Socialism.* New York: Pathfinder, 1972.

Jensen, Joan M. *With These Hands: Women Working on the Land.* Old Westbury: Feminist Press, 1981.

Johnston, Jill. *Lesbian Nation: The Feminist Solution.* New York: Simon and Schuster, 1973.

———. *Marmalade Me.* New York: E. P. Dutton, 1971.

Jones, Jacqueline. *Labor of Love, Labor of Sorrow: Black Women, Work, and the Family from Slavery to the Present.* New York: Basic Books, 1985.

Jordan, June. *Civil Wars.* Boston: Beacon, 1981.

Kahn–Hut, Rachel, et al., eds. *Women and Work.* New York: Oxford University Press, 1982.

Kaledin, Eugenia. *Mothers and More: American Women in the 1950s.* Boston: Twayne, 1984.

Kanowitz, Leo. *Women and the Law: The Unfinished Revolution.* Albuquerque: University of New Mexico Press, 1969.

Kaplan, Samuel. *The Dream Deferred: People, Politics, and Planning in Suburbia.* New York: Seabury, 1976.

Katz, Jonathan, ed. *Gay American History: Lesbians and Gay Men in the U.S.A.* New York: Thomas Crowell, 1976.

Katz, Jonathan. *Gay/Lesbian Almanac: A New Documentary.* New York: Harper and Row, 1983.

Katz, Joseph, et al. *No Time for Youth: Growth and Constraint in College Students.* San Francisco: Jossey Bass, 1968.

Kayden, X. *Report on Women in Continuing Education.* Washington: U.S. Office of Education, Sept. 1970.

Kearns, Doris. *Lyndon Johnson and the American Dream.* New York: N.A.L., 1976.

Keenan, Brigid. *The Women We Wanted To Look Like.* New York: St. Martin's, 1977.

Keller, Rosemary Skinner, Louise L. Queen, and Hilah F. Thomas, eds. *Women in New Worlds*, vol. 2. Nashville: Abingdon, 1982.

Keniston, Kenneth. *The Uncommitted: Alienated Youth in American Society.* New York: Harcourt Brace Jovanovich, 1960.

Kennedy, David M. *Birth Control in America: The Career of Margaret Sanger.* New Haven: Yale University Press, 1970.

Kennedy, Florynce. *Color Me Flo: My Life and Good Times*. Englewood Cliffs: Prentice–Hall, 1976.

———and Diane Schulder. *Abortion Rap*. New York: McGraw-Hill, 1971.

Kennedy, Susan Estabrook. *If All We Did Was Weep at Home: A History of White Working–Class Women in America*. Bloomington: Indiana University Press, 1979.

Kennelly, Karen, ed. *American Catholic Women: A Historical Exploration*. New York: Macmillan, 1989.

Kent, Sister Mary Corita. *Sister Corita*. Philadelphia: Pilgrim, 1970.

Kessler–Harris, Alice. *Out to Work: A History of Wage Earning Women in the United States*. New York: Oxford University Press, 1982.

———. *Women's Wage: Historical Meanings and Social Consequences*. Lexington: University of Kentucky Press, 1990.

Kett, Joseph F. *Rites of Passage: Adolescence in America, 1790 to the Present*. New York: Basic, 1977.

Keyssar, Helene. *The Curtain and the Veil: Strategies in Black Drama*. New York: Burt Franklin, 1982.

———. *Feminist Theatre: An Introduction to Plays of Contemporary British and American Women*. New York: Grove, 1985.

King, Billie Jean. *Billie Jean*. New York: Harper and Row, 1974.

King, Mary. *Freedom Song: A Personal Story of the 1960s Civil Rights Movement*. New York: William Morrow, 1987.

Kirby, Michael. *Happenings*. New York: E. P. Dutton, 1965.

Klein, Ethel. *Gender Politics: From Consciousness to Mass Politics*. Cambridge: Harvard University Press, 1984.

Koedt, Anne, Ellen Levine, and Anita Rapone, eds. Compiled from *Notes of the New York Radical Women*. In *Radical Feminism*. New York: Quadrangle, 1973.

Koltun, Elizabeth, ed. *The Jewish Woman: New Perspectives*. New York: Schocken, 1976.

Komarovsky, Mirra. *Blue-Collar Marriage*. 1962. Reprint. New York: Random House, 1964.

Komisar, Lucy. *The New Feminism*. New York: Franklin Watts, 1971.

Komisar, Lucy and Ann Scott. *And Justice for All*. Chicago: National Organization for Women, 1971.

Kotz, Nick, and Mary Lynn Kotz. *A Passion for Equality: George A. Wiley and the Movement*. New York: W. W. Norton, 1977.

Kraditor, Aileen. *The Ideas of The Woman Suffrage Movement, 1890–1920*. New York: Columbia University Press, 1965.

Kreps, Juanita. *Sex in the Marketplace: American Women at Work*. Baltimore: Johns Hopkins University Press, 1971.

Lader, Lawrence. *Abortion*. Boston: Beacon, 1966.

———. *Abortion II: Making the Revolution*. Boston: Beacon, 1973.

Ladner, Joyce A. *Tomorrow's Tomorrow: The Black Woman*. Garden City: Doubleday, 1971.

LaGuardia, Robert. *Ma Perkins to Mary Hartman: The Illustrated History of Soap Operas*. New York: Ballantine, 1977.

Laing, R. D. *The Politics of the Family and Other Essays*. New York: Random House, 1969.

Lamson, Peggy. *Few Are Chosen: American Women in Political Life Today*. Boston: Houghton Mifflin, 1968.

Landau, Deborah. *Janis Joplin: Her Life and Times*. New York: Paperback Library, 1971.

Lanker, Brian. *I Dream a World: Portraits of Black Women Who Changed America*. New York: Stewart, Tabori and Chang, 1989.

Lasch, Christopher. *Haven in a Heartless World: The Family Besieged*. New York: Basic, 1977.

Lash, Joseph P. *Eleanor: The Years Alone*. New York: Norton, 1977.

Lauter, Paul, and Florence Howe. *The Conspiracy of the Young*. New York: World Publishing, 1970.

Leach, William. *True Love and Perfect Union: the Feminist Reform of Sex and Society*. New York: Basic Books, 1980.

Lederer, W. H., and Don D. Jackson. *The Mirages of Marriage*. New York: W. W. Norton, 1968.

Lee, Nancy Howell. *The Search for an Abortionist*. Chicago: University of Chicago Press, 1969.

Lehman, Edward C. *Women Clergy: Breaking Through the Gender Barriers*. New Brunswick: Transaction Books, 1985.

Lerner, Gerda, ed. *Black Women in White America: A Documentary History*. New York: Vintage, 1973.

Lerner, Gerda. *The Majority Finds Its Past: Placing Women in History*. New York: Oxford University Press, 1979.

Lester, Julius. *Look Out, Whitey! Black Power's Gon Get Your Mama!* New York: Grove, 1968.

Leuchtenburg, William. *A Troubled Feast: American Society Since 1945*. Boston: Little, Brown & Co., 1983.

———. *In the Shadow of FDR: From Harry Truman to Ronald Reagan*. Ithaca: Cornell University Press, 1983.

Levine, Arthur. *When Dreams and Heroines Died: A Portrait of Today's College Student*. San Francisco: Jossey–Bass, 1980.

Levertov, Denise. *The Poet in the World*. New York: New Directions, 1973.

Levitan, Sar A., ed. *Blue-Collar Workers: A Symposium on Middle America*. New York: McGraw–Hill, 1970.

Levitan, Sar A. and Garth L. Mangum, *Federal Training and Work Programs in the Sixties*. Ann Arbor: Institute of Labor and Industrial Relations, 1969.

Lifton, Robert Jay, ed. *The Woman in America*. Boston: Beacon, 1967.

Lincoln, C. Eric. *The Black Muslims in America*. Boston: Beacon, 1973.

Lindenfeld, Frank, and Joyce Rotschild–Whitt, eds. *Workplace Democracy and Social Change*. Boston: Porter–Sargent, 1980.

Ling, Amy. *Between Worlds: Women Writers of Chinese Ancestry*. New York: Pergamon, 1990.

Lippard, Lucy R. *A Different War: Vietnam in Art*. Bellingham, WA: Whatcom Museum of Art, 1991.

———. *Eva Hesse*. New York: New York University Press, 1976.

———. *Get The Message: A Decade of Art for Social Change*. New York: E. P. Dutton, 1984.

———. *Overlay: Contemporary Art and the Art of Prehistory*. New York: Pantheon, 1983.

———. *Six Years: The Dematerialization of the Object*. New York: Praeger, 1973.

Lisle, Laurie. *Portrait of an Artist: A Biography of Georgia O'Keeffe*. New York: Washington Square Press, 1980.

Litoff, Judy Barrett. *American Midwives: 1860 to the Present*. Westport, Conn.: Greenwood Press, 1978.

Llewellyn–Jones, Derek. *Everywoman and Her Body*. New York: Lancer, 1971.

Lloyd, Cynthis B., Emily S. Andrews, and Curtis L. Gilroy. *Women in the Labor Market*. New York: Columbia University Press, 1979.

Lopata, Helena Z. *Occupation Housewife*. New York: Oxford University Press, 1971.

Lopate, Carole. *Women in Medicine*. Baltimore: Johns Hopkins University Press, 1968.

López y Rivas, Gilberto. *The Chicanos: Life and Struggles of the Mexican Minority in the United States*. New York: Monthly Review Press, 1973.

Lukas, J. Anthony. *Don't Shoot, We Are Your Children*. New York: Random House, 1971.

Luker, Kristen. *Abortion and the Politics of Motherhood*. Berkeley: University of California Press, 1984.

Lundberg, Ferdinand and Marynia F. Farnham. *Modern Women: The Lost Sex*. New York: Grosset and Dunlap, 1947.

Lynd, Staughton, ed. *Nonviolence in America: A Documentary History*. Indianapolis: Bobbs Merrill, 1966.

Maccoby, Eleanor E., ed. *The Development of Sex Differences*. Stanford: Stanford University Press, 1966.

Maccoby, Eleanor E., and Carol N. Jacklin. *The Psychology of Sex Differences*. Stanford: Stanford University Press, 1974.

Macdonald, Dwight. *On Movies*. New York: Berkeley-Medallion, 1971.

MacPherson, Myra. *Long Time Passing: Vietnam and the Haunted Generation*. New York: New American Library, 1984.

Maggs, Christopher, ed. *Nursing History: The State of the Art*. London: Croom Helm, 1985.

Makeba, Miriam. *Makeba: My Story.* New York: New American Library, 1987.

Malone, Bill C. *Country Music U.S.A.: A Fifty-Year History.* Austin: University of Texas Press, 1968.

Mangan, J. A., and Roberta, J. Park. *From "Fair Sex" to Feminism: Sport and the Socialization of Women in the Industrial and Post–Industrial Eras.* London: Frank Cass, 1987.

Mansbridge, Jane. *Why We Lost the ERA.* Chicago: University of Chicago Press, 1986.

Margolis, Maxine. *Mothers and Such: Views of American Women and Why They Changed.* Berkeley: University of California Press, 1984.

Marcus, Eric. *Making History: The Struggle for Gay and Lesbian Equal Rights, 1945–1990: An Oral History.* New York: Harper Collins, 1992.

Marotta, Toby. *The Politics of Homosexuality.* Boston: Houghton Mifflin, 1981.

Martin, Del and Phyllis Lyon. *Lesbian/Woman.* San Francisco: Glide Publications, 1972.

Martin, Wendy, ed. *American Sisterhood: Writings of the Feminist Movement from Colonial Times to the Present.* New York: Harper and Row, 1972.

Martinez, Elizabeth Sutherland, ed. *Letters from Mississippi.* New York: Mc-Graw–Hill, 1965.

Marzolf, Marion. *Up from the Footnote: A History of Women Journalists.* New York: Hastings House, 1977.

Masotti, Louis H., and Jeffrey K. Hadden, eds. *Suburbia in Transition.* New York: New Viewpoints, 1974.

Masters, William H., and Virginia E. Johnson. *Human Sexual Response.* Boston: Little, Brown, 1966.

———. *Human Sexual Inadequacy.* Boston: Little, Brown, 1970.

Mattfeld, Jacqueline A., and Carol G. Van Aken. *Women and the Scientific Professions.* Cambridge: MIT Press, 1965.

Matthiessen, P. *Sal si Puedes—Escape If you Can: César Chávez and the New American Revolution.* New York: Random House, 1970.

Maurer, Harry. *Strange Ground: Americans in Vietnam, 1945–1975: An Oral History.* New York: Henry Holt, 1989.

May, Elaine Tyler. *Great Expectations: Marriage and Divorce in Post–Victorian America.* Chicago: University of Chicago Press, 1980.

———. *Homeward Bound: American Families in the Cold War Era.* New York: Basic, 1988.

McCarthy, Mary. *The Seventeenth Degree: How It Went, Vietnam, Hanoi, Medina, Sons of the Morning.* New York: Harcourt Brace Jovanovich, 1974.

———. *Vietnam.* London: Weidenfeld and Nicholson, 1967.

McDonagh, Don. *Martha Graham.* New York: Praeger, 1973.

McLaughlin, Loretta. *The Pill, John Rock, and the Church: The Biography of a Revolution.* Boston: Little, Brown, 1982.

McLoughlin, William G., and Robert N. Bellan, eds. *Religion in America*. Boston: Houghton Mifflin, 1968.

Mead, Margaret, and Frances Bagley Kaplan, eds. *American Women: Report of the President's Commission on the Status of Women*. New York: Scribner's, 1965.

Meconis, Charles. *With Clumsy Grace: The American Catholic Left, 1961–1975*. New York: Seabury, 1979.

Melhem, D. H. *Gwendolyn Brooks: Poetry and the Heroic Voice*. Lexington: University Press of Kentucky, 1987.

———. *Heroism in the New Black Poetry: Introductions and Interviews*. Lexington: University Press of Kentucky, 1990.

Melinkoff, Ellen. *What We Wore: An Offbeat Social History of Women's Clothing 1950–1980*. New York: Quill, 1984.

Melosh, Barbara. *"The Physician's Hand": Work, Culture, and Conflict in American Nursing*. Philadelphia: Temple University Press, 1982.

Melville, Thomas, and Marjorie Melville. *Whose Heaven, Whose Earth?* New York: Knopf, 1971.

Meriwether, Louise. *Don't Ride the Bus on Monday: The Rosa Parks Story*. Englewood Cliffs: Prentice–Hall, 1973.

Merriam, Eve. *After Nora Slammed the Door: American Women in the 1960s, The Unfinished Revolution*. Cleveland: World Publishing, 1964.

Merriam, Eve, ed. *Growing Up Female in America: Ten Lives*. New York: Dell, 1971.

Mersmann, James. *Out of the Vortex: A Study of Poets and Poetry Against the War*. Kansas City: University Press of Kansas, 1974.

Merton, Andrew H. *Enemies of Choice: The Right–to–Life Movement and Its Threat to Abortion*. Boston: Beacon, 1981.

Middlebrook, Diane Wood. *Anne Sexton: A Biography*. Boston: Houghton Mifflin, 1991.

Miller, Herman P. *Rich Man, Poor Man*. New York: Thomas Y. Crowell, 1971.

Miller, James. *Democracy Is in the Streets*. New York: Simon and Schuster, 1987.

Miller, Jean Baker. *Toward a New Psychology of Women*. Boston: Beacon, 1976.

Miller, William. *Dorothy Day: A Biography*. New York: Harper and Row, 1982.

Millett, Kate. *Sexual Politics*. Garden City: Doubleday, 1970.

Mills, Kay. *A Place in the News: From the Women's Pages to the Front Page*. New York: Dodd, Mead, 1988.

Minnich, Elizabeth, Jean O'Barr, and Rachel Rosenfeld, eds. *Reconstructing the Academy: Women's Education and Women's Studies*. Chicago: University of Chicago Press, 1988.

Mintz, Morton. *By Prescription Only*. Originally, *The Therapeutic Nightmare* 1965; Boston: Beacon, 1967.

Mitchell, Juliet. *Woman's Estate*. New York: Pantheon, 1971.

Modleski, Tania. *Loving with a Vengeance: Mass–Produced Fantasies for Women*. New York: Methuen, 1982.

Mohr, James C. *Abortion in America*. New York: Oxford University Press, 1978.

Moody, Anne. *Coming of Age in Mississippi*. New York: Dial, 1968.

Moore, E. C. *Abortion and Public Policy: What Are the Issues?* Washington: Population Association of America, 1971.

Mootry, Maria K., and Gary Smith, eds. *A Life Distilled: Gwendolyn Brooks, Her Poetry and Fiction*. Urbana: University of Illinois Press, 1989.

Morantz, Regina Markell, Cynthia Stodola Pomerleau, and Carol Hansen Fenichel, eds. *In Her Own Words: Oral Histories of Women Physicians*. New Haven: Yale University Press, 1982.

Morantz–Sanchez, Regina Markell. *Sympathy and Science: Women Physicians in American Medicine*. New York: Oxford University Press, 1985.

Mordden, Ethan. *Movie Star: A Look at the Women Who Made Hollywood*. New York: St. Martin's, 1983.

Morello, Karen Berger. *The Invisible Bar: The Woman Lawyer in America, 1628 to the Present*. Boston: Beacon, 1986.

Morgan, Robin. *Going Too Far: The Personal Chronicle of a Feminist*. New York: Random House, 1977.

Morgan, Robin, ed. *Sisterhood is Powerful: An Anthology of Writing from the Women's Liberation Movement*. New York: Vintage, 1970.

Morgenstern, Dan. *Jazz People*. New York: Abrams, 1976.

Morris, Aldon. *The Origins of the Civil Rights Movement: Black Communities Organizing for Change*. New York: Free Press, 1984.

Morrison, Donald, ed. *1968: A Pictorial History*. New York: Time, Inc., 1989.

Mosqueda, Lawrence, J. *Chicanos, Catholicism, and Political Ideology*. Lanham, MD.: University Press of America, 1986.

Moynihan, Daniel P. *The Negro Family: The Case for National Action*. Washington: GPO, 1965.

Muckenhirn, Mary Ellen [Sister Mary Charles Borromeo, O.S.C.]. *The New Nuns*. New York: New American Library, 1967.

Munro, Eleanor. *Originals: American Women Artists*. New York: Simon and Schuster, 1979.

Myron, Nancy, and Charlotte Bunch, eds. *Lesbianism and the Women's Movement*. Baltimore: Diana Press, 1975.

Neal, Sister Marie Augusta, S.N.D. *Catholic Sisters in Transition: From the 1960s to the 1980s*. Wilmington: Michael Glazier, 1984.

Nemser, Cindy. *Art Talk: Conversations with 12 Women Artists*. New York: Scribner, 1975.

Newcomer, Mabel. "A Century of Higher Education for Women." 1959. In *Perspectives on Working Women: A Datebook, Bulletin 2080*, U.S. Department of Labor, Bureau of Labor Statistics. October 1980. Washington: GPO, 1980.

Nielsen, Georgia Panter. *From Sky Girl to Flight Attendant: Women and the Making of a Union.* Ithaca: New York: State School of Industrial and Labor Relations, 1984.

Nies, Judith. *Seven Women: Portraits from the American Radical Tradition.* New York: Viking, 1979.

Norman, Beth. *Women at War.* Philadelphia: University of Pennsylvania Press, 1991.

Notes from the First Year: Women's Liberation. Edited by Shulamith Firestone. New York: New York Radical Women, 1968.

Notes from the Second Year: Women's Liberation—Major Writings of the Radical Feminists. Edited by Shulamith Firestone and Anne Koedt. New York: New York Radical Women, 1970.

Notes from the Third Year: Women's Liberation. Edited by Anne Koedt, Anita Rapone, and Ellen Levine. New York: New York Radical Feminists, 1971.

Nye, Ivan F., and Lois W. Hoffman, eds. *The Employed Mother in America.* Chicago: Rand McNally, 1963.

Obst, Lynda Rosen, ed. *The Sixties: The Decade Remembered Now, By the People Who Lived It Then.* New York: Random House/Rolling Stone, 1977.

O'Connor, Flannery. *Mystery and Manners: Occasional Prose.* Sally and Robert Fitzgerald, eds. New York: Farrar, Straus and Giroux, 1969.

Oltman, R. M. *Campus 1970: Where Do We Stand?* Washington: American Association of University Professors, 1971.

O'Neill, William L. *Everyone Was Brave.* New York: Quadrangle, 1969.

———. *The Woman's Movement: Feminism in the United States and England.* Chicago: Quadrangle, 1971.

———. *Women at Work.* New York: Quadrangle, 1972.

Oppenheimer, Valerie Kincade. *The Female Labor Force in the United States: Demographic and Economic Factors Governing its Growth and Changing Composition.* Population Monograph Series, no. 5. Berkeley: University of California Press, 1970.

———. *Work and the Family: A Study in Social Demography.* New York: Academic Press, 1982.

Orbansky, Mollie. *Who Was Poor in 1966, Research and Statistics* note no. 23. December 1967. Prepared for the Department of Health, Education and Welfare. Washington: GPO, 1967.

Owings, Nathaniel. *The Spaces in Between.* Boston: Houghton Mifflin, 1973.

Papachristou, Judith. *Women Together: A History in Documents of the Women's Movement in the United States.* New York: Knopf, 1976.

Peck, Abe. *Uncovering the Sixties: The Life and Times of the Underground Press.* New York: Pantheon, 1975.

Peck, Ellen. *The Baby Trap.* New York: Bernard Geis, 1971.

Peck, Ellen, and Judith Senderowitz. *Pronatalism: The Myth of Mom and Apple Pie.* New York: Crowell, 1974.

Perry, Charles. *The Haight–Ashbury: A History.* New York: Random House/Rolling Stone, 1984.

Perry, Paul. *On the Bus: The Complete Guide to the Legendary Trip of Ken Kesey and the Merry Pranksters and the Birth of the Counterculture.* New York: Thunder's Mouth, 1990.

Petchesky, Rosalind Pollack. *Abortion and Woman's Choice: The State, Sexuality, and Reproductive Freedom.* Boston: Northeastern University Press, 1984.

Piven, Frances Fox, and Richard A. Cloward. *Poor People's Movements: Why They Succeed, How They Fail.* New York: Vintage, 1979.

———. *Regulating the Poor: The Functions of Public Welfare.* New York: Random House, 1971.

Placksin, Sally. *American Women in Jazz: 1900 to the Present: Their Words, Lives and Music.* New York: Seaview, 1982.

Plaskow, Judith, and Joan Arnold, eds. *Women and Religion.* Missoula: Scholar Press for the American Academy of Religion, 1974.

Plath, Aurelia Schober, ed. *Letters Home by Sylvia Plath: Correspondence 1950–1963.* New York: Harper and Row, 1975.

Powers, Thomas. *Diana: The Making of a Terrorist.* Boston: Houghton Mifflin, 1971.

Preisand, Sally. *Judaism and the New Woman.* New York: Berckman, 1975.

President's Commission on Obscenity and Pornography. *Report.* 1970. Washington: GPO.

President's Task Force on Women's Rights and Responsibilities. *A Matter of Simple Justice.* Washington, D.C.: Government Publishing Office, 636 1969.

Quant, Mary. *Quant by Quant.* London: Pan, 1965.

Quiñoñez, Lora Ann, CDP, and Mary Daniel Turner, SND de N. *The Transformation of American Catholic Sisters.* Philadelphia: Temple University Press, 1992.

Radl, Shirley. *Mother's Day Is Over.* New York: Charterhouse, 1973.

Radway, Janice A. *Reading the Romance: Women, Patriarchy, and Popular Literature.* Chapel Hill: University of North Carolina Press, 1984.

Raines, Howell. *My Soul Is Rested: The Story of the Civil Rights Movement in the Deep South.* New York: Putnam, 1977.

Rainwater, Lee, and William L. Yancey. *The Moynihan Report and the Politics of Controversy.* Cambridge: MIT Press, 1967.

Rainwater, Lee, Richard Coleman, and Gerald Handel. *Workingman's Wife.* Dobbs Ferry, N.Y.: Oceana, 1959.

Rayner, William. *Wise Women.* New York: St. Martin's Press, 1983.

Reagon, Bernice Johnson. "Songs of the Civil Rights Movement, 1955–1965: A Study in Cultural History." Ph.D. diss., Howard University, 1975.

Redstockings, eds. *Feminist Revolution.* New Paltz: Redstockings, 1975.

Reed, Evelyn. *Problems of Women's Liberation.* New York: Pathfinder, 1969.

Reed, James. *From Private Vice to Public Virtue: The Birth Control Movement and American Society Since 1830.* New York: Basic Books, 1978.

Reimers, David. *Still the Golden Door: The Third World Comes to America.* New York: Columbia University Press, 1985.

Reiss, Ira. *The Social Context of Premarital Sexual Permissiveness*. New York: Holt, Rinehart and Winston, 1967.

Rendon, Armando B. *Chicano Manifesto*. New York: Macmillan, 1971.

Report of the President's Commission on Campus Unrest. 1970. Washington: GPO.

Ribble, Margaret. *Rights of Infants*. 1943, rev. ed. New York: Columbia University Press, 1964.

Rich, Adrienne. *On Lies, Secrets, and Silences: Selected Prose, 1966–1978*. New York: W. W. Norton, 1979.

Rieff, Philip. *Freud: The Mind of the Moralist*. New York: Anchor, 1961.

Rimmer, Robert H. *The Harrad Experiment*. New York: Bantam, 1966.

Rindfuss, Ronald R., and James A. Sweet. *Postwar Fertility Trends and Differentials in the United States*. New York: Academic, 1977.

Robins, Corinne. *The Pluralist Era: American Art, 1968–1981*. New York: Harper and Row, 1984.

Robinson, Jo Ann Gibson. *The Montgomery Bus Boycott and the Women Who Started It*, ed. David Garrow. Knoxville: University of Tennessee Press, 1987.

Robinson, Paul. *The Modernization of Sex: Havelock Ellis, Alfred Kinsey, William Masters, and Virginia Johnson*. New York: Harper and Row, 1976.

Robinson, Roxanne. *Georgia O'Keeffe: A Life*. New York: Harper and Row, 1989.

Rodgers–Rose, La France. *The Black Woman*. Beverly Hills: Sage, 1980.

Rogan, Helen. *Mixed Company: Women in the Modern Army*. Boston: Beacon, 1981.

Rose, Barbara. *Helen Frankenthaler*. New York: Harry N. Abrams, 1971.

Rosen, Marjorie. *Popcorn Venus: Women, Movies and the American Dream*. New York: Coward, McCann and Geohegan, 1973.

Rosen, Harold. *Abortion in America*. Originally *Therapeutic Abortion*. 1954, rev. ed. Boston: Beacon, 1967.

Rossi, Alice S., and Ann Calderwood, eds. *Academic Women on the Move*. New York: Russell Sage, 1973.

Rossi, Alice S. *Feminists in Politics: A Panel Analysis of the First National Women's Conference*. New York: Academic Press, 1982.

Rostagno, Aldo, with Julian Beck and Judith Malina. *We, The Living Theatre*. New York: Ballantine, 1970.

Roszak, Betty, and Theodore Roszak, eds. *Masculine/Feminine: Readings in Sexual Mythology and the Liberation of Women*. New York: Harper and Row, 1969.

Rothman, Sheila. *Woman's Proper Place: A History of Changing Ideals and Practices, 1870 to the Present*. New York: Basic, 1978.

Rothschild, Mary Aickin. *A Case of Black and White: Northern Volunteers and the Southern Freedom Summers, 1964–1965*. Westport, Conn.: Greenwood, 1982.

Roy, Rustum, and Della Roy. *Honest Sex*. New York: N.A.L., 1968.

Rubin, Lillian Breslow. *Worlds of Pain: Life in the Working–Class Family*. New York: Basic Books, 1976.

Rubinstein, Charlotte Streifer. *American Women Artists: From Early Indian Times to the Present*. Boston: G. K. Hall, 1982.

Ruddick, Sara, and Pamela Daniels, eds. *Working It Out: 23 Women Writers, Artists, Scientists, and Scholars Talk About Their Lives*. New York: Pantheon, 1977.

Ruether, Rosemary Radford, ed. *Religion and Sexism: Images of Women in the Jewish and Christian Traditions*. New York: Simon and Schuster, 1974.

Ruether, Rosemary, and Eleanor McLaughlin, eds., *Women of Spirit: Female Leadership in the Jewish and Christian Traditions*. New York: Simon and Schuster, 1979.

Rupp, Leila and Verta Taylor. *Survival in the Doldrums: The American Women's Rights Movement, 1945 to the 1960s*. New York: Oxford, 1987.

Ruzek, Sheryl Burt. *The Women's Health Movement: Feminist Alternatives to Medical Control*. New York: Praeger Special Studies, 1978.

Ryan, Mary. *Womanhood in America*. New York: Franklin Watts, 1975.

Ryan, William. *Blaming the Victim*. New York: Vintage, 1972.

Sale, Kirkpatrick. *SDS*. New York: Random House, 1972.

Salper, Roberta, ed. *Female Liberation: History and Politics*. New York: Knopf, 1972.

Sandler, Bernice. *Equal Rights for Men and Women*. Hearings Before Subcommittee No. 4 of the House Committee on the judiciary. sec. no. 2, 1971. Washington: GPO.

Sandler, Irving. *American Art of the 1960s*. New York: Harper & Row, 1988.

Sapiro, Virginia. *Women in American Society*. Mountain View, CA: Mayfield Publishing, 1990.

Sargent, Lydia, ed. *Women and Revolution: A Discussion of the Unhappy Marriage of Marxism and Feminism*. Boston: South End, 1981.

Sausmarez, Maurice de. *Bridget Riley*. London: Studio Vista, 1970.

Savan, David. *In Their Own Words: Contemporary American Playwrights*. New York: Theatre Communications Group, 1988.

Sayre, Nora. *Sixties Going on Seventies*. New York: Arbor House, 1973.

Sayres, Sohnya, Anders Stephanson, Stanley Aronowitz, and Fredric Jameson, eds. *The 60s Without Apology*. Minneapolis: University of Minnesota Press, 1984.

Schneider, Susan Weidman. *Jewish and Female: Choices and Changes in Our Lives Today*. New York: Simon and Schuster, 1984.

Schulder, Diane, and Florynce Kennedy. *Abortion Rap*. New York: McGraw–Hill, 1971.

Schwartz, Hillel. *Never Satisfied: A Cultural History of Diets, Fantasies, and Fat*. New York: Free Press, 1986.

Schwartz, Judith. *The Radical Feminists of Heterodoxy*. Lebanon, N.H.: New Victoria, 1982.

Scott, Anne Firor. *Making the Invisible Woman Visible*. Urbana: University of Illinois Press, 1984.

Scott, Joan Wallach. *Gender and the Politics of History*. New York: Columbia University Press, 1988.

Seaman, Barbara. *The Doctors' Case Against the Pill*. New York: D. H. Wyden, 1969.

———. *Free and Female: The New Sexual Role of Women*. New York: Fawcett/ Crest, 1973.

———. *Women and the Crisis of Sex Hormones*. New York: Rawson, 1977.

Seifer, Nancy. *Absent from the Majority: Working Class Women in America*. Introduction by Barbara Mikulski. New York: National Project on Ethnic America of the American Jewish Committee, 1973.

Semple, John. *Call Me Jock*. Waterford, Ct.: Waterford Publishing Co., 1981.

Sennett, Richard, and Jonathan Cobb. *The Hidden Injuries of Class*. New York: Knopf, 1972.

Seward, Georgene and Robert Williamson, eds. *Sex Roles in Changing Society*. New York: Random House, 1970.

Sexton, Patricia Cayo. *Blue Collars and Hard Hats: The Working Class and the Future of American Politics*. New York: Random House, 1971.

Shafer, Byron E. *Quiet Revolution: The Struggle for the Democratic Party and the Shaping of Post-Reform Politics*. New York: Russell Sage, 1983.

Sheehan, Neil. *A Bright Shining Lie: John Paul Vann and America in Vietnam*. New York: Random House, 1988.

Shepherd, J. *Automation and Alienation: A Study of Office and Factory Workers*. Cambridge: MIT Press, 1971.

Sherman, Claire Richter, ed. *Women as Interpreters of the Visual Arts, 1820–1979*. Westport, Conn.: Greenwood, 1981.

Shore, Michael, with Dick Clark. *The History of American Bandstand*. New York: Ballantine, 1985.

Shoulders, J. *Junior College: An Attraction to Women*. Columbia, MO.: University of Missouri, 1968.

Shreve, Anita. *Women Together, Women Alone: The Legacy of the Consciousness– Raising Movement*. New York: Viking, 1989.

Shrimpton, Jean. *The Truth about Modelling*. London: W. H. Allen, 1964.

Slater, Philip E. *The Pursuit of Loneliness: American Culture at the Breaking Point*. Boston: Beacon, 1970.

Smith, Hilda. "CCWHP: The First Decade." 1979. Unpublished history of the Coordinating Committee on Women in the Historical Profession.

Smith, Joe, with Mitchell Fink, ed. *Off the Record: An Oral History of Popular Music*. New York: Warner, 1988.

Smith, Lillian. *Our Faces, Our Words*. New York: W. W. Norton, 1964.

Smuts, Robert W. *Women and Work in America*. New York: Schocken, 1971.

Sochen, June. *Consecrate Every Day: The Public Lives of Jewish American Women, 1880–1980*. Albany: State University of New York Press, 1981.

———. *Movers and Shakers: American Women Thinkers and Activists 1900–1970.* New York: Quadrangle, 1973.

Solanas, Valerie. *SCUM Manifesto.* New York: Olympia, 1968.

Solomon, Barbara Miller. *In the Company of Educated Women: A History of Women and Higher Education in America.* New Haven: Yale University Press, 1985.

Solotaroff, Ted. *Red Hot Vacuum and Other Pieces of the Writing of the Sixties.* New York: Atheneum, 1970.

Sontag, Susan. *On Photography.* New York: Dell, 1973.

———. *Styles of Radical Will.* New York: Farrar, Straus and Giroux, 1969.

Southern, Terry, and Mason Hoffenberg. *Candy.* New York: Putnam, 1964.

Spender, Dale. *Women of Ideas (And What Men Have Done to Them).* London: Routledge and Kegan, 1982.

Spitz, René. *The First Year of Life: A Psychoanalytic Study of Normal and Deviant Development of Object Relations.* New York: International Universities Press, 1965.

Spivack, Charlotte. *Merlin's Daughters: Contemporary Women Writers of Fantasy.* New York: Greenwood, 1987.

Spock, Benjamin. *Baby and Child Care.* rev. ed. New York: Pocket Books, 1968. The first edition of Dr. Spock appeared in 1946 and revised editions were published at regular intervals thereafter.

Stambler, Sookie. *Women's Liberation: Blueprint for the Future.* New York: Ace Books, 1970.

Stanford, Barbara, ed. *On Being Female.* New York: Washington Square Press, 1974.

Staples, Robert. *The Black Family: Essays and Studies.* Belmont, CA: Wadsworth, 1971.

Stein, Jean. *Edie: An American Biography.* New York: Dell, 1983.

Stein, Robert, ed. *Why Young Mothers Feel Trapped: A Redbook Documentary.* New York: Redbook, 1965.

Steinberg, Ira S. *The New Lost Generation: The Population Bomb and Public Policy.* New York: St. Martin's, 1982.

Steinem, Gloria. *Outrageous Acts and Everyday Rebellions.* New York: Holt, Rinehart and Winston, 1983.

Steiner, Stan. *La Raza: The Mexican–Americans.* New York: Harper and Row, 1970.

Stern, Jane, and Michael Stern. *Sixties People: Perky Girls, Playboys, Hippies, Party Animals.* New York: Alfred A. Knopf, 1990.

Stern, Susan. *With the Weatherman: The Personal Journal of a Revolutionary Woman.* Garden City: Doubleday, 1975.

Stetson, Erlene, ed. *Black Sister: Poetry by Black American Women, 1746–1980.* Bloomington: University of Indiana Press, 1981.

Stevens, Jay. *Storming Heaven: LSD and the American Dream.* New York: Harper and Row, 1987.

Stevenson, Anne. *Bitter Fame: A Life of Sylvia Plath*. Boston: Houghton Mifflin, 1989.

Steward, Sue, and Sheryl Garratt. *Signed, Sealed, and Delivered: True Life Stories of Women in Pop*. London: Pluto, 1984.

Stoehr, Taylor. *Free Love in America: A Documentary History*. New York: AMS Press, 1979.

Strainchamps, Ethel, ed. *Rooms with No View: A Women's Guide to a Man's World of the Media*. New York: Harper and Row, 1974.

Sutherland, Elizabeth, ed. *Letters from Mississippi*. New York: McGraw–Hill, 1965.

Takaki, Ronald. *Strangers from a Different Shore: A History of Asian Americans*. Boston: Little, Brown, 1989.

Tanner, Leslie, ed. *Voices from Women's Liberation*. New York: Signet, 1971.

Tate, Claudia, ed. *Black Women Writers at Work*. New York: Continuum, 1983.

Teal, Donn. *The Gay Militants*. New York: Stein and Day, 1971.

Terkel, Studs. *Working*. New York: Avon, 1972.

Theodore, Athena. *The Professional Woman*. Cambridge: Schenkman, 1971.

Thompson, Mary Lou, ed. *Voices of the New Feminism*. Boston: Beacon, 1970.

Tiger, Lionel. *Men in Groups*. New York: Random House, 1969.

Tinker, Irene, ed. *Women in Washington: Advocates for Public Policy*. Sage Yearbooks in Women's Policy Studies, vol. 7. Beverly Hills: Sage, 1963.

Tischler, Barbara, ed. *Sights on the Sixties*. New Brunswick: Rutgers University Press, 1992.

Tobin, Sister Mary Luke, *Hope Is An Open Door*. Nashville: Abingdon, 1982.

Toffler, Alvin. *Future Shock*. New York: Random House, 1970.

Toren, N. *Social Work: The Case of a Semi-Profession*. Beverly Hills: Sage, 1972.

Torre, Susana. *Women in American Architecture: An Historic and Contemporary Perspective*. New York: Whitney Library, 1977.

Tracy, Robert with Sharon DeLano. *Balanchine's Ballerinas: Conversations with the Muses*. New York: Linden/Simon and Schuster, 1983.

Traxler, Mary Peter, S.S.N.D. *New Works for New Nuns*. Saint Lousi: B. Herder, 1968.

Trent, James, with Jenette Golds. *Catholics in College: Religious Commitment and the Intellectual Life*. Chicago: University of Chicago Press, 1967.

Turk, Midge. *The Buried Life: A Nun's Journey*. New York: World Publishing, 1971.

Turner, Florence. *At the Chelsea*. New York: Harcourt Brace Jovanovich, 1987.

Twiggy [Lesley Hornby.] *Twiggy: An Autobiography*. London: Hart Davies MacGibbon, 1975.

Twin, Stephanie L. *Out of the Bleachers: Writings on Women and Sport*. Old Westbury, NY: Feminist Press, 1979.

Tuchman, Gaye, Arlene Kaplan Daniels, and James Benét, eds. *Hearth and Home: Images of Women in the Mass Media*. New York: Oxford University Press, 1978.

Tucker, Anne, ed. *The Woman's Eye*. New York: Knopf, 1973.

Ultra Violet [Isabelle Collin Dufresne]. *Famous for Fifteen Minutes: My Years with Andy Warhol*. New York: Harcourt Brace Jovanovich, 1988.

Unger, Irwin, and Debi Unger. *The Movement: A History of the American New Left, 1959–1972*. New York: Harper & Row, 1974.

Valentine, [Sister] M. Hester. *The Post–Conciliar Nun*. New York: Hawthorne, 1968.

VanDevanter, Lynda V. *Home By Morning*. New York: Beaufort, 1983.

Verdesi, Elizabeth. *In But Still Out: Women in the Church*. Philadelphia: Westminster, 1983.

Veroff, Joseph, Richard A. Kulka, and Elizabeth Douvan. *The Inner American: A Self-Portrait from 1957 to 1976*. New York: Basic, 1981.

Veroff, Joseph, Richard A. Kulka, and Elizabeth Douvan. *Mental Health in America: Patterns of Help–Seeking 1957–1976*. New York: Basic, 1981.

Walker, Margaret. *How I Wrote Jubilee*. New York: Feminist Press of the City University of New York, 1990.

Wall, Cheryl, ed. *Changing Our Own Words: Essays on Criticism, Theory, and Writing by Black Women*. New Brunswick: Rutgers University Press, 1989.

Walsh, Mary Roth. *Doctors Wanted, No Women Need Apply: Sexual Barriers in the Medical Profession, 1835–1975*. New Haven: Yale University Press, 1977.

Walsh, Mary Roth, ed. *The Psychology of Women: Ongoing Debates*. New Haven: Yale University Press, 1987.

Wandersee, Winifred D. *On the Move: American Women in the 1970s*. Boston: Twayne/G. K. Hall, 1988.

Ward, Ed, Geoffrey Stokes, and Ken Tucker. *Rock of Ages: The Rolling Stone History of Rock and Roll*. New York: Rolling Stone, 1986.

Ware, Cellestine. *Woman Power: The Movement for Women's Liberation*. New York: Tower, 1970.

Warhol, Andy, and Pat Hackett. *POPism*. New York: Harcourt Brace Jovanovich, 1980.

Watters, Pat. *Down to Now: Recollections of the Civil Rights Movement*. New York: Pantheon, 1972.

Weibel, Kathryn. *Mirror, Mirror: Images of Women Reflected in Popular Culture*. Garden City: Anchor, 1977.

Weinbaum, Batya. *The Curious Courtship of Women's Liberation and Socialism*. Boston: South End, 1978.

Weiner, Lynn. *From Working Girl to Working Mother: The Female Labor Force in the United States, 1820–1980*. Chapel Hill: University of North Carolina Press, 1985.

Wenner, Jann S., ed. *Twenty Years of Rolling Stone: What a Long, Strange Trip It's Been*. New York: Straight Arrow, 1987.

Wertz, Richard W., and Dorothy C. Wertz. *Lying-In: A History of Childbirth in America*. New York: Schocken, 1979.

Westoff, Charles F., and Norman B. Ryder. *The Contraceptive Revolution*. Princeton: Princeton University Press, 1977.

Westoff, Leslie Aldridge, and Charles F. Westoff. *From Now to Zero: Fertility, Contraception, and Abortion in America*. Boston: Little, Brown, 1971.

Williams, Juan. *Eyes on the Prize: America's Civil Rights Years, 1954–1965*. New York: Viking, 1987.

Wilson, Mary. *Dreamgirl: My Life as a Supreme*. London: Sidgwick and Jackson, 1987.

Wilson, Robert A. *Feminine Forever*. New York: M. Evans, 1966.

Wolfe, Tom. *The Purple Decades: A Reader*. New York: Farrar, Straus and Giroux, 1982.

Woliver, Robbie. *Bringing It All Back Home: 25 Years of American Folk Music at Folk City*. New York: Pantheon, 1986.

Woloch, Nancy. *Women and the American Experience*. New York: Knopf, 1984.

Wong, Mary Gilligan. *Nun: A Memoir*. New York: Harcourt Brace Jovanovich, 1983.

Wright, Gwendolyn. *Building the Dream: A Social History of Housing in America*. Cambridge: MIT Press, 1981.

Yates, Gayle. *What Women Want: The Ideas of the Movement*. Cambridge: Harvard University Press, 1975.

Yntema, Sharon. *More than 100 Women Science Fiction Writers: An Annotated Bibliography*. Freedom, CA: Crossing Press, 1988.

Zaroulis, Nancy and Gerald Sullivan. *Who Spoke Up? American Protest Against the War in Vietnam, 1963–1975*. Garden City: Doubleday, 1984.

Zimmerman, Bonnie. *The Safe Sea of Women: Lesbian Fiction, 1969–1989*. Boston: Beacon, 1990.

Zinn, Howard. *SNCC: The New Abolitionists*. Boston: Beacon, 1964.

Articles

Adams, Velma A. "Room at the Top in Sales." *National Business Woman* (June 1966): 9–10.

Adelson, Joseph. "Is Women's Lib a Passing Fad?" *New York Times Magazine* (19 March 1972): 94.

Ademeck, R. J. "College Major, Work Commitment and Female Perceptions of Self, Ideal Woman, and Men's Ideal Woman." *Sociology Focus* 3 (1970): 97–112.

Ademeck, R. J., and W. J. Goudy. "Identification, Sex, and Change in College Major." *Sociology of Education* 39:2 (1966): 183–99.

Albjerg, M. H. "Why Do Bright Girls Not Take Stiff Courses?" *Educational Forum* 25 (1961): 141–44.

Alexander, Shana. "The Politics of Abortion." *Newsweek* (2 October 1972).

Alloway, Lawrence. "Marilyn as Subject Matter." *Arts Magazine* 42:3 (September–October 1967): 27–30.

Almquist, E. M., and S. S. Angrist. "Career Salience and Atypicality of Occupational Choice Among College Women." *Journal of Marriage and the Family* 32:2 (1970): 242–49.

———. "Role Model Influences on College Women's Career Aspirations." *Merrill-Palmer Quarterly* 17 (1971): 263–79.

Alpert, Jane. "Mother Right," *Ms* (August 1973).

Angelou, Maya. "Interview," *New York Post* (26 December 1970).

Aptheker, Bettina. "The Matriarchal Mirage: The Moynihan Connection in Historical Perspective," in *Women's Legacy: Essays on Race, Sex, and Class in American History*. Amherst: University of Massachusetts Press, 1982.

Austin, J. Ellen, and Mickey C. Smith. "Women in Hospital Pharmacy: A Study of Eight States." *American Journal of Hospital Pharmacy* (January 1971).

Babchuk, N., and A. Booth. "Voluntary Association Membership: A Longitudinal Analysis." *American Sociological Review* 34:1 (1969): 31–45.

Bart, Pauline and Melinda Bart Schlesinger. "Collective Work and Self-Identity: The Effect of Working in a Feminist Illegal Abortion Collective." In *Workplace Democracy and Social Change*. Frank Lindenfeld and Joyce Rothschild-Whitt, eds. Boston: Porter–Sargent, 1980.

Bell, Robert and Jay Chaskes. "Premarital Experience Among Coeds, 1958 and 1968." *Journal of Marriage and the Family* 32 (February 1970): 81–84.

Bender, Marilyn. "College Girl Sees No Future But Marriage." *New York Times* (26 March 1962).

Bender, Marilyn. "Once Sheltered Wives, They're Marching to a Different Drum." *New York Times* (11 November 1969).

Benne, Kenneth, and Warren Bennis. "Role Confusion and Role Conflict in Nursing." *American Journal of Nursing* 59:2 (1959).

Berry, Jane. "Effects of Poverty on Culturally Disadvantaged Women." *Adult Leadership* (May 1969): 10–14.

Bergquist, Virginia A. "Women's Participation in Labor Organizations." *Monthly Labor Review* (October 1974): 3–9.

Berman, Saul. "The Status of Women in Salakhic Judaism" In *The Jewish Woman: New Perspectives*. Elizabeth Koltun, ed. New York: Schocken, 1976, 121–22.

Bettelheim, Bruno. "Growing Up Female." *Harper's Magazine* 225 (October 1962), 124.

Bibb, Robert. "Blue-Collar Women in Low-Wage Industries: A Dual-Market Interpretation." In *The American Working Class: Prospects for the 1980s*. Ed. Irving Lewis Horowitz et al. New Brunswick: Transaction Books, 1979, 125–49.

Bird, Caroline. "Women's Colleges and Women's Lib." *Change* 4:3 (1 April 1972): 64.

Black, Cobey. "Women in the Peace Corps." *National Business Woman* (May 1962): 4.

Blake, Judith. "Abortion and Public Opinion: The 1960–1970 Decade." *Science* 171 (2 December 1971): 546.

Blau, Francine D. "Women in the Labor Force: An Overview," in *Women: A Feminist Perspective*. 2nd ed. Jo Freeman, ed. Palo Alto: Mayfield, 1979.

Blitz, Rudolph C. "Women in the Professions, 1870–1970." *Monthly Labor Review* 97:5 (May 1974): 34–39.

Bowers, J. Z. "Women in Medicine: An International Study." *New England Journal of Medicine* 275 (1966): 362–65.

Bowman, Garda W., Beatrice N. Worthy, and Stephen A. Greyser. "Are Women Executives People?: Survey of 2000 Executives." *Harvard Business Review* 43 (July 1965): 15.

Brandwein, Ruth A., Carol A., Brown, and Elizabeth Maury Fox. "Women and Children Last: The Social Situation of Divorced Mothers and Their Families." *Journal of Marriage and the Family* 36 (August 1974): 498–514.

Broverman, Inge K., D. M. Broverman, F. E. Rosenkrantz, and S. R. Vogel. "Sex-Role Stereotypes and Clinical Judgments of Mental Health." *Journal of Consulting and Clinical Psychology* 34:1 (1970): 1–7.

Buber, Judith. "Women Who Work in Factories." *Dissent* 19:1 (Winter 1972).

Bunting, Mary I. "The Radcliffe Institute for Independent Study." *Educational Record* 42 (October 1961): 179–86.

———. "The Radcliffe Institute: Is There Life After Birth?" *Change* 7:7 (September 1975): 13.

Cade, Toni. "The Pill: Genocide or Liberation?" in Cade, ed. *The Black Woman: An Anthology*. New York: Mentor, 1970.

Callwood, June. "Infidelity." *Ladies' Home Journal* 82 (April 1965): 76–77, 132–34.

Cannon, Kenneth L., and Richard Long. "Premarital Sex and Behavior in the Sixties." *Journal of Marriage and the Family* (February 1971): 39–40.

Carter, Norene. "The Episcopalian Story." In *Women of Spirit*. Rosemary Ruether and Eleanor McLaughlin, eds. New York: Simon and Schuster, 1979.

Cartwright, L. W. "Conscious Factors Entering into Decisions of Women to Study Medicine." *Journal of Social Issues* 28:2 (1972): 210–15.

Chambers, Carl D. and Dodi Schultz. "Women and Drugs." *Ladies' Home Journal* 88:1 (November 1971): 131.

Chevalier, Lois R., and Leonard Cohen. "The Terrible Trouble with the Birth-Control Pill." *Ladies' Home Journal* 84:7 (July 1967): 44.

Clarke, Mary. "Let's Keep on Keepin' On." Women Strike for Peace. *Memo* 22.

Cleland, Virginia. "Sex Discrimination: Nursing's Most Pervasive Problem." *American Journal of Nursing* 71:8 (August 1971): 1142–47.

Cless, Elizabeth. "A Modest Proposal for the Educating of Women." *American Scholar* 36 (1969): 618–27.

Clinas, B. "Women on College Faculties." *Science* 168 (1970): 917–18.

Cohen, M. "You've Come a Long Way, Baby . . . or Have You?" *Sexual Behavior* 2:6 (1972): 48–51.

Collins, A. M., and W. E. Sedlacek. "Counselor Perceptions of Sexual Attitudes of Female University Students. *College Student Journal* 6:3 (1973): 13–16.

Cook, Alice B. "Women and the American Trade Unions." *Annals of the American Academy of Political and Social Sciences* 37 (1968): 124–32.

Cook, Joan. "The Troubled, Uneasy World of the Women in the Berrigan Case." *New York Times* (26 May 1971): 48.

Cooke, Joanne. "Editorial: Here's To You Mrs. Robinson." *Motive* 29:6–7 (March–April 1962).

Cooper, Judy. "It Could Have Happened Twenty Years Ago." *Equal Times* (31 July 1983).

Cooperstock, Ruth. "Sex Differences in the Use of Mood-Modifying Drugs: An Explanatory Model," *Journal of Health and Social Behavior* 12:3 (September 1971): 238–44.

Costantini, Edmond, and Kenneth H. Craik. "Women as Politicians: The Social Background, Personality, and Political Careers of Female Party Leaders." *Journal of Social Issues* 28:2 (1972): 217–236.

Costello, Mary. "Legalization of Prostitution." [25 August 1971]. In *Editorial Research Reports on the Women's Movement*. Washington: Congressional Quarterly (1973), 127–142.

Cox, Harvey. "The 'New Breed' in American Churches: Sources of Social Activision in American Religion." In *Religion in America*. William G. McLoughlin and Robert N. Bellah, eds. Boston; Houghton Mifflin, 1968.

Cremin, Lawrence A. "Focus on Education." *The 1964 World Book Year Book: Reviewing Events of 1964*. Chicago: Field Enterprises, 1964, 39–40. See also Cremin. "Focus on Education." *The 1965 World Book Year Book:* 40–41.

Cugat, Lorraine. "Mrs. Cugat Can't See Gals as Tooters: Kills Glamour." *Down Beat* (4 May 1959), 13.

Cunningham, R. M., Jr. "Women Who Made It Offer Insights into Their Problems." *College and University Business* 48 (1970): 56–61.

Curtis, Charlotte. "Miss America Pageant is Picketed by 100 Women." *New York Times* (8 September 1968).

Dainton, P. M. "Women Executives: Is There Room at the Top?" *Personnel Management* 49 (1967): 15–19.

Davidson, Carl. "Whither the Weathermen." *Guardian* (26 December 1970).

Davidson, Sara. "An 'Oppressed Majority' Demands Its Rights." *Life* 67 (12 December 1969): 66–70.

Davies, Marjorie. "Women's Place Is at the Typewriter: The Feminization of the Clerical Labor Force." *Radical America* 8 (1974): 1–37.

Davis, Douglas. "Cockroach or Queen." *Newsweek* (15 January 1973): 73.

Decter, Midge. "The Peace Ladies." *Harper's* 226 (March 1963): 49.

Degler, Carl N. "Revolution without Ideology: The Changing Place of Women in America." *Daedalus* 93:2 (1964): 653–70. And in *The Woman in America.* Robert Jay Lifton, ed. Boston: Beacon, 1967.

Deming, Barbara. "Prison Notes." *Liberation* 1–6 (August 1964–March 1965).

Derr, Jull Mulvay. "Strength in Our Union: The Making of Mormon Sisterhood." In *Sisters in Spirit: Mormon Women in Historical and Cultural Perspective.* Maureen Ursenbach Beecher and Lavinia Fielding Anderson, eds. Urbana: University of Illinois Press, 1987.

Dewey, Lucretia M. "Women in Labor Unions." *Monthly Labor Review* 94 (February 1971): 42–48.

Didion, Joan. "The Great Reprieve." *Mademoiselle* (February 1961).

Dinerman, B. "Sex Discrimination in Academia." *Journal of Higher Education* 42 (1971): 253–64.

———. "Women in Architecture." *Architectural Forum* (December 1969): 50–51.

Dixon, Marlene. "On Women's Liberation." *Radical America* (February 1970): 27–28.

———. "The Rise of Women's Liberation." *Ramparts* 8:6 (December 1969): 57–64.

Dixon, R. B. "Halleluja the Pill?" *Transaction* 8: 1–2 (1970).

Dolan, E. "Higher Education for Women." *Higher Education* 20:1 (1963).

———, "Q.E.D." *AAUW Journal* (October 1964): 136–37.

Duffett, Judith. "Atlantic City is a Town with Class—They Raise Your Morals While They Judge Your Ass." *VWLM* [Voice of the Women's Liberation Movement] 1:3 (October 1968).

Duffey, Mary Beth Dakoske. "Fidelity to a Promise of Service." *Catholic Rural Life* 31:4 (July 1964): 16–18.

Dworkin, A. G. "Stereotypes and Self-Images Held by Native-Born and Foreign-Born Mexican Americans." *Sociology and Social Research* 49:2 (1965): 214–24.

Edwards, C. N. "The Student Nurse: A Study in Sex Role Transition." *Psychological Reports* 25:3 (1969): 975–90.

English, Deirdre. "What a Long, Strange Trip It Was." *New York Times Book Review* (Dec. 9, 1990): 3, 41.

Epstein, Cynthia. "Encountering the Male Establishment: Sex Status Limits on Women's Careers in the Professions." *American Journal of Sociology* 75 (1970): 965–82.

Epstein, Gilda F., and Arline L. Bronzaft. "Female Freshmen View Their Roles as Women." *Journal of Marriage and the Family* 34 (November 1972): 671–84.

Erikson, Erik. "Inner and Outer Space: Reflections on Womanhood." In *Woman in America.* Robert Jay Lifton, ed. Boston: Beacon Press, 1967.

Erskine, Helen Gaudit. "The Polls: Women's Role." *Public Opinion Quarterly* 34 (1971): 275–90.

Etzioni, Amitai. "Sex Control, Science and Society." *Science* 161 (13 September 1968): 1107–12.

Farians, Elizabeth. "Phallic Worship: The Ultimate Idolatry." In *Women and Religion*. rev. ed. Judith Plaskow and Joan Arnold, eds. Missoula, Mont.: Scholars Press for the American Academy of Religion, 1974.

Faunce, William, Einar Hardin, and Eugene H. Jacobson. "Automation and the Employee." *Annals of the American Academy of Political and Social Science* (1962): 340.

Ferguson, R. "Women's Liberation Has Different Meaning for Blacks." *Washington Post* (3 October 1970).

Fischer, A., and P. Golde. "The Position of Women in Anthropology." *American Anthropologist* 70:2 (1968): 337–43.

Fitzgerald, Laurine E., and Joanne B. Lantz. "The Adult Coed: A Personal Vocational Profile." *National Business Woman* (October 1968): 8.

Fox, Greer Litton. "Sex Role Attitudes as Predictors of Contraceptive Use Among Unmarried University Students." *Sex Roles* 33 (1977): 265–83.

———. "The Woman Graduate Student in Sociology." In *Women on Campus: Proceedings of the Symposium, Oct. 14, 1970.* (Ann Arbor: University of Michigan, 1970): 33–35.

Freeman, Jo. "Growing Up Girlish." *Transaction* 8:1 (November–December 1970): 1–2.

———. "Women's Liberation and its Impact on the Campus." *Liberal Education* 57:4 (1971): 468–78.

Frisof, Jamie Kelem. "Textbooks and Channeling." *Women: A Journal of Liberation* 1:1 (Fall 1968): 26–28.

Fruchter, Norman. "SDS: In and Out of Context." *Liberation* (February 1972).

Gagnon, John, and William Simon. "Is a Women's Revolution Really Possible?" *McCall's* 76 (October 1969): 76, 126–29.

Gallagher, Teresa. "Women's Entry into Pharmacy: Professionalization, Expansion, and Interoccupational Competition for Men." Unpublished paper from the American Educational Research Association annual meeting (5–9 April 1988).

Gallup, George H., and Evan Hill. "The American Woman." *Saturday Evening Post* 233 (22 December 1962): 15–32.

Gannon, Martin J. "A Profile of the Temporary Help Industry and its Workers." *Monthly Labor Review* 97:5 (May 1974), 44–49.

Garland, Phyl. "Builders of a New South." *Ebony* 21:10 (August 1966): 32–36.

Gellhorn, Martha. "Suffer the Little Children." *Ladies' Home Journal* (January 1967).

Gent, George. "Women Filmmakers: Doors Opening." *New York Times* (15 June 1972).

Gervis, Stephanie. "Women Speak Out for Peace." *The Nation* 193 (30 December 1961): 523–36.

Gilder, George. "The Suicide of the Sexes." *Harper's* (June 1973): 42–54.

Gilkes, Cheryl. "'Together and in Harness': Women's Traditions in the Sanctified Church." *Signs* 10:4 (Summer 1985), 679.

Gill, Gerald. "From Maternal Pacifism to Revolutionary Solidarity: African-American Women's Opposition to the War in Vietnam." In *Sights on the Sixties*. Barbara Tischler, ed. New Brunswick: Rutgers University Press, 1992.

Gilman, Richard. "There's a Wave of Pornography/Obscenity/Sexual Expression." *New York Times Magazine* (8 September 1968): 36–37, 39–82.

Gleazer, Edmund J., Jr. "Growth and Status of the Junior College." In *The Encyclopedia of Education*. Lee C. Deighton, ed. (New York: Macmillan, 1971), 321–24.

Glenn, Evelyn Nakano, and Roslyn L. Feldberg. "Degraded and Deskilled: The Proletarianization of Clerical Work." In *Women and Work*. Rachel Kahn-Hut et al., eds. New York: Oxford University Press, 1982.

Glueck, Grace. "Women Artists Demonstrate at Whitney." *New York Times* (12 December 1970).

Gold, Ivan. "On Having Grace Paley Once More Among Us." *Commonweal* 89 (25 October 1968): 111–12.

Goldberg, P. "Are Women Prejudiced Against Women?" *Transaction* 5 (November 1968): 28–30.

Gordon, Ann D., Mari Jo Buhle, and Nancy E. Schrom. "Women in American Society." *Radical America* 5 (July–August 1971): 11.

Gornick, Vivian. "The Next Great Moment in History is Theirs." *Village Voice* (27 November 1969).

———. "Who Says We Haven't Made a Revolution?" *New York Times Magazine* (15 April 1990): 24–27, 52–53.

———. "Why Women Fear Success." *Ms* (Spring 1972), 50–53.

Graham, Dorothy Lockwood. "The Double Life of a Woman Executive." *National Business Women* (February 1962): 8–9, 29.

Graham, Patricia Albjerg. "Status Transitions of Women Students, Faculty, and Administrators." In *Academic Women on the Move*. Alice S. Rossi and Ann Calderwood, eds. New York: Russell Sage, 1973.

Green, Carol Hurd. "The Writer Is a Spy." *Boston Review of the Arts* (August 1972), 24.

Green, George N. "ILGWU in Texas, 1930–1970." *The Journal of Mexican American History* 1 (Spring 1971): 144–69.

Grenier, Cynthia. "Lillian Hellman: A Lying Legend in Her Own Time." *The World and I: A Chronicle of Our Changing Era* (May 1987): 417–19.

Grimm, James W., and Robert N. Stern. "Sex Roles and Internal Labor Market Structures: The 'Female' Semi-Professions." *Social Problems* 21 (June 1974): 694.

Gross, Edward. "*Plus sa* [sic] *change* . . .: The Sexual Structure of Occupations Over Time." *Social Problems* 16 (1968): 198–208.

Harlacher, Ervin L. "Community Services in Community Colleges." In *The Encyclopedia of Education* (New York: Macmillan, 1971): 324–29.

Harrison, Cynthia E. "A 'New Frontier' for Women: The Public Policy of the Kennedy Administration." *Journal of American History* 67 (December 1980): 630–46.

Hartley, Ruth E. "Women's Roles: How Girls See Them." *American Association of University Women Journal* (May 1962).

Haskell, Molly. "French Lesson." *Lears* 3:5 (July 1990): 71–72.

Hayden, Dolores. "Catharine Beecher and the Politics of Housework." In Susana Torre. *Women in American Architecture: An Historic and Contemporary Perspective*. New York: Whitney Library of Design, 1977.

Hechlinger, Grace, and Fred M. Hechlinger. "College Morals Mirror Our Society." *New York Times Magazine* (14 April 1963): 108–120.

Hedges, J. N., and S. E. Bemis. "Sex Stereotyping: Its Decline in Skilled Trades." *Monthly Labor Review* 97:5 (May 1974): 14–22.

Hershey, Leonore. "Echoes of Heros." *McCalls* 91 (July 1964).

Hillman, Bessie. "Gifted Women in the Trade Union." In *American Women: The Changing Image*. Beverly Cassara, ed. Boston: Beacon Press, 1962.

Hinckle, Warren and Marianne Hinckle. "A History of the Rise of the Unusual Movement for Women Power in the United States, 1961–1968." *Ramparts* 6:7 (February 1968): 28.

Hoffman, Betty Hannah. "Coeds in Rebellion." *Ladies' Home Journal* 82 (October 1965): 168.

———. "Through All My Housework in an Hour." *Ladies' Home Journal* (October 1960): 184–90.

Hoge, Dean R., Cynthia L. Luna, and David K. Miller. "Trends in College Students' Values between 1952 and 1979: A Return of the Fifties?" *Sociology of Education* 54 (1981): 266–173.

Holden, Stephen. "Ellie Greenwich: Her Life and Her Songs at the Bottom Line." *New York Times* (20 January 1984): sec. Y, 12.

Horner, Matina S. "Fail: Bright Women." *Psychology Today* 3 (November 1969): 36.

Howard, Jane. "Is Women's Lib a Dirty Word in Milwaukee?" *Life* (27 August 1971): 46–51.

Howe, Florence. "Sexual Stereotypes Start Early." In *The Women, Yes!* Marie B. Hecht et al., eds. New York: Holt, Rinehart, and Winston, 1973.

Howe, Irving. "The Middle Class Mind of Kate Millett." *Harper's* 241 (December 1970): 124–29.

Hunter, Jane E. "A Daring New Concept: *The Ladies' Home Journal* and Modern Feminism." *NWSA Journal*, 2:4 (1972): 583–602.

Hussain, Margary. "Muhammad Speaks." In *Black Muslims in America*. A. Lincoln, ed. Boston: Beacon Press, 1971.

Ingalls, Zoe. "Women's Colleges Show Renewed Vigor After Long, Painful

Self-Examination." *Chronicle of Higher Education* 29:3 (12 September 1984): 1, 18–19.

James, David. "Carolee Schneemann's Fuses." *Cinematograph* 3 (1988): 314–20.

Johnson, Davis G. and Edwin B. Hutchins. "Doctor or Dropout? A Study of Medical Student Attrition." *Journal of Medical Education* 41:12 (1966).

Kane, Christine L. "Inside the Death Factory." *New Boston Review* (June 1981).

Kaufman, Debra Renee. "Professional Women: How Real Are the Recent Gains?" In *Women: A Feminist Perspective.* Jo Freeman, ed. Mountain View, Calif.: Mayfield, 1989.

Kempton, Sally. "Cutting Loose: A Private View of the Women's Uprising." *Esquire* 74 (July 1970): 56–57.

Keniston, Ellen, and Kenneth Keniston. "An American Anachronism: The Image of Women and Work." *American Scholar* 33 (Summer 1964): 355–75.

Kenneally, James J. "A Question of Equality." In *American Catholic Women: A Historical Exploration.* Karen Kennelly, ed. New York: Macmillan, 1989.

Kernan, J. B. "Her Mother's Daughter? The Case of Clothing and Cosmetic Fashions." *Adolescence* 8:31 (1973): 343–50.

King, Mary, and Casey Hayden. "Sex and Caste: A Kind of Memo." *Liberation* (1966).

Knudson, E. D. "Public Health Nurses' Interest in Occupational Achievement." *Nursing Research* 17:4 (1968): 327–35.

Kobrin, Frances E. "The American Midwife Controversy: A Crisis in Professionalism." *Bulletin of the History of Medicine* 40 (1966): 350–63.

Koedt, Anne. "Myth of the Vaginal Orgasm." *Notes from the First Year.* In Koedt, Ellen Levine, and Anita Rapone. *Radical Feminism.* New York: Quadrangle, 1973.

Komarovsky, Mirra. "The Homemaker: A Comparative View." *AAUW Journal* (May 1962): 226–29.

Koontz, Elizabeth Duncan. Foreword to "Day Care Facts." U.S. Department of Labor, Women's Bureau. Washington: GPO, 1970.

———. "Voluntarism: A Vital Contribution." *AAUW Journal* (January 1970).

Kosa, J., and R. E. Coke, Jr. "The Female Physician in Public Health Conflict and Reconciliation of the Sex and Professional Roles." *Sociology and Social Research* 49:3 (1965): 294–305.

Kramer, Noel Anketell. "Discrimination and the Woman Law Student." In *Women on Campus: Proceedings of the Symposium, Oct. 14, 1970.* (Ann Arbor: University of Michigan, 1970): 39–41.

Kuhn, Irene Corbally. "Lysistratas of the Bomb." *National Review* 14:24 (15 June 1963): 24.

Kurman, George. "What Does Girls' Cheerleading Communicate?" *Journal of Popular Culture* 20:2 (Fall 1986): 57–63.

Kurtz, R. "Body Image—Male and Female." *Transaction* 6 (1968): 25–27.

Langer, Elinor. "Notes for the Next Time." *Working Papers for a New Society* (Fall 1973): 39–81.

Lanier, A. R. "Women in Rural Areas." *Annals of the American Academy of Political and Social Science* 375 (1968): 115–43.

Lanker, Brian, and Maya Angelou. "I Dream a World." *National Geographic* 176:2 (August 1989): 209–225.

La Rue, L. "Black Liberation and Women's Lib." *Transaction* 8:1–2 (1970): 280–85.

Lazarre, Jane. "What Feminists and Freudians Can Learn from Each Other." In *Women in a Changing World*. Uta West, ed. New York: McGraw Hill, 1975.

Lennane, K. Jean, and R. John Lennane. "Alleged Psychogenic Disorders in Women: A Possible Manifestation of Sexual Prejudice." *The New England Journal of Medicine* 288 (3 February 1973): 288–92.

Lerner, Gerda. "New Approaches to the Study of Women in American History." *Journal of Social History* 3 (Fall 1969): 333–56.

Lewis, E. C. "Women in Graduate School." *Graduate Comment* 12:1 (1969): 29–35.

Lewis, M., and R. N. Butler. "Why Is Women's Lib Ignoring Old Women?" *Aging and Human Development* 3:3 (1972): 223–31.

Linden-Ward, Blanche. "The ERA and Kennedy's Presidential Commission on the Status of Women," in *John F. Kennedy*. Paul Harper and Joann P. Kreig, eds. (New York: Greenwood, 1988).

———. "Kate Millett." In *Contemporary Cultural Criticism*. Hartmann Heuermann and Berndt-Peter Lange, eds. Frankfort-am-Main: Peter Lang, 1992.

Linn, E. L. "Women Dental Students: Women in a Man's World." *Milbank Memorial Fund Quarterly* 49:3 pt 2 (1971): 63–76.

Linn, Lawrence S., and Milton S. Davis. "The Use of Psychotherapeutic Drugs by Middle-Aged Women." *Journal of Health and Social Behavior* 12 (December 1971): 331.

Logan, Gary J. "Fighting Loneliness: A Woman Veteran's Vietnam Experience." *Mettro* (Washington, D.C.) (22 January 1981).

Longcope, Kay. "Mary Kay's Cosmetic Family." *Boston Globe* (14 January 1982): 39, 42.

Lopata, Helena Z. "Living Arrangements of American Urban Widows." *Sociological Forces* 5:1 (1971): 41–61.

———. "The Social Involvement of American Widows." *American Behavioral Scientist* 14 (1970): 41–58.

Lovelace, C. "Gender and the Case of Carolee Schneemann." *Millenium* (Fall/Winter 1986–87).

Lowenstein, L. "Who Wants Lady Interns?" *New England Journal of Medicine* 284 (1971): 735.

Lublin, J. S. "Discrimination Against Women in Newsrooms: Fact or Fantasy." *Journalism Quarterly* 49:2 (1972): 357–61.

Ludeman, W. W. "Declining Female College Attendance: Causes and Implications." *Educational Forum* 25 (1971): 505–07.

Lyness, Judith L., Milton E. Lipetz, and Keith E. Davis. "Living Together: An Alternative to Marriage." *Journal of Marriage and the Family* 34 (May 1972): 305–11.

Lyon, Bonnie. "Tillie Olsen: The Writer as a Jewish Woman." *Studies in American Jewish Literature* 5 (1986), 91.

MacDonald, S. "Carolee Schneemann: Autobiographical Trilogy." *Film Quarterly* 34 (1980).

Mack, Grace E. "The Black Woman Graduate Student." In *Women on Campus: Proceedings of the Symposium, Oct. 14, 1970.* (Ann Arbor: Univ. of Michigan, 1970): 42–45.

Mahoney, Caroline. "Constitutional Lawyer: Eleanor Holmes Norton." In *On Being Female.* Barbara Stanford, ed. New York: Washington Square Press, 1974.

Mailer, Norman. "The Prisoner of Sex." *Harper's* (March 1971). (Reprinted as *The Prisoner of Sex.* New York: Little, Brown, 1971.)

Mainardi, Pat. "The Politics of Housework." In *Sisterhood is Powerful: An Anthology of Writings from the Women's Liberation Movement.* Robin Morgan, ed. New York: Random House, 1970.

Marling, Karal Ann, and John Wetenhall. "The Sexual Politics of Memory: The Vietnam Women's Memorial Project and 'The Wall.'" *Prospects* 14 (1989): 341–72.

Martin, Del, and Phyllis Lyon. "The Realities of Lesbianism." In Joanne Cooke, Charlotte Bunch Weeks, and Robin Morgan, eds. *The New Woman: MOTIVE Anthology on Women Liberation.* Indianapolis: Motive, 1970.

Maslow, Abraham H. "Self-Esteem (Dominance-Feeling) and Sexuality in Women." In *Journal of Social Psychology* 16 (1942). (Reprinted in *Psychoanalysis and Female Sexuality.* Hendrik M. Ruitenbeek, ed. New Haven: College and Univ. Press, 1966: 161–197.)

Maslow, Abraham H., H. Rand, and S. Newman. "Some Parallels Between Sexual and Dominant Behavior of Infra-Human Primates and the Fantasies of Patients in Psychotherapy." *Journal of Nervous and Mental Disease* 131 (1960): 202–212.

McAfee, Kathy, and Myrna Wood. "Bread and Roses." *Leviathan* 1:3 (June 1969).

McCain, Nina. "As Daughters Grow Up and Moms Grow Old." *Boston Globe* (10 May 1990).

McDaniel, C. O., Jr. "Dating Roles and Reasons for Dating." *Journal of Marriage and the Family* 31:1 (1969): 97–107.

McNally, Gertrude B. "Patterns of Female Labor Force Activity." *Industrial Relations* 7 (May 1968).

Mead, Margaret. "The American Woman Today." *The World Book Year Book: Annual Supplement to The World Book Encyclopedia.* Chicago: Field Enterprises, 1969, 78–95.

Meier, Harold C. "Mother-Centeredness and College Youths' Attitudes Toward Social Equality for Women: Some Empirical Findings." *Journal of Marriage and the Family* 34 (February 1972): 115–21.

Menkes, Suzy. "Oleg Cassini and the Value of Jackie Kennedy." *International Herald Tribune* (5 June 1990).

Mikulski, Barbara. Introduction to Nancy Seifer, *Absent from the Majority: Working Class Women in America.* New York: National Project on Ethnic America of the American Jewish Committee, 1973.

Millett, Kate. "Libbies, Smithies, Vassarites." *Change* 2:5 (September–October 1970): 42–50.

Mitchell, Juliet. "Women: The Longest Revolution." *New Left Review* (November–December 1966), 11–37.

Modell, John. "Dating Becomes the Way of American Youth." In *Essays on the Family and Historical Change.* Leslie Page Moch and Gary D. Stark, eds. Arlington: Texas A and M University Press, 1983: 91–126.

Modell, John, Frank F. Furstenberg, and Douglas Strong. "The Timing of Marriage in the Transition to Adulthood: Continuity and Change." In *Turning Points: Historical and Sociological Essays on the Family.* Supplement to *American Journal of Sociology* 84 (1978): 120–50.

Moore, Margaret. "How to Succeed at Crime-Fighting by Really Trying." *National Business Woman* (July 1967).

Moran, Robert D. "Reducing Discrimination: Role of the Equal Pay Act." *Monthly Labor Review* (June 1970): 32–37.

Morgan, Robin. "Lesbianism and Feminism: Synonyms or Contradictions?" *Second Wave* 2:4 (1973): 14–23.

Motz, A. "The Roles of the Married Woman in Science." *Marriage and Family Living* 23:4 (1961): 374–76.

Mudd, Emily Hartshorne. "The Impact on Family Life." *AAUW Journal* (March 1964), 123.

Mueller, Kate Hevner. "American Women and Their Work: The Need for Commitment" *AAUW Journal* (March 1964): 122–24.

Murray, P., and M. O. Eastwood. "Jane Crow and the Law: Sex Discrimination and Title VII." *The George Washington Law Review* 34:2 (1965): 232–56.

Nadelson, C., and M. T. Notman. "The Woman Physician." *Journal of Medical Education* 47 (1972): 176–83.

Nash, Diane. "Inside the Sit-Ins and Freedom Rides: Testimony of a Southern Student," in *The New Negro,* edited by Matthew Ahmann. Notre Dame: Fides, 1961.

North, Caroline P. "The New Education is 100 Years Old." *National Business Women* (February 1962): 28.

O'Gara, James. "The Archbishop and the Sisters." *Commonweal* 85:2 (14 October 1966), 47.

Ohvall, Richard A., and Surinder K. Sehgal, "Practice Continuity and Longevity of . . . Women Pharmacists," *Journal of the American Pharmaceutical Association, Practical Pharmacy Edition* ns 9:10 (October 1969), 518–20.

Ostrofsky, M. "Women Mathematicians in Industry: The Road to Success is Difficult." *AAUW Journal* (March 1964).

Pareles, Jon. "On-Again Off-Again Jefferson Airplane Is On Again." *New York Times* (September 1989): C10, 12.

Parrish, John B. "Professional Womanpower as a National Resource," *Quarterly Review of Economics and Business* 1 (February 1961).

Pfeil, E. "Role Expectations When Entering into Marriage." *Journal of Marriage and the Family* 30:1 (1968): 161–65.

Piercy, Marge. "The Grand Coolie Damn." In *Leviathan* 1:6 (October/November 1969): 16–22. Reprinted in *Sisterhood is Powerful*. Robin Morgan, ed. New York: Vintage, 1970.

Pohl, M. L. "Baccalaureate for Nursing." *National Association of Women Deans and Counselors Journal* 29 (1966): 18–83.

Pollitt, Katha. "The Three Selves of Cynthia Ozick." *New York Times Book Review* (22 May 1983): 7.

Potter, David M. "American Women and the American Character." *Stetson University Bulletin* 62 (January 1962): 1–22.

Poussaint, A. F. "The Stresses of the White Female Worker in the Civil Rights Movement in the South." *American Journal of Psychiatry* 123:4 (1966): 401–407.

Rachlin, Helen. "Urban Institutions and Women's Leadership." *Adult Leadership* (May 1969): 22–23.

Ramey, James, W. "Communes, Group Marriages, and the Upper-Middle Class." *Journal of Marriage and the Family* 34 (November 1972): 647–55.

Raphael, Edna E. "Working Women and Their Membership in Labor Unions." *Monthly Labor Review* 97:5 (May 1974): 27–33.

Reagon, Bernice Johnson. "My Black Mothers and Sisters, or On Beginning a Cultural Autobiography." *Feminist Studies* 8:1 (Spring 1982): 95.

"Rebelling Women—The Reason." *U.S. News and World Report* (13 April 1970): 35.

Rice, Joy K. "Continuing Education for Women, 1960–75: A Critical Appraisal." *Educational Record* 56:4 (Fall 1975): 241–42.

Rich, Adrienne. "When We Dead Awaken: Writing as Re-Vision." *College English* 34 (October 1972): 18–25.

Richie, Jeanne. "Church, Caste and Women." *Christian Century* 87:3 (21 January 1970): 73–77.

Rivlin, Alice M. "American Women and Their Work: What Do They Work At?" *AAUW Journal* (March 1964): 120–23.

Robbins, Jhan. "The Women Who Stayed." *McCalls* 92 (September 1965).

Roberts, Barbara. "Psychosurgery: The 'Final Solution' to the 'Woman Problem'?" *Second Wave* 2 (1972): 14–43.

Robin, S. S. "The Female in Engineering." In *Engineers and the Social System.* R. Perucci and S. E. Gerstl, eds. New York: John Wiley, 1964. 203–10.

Robinson, Ira E., and Davor Jedlicka. "Change in Sexual Attitudes and Behavior of College Students from 1965 to 1980: A Research Note." *Journal of Marriage and the Family* 44 (February 1982): 137–40.

Rogth, Robert T., and Judith Lerner. "Sex-Based Discrimination in the Mental Institutionalization of Women." *California Law Review* 63 (1964): 753–801.

Rosen, Ruth. "Sexism in History; or, Writing Women's History Is a Tricky Business." *Journal of Marriage and the Family* 33:3 (1971): 541–44.

Rossi, Alice S. "Abortion and Social Change." *Dissent* 16 (July–August 1969).

———. "Equality Between the Sexes: An Immodest Proposal." In *Woman in America.* R. Lifton, ed. Boston: Houghton Mifflin, 1965.

———. "Sex Equality: The Beginning of Ideology." *The Humanist* 29:5 (September–October 1969): 3, 6, 16.

———. "Women in Sciences: Why So Few?" *Science* 148 (28 May 1965): 1196–1202.

Roth, Robert T. and Judith Lerner. "Sex-based Discrimination in the Mental Institutionalization of Women." *California Law Review* 63 (753): 796–801.

Rothschild, Mary Aickin. "White Women Volunteers in the Freedom Summers: Their Life and Work in a Movement for Social Change." *Feminist Studies* 5:3 (Fall 1979): 466–94.

Roy, Rustum. "Is Monogamy Outdated?" *The Humanist* (March–April 1970): 19.

Ruether, Rosemary. "Are Women's Colleges Obsolete?" *The Critic* 27:2 (October–November 1968): 63.

Rush, Tom. "How Success Spoiled the Folkies." In *The Sixties.* Lynda Rosen Obst, ed. New York: Random House/Rolling Stone Press, 1977.

Russ, Joanna. "Somebody is Trying to Kill Me and I Think It's My Husband: The Modern Gothic." *Journal of Popular Culture* 6 (1973): 666–91.

Sarachild, Kathie. "Consciousness-Raising: A Radical Weapon." In Redstockings, eds. *Feminist Revolution.* New York: Redstockings, 1970.

———. "Feminist Consciousness-Raising and Organizing." In *Voices from Women's Liberation.* Leslie B. Tanner, ed. New York: Signet, 1970.

Sassower, Doris L. "Women in the Law: The Second Hundred Years." *ABA Journal* 57 (April 1970): 329–32.

Saucier, Karen A. "Healers and Heartbreakers." *Journal of Popular Culture* 20:3 (Winter 1986): 147–66.

Scarlett, John H. "Undergraduate Attitudes Toward Birth Control: New Perspectives." *Journal of Marriage and the Family* 34 (May 1974): 312–22.

Scher, M. "Women Psychiatrists in the United States." *American Journal of Psychiatry* 130:10 (1973): 1118–22.

Schneemann, Carolee. "A Feminist Pornographer in Moscow." *Independent* (March 1992).

Schonberger, Richard J. "Ten Million Housewives Want to Work." *Labor Law Journal* 21:6 (June 1970): 374–79.

Schwartz, J. J. "Medicine as a Vocation Choice Among Undergraduate Women." *National Association of Women Deans and Counselors Journal* 33:1 (1969): 7–12.

Scott, Joseph E., and Jack L. Franklin. "The Changing Nature of Sex References in Mass Circulation Magazines." *Public Opinion Quarterly* 36 (Spring 1972): 80–86.

Scully, M. G. "Women in Higher Education Challenging the Status Quo." *Chronicle of Higher Education* 4 (1970): 2–5.

Shaffer, Helen B. "Women's Consciousness Raising." [5 July 1973]. In *Editorial Research Reports on the Women's Movement*. Washington: Congressional Quarterly (1973), 3–20.

Shapiro, Harriet. "Grace Paley: 'Art Is On the Side of the Underdog.'" *Ms* 2:11 (May 1974): 43.

Shaw, Bynum. "Nevertheless, God Probably Loves Mrs. Murray." *Esquire* (October 1964): 110–12, 168–71.

Sheehy, Gail. "The New Breed." *New York* (July 16, 1971): 22.

Simon, R. J. "The Woman Ph.D.: A Recent Profile." *Social Problems* 15:2 (1967): 221–36.

Simon, William, and John Gagnon. "Psychosexual Development." *Transaction* 6 (March 1969): 9–17.

Simon, William, and John Gagnon. "Femininity in the Lesbian Community." *Social Problems* 15:2 (1967): 212–21.

Smith, C. P., and C. H. Smith. "Why Don't Women Succeed?" *New Society* 16 (1970): 577–79.

Smith, D. C., and K. Harwood. "Women in Broadcasting." *Journal of Broadcasting* 10:4 (1966): 339–56.

Soloman, Alan. "The Green Mountain Boys." *Vogue* (1 August 1966).

Spires, Elizabeth. "The Art of Poetry XXVII: Elizabeth Bishop." *The Paris Review* 80 (Summer 1981).

Stapen, Nancy. "Abstract Expressionism of the 60s Revisited." *Boston Globe* (18 February 1991): 69.

Stebbings, Elsie L. "Underestimated by Chance or by Choice." *National Business Woman* (February 1968): 6–8.

Stein, L. I. "Male and Female: The Doctor-Nurse Game." In J. P. Spradley and D. McLundy. *Conformity and Conflict—Readings in Cultural Anthropology*. New York: Oxford University Press, 1971.

Stein, Robert L. "Women At Work." *Monthly Labor Review* (June 1970): 17.

Steinmann, A., and D. J. Fox. "Male-Female Perceptions of the Female Role in the United States." *Journal of Psychology* 642 (1966): 265–76.

Stimpson, Catharine R. "Literature as Radical Statement." In *Columbia Literary*

History of the United States. Emory Elliot, ed. New York: Columbia Univ. Press, 1988.

Stimpson, Catharine R. "The New Feminism and Women's Studies." In *Women on Campus: The Unfinished Liberation.* New Rochelle, N.Y.: Change, 1975.

Stokes, Sybil L. "Women Graduate Students in Political Science." In *Women on Campus: Proceedings of the Symposium, October 14, 1970.* Ann Arbor: University of Michigan, 1970: 36.

Stricker, Frank. "Cookbooks and Law Books: The Hidden History of Career Women in 20th-Century America." *Journal of Social History* 10 (Fall 1976): 1–19.

Strong, Leslie D. "Alternative Marital and Family Forms: Their Relative Attractiveness to College Students and Correlatives of Willingness to Participate in Nontraditional Forms." *Journal of Marriage and the Family* 40 (August 1978): 493–503.

Suelzle, Marigean. "Women in Labor." In *Women's Liberation.* Michael E. Adelstein and Jen G. Pival, eds. New York: St. Martin's, 1972.

Swerdlow, Amy. "Ladies' Day at the Capitol: Women Strike for Peace Versus HUAC." *Feminist Studies* 8 (1982): 493–520.

Tallman, I. "Working-Class Wives in Suburbia: Fulfillment or Crisis?" *Journal of Marriage and the Family* 31:1 (1969): 65–72.

Taussig, Helen B. "The Evils of Camouflage as Illustrated by Thalidomide." *New England Journal of Medicine* (11 July 1963).

Tornabee, Lyn. "The Bored Housewife." *Ladies' Home Journal* 83 (November 1966): 97–99, 115.

Trecker, Janice Law. "Women's Place Is in the Curriculum." *Saturday Review* (16 October 1971): 83–86, 92.

Treen, Joseph. "Discreet Charm of Louise Bourgeois: After Years of Obscurity, She Emerges as Grande Dame of the Art World." *Boston Globe* (13 August 1990): 35.

Trilling, Diana. "The Death of Marilyn Monroe." In *Claremont Essays.* New York: Harcourt Brace and World, 1964.

Tyler, L. E. "Must University Administration Remain a Man's World?" *Graduate Comment* 12:1 (1969): 6–12.

Veevers, J. E. "Voluntarily Childless Wives: An Explanatory Study." *Sociology and Social Research* 57:3 (1973): 356–66.

Viorst, Hilton. "Javits Scolds Women Peace Marchers." *New York Post* (8 May 1963): 7.

Vogel, Alfred. "Your Clerical Workers Are Ripe for Unionization." *Harvard Business Review* 49 (March–April 1971).

Waldman, E., and B. J. McEaddy. "Where Women Work: An Analysis by Industry and Occupation." *Monthly Labor Review* 97:5 (May 1964): 3–23.

Walsh, R. H. "The Generation Gap in Sexual Beliefs." *Sexual Behavior* 2:1 (1972): 4–11.

Warrior, Betsy. "Man As an Obsolete Life Form." In *Women's Liberation: Blueprint for the Future*. New York: Ace, 1970, 45–47.

Weiss, Nancy Pottishman. "Mother, the Invention of Necessity: Dr. Benjamin Spock's *Baby and Child Care*." *American Quarterly* 29 (Winter 1977): 519–46.

Weisstein, Naomi. "'Kinder, Küche, Kirche' as Scientific Law: Psychology Constructs the Female." In *Sisterhood is Powerful: An Anthology of Writings from the Women's Liberation Movement*. Robin Morgan, ed. New York: Vintage, 1970.

Weisstein, Naomi. "Psychology Constructs the Female." In *Women in Sexist Society*. Vivian Gornick and B. K. Moran, eds. New York: New American Library, 1971. Also in *From Feminism to Liberation*. Edith Hoshino Altbach, ed. Cambridge: Schenkman, 1971.

Wells, Jean A. "Women's Job Prospects." *AAUW Journal* (October 1964): 20–24.

Wells, Theodora. "Women—Which Includes Men, Of course , . . . An Experience in Awareness." *Association for Humanistic Psychology Newsletter* 7:3 (December 1970).

———. "Women in Congress: 1917–1964." *The Western Political Quarterly* 19:1 (1966): 16–30.

———. "Women in State Legislatures." *The Western Political Quarterly* 21:1 (1968): 40–50.

Whitbread, Jane. "The Families of the Men in Vietnam." *Parents' Magazine and Better Homemaking* 42 (October 1967): 53–55, 113–15.

———. "How Servicemen's Marriages Survive Separation." *Redbook* 132 (April 1969): 94, 146.

White, J. J. "Women in the Law." *Michigan Law Review* 65:6 (1967): 1051–1123.

White, Peggy, and Starr Goode. "The Small Group in Women's Liberation." *Women: A Journal of Liberation* (Fall 1969): 56–57.

Whitney, Phyllis. "Writing the Gothic Novel." *Writer* 80 (February 1967): 9–13, 42–43.

Whyte, William H., Jr. "The Wives of Management," in *Man, Work, and Society*. Sigmund Noscow and William H. Form, eds. New York: Basic Books, 1962.

Willett, Roslyn S. "Working in 'A Man's World': The Woman Executive." In *Women in Sexist Society: Studies in Power and Powerlessness*. Vivian Gornick and Barbara K. Moran, eds. New York: Mentor, 1971, 518–19.

Willis, Ellen. "Sister Under the Skin? Confronting Race and Sex." *Village Voice Literary Supplement* 8 (June 1982).

———. "Declaration of Independence." *The Voice of the Women's Liberation Movement*. #6 (1969).

———. "Women and the Left." *Notes from the Second Year*. (1970).

Winch, R. "Permanence and Change in the History of the American Family and Some Speculations as to its Future." *Journal of Marriage and the Family* 32:1 (1970): 6–15.

Winick, Charles. "The Beige Epoch: Depolarization of Sex Roles." *Annals* 376 (March 1968), 24.

Wohl, Lisa Cronin. "What's So Rare as a Woman on Wall Street." *Ms* (June 1973).

Wolfe, Tom. "The Pumphouse Gang." In *The Sixties*. Lynda Rosen Obst, ed. New York: Random House/Rolling Stone Press, 1977.

Woods, Cynthia. "From Individual Dedication to Social Activism: Historical Development of Nursing Professionalism." In *Nursing History: The State of the Art*. Christopher Maggs, ed. London: Croom Helm, 1985.

Wyer, R. S., Jr., D. A. Weatherly, and G. Terrell. "Social Role, Aggression, and Academic Achievement." *Journal of Personality and Social Psychology* 1:6 (1965): 645–49.

Zelinsky, Wilbur. "The Strange Case of the Missing Female Geographer." *Journal of American Geography* 25:2 (1973): 101–05.

Zigas, Irma. "Hell, No! We Won't Let Them Go." [Women Strike for Peace] *Memo* 19 (1966).

Index